ENGLISH GRAMMATICAL CATEGORIES

ENGLISH
GRAMMATICAL
CATEGORIES

AND THE TRADITION
TO 1800

IAN MICHAEL
Vice-Chancellor University of Malawi

CAMBRIDGE
AT THE UNIVERSITY PRESS
1970

Published by the Syndics of the Cambridge University Press
Bentley House, 200 Euston Road, London N.W.1
American Branch: 32 East 57th Street, New York, N.Y.10022

© Cambridge University Press 1970

Library of Congress Catalogue Card Number: 77–111133

Standard Book Number: 521 07634 x

Printed in Great Britain
at the University Printing House, Cambridge
(Brooke Crutchley, University Printer)

To my wife
MOLLY
and to our friend and colleague
DORA PYM

PREFACE

To say that this book is a record of discovery would rouse misleading expectations, an excitement out of keeping with the sobriety (to use no stronger word) of its title. Nevertheless it is the findings of an expedition into little-known country, and its growth helps to explain its purpose. It began in an enquiry about what effect Latin had had on the early development of English grammar. This question raised another: what, in such a context, was Latin? Sixteenth-century grammars? Priscian? It seemed that the whole grammatical tradition, both Greek and Latin, was inescapably relevant to the enquiry. It seemed also that the very little which had so far been written about these questions relied too much on 'influence'—the assumed influence of one writer on another—as an organising concept; that the evidence was thin and the generalisations robust but unproductive. Stronger evidence would be found in a study of some of the categories, especially the parts of speech, which appeared in both the English and the classical tradition. Any review of the main classical categories meant relying on the texts, not on modern historians and philologists, who had written with other purposes. For the English grammars there were few historians and no body of texts. In the eighteenth century, especially, all but the major texts had to be rediscovered. To this already arrogant undertaking were added two expansive temptations. The English grammars were largely unknown; although most of them were unimportant works individually, together they formed part of the educational history of the country, and it was tempting to find and survey them all for the sake of the comprehensive evidence which was not available for any other kind of textbook. This temptation was readily accepted. All known grammars have been studied, but only for their main categories. They contain also much valuable information about the early history of English studies and English teaching. It was also tempting to try to place the grammars in the intellectual history of the country, especially among the ideas about language by which they were (or, more often, were not) influenced.

This temptation was resisted: writing the history of ideas is no job for the intermittent and nocturnal scholar.

The heart of the book is in Part Two, and for many readers that may be the point of entry. The Greek and Latin tradition is an essential part of the long development of English teaching, but the categorical summary of it which is given here cannot be high-spirited, and may, if wished, be used for reference only.

A great many people have helped: too many to thank. But particular acknowledgment should be made to my former colleagues in the University of Bristol, where most of this work was done, and especially to Miss Susie Tucker, to the staff of the library, to Lewis Hull (who really started it) and to Mrs Dora Pym (without whom it would have died among the adverbs). Dr Robin Alston, of the University of Leeds, has been most generous not only in telling me about newly located works in advance of the publication of his *Bibliography of the English Language* but also in arranging for photocopies of them to be sent to me in Malawi. I am also most grateful to the Keeper of the Brotherton Collection in the University of Leeds for permission to use the manuscript grammar *The Practice of Speaking and Writing English*, and to the Librarian of the University of Glasgow for permission to quote from the grammatical manuscripts of James Douglas. I still look forward to renewing discussion with Dr Ivan Poldauf, of the Palacký University, Olomouc, who introduced me to that fine eccentric, William Ward.

In quotations the punctuation, spelling and capitalisation of the original text have been retained, but italics have been preserved only when their emphasis was relevant. In most cases the titles of works noted in Alston's bibliography are here given in a short form; other titles are given in full if they are interesting, but only the short title is italicised. The English grammars are cited by author and date only.

I. M.

Blantyre, Malawi
June, 1970

CONTENTS

Contents

Contents

Contents

Contents

L'art d'analyser la pensée, est le premier fondement de l'art de parler, ou en d'autres termes...une saine Logique est le fondement de la Grammaire.

Encyclopédie, vol. 7, 1757, *s.v.* Grammaire

ABBREVIATIONS

K.   H. Keil, *Grammatici Latini*, 6 vols. Leipzig, 1855–74

S & U   R. Schneider and G. Uhlig, *Apollonius Dyscolus*, 4 vols. Leipzig, 1878–1910 (vol. I. i, *De Pronomine*; *De Adverbio*; *De Coniunctione*; vol. I. ii, *Commentary*; vol. II, *De Constructione*; vol. III, *Fragmenta*)

SVF   von Arnim, *Stoicorum Veterum Fragmenta*, 4 vols. Leipzig, 1905–24.

TE   Thomas of Erfurt, *Grammatica Speculativa*, ed. P. Fr. Mariani Fernandez Garcia, Quaracchi, 1902.

INTRODUCTION

Do we not every day meet with scholars, who after having finished an English course of instruction, can neither spell, pronounce, read, speak, nor write their own language without violating...its principles of expression, or grammatical construction?

Henry Macnab, *A Plan of Reform, 1766*

The cry is still raised, as it was in 1766 and earlier, that apprentices and undergraduates express themselves badly: that they cannot control their own language. It is not generally realised, even in the schools, how difficult it is for anyone to control the expression and interpretation of language, and that control is as difficult to teach as it is to achieve. The traditional means of teaching control, to pupils at all levels, in their own language as well as in foreign languages, is the set of analytical procedures called grammar. The discipline called English grammar, as taught to schoolchildren, is widely, if vaguely, said to be ineffective—for various reasons. The best reason, and the only one relevant here, is that it is not the right kind of grammar. In what way is conventional English grammar inappropriate to the purpose of teaching linguistic control to native speakers of English? Here the critics, understandably, falter. The nearest they get to an agreed answer is to say that English grammar has merely been taken over from Latin grammar, that Latin is more richly inflected than English, and therefore much of the old grammar is inappropriate. Some critics go further and say that the trouble lies not only in this difference between English and Latin but in the deeper reason that the old grammar was used to teach a foreign language, whereas we need a grammar which will give full weight to the distinctive characteristics of a vernacular.

The present work arises directly out of the teacher's problems. It seems obvious that English grammar at the elementary level (and that is where the urgent pressures lie) is just the application to English of Latin grammar. Yet this fact, which the critics have for long made their chief reason for the inappropriateness of our grammar, also supports one of the chief resistances to any real reform: 'Who are you to change the system of centuries, compact, agreed, established?' The acceptance of any effective reform is, in this situation, closely related to our understanding of the past.

In order to gain the relevant understanding certain questions need to be answered: Just what *is* the compact, agreed and established grammatical tradition which we are said to have inherited? What is meant by saying that Latin grammar was 'applied' to English? In what circumstances, with what deliberation and agreement, was it applied? Was there any protest, any anticipation of our own criticisms?

The continuity of the classical tradition is most clearly apparent in the names of the parts of speech: noun and verb seem unquestionable; the pronoun is inescapable; the adjective and adverb are presumably necessary attendants; the conjunction and preposition jostle each other, but long familiarity seems to have established the role of each. If questions are to be asked about a set of analytical procedures the best evidence on which to base the answers must be the different categories into which the primary material (in this case language) is being analysed; and the traditionally most important of these categories are the parts of speech. This enquiry has therefore been shaped as an examination of certain grammatical categories. The nature and development of the categories is the only adequate evidence on which to base answers to the original questions. Behind a superficial appearance of uniformity, imitativeness and dullness the English grammars in fact contain a most surprising diversity of outlook and of categories. This diversity is new and important evidence, but can be adequately displayed only by extensive quotation.

The texts themselves are little known. The present work uses all the extant English grammars which had been written by 1800. There are 272 of them, but the exact number will depend on the way an English grammar is defined; and new grammars will still be discovered. Of these 272 grammars about 140 have not been studied before. Ivan Poldauf, in his *On the History of some Problems of English Grammar before 1800*, used about a hundred of them. No other study has used more than thirty. Besides Poldauf's the only other strict examination of grammatical categories is Emma Vorlat's *Progress in*

Introduction

English Grammar, 1585–1735, which is based on a detailed study of fourteen grammars. Otherwise attention has been hitherto paid almost exclusively to matters of phonology and usage.

The criteria used in selecting the works studied here are that they should be written by a native speaker of English, should discuss the parts of speech, and should have been written or printed in England by 1800. Strict consistency has not been attempted. John Dalton's grammar was not published until 1801 and is strictly out of time, making the number of grammars studied 273. But it is included because it is interesting. The anonymous *An English Grammar* printed in Antigua about 1750 is strictly out of place, but is included for the same reason. Mark Lewis's *Plain and Short Rules* refers chiefly to punctuation, but is included because it contains a discussion of syntax which does not appear in his other writings. John Ward's *Four Essays*, W. R.'s *Letters*, Anderson's *The Bee* and 'Mica's' articles do not discuss all the parts of speech. Mrs Lovechild's *Parsing Lessons* cannot be separated from their companion grammars. White, Pickbourn and Warren Hastings discuss only the verb, but this part of speech is so important that some inconsistency of treatment may be excused. Alderson's *English Grammatical Exercises* and the anonymous *English Syntax Rules* refer to the parts of speech only indirectly, but are evidence for particular systems of classification. The seventeenth-century basic grammars, discussed in chapter 7, are by definition equally grammars of Latin.

Of the 273 works listed in Appendix VI, 167 were written as distinct English grammars. A further twenty-nine were published on their own but were basic grammars or universal works like Harris's *Hermes*. Twenty-six were attached to dictionaries, the first in 1735. Eleven were attached to spelling books, the first in 1704, the latest in 1788. Thirty-one were included in works of wider scope, ranging from *The Ladies' Polite Secretary* by 'the Right Honourable Lady Dorothea Du Bois' and Thomas Wise's *The Newest Young Man's Companion* to the *Encyclopaedia Britannica*.

The authors are equally varied. The Royal Society is represented by Wallis and Wilkins; literature by Evelyn, Ben Jonson and Samuel Johnson; chemistry by Priestley and Dalton; the church by Lowth, John Wesley and many others. Most of the authors were teachers. Gill was High Master of St Paul's and Greenwood second master; Maittaire was second master at Westminster. Cooper, Cave Beck,

3

William Ward, Rothwell and many more were masters of grammar schools; many were masters or ushers in academies; some, like Angus, Nicholson and Groombridge, private teachers of particular subjects. Of the recorded grammars 222 are by named authors, of whom 140 are known to have been teachers; about many there is no information.

In order to make comparison possible it has been necessary to summarise the classical grammatical tradition, using the same categorical approach as is used for the English. The difficulties of present-day teachers of English, both conservative and radical, are accentuated by misconceptions about the tradition: its unanimity and credentials. It has been necessary to show, in outline, its whole range. It would have been misleadingly incomplete to discuss only the renaissance grammars out of which Lily and the first English grammars directly emerged. A possible outline was provided by R. H. Robins's excellent *Ancient and Medieval Grammatical Theory in Europe*, but this concise survey is concerned primarily with ideas about language, and does not profess to examine the development of particular categories—an essential part of the present study. A categorical summary was therefore necessary, something stark: a quarry, not a landscape. In the event it could not be even ideally stark: unfamiliar lines of thought, anticipations of modern themes and the hitherto unremarked appearance of features later found in the English tradition, all needed comment. The speculative grammarians, in particular, are so little known that a bare list of their categories would have been meaningless. Part One, therefore, is a compromise, unsatisfactory except in relation to this study. It is based directly on the sixty-six texts listed in Appendix IV, and is meant to summarise not only the principal categories in the tradition but something of the writers' points of view. The proliferation of subordinate categories, for example, in long lists, is a feature which can be mentioned in a sentence, but its real nature, and the force of its resemblance to aspects of elementary English teaching today, can be appreciated only if some such lists are given in full.

The categories discussed in the following chapters have often to be related to the criteria by which they are formed. This involves the frequent use of three terms which, though familiar, are used in different ways by different modern writers. They have here the following senses:

Introduction

Formal. To say that *neatness* must be a noun because it ends in -*ness* is to use a formal criterion.

Semantic. To say that *neatness* must be a noun because it is the name of something is to use the criterion of meaning: a semantic criterion.

Syntactic. To say that *neatness* must be a noun because it makes sense when put before the words 'pleases me' is to use a syntactic criterion.

PART I

THE TRADITION

1. THE SOURCES

The categories used by the early writers of English grammars were seldom chosen as the result of independent thought. They were, and have remained, the categories not only of the renaissance grammarians but to a very large extent those of the Stoic and Alexandrian grammarians of the first and second centuries B.C. The full force of this elaborate, compacted, and overwhelmingly authoritative tradition has been appreciated only in comparatively modern times. Its influence was immense and inescapable. Till recently it has determined most of the categories used in English grammars, and a summary of it is needed to set them in perspective. A summary it must be, however, and not a history. Even as a summary it should illustrate the continuity of the tradition, and its apparent stability; it should illustrate also its astonishing variety, and the uncertainties which make its stability only apparent. The continuity and the uncertainty still affect our daily lives. We try to teach schoolchildren what a verb is, what a sentence is; but we cannot agree amongst ourselves. We have traditional formulae, but we are uncertain how far they are valid and useful. We have done what a bird's-eye view of the tradition shows all our predecessors to have done. We have accepted many traditional grammatical categories without thinking enough about the varying purposes for which such categories would be appropriate, and about the criteria which would properly relate a given category to a given purpose.

To speak of a tradition is perhaps to simplify too much those overlapping processes of philosophical, logical, rhetorical and verbal study which were never entirely static, however sluggish they may have been for centuries at a time. Of the complex historical influences which kept these studies narrow and gave them the authority of tradition by far the most important is the cultural dominance of Latin. Linguistic study was confined to two languages, structurally similar: Greek, from which the first categories had been drawn, and

Latin, from which they had been finally systematised. Broadly speaking, the classical languages, with no real rivalry from Hebrew, were Language, and their grammar was Grammar. It is thus difficult to summarise the tradition barely, in terms of its chief categories, without becoming closely involved in the wider issues which could be discussed only in a history of linguistic thought. In order to preserve the advantages of a summary (if for no other reason) this introductory conspectus is planned as a list of categories, with a commentary intended to clarify, as far as possible, the nature of the category rather than to place it in the intellectual thought of its time or to describe the details of its subsequent development.

The list includes those categories which have remained till the present day part of the traditional system of English grammar, and also some of those which were at one time established in the traditional system but later dropped out. The decision as to what is or is not a grammatical category has therefore had to take into account both modern and ancient interpretations of the term *grammar*.

The list illustrates, but not exhaustively, the zeal for classification which animated the Stoics and most later systematisers. It excludes most phonetic categories, as well as many logical concepts which, though of great linguistic importance, were not incorporated into the traditional grammatical system.

The writers who have been used as sources for this summary are listed in Appendix IV. It is sometimes convenient to regard them as falling into groups: those in whom we see the beginning of the tradition, up to and including Aristotle; the Stoic and Alexandrian grammarians, up to and including Apollonius Dyscolus in the second century B.C., who first systematised the tradition; those, especially Priscian, about A.D. 500, by whom the tradition was consolidated; the speculative grammarians of the thirteenth and fourteenth centuries; the renaissance grammarians up to and including Lily and Ramus in the sixteenth century.

CLASSICAL SOURCES

By the middle of the fourth century B.C. some fundamental categories had been described or suggested with various degrees of precision. Their interpretation is almost always difficult, not only, or even chiefly, because our texts are incomplete, but because the categories are usually formed according to logical or psychological criteria different from, but easily confused with, the traditional grammatical criteria which we have come to take for granted. It is therefore dangerously easy to attribute too precise and ancient an origin to grammatical categories which have evolved, in ways which cannot be exactly documented, out of many different kinds of speculation. Yet the line of development is real and important. Our traditional system bears countless marks of its origin, not least the logical, or pseudo-logical, air which it has at times flaunted, at times sought to suppress. Contemporary linguistic philosophers are, to a large extent, asking again questions put by Aristotle, by the Stoics, and by the schoolmen about the relations between things, concepts and words.

The categories described here are those of Dionysius Thrax, who drew on the work of previous, especially Alexandrian, grammarians[1] to produce in the second century B.C. the earliest extant systematic grammar in the western world: one which had an active life long enough for it to be used at Merchant Taylors' School, London, during the boyhood of an uncle of Gilbert Murray's.[2] Stoic variations are noted when necessary, although the exact meaning of many Stoic terms is uncertain, and syntactical categories are taken from Apollonius Dyscolus, of the second century A.D.

Donatus, of the fourth century A.D., and Priscian are the basic sources for the next group, but use is also made of Varro, of the first century B.C., and Quintilian, first century A.D. They both belong chronologically to the earlier period but are included here because they wrote in and about Latin. Sacerdos, third century A.D., has also been used, and the fourth-century grammarians Diomedes and Charisius. Of these seven writers, the five grammarians were certainly drawing on earlier work. Latin and Greek are sufficiently alike in structure for it to have been natural, and on the whole appropriate, that the Roman grammarians should have adopted most of the categories established in Greek. The Romans made their grammars more systematic but, apart perhaps from Varro, added little in subtlety. Priscian was subtle, but no Roman: he was born in Africa and taught in Constantinople. The transition from Greek grammar to Latin was unbroken: the first interest of the Romans in

[1] K. Barwick, 'Remmius Palaemon und die römische ars grammatica', *Philologus*, Suppl. xv. 2, 1922, 94f. emphasises the use made by Dionysius of Stoic work on phonology.
[2] Gilbert Murray, 'The Beginnings of Grammar', *Proc. Class. Assoc.* 1931, reprinted in *Greek Studies*, 1946, pp. 181 f.

grammar is said to have been aroused by Crates, who was lecturing in Rome on poetical texts about 168 B.C.;[1] Varro, born fifty years after Crates' visit and, roughly, a contemporary of Dionysius Thrax, wrote copiously about Latin and its grammar with, apparently, a wide knowledge of the Greek grammarians. Priscian describes himself as applying the fruits of Greek scholarship to Latin, and frequently acknowledges his indebtedness to Apollonius Dyscolus.[2]

Priscian, Lily and Lindley Murray have probably influenced the ordinary teaching of English grammar more than any other grammarians, and they all claimed to be little more than compilers and systematisers.

MEDIEVAL SOURCES

It is not possible to choose with any certainty representative medieval grammatical works. At least sixty grammars are known, but more than half of them have not yet been printed in full. As this is such an unfamiliar part of the tradition it is described here briefly.

There seem to be three types of grammar. The first can be labelled 'literary' because it follows, very weakly, the literary rather than the logical parts of Priscian's outlook; the second can be labelled 'logical', for the converse reason. The third type, quite different from the other two, has been called 'speculative'.

Literary grammars. Most of the literary grammars are elementary manuals, based on Donatus and Priscian, from which the specific literary references have increasingly vanished. I have used Bede (d. 735) whose authorship is doubtful, Alcuin (d. 804), Aelfric (d. 1020) and Hugo of St Victor (d. 1141), together with two versified manuals, the *Doctrinale* of Alexander of Villedieu (1199), and the *Graecismus* of Eberhard of Bethune (*c.* 1200). A higher proportion of literary grammars has been printed than of either of the other two types. The principal works yet unprinted seem to be Remigius of Auxerre's commentaries on Donatus, Priscian and Martianus Capella,[3] and John Garland's *Compendium grammatice* (written before 1236).[4]

Logical grammars. For the second type, roughly labelled 'logical', I have been largely dependent on brief quotations and descriptions.

---

[1] Sextus Empiricus, *Adv. Math.* I. 11.
[2] Priscian, xvii. 1, for example.
[3] Hauréau, 1890, I. 78; Grabmann, MG, III. 245.
[4] MSS. in Hauréau.

It is difficult, therefore, to know what works are relevant. The dialectical exercises known as *sophismata* interweave logical and linguistic considerations so closely that they would be a necessary part of any general survey.[1] But as they are not conceived primarily as grammars, and as they seem to leave purely grammatical categories untouched, I have excluded them, together with the logical works of Boethius, Abelard and William of Sherwood, all of whom discuss the linguistic expression of logical concepts such as quantification (*omnes*) and indefiniteness (*aliquis*). It is, however, worth quoting two topics from Siger of Courtrai's *Sophismata* as illustrations of an approach to language which is characteristic of the period. The first topic he considers is: '"Amo est verbum", hoc est sophisma propositum circa quod unum quaeratur, scilicet: utrum haec oratio sit congrua.'[2] The second is the familiar *Magistro legente pueri proficiunt*, about which he asks 'utrum ablativus qui dicitur poni absolute, ab alio regatur'.[3]

From a strictly grammatical point of view (which is not the one Siger is here adopting) this last seems an almost perverse attempt to create difficulties. But the treatment of both texts shows something of that wrestling with words which was the new skill of the scholastic logicians. We naturally regard *amo* as a word about which, in this context, it is irrelevant to ask whether it is first person or third. It is a second-order word. Its status is that of 'the word *amo*', not that of a sign referring to the speaker. This may be a common-sense distinction, but it has been achieved only with difficulty. To Siger there was a contradiction to be removed if the subject of a sentence (*amo*) was in the first person and its verb in the third.

The two positions to be debated about *magistro legente* are, broadly, (i) that if *magistro legente* is absolute it cannot be governed by anything, and as there are no words, present or understood, by which it could be governed, it must be absolute. On the other hand, it is argued, (ii) any expression has a structure; in any structure there are degrees: there is a hierarchy in which the more important elements have authority over the less important; this expression is a structure, so its elements must be under authority, that is under *regimen*. The

---

[1] The most accessible example of the *sophismata* is that of Siger of Courtrai, in Wallerand, 129–65. See also M. Grabmann, 'Die Sophismataliteratur des 12. und 13. Jahrhunderts mit Textausgabe eines Sophisma des Boetius von Dacien', *Beitr. zur Gesch. des Philosophie des Mittelalters*, 36. 1940. I.

[2] Wallerand, p. 129.　　　　　　　　　　[3] op. cit. p. 137.

wrestling here is not so much over the text as with the terms of the solution. To our common sense a metaphor drawn from a social structure carries no necessary logical authority when applied to a linguistic structure. We regard words as our servants more confidently, perhaps, than Siger could, but it is doubtful if we have any greater authority over them.

Apart from the sophismata and the manuals of letter-writing (*artes dictaminis*) there are a number of other 'logical' grammars and grammatical works (few of which have been published in full) such as Anselm's *Dialogus de 'grammatico'*.[1] These include the grammars of Johannes de Pigna (twelfth century),[2] Ralph of Beauvais (twelfth century),[3] Robert Grosseteste (d. 1253)[4] and Petrus Ysolella (thirteenth century),[5] the Commentary on Priscian by William of Conches (twelfth century)[6] and many anonymous commentaries such as the three belonging to the late twelfth and early thirteenth centuries which are discussed by R. W. Hunt.[7]

Speculative grammars. The third type of grammar in the medieval period, and the most distinctive, is the speculative grammar.[8] The writers of these grammars accepted Priscian's system of categories, but roofed it over with a theory of language derived from scholastic logic and philosophy. Their fundamental question, old in their day and one we are still asking, was: 'What is the relation between words and things?' Their answers were based on the assumption that words possessed modes of signification (*modi significandi*). The grammars were frequently entitled *De Modis Significandi Tractatus* and the writers accordingly known as *modistae*.

The earliest speculative grammars are the *Summa Gramatica* of Roger Bacon and the *De Modis Significandi* attributed to Albertus

---

[1] Appendix IV, below. See also D. P. Henry, 'Why "grammaticus"', *Archiv. Lat. Med. Aevi*, 28. 1958. 165–80, and 'Saint Anselm's De "grammatico"', *Philos. Quart.*, x. 1960. 115–26.

[2] Johannes De Pigna, *Summa Grammatice*, Grabmann, MG, I. 112.

[3] Ralph of Beauvais, *Summa super Donatum*, Hunt, II. 11 ff.

[4] Robert Grosseteste, *Grammatica*: MSS. in S. Harrison Thomson, *The Writings of Robert Grosseteste, Bishop of Lincoln*, 1940, pp. 100–1.

[5] Petrus Ysolella, *Summa Grammatice*, Grabmann, MG, I. 112; Hunt, II. 177 n.

[6] William of Conches, *Commentary on Priscian*, Grabmann, MG, I. 113; extracts in Thurot. Text in PL unreliable.   [7] Hunt, II. 1–3.

[8] A brief account is given in Robins, chap. 3; the fullest account of the grammars is in Grabmann, *Die Entwicklung der mittelalterlichen Sprachlogik*, MG, I. 104–46. See also Roos, chaps. 4 and 5; Wallerand, chap. 5; Grabmann, TE, pp. 57–98; Grabmann, MG, III. 243–53.

Magnus, both written about the middle of the thirteenth century. The latest ones seem to be the unpublished grammars of Joannes Josse de Marville, written in 1322,[1] and Johannes Aurifaber, written in 1332.[2]

The grammars fell into disrepute during the early period of the renaissance. The literary tradition in grammatical studies had never been completely dead, and with reviving interest in 'the authors' the speculative grammars seemed uncongenial and irrelevant to literary studies. Grabmann quotes one German humanist who says that such grammars should never be used with children and that preoccupation with them has sent even mature scholars mad.[3] Only Thomas of Erfurt's, on the strength of its attribution to Duns Scotus, and the grammar attributed to Albertus Magnus, seem to have been printed during the fifteenth or sixteenth centuries. In modern times the importance of the speculative grammars was first realised by H. A. F. Haase;[4] Thurot printed extracts from them in 1868, but it was not until 1878 that Johann Müller properly interpreted the term *modista*.[5] Present interest in the grammars is strengthened by the logical and linguistic preoccupations of modern philosophers, but its strongest impetus has come from the researches during the last forty years of the late Professor Martin Grabmann of Munich.

The type of question discussed in the speculative grammars can be illustrated more fully than can the arguments themselves. Few of the grammars have been printed, and it is as much from the questions quoted by Grabmann and Roos as from the grammars of Siger and Thomas that we gain an impression of the type as a whole. The following are typical of the most general kind of question:

(i) Utrum possibile sit vocem imponi ad significandum.[6]

(ii) Quis grammaticam invenit, an scilicet grammaticus an philosophus[7]

(iii) Utrum grammatica sit eadem in omnibus ydiomatibus in quibus inventa est, et scilicet in ydiomate greco ebrayco et latino.[8]

---

[1] Joannes Josse, *Tractatus*, Roos, p. 21; Grabmann, TE, pp. 89 f. For MSS. see Lehmann, pp. 32–3.

[2] Johannes Aurifaber, *Tractatus*, Grabmann, TE, p. 93. For MSS. see Lehmann, pp. 18–19.　　　　　　　　　　　　　　　[3] Grabmann, MG, I. 142.

[4] H. A. F. Haase, *De medii aevi studiis philologicis disputatio*, Breslau 1856.

[5] Grabmann, MG, I. 117.　　　　　　　　[6] Albertus Magnus, Qu. 4.

[7] Boethius of Dacia, quoted by Grabmann, TE, p. 81.

[8] Anon. commentary: Breslau Univ. Lib., Cod. IV.Q.9, quoted by Grabmann, TE, p. 25. Boethius of Dacia has the same question.

(iv) Utrum in verbis primae et secundae personae intelligitur nominativus casus.[1]

(v) Quid primum sit et minimum ex quo incipit consideratio grammatice.[2]

(vi) Quid sit subiectum (the fundamental subject matter) in grammatica.[3]

These were questions of a new kind. They are not like the questions of antiquity, which seldom reached behind the words, except in making etymologies. These questions are probing into the nature and functioning of language itself.

In discussing these and consequent questions a number of categories are used which are philosophical rather than grammatical, and need to be described briefly before the speculative grammarians' treatment of the traditional categories can be understood.

The relation between words and things is referred to by the term *impositio*. Words have meaning (*significatio*) by being 'imposed' on things (*per impositionem*) by the inventor of language. This is not far from the belief that language is arbitrary and conventional, which belief is sometimes explicitly expressed when words are said to signify *ad placitum*.

The question was frequently asked whether grammar was invented by a philosopher or by a grammarian. This was equivalent to asking whether language was, by its structure, systematically related to reality, or whether it was random and ad hoc. The accepted answer was that grammar was invented by a philosopher, and thus, by implication, logical. This would seem inconsistent with any belief that language was a purely conventional system, but the contradiction is not complete. The relation between a single word and a single thing may be arbitrary and conventional, while the relations between the words, that is the *structure* of language, may logically reflect the *structure* of reality. But for the speculative, as distinct from the logical, writers *inventio* was directly related to the concept of essence, and the relation between word and thing was not, in fact, regarded as arbitrary, but determined by the essence of the thing. Hunt, in his summary description of *inventio*, brings out clearly the extent to which linguistic considerations were subordinated to, in fact obscured by, metaphysical ones:

---

[1] Albertus Magnus, Qu. 11.   [2] Albertus Magnus, Qu. 3.
[3] Radulphus Brito, quoted by Grabmann, TE, p. 92.

It is possible in examining the parts of speech to look for the cause of their invention. When this has been found it can be used as a criterion for determining the proper grammatical function of a word. Further, the nature of its invention, that is the purpose for which it was principally or properly invented, is the criterion by which we ought to judge a word, not the way it is used in the construction of a sentence.[1]

An extreme example of how concentration on logic can obscure an obvious truth is given by Richard Kilwardby (d. 1279) in his Commentary on the first book of Priscian's *Ars Minor* (i.e. Priscian, Bk xvii). His argument that there is only one science of grammar, equally appropriate to all languages, leads him to the conclusion that grammar does not deal with words in use:

Since science remains the same in any part of the world, and its subject matter remains the same, the subject-matter of grammar ought to be the same in all parts of the world. But discourse, or words in order and agreement, does not remain the same in all parts of the world. Therefore discourse is not the subject-matter of grammar.[2]

As Wallerand points out, Kilwardby is wanting to restrict grammar to the study of the expression of the relations between concepts, to incorporate it within logic.

The modal framework as it appears in Siger and Thomas (there are slight differences between them) is highly schematic. It is applied to things, minds and words. Things in themselves are what they uniquely are by virtue of 'modes of being' (*modi essendi*). The *modus essendi* of a thing is the union of its defining properties. Minds have the property of apprehending things. This property is the *modus intelligendi activi*. Things as apprehended by minds have the correlative property of being apprehended: *modus intelligendi passivi*. Words (through the operation of *impositio*) have the property of signifying things: *modus significandi activi*. Things as signified by words have the correlative property, *modus significandi passivi*, which enables them to be represented by language.

Described in terms of the modes the schema has three levels:

(i) *Modus essendi*, that is, according to Siger, 'proprietates rerum seu entium', a mode belonging to things.[3]

---

[1] R. W. Hunt, I. 212.

[2] Kilwardby, quoted by Wallerand, p. 44: 'Cum scientia maneat eadem apud omnes, et subiectum eius idem manet, quare subiectum grammaticae debet manere idem in omnibus. Sed oratio constructa vel vox literata ordinabilis propter congruum non idem manet apud omnes; quare non erit subjectum grammaticae.'

[3] Siger, p. 93.

(ii) *Modus intelligendi*, of which the active form belongs to minds and the passive to things. Siger describes the active mode as: 'modus quo intellectus comprehendit modum essendi seu proprietatem ipsius rei'.[1]

Thomas defines the active mode as, 'ratio concipiendi, qua mediante, intellectus rei proprietates significat, concipit vel apprehendit'.[2] For the passive mode Thomas has the simpler and more effective definition: '...proprietas rei, prout est ab intellectu apprehensa'.[3] Siger's definition makes it reassuringly clear (though it is only Thomas who discusses the question directly) that the modes are relative to each other and, in a sense, merely different aspects of the same reality. He says of the passive mode that it is 'ipse modus essendi ab ipso intellectu apprehensus seu modus intelligendi relatus ad modum essendi'.[4]

(iii) *Modus significandi*, of which the active form belongs to words and the passive to things. Thomas defines the active form as 'modus, sive proprietas vocis, ab intellectu sibi concessa, mediante qua, vox proprietatem rei significat', and the passive as 'modus, sive proprietas rei, prout est per vocem significata'.[5]

Siger distinguishes further between the mode (which he calls *modus signandi*) which permits a word to have meaning, that is permits the vocal sound (*vox*) to become a word (*dictio*), and the mode which permits a word to function as a part of speech, that is in relation to other words, syntactically: 'vox autem formaliter dicitur pars orationis per modum significandi activum'.[6]

In discussing the relationship of these modes to each other Thomas makes use of the distinction between material and formal modes. The active and passive modes are the same materially but differ formally; the modes of conceiving and signifying are the same formally but differ materially. By the time he has developed this argument in its most patterned form it is difficult to remember (and perhaps to believe) that it has any connection with language. A short quotation will suffice. The *modus intelligendi activus* and the *modus intelligendi passivus* agree *formaliter* and differ *materialiter*:

because the *modus intelligendi passivus* expresses the property of the thing according to the passive power of conceiving, but the *modus intelligendi*

---

[1] Siger, p. 94. [2] TE, p. 14. [3] ibid.
[4] Siger, p. 94. [5] TE, p. 7.
[6] Robins, p. 82 n. Siger, p. 94.

activus expresses the property of the mind, which is the active power of conceiving. The power of conceiving by means of which the mind actively conceives the property of the thing is the same as that by means of which the property of the thing is conceived passively. Therefore the properties are different, and the power is the same. Therefore they differ materially but are the same formally.[1]

It is clear even from this stark summary that the most important category for grammar is the *modus significandi activus*. Thomas subdivides this mode into *modus significandi essentialis* and *modus significandi accidentalis*, the first of which he further divides into three subdivisions and the second into two. The schema is as follows, with Thomas's definitions:

I. *Modus significandi essentialis*
    1 *a. modus significandi essentialis generalissimus*
    1 *b. modus significandi essentialis specialissimus*
    1 *c. modus significandi essentialis subalternus*
II. *Modus significandi accidentalis*
    2 *a. Modus significandi accidentalis absolutus*
    2 *b. modus significandi accidentalis respectivus*

I. *Modus significandi essentialis*: 'That by means of which a part of speech merely has being, either as genus or as species' (*per quem pars orationis habet simpliciter esse, vel secundum genus, vel secundum speciem*; TE, p. 24).

I *a* ... *generalissimus*: 'the mode of the essence of a given part of speech and of any subdivision of that part of speech contained within it' (*qui est de essentia partis orationis et cuiuslibet suppositi sub se contenti*; TE, p. 24).

I *b* ... *specialissimus*: 'the mode of the essence of any subject at all of that part of speech' (*qui est de essentia quorumdam suppositorum illius partis*; TE, p. 24).

I *c.* ... *subalternus*: 'the mode of the essence of the subjects of a given part of speech considered neither in very general nor in very specific terms, but occupying a middle mode' (*qui est de essentia suppositorum illius partis, nec generalissime, nec specialissime, sed medio modo se habens*; TE, p. 25).

---

[1] TE, p. 18: 'quia modus intelligendi passivus dicit rei proprietatem sub ratione intelligendi passiva; sed modus intelligendi activus dicit proprietatem intellectus, quae est ratio intelligendi activa; sed eadem est ratio intelligendi, per quam intellectus proprietatem rei intelligit active, et per quam rei proprietas intelligitur passive; ergo proprietates sunt diversae, et ratio est eadem; ergo materialiter differunt, et sunt formaliter idem.'

II. *Modus significandi accidentalis*: 'What comes to a part of speech after its being is complete. This mode does not give mere being to a part of speech, neither as genus nor as species' (*qui advenit parti post eius esse completum, non dans esse simpliciter parti, nec secundum genus, nec secundum speciem*; TE, p. 24).

II*a*. ... *absolutus*: 'is said to be that by means of which one syntactical unit is related not to another unit but solely to the property of the thing [it refers to]' (*dicitur ille, per quem unum constructibile non habet respectum ad alterum, sed solum ad rei proprietatem*; TE, p. 26).

II*b*. ... *respectivus*: 'that by means of which one syntactical unit is related not only to the property of the thing [it refers to] but also to another syntactical unit' (*per quem unum constructibile habet respectum non solum ad rei proprietatem, sed etiam per quem unum constrictibile habet respectum ad alterum*; TE, p. 26).

The weakness of this aspect of the speculative approach is fully apparent:[1] the modal framework adds nothing to the categories over which it is erected, and many of the definitions are circular. Nevertheless it is difficult to draw a line between these extravagances of analysis and the genuinely original and constructive approach to syntax which some of the speculative grammarians showed. The subtlety which threw fresh light on, for example, the notion of transitivity sprang from the same way of thinking as that which produced the *modus significandi essentialis subalternus*.

Roger Bacon, during a discussion of whether the gerund can act as the subject of a verb, refers to the accusative case:

Every accusative, by virtue of its accusativeness, expresses a thing under the idea of finality, not under the idea of causation. This is shown inductively, as in *video Sortem; percutio Platonem; vado ad ecclesiam;* for in these and similar expressions the accusative expresses nothing but the thing under the idea of finality. (*Summa Gramatica*, p. 92.)[2]

What is significant here is not the hypostatisation of *ratio accusativi* but that Bacon was returning to the Greek description of the accusa-

---

[1] Horne Tooke's judgment is too harsh, but there are times when one must sympathise with him. He says of Thomas's grammar (believing it to be by Duns Scotus) that it 'should be intitled, not *Grammatica Speculativa*, but—an Exemplar of the subtle art of saving appearances, and of discoursing deeply and learnedly on a subject with which we are totally unacquainted'. Tooke, 1786, 1, 8 n.

[2] 'Omnis acusativus de racione acusativi dicit rem sub racione finis, set non sub racione cause, et hoc patet inductive, ut "video Sortem", "percucio Platonem", "vado ad ecclesiam"; in hiis eciam et consimilibus acusativus nichil dicit nisi rem in racione finis.'

tive—αἰτιατική, causal, mistranslated *accusativus*—and finding even there a possible ambiguity between the active view of causation (proceeding from the cause to the effect) and the static view (regarding the effect alone, as a thing-caused). It is the latter sense he is asserting. The point is developed in the idea of transitivity as a feature of nouns.

On the modal framework which has been outlined are based several of the more detailed questions which the speculative grammarians pose for discussion. Some examples follow:

(i) Utrum modi significandi sint in voce tanquam in subiecto vel in ipsa re. (Albertus Magnus, Qu. 5.)

(ii) Utrum partes orationis distinguuntur per significatum (the thing signified) vel per modum significandi. (Albertus Magnus, Qu. 7.)[1]

(iii) As the modes of signification are the principles governing words, by means of which words are joined in a structure of parts of speech so as to express (in a correct manner) what has been purposively conceived—do all the modes of signification have their origin in the properties of things? (Boethius of Dacia.)[2]

(iv) Utrum modi significandi sint principia constructionis (Radulphus Brito.)[3]

(v) Utrum modi significandi intelligendi ei essendi sint idem. (Ibid.)

(vi) Utrum modi significandi sint in voce vel in re vel in intellectu. (Ibid.)

It is a pity that the grammar of Johannes Avicula has not yet been printed. Grabmann praises it highly as the most significant and philosophically valuable of all the speculative grammars known to him. He quotes from Johannes' statement of his intentions words which are not only of interest in themselves but suggest some reassurance for the sceptical reader:

Let no one think that I am undertaking this work through...envy, but in the cause of truth. By discussing propositions and by removing uncertainty if any of them are empty or unnecessary I hope to give a helping hand to those who do not understand about the modes of signification. I shall support my own opinions with explanations as well as with probable

---

[1] Martin of Dacia has the same question: Roos, p. 141.

[2] Quoted by Grabmann, TE, p. 82: 'Cum modi significandi dictionum sint principia, per que fit iunctura dictionum in contextu partium orationum ad exprimendum debito modo conceptum intentum, queritur, utrum omnes modi significandi debeant habere ortum a proprietatibus rerum.' The same question is put by Johannes Avicula (Grabmann, MG, I. 137).   [3] Quoted by Grabmann, TE, p. 92.

reasons. Finally I shall clarify the obscure comments (those that are at all well known) of others about the modes of signification. (Johannes Avicula, in Grabmann, MG, I. 136.)[1]

The richness of the material still to be studied is shown by the number of manuscripts of speculative grammars and commentaries given by Paul Lehmann in his expansion of Grabmann's original list. Lehmann records about ninety separate works, over thirty of which are by named authors. Before the work of the modistae can be judged as a whole and any final evaluation made of the speculative approach we need the texts not only of authors mentioned already, and the commentaries on Priscian by Peter Helias (especially), Robert Kilwardby and Jordan of Saxony, but the grammars of virtually unknown authors such as Huguccio of Pisa, Johannes Rus, Vincent the Hermit, Johannes de Tarteis, Hubertus Hoygensis, Simon of Dacia, Gosvinus de Marbais, Henricus de Crisseyo, George Nigri of Kaaden, and Erhardus Knab of Zwiefalten, together with a score of anonymous works.

RENAISSANCE SOURCES

The renaissance grammatical tradition in England can almost be summed up in Lily's Latin grammar. This is not because his work is comprehensive, but because it was from 1540 the only Latin grammar developed during the seventeenth century and many versions of 'Lily' were produced, professing to reproduce, but actually modifying, the authorised text. These modifications, however, were made from the point of view of practical schoolmasters, and affected the presentation of the material more than the grammatical categories themselves.[2]

Two grammarians are included here from among those later than Lily: the Frenchman Peter Ramus, whose Latin grammar was published in 1559, and the Spaniard Sanctius, whose *Minerva* was published in 1587, a year after the appearance of the first English grammar and therefore strictly outside present consideration. Sanctius, however, is forthrightly undogmatic about the categories

---

[1] 'Nec nos aliquis existimet hoc opus assumere ratione...livoris sed veritatis ratione modorum significandi naturam ignorantibus propellare dicentes de propositis opiniones versipellium abolendo si que sint inanes et supervacue, nostras quidem rationibus probabilibus nec non sermonibus ermineticis fulciendo, dicta ceterorum enimathica de modis significandi in per se nota finaliter resolvendo.'

[2] For the development between 1510 and 1557 of the composite work known as Lily's or the Royal Grammar see Appendix IV.

of grammar and too refreshing to exclude on a technicality. It is not until 1751, in James Harris's *Hermes*, that Sanctius is given the respect he deserves. Ramus is included because the attention he pays to formal criteria is an important but undeveloped part of the tradition.

Three contemporaries of Lily are included also: the Englishmen Robert Whittinton, whose *De octo partibus orationum opusculum* (1515?) is a similar but independent work; Thomas Linacre, whose grammars were too difficult in their full form (and perhaps too austere in any form) to be popular; and the Dutchman, Jan van Pauteren, known as Despauter, whose *Rudimenta* was first printed in 1512.

The earlier renaissance grammarians are represented by two Italians, Perottus, whose *Rudimenta Grammatices*, written in 1468, is referred to by Sandys[1] as 'the first modern Latin Grammar', and Sulpitius, who published his grammar in 1475 and is in his turn referred to by Paetow as 'the first humanistic grammarian',[2] and also by Theodore of Gaza, the authoritative form of whose Greek grammar appeared in 1495, twenty years after his death.[3]

The range of renaissance grammars is very wide, but by the time the English grammars begin to appear most of the tradition has been channelled through Lily's grammar and it is in this form that it was influential.

[1] Sandys, II. 54.   [2] Paetow, p. 44.   [3] Sandys, II. 64.

2. GRAMMAR, DIVISIONS OF GRAMMAR AND PARTS OF DISCOURSE

General and particular. At first ἡ γραμματική (τέχνη) had two principal meanings. It could mean consideration of the phonetic and other, often metaphysical, values of letters (discussed in the *Cratylus*, for example, as part of the problem of the relation between words and things). This consideration included also accentuation, and was closely related to the study of metre and music. Pronunciation and versification being naturally associated with each other, and both being part of γραμματική, it is not surprising that, as prosody, they remained part of grammar, in England, until well into the nineteenth century. Γραμματική could also mean the skill required to know your letters, to read and write. Plato describes grammar as 'the art of knowing which letters will combine with which',[1] and Aristotle says, 'Grammar considers all speech sounds'.[2] The sense of γραμματική was gradually extended to include 'the systematic study of (the Greek) language', but it did not lose its strong early association with phonetic studies and the classification of individual letters of the alphabet.

Dionysius Thrax defines grammar as: 'acquaintance (ἐμπειρία) with the general usage of poets and prose-writers'.[3] The significance of ἐμπειρία is hard to assess. Steinthal discusses the relation between ἐμπειρία and τέχνη, the more frequent term.[4] He sees three stages in the development of the terms. At first τέχνη stood for the study of particulars; it implied no attempt to generalise, and was fallible; it was more than unthinking routine (τρίβη) but less than pure, and

---

[1] *Sophist*, 253 a. [2] *Metaph.* 1003 b.
[3] Dionysius Thrax, p. 5: ἐμπειρία τῶν παρὰ ποιηταῖς τε καὶ συγγραφεῦσιν ὡς ἐπὶ τὸ πολὺ λεγομένων. Sextus Empiricus quotes this definition (*Adv. Math.* I. 57) where Bury translates ἐμπειρία as 'expertness'.
[4] Steinthal, II. 169 ff.

therefore infallible, knowledge (ἐπιστήμη). In a second stage ἐμπειρία referred to the particulars of experience considered as the result of action, and τέχνη to experience considered as the mode of action rationally examined and analysed.[1] In the third stage the upgrading of τέχνη, evident already in Plato, had made it more or less the equivalent of ἐπιστήμη, the higher levels of generalisation; whereas ἐμπειρία referred only to the comparison of particulars and to the first levels of generalisation. Steinthal summarises the change by saying that τέχνη originally meant a practical activity and then came to mean the theory and method of such an activity.

The significance of this for grammar is that the labelling of grammar as either ἐμπειρία or τέχνη represented the same kind of tension as exists today between those who restrict the term *grammar* to a purely structural treatment of language and those who wish it to include considerations of meaning. Crates distinguished between γραμματικός, who dealt with words, inflection and accentuation, and κριτικός, who dealt with the truth of ideas, the logical treatment of linguistic categories, and with rhetoric and poetry. For Crates the grammarian was merely a labourer in the service of the critic.[2]

One scholiast on Dionysius,[3] in setting out his eight divisions of any τέχνη, and therefore of grammar, makes a comment of the greatest importance. That which makes grammar necessary (αἴτιον), he says, is unintelligibility (ἀσάφεια), either of writer or speaker, in one's own language (especially when used figuratively) or in a foreign language. The aim of grammar is therefore to promote clarity (σαφήνεια). Later he adds: the material to which grammar, along with rhetoric and dialectic, is applied is ordinary (γενικόν) speech, but whereas the aim of dialectic is truth, and of rhetoric persuasion, the aim of grammar is understanding (κατάληψις τοῦ λόγου).[4] One of the defects of the traditional system is that it has obscured this close connection between grammar and language-in-use.

Dionysius describes grammar under six heads:[5]

   (i) reading aloud correctly;

   (ii) explanation of the figurative language used by poets;

   (iii) explanation of difficult words, especially those used in historical writing;

---

[1] cf. Plato, *Gorgias*, 465 b.   [2] Sextus Empiricus, *Adv. Math.* 1. 79.
[3] Bekker, p. 656.   [4] op. cit. p. 658.
[5] Dionysius Thrax, pp. 5–6.

(iv) tracing the original (inner) significance of words (ἐτυμολογίας εὕρεσις);

(v) demonstration of grammatical analogies (i.e. classifying of words which resemble each other in form);

(vi) literary criticism (κρίσις ποιημάτων).

These divisions are made in varying forms by grammarians and commentators, with much overlapping of terminology and only occasional recognition, as by Sextus Empiricus,[1] that the divisions are all interrelated. The three constant divisions are reading, explanation, and criticism.[2]

In few of the detailed Latin grammars before Priscian is there any discussion of the term *grammar*. Presumably the writers take it for granted: grammar is what they are writing about. There is certainly little variation in the broad contents of their books. The opening sections of both Sacerdos and Charisius are lost, but there is no evidence that they differed from the others. Diomedes, however, seems to have felt that his own attitude differed from that of his predecessors. He does not define grammar at the beginning of his work but gives a list of the starting-points taken by different writers of an *Ars Grammatica*. Some, he says, begin by discussing *ars* itself (Marius Victorinus, for example, described *ars* as, 'the comprehensive theory of any activity viewed as a whole and directed towards some practical purpose');[3] some start with the elements (*ab elementis*), that is, the sounds of which letters are signs; some with the letters themselves, or with words (*a voce*); many start with the cases, a few with the declension of nouns. Most, however, start with the parts of speech. He himself is going to start with discourse (*oratio*), and he proceeds to describe the formation of an articulate sound 'velut internuntius ac proditor humanae mentis'.[4] It is not reading too much into this to say that, while accepting what seems, in spite of his analysis, to have been the customary starting-point in some aspect of phonology, Diomedes is anxious to keep that part of grammar, if not the rest, in close relation with the *use* of language: a praiseworthy point of view at a time when grammar was becoming increasingly standardised and formal.

This interpretation is supported by the description given in Bk II

---

[1] Sextus Empiricus, *Adv. Math.* I. 91.   [2] Scholiast, in Bekker, pp. 659, 728 and 736.
[3] Marius Victorinus, Bk I (K. VI. 3): 'Summa rerum ratio comprehensarum atque exercitatarum ad aliquem vitae finem.'   [4] Diomedes, Bk I (K. I. 300).

of what Diomedes means by grammar.[1] It is particularly the 'applied science' (*scientia exercitata*) of reading and expounding the work of poets, historians and other writers. It is also the rules of speaking and writing correctly (*recte loquendi et scribendi ratio*). That is to say, grammar covers the whole field of literary and linguistic study. Similarly, Martianus Capella, in the first half of the fifth century A.D., makes the personification of grammar say that her responsibility used to be for *docte scribere legereque*; now it includes *erudite intelligere probareque*—'the same work as the philosophers and critics do'.[2]

Diomedes puts the widest interpretation on the term *grammar*. Servius, his older contemporary, was anxious to restrict it to linguistic studies, and Maximus Victorinus to restrict it to literature. The four constituents, for Maximus, are *lectio* (correct reading aloud); *enarratio* (explanation of the text); *emendatio* (correction of errors in the subject matter); *iudicium* (expressing approval: 'bene dictorum comprobatio').[3] Servius, like Ramus in sixteenth-century France, says that grammar must be distinguished from logic, rhetoric and philosophy. After referring to the different starting-points chosen by writers of grammars he continues:

But they are all mistaken: they have not assigned each matter to its proper sphere, but have dealt with everything together, including what concerns the orator and the philosopher. The orator can deal with the letters; no one can deal better than the philosopher with the speech-sounds; definition is for the Aristotelians. Donatus was correct, and more scholarly, in beginning with the eight parts of speech, which are the particular concern of grammarians—[quae specialiter ad grammaticos pertinent].[4]

It is difficult for us to feel that this disagreement about the nature of grammar means very much. We say, when we speak with consideration, that grammar 'is' what we choose to make it. If one writer extends the term to cover literary criticism and another restricts it to the correct use of the vernacular we find it inconvenient only if they fail to define their terms. We tend to think that we have freed ourselves from the power of words to control our thinking; certainly we suppose that we have freed ourselves from any belief that the word *grammar* means, absolutely, something towards which our understanding can approach with greater or less accuracy. But our belief is only partly justified. The struggle of the ancient and medieval world to define grammar is only one insignificant example

---

[1] Diomedes, Bk II. (K. I. 426.) [2] Martianus Capella, Bk III. § 230.
[3] Maximus Victorinus (K. VI. 188). [4] Servius, *In Artem Donati* (K. IV. 405).

27

of our permanent struggle with the problem of universals. There may seem to be no problem now over technical terms like grammar, but the fashionable nominalism of our times has not affected the schools. There rubbishy definitions of the parts of speech are often taught to young children by teachers who admit they are rubbish but profess to be bound by the syllogism, 'Grammar is important: the definitions are part of grammar; the definitions are important.' The concept 'grammar' is unanalysed. Accordingly there is still some point in demonstrating that grammar has always been a multiple, and not a simple, category, whose components have varied with the pre-occupations of the writer and his times.

Among the early Latin grammarians there were two extremes of emphasis: on the one hand the study (usually phonological) of the letters of the alphabet, and on the other the study of literature, of letters in the extended sense. Between these two lay the elementary skills of reading and writing correctly. Development did not take the form of favouring one emphasis more than another, but of making each emphasis more explicit. Cicero, writing in 46 B.C., had described grammar as, 'poetarum pertractatio, historiarum cognitio, verborum interpretatio, pronuntiandi quidam sonus'.[1] Suetonius refers to the early grammarians in Rome, contemporary with Cicero, as teaching rhetoric as well as the literary study which was their principal skill and for which they had been named *litterati* before the Greek term *grammaticus* became fashionable.[2] Quintilian, writing about twenty years before Suetonius, similarly treats grammar as the undifferentiated study of both literature and language:[3] the main work of the *grammaticus* is to teach spelling, writing and the interpretation of literature. But the *elementa grammatices* included learning the difference between consonants and vowels; the use of the letters of the alphabet; the parts of speech; the origin of proper names. Maximus Victorinus, who is later than Suetonius, also includes literary and linguistic studies in his definition of grammar, but distinguishes them sharply as on the one hand, 'Scientia interpretandi poetas atque historicos' and on the other 'recte scribendi loquendique ratio'.[4]

At least as early as the second century A.D. the term *grammar* had been associated, by one writer or another, with a far wider range of

---

[1] Cicero, *De Oratore*, I. chap. 42.
[2] Suetonius, *De Grammaticis*, IV.
[3] Quintilian, I. iv. 1–2; 6–29.
[4] Maximus Victorinus (K. VI. 188).

activities than is suggested by the surviving grammatical texts. It could include phonology, etymology (in the modern sense), the mechanics of reading, correctness of usage, clarity of interpretation, literary judgment. There seem to have been two tendencies, then as now: on the one hand to keep the study of words closely associated with the study of literature, by which alone it would be justified; on the other hand to regard the study of words as an analytical pursuit which needs no justification: words are part of human experience and therefore should be ordered and classified.

Usage. During the medieval period the range of emphasis shifts. From receiving most emphasis the study of literature now receives least; even those grammars labelled earlier as 'literary' are so only by virtue of their occasional references to authors: the study of literature disappears from their formal definitions of grammar. Increasingly writers take only one point of view, that of usage. Alcuin refers only to correctness: 'Grammar is the art of letters, and the guardian of correct speaking and writing: it is fixed by nature, reason, authority and custom.'[1] Ælfric alone emphasises the study of literature, though with a side glance at correctness: 'Grammar... makes Latin accessible, and guards it, and no man has properly grasped the meaning of Latin books unless he is master of this branch of learning.'[2]

Hugo of St Victor, writing before 1141, borrows from Isidore the conventional basis of his description but puts it in his own words. He compresses into this short description of grammar much that is characteristic of medieval thought about language. Grammar, according to Hugo, is: '...knowing how to speak correctly in accordance with what is customary among educated people. Among the subjects of instruction grammar was invented after the letters of the alphabet; it was made the source of the other subjects and prescribed rules for them.'[3]

For John of Salisbury, also, in the middle of the twelfth century, correctness is the traditional concern of grammar: 'Traditum

[1] Alcuin, col. 857: 'Grammatica est litteralis scientia, et est custos recte loquendi et scribendi; quae constat natura, ratione, auctoritate, consuetudine.'

[2] Ælfric, p. 289: 'Grammatica...geopenað and gehylt lêdensprâece, and nân man naefð lêdenbôca andgit befullon, bûton he þone craeft cunne.'

[3] Hugo, p 268: 'scientia recte loquendi secundum liberalium litterarum instituta, quae in disciplinis post litteras communes inventa caeteris regula facta est et origo'.

quidem est gramaticam esse recte scribendi recteque loquendi scientiam.' But his own prescription is a little wider. He says the grammarian must master three subjects: *ars* (school-grammar); *vitium* (by inversion, 'correctness'); *figura* (figures of speech).[1] Correctness is described by Peter Helias (in rather circular terms) at about the same time: 'Grammar is expert knowledge of how to speak and write correctly. It is the function of this branch of learning to arrange letters properly into syllables, and syllables into words, and words into discourse; to pronounce them correctly so as to avoid mistakes in vocabulary or in phraseology.'[2] A twelfth-century commentator on Priscian is even more explicit. The grammarian's purpose is, 'to teach his readers to be well able to speak grammatically, that is, to know how to fit case to case, number to number, gender to gender'.[3]

Universal grammar. This simple and long-standing conception of grammar is taken for granted by the speculative grammarians. They are less concerned with the forms of a given language than with universal grammar, that is, with language as such. Universal grammar is one of their distinctive and original notions. Peter Helias, in the middle of the twelfth century, had given the idea no support, saying there were as many grammars as there were languages,[4] but Roger Bacon, a century later, was stating emphatically, 'Grammatica una et eadem est secundum substanciam in omnibus linguis, licet accidentaliter varietur'.[5] The speculative grammarians, however, use the term *grammar* in as great a variety of senses as every writer before them (and since). One of their customary questions was whether grammar was a science (*scientia*). Albertus Magnus debates this, using Priscian, Donatus and Peter Helias as his opponents.[6] Albertus maintains that grammar is not a science. His argument is not easy to follow with certainty. He bases it on the view that scientific reasoning is determined (*ex necessariis*) and cannot be affected by

[1] John of Salisbury, *Metalogicon*, ed. C. C. J. Webb, 1929, I. chap. 18.

[2] Peter Helias, in Thurot, p. 121. 'Grammatica est scientia gnara recte scribendi et recte loquendi. Huius...artis officium est litteras congrue in sillabas, sillabas in dictiones, dictiones in orationes ordinare et easdem competenter pronunciare ad evitationem soloecismi et barbarismi.'

[3] R. W. Hunt, I. 211 n.: 'lectores instruere ut sint periti gramatice loqui, scilicet ut sciant reddere casum casui, numerum numero, genus generi'.

[4] Thurot, p. 126.   [5] Roger Bacon, *Greek Grammar*, p. 27.

[6] The question is also put by Boethius of Dacia and by Radulphus Brito.

human desires: this is not so with grammar, which proceeds 'a voluntate nostra'.[1]

Similarly Albertus discusses what is the subject matter of grammar.[2] He rejects the obvious answers—words or sentences— saying that the true subject matter is the mode of construction (*modus construendi*), contrasted with the mode of knowledge (*modus sciendi*) which is the subject matter of logic. This again illustrates both the strength and the weakness of the speculative approach: the strength that it puts a new emphasis on the importance of syntax, of the relational aspects of language; its weakness that it misleads us in seeming to introduce not just a new emphasis but new linguistic concepts.

One feature of the early speculative writers' conception of grammar is their repudiation of phonology. Roger Bacon is discussing the proper bounds of grammar. His discussion is part of an attack on a grammar purporting to be a translation of a work of Aristotle's. It cannot, Bacon argues, be the work of Aristotle—'nec alicuius sapientis'—because the author admits that he 'is exceeding the bounds of art and the limits of science by discussing, in a metaphysical way, the nature of speech and sound'. This is, Bacon says,

without doubt to go beyond the sphere of grammar...for since grammar is the first of those branches of knowledge which lead to learning, one who is learning grammar cannot understand what belongs to more advanced branches of knowledge, of which he is more ignorant than he is of grammar...To explain the production of sound and of speech belongs to natural philosophy, to metaphysics and to music...the grammarian cannot and should not push himself into such profound enquiries.

Bacon then proceeds to illustrate his argument:

A grammarian can say that there are so many letters in such and such a language; he can show how they resemble each other and how they differ in different languages. But he cannot teach why it is impossible for there to be more letters, whether vowels or consonants. We know that in every language there are only five vowels which differ in their substantial capacity for sound. But to say why there cannot be more or fewer will always be impossible for the grammarian, as such, out of the resources of his own branch of knowledge. (*Greek Grammar*, pp. 57–8.)[3]

---

[1] Albertus Magnus, Qu. 1.   [2] Albertus Magnus, Qu. 2.
[3] '...procul dubio excedit statum artis grammatice...quia cum grammatica sit prima scienciarum in via doctrine, non potest discipulus in grammatica intelligere proprietates scienciarum posteriorum que adhuc sunt ei ignociores quam grammatica...Pertinet eciam ad naturalem philosophum et ad metaphysicum et ad musicum dare causas in

A later reference of Bacon's to the work of the grammarian shows something of the difference between the early speculative grammarians, of whom Bacon is regarded as the first, and the later grammarians of the fourteenth century. Bacon is discussing whether one should say *pars est*... or *pars sunt*... Doubt arises because the thing to which *pars* refers may in fact be plural, as a part of a crowd is composed of many people. So far as the grammarian is concerned, Bacon argues, it is better to advocate *pars est*, because the principal function of the grammarian is not to consider the things to which words refer in the most fundamental sense (*significata*) but the acquired, secondary meaning of words (*consignificata*). *Pars*, that is, is to be regarded as grammatically singular whether or not it refers to a plurality of objects.[1] This linguistic conception of grammar was weakened in later speculative writers.

Communication. It is their emphasis on speech which is important in the speculative grammarians' definitions of what they mean by grammar. Grammar is not so much *scientia litterarum* as *sermocinalis scientia*.[2] Grammar is fundamentally concerned with the expression and communication of ideas, but this central position given to communication derives not from psychological thinking about language, but from logical.[3] Speculative thinking at its best can be illustrated from Martin of Dacia's definition of grammar: 'Grammatica docet exprimere mentis conceptum per sermonem congruum' which he supplements later by saying, 'finis perfectae orationis est perfectus sensus in animo auditoris'.[4] It is statements of this kind which surprise the modern reader. We do not expect a medieval grammarian to emphasise the importance of communication.

In spite of their sometimes ridiculously schematic approach the medieval grammarians made two important additions to the range

generacione soni et vocum... et ideo grammaticus non potest nec debet se intromittere de tanta sonorum et vocum profunda inquisicione... grammaticus potest declarare quod tot littere sunt in lingua tali vel tali et dare convenienciam et diversitatem earum secundum diversas linguas. Sed non potest docere causam quare non est possibile ut plures littere sint sive de vocalibus sive de consonantibus conferamus. Scimus enim quod in nulla lingua sunt nisi quinque vocales differentes in soni potestate substanciali. Sed causam dare quare non possunt esse pauciores nec plures nuncquam purus grammaticus poterit ex sue sciencie potestate.'

[1] Roger Bacon, *Summa Gramatica*, p. 32.
[2] Siger, p. 93; Boethius of Dacia, in Grabmann, TE, p. 81.
[3] Roos, p. 137. For the origin of logic in communication (disputation, dialectic) see Ernst Kapp, *Greek Foundations of Traditional Logic*, New York 1942.
[4] Roos, ibid.

of ideas associated with grammar: the study of language in general, and the logical analysis of a grammatical structure. Logical processes, like those of mathematics, were of universal validity. When a particular language was examined from a logical point of view the tendency was for its characteristics to be generalised: its grammar became Grammar, that, is universal grammar. So in the hands of a logician the study of grammar tended to include statements (not, of course, historical statements) about language in general. But as language 'in general' can be illustrated only through instances drawn from particular languages, the generalising tendency of the logicians' approach also focused attention on the structure of Latin in particular. To the already established idea of grammatical structure (syntax) the medieval grammarians added the first suggestions of the logical analysis of language. Aristotle had drawn logic out of natural language, had set it apart and had given it its own structure and laws. The medieval grammarians seem at times to be asking whether the working of these laws throws any light on the working of natural language.

Usage again. The renaissance grammarians, repudiating scholasticism, of course readmitted literature into their conception of grammar, but not in the old way. The separate disciplines of language and literature were evolving, as appears even in their formal, conventional definitions. Perottus, one of the earliest, is the only grammarian to refer directly to literature: 'ars recte loquendi recteque scribendi scriptorum et poetarum lectionibus observata'.[1] For those of the others who mention it at all the emphasis is wholly on correctness:

recte loquele recteque scripture scientia (Sulpitius, sig. a 2.)

congrue loquendi scientia: recteque scribere docens: usu, ratione, auctoritateque constans. (Whittington, sig. A ii.)

recte scribendi atque loquendi ars. (Lily, *Brev. Inst.*, 1567, sig. A ii.)

ars bene loquendi. (Ramus, Bk i. chap. 1.)

ars recte loquendi cuius finis est congruens oratio .(Sanctius, Bk i. chap. 2, 18.)

Sanctius restricts grammar so fiercely to the study of words that he makes the characteristically extreme claim that a grammarian can study the words even without knowing what they mean:

[1] Perottus, sig. a 2 verso.

For me the complete and absolute grammarian is he who can understand, in Cicero and Virgil, which word is a noun, which a verb, and other purely grammatical matters, even if he does not understand the meaning of the words. The reading of orators and poets involves various branches of learning; if your school-master is experienced in them that does not make him a grammarian, for while he is explaining astrology he is an astrologer. (Bk I. chap. 2, 15.)[1]

Sanctius agrees in making correctness the first aim in studying grammar but he differs from the others in treating usage as a lesser authority than reason. He says he is going to discuss the whole question of grammar 'ratione primum, deinde de testimoniis et usu', but he almost immediately goes on to gesture aggressively at usage:

However great the authority which a prosperous grammarian flourishes at me, unless he can support what he says by reason and by quoting examples grammar will have no particular claim on my confidence. Any custom which forces the laws of reason to cry out in protest should be done away with: it is not custom but corruption. (Bk I. chap. 2, 14.)[2]

The renaissance grammarians were right in repudiating the excesses of a logical and *a priori* approach to grammar; they were right in returning to the actual behaviour of words. What they lacked (and it is the great merit of Sanctius that he realised this) was a robustly empirical outlook which would enable them to ask how best to describe the observed behaviour of words. Sanctius is continually questioning the usefulness of the traditional categories: to what features of Latin do they in fact correspond? He demands evidence, in the name not of logic but of reason, that is, of a genuinely scientific approach to language. *Minerva* is one of the most invigorating grammatical works ever written, and tempts one to join in the trivial game of credits and label Sanctius 'the first modern grammarian'.

---

[1] 'Mihi perfectus absolutusque Grammaticus est ille, qui in Ciceronis, vel Virgilii libris intelligit, quae dictio sit Nomen, quae Verbum, & caetera, quae ad solam Grammaticam spectant, etiamsi sensum verborum non intelligat: est enim oratorum & poetarum lectio variis artibus referta, quas si magister iste callet, iam non grammaticus dicendus est; sed dum explanat Astrologiam, astrologus'.

[2] 'Quantacunque auctoritate mihi Grammaticus polleat, nisi ratione propositisque exemplis, quod dixerit, confirmaverit, nullam in re praesertim grammatica fidem faciet... extirpanda est consuetudo, quae legem habeat reclamantem, quae potius corruptela vocanda est.'

THE PARTS OF GRAMMAR

During the medieval period, as has been already illustrated, the reference of the term *grammar* was increasingly restricted to linguistic rather than literary studies. This led to a more formal treatment of the linguistic 'parts of grammar', which became relatively fixed categories enumerated by most grammarians of Latin or English. Until the twelfth century, however, the earlier, undifferentiated sense of the term prevailed: literary and linguistic studies were considered part of the same discipline.

Isidore, early in the seventh century, Alcuin in the eighth, Ælfric at the end of the tenth and Hugo of St Victor early in the twelfth, all enumerate what they call the divisions of grammar. This is Isidore's list:

the eight parts of speech	unusual words (*glossae*)
word (*vox articulata*)	shades of meaning (*differentiae*)
letter	barbarism
syllable	solecism
metrical foot	errors (*vitia*)
accentuation	irregularities (*metaplasmi*)
punctuation (*positura*)	grammatical figures (*schemata*)
critical marks and abbreviations	rhetorical figures (*tropi*)
(*notae*)	prose literature
spelling	metrical literature
analogy	fiction (*fabulae*)
etymology	history

(Isidore, I, 5.)

Alcuin and Ælfric, whose lists are identical, add *oratio* (discourse or sentence), *dictio* (*word* as a semantic unit, whereas *vox* is a phonetic unit) and *definitiones*.[1] Hugo's list of twenty-two parts is also based on Isidore. He comments, with justice, 'de numero partium grammaticae artis alii vel alii ut libuit vel visum est diffinierunt'.[2] Such a hotch-potch, by including a little of everything, tells us nothing about grammar. It is just an itemisation of the literary and linguistic studies which earlier writers mentioned in their descriptions of grammar.

The first writer explicitly to make purely linguistic divisions of grammar seems to have been Peter Helias (*c.* 1150): he certainly claims to be naming them for the first time: 'Partes huius artis sunt

---

[1] Alcuin, col. 858; Ælfric, p. 289. [2] Hugo of St Victor, p. 268.

quatuor: quarum nomina quoniam non habemus, dicatur prima pars scientia de litteris, secunda de sillabis, tertia de dictionibus, quarta de oratione'.[1] This fourfold division into elements was still current in English grammars during the eighteenth century. Thurot says it is derived from Priscian,[2] but this is true only in the sense that Priscian covers these topics in this order. He does not single them out from other topics as being the primary divisions of grammar. The fourfold division frequently appears as a threefold one, when letters and syllables are taken together.

More frequently the divisions are made not in terms of elements but of processes:

Orthographia includes consideration of the letters of the alphabet, syllables and spelling.

Etymologia includes the parts of speech and other classifications of words.

Oratio or *Diasynthetica* or *Sintasis*[3] includes discourse, the sentence and syntax.

Prosodia covers pronunciation.

It is not clear when this long-lasting classification first appeared. Roos puts it at the beginning of the thirteenth century but quotes no examples.[4] In the medieval period, as later, it took many forms. Orthography seems to have been the most elastic term. Eberhard made a threefold division into Orthography, Prosody and Syntax, where orthography includes the parts of speech,[5] and Thurot quotes a gloss which makes a division into two, orthography and syntax only.[6] The *Doctrinale* of Alexander of Villedieu, on the other hand, composed in twelve sections, was by the beginning of the fourteenth century arranged in most manuscripts into three parts, Etymology, Syntax and a mixture of prosodic and rhetorical categories.[7] The speculative grammarians seem to have kept to a strictly twofold division into Etymology and Syntax, though neither Thomas nor Siger uses the former term.

Those of the early renaissance grammarians who make these divisions in grammar—Perottus, Sulpitius, Despauter and Whittinton—call them Letter, Syllable, Word and Expression or Discourse (*oratio*). Despauter's examples of the four categories are (i) *a*,

---

[1] Thurot, p. 132.
[2] Thurot, p. 131; Funke, *Frühzeit*, p. 42, makes the same attribution, but vaguely.
[3] Roos, p. 138.   [4] ibid.   [5] Eberhard, Bk iii. chap. 7. 1. 62.
[6] Thurot, p. 132.   [7] Reichling, p. lxxi.

Grammar, divisions of grammar, etc.

(ii) *pa*, (iii) *pater*, (iv) *pater noster*.[1] Lily calls them Orthography, Etymology, Syntax and Prosody, and this was the standard arrangement until Ramus, insisting that orthography and prosody were categories of a different kind, made only a twofold division into Etymology and Syntax. Sanctius rejects all divisions: Syntax is what the whole of grammar is directed to (*'finis Grammaticae'*) and therefore cannot be part of it; it is not easy to make any divisions in grammar, so it is best to make none.[2] The significance of these fluctuations is that those grammarians who were strongly influenced by logic—especially the speculative grammarians and Ramus—made one essential distinction: between words themselves and words in combination. Other grammarians, wishing also to emphasise phonological, rhetorical or literary features, made their divisions accordingly.

Literary and linguistic. It can be seen within the tradition, and more clearly within the development of the English grammars, how the term *grammar*, originally (however it was defined) the name of a group of related literary and linguistic studies, was increasingly restricted in its application, but never entirely confined, to a system of categories used in linguistic analysis. Nevertheless it carried, and still carries, much of its original connotation: it is felt to be a term with a far wider meaning than that which a considered definition would propose or an elementary textbook illustrate. *Grammar*, in fact, is thought of in some contexts as applying solely to the analysis of linguistic structure, in others to wider questions of usage, tone and style. It is perhaps the vaguest term in the schoolmaster's, if not the scholar's, vocabulary. This condition leads to confused teaching.

The tradition illustrates two truths. On the one hand it is apparent not only that literary and linguistic studies cannot be divorced from each other, but that they are inseparable from rhetoric, and closely related to logic. On the other hand, these disciplines need a life of their own: grammar, logic and literary criticism are concerned with different aspects of the use of language. These are complementary, not contradictory truths, but their reconciliation was not achieved within the tradition.[3] The unity of grammar, logic and rhetoric was

---

[1] Despauter, fol. 3.   [2] Sanctius, Bk I. chap. 2. 17–18.

[3] R. R. Bolgar (*The Classical Heritage and its Beneficiaries*, Cambridge, 1958, pp. 39–40) expresses surprise that the attention paid to 'the writer's art' by Aristotle, Cicero, "Long-

implicit in the trivium, but could not be more fully achieved because the trivium was conceived within the setting of a foreign language. This meant that grammar was not the study of one's own language, but of Latin; it was not linguistic analysis, but linguistic description and drill.

The unifying concept, which relates grammar, rhetoric and logic without destroying their autonomy, is *structure*. Each is concerned with patterns, with structures, built on relations of different kinds, and each kind of structure requires analysis of a different kind. These different kinds of analysis can reinforce each other only if they are conducted in a language known so well that subtleties of meaning, emphasis, word-order and sentence-pattern can be discussed without difficulty. That language can only be the mother tongue. One of the great challenges to English studies at the present time is to achieve that mutually supporting partnership between grammatical, logical and literary analysis. One of the lessons of the tradition is that such an alliance is desirable and, however gropingly, long-sought.

THE PARTS OF DISCOURSE

It was only with the decline of rhetoric and logic as formal teaching subjects that categories such as question, sentence and clause came to have a distinctive connection with grammar. Even now most attempts to define a sentence fail because they are misconceived: they do not separate rhetorical criteria (e.g. the intentions of the speaker) from logical (e.g. predication) and grammatical criteria (e.g. the presence of a finite verb). This part of the tradition, therefore, can be only thinly represented from purely grammatical sources.

Sentence. Statement (λόγος) is discussed by Plato[1] in terms which do not distinguish it from the sentence, and by the author of chapter 20 of the *Poetics* in terms which do not distinguish it from the phrase. It is widely used by Aristotle as a logical term, but not as a grammatical one, as are also *affirmation* (κατάφασις) and *negation* (ἀπόφασις), *wish* (εὐχωλή), *question* (ἐρώτησις) and *command*

inus" and Dionysius of Halicarnassus 'remained without influence, if not wholly unknown, until the sixteenth century... In no other field was Europe so tardy about taking the best that the past had to offer.'
[1] Plato, *Sophist*, 262.

Grammar, divisions of grammar, etc.

(ἐντολή). According to Diogenes Laertius[1] these categories were first distinguished by Protagoras, who included also *answer* (ἀπόκρισις), a purely rhetorical and not a grammatical category. They are referred to by Aristotle as τὰ σχήματα τῆς λέξεως—the modes of discourse.[2] Their formal and rhetorical aspects were not yet distinguished, and it seems often to be extremely difficult to say how these terms are to be interpreted. It is easy to make them too precise.

Plato speaks of sentences (λόγοι) being composed of nouns and verbs,[3] and a sentence is distinguished by Aristotle from a statement (proposition), which is alone capable of truth or falsehood, but not from the word or phrase.[4] Elsewhere Aristotle distinguishes simple from composite speech. His examples of the former are, in fact, single words, and his examples of the latter sentences, but he does not make his distinction explicit in these terms. He is discussing the logical, and not what we would now consider the grammatical aspect of predication.[5] In the reference of Plato and Aristotle to language λόγος can seldom be more precisely rendered than by 'form of speech'. The concepts of phrase and sentence are formed, but have yet to be separated from the concept of discourse, which can also be expressed by λόγος.

Dionysius Thrax gives a formal definition of λόγος, but here also it is not clear that he means by it only what we mean by the sentence. λόγος certainly includes the sentence, but it seems also to include more. It is not yet possible to say that the category of sentence is unambiguously formed: we have rather something which corresponds to 'small unit of discourse'. Dionysius' definition runs: 'A combination of words, in prose [or metre] expressing a complete thought' (πεзῆς λέξεως σύνθεσις διάνοιαν αὐτοτελῆ δηλοῦσα).[6] Sir Alan Gardiner questions the translation of αὐτοτελῆ as 'complete'. He prefers 'self-sufficient', and blames Priscian's translation *perfectum* for introducing into linguistic theory a misleading conception of the sentence.[7] The ambiguity of 'complete' has certainly caused much trouble. It is usually not made clear whether an expression is to be regarded as complete if it contains all the words it could contain, so that the cry 'Fire!' would be incomplete because it could be

---

[1] Diogenes Laertius, IX, 54. [2] Aristotle, *Poetics*, 1456 b.
[3] Plato, *Crat.* 431 b. [4] Aristotle, *Int.* 17 a. [5] Aristotle, *Cat.* 1 a.
[6] Dionysius Thrax, p. 22. Several MSS. read:'…πεзῆς τε καὶ ἐμμέτρου…'.
[7] A. H. Gardiner, *The Theory of Speech and Language*, 2nd edn, Oxford, 1951, p. 99.

expressed, 'There is a fire in my house', or if it satisfies the speaker, who stops speaking because he does not wish to say anything more. By the latter criterion 'Fire!' would be complete. 'Self-sufficient' removes the ambiguity in this instance because it could indicate only the latter alternative, but it remains ambiguous when applied to an expression like 'the biggest aspidistra in the world' which may be said to have a measure of both completeness and self-sufficiency.

A commentator on Dionysius gives a version of his definition in which the idea of completeness is even more fully brought out: 'A combination of words, giving full expression—no more and no less— to a complete thought' (λέξεων σύνθεσις, διάνοιαν αὐτοτελῆ κατὰ σύμμετρον περιγραφὴν ἀπαρτίζουσα).[1]

Dionysius makes a distinction between λέξις and λόγος, between words as minimum units of discourse and words combined as discourse, which is almost the same as the Stoic distinction between the same two terms. The Stoics distinguished between nonsense, mere articulation of meaningless words, and discourse: 'λέξις differs from λόγος in that λόγος is always meaningful but λέξις includes what does not make sense' (λέξις δὲ λόγου διαφέρει, ὅτι λόγος ἀεὶ σημαντικός ἐστι, λέξις δὲ καὶ ἄσημος).[2] The two points of view are together equivalent to the important distinction between words in use and words out of a context.

Priscian clearly uses three categories: (i) discourse (*oratio*); (ii) complete discourse (*oratio perfecta* or *oratio plena*); (iii) expression of opinion, statement (*sententia*). What is not clear is how far any of these is equivalent to our own (still indeterminate) concept of the sentence.

Priscian's definition of *oratio* is: 'a proper arrangement of words, expressing fully what the speaker wants to say' (ordinatio dictionum congrua, sententiam perfectam demonstrans).[3] He continues:

But this definition of *oratio* is in purely general terms:. . .a book of rhetoric is called *oratio*, and the term is often used to refer even to a single word, such as imperatives, and to answers which are complete in one word. When, for example, I say 'What is the greatest good in life?' and someone replies 'honesty', I say he has replied 'bona oratione'.

In Bk xvii Priscian is comparing the variations of order which are possible not only among letters (*Teucer and Teucre*) and syllables

---

[1] Steinthal, ii. 181.   [2] Diogenes Laertius, vii. 57.
[3] Priscian, Bk ii. 15 (K. ii. 53).

(*displicina* and *disciplina*), but among words (*publica res* and *res publica*) and among *orationes*, as *nutrivit filios ac peperit* and *peperit ac nutrivit*.[1]

In this last passage *oratio* is, as it happens, equivalent to our loose use of *sentence*, but the preceding quotation shows that, in so far as it 'plenam ostendit sententiam', it could apply to a paragraph as well as to a sentence. All we can say is that *oratio*, like λόγος, is used either for discourse in general or for a quantity of discourse which has some measure of wholeness. It is not clear how far *congrua* means 'harmonious' and how far it means 'agreeing grammatically'. The latter sense Priscian usually expresses by *oratio perfecta*.[2]

Quintilian, discussing the meaning of *sententia*, in his day, said that in rhetoric it meant 'epigram or maxim' (*lumen*) and he quotes a list of rhetorical elements which includes, and implies a difference between, *sententia, membrum* and *articulus*—that is, sentence, clause and one-word sentence, regarded, however, as rhetorical and not as grammatical units.[3] Priscian uses *sententia* similarly as a rhetorical term, but his discussion of it is conducted partly in grammatical terms, and illustrates one step in the development of *sententia* into sentence, for in describing how *usus* differs from *sententia* he says that *sententia* is always a statement (*indicative profertur*) whereas *usus* often takes the form of a question.[4]

With Priscian the term *sententia* and the concept of 'uttering a complete thought', which is implicit in *oratio perfecta*, are very closely connected.

During the medieval period *oratio* continues to cover both sentence and unit of discourse. Siger, for example, uses *oratio* for what is expressed by *sermo compositus* and discussed by Priscian in his two books on syntax.[5] The opening words of Roger Bacon's *Summa Gramatica* are 'oracio gramatica aut sit mediante verbo prime persone vel secunde vel tercie', where both senses of *oratio* are needed,[6] and in two consecutive paragraphs later in the work he uses *oratio* to indicate the sentence *lupus est in fabula* and the phrase *idem sibi*.[7] Ries quotes Peter Helias, who is using *perfecta oratio* as the equivalent of our 'sentence', in a definition which is still current:

[1] K. III. 114.　　　　　　　　　[2] e.g. Bk XVII. 3 (K. III. 108).
[3] Quintilian, VIII. v.
[4] Priscian, *Praeexercitamina*, § 8 (K. III. 432).
[5] Wallerand, p. 93.　　　　　　[6] Bacon, *Summa Gramatica*, p. 1.
[7] ibid. p. 161.

In omni perfecta oratione dicitur aliquid et de aliquo. Fuit igitur repertum nomen ad discernendum, de quo est sermo, verbum vero ad discernendum, quid dicitur de eo.[1]

The idea of completeness, on the other hand, is very fully discussed, especially by Bacon.[2] He analyses it in three different ways, according to three pairs of distinctions: (i) between what is expressed and what is understood (*perfecta quoad vocem vel intellectum*); (ii) between what is comprehended by the mind (*intellectum*) and what is perceived by the senses (*sensum*); (iii) between first and second intellection (*quantum ad intellectum primum vel secundum*). First intellection is our understanding of the thing-signified (*significatum*), that is, the formation and expression of concepts; secondary intellection is our understanding of concepts in relation to each other, especially by means of logical words (*consignificativa*) such as *all*, and by means of the modes of signification. Bacon assumes that his reader is completely familiar with his terminology (though even he seems uncertain which should be called first and which second intellection). His discussion is lengthy, complex and compressed.

Of the renaissance grammarians considered here only Perottus,[3] Whittinton[4] and Despauter[5] define *oratio*, and then only by repeating Priscian. But whereas Priscian had made *congrua* (correct or harmonious) apply to the arrangement of the words (*ordinatio*),[6] Perottus and Whittinton read *congruam*, making it apply to the sense of the words (*sententiam*). Despauter gives only the first part of Priscian's definition—*dictionum congrua ordinatio*—and shows by his example—'*ut homo albus*'—that it is as 'expression' rather than 'sentence' that *oratio* must be understood.

Period (περίοδος). This is always a term of rhetoric. Aristotle describes it as an expression (λέξις) 'having a beginning and end in itself and a magnitude that can be easily grasped'.[7] It is defined, that is, not so much by its form as by the speaker's intuitive feeling for a manageable unit of words. The period refers to an expression as if it were a journey in which it is important only to arrive, provided one has travelled stylishly, visiting the best places en route, even if a detour

---

[1] Peter Helias, quoted by Ries, *Was ist ein Satz*, 2nd edn, 1931, from Golling, Intro. to Landgraf, *Hist gram. Lat. Sprache*, 1903, III. 30.

[2] Bacon, op. cit. pp. 17–27.
[3] Perottus, sig. a 3 verso.
[4] Whittinton, sig. A ii,
[5] Despauter, fol. 3 verso.
[6] See above, p. 40.
[7] Aristotle, *Rhet.* 1409 a (transl. Freese).

is needed. The sentence is concerned at least as much with the route as with the fact of arrival, and assumes, on the whole, that the journey will be direct and economical. Steinthal quotes a definition by Herodian,[1] a son of Apollonius Dyscolus: a period is 'an expression made from an easily encompassed arrangement of clauses, completing an independent thought'—λόγος ἐν εὐπεριγράφῳ συνθέσει κώλων αὐτοτελῆ διάνοιαν ἀποτελῶν. According to Steinthal this definition was often used for the sentence also, with λέξεων substituted for κώλων, a term not fully understood. This would again indicate that the sentence was not yet a fully defined category.

Clause. This was a rhetorical term at first. Aristotle uses κῶλον for a part of a period, with the implication that it is not to be an arbitrary part, but one with its own unity.[2] The Latin term is *membrum*,[3] but it seems to have been little used by the grammarians. It does not appear in Priscian. The category appears most explicitly in Peter of Spain's logic. His fourth type of restriction, *per implicitationem*, corresponds exactly with the relative clause. Mullally translates *implicatio* as 'subordinate clause', but this is too wide. Peter's account of restriction shows that he regards adjective and adjectival clause as logically equivalent but grammatically distinct. The first type of restriction is *per nomen*, as in *homo albus*;[4] the fourth type, *per implicationem*, as in *homo qui est albus*. Of the latter Peter says:

Omnis implicatio immediate coniuncta termino communi restringit ipsum sicut suum adiectivum, ut cum dicitur: 'Homo, qui est albus, currit', iste terminus 'homo' restringitur ad albos per hanc implicationem, scilicet 'qui est albus'.[5]

It is clear also that *implicatio* refers to a type of expression and not to a logical process, for Peter later gives a rule governing cases:

quotienscunque signum universale et implicatio ponuntur in eadem locutione...ut cum dicitur: 'omnis homo currit qui est albus.'[6]

---

[1] Steinthal, II. 347, quoting Walz, *Rhet. graec.* VIII. 592.
[2] Aristotle, *Rhet.* 1409 b.
[3] Cicero, *Orator ad Brutum*, ed. C. F. A. Nobbe, Leipzig 1869, 62, 211: he refers to units 'quae nescio cur, quum Graeci κόμματα et κῶλα nominent, nos non recte incisa et membra dicamus'.
[4] Peter of Spain, *Summulae Logicales*, Tractatus VII, ed. and transl. J. P. Mullally, Notre Dame, Indiana 1945, p. 46.
[5] Peter of Spain, op. cit. p. 50.
[6] ibid.

Roger Bacon uses *clausula*, in his treatment of syllepsis and zeugma, to refer to expressions which are, in fact, sentences;[1] but he does not define the term and it is not certain how narrowly he is using it. By the time of Lily's grammar *clausula* certainly refers to parts of sentences, but there is no certain evidence that it means more than that. The section *De Sententiarum Punctis* is also *de clausularum distinctionibus*, but the examples after which punctuation is required include words, phrases and sentences.[2] The clause has no distinctive status.

Phrase is a category which cannot be said to exist, in grammar, until modern times. Aristotle sometimes touches on the question of what it is that gives unity to an expression which is not a statement, and in one place he seems to distinguish between noun and what we should call noun-phrase (λόγος ὀνοματωδῆς).[3] This is however, merely another instance of the variable term λόγος in the general sense *expression*: it does not indicate the modern distinction between phrase and clause.

In Greek, Latin and English *phrase* has, until recently, kept close to its etymological sense of 'way of speaking', and has thus been a stylistic rather than a grammatical term. What we understand as a phrase was covered by the terms *oratio* or *dictio*.[4]

Word (λόγος, ἔπος): the definition of a word as a minimal meaningful unit is suggested by Aristotle's description of the noun and the verb (the only units he recognised as words in any full sense): both (*a*) 'have meaning' (φωνὴ σημαντική) and (*b*) 'are composed of parts which by themselves have no meaning' (ἧς μηδεν μέρος ἐττὶ σημαντικὸν κεχωρισμένον).[5] Dionysius defines the word as 'the smallest unit of discourse' (μέρος ἐλάχιστον τοῦ κατα σύνταξιν λόγου).[6] One scholiast objects that this definition applies also to letters and speech-sounds (στοιχεῖα) and should read 'the smallest unit of meaning (διανοιάς)'.[7] Apollonius has a similar definition but without any reference to the word being a *minimim* unit: μέρος... τοῦ κατα σύνταξιν αὐτοτελοῦς λόγου.[8] Only Varro and Priscian,

---

[1] Roger Bacon, *Summa Gramatica*, pp. 64, 71, 73.
[2] Lily, *Brev. Instit.*, 1567, sig. A iv.   [3] Aristotle, *Anal. Post.* 93 b.
[4] Cf. R. Bacon, *Greek Grammar*, p. 28: 'diccio non significat lexin in greco sed phrasin, ut ait Boecius'. Later grammarians did not agree with him.
[5] Aristotle, *Int.*, 16 a, b.   [6] Dionysius Thrax, p. 22.
[7] Bekker, *Anecdota Graeca*, p. 836.   [8] Apollonius Dyscolus, *Synt.*, IV, 2.

who here translates Dionysius, keep this important idea of the word
(*verbum; dictio; locutio*) as a *minimum* unit: Varro defines it as: ' . . .ora-
tionis vocalis partem quae sit indivisa et minima',[1] and Priscian as
' . . .pars minima orationis constructae'.[2] Charisius says merely that a
word is a finite expression (*locutio finita*) with a definite meaning.[3]
Diomedes repeats this and gives as an alternative definition: 'Words
are articulate sounds with some meaning, out of which speech is
constructed and into which it is resolved.'[4]

Of the medieval grammarians only the speculative writers have
anything to add to the category. Alcuin underlines Priscian's
definition, which he repeats, by adding to it unhelpfully ' . . .ple-
numque sensum habentis'.[5] Unhelpfully because a word does not,
presumably, according to Priscian's definition, cease to be a word if
the expression in which it occurs does not make *complete* sense
(however that is defined).

The speculative grammarians take up Priscian's formulation of the
Stoic distinction between merely organic (inarticulate) sounds and
speech (articulate) sounds. Martin of Dacia keeps to the twofold
distinction between *dictio* and *vox*: 'Dictio est vox habens rationem,
significandi aliquid ut haec dictio "homo". Dicit enim mihi aliquid
compositum ex voce significante et re significata.'[6] Siger[7] and
Thomas of Erfurt base their analyses on a threefold distinction
between *vox*, the mere speech-sound; *dictio*, the word regarded as a
meaningful speech-sound; *pars*, the word regarded as a syntactical
unit.

Thomas explains, in strikingly 'modern' language, why the
grammarian, as such, is not concerned with *vox*:

You must understand that a word, regarded merely as a sound, is no
concern of the grammarian; as a sign, it is his concern. Grammar deals
with signs of things, and the spoken word is considered as a sign before other
signs of things because it is the most easily used of them all. But functioning
as a sign is an accident of the word, and the grammarian, therefore, when
he is discussing the word is discussing it *per accidens*. (TE, p. 21.)[8]

---

[1] Varro, x. 77.   [2] Priscian, II. 14 (K. II. 53).
[3] Charisius, I. 6 (K. I. 16).
[4] Diomedes, II (K. I. 436): ' Dictio est vox articulata cum aliqua significatione ex qua instruitur oratio et in quam resolvitur.'
[5] Alcuin, col. 858.   [6] Roos, p. 143.
[7] Siger, p. 95.
[8] 'Sciendum est, quod vox, inquantum vox, non consideratur a Grammatico, sed inquantum signum, quia Grammatica est de signis rerum; et quia vox est habilissimum

What distinguishes *vox* as *dictio* and as *pars* he explains as follows:

When the mind imposes an articulate sound (*vox*) [on a thing] so as to make it directly or indirectly meaningful it gives the sound a double power: the power of signifying directly (called *significatio*) by means of which the articulate sound is made a sign, something which signifies, and thus, considered formally, a word (*dictio*).

The second power is that of signifying indirectly, which is called the active mode of signification, by means of which the significant articulate sound is made a secondary sign, something which signifies indirectly and is thus, considered formally, a part of speech (*pars*). For a part of speech is a part of speech in itself because of this power of indirect signification...as if by means of some formal principle. But a part of speech is a part of speech in its relation to other parts by means of the same active power of signifying indirectly, but as if by an inherent efficient principle. (TE, pp. 8–10.)[1]

Thomas is referring, presumably, to a feature of language which is more easily recognisable in English than in Latin: that the syntactical function of a word is part of its meaning. In *He is wearing a green jacket* the word *green* is *dictio* in so far as it 'means' the colour and *pars* in so far as it attributes the colour to the jacket.

Apart from Ramus, the renaissance grammarians, if they give any attention to the word, repeat Priscian, as do Perottus, Sulpitius, Despauter and Whittinton. Lily does not discuss it. Ramus alone ignores the structural criterion; he says merely, 'Vox est nota qua unumquodque vocatur',[2] which is derived more from the logicians than from Priscian.

Sulpitius and Whittinton define *pars orationis* in terms which recall the speculative grammarians' definition of *dictio*: 'Pars orationis est vox indicans mentis conceptum.'[3] It would seem that the structural and

signum inter alia signa, ideo vox inquantum signum prius consideratur a Grammatico, quam alia signa rerum. Sed quia esse signum accidit voci, ideo Grammaticus considerans vocem, considerat eam per accidens.'
[1] 'Cum intellectus vocem ad significandum, et consignificandum imponit, duplicem ei rationem tribuit, scilicet, rationem significandi, quae vocatur significatio, per quam efficitur signum, vel significans; et sic formaliter est dictio; et rationem consignificandi, quae vocatur modus significandi activus, per quam vox significans fit consignum, vel consignificans; et sic formaliter est pars orationis; ita quod pars est pars secundum se per hanc rationem consignificandi...tanquam per principium formale; sed est pars relata ad aliam per eamdem rationem consignificandi activam, tanquam per principium efficiens intrinsecum.'
[2] Ramus, Bk I, chap. I.
[3] Sulpitius, sig. a 2 verso; Whittinton, sig. A ii verso.

syntactic criteria which distinguished *pars* from *dictio* have been lost sight of. The renaissance grammarians made no use of the two most important ideas about the word which were available to them: Dionysius Thrax's description of it as a minimum unit of discourse, and the speculative grammarians' distinction between semantic and syntactic units.

3. PARTS OF SPEECH

The beginning of system. In chapter 20 of the *Poetics* occurs the expression τὰ μέρη τῆς λέξεως, which is sometimes taken as equivalent to our 'parts of speech', but the context shows that it is an altogether wider category, including phonetic elements and inflexions. The logical and rhetorical classification of words had by then distinguished the categories noun and verb, but no grammatical classification had been made.

The early Stoic classification was into: noun, verb, article (including the pronoun) and conjunctive particle (broadly, the conjunction and preposition treated as a single category). Diogenes Babylonius and the later Stoics treated common nouns and proper nouns as separate parts of speech, and Antipater of Tarsus is said to have added a sixth, μέσοτης;[1] but it is not certain to what this term refers. It is probably the adverb.

Dionysius classifies words as noun, verb, participle, article, pronoun, preposition, adverb and conjunction.[2] This is the first appearance of a systematic classification, very close to the one we still use.

A century after Dionysius, Varro proposed a fourfold classification which was unique in using only formal criteria:

   (i)   words which have cases (nouns)
   (ii) words which have tenses (verbs)
  (iii) words which have both cases and tenses (participles)
  (iv) words which have neither (all other words)

This classification he relates, but not clearly, to a notional classification into words which:

   (i)   name (*appellandi*)
   (ii) say (*dicendi*)
  (iii) join (*iungendi*—the relation of this group to participles is particularly obscure)
  (iv) support (*adminiculandi*).[3]

---

[1] Diogenes Laertius, VII. 57; Steinthal, I. 298; P. B. R. Forbes in OCD, s.v. *Grammar*, §§ 6 and 7.   [2] Dionysius Thrax, p. 23.   [3] Varro, VIII. 44.

This classification seems to have found little, if any, support. The Latin grammarians of the period all adopt Dionysius' categories, except that they separate the interjection—hesitantly—from the adverb, within which the Greeks had classified it, and exclude the article.

Quintilian refers shortly to other systems of parts of speech which he says have been put forward.[1] These involve treating as distinct parts of speech not only the interjection but also (*a*) the common noun; (*b*) words like *eheu*, which Quintilian says are classed as *adseveratio*; (*c*) words like *fasciatim*—'in bundles'—which form a class of words, called *tractio*, indicating how things are handled. He does not himself support these last two suggestions.

Donatus emphasises the logician's view that the noun and verb are the principal parts of speech. He also says that many people think there are more, and many think there are fewer, than eight parts.[2] Priscian discusses the parts of speech at greater length. He gives the same primacy to the noun and verb '*secundum dialecticos*' and introduces[3] the term *syncategoremata* (which he latinises as *consignificantia*) for all words which do not by themselves make a complete utterance, that is all words other than noun and verb. The distinctive position assigned to the noun and verb is one of the few matters of joint interest about which grammar and logic did not quarrel.

Grammarians, in Latin and English, were clearer about the primacy of the noun and verb than about the correlative category of syncategoremata. Priscian had introduced the category in negative terms: 'According to the dialecticians, therefore, there are two parts of speech, noun and verb, because these make complete sense when alone as well as when they are joined together. The other parts of speech they used to call "syncategoremata", that is words which have meaning only when joined with other words.'[4] Later, however, Priscian makes it much clearer that he is not really accepting the logicians' view that there are only two parts of speech and that all except the noun and verb are just *adminicula vel iuncturae*. He is quite explicit: 'What else is a part of speech but a word indicating a

---

[1] Quintilian, I. chap. 4.   [2] Donatus, *Ars Grammatica*, II. I (K. IV. 372).

[3] The term is not in Aristotle (Roos, p. 110) but Priscian seems to be adopting it from someone. Apollonius uses συγκαταγορέω for 'to predicate jointly' (Liddell and Scott, s.v.).

[4] Priscian, II. 15 (K. II. 54): 'Partes igitur orationis sunt secundum dialecticos duae, nomen et verbum, quia hae solae etiam per se conjunctae plenam faciunt orationem, alias autem partes "syncategoremata", hoc est consignificantia appellabant.'

concept, that is a thought? Accordingly, any sound made by the voice, which means something and can be written down, ought rightly to be called a part of speech.'[1]

In his discussion of words like *quis, qui, qualis*, Priscian had already made it clear that he was rejecting not only logical but also purely formal criteria in establishing parts of speech. Because such words express substance, however indefinitely, and quality, however generally, 'they should therefore be called nouns, although some of them have the declension of pronouns. For it is not declension, but the function and meaning of every single part of speech, which is to be considered.'[2] This is a particular application of the principle he previously laid down: 'The parts of speech cannot be distinguished from each other unless we have regard to their individual capacities for expressing meaning.'[3] Meaning, not form, is to be the criterion.

Over syncategoremata Peter of Spain followed Priscian closely,[4] but it was not till the term was given a more narrowly logical interpretation that it was defined positively. Roos quotes Thomas Aquinas: 'A word is said to be syncategorematic when it attaches to the subject the quantifying of the predicate, as the words *all* or *no*, and likewise. . .*alone*, because they exclude everything else to which reference might be made from having a place in the predicate.'[5] A similar definition is given by William of Sherwood, but he makes explicit the feature of syncategoremata which was seized on by later grammarians, who had perhaps never heard of the category: '*semper*. . .*cum alio iungitur in sermone*'.[6] It was as 'consignificatives' that syncategoremata entered the English grammars.

Priscian also refers to other systems of nine, ten or eleven parts of speech, in which the common noun, the infinitive forms of the verb, and pronouns which cannot be used with articles are separately or together made distinct parts of speech.[7]

---

[1] Priscian, XI. 7 (K. II. 552): 'Quid enim est aliud pars orationis nisi vox indicans mentis conceptum, id est cogitationem? Quaecumque igitur vox literata profertur significans aliquid, iure pars orationis est dicenda.'

[2] Priscian, II. 19 (K. II. 55): 'Nomina sunt igitur dicenda, quamvis declinationem pronominum habeant quaedam ex eis. Non enim declinatio, sed vis et significatio uniuscuiusque partis est contemplanda.'

[3] Priscian, II. 17 (ibid.): 'Non aliter possunt discerni a se partes orationis nisi uniuscuiusque proprietates significationum attendamus.'

[4] Peter of Spain, ed. Bochenski, I. 5 (quoted by Roos, p. 110).

[5] Thomas Aquinas, I. 31. 3 c (quoted by Roos, p. 110).

[6] William of Sherwood, *Syncategoremata*, ed. J. R. O'Donnell, *Med. Stud.*, III. 1941. 48.

[7] Priscian, II. 16 (K. II. 54).

Medieval systems. In the medieval period the classification of Donatus and Priscian was accepted without question, though Smaragdus felt it necessary to reinforce their authority: after repeating what Donatus says about the varying opinions over the number of the parts of speech Smaragdus adds: 'The whole church, however, holds that there are only eight, and I have no doubt that this view is divinely inspired.'[1]

The logical treatment of the parts of speech cannot be described here, but an illustration from Roger Bacon will show how fruitful a source of confusion could be the use of the same terms for what were not always seen to be different categories—a confusion which we ourselves still find it difficult to avoid. Bacon, keeping close to Boethius, whom he often quotes, establishes first that there are two parts of speech (noun and verb) in logic and eight in grammar.[2] He then distributes the grammatical parts under one or other of the two logical ones.

The pronoun is included within the noun 'because it refers to the thing which the noun signifies, and because of its function, which is to act as the subject of the verb'.[3] The adverb also is included within the noun because, according to Boethius, 'its meaning is finite and it does not express time'.[4] If it is objected that the adverb, because it is uninflected, cannot be a noun, it is argued that inflection cannot be a defining property of the noun because there exist indeclinable nouns, the *monoptota* of the grammarians (e.g. Latin *astu*, though Bacon gives no examples). The interjection is included within the adverb. The only reason Bacon gives is 'ut vult Priscianus', which is only partly true, for Priscian's enumeration of the parts of speech does include the interjection, though he clearly thinks there is a strong case for keeping it within the adverb. The participle is included within the verb because 'temporis demonstrativum est'. The participle also 'participat naturam nominis, ideo aliquando accipitur loco nominis'. This obstacle to a tidy classification is passed over without discussion. The conjunction and preposition are not to be regarded as parts of speech 'simpliciter quantum ad significacionem, sed quantum ad officium'. They are in fact, in Bacon's classification, excluded altogether,

[1] Smaragdus, quoted by Thurot, p. 65: 'Multi plures, multi vero pauciores partes esse dixerunt. Modo autem octo universalis tenet ecclesia. Quod divinitus inspiratum esse non dubito.'   [2] Roger Bacon, *Sumule Dialectices*, pp. 232 and 239.
[3] loc. cit. p. 239: '...propter significati convenienciam et officium ejus, quod est quod suppositum reddit verbo'.
[4] ibid.: '...cuiusdam finite significacionis est sine tempore'.

because they cannot be levelled under either noun or verb. This is virtually a recognition of the logical status of the conjunction and preposition, and a tacit recognition that the criteria by which other parts of speech are determined (largely that of meaning) are not adequate for these two, at any rate. Bacon goes on to quote Boethius: just as the reins and the bridle are not part of the chariot but as it were ligatures and accessories, so the preposition and conjunction are not parts of speech but connectives (*calligata quedam*).[1]

Renaissance systems. Of the renaissance grammarians considered here all those before Ramus follow Priscian's enumeration of the parts of speech. It is difficult to know how Ramus classified them, even how far he wished to classify them. Funke writes as if Ramus enumerated a classification in the traditional way, but this is not the case. Ramus does not *discuss* the parts of speech; the only classification he makes is into two groups: those which have number and those which do not. But he continues also to use the traditional names even when he is repudiating some of the traditional divisions, as he repudiates the preposition and interjection. His primary division into two classes is quite explicit:

Words are classified according to number, for a word either has number, or it has not. Number is a distinguishing feature of words in terms of unity or multiplicity, whereby they can be expressed as singular or plural...There are distinctive signs for each number, by means of which a word which has number can be inflected...A word which has number is a noun or a verb. (Bk I. chap. 3.)[2]

He then proceeds straight into the next chapter, *De Nomine.*

Sanctius makes great play with the classification of the parts of speech, 'in quibus tanta est inconstantia Grammaticorum, ut nihil certi nobis adhuc potuerint constituere'. He quotes the views of Varro and Quintilian, misquotes Servius, refers to Antonio of Lebrixa and then gives his own opinion: there are only three parts of speech, noun, verb and particle. He uses Plato as his authority, referring especially to his 'Liber de Ente'—i.e., the *Sophist.* He also claims that Hebrew,

---

[1] Roger Bacon, op. cit. p. 239.

[2] (Of *Vox*) 'Species ejus, numero dividuntur: Vox enim particeps est numeri aut expers. Numerus est differentia vocis secundum unitatem aut multitudinem, unde vox singularis aut pluralis exprimi potest...Utriusque numeri speciales differentiae sunt, quibus vox numeri particeps flecti potest...Vox particeps numeri est nomen, aut verbum.' Cf. Funke, *Frühzeit,* p. 54.

Parts of speech

Arabic, Greek and Latin all had at one time only three parts.[1] Sanctius' classification is:

(i) Noun (including participle)
(ii) Verb
(iii) Particle (including preposition, adverb, conjunction)

The pronoun and the interjection are excluded altogether, the interjection on the long-standing reason that it is only a 'natural' noise, not a significant word. The pronoun is excluded for the probably unique reason that it cannot be given a definition which does not apply also to the noun. 'Nullum igitur Pronomen est.'[2]

In his own Latin grammar, however, he enumerates six parts of speech: noun, verb, participle, preposition, adverb, conjunction. The pronoun and the interjection are still denied the status of parts of speech, but the category of particle has not stood up to the practical requirements of a detailed teaching grammar and, as it so often does in the English grammars, has had to divide into its constituent parts.[3]

INDIVIDUAL PARTS OF SPEECH

Noun. Noun (ὄνομα) and verb are distinguished by Plato,[4] though the distinction is conceived from the point of view of a speaker and not according to the form of the words. The distinction between noun and verb therefore serves also to distinguish designation from predicate. The first definition of the noun we have is that of Dionysius Thrax, which sets the pattern for all later grammarians: 'A noun is an inflected part of speech indicating a person, thing or action.' Dionysius uses three criteria:

(i) the noun is inflected (πτωτικόν)

(ii) it indicates a person (σῶμα) or a thing (πρᾶγμα, which also carries the sense of 'action')

(iii) it names either a class (κοινῶς) or an individual (ἰδίως).[5]

---

[1] Sanctius, Bk I. chap. 2. Cf. P. K. Hitti, *The Arabs*, 7th edn. 1960, p. 241: 'According to the famous biographer ibn-Khallikan it was 'Ali who laid down...this principle: The parts of speech are three—noun, verb and particle, and told him to found a complete treatise thereon.'   [2] op. cit. pp. 19–23.
[3] Sanctius, *Grammatica Latina*, included in 5th edn of *Minerva*, 1795, p. 2.
[4] Plato, *Soph.* 261 d, e; *Crat.* 431 b.
[5] Dionysius Thrax, p. 24: 'ὄνομα ἔστι μέρος λόγου πτωτικόν, σῶμα ἢ πρᾶγμα σημαῖνον'. Bekker, p. 634, accepts the addition of some MSS.: 'κοινῶς τε κἀι ἰδίως λεγόμενον'.

53

Donatus uses the same criteria: 'pars orationis cum casu corpus aut rem proprie communiterve significans'.[1] Charisius and Diomedes have the same definition but add 'sine tempore', so as to exclude the participle and keep sharp the distinction between noun and verb. Priscian omits the formal criteria: 'pars orationis quae unicuique subjectorum corporum seu rerum communem vel propriam qualitatem distribuit'.[2]

In the medieval period those grammarians who define the noun repeat either Donatus or Priscian. Alcuin makes his pupil Saxo repeat Priscian, but the master supplements the definition himself: 'Nomen est vox significativa secundum placitum, sine tempore, definitum aliquid significans in nominativo.'[3] He then goes on to explain that the form of a noun is conventional because different languages have different names for the same thing: 'una est substantia, sed diversa nomina'. This reference to substance Thurot says is characteristic of the early medieval definitions of the noun but was replaced in the thirteenth century by an emphasis on permanence.[4] The two concepts are very closely allied. Bacon does not discuss the parts of speech directly in the *Summa Gramatica*. In the *Sumule Dialectices* he defines the noun almost in the words of Alcuin's schoolmaster, but adds to *vox significativa*: '...cuius nulla pars separata [aliquid] significat' because, he says, the definition would otherwise fit the sentence also. Bacon's complete definition runs as follows: 'Nomen...est vox significativa ad placitum sine tempore, cujus nulla pars separata [aliquid] significat, finita, recta.'[5]

The other speculative grammarians define the noun in terms of being, substance, permanence, condition and individuality (*determinata apprehensio*):

Modus significandi essentialis generalis nominis est modus significandi substantiae, permanentis habitus seu entis. (Siger, p. 95.)

Nomen ergo est pars orationis significans per modum entis, vel determinatae apprehensionis...Modus entis est modus habitus et permanentis, rei inhaerens, ex hoc quod habet esse. (TE, pp. 29 and 27.)

The range of criteria which might be used in defining the noun was already wide. The scholastic grammarians alone ignored all formal criteria, and in this respect they had no followers. Despauter

---

[1] Donatus, *Ars Minor* (K. IV. 355).   [2] Priscian, Bk II. 22 (K. II. 56).
[3] Alcuin, col. 859.   [4] Thurot, p. 160.
[5] Roger Bacon, *Sumule Dialectices*, p. 234. (See below, p. 58.)

is the only one of the renaissance grammarians noticed here who seems to echo them; the noun, according to him, 'significat substantiam cum qualitate propria vel communi'.[1] Some grammarians reproduced verbatim Donatus (as did Perottus and Whittinton) or Priscian (as did Sulpitius); others made a selection from established criteria; a few introduced fresh criteria of their own. The general tendency is to rely more on formal criteria than on meaning. The opposite tendency, which is very marked in the English grammars, comes from the lack of inflections in English and partly, one must suppose, from the often-repeated definition given in the elementary part of Lily's grammar: 'the name of a thynge that is and may be seen, felte, herde, or understande'.[2] Formal criteria which had not previously been used are the expression of gender and number, and the negative criterion that the noun does not express person. These all seem to have been first brought into the definition by Linacre, who is followed by Ramus and Sanctius and, in the last instance only, by Lily. Some representative definitions are:

μέρος λόγου πτωτικὸν σημαντικὸν ἄνευ χρόνου (a part of speech with case and meaning and without tense). (Theodore of Gaza, Bk iv.)

'...quod declinatur per casus et non significat cum tempore.' (Antonio of Lebrixa, fol. xvii.)

...rem significat, sine ulla temporis aut personae differentia. (Lily, *Brev. Inst.*, 1567, Sig. A v.)

'...vox numeri casualis cum genere.' (Ramus, Bk i).[3]

Funke draws attention to the clear and deliberate way in which by means of separate definitions, Linacre distinguishes formal from semantic criteria, a feature not found in any other humanist grammar known to him.[4] Linacre's method, most clearly seen in the *Rudimenta*, is to list the formal properties in a section called *rudimenta declinationum*, and in a later section, *rudimenta definitionum*, to combine them with an explanation in terms of meaning. In the *Progymnasmata* he accordingly says first that the noun is declined with gender, number and case,[5] and subsequently expands this into: 'A nowne is: that betokeneth a thynge wyth oute ony dyfference of tyme or person and is declyned with case.'[6] It is not as certain as Funke seems to

---

[1] Despauter, fol. 3 verso. [2] Lily, 1527, p. 11.
[3] Also Sanctius, Bk i. chap. 5. 72 where he attributes the definition to Scaliger.
[4] Funke, *Frühzeit*, pp. 88–90. [5] Linacre, *Progymnasmata*, sig. A ii.
[6] op. cit. sig. B v verso.

suggest that this arrangement of Linacre's arises from any linguistic theory: he does not keep to it in his most substantial work, *De Emendata Structura latini sermonis*. It seems more probable that Linacre viewed it as an expository device, appropriate only for his two elementary grammars, for in *De Emendata Structura* he gives just the one combined definition: 'Nomen est pars orationis, quae casibus inflexa significat aliquid sine ulla temporis, aut certae personae adsignificantia.'[1] It is in the classification of nouns that he takes care to separate considerations of form from those of meaning.

Verb. Plato, with much effect for the future, describes the verb (ῥῆμα) as denoting action: τὸ μὲν ἐπὶ ταῖς πράξειν ὂν δήλωμα ῥῆμα που λέγομεν.[2] Aristotle describes the essential features of a verb as the expression of time and predication, but he restricts the term to affirmative forms of the present tense.[3] The Stoic definition, according to Diogenes Babylonius, was, '...a part of speech signifying an uncombined predicate (...σημαῖνον ἀσύνθετον κατηγόρημα)'.[4] Just what ἀσύνθετον means here is not clear: it may refer to the difference in syntactical relationship between *man hungry* and *man sings*, in which *sings* would be held to be more independent of *man* than *hungry* is.

The first formal definition of the verb comes from Dionysius Thrax: '...a word without case-inflexions; admitting distinctions of time, person and number; with active and passive force'.[5] To the second section of this definition Apollonius Dyscolus added 'when it expresses states of mind' (τῆς ψυχῆς διαθέσεις) so as to include the infinitive, which does not express number or person.[6] The Latin grammarians of the Byzantine period keep close to Dionysius. Donatus adds the category neuter to active and passive, and omits the reference to number. Priscian adds a reference to mood, and omits person and number. The omissions are not significant, as the omitted categories are of course included among the accidents. The definitions follow:

[1] Linacre. *De Emendata Structura*, Bk I, fol. I recto.
[2] Plato, *Soph.* 262 a.
[3] Aristotle, *Int.* 16 b.
[4] Diogenes Babylonius, quoted by Diogenes Laertius, VII. 58.
[5] Dionysius Thrax, p. 46: ῥῆμά ἐστι λέξις ἄπτωτος, ἐπιδεκτικὴ χρόνων τε καὶ προσώπων καὶ ἀριθμῶν, ἐνέργειαν ἢ πάθος παριστᾶσα.
[6] Schol. on Dionysius, Bekker, p. 882.

Parts of speech

'Verbum est pars orationis cum tempore et persona sine casu aut agere aliquid aut pati aut neutrum significans.' (Donatus, *Ars Grammatica*, II. 12; K. IV. 381.)

'...pars orationis cum temporibus et modis, sine casu, agendi vel patiendi significativum.' (Priscian, VIII. 1; K. II. 369.)

The renaissance grammarians based their treatment of the verb so often on one or other of these definitions that the varied treatment which the category received in medieval grammars tends to be lost sight of. There was much verbatim reproduction—by Bede of Donatus, by Hugo of Priscian—but Ælfric, in the tenth century, offers an apparently novel description of the verb, although he professes in the grammar as a whole merely to be giving extracts from Priscian: '*Verbum* means verb, and the verb signifies action, or passion, or assent. Action is when you say *aro*, I plough...passion is when you say *verberor*, I am beaten...assent is when you say, *amor*, I am loved.'[1]

The verb seems to move Alcuin to a warmth and eloquence which are as welcome as they are rare in this dryly analytical atmosphere. The two pupils Franco and Saxo are putting questions to each other in the presence of their master, but on this occasion Saxo tactfully gives the master an opening.

Franco: Primo omnium verbi definitionem dic mihi.

Saxo: Magis interrogemus magistrum, quae sit verbi definitio secundum philosophiam.

Magister: Habet subtilem definitionem et nobilem, et est huiusmodi: Verbum est vox significativa secundum placitum, cum tempore, definitum aliquid significans et accidens. (Alcuin, col. 874.)

The words *et accidens* are explained by 'accidit enim actio vel passio homini'. Noble this may be, but there was greater subtlety to come. Nobility of approach, however, is suggested by all that is accessible of Smaragdus' treatment of the verb: according to him, in the same way as the meadows shine with flowers so do the scriptures with verbs.[2] Subtlety is introduced by Peter Helias. His treatment of the verb combines the customary description in terms of action and passion with a definite reference to the idea of communication. This latter is introduced, apparently, as a category from logic, and is

---

[1] Ælfric, p. 9. '*Verbum* is word, and word getâcnað weorc oððe prôwunge oððe geþafunge. Weorc byð, þonne ðu cwest: *aro* ic erige...þrôwunge byð, þonne ðu cwyst: *verberor* ic eom beswungen...geðâfung byþ, ðonne ðu cwyst: *amor* ic eom gelufod.'

[2] Smaragdus, p, 612.

therefore all the more a close parallel to the emphasis placed in the Port Royal grammar of 1660, and in its companion logic of 1662, on the verb as the means of affirmation. Peter Helias' definition is as follows:

Every verb signifies action or passion, not because every verb signifies that which *is* action or passion but because every verb signifies either what is (actually) action or passion, or something different which is in the manner of action or passion: that is, with tense, with verbal terminations, and by way of being spoken about something else.'[1]

Many other writers at this period were concerned to distinguish more clearly between verb and noun than was possible by following either Priscian's emphasis on action and passion or the formal criteria used, for example, by Roger Bacon. For Bacon's definition of the verb is virtually identical with his definition of the noun, quoted earlier, except for the reference to tense: 'Verbum est vox significativa ad placitum cum tempore, cuius nulla pars per se significat, finita, recta.'[2] If the verb and the noun were the two primary and fundamental parts of speech, as was generally accepted, a firm distinction should be possible in terms either of meaning or of form, if not both; R. W. Hunt quotes one attempt from a twelfth-century commentary on Priscian. The commentator's argument, as summarised by Hunt, runs:

If the verb is said to signify pure action and passion, its signification will be that of the noun, because the nouns 'action' and 'passion' signify all actions and passions. We say therefore that it signifies neither action simply, nor a person acting, but that action is in a person acting, as for example 'He runs'. But the noun, e.g. 'a run', though it signifies an action, signifies it simply and does not say it is in something. The verb signifies the inherence of both action and substance, and so may be said to signify action and substance, but in a different way from the noun. (I. 1941. 217–18.)

This use of the notion of inherency is not unlike the later speculative grammarians' mode of signifying being. Both Siger and Thomas discuss the verb at great length. Siger proceeds by a series of defini-

---

[1] 'Omne verbum significat actionem vel passionem, non quod omne verbum significet id quod est actio vel passio, sed quod omne verbum vel id quod est actio vel passio significet vel aliquid aliud modo actionis vel passionis, id est cum tempore, in verbali terminatione et ut de altero dicitur.' Quoted by R. W. Hunt, I. 1941. 220 n.

[2] Roger Bacon, *Sumule Dialectices*, p. 237.

tions of decreasing generality. In most general terms the verb signifies 'through the mode of signifying being or becoming'.[1] This establishes its difference from the noun. According to the second stage of his definition 'the general mode of signifying being is the mode of signifying through the mode of change (becoming or moving) or being'.[2] This the verb shares with the participle. The last stage excludes the participle. 'The specific mode of the verb is the mode of signifying being about something.'[3] The words 'about something' distinguish the verb from the participle and refer to the difference between finite and non-finite forms: the verb is making an assertion, the participle is not.

Siger then proceeds to show that the verb must be dependent on something that is not itself a verb. In the course of this argument he refers to more familiar criteria. The verb 'signifies both action and passion...carries the secondary signification of time and is always the mark of what is said about something else'.[4] It is apparent that he attaches less importance to these traditional criteria than to the metaphysical terms in which he frames his definitions.

Thomas reaches an equally speculative conclusion but without even the slight reference to communication which gives Siger's definition some connection with the facts of language: The verb is a part of speech 'signifying through the mode of being and of differing-from-substance'.[5]

Much of the difficulty which the verb caused both logical and speculative writers comes from the substantive verb *to be*. Any definition of the verb as a whole had to cover it, but its special status was well recognised. Although the philosophical and logical questions which it provoked belonged to a far wider field than grammar it would have been quite impossible for any writer of the time to have prevented himself (in the unlikely event of his even wishing to) from becoming involved in them.

The varying practice of the renaissance grammarians can best be illustrated in terms of the distinction between formal and semantic

[1] Siger, p. 108: '...per modum significandi fieri seu esse'.
[2] ibid. 'Modus significandi generalis essentialis verbi est modus significandi per modum fluxus, fieri seu motus, seu esse.'
[3] ibid. 'Modus specificus verbi est modus significandi essentialis de aliquo.'
[4] ibid. '...actionis simul et passionis est significativum...verbum est quod consignificat tempus et est semper nota eorum quae de altero dicuntur'.
[5] TE, p. 90: '...pars orationis significans per modum esse distantis a substantia'.

59

criteria. Those who define the verb solely in formal terms are a minority, but a continuing and, latterly, an emphatic minority.

Theodore of Gaza, in the middle of the fifteenth century, makes only a slight reference to meaning; Antonio of Lebrixa, at the end of the fifteenth century, makes none: 'verbum est quod declinatur per modos et tempora sine casu'.[1] Ramus, in the middle of the sixteenth century, uses number and person, but not mood: 'vox numeri personalis cum tempore'.[2] Sanctius, at the end of the century, has almost the same definition as Ramus—'vox particeps numeri personalis cum tempore'—which he defends aggressively: it is a 'true and perfect definition...*reliquae omnes Grammaticorum ineptae*'.[3]

Most grammarians used criteria of both form and meaning: Linacre with obvious discrimination, the others showing by the structure of their definitions that they were aware of the difference between them but had no wish to treat them separately. Linacre's formal definition says that the verb is declined with mood, tense, person and number;[4] his combined definition omits the last two: ...'declyned: wyth mode and tens, and betokeneth to be, to doo or to suffre, with some dyfference of tyme'.[5] Other mixed definitions are:

pars orationis cum tempore et persona sine casu aut agere aliquid, aut pati, aut neutrum significans.[6]

pars orationis declinabilis cum modis et temporibus sine casu agendi vel patiendi significativa.[7]

pars orationis declinabilis cum modo, tempore, persona, sine casu, agere vel pati vel neutrum significans.[8]

Lily's grammar is the only one considered here to bring into its definition any reference to the verb as a means of assertion, and to its place in the sentence: '...a specyall parte of speche that cometh in every perfyt reason and in every sentence. And it is a worde that eyther betokeneth beynge of a thynge...or doynge of a thynge...or sufferynge of a thynge.'[9] His practice is the reverse of Linacre's: Lily makes this elementary definition in semantic or syntactic terms only, and the later, Latin, definition to include formal criteria: '...quae modis et temporibus inflexa, esse aliquid...significat.'[10]

---

[1] Antonio of Lebrixa, sig. xvii verso.   [2] Ramus, Bk ii. chap. i.
[3] Sanctius, Bk i. chap. 12. ad init.   [4] Linacre, *Progymnasmata*, sig. A iv verso.
[5] ibid. sig. C ii verso.   [6] Despauter, fol. 6 verso.
[7] Perottus, sig. b 6; Sulpitius, sig. A iv.   [8] Whittinton, sig. B ii verso.
[9] Lily, 1527, p. 25.   [10] Lily, *Brev. Inst.* 1567, sig. C iii verso.

Parts of speech

The most noticeable feature of the definitions of the renaissance grammarians is the agreement among them about the kind and style of definition which is appropriate and the disagreement about its detailed contents. They—the ten discussed here—are agreed only in including tense; two of them add person, two add mood, two add both; two add person and number; four include the negative criterion that the verb lacks case. Those who give semantic criteria agree on doing and suffering; what is not either of these is described either as 'being', or negatively as 'neither doing nor suffering.'

Conjunction. Aristotle[1] and the author of chapter 20 of the *Poetics* use the term σύνδεσμος, for which there is no single equivalent in English. The usual translation is *conjunction* or *particle*; Potts calls it *ligature*;[2] I prefer *conjunctive particle* here because σύνδεσμος is the term which was later translated *coniunctio*.[3]

The Stoic grammarians continued to combine conjunctive words and particles into one category. Their definition, as given by Diogenes Laertius, was: 'an indeclinable part of speech binding together (other) parts of speech'.[4] The Alexandrian grammarians, represented by Dionysius Thrax, divided the conjunctive word from the conjunctive particle, thus forming the categories conjunction and preposition. Dionysius' definition of the conjunction is: 'a word linking thoughts in an orderly arrangement and filling up gaps in expression'.[5] The weakness of this, compared with the Stoic definition, is that it makes the conjunction join thoughts instead of words.

The two characteristics of the conjunction on which emphasis comes to be placed are (i) that it joins or subordinates; (ii) that it joins either sentences or smaller units. Except for Priscian, all the grammarians of the Byzantine period have in effect the same definition as that attributed to Cominianus by Charisius, and to Palaemon by Diomedes: 'pars orationis adnectens ordinansque sententiam'.[6] It is, as always in this period, difficult to know how closely *sententiam*

---

[1] Aristotle, *Rhet.* 1407 a.
[2] L. J. Potts, *Aristotle on the Art of Fiction*, 1953, p. 44.
[3] There seems to have been little, if any, support for Quintilian's view that a better translation would be *convinctio.* (*Inst. Orat.* I. iv. 18.)
[4] Diogenes Laertius, Bk VII. 58: 'μέρος λόγου ἄπτωτον, συνδοῦν τὰ μέρη τοῦ λόγου.'
[5] Dionysius Thrax, p. 86: 'σύνδεσμός ἐστι λέξις συνδέουσα διάνοιαν μετὰ τάξεως καὶ το τῆς ἑρμηνείας κεχηνὸς δηλοῦσα.'
[6] Donatus, *Ars Grammatica*, II. 15 (K. IV. 388).

should be translated *sentence*. Priscian (and Diomedes, who gives an alternative definition closely resembling Priscian's) distinguishes clearly the two characteristics joining and ordering:

pars orationis indeclinabilis, conjunctiva aliarum partium orationis, quibus consignificat, vim vel ordinationem demonstrans: vim, quando simul esse res aliquas significat, ut '*et pius et fortis fuit Aeneas*': ordinem, quando consequentiam aliquarum demonstrat rerum, ut, '*si ambulat, movetur*'. (XVI. I and 2; K. III. 93.)

In the following section Priscian complicates his discussion by saying that copulative conjunctions join 'tam verba quam sensum'. This is not a distinction between word and meaning, for *verbum* with Priscian always means 'verb': he uses *dictio* for 'word'. *Sensum* must be taken to mean 'noun or noun equivalent'; it cannot here mean 'sense, meaning'; it cannot mean just 'word', or there is no contrast with *verbum*. Even so it is not easy to see why Priscian did not use it in the plural as Isidore uses it in the same connection. Isidore says the conjunction is so called 'quod sensus sententiasque conjungat' and gives as examples *Augustinus et Hieronymus* and *scribit et legit*.[1]

By the time of Priscian, at the beginning of the sixth century, the category conjunction was formed: it was indeclinable, and it joined. The question was just what exactly it did join: or rather, for everyone knew what it joined, how to express in a definition what everyone knew. The difficulty is in fact nothing to do with the conjunction at all: it is part of our real difficulty with the sentence. When the modern schoolmaster shackles himself with the rule that a conjunction joins only sentences he is trying to save his pupils, and himself, from the consequences of permitting it to join words also. For if the conjunction may be said to join words he will have to explain that the joining word in 'Pig and Whistle' is a conjunction whereas the joining word in 'Puss in Boots' is not. If he is prepared to attempt such an explanation he is usually pushed into confining himself to examples such as 'Jack and Jill went up the hill' where he feels it is permissible to show that the conjunction *and* is 'really' joining sentences because what the speaker 'really' says is 'Jack went up the hill and Jill went up the hill'. He is indeed a fortunate and successful schoolmaster if one of his pupils will press the point and ask whether, when a speaker says, 'This is the Pig and Whistle', he is 'really' saying, 'This is the Pig and this is the Whistle'.

[1] Isidore, I. xii.

62

Parts of speech

This is not the place to discuss these difficulties. They have a long history, which can be seen, during the medieval and renaissance periods, in the very process of coagulation.

The existence of the category (it can scarcely be said to have a development) after Priscian can best be described according to what the conjunction is said to join. Apart from those grammarians who repeat Donatus or Priscian verbatim the medieval and renaissance writers considered here suggest six answers.

(i) *Conjunctions join 'terms'*. Martin of Dacia describes the conjunction as joining substances and actions, and he uses also the word *extrema*, on which Thomas bases his definition. Thomas defines it as, '*Pars orationis per modum coniungentis duo extrema significans.*'[1] The logical, non-linguistic tone of *extrema* can be translated only by some such word as 'term'.

(ii) *Conjunctions join 'things which differ from each other'*. Alexander of Villedieu, at the end of the twelfth century, is as non-committal as Thomas and his metaphor suggests a linguistic theory which is quite as speculative: Iungere non poterit coniunctio mobile fixo;
Iungit diversa coniunctio significata.[2]

Reichling explains *mobile* as referring to the adjective and *fixo* to the substantive, but the implied argument is obscure. If Alexander would count two adjectives joined by *et* as being joined by a conjunction, what is the force of *diversa*? From his subsequent hexameters it would seem that Alexander is pointing to the difference between *homo grammaticus* (where two words are juxtaposed, thereby showing that they refer to one thing) and *homo et grammaticus* where the same two words are joined by a conjunction, thereby showing that they are to be regarded as *diversa* and therefore referring to two things.

(iii) *Conjunctions join 'parts of speech'*. Several grammarians, all in the renaissance period, say merely that the conjunction joins parts of speech. Amongst the parts of speech is the verb; any instance of two finite verbs being joined will necessarily involve the joining of two sentences. The sentence as such, therefore, need not be mentioned. Two examples suffice:

'...diversas partes orationis coniungit: ut *Pompeius et Caesar*; *amat et docet*.' (Antonio of Lebrixa, fol. xvii verso.)
'...vox expers numeri, qua orationis multiplicis partes coniunguntur.' (Ramus, Bk II. chap. 9.)

[1] TE, p. 129.   [2] Alexander of Villedieu, lines 1531–2.

63

The Tradition

(iv) *Conjunctions join 'nouns and verbs'*. Just as Antonio chose nouns and verbs for his examples of the parts of speech, so a number of grammarians define the conjunction as joining specifically these two kinds of word:

> *Coniunctio* is association or joining. This part of speech can do nothing by itself but joins together both the noun and the verb. (Ælfric, p. 10.)

> A *iungo iungis* coniunctio dicitur esse,
> Nam iungit partes nomina verba simul.
> (Eberhard of Bethune, chap. 22. 201.)

(v) *Conjunctions join 'words and sentences'*. It is only among the later renaissance grammarians that the conjunction's part in joining sentences is clearly, and increasingly, stressed. Lily's elementary definition gives words and sentences equal weight: '...byndeth wordes and sentences togyder'.[1] In his Latin accidence it is the phrase or clause which is stressed: '...pars orationis, quae sententiarum clausulas apte connectit.'[2] Linacre's first definition, perhaps written about 1512, stresses the sentence more than the word: '...a part undeclyned that knyttyth and ordryth sentencys to gydre and some tyme wordys'.[3] In the *De Emendata Structura*, first published in 1524, where he seems to have drawn on Lily, Linacre gives no fewer than three definitions of the conjunction, all in terms of 'clausulae': '...pars orationis, quae clausulas in sermone apte coniungit. Aliter, coniunctio est pars orationis, quae clausularum inter se connexum declarans, plurimum ad orationis claritatem confert. Aliter, quae tantum habitudinem clausularum inter se in sermone definit.'[4]

(vi) *Conjunctions join 'sentences only'*. The extreme position that the conjunction joins only sentences makes its first appearance (among the grammars considered here) in Sanctius, but has supporters during the whole history of English grammar. The conjunction is one of Sanctius' class of particles. His formal definition runs: 'Coniunctio orationes inter se coniungit',[5] but eleswhere he is even more explicit: 'Coniunctio...tantum iungit sententias.'[6]

---

[1] Lily, 1527, p. 58.   [2] Lily, *Brev. Inst.*, 1567, sig. D vii verso.
[3] Linacre, *Progymnasmata*, sig. C iii verso.
[4] Linacre, *De Emendata Structura*, fol. 32 verso.
[5] Sanctius, Bk I, chap. 14. *ad init.*
[6] ibid. Bk I. chap. 18. 220. Scaliger had taken the same position: 'Coniunctionis autem notionem veteres paullo inconsultius prodidere; neque enim, quod aiunt, partes alias coniungit...sed coniunctio est, quae coniungit orationes plures.' *De causis linguae latinae*, chap. 165 (quoted by Harris, *Hermes*, 1751, Bk II. chap. 2. 238 n.).

Parts of speech

Preposition. The Alexandrian grammarians, represented by Dionysius Thrax, were the first to distinguish the preposition (πρόθεσις) as a part of speech. Hitherto words of the kind had been included within the category of conjunctive particle or, by the Stoics, treated as a subclass of it (προθέτικος σύνδεσμος). Dionysius says the preposition is 'put before all parts of speech both in compound and in syntactical construction (ἐν τε συνθέσει καὶ συντάξει)',[1] and later writers within the tradition had little more to say.

The distinction between separable and inseparable forms is the characteristic with which the early Latin grammarians mostly deal, especially the fact that prepositions 'make adverbs if they are not followed by inflected forms'.[2] Donatus introduced into his definition a reference to meaning which Priscian, and most of the other grammarians, excluded:

pars orationis, quae praeposita aliis partibus orationis significationem earum aut mutat aut complet aut minuit. (Donatus, *Ars Grammatica*, II. 16; K. IV. 389.)

pars orationis indeclinabilis, quae praeponitur aliis partibus vel appositione vel compositione. (Priscian, XIV. i; K. III. 24.)

In formal terms there was little else to be said, and it is noticeable that many more of the medieval and renaissance grammarians repeat Donatus or Priscian verbatim, for this part of speech, than for any of the others so far considered. Donatus is repeated by Bede, Hugo, Despauter and Linacre (in an alternative definition): Priscian by Alcuin, Perottus, Sulpitius, Whittinton and Lily (in the Latin accidence). Antonio of Lebrixa at the end of the fifteenth century makes explicit one point which Priscian and the others merely imply: that the separable forms are used only before substantives, whereas the inseparable forms can be attached to other parts of speech: '...praeponitur nomini per appositionem et aliis etiam partibus per compositionem'.[3]

Those who attempt to introduce criteria of meaning are at once involved in analysing the relation between the preposition and what it governs. The speculative grammarians frame their explanations in terms of the modes of signification:

[1] Dionysius Thrax, p. 70.
[2] Diomedes, Bk I (K. I. 409): 'adverbia faciunt, si quando illas non subsecuntur casus'.
[3] Antonio of Lebrixa, fol. xvii verso.

The preposition...was invented in order to designate, in relation to an action, some characteristic of substance [considered as] beginning or ending and receiving...The preposition is therefore a part of speech signifying though the mode of relating substance to action. (Michel de Marbais.)[1]

Thomas of Erfurt bases his definition on the view that the preposition was invented 'at first so as to control the mode of cases, and compress it; then to relate to action what is expressed by case'.[2] His formal definition runs: '...a part of speech signifying through the mode of adjoining another inflected word, which it attracts and brings into relation with an action.'[3] The interpretation of anything put in such general terms is not easy, but it does not seem as though either writer says anything more than was already in the customary formal definition.

Linacre is the only renaissance writer to frame his definition in terms of meaning: '...a part of spech undeclyned which sygnyfieth respecte or havyour of a thyng in place, ordre, or cause'.[4] His later definition in the *De Emendata Structura* is an expansion of this: '...pars orationis, quae certam eorum, quibus additur, habitudinem, ut loci, termini, ordinis, causae, vel actionis determinat'.[5]

Enumeration of this kind was as a rule, rightly, kept out of the definitions. A great many grammarians, English and Latin, attach more importance to their classified lists of prepositions (and of adverbs and conjunctions) than to the definitions. Very few question the value of definitions, but their experience of teaching would be likely to show that the lists were more useful, and acted, in fact, as ostensive definitions.

Ramus alone denies the preposition any standing as a part of speech. He discusses it only in his chapters on syntax, where he treats such words as adverbs.[6] His classification of the preposition is quite explicit: 'Adverbii porro definitione comprehenduntur praepositiones et interiectiones'.[7]

---

[1] In Thurot, p. 195. 'Prepositio...fuit inventa ad designandum aliquam habitudinem substantie initiantis vel terminantis et recipientis ad actum...Prepositio igitur est pars orationis significans per modum retorquentis substantiam ad actum.'

[2] TE, p. 134: '...ut primo modum casualem contrahat, et coarctet; et deinde casualem ad actum reducat'.

[3] TE, p. 135: '...pars orationis significans per modum adiacentis alteri casuali, ipsum contrahens, et ad actum reducens.'

[4] Linacre, *Progymnasmata*, sig. C iii verso.

[5] Linacre, *De Emendata Structura*, fol. 24 verso.

[6] Ramus, Bk IV, chaps. 14–17.   [7] Ramus, Bk 2. chap. 8.

Parts of speech

The last word on the preposition should be Lily's, whose English definition was too influential not to be quoted: '...a parte of speche put before other wordes, other [sic] ioyneth to the wordes in compoundes, as *Indoctus*, or asondre from the wordes, as *Coram Deo*'.[1]

Article. Early references to the article (ἄρθρον) give no information about the significance of the term. The reference in chapter 20 of the *Poetics* is obscure, if not textually corrupt, and the reference to the 'so-called articles' (τοῖς καλουμενοῖς ἄρθροις) in the *Rhetorica ad Alexandrum* is uninformative.[2] The category is first met clearly in Stoic writings. Chrysippus defined it as 'an inflected part of speech which distinguishes the genders and numbers of nouns'.[3] This seems to have covered also the relative pronoun, as it certainly did with Dionysius Thrax, whose definition runs: 'a declinable part of speech placed before or after the inflection of nouns; before it, as ὁ, or after it, as ὅς';[4] to which a scholiast adds 'so as to indicate a pre-existing notion (a process) which is called "reference" (ἀναφορά)'.[5] This is the same category as that which the Stoics called ἄρθρα ἀοριστώδη—*indefinite* (that is, 'unrestricted as to personal reference')[6] and included also what we should call indefinite and interrogative pronouns.[7] The relation between article and pronoun at this stage of their development is too complex to discuss here. Apollonius Dyscolus sums up the eventual relationship: 'the article with the noun and the pronoun instead of it' (τὸ ἄρθρον μετ ὀνόματον, καὶ ἡ ἀντωνυμία ἀντ' ὀνόματου).[8]

Among the Latin grammarians Varro alone, according to one of his classifications, counts the article as a separate part of speech. In his terminology *articulus* means a word with case-inflections which is not a noun. *Articuli* may be definite (*finiti*) like *hic*, or indefinite (*infiniti*) like *quis*. He quotes, apparently with approval, the term *pronomen* for the former and *provocabulum* for the latter. Varro's terminology, therefore, makes the pronoun a kind of article.[9] Servius, reversing the terms, calls *hic* an article, but classifies it among the pronouns.[10] Similarly, according to Donatus, the difference

---

[1] Lily, 1527, p. 58.   [2] (Aristotle), *Rhet. ad Alex.*, 1435 a, b.   [3] Steinthal, I. 298.
[4] Dionysius Thrax, p. 61: '...μέρος λόγου πτωτικόν, προτασσόμενον καὶ ὑποτασσόμενον τῆς κλίσεως τῶν ὀνομάτων'.
[5] Bekker, p. 899: 'εἰς γνῶσιν προϋποκειμενην, ὅπερ καλεῖται ἀναφορά.'
[6] Robins, p. 30.   [7] Steinthal, II, 214.
[8] Apollonius, *De Constr.*, Bk I. §24 (S & U. II. 25).
Varro, Bk VIII. 45; Bk X. 18.   [10] Servius, *Comm. in Donatum* (K. IV. 428).

between pronoun and article is that the former can stand alone, as *quis, iste* (Varro's *provocabulum*) whereas the latter must be joined to a noun or participle, as *hic* (Varro's *pronomen*).[1] Priscian denies Latin any articles,[2] but speaks as though some writers considered *idem* and *qui* as articles.[3] The word *O* is discussed by Servius and Priscian, but rejected as an article because it does not change its form.

No subsequent Latin grammars include the article as a part of speech, though *hic* and *ille* are often referred to as articles, and used in distinguishing substantive from adjective. A word which can have before it only one out of *hic, haec* and *hoc* is a substantive; a word which can have any of the three before it is an adjective.[4] Roger Bacon, in his Greek Grammar, speaks with apparent regret of the absence of articles in Latin, though 'omnes fere naciones habeant eos, et lingua gallica habet eos ut li le las et huius modi...' *Hic, haec* and *hoc* he calls 'pronomina articularia'.[5]

Pronoun. Five leading ideas are apparent, in various combinations, in the tangle of description which surrounds the pronoun:

(i) that it is used instead of a noun, especially a proper noun;

(ii) that it indicates a thing without reference to any of its qualities except individuality;

(iii) that it expresses indefiniteness;

(iv) that it is a means of expressing the first and second persons, all nouns being of the third person;

(v) that it saves tedious repetition of the noun.

Latin and Greek pronouns are so varied ('irregular') in form that most grammarians frame their definitions in terms of meaning or function.

The category had not yet taken form among the Stoic grammarians. They classified what we now call personal pronouns among their definite articles (ἄρθρα ὡρισμένα) and our definite article and relative pronoun among their indefinite articles (ἄρθρα ἀοριστώδη). This was because there was no general category of pronoun; the personal pronouns were felt to be more precise in their reference than were the relative pronouns and our definite article; the former were

---

[1] Donatus, *Ars Grammatica*, Bk II. 11 (K. IV. 381).
[2] Priscian, XVII. 27 (K. III. 124).   [3] Priscian, XIII. 17 (K. III. 11).
[4] e.g. Perottus, sig. a 3 verso; Sulpitius, sig. a 3 verso.
[5] Roger Bacon, *Greek Grammar*, pp. 13–14.

therefore classified along with the more definite, and the latter with the less definite ἄρθρα.[1]

The category first appears in Dionysius Thrax, as ἀντωνυμία (noun-substitute), where it is equivalent to the Stoic definite article; that is, it still excludes the relative pronoun, which Dionysius continued to treat as an indefinite article. His definition of the pronoun is, 'λέξις ἀντὶ ὀνόματος παραλαμβανομένη, προσώπων ὡρισμένων δηλωτική' (a word used instead of a noun to indicate a definite person).'[2] This gradual separation of pronoun from article is discussed at length and with subtlety by Apollonius Dyscolus *De Pronomine*. Several of his opinions are summed up in his discussion of the appropriate name for the category. He disapproves of Dionysius' ἀντωνυμία (though he uses it himself) and its variant ἀντώνυμον, because not all pronouns are used instead of nouns. He rejects Tyrannio's interesting suggestion of σημείωσις (sign or signal), apparently misunderstanding what Tyrannio meant by it,[3] and also a suggested ἰσωνυμία, because the pronoun has not meaning *equal* to that of the noun.[4] His own definition of the pronoun, though slightly different in wording, is the same as that of Dionysius.

Among the Latin grammarians there is agreement that the pronoun is put 'instead of' a noun, but on little else. Varro has his own classification, in which words like *quis* and *qui* (the least definite of his four degrees) which he calls *provocabula*, are distinguished from words like *hic, haec, hoc* (the most definite) which he calls *pronomina*.[5] Donatus says the pronoun means almost exactly the same as the noun: '...pro nomine posita tantundem paene significat personamque interdum recipit'.[6] Diomedes and Charisius say it means 'less than the noun but almost the same'. Priscian alone restricts the pronoun to being used for a proper noun: '...pars orationis, quae pro nomine proprio uniuscuiusque accipitur personasque finitas recipit'.[7] He is emphatic in rejecting the view that we use pronouns because we do not know the name of the thing we are referring to; he recognises the expression of indefiniteness, but the main reason for the existence of pronouns is the fact, as he conceives it, that nouns 'are' of the third person only.[8] Isidore is the first writer to give prominence to the idea

[1] Robins, pp. 29–30. [2] Dionysius Thrax, p. 63.
[3] Apollonius Dyscolus, *De Pronomine*, Bk I (S & U, I, i. 4).
[4] Apollonius Dyscolus, op. cit. p. 9. [5] Varro, VIII. 45.
[6] Donatus, *Ars Grammatica*, II. 11 (K. IV. 379).
[7] Priscian, XII. I (K. II. 577). [8] Priscian, XVII. 69 (K. III. 148).

of repetition: 'the pronoun is so called because it is put in place of a noun so that repetition of the noun itself should not cause weariness (*ne fastidium faciat nomen ipsum dum iteratur*)'.[1]

The medieval and renaissance grammarians adopt, broadly, one or other of two approaches: they treat the pronoun either as standing for the noun and expressing person, or as expressing substance without quality. Linacre, Ramus and Sanctius differ from the rest and from each other. Tatwine speaks of the pronoun being used for the noun, 'cuius minister est et obsequio fungitur'.[2] Bede keeps close to Donatus; Alcuin and Ælfric repeat Isidore's reference to avoiding repetition, an idea not directly mentioned by either Donatus or Priscian, nor given any prominence by the renaissance grammarians. Lily does not mention it, but it is a commonplace in the English grammars. Perottus, Sulpitius, Despauter and Antonio follow Priscian in emphasising, if not in prescribing, the reference of the pronoun to the proper noun. The usual formula is: '...ponitur loco nominis proprii'.[3]

Peter Helias is concerned with two questions especially. The first is the difference between substantive and pronoun, to which he gives the customary answer: 'The pronoun signifies substance without quality, that is, it signifies a thing in itself.'[4] The second question is how a pronoun can refer to a thing when you know nothing about the thing. In this connection he quotes an anonymous gloss on Priscian, which reads:

When I say, 'I met some man or other and he stole my cloak', does the pronoun *he* in this sentence signify a definite individual, seeing that it refers to an unknown man? To which the answer is that in this sentence *he* signifies a definite person, namely an unknown man—'definite' not because *he* tells us any quality of the man, but because in that context it cannot be applied significantly to anything else, and it is applied in personal terms.[5]

Until a full text of Peter Helias is published it is premature to say exactly how he treated the pronoun, but it is clear from this that he is

---

[1] Isidore, I. viii.   [2] Tatwine, p. 398.   [3] Antonio of Lebrixa, fol. xvii.
[4] Peter Helias, *Summa super Priscianum* (Hunt, I. 201): 'Pronomen vero significat substantiam sine qualitate, id est significat rem ut substat...'
[5] 'Queritur cum dico "Nescio quem hominem inveni et is abstulit michi cappam", an certam et finitam personam hoc pronomen *is* in hac oratione significet, cum ad ignotum hominem referatur. Ad quod dicimus quia in hac oratione *is* certam personam significet, scilicet ignotum hominem, nec dico certam quod *is* eius qualitatem nobis notificet, sed certam quia *is* ad nullam aliam rem significandam ibi potest dirigi.' (ibid.)

regarding it more as Tyrannio's σημείωσις than as the noun-substitute of Dionysius, Priscian and the central tradition.

Roger Bacon refers both to Priscian and to the scholastic definition. The latter he formulates: 'Pronouns signify the substance of nouns, though they differ in their mode of signification: nouns are said to signify substance with quality, and pronouns without quality.'[1] Bacon also explains why Priscian discusses the pronoun after the verb: pronouns were invented after verbs 'to make up for the absence of the first and second person'. This is Eberhard's reason also: 'Causa duplex igitur pronominibus reperitur Cur sunt inventa, quarum tibi prima necesse est, Altera commoditas.'[2] Pronouns of the first and second person, he goes on to explain, were invented because they were *necessary* for the speaker; the third-person pronouns were invented for the *convenience* of other people: 'Quae sunt alterius personae commoditate...inventa.'

The modal definitions of the speculative grammarians in this instance closely resemble Peter Helias. Siger first gives the customary '...pars est declinabilis et pro nomine ponitur'; he continues:

The mode of signification by means of which a pronoun is a pronoun is the mode of signification of substance, unchanging condition, or being, which is the same, so that the pronoun has only one mode of signification, as has been said. There belongs to the pronoun (and it is this which makes it a pronoun) a mode of signification which is indeterminate, indefinite, merely of substance, without quality. (Pp. 124–5.)[3]

Thomas of Erfurt makes the same point, more tersely: '...pars orationis significans per modum entis, et indeterminatae apprehentionis'.[4]

Of the humanist grammarians only three have a fresh contribution to make, the most interesting being Linacre's attempt to define the pronoun in largely formal terms: 'A pronowne is a part of spech declinyd with case, which sygnyfieth a thing with out any dyfference of tyme, and ever with certeyne difference of parson.'[5] Ramus does

---

[1] Roger Bacon, *Greek Grammar*, p. 158: 'Quoniam (pronomina) substanciam significant nominum, licet differant in modo significandi, secundum quod dicuntur nomina signifi-care substanciam cum qualitate et pronomina sine qualitate.'
[2] Eberhard of Bethune, Bk iii. chap. 14 (Wrobel, p. 144).
[3] 'Modus autem significandi per quem pronomen est pronomen est modus significandi substantiae, habitus permanentis, seu entis, quod idem est; ita quod pronomen non habet nisi unum modum significandi qui dictus est. Modus autem significandi indeterminati, confusi, substantiae mere seu sine qualitate, accidit pronomini, unde pronomen est.'
[4] TE, p. 73.   [5] Linacre, *Progymnasmata*, sig. C i verso.

71

not consider the pronoun a part of speech at all, but treats it as an 'irregular parisyllabic adjective',[1] and Sanctius' total abolition of the category has already been quoted.[2] Lily's grammar contains two quite different criteria. In the English accidence the definition is framed in syntactic terms; a pronoun can be substituted for a noun without changing the structure of the sentence: '...is moche lyke a nowne and in reason[3] standeth for a nowne'.[4] In the Latin accidence a distinction is made which is not part of the older tradition: '...qua in demonstranda aut repetenda re aliqua utimur'.[5] Lily does not explain or illustrate this definition, but it is taken by later writers of Latin and English grammars as pointing to the difference between the use (*demonstrare*) of a pronoun which has no *verbal* antecedent or referent, such as the use of *I* or *this* in conversation, and on the other hand the use (*repetere*) of *he* or *which* to refer to some *noun* previously mentioned. The distinction is discussed further in chapter 12, below.

Within the tradition, as later in the English grammars, the category *pronoun* is held together virtually by its name. The words which it may include cover a wide range of subtle, overlapping functions, of which 'standing instead of a noun' may be the least important. We cannot say that these functions were unrecognised within the tradition (although our own perception of them has been made easier by subsequent developments in logical and linguistic analysis). They were recognised fitfully and unsystematically, according to the particular line of thought of individual grammarians. Recognition was neither wide enough nor sustained enough to produce the imaginative energy needed to form fresh parts of speech. For the renaissance grammarians, as for ourselves, there had been pronouns for so long that it was (almost literally) unthinkable that the category should be recast. This inertia, which makes for stability, has so far proved even more powerful than the (at times forceful) recognition that the traditional category of pronoun is an inconsistent combination of sometimes unrelated functions which, if it is not unstable, ought to be.

Adverb. The early treatment of the adverb is obscure. A form such as καλῶς seems to have been classed sometimes with the noun, some-

---

[1] Ramus, Bk I. chap. 9: 'de parasyllabis adiectivis anomalis, quae pronomina dicuntur'.
[2] See above, p. 53.
[3] 'Reason' = discourse; the earlier name for the parts of speech was 'parts of reason'.
[4] Lily, 1527, p. 21. [5] Lily, *Brev. Inst.* 1567, sig. C i verso.

times with the verb. For this reason Antipater called it μεσότης, a term later transferred to the participle.[1] The term πανδέκτης was then used for the adverb on the grounds that it was the 'mediator' of the parts of speech, having something in common with them all. Dionysius Thrax uses the Alexandrian term ἐπίρρημα, and provides the first definition: 'an indeclinable part of speech used to amplify or qualify a verb'.[2] The adverb had taken shape as a distinct part of speech by the time of the later Stoics, but it was a cause of great uncertainty: formally it was related to the noun (adjective), as καλῶς to κάλος; structurally it was linked with the verb, but it could also stand alone as a sentence-equivalent: a feature it shared with those words which we call interjections but the Greeks did not distinguish from adverbs; semantically the adverb had a reference so wide that it seemed to cover every activity of the human mind.

This uncertainty about the adverb is expressed particularly by Donatus, who gives instances of words from every part of speech which might be considered adverbs: there is uncertainty as between adverb and noun (*falso*): between adverb and pronoun (*qui*); between adverb and verb (*pone*); between adverb and participle (*profecto*); and conjunction (*quando*); and preposition (*propter*); and interjection (*heu*).[3]

Smaragdus, in the verse preface to his chapter on the adverb, expresses apprehension not only on this score but also at the semantic range of the adverb:

Although adverbs arise from other parts of speech they flow from their own spring also in vast numbers. The range of this part of speech is altogether too vast; its heart is abundant, its hand powerful. If in the end the parts of speech lost their own proper functions they would lie drowned in the vast whirlpool of adverbs. The adverb draws to itself parts of speech like the all-absorbing sea, and violently forces them to obey its laws. (p. 613.)[4]

---

[1] Steinthal, I. 298; Robins, p. 33.
[2] Dionysius Thrax, p. 72: 'κατὰ ῥήματος λεγόμενον ἢ ἐπιλεγόμενον ῥήματι'.
[3] Donatus, *Ars Grammatica*, II. 13 (K. IV. 387).
[4] 'Quamvis a reliquis adverbia partibus orta
Sint, tamen a proprio plurima fonte fluunt.
Est huius partis nimium latissimus ordo,
Multifer est pectus et violenta manus.
Pars omnis proprium tandem si perderit actum,
Istius in vasto gurgite mersa iacet,
Adgregat ut pelagus partes sorbendo marinum,
Et violenter eas ad sua iura trahit.'

73

The Tradition

Donatus and Priscian, and the other Latin grammarians of the Byzantine period, agree closely with Dionysius, especially in relating the adverb only to the verb:

pars orationis, quae adiecta verbo significationem eius explanat atque inplet. (Donatus, *Ars Grammatica*, II. 13; K. IV. 385.)

pars orationis indeclinabilis, cuius significatio verbis adicitur. Hoc enim perficit adverbium verbis additum, quod adiectiva nomina appellativis nominibus adiuncta, ut 'prudens homo prudenter agit'. (Priscian, xv. 1; K. III. 60.)

It is not until the renaissance period that the definitions refer to the possibility of the adverb limiting any part of speech other than the verb. Amongst the grammarians considered here the earliest to make this extension is Antonio of Lebrixa, who says it can limit the noun (adjective) and participle: '...est quod additum verbo nomini aut participio significationem eius auget aut minuit aut mutat'.[1] Whittinton includes the participle, gerund and supine, but the only grammar besides Antonio's to include the noun adjective is Lily's, in the Latin accidence: '...pars orationis non flexa, quae adiecta verbo, sensum eius perficit atque explanat. Explanat etiam interdum et nomen: ut "Homo egregie impudens".'[2]

The English accidence in Lily's grammar, however, contains a definition of the adverb in which no mention is made of any part of speech except the verb.[3] This is one of the most striking discrepancies caused by its varied authorship and piecemeal development.

Definitions of the adverb sometimes can be misleading. In spite of his definition Priscian did in fact recognise as comparative adverbs words like *magis, minus, maxime*, which regularly limit adjectives or adverbs.[4] A question frequently discussed is whether the adverb (as also the interjection) can properly be so called when it is used alone, in a one-word sentence; or, alternatively, whether it is proper to make a one-word sentence out of an adverb, as '*non*' or '*bene*'. This question is referred to on page 136, below.

Thomas of Erfurt and Martin of Dacia are the only speculative grammarians whose discussion of the adverb is accessible: Siger's chapter on the adverb has not survived. Martin says that the adverb 'signifies, through the mode of limitation or through the mode of adjacency-to-another, what signifies through the mode of

---

[1] Antonio of Lebrixa, fol. xvii verso. [2] Lily, *Brev. Inst.* 1567, sig. D vi.
[3] Lily, 1527, p. 57. [4] Priscian, xv. 36 (K. III. 88).

becoming'.[1] That is, the adverb limits the verb and participle. Thomas's definition is to the same effect.[2] By far the most satisfactory definition within the tradition is the purely formal one of Ramus, '*vox expers numeri quae voci alii adiungitur*'.[3] It is deliberately so wide that it covers the preposition also, which Ramus treats separately in his syntax, but apparently as a sub-class of the adverb.[4] The strength of the definition is that it bypasses all the uncertainty which worried Donatus: it is no longer necessary to make difficult judgments about what the adverb means and what kind of word it is limiting.

Participle. The early Stoics had treated the participle as a kind of reciprocal common noun, or form of the verb with case-inflection. Priscian explains this by examples such as '*amator est amans*' and '*amans amator*', to which we would apply the term 'cognate' rather than reciprocal.[5] The later Stoics treated the participle as a special form of the verb (μετοχή) but not as a separate part of speech. By the time of Dionysius Thrax it is treated as a part of speech which '...partakes of the nature of verbs and nouns',[6] and this is how it is described by practically every grammarian after him, with the exception of the modistae. The nature of the relationship which the participle has to both noun and verb is analysed by Donatus: '...pars orationis dicta, quod partem capiat nominis, partem verbi. Recipit enim a nomine genera et casus, a verbo tempora et significationes, ab utroque numerum et figuram'.[7]

Priscian and his followers keep to the substance of this,[8] and the slight difference in emphasis made by some of the renaissance grammarians can be shown by quotation. The speculative grammarians, represented by Siger and Thomas, begin with Donatus, but are compelled by their system to cast their definitions eventually in modal terms. Siger's conclusion is:

The specific mode of signification of the participle is the mode of signifying not-other-than, or united with, substance; so that the participle does not signify an action as other than substance, but as united with substance;

---

[1] Martin of Dacia, chap. xliv. 66: 'Adverbium significat per modum determinantis sive per modum adiacentis alteri quod significat per modum fieri.'
[2] TE, p. 113.   [3] Ramus, Bk ii. chap. 8.   [4] cf. p. 66, above.
[5] Dionysius of Halicarnassus, *De Compositione Verborum*, chap. 2; Priscian, xi. 1 (K. ii. 548).
[6] Dionysius Thrax, p. 60: '...μετέχουσα τῆς τῶν ῥημάτων καὶ τῆς τῶν ὀνομάτων ἰδιότητος'.
[7] Donatus, *Ars Grammatica*, ii. 14 (K. iv. 387).   [8] Priscian, xi. 7 (K. ii. 552.)

accordingly one must think of the participle in almost the same way as one thinks of action mixed with potentiality. (p. 123.)[1]

Thomas of Erfurt agrees with this closely.[2] Neither improves on Bacon, whose definition is still so wide that it would include the infinitive, but seems intended to keep the participle firmly linked to the verb and distinct from the adjective: '...*significat substanciam cum actu et non cum qualitate*'.[3]

Some of the renaissance grammarians are quoted here to show their agreement. The treatment of the participle during the whole course of the tradition is more uniform than the treatment of any other part of speech. This is because a definition in formal terms was almost inescapable, and the formal criteria were obvious. A definition in terms of meaning would be inadequate because the 'meaning' of the participle was the same as the meaning of the verb. The formal criteria lay to hand, in the accidents of case and tense especially. Case neatly distinguished the participle from the finite verb; tense and voice neatly distinguished it from the noun adjective. In English, as will appear, it was less clear what to do with the participle.

pars orationis indeclinabilis quae pro verbo ponitur ex quo derivatur, genus et casum habens ad similitudinem nominis. (Perottus, sig. d 7 verso.)

quod declinat per casus cum tempore. (Antonio of Lebrixa, fol. xvii verso.)

pars orationis partem capiens nominis, partemque verbi. (Despauter, fol. 9.)

a part of speech declined with case which signifieth a dede with some difference of time. (Linacre, *Progymnasmata*, sig. C iii verso.)

cometh deryved of a verbe, and hath in sygnificacyon moche the maner of his verbe that he cometh of, and is declyned with case as a nowne. (Lily, 1527, p. 53.)

a verbo personali nomina verbalia oriuntur, significationem et tempus a verbo ducentia. (Ramus, Bk II. chap. 2. 52.)

Ramus, as is apparent, made the participle a secondary part of speech, within the noun.

Interjection. Words which were later called interjections were classed by Greek grammarians among the adverbs because, as Priscian explains,[4]

---

[1] 'Modus autem significandi specificus participii est modus significandi indistantis seu uniti substantiae; ita quod participium non significat actum ut alterum a substantia sed unitum substantiae; ita quod quasi eodem modo imaginandum est de participio sicut de actu permixto potentiae.' [2] TE, p. 123.
[3] Roger Bacon, *Summa Gramatica*, p. 7. [4] Priscian, xv. 40 (K. III. 90).

they could either be attached to verbs or verbs could be understood with them. That is to say, if a man exclaims, 'Alas, my
horse has been beaten!' the word 'alas' is functioning just like
'unfortunately' in 'My horse has been unfortunately beaten'. In
this example (which is not Priscian's) the resemblance can seem even
closer, because the man might also say, 'Unfortunately, my horse has
been beaten', where 'unfortunately' has the same sort of independence that 'alas' had. This independence is even more apparent if
the man, in answer to the question, 'What happened to your horse?
Was it beaten?' replies just, 'Unfortunately', as he might (given a
sheltered and rather literary upbringing) reply, 'Alas!'.

In Latin grammars the interjection came to be treated as a
separate part of speech because, according to Priscian, its real
independence of the verb, and its self-sufficient expression of emotion,
could not be denied.[1] Varro makes no mention of it. Quintilian says
that it must be added to the parts of speech, but gives no definition.[2]
In the grammars proper three criteria are used, in various combinations, to define the interjection:

(i) morphological: that it has no formal relation to other words
and no variations in form itself; it lacks family and is therefore
suspect. The common term is *incondita*, usually translated 'rude'.

(ii) psychological: that it expresses emotion; *animi affectum
significat.*

(iii) syntactical: that it has no relation in construction with
other words; it is *interiecta.*

Before the renaissance only one writer, Archbishop Tatwine in the
eighth century, omits all reference to the interjection's expressing
emotion,[3] and only two, Maximus Victorinus[4] and Cominianus,[5]
make that their sole criterion. Diomedes combines (i) and (ii):
'...pars orationis affectum mentis singificans voce incondita.'[6]
Donatus combines (ii) and (iii): '... pars orationis interiecta aliis
partibus orationis ad exprimendos animi affectus ',[7] and most later
writers follow him.

---

[1] ibid.; Charisius, Bk II (K. I. 190) makes the same point adding that the wish to keep
the number of the parts of speech at eight (Latin having no article)was not a motive.

[2] Quintilian, I. iv. 19.

[3] Tatwine, p. 398: '...sola separatim posita, nullae subiecta regulae, aliis partibus
non adhaeret'.   [4] Max. Victorinus (K. VI. 204).

[5] Cominianus, quoted by Charisius, Bk II (K. I. 238).

[6] Diomedes, Bk I (K. I. 419)   [7] Donatus, *Ars Grammatica*, Bk II (K. IV. 391).

The independence of the interjection is much discussed, especially in relation to the stock example, 'pro dolor', which phrase Servius and Priscian saw could have the force of an interjection. Alcuin makes a simple point, ignored by the grammarians of Latin and English who cumber their work with long lists of the possible kinds of interjections: 'I think there are as many different kinds of interjection as there are different emotions.'[1]

Apart from the speculative grammarians only two of the medieval writers need comment: Hugo of St Victor for the fullness of his definition (he is one of the very few writers to include all three criteria) and Eberhard of Bethune for his unusual practice in returning to the Greek classification and including the interjection among the adverbs:

pars orationis qua interiecta aliis partibus orationis animi tantum exprimit affectus voce incondita quae ex natura magis quam institutione profecta videtur. (Hugo of St Victor, p. 288.)

> Interiectivas dicunt adverbia vere,
> Vel quoniam verbis iunguntur vel quia saepe
> Verba subaudiri soleant in vocibus harum.
> (Eberhard of Bethune, chap. 24, 214.)

The most interesting feature of the interjection is not the one on which the definitions, in Latin and English grammars, most concentrate—the expression of emotion. The speculative grammarians, and especially Roger Bacon, are alone in giving a great deal of attention to the more important question of the status of the interjection as an utterance and to its syntactical relations.

Roger Bacon takes up Priscian's example of the exclamation *pro dolor* and discusses whether it is a word or a sentence. His discussion is of great interest. It shows the scholastic approach unencumbered by doctrinaire modal machinery, and it is characteristic of its strength—the perceptive analysis of the structure of an expression—and of the weakness which belongs to almost all grammatical study before modern times: the failure to see that the only laws which can be said to govern language are those derived from the working of language itself, and not from outside it. Bacon's discussion is worth quoting at length:

One can ask first about the expression *pro dolor* whether it is a word or a sentence. It is clearly not a word. Interjections signify an emotion, nouns

---

[1] Alcuin, col. 902: 'Reor diversas esse interiectionum significationes, sicut diversi sunt motus animi.'

and all other parts of speech a concept, and as no unity can be formed out of an emotion and a concept (because they just do not combine or agree with each other) it is clear that an interjection cannot be compounded with any other word.

Similarly, if this interjection *pro* is compounded with the noun *dolor* something will result from their union: not purely an expression of emotion, because then the thing signified by the noun would have no influence; not purely the expression of a concept, because then the thing signified by the interjection would have no influence. What will result, therefore, is a combination formed from an emotion and a concept. But this can be proved impossible: I ask whether the combination is an interjection, or a noun, or some other part of speech. It is not an interjection, because the interjection expresses only emotion; not a noun, because every noun signifies only a concept, and no emotion; for the same reason it cannot be any other part of speech, because every part of speech signifies through the mode of conception. Therefore if this expression *pro dolor* is a compound word it is not a part of speech. But this is absurd, because it would not then be a conventionally meaningful expression; therefore the first statement is absurd, that it is a compound word.

The opposite point of view: because the interjection is, like the adverb, a disposition to action, it can therefore be compounded with another part of speech as the adverb can; the adverb can be compounded as in '*benedictus, benedico*', therefore, etc.

Similarly, the parts out of which a compound is made must themselves be incomplete, because the whole is complete; the parts, however, are subject to imperfection and inadequacy...Since the interjection is itself quite incomplete before it is put into the compound, and is uttered as a crude and imperfect expression, it is very well suited to make a compound through having in itself the incompleteness which is the condition of making compounds.

The conclusion of all this is that the expression under discussion is not a compound word but a sentence. (*Summa Gramatica* pp. 95–7.)[1]

[1] 'Queritur primo de hoc quod dico "Proch dolor", an sit diccio vel oracio. Quod non sit diccio videtur: interjeccio significat affectum animi, nomen et quelibet alia pars oracionis conceptum, quare cum nichil unum possit fieri ex affectu et conceptu, cum simpliciter disconveniant et repugnant, videtur quod non possit interjeccio componi cum aliquo.

'Item, si componatur hec interjeccio "proch", cum isto nomine "dolor" aliquid resultabit ex eorum unione; istud autem non erit affectus purus, quia tunc nichil operabitur significatum nominis; nec conceptus purus, quia tunc nichil operabitur significatum interjeccionis, quare erit aggregatum ex affectu et conceptu. Set probacio (est) quod non: quia tunc quero, aut erit interjeccio aut nomen aut aliqua alia pars oracionis. Non interjeccio, quia interjeccio solum affectum demonstrat; non nomen quia omne nomen solum conceptum significat et nullum affectum; et eadem racione nec aliqua alia pars, quia nulla significat nisi solum per modum conceptus; quare si hec vox "proch dolor" esset composita, non esset pars oracionis. Hoc autem est inconveniens, quia non esset vox significativa ad placitum, quare primum est inconveniens, scilicet quod sit vox composita.

'Oppositum videtur: quia interjeccio est disposicio actus sicut adverbium, potest igitur

Bacon then repeats his objection to the argument that the inter-jection is a kind of adverb, and gives his objection to the argument that the incompleteness of the interjection makes its proper place to be within a compound:

If an expression is suited to the formation of compounds by virtue of its incompleteness, nevertheless its meaning is obstructed. Granted a word may be incomplete, and incompleteness may have some small share in the nature of compounds; yet when a word is uttered suddenly, without deliberation, and is met in no regular or customary pattern (and for this reason is more of a hindrance than a help in forming a compound word, because these conditions apply to every part of speech besides the inter-jection): and because it is agreed that the whole cannot be an interjection because of the regular formation of the word forming the other component ...therefore these words do not form any kind of compound. (*Summa Gramatica*, pp. 95–7.)[1]

We can now see that Bacon is using logical techniques inappropri-ately, but he is aware all the time of the speaker behind the expression he is analysing; it is this which makes his work distinctive and, in this instance, superior to Thomas of Erfurt, in whom new philosophy and old grammar combine most uneasily: 'The interjection's most general essential mode is the mode of signifying through the mode of limiting another [word], in this case a verb or participle, and expressing emotions.'[2]

The renaissance grammarians, almost without exception, repeat, verbatim or in substance, the definitions of Diomedes or Donatus. Linacre's translation of Diomedes (whether direct or indirect) is worth quoting because it introduces two terms with a long history

componi cum alia parte oracionis sicut adverbium, set adverbium potest ut "benedictus", "benedico", quare etc.

'Item, cum ad composicionem exigatur parcium compositarum inperfeccio, quia totum completum et perfectum est, partes autem sub inperfeccione et corrupcione...cum ergo ipsa interjeccio sit de se ante conjunccionem maxime inperfecta et voce incondita et inperfecta proferatur, quare maxime nata est ad composicionem, cum inperfeccionem habeat de se que est racio composicionis.

'Et soluciones istorum sunt quod ista vox non est diccio set oracio.'

[1] '...si vox conferret ad composicionem propter inperfeccionem, tamen inpediret ejus significatum; et licet sit inperfecta, et inperfeccio aliquantulum operetur ad composicionis naturam, cum sua vox subito et sine deliberacione proferatur et indisposita et non regu-lariter accendenda, et propter hoc magis inpedit composicionem vocis quam ad hoc operetur, quia ille condiciones exiguntur ad quamlibet partem oracionis preterquam ad interjeccionem, et quia interjeccio esse non potest constat propter regulatam formacionem vocis alterius componencium, quare nullo modo erit composicio eorum.'

[2] TE, p. 139: 'Modus significandi essentialis generalissimus interjectionis est modus significandi per modum determinantis alterum, quod est verbum, vel participium, affectiones animi repraesentans.'

in English and Latin grammars: 'rude' and 'passion of the mind':
'a part undeclynyd the which undre a rude voyce betokeneth some
passyon of the mynde'·[1] Lily's equivalent is: 'a sounde or a voyce
that brasteth out in speche, betokenynge the affecyon of the mynde'.[2]

Ramus and Sanctius both fall outside the normal pattern; Ramus
because he keeps to the old classification and treats the interjection
among the adverbs,[3] Sanctius because he excludes it altogether from
the parts of speech on the grounds that it is not a word at all, but
only a natural noise.[4]

[1] Linacre, *Progymnasmata*, sig. C iii verso. [2] Lily, 1527, p. 60.
[3] Ramus, Bk ii. chap. 8. [4] Sanctius, Bk i. chap. 2.

4. CLASSIFICATION WITHIN THE PARTS OF SPEECH

One of the most distinctive, but wearisome, features of the tradition is the elaboration with which the various parts of speech are subdivided and classified. Most, but not all, grammarians attach considerable importance to classification; some undertake it with zeal, some as a routine. The practice is as old as Dionysius Thrax, and he was presumably following, even if also elaborating, what was customary before him, especially among the Stoics. Classification is a prominent feature of the early English grammars and appears still, in something very like its full Alexandrian form, in some of the more indiscriminatingly analytical school grammars of today.

This elaborate classification is of interest not only as the model for the English grammars, but as an expression of the outlook upon language of the ancient and medieval world. For them, as for us, the study of language is a meeting-ground for logic, philosophy and grammar. The first classifications of the noun contain subdivisions in which logical, formal, rhetorical and semantic criteria are jumbled together, and something can be seen during the development of the tradition of the first, and most difficult, stages of sorting them out.

NOUN

Dionysius makes two classifications. His first[1] is into:
Primitive (πρωτότυπον, *primitivum*) : 'having no simpler form.'
Derivative (παράγωγον, *derivativum*).

The derivatives are grouped into seven classes:
Comparative (συγκριτικόν, *comparativum*)
Superlative (ὑπερθετικόν, *superlativum*)
Diminutive (ὑποκοριστικόν, *diminutivum*)

---

[1] Dionysius Thrax, p. 25. The Latin terms are those used by Priscian or Donatus.

and a group of four which express different kinds of personal names.

The passage containing Dionysius' second classification, into twenty-four groups, is suspected by Steinthal.[1] It begins[2] with the distinction first made, apparently, by Zeno[3] and Chrysippus,[4] between proper and common nouns:

Proper (ὄνομα κύριον, ὄνομα ἰδίως λεγόμενον, *proprium*): 'what signifies individual being—τὸ τὴν ἰδίαν οὐσίαν σημαῖνον—e.g. *Homer*'.

Common (ὄνομα προσηγορικόν, ὄνομα κοινῶς λεγόμενον, *appellativum*): 'what signifies common being—τὸ τὴν κοινὴν οὐσίαν σημαῖνον— e.g. '*man, horse*'.

Dionysius does not follow the later Stoics in making proper and common nouns into separate parts of speech, though one commentator[5] records a tradition also referred to by Quintilian, that he did treat the common noun as a separate part of speech, and argues that the grammar in his name must therefore be by a different Dionysius.

Indefinite (ἀόριστον, *infinitum*): 'the opposite of the interrogative', e.g. ὁπόσος, *quantus*.

Collective (περιληπτικόν, *collectivum*): e.g. 'crowd'.

Distributive (ἐπιμεριζομενόν, *distributivum* or *dividuum*): e.g. 'each'.

Ordinal (τακτικόν, *ordinale*): e.g. 'first'.

Cardinal (ἀριθμητικόν, *numerale, numeri*): e.g. 'one'.

Local (περιεκτικόν, *locale*): 'denoting a place in which a number are collected, as a grove, the Parthenon'. Priscian's examples are of the type *propinquus, longinquus*.

Onomatopoeic (πεποιημενόν, *factitium*): e.g. φλοῖσβος, *tintinnabulum*.

Generic (γενικόν, *generale*): 'can be divided into many species, e.g. plant, animal'.

Epithet (ἐπίθετον): Diomedes calls it *adiectum* or *adiectio*; Donatus calls it *epitheton, adiectum nominis, adiectivum* and '[a word] *mediae significationis*': 'A word used with a proper noun or common noun to indicate with equal appropriateness either praise or blame... e.g. *temperate, licentious.*'[6]

---

[1] Steinthal, II. 250.   [2] Dionysius Thrax, pp. 33 f.   [3] Zeno, SVF, I. 19. No. 65.
[4] Diog. Laertius, VII. 192.   [5] Bekker, p. 672.
[6] Dionysius Thrax, p. 34.

Relational (πρός τι ἔχον, *ad aliquid dictum*): applied to correlative terms like *father, son; slave, master.*

Quasi-relational (ὡς πρός τι ἔχον, *quasi ad aliquid dictum*): e.g. *day, night.*

Relative (ἀναφορικόν, ὁμοιωματικόν, *relativum*): 'indicating a resemblance', e.g. *qui, qualis.*

Interrogative (ἐρωτηματικόν, *interrogativum*): Priscian's examples include *quis* and *qualis.*

Specific (εἰδικόν, *speciale*): e.g. *vine, horse.*

Absolute (ἀπολελυμενόν, *absolutum*): 'what is known through itself alone', e.g. *god, reason.*

Participatory (μετουσιαστικόν): 'what shares in the nature of something'. e.g. *golden, silvery.*

Homonym (ὁμώνυμον, *homonymon*): 'applied equivocally to several things', e.g. Ajax the son of Telamon and Ajax the son of Oileus; μῦς θαλάσσιος (mussel) and μῦς γηγενής (mouse).

Synonym (συνώνυμον, *synonymon*): 'different names applied to the same thing'. Priscian follows Dionysius in giving as examples different words all meaning 'sword'.

Suffered (φερώνυμον); 'applied because of what has happened to one: τὸ ἀπό τινος συμβεβηκότος τεθέν', e.g. *Megapenthes*, literally 'great mourner'.

Twin (διώνυμον): two names acting as one proper noun, naming one person.

Appropriate (ἐπώνυμον): a kind of 'twin' name, considered as intrinsically appropriate and accompanying a proper name as *Earthshaker* accompanies Poseidon.

Ethnic (ἐθνικόν, *gentile*): e.g. *Phrygian, Greek.*

Donatus, Diomedes and Priscian between them include all in Dionysius' list except the four for which no Latin equivalent is given above. They make a number of additions:

Substantive (*substantivum, nomen substantivum, nomen substantiae infinitae, nomen substantivum infinitum*): Priscian uses the term, but does not make a formal category of it. It refers always to forms of *quis* and *qui.*

Material (*corporale*): e.g. *homo, terra* (Donatus).

Abstract (*incorporale*): e.g. *pietas*; defined by Charisius as 'quae intellectu tantum modo percipiuntur, verum neque videri neque tangi possunt'.[1]

---

[1] Charisius, Bk II (K. I. 153). Donatus has the same category.

Classification within the parts of speech

Quality (*qualitatis*): e.g. *bonus* (Donatus).

Quantity (*quantitatis*): e.g. *magnus* (Donatus).

Redditive (*redditiva*): e.g. *talis, tantus* (Priscian).

Temporal (*temporale*): e.g. *mensis* (Priscian).

Fixed (*fixum*): e.g. *mater, soror*, which cannot be put into another gender (Donatus).

Movable (*mobile*): e.g. proper nouns which have masculine and feminine forms: *Gaius, Gaia*; and nouns like *bonus* which have a form for each gender (Donatus).

Quasi-participial (*participiis simile*): e.g. *sapiens, demens* (Donatus).

Verbal (*verbale*): e.g. *doctor*: nouns which are 'facta de verbo' (Donatus).

The convention of classifying nouns with this wholehearted comprehensiveness did not last into the renaissance period. The medieval grammarians who were following Priscian and Donatus closely took over the lists as they stood. Isidore makes a classification into thirty-two kinds, closely following Priscian; Bede into twenty and Tatwine into twenty-seven kinds, taken from Donatus; Alcuin and Ælfric into thirty kinds, taken from Priscian; Bacon also follows Priscian, restricting himself in the *Greek Grammar* to a list of nine, but in the *Sumule* attributing 'apud grammaticos' thirty-three differentiae to the noun;[1] and Hugo of St Victor achieves a list of thirty-seven.[2] Thomas of Erfurt similarly lists twenty-four, and Eberhard twenty-seven, types of noun adjective, almost all of them the same as Priscian's.[3] The renaissance grammarians restrict their classification to the main subdivisions: proper and common, substantive and adjective, the development of which is important enough to justify closer attention.

Proper noun. The two approaches of our school grammars are already apparent, though very closely related. The logical approach would define the proper noun as 'the name of a unique object'; the material approach treats it as 'the name of a person, place or thing'. The logical approach, apparent in Dionysius Thrax and reinforced by Priscian, is the central one of the tradition; the material approach is a weakened, pragmatic and didactic modification, derived from a feature of naming which has nothing to do with logic. We give names

---

[1] Roger Bacon, *Sumule Dialectices*, p. 236.
[2] Hugo of St Victor, p. 274.   [3] TE, pp. 37 f.

of a particular kind to people, places and (sometimes) to objects whose individuality we wish to emphasise in the way our own names give individuality to us. Two processes are being operated; the logical one of expressing uniqueness, the psychological one of personalising. When a man calls his car 'Daisy' he is primarily concerned to personalise it, but he also gives it a name which singles it out from other cars. A man who says to his wife, 'Shall we take the car?' is, if he has only one car, primarily concerned to single it out from all other cars, especially from the taxi or the neighbour's car which would be the alternatives. The words *the car*, in this context, form a logically proper noun, but the tradition could not so regard them. Perhaps if Latin had articles it would have been easier to see that 'Rome' and 'the city', in a given context, are logically equivalent, and a useful separation could have been made between personalising names and (logically) proper names.

As it is, the traditional category of proper noun has these two elements confused in it. The definition is often expressed in logical terms, but personalising is tacitly made the criterion, as the examples show. Donatus defines the proper noun as '*unius nomen*',[1] but the only examples he gives are *Roma and Tiberis*.[2] Diomedes, who follows Donatus closely, is unusual here in restricting proper nouns to the names of gods, men and places, thereby recognising even in his definition the primacy of the personalising criterion.[3] Priscian defines the proper noun in almost purely logical terms: 'Proprium vero naturaliter uniuscuiusque privatam substantiam et qualitatem significat et in rebus est individuis, quas philosophi atomos vocant, ut "Plato", "Socrates"'.[4] He also recognises that the same proper name is used to refer to many people. This he explains, not, as we do now, in terms of context or universe of discourse, but (truly, so far as it goes) as being accidental (*fortuitu*) and not due to the perception of any quality common to all the people.

With the renaissance grammarians the proper noun is usually left undefined; those who do give a definition—Perottus, Linacre and Lily—keep close to Donatus. Lily can represent them: 'Proprium, est quod rem uni individuo propriam significat'.[5]

---

[1] Donatus, *Ars Minor* (K. IV. 355).
[2] Donatus, *Ars Grammatica*, II. 2 (K. IV. 373).
[3] Diomedes, Bk I (K. I. 320).   [4] Priscian, II. 25 (K. II. 58).
[5] Lily, *Brev. Inst.*, 1567, sig. A v.

Classification within the parts of speech

Common noun. Donatus defines the common noun as '*multorum nomen*';[1] Charisius[2] and Diomedes[3] define it as being used '*generaliter communiterve*'. Varro's classification of nouns had probably allowed greater precision than this, but he gives us too little information. He calls the common noun *vocabulum*, in his second degree of definiteness (which he calls *ut infinitum*).[4] Priscian attempts a more precise definition: 'The difference between proper nouns and common nouns is that common nouns naturally apply to many things, which have in common either substance or quality or quantity, and these may belong either to the genus or to the species: to the genus names like 'animal, body, courage;' to the species 'man, stone, white, short'.[5] This is the most that anyone except Siger has to say about the common noun within the tradition. Thomas of Erfurt merely transposes the same idea into a mode: 'The common or appellative noun signifies by means of a mode which can be communicated to several subjects.'[6] The renaissance grammarians, if they define the common noun at all, repeat Donatus. The only writer to have suggested a fresh approach is Siger of Courtrai, who introduces from logic the definition of the common noun as one that can be preceded by universal signs such as *all* and *no*, it being a defining property of the proper noun that it cannot be so preceded: 'Ista autem qualitas appellativa est principium constructionis cum signis universalibus ut: omnis, quilibet, nullus, etc. quae cum propriis nominibus, unde propria sunt, congrue non ordinantur.'[7]

Thomas is unusual in preferring the term *commune* to *appellativum* which was the term generally used, as was *appellative* in the early English grammars. The adverb *communiter*, however, often appears in the definitions, and as early as the sixth century Isidore's use of *communia* showed how the term 'common' was ready to develop: 'Appellativa nomina inde vocantur quia communia sunt et in multorum significatione consistunt.'[8]

---

[1] Donatus, *Ars Minor* (K. IV. 355).   [2] Charisius, II. 6 (K. I. 153).
[3] Diomedes, I (K. I. 322).
[4] Varro, VIII. 45.
[5] Priscian, II. 24 (K. II. 58): 'Hoc autem interest inter proprium et appellativum, quod appellativum naturaliter commune est multorum, quos eadem substantia sive qualitas vel quantitas generalis specialisve iungit.'
[6] TE, p. 31: 'Nomen ergo commune vel appellativum significat per modum communicabilis [sic] pluribus suppositis.'
[7] Siger, p. 97.
[8] Isidore of Seville, I. vii.

Noun substantive. The early development of the category noun substantive, to which the term *noun* was eventually restricted, cannot be fully illustrated from the grammars. The category was adumbrated by Priscian and is suggested by grammarians who follow him. Alcuin, for example, gives the property of the noun as being 'to signify substance or quality or quantity',[1] but his definition includes no reference to substance, nor is the substantive one of his explicit categories. In the middle of the twelfth century it is defined by John of Salisbury: 'Quod casualiter flectitur et temporis expers est, dictum est nomen substantivum, si substantiam significat aut substantive.'[2] But there is no similar treatment in the grammars until the later speculative approach of Siger and Thomas of Erfurt. According to Thomas the noun substantive is determined by the mode of independence—'*per se stantis*'.

Just as the most general mode of signification of the noun derives from its property of absolute being, so the mode *per se stantis* derives from its property of limited being, and this mode determines the substantival mode. A noun substantive, therefore, signifies through the mode of (the thing) determined, according to its essence, as *whiteness*. (TE, p. 32.)[3]

Siger's account of the noun substantive is on similar lines, though he varies his terms slightly. The mode through which the substantive signifies is, according to him, '*modus per se entis et abstracti*'. The *modus per se entis* is the mode of substance and (though he does not take the argument as far as this) is expressed in material nouns; the *modus abstracti* is the mode of '*entia per se distincta ab illo in quo sunt*' and is expressed '*in accidentibus abstractis*'.[4]

By the time of the renaissance grammarians a change has occurred. They all (except Linacre, who seems to ignore it) make the substantive one of the sub-classes of the noun, but define it in formal or structural terms. Perottus and Sulpitius make the criterion of a noun substantive that it is declined 'with one article',[5] meaning that it has only one gender and will therefore be correctly preceded by only one form of *hic* or *ille*. By this criterion a word like *bonus*, which may be preceded by *hic* in any of its three forms or, in another way of

---

[1] Alcuin, col. 858. [2] John of Salisbury, *Metalogicon*, 1. chap. 15.
[3] 'Sicut enim modus significandi generalissimus Nominis sumitur a proprietate essentiae absolutae, sic modus significandi per modum se stantis sumitur a proprietate ipsius essentiae determinatae; et hic modus constituit nomen substantivum. Nomen ergo substantivum significat per modum determinati secundum essentiam ut *albedo*.'
[4] Siger, p. 98. [5] Perottus, sig. a 3 verso.

putting it, '*variatur per tres diversas voces*', is a noun adjective.[1] Ramus similarly says the substantive has one gender, or at the most two, whereas the adjective has three.[2]

The definitions of Despauter and Lily use quite different criteria, which were generally followed in the English grammars. They provide a definition in syntactic terms:

potest per se stare cum verbo in sensu perfecto. (Despauter, fol. 3 verso.) Substantive standeth by hym selfe, and loketh not for an other worde to be joyned with hym. (Lily, 1527, p. 12.)

and similarly in the Latin accidence:

quod nihil addi postulat ad suam significationem exprimendam. (Lily, *Brev. Inst.*, 1567, sig. A verso.)

The substantive illustrates, more clearly perhaps than any other part of speech, the operation of the three distinct criteria by which the parts of speech could be defined. It could be defined in terms of meaning: a substantive signified substance, however that was interpreted. It could be partially defined in formal terms, as having case-endings but no tense; but this did not distinguish substantive from adjective. To do that it was necessary to introduce one or other of two syntactic criteria: that the substantive could be preceded by a demonstrative of only one gender, whereas the adjective could be preceded by one of any gender; or that it could stand alone in a sentence, whereas an adjective could not. None of these criteria was entirely adequate, either for Latin or English, but they indicate that the tradition developed and permitted greater flexibility and ingenuity of approach than it is usually given credit for.

Noun adjective. 'Epithet' is still, as it was for Plato,[3] a stylistic and not a grammatical term. It is restricted to adjectives which contain, or are used so as to carry, some kind of judgment, though we would probably hesitate to apply it, as Aristotle does, to a noun or noun phrase in apposition.[4] The notion of judgment is central to the definition of Dionysius Thrax also, and persists in Priscian, though he gives equal weight to the more general concept of expressing quality. When he is discussing the kinds of common noun Priscian says *adiectiva* are so called 'because they are put with other common

---

[1] Sulpitius, sig. a 3 verso. [2] Ramus, p. 18.
[3] Plato, e.g. *Soph.*, 225 d; *Phaedr.*, 238 a, c. [4] Aristotle, *Rhet.*, 1405 a; 1406 a.

nouns which indicate substance, or even with proper nouns, to show their quality or quantity... as "good animal... wise grammarian"".[1] Later he says that adjectives are used to express praise (e.g., 'just') or blame (e.g., 'unjust') or a neutral judgment, as when *magnus* is applied either to a general or to a thief, as well as to express qualities without any judgment, as in 'black crow'.[2] The adjective has become a grammatical category, nevertheless, as it was not for Donatus. For Donatus the adjective was primarily *epitheton*, a kind of noun which expressed a judgment; qualities were expressed by other kinds of nouns. Priscian brings together the expression of judgment and the expression of quality under the common category of adjective, whose property it is—and this is the grammatical criterion—to be compared.

Substantive and adjective. The separation of adjective and substantive, which we take as a matter of course, is simple and necessary only if one regards grammatical considerations—as, for example, that the adjective can be compared, the substantive not; that the substantive can be used without an adjective but the adjective cannot be used without a substantive (though expressions like 'the rich' have caused argument). If a separation is attempted in terms of meaning it appears less simple and less necessary. Both 'rich' and 'richness' unmistakably refer to some thing: the referential or nominal element in both is so strong that the grammarians within the tradition, and all the early English grammarians, called them both nouns. When the difference between noun substantive and noun adjective was not described in grammatical terms it was described in metaphysical ones: as an expression of the difference between substance and quality.[3] This made for difficulties which cannot be discussed here, but can be illustrated from Roger Bacon's initial consideration of syntax in the *Summa Gramatica*. His discussion of the adjective, in spite of its difficulty, is a good example of the interaction between logical and grammatical thinking. The point he makes is simply that the 'pure' adjective is one which has no substantival content (in metaphysical terms) and cannot act as the subject of a verb (in

---

[1] Priscian, II. 25 (K. II. 58).   [2] Priscian, II. 28 (K. II. 60).

[3] D. P. Henry shows ('St Anselm's *De grammatico*', *Philos Quart.*, 1960, pp. 115–26) that Anselm's dialogue is largely concerned with whether words like *grammaticus* are to be taken as signifying substance and quality (because they are names) or as signifying quality alone (because they are derivative names). This is equivalent to asking whether substantive and adjective are distinct categories.

syntactical terms). The uneasy association of these two points of view is apparent throughout the whole development of English grammar. Bacon argues:[1]

Every noun is said to signify substance with quality, whence, according to the grammarian, an adjective, like 'white', signifies substance with quality. Although Boethius says that an adjective signifies quality alone this is not inconsistent with what I have just said, because 'white' signifies whiteness alone, which, according to logic, is a quality only. From a grammatical point of view whiteness may be composed of substance and quality, because in general the genus of a thing is, from a grammatical point of view, its own substance; its differentia is its own quality or aggregate composed of substance and form, and consequently the composite structure (and not the form, which is only one part of the composite structure) is the quality. Also, from the point of view of the grammarian and the logician that substance to which the quality signified by the noun adjective is directed is not signified by the pure adjective, but is only understood; and because this is so the adjective is pure, having in no way the nature of a substantive and therefore being unable to act as a subject.

The context within which Bacon was discussing the adjective and the substantive was not that to which the systematic grammarian would have turned first. Bacon was discussing the syntactical question whether an adjective could be the subject of a sentence, or whether a substantive had always to be understood. It was not necessary for him to define an adjective. Siger and Thomas of Erfurt are more directly concerned to define the relation between adjective and substantive. The modal terms in which they frame their definitions are, however, tautologous when they are not obscure:

The mode of adjacency in a noun is derived from its property of attaching itself to some other [word] in conformity with its own being, and this mode forms the noun adjective. (TE, p. 33.)[2]

[1] Roger Bacon, *Summa Gramatica*, p. 6: '...quod omne nomen significat substanciam cum qualitate, unde diccio adjectiva, ut *album*, significat substanciam cum qualitate secundum gramaticum, [et] licet dicat Boetius quod solum significat qualitatem, non contradicit, quia *album* significat albedinem solum, que qualitas est tantum secundum logicum, licet componatur ex substancia et qualitate secundum gramatici consideracionem, quia generaliter genus cujuslibet est sua substancia secundum gramaticum, differencia sua qualitas sive aggregatum totum ex substancia et forma, et per consequens compositum, et non [forma] que est altera pars compositi, est qualitas. Secundum eciam gramatici et logici consideracionem, illa substancia ad quam qualitas significata per nomen adjectivum inclinatur non significatur per adjectivum purum, set solum intelligitur; et quia sic est, ideo purum adjectivum est, et nullo modo habens naturam substantivi, et propter hoc supponere non potest.'

[2] 'Modus adiacentis in nomine sumitur a proprietate ipsius esse inhaerentis alteri secundum esse; et hic modus constituit nomen adjectivum.'

The adjective is a mode of signification expressing an accident of the noun. It designates, with regard to any given thing, its mode of being [in its aspect of] adjacency regarded purely as such, or else it is adjacent to a proper noun, as 'white' and words like it, or, less often with proper nouns, 'inclined' and words like it. (Siger, p. 97.)[1]

The treatment by the renaissance grammarian sof the adjective is complementary to their treatment of the substantive. Perottus, Sulpitius and Ramus define it as a noun which has three forms, for the three genders; Despauter and Lily as being unable to stand alone in a sentence:

non potest per se stare cum verbo in sensu perfecto. (Despauter, fol. 3 verso.)

quod substantivo indiget, cui in oratione adhaereat. (Lily, *Brev. Inst.* 1567, sig. A verso.)

The adjective was still the noun adjective. It had not yet been given, by any grammarian, the status of a part of speech, and it was not to achieve this status with any certainty, even in the English grammars, until the very end of the seventeenth century.

VERB

There is within the tradition no standard classification of verbs, although many kinds of verb are mentioned in various contexts. Differences such as that between active and passive verbs are treated sometimes formally (the difference between -o and -or), sometimes in terms of meaning. Differences which appear only in meaning, as between verbs which have to do with the body (like *wash*, *shave*) and those which have to do with the mind (like *teach*, *persuade*) are not given the systematic treatment received by similar differences in the meaning of adverbs and conjunctions. The formal differences are mostly treated as accidents of the verb, but as the English grammars frequently treat active, passive and neuter as kinds of verbs these categories are here treated separately. Transitive and intransitive verbs are so closely related to active and neuter verbs that they are never clearly separated from them. The only sub-class of verb which is always given a distinctive status is the substantive verb, and it is the only class which developed, and need be followed, beyond Priscian.

---

1 'Adiectivum est modus significandi accidentalis nominis designans circa rem modum essendi adiacentis, ut adiacens, sive proprie adiaceat, ut: "albus", et consimilia, sive improprie magis, ut: "animatum", et similia.'

Classification within the parts of speech

Active and transitive; neuter and intransitive. The Stoics classified verbs in at least two ways, but we do not know for certain what they were. They seem to have made one classification in logical terms, corresponding to our distinction between transitive and intransitive (but perhaps referring to the whole expression and not just to the verb) and another classification in terms of voice, corresponding to our distinction between active and passive. If, as seems likely, this second classification was not made strictly on a morphological basis the categories active and transitive would tend to merge into each other, with confusing results. The category of neuter verbs (οὐδέτερα), of which ζῶ, *I live*, is a frequent example, relates to this first classification rather than to the second: that is, to verbs which are not transitive, but because they are self-sufficient cannot meaningfully be said to be intransitive either: the category of object is irrelevant, so they cannot be said *not* to have one, any more than they can be said to have one.

The classification of Dionysius Thrax was on a formal basis, and he makes no reference to categories such as transitive and intransitive. He makes voice (διάθεσις) an accident of the verb (and also of the noun) and defines it ostensively:

Active (ἐνεργήτικος): 'as τύπτω, I strike'.
Passive (παθήτικος): 'as τύπτομαι, I am struck'.[1]

According to Steinthal[2] the confusion of categories was increased by later grammarians, who added to Dionysius' morphological classification the Stoic category *neuter*, which had been introduced as part of a logical classification. It is possible to point to verbs which are neither transitive nor intransitive, but it is difficult to say, even in Greek, what kind of a verb is, *on a morphological basis*, neither active nor passive: ζῶ is neuter on a logical basis, but is active in form. The addition of the category neuter made it all the more difficult to separate the verb which was (morphologically) active from the verb which was (logically) transitive. The confusion of criteria persists well into modern times.

Apollonius discusses the active voice and our transitive verbs in such a way as to make it almost certain that he distinguished the two categories, even though he refers to the latter usually by a description,

---

[1] Dionysius Thrax, p. 48. The ancient treatment of the middle voice is disregarded here.
[2] Steinthal, II. 293.

and seldom by the term 'transitive' (διαβιβαστικός). He says clearly that not all verbs signify action,[1] and he refers to action as 'passing across' as if to some object—ἡ ἐνεργέια ὡς πρὸς ὑποκείμενον τι διαβιβάζεται'.[2] He refers to the 'transitive force' (διαβιβάσμος) of verbs, and pictures it as being a movement of the person of the verb: transitive verbs are τὰ ἐν διάβασει τοῦ προσώπου ῥήματα. Our transitive verbs he calls 'verbs followed by an oblique case' and our intransitives 'verbs accompanied by a nominative only'.[3] He thus uses both psychological and syntactic criteria in discussing the relation between subject, verb and object, but his emphasis here (not always elsewhere) is on syntactic criteria.

In view of Priscian's admiration for Apollonius, whom he calls 'maximus auctor artis grammaticae[4]. . .cuius auctoritatem in omnibus sequendam putavi',[5] it is probable that his treatment of the verb follows Apollonius closely; but as Apollonius' book devoted specially to the verb is lost it is not always possible to say with whom a particular innovation begins. Priscian defines the active use of a verb as follows: 'Activa (significatio) semper actum significat et facit ex se passivam'—that is, active implies passive and passive active: 'for when I say, "I hear you" I show that my ears are receiving (*patiuntur*) the action of your voice; and vice versa: I say, "I am heard by you" when my voice acts on your ears'.[6] The other Latin grammarians define active and passive primarily in formal terms: 'Activa sunt quae o littera terminantur et accepta r littera faciunt ex se passiva. . .passiva sunt quae r littera terminantur et ea amissa redeunt in activa.'[7]

Neuter verbs (*neutra* or *neutralia*) are defined by both Donatus and Priscian in formal terms: those which end in -o but have no passive form.[8] Donatus does not mention transitive verbs, but Priscian refers to them in the same terms as Apollonius has used: '. . .transitiva, quae ab alia ad aliam transeunt personam, in quibus solent obliqui

---

[1] Apollonius Dyscolus, *Synt.* III. 148 (S & U, II, 395).

[2] ibid. Gilbert Murray quotes this sentence and points out that ὑποκείμενον means 'the thing spoken about' which may be subject or object grammatically. Neither 'subject' nor 'object' is, therefore, a satisfactory translation, because to us the two terms are mutually exclusive (G. Murray, 'The Beginnings of Grammar', *Proc. Class. Assoc.* 1931, reprinted in *Greek Studies*, 1946, p. 184).

[3] Apollonius Dyscolus, *Synt*, III. 155–6.   [4] Priscian, XI. 1 (K. II. 548).

[5] Priscian, XIV. 1 (K. III. 24).   [6] Priscian, VIII. 7 (K. II. 373).

[7] Donatus, *Ars Grammatica*, II. 12 (K. IV. 383).

[8] Priscian, VIII. 7 (K. II. 373); Donatus, *Ars Grammatica*, II. 12 (K. IV. 383.)

casus, adiungi verbis;...ab alia persona ad aliam transit verbi significatio'. [1]Intransitive verbs (*intransitiva* or *absoluta*) are correspondingly defined as those in which there is no movement between persons: '*Intransitivum...hoc est in sua manens persona.*'[2] Priscian gives as examples *morior* and *vagor*, *spiror* and *ambulo*;[3] these are *absoluta*, which, because there is no 'transition', 'do not need cases after them'. As neuter and intransitive verbs, which later came to be identified, are by Priscian defined according to different criteria it is possible without contradiction for a neuter verb to be used transitively. As examples of this he gives *eo iter* and *navigo Pontum*.[4]

During the medieval period, and particularly among the speculative writers, the transitive verb is treated as only one instance of the wider category of transitive constructions, which would include also, for example, the relation between two nouns in apposition—'Rome, the Eternal City', an intransitive construction—and between two nouns, one of which is in the genitive—'*filius Marci*', a transitive construction. Thurot[5] suggests that the earliest grammarian to make this extension of the category is Hugo of St Victor (d. 1141); it is certainly established in Roger Bacon's *Summa Gramatica*, and explicitly discussed by Thomas of Erfurt.[6] Thomas says that grammarians have posited certain '*verba transitiva*' which have a '*modum transeuntis*', and other verbs which are '*absoluta*', that is '*transitione privata*', such as *sto* and *curro*. He does not want such a category himself, on the grounds that there are many '*constructiones transitivae*'. Thurot points out that this extension of the term 'transitive' did not last, although later grammarians kept for a time the scholastic distinction between *transitio personarum* and *transitio actuum*. The latter was a function only of the verb or participle and is discussed in the syntactical part of the grammars; the former weakened and is little mentioned by the renaissance grammarians.

By the renaissance period all the ways of classifying verbs had made their appearance. Different combinations were adopted by different grammarians. Formal or syntactic criteria were often favoured, and transitive verbs were consequently levelled under active, and intransitive under neuter, verbs. Linacre and Lily, however, both define the transitive verb:

---

[1] Priscian, xi. 8 (K. ii. 552).   [2] ibid.
[3] Priscian, viii. 22 (K. ii. 389) and xvii. 93 (K. iii. 159).
[4] Priscian, xviii. 128 (K. iii. 267).   [5] Thurot, p. 83.   [6] TE, pp. 108–9.

95

Transitivum id dicimus, quad in aliquem casum fertur, diversum ab eo, qui ipsum praecessit... (Linacre, *De Emendata Structura*, fol. 10.)

Verbes transitives, are all suche as have after them an accusative case of the doer or sufferer, whether they be actives, commune, or deponent. (Lily, *Shorte Intro.*, 1567, sig. D i verso.)

In the Latin accidence of Lily's grammar transitive verbs are not mentioned, but intransitives are made a sub-class of neuter verbs.

Linacre's classification of the verb is one of the rare places within the tradition where an explicit distinction is made between semantic, formal and syntactic features. Verbs, according to Linacre, are in respect of meaning active, passive or neuter; in respect of meaning and termination they are common or deponent; in respect of construction they are transitive or intransitive.[1]

In its treatment of the five types of verb—active, passive, neuter, common and deponent—Lily's grammar follows both Donatus and Priscian. In its early forms Lily's English accidence resembles Donatus: an active verb is one which ends in -o and can (in the passive) end in -r; a neuter verb is one which ends in -o and cannot end in -r.[2] The later forms of the English accidence, however, and the Latin accidence, add considerations of meaning:

A verbe active endeth in o, and betokeneth to do...
A verb passive endeth in or, and betokeneth to suffer... (*Shorte Intro.* 1567, sig. B ii.)
Activum, est quod agere significat, et in o finitum, passivum in or formare potest.
Passivum, est quod pati significat... (*Brev. Inst.* 1567, sig. C iii verso.)

The confusion between form, meaning and structure is reflected in the fluctuating treatment of the categories in the authorised grammar, and made their transfer to English even more difficult than it would have been in any case. Even Sanctius' forthright sense can give little help in such a situation.[3] He accepts only the categories active, passive and substantive. Deponents he classifies as active; neuter verbs are also active, but a special kind of active verb: they require an accusative, but as there is for each of these verbs only one accusative which can follow it (*accusativus cognatus*) it is not expressed. His examples include *ambulare* (*viam*).

---

[1] Linacre, *De Emendata Structura*, fol. 9.   [2] Lily, 1527, p. 25.
[3] Sanctius, Bk III. chaps. 2 and 3.

Classification within the parts of speech

The confused development of these categories may be summed up as follows:

Active and passive: Distinguished in some sense by the Stoics; defined ostensively by Dionysius Thrax, formally by Donatus, semantically by Priscian and (in effect) by Thomas of Erfurt; thereafter defined in any of these ways.

Neuter: used by the Stoics with reference to the logical distinction between transitive and intransitive; applied later to the grammatical distinction between active and passive; defined by Donatus, Priscian and later grammarians in formal terms.

Transitive and intransitive: Distinguished in some sense by the Stoics; described by Apollonius Dyscolus, Priscian and the scholastic grammarians in terms of person; by the renaissance grammarians increasingly equated with active and neuter.

The verb 'be'. The verb 'be' tops an eminence on the battlefield over which grammar and logic still skirmish. Here it is ceded to the logicians, but the grammarians' treatment of the verb must be briefly noted.

For Aristotle, the verb 'be' is purely logical. He is not concerned with any meaning apart from its copulative function,[1] and seems to have no special name for it. Dionysius does not mention the verb. Apollonius refers to it as 'the verb of existence'—ῥῆμα ὑπαρκτικόν—[2] which Priscian translates, not altogether happily, as *verbum substantivum*: '"sum" verb[um], quod ὑπαρκτικόν Graeci vocant, quod nos possumus 'substantivum' nominare; id enim omnium semper est perfectissimum, cui nihil deest.'[3] The suggestion that the verb 'be' signified substance opened the way to speculation of great intensity. One question, of importance to the grammarians, was, 'If the verb substantive is a verb, what action or passion does it signify?'[4] The conclusion of Peter Helias, which was influential, was that the verb substantive signified substance 'in the manner of action':

We say, therefore, that *sum, es* signifies substance: about something other than itself, with tense, and with verb endings. And since substance unites and joins all other things, for it unites and joins accidents in itself, *sum, es* is copulative, because it signifies substance which unites and joins other

---

[1] Aristotle, *Int.* 16 b.
[2] Apollonius Dyscolus, v. S & U, I. i. 48, note on 25. 2 for refs.
[3] Priscian, VIII. 51 (K. II. 414).   [4] Hunt, I. 221.

things in itself...The verb substantive does not signify action directly, but only substance. It is said to signify action because, although it signifies substance, it signifies it in the mode of action. (Peter Helias, *Summa super Priscianum.*)[1]

To regard the verb *be* as signifying substance would have been incompatible with the speculative grammarians' definition of the verb. This perhaps explains why Thomas of Erfurt's definition of the substantive verb (which he calls by that name) is expressed in terms of such cosmic generality as to be virtually meaningless: '...significat per modum esse generaliter, specificabile per quodlibet esse speciale.'[2] For Martin of Dacia, similarly, the verb substantive is 'verbum significans per modum generalem respectu cuiuslibet praedicamenti'.[3]

Thomas discusses at great length[4] a view of the verb which he says the ancient grammarians did not mention: the view that every verb is reducible, in terms of logic, to a form containing the verb *be*, so that 'a dog runs' can be expressed as 'a dog is running'. This process of logical translation, called *compositio*, was thought to display the real structure of the verb and was a commonplace of scholastic logic. It is the re-introduction of the copula, masquerading rather halfheartedly as a quasi-grammatical category. The frequent tag, smoothing over the difference between the logical and the grammatical approaches, was to call the verb *be* '*radix omnium verborum*',[5] an expression which appears again in Sanctius.[6]

All the renaissance grammarians who are considered here treat the verb substantive, usually by that name, as a neuter verb. This (because *sum* does not end in -o) conflicts with the formal criteria of Donatus and Priscian, but *sum* was so obviously neither active nor passive that considerations of meaning were implicitly introduced: the old triad 'active, passive or neither' was replaced by 'signifying doing, suffering or neither', derived from Donatus.[7] But the compromise was not comfortable. A verb like *curro*, which on the old

---

[1] Quoted by R. W. Hunt, I. 231. 'Dicimus ergo quod "sum, es" significat substantiam, scilicet ut de altero, scilicet cum tempore, et in verbali terminatione. Et quoniam substantia est unitiva omnium aliarum rerum accidentia namque sibi unit et copulat, inde est quod "sum, es" copulativum est, eo quod substantiam que sibi cetera unit et copulat significet...Verbum enim substantivum non id quod est actio significat, sed solam substantiam. Iccirco tamen actionem dicitur significare, quia licet substantiam significet, modo tamen actionis eam significat.'

[2] TE, p. 91.

[3] Martin of Dacia, in Roos, p. 156, and *De Modis Significandi*, chap. 36 (*Opera*, p. 54).

[4] TE, pp. 94 f.   [5] ibid. Bacon, *Summa Gramatica*, p. 81.

[6] Sanctius, Bk III. chap. 5. 524.   [7] Above, pp. 56–7

criterion had been neuter, because it ended in -o and had no passive form, could scarcely be said not to 'signify doing'. The change which let *sum* in pushed *curro* out. The solution was simple, and can be illustrated from Lily. The formal criterion was extended to include verbs (there is only one) ending in -m: 'Neutrum, est quod in o, vel in m, finitum, nec activam, nec passivam formam integre induere potest: ut Curro, ambulo, iaceo, sum.'[1] Similarly the semantic definition of the verb was changed so as to include the expression of being: 'signifying being, doing or suffering'.[2]

Lily groups neuter verbs into three classes:

    (i) The Verb substantive

    (ii) The Verb absolute: '*quod ipsum per se sensum absolvat*'

    (iii) Verbs with a cognate object, e.g. *Bibo vinum*: '*cuius actio in rem cognatae significationis transit*'.[3]

The second group, absolute verbs, he divides into two: those which signify an action complete in the verb itself, as *dormio*; those which signify a 'passion' complete in the verb itself, as *rubeo, nigresco*. The first of these sub-groups corresponds to Priscian's intransitive or absolute verbs,[4] the second to his reciprocal verbs. Lily's third class of neuter verbs corresponds to Priscian's transitive neuter verbs.[5]

PRONOUN

Dionysius makes one explicit classification of all pronouns:[6] into those with articles, as ὁ ἐμός, and those without, as ἐγώ. He also applies to pronouns the classification of all words as either primitive or derivative, according to which ἡμεῖς, for example is primitive and ἡμέτερος derivative. This second criterion enables him to indicate the distinction represented in English by the forms 'we:our'. The criterion of the article would have enabled him to indicate the distinction represented by 'our:ours'. He uses the term possessive (κτητικός) but all he clearly says about possessive pronouns is that they are all derivatives. He does not make explicit the distinction, implicit in his linked criteria, between the conjunctive and disjunctive forms (our:ours) of what we traditionally call the possessive pronoun.

---

[1] Lily, *Brev. Inst.* 1567, sig. C iv.
[2] For Lily's definition in these terms see above, p. 60. [3] Lily, ibid.
[4] p. 95, above. [5] p. 94, above.
[6] Dionysius Thrax, pp. 65–6.

4-2

It is not easy to say what classes of pronoun are recognised by Apollonius. His work is so extensive and refined in its analysis that it seems at first disrespectful to suggest that categories which we take so much for granted are not yet fully formed in it. But it is unwise to take anything for granted concerning the pronoun, and one sign of Apollonius' strength is that he is less concerned than perhaps any other ancient grammarian with the business of classification and labelling: he concentrates on the way in which individual words are used.

The classification of the pronouns among the Latin grammarians is too complicated to display adequately here, even in outline. Among the many criteria used, which overlap and interlock, are:

(i) the difference between, for example, *me* and *meus*, which is sometimes described in formal terms as a difference between primitives and derivatives, and sometimes in structural terms as a difference between those pronouns which can stand alone (*absoluta*), those which are dependent on another word (*respectiva*) and those which are attached to another word (*enclitica*)

(ii) the difference between definite (*finitum*) and indefinite (*infinitum*) reference

(iii) how a word is related to the expression of person; is *ille*, for example, more closely related to the expression of person than is *qui*?

(iv) the use of (correlative) words in question and answer: *praepositiva* such as *quantus*, *quis* or *hic*, and *subiunctiva* or *relativa*, such as *tantus*, *is*

(v) the distinction between *extrinsecus* and *intrinsecus*, which is explained by Servius: '*Intrinsecus* is so called because it relates to the person of the possessor; *extrinsecus* because it relates to the person of the thing possessed.'[1] That is to say, in an expression like *noster hortus* the word *noster* is intrinsically plural, because it relates to the group of people owning the garden, and extrinsically singular, because it relates to the one garden which they own.

The principal kinds of pronoun discussed by Apollonius are all discussed by the Latin grammarians. The term *relativus* does not yet carry its restricted modern meaning, but is used in any context in which the reference of pronouns is discussed. One of the most

---

[1] Servius, *Comment. in artem Donati* (K. IV. 410): 'Intrinsecus autem dicitur quod pertinet ad personam possidentis, extrinsecus quod pertinet ad personam possessi.'

influential of all Priscian's comments on the pronoun is his list of fifteen words which are pronouns 'without argument': 'In his igitur quindecim pronominibus nulla fit controversia, quin omnes fateantur, ea esse pronomina...ego, tu; ille, ipse, iste, hic, is, sui; meus, tuus, suus, noster, vester, nostras, vestras.'[1] This list, with its open admission that there could be several opinions as to what was or was not a pronoun, was the refuge of many bewildered grammarians in subsequent centuries, and the honoured number fifteen appears also in the enumeration of the English pronouns. Priscian's enumeration is scarcely varied by any of the medieval or renaissance grammarians who attempt any classification of the pronoun. The term *relative*, at first used to indicate any kind of pronominal reference, becomes more firmly attached to *qui*, but is a source of great uncertainty. The classification in Lily's grammar illustrates this, even if it is in part a consequence of mixed authorship. The tone is confident: 'There be fiftene pronounes.'[2] Priscian's list then follows. The fifteen pronouns are classified as either primitive or derivative: the first eight on the list are primitive, the rest derivative. Primitives are then said to be identical with demonstratives 'bicause they shew a thing not spoken of before'.[3] Immediately after, six pronouns are enumerated as being relatives 'bicause they rehearse a thing that was spoken of before'. These six are *hic, ille, iste, is, idem, qui*. But the first four of these had already been included among the demonstratives. For a categorical system to tolerate, and authoritatively preserve, such inconsistencies of classification, it must command respect which is not only unthinking, but tightly shuts its eyes to the problems which thought would unleash.

ADVERB

The classification of the adverb was one of the most elaborate features of the tradition, and is still a burden to schoolchildren. Dionysius Thrax lists twenty-eight kinds of adverb. The list shows not only the usual overlapping of formal and semantic criteria, but the natural way in which what we would call interjections take their place among the adverbs. From one point of view these lists are an attempt, so many times made in the following centuries, to enumerate the ways of thought. Because questions of vocabulary had not yet

[1] Priscian, XII. 1 (K. II. 577).　　　[2] Lily, *Shorte Intro.* 1567, sig. A viii verso.
[3] loc. cit. Cf. *Brev. Inst.* sig. C ii: 'Demonstrativa dicuntur eadem quae et primitiva'.

been separated from questions which are grammatical in a narrower sense a formal classification, with which the lists usually begin, slides naturally into a display of meanings, in which there can be no certitude and no finality. This is so obvious that one wonders why the lists were gladly repeated long after the time when the clashing of categories must have been palpably discordant. Any student of language will suggest an answer: when everything you handle is elusive, when everything you wish to isolate is inseparably related to something else, when several points of view need to be maintained simultaneously—then even the illusion of order and system becomes a necessary comfort, and the breathless grammarian props himself against a good long list.

Dionysius divides the adverb into the following classes:

(i) simple   (ii) compound

(iii) temporal

(iv) relative to a standard: of manner (μεσότητος), e.g. *sensibly* (σοφῶς)

(v) of quality   (vi) of quantity

(vii) of number   (viii) of place

(ix) of wishing   (x) negative

(xi) affirmative

(xii) illustrative, e.g. *as, as if* (ὥς, ὥσπερ)

(xiii) hypothetical   (xiv) of order

(xv) collective, e.g. *totally* (ἄρδην), *abundantly* (ἤλιθα)

(xvi) exhortatory, e.g. *come on!* (ἄγε)

(xvii) comparative   (xviii) interrogative

(xix) intensifying (ἐπιτάσεως), e.g. *very* (σφόδρα), *very much* (ἄγαν)

(xx) of affirmation on oath (κατωμοτικά)

(xxi) of confirmation   (xxii) of anger

(xxiii) prohibitive   (xxiv) of astonishment

(xxv) of combination (συλλήψεως), e.g. *at the same time* (ἅμα)

(xxvi) of denial on oath (ἀπωμοτικά)

(xxvii) of obligation

(xxviii) expressing inspiration (θειασμοῦ), e.g. εὐοῖ[1]

Priscian repeats these, except the last seven, and adds a further nine:

(xxix) *deortativum*, e.g. *ne* for *neque*

(xxx) *remissivum*, e.g. 'to slow down *paulatim*'

---

[1] Dionysius Thrax, pp. 73–86.

Classification within the parts of speech

(xxxi) *discretivum*, e.g. *separatim*
(xxxii) *superlativum*, e.g. *maxime*
(xxxiii) *diminutiva*, e.g. *clanculum*, from *clam*
(xxxiv) *demonstrativa*, e.g. *ecce*
(xxxv) *relativa*, e.g. *quando*
(xxxvi) *vocandi*, e.g. *O*[1]

Most medieval grammarians give similar lists. The renaissance grammarians do not give such elaborate classifications, though Lily, in the English accidence, gives a list of twenty. In the Latin accidence he confines the list to adverbs of quantity, time and place. Even Sanctius, who says with justice: 'Significationes vero abverbiorum enumerare magis Philosophi est, quam Grammatici', enumerates seventeen kinds of adverb 'in case anyone wants them'.[2]

CONJUNCTIVE PARTICLE AND CONJUNCTION

Chrysippus, in the third century B.C., had classified conjunctive particles as, at least, copulative, disjunctive and hypothetical,[3] but the first complete classification we know is that of Dionysius Thrax in the following century:[4]

(i) copulative (συμπλεκτικός): 'such as articulate an explanation which is produced with no fixed limits',[5] e.g. *and, but* (καί, ἀλλά, μέν, δέ)

(ii) disjunctive (διαγευκτικός): 'such as join words but separate facts',[6] e.g. *or* (ἤ)

(iii) hypothetical (συναπτικός): 'such as do not indicate existence, but sequence',[7] e.g. *if* (εἴ)

(iv) causal (παρασυναπτικός): 'such as express both existence and sequence',[8] e.g. *since, seeing that* (ἐπεί)

(v) final (αἰτιολογικός): 'such as are used with a sentence which answers to one in which a cause is expressed',[9] e.g. *in order that* (ἵνα)

(vi) dubitative (ἀπορηματικός), e.g. ἄρα

---

[1] Priscian, xv and passim.
[2] Sanctius, Bk I. chap. 18. p. 219: 'ne hic aliquis forte ea desideret'.
[3] Chrysippus, SVF, II. 68, 15; 68, 19; 68, 21.
[4] Dionysius Thrax, pp. 87–100.
[5] ὅσοι τὴν ἑρμηνείαν ἐπ' ἄπειρον ἐκφερομένην συνδέουσιν, p. 88.
[6] ὅσοι τὴν μὲν φράσιν ἐπισυνδέουσιν, ἀπὸ δὲ πράγματος εἰς πρᾶγμα διιστᾶσιν, p. 90.   [7] ὅσοι ὕπαρξιν μὲν οὐ δηλοῦσι, σημαίνουσι δὲ ἀκολουθίαν, p. 91.
[8] ὅσοι μεθ' ὑπάρξεως καὶ τάξιν δηλοῦσιν, p. 92.
[9] ὅσοι ἐπ' ἀποδόσει αἰτίας ἕνεκεν παραλαμβανόνται, p. 93.

The Tradition

(vii) inferential (συλλογιστικός), e.g. ἀλλὰ μήν
(viii) expletive (παραπληρωματικός), e.g. δή, γέ
(ix) adversative[1] (ἐναντιωματικός), e.g. *nevertheless* (ὅμως).

Apollonius does not define the conjunction, but the examples he gives all join sentences. He repeats the classification of Dionysius and adds six classes of his own,[2] given here with Priscian's translation.

(x) confirmatory (βεβαιωτικός, *approbativa*)
(xi) subdisjunctive (παραδιαζευκτικός, *subdisiunctiva*) i.e. either A or B *or* A and B
(xii) affirmative (διασαφητικός, *disertiva*)
(xiii) negative-conditional (ἀναιρετικός, *abnegativa*), e.g. ἄν
(xiv) of result (ἀποτελεστικός, *effectiva*)
(xv) connective (ἐπιζευκτικός, *adiunctiva*), e.g. *ut* final.

The classification of conjunctions continued as a customary practice, though its inadequacy was recognised. Diomedes and Charisius both discuss whether some kinds of conjunction are not adverbs. The difficulty of distinguishing between the two parts of speech leads them both to give the rather despairing comfort: 'Do not be upset if you find you have judged some words to be both adverbs and conjunctions.'[3] Whose consolation this originally was we do not know. Sacerdos, Charisius and Donatus classify conjunctions under five heads, Priscian under seventeen. Donatus comments: 'There are also words about which we cannot say with certainty whether they are conjunctions, prepositions or adverbs unless we consider the context (*sententiam*) e.g. *ut, cum*.'[4] His own classification is that most widely followed in the medieval period:

(i) *Copulativae*, e.g. *et, atque*
(ii) *disiunctivae*, e.g. *vel, neque*
(iii) *expletivae*, e.g. *videlicet, quoque*
(iv) *causales*, e.g. *si, quando, sed, preterea*
(v) *rationales*, e.g. *ita, quia, ergo*[5]

This is followed by Alcuin, Bede, Hugo, Martin of Dacia and Thomas of Erfurt. The comments of the last two are of particular

---

[1] Nos. vi–ix appear only in Bekker's text, p. 643.
[2] Apollonius Dyscolus, *De Conj.* (S & U, i. ii. 220).
[3] Charisius, ii (K. i. 226); Diomedes, i (K. i. 416): 'Nec te moveat si quaedam esse adverbia et coniunctiones recognoveris.'
[4] Donatus, *Ars Grammatica*, ii (K. iv. 389).   [5] Donatus, loc. cit.

interest. Martin rejects Priscian's view that the disjunctive conjunction joins words but separates meanings; he says it joins both.[1]

Logical considerations. Thomas distinguishes causal and rational conjunctions on grounds which illustrate very neatly the extent to which logical considerations can come to dominate grammatical ones. Thomas's illustrations of the two types of conjunction use the same word, *ergo,* and the same grammatical construction.

> causal: *Socrates currit,* ergo *movetur.*
> rational: *Terra interponitur inter solem et lunam;* ergo *eclipsatur.*[2]

Thomas is making an important distinction, though we should describe it in different terms. He sees Socrates' running as the *cause* of his being moved. Socrates cannot help being moved if he runs. There is no such necessary connection between the moon's eclipse (i.e. its being darkened) and the earth's position between sun and moon. The earth's position is one possible reason for the darkening of the moon, but it is not necessary and undeniable: other reasons could be, and have been, imagined. We should nowadays refer the idea of causation to Thomas's second sentence rather than to his first. His first sentence is analytic; running entails moving; the second verb adds no new information to the first. The second sentence is synthetic (so long as *eclipsatur* means only 'is darkened' and does not itself imply the interposition of the earth) because the idea of darkening is not already contained in the idea of interposition. *Ergo* expresses not the logical relation of entailment but the empirical relation of causation.

Both sentences undoubtedly give instances of the correct use of *ergo,* and therefore (for such a word) of its meaning. Can any sense of 'grammar' which seeks to exclude such considerations be of interest to those who *use* a language? Thomas, referring to his definition of the conjunction,[3] proceeds to his last category, the expletive conjunction: 'Si autem coniunctio extrema non coniungit, sed coniuncta adornat, sic tunc sunt coniunctiones *expletivae,* quia extra plenum sensum orationis sunt positae.'[4] The explanation for this seems to be that conjunctions are considered to join (as he had said earlier) either by virtue of a conjunctive power (*per vim*) or by

---

[1] Martin of Dacia, *De Modis Significandi,* chap. 51 (*Opera,* p. 77).
[2] TE, pp. 130–1.   [3] See above, p. 63.   [4] TE, p. 132.

their position between the elements they join (*per ordinem*). Words like 'also' are not fixed in their position in the sentence, but have a joining power of some kind ('He plays the piano; also he sings'). Thomas's explanation of the expletive conjunctions seems to be based on the assumption that they have so little joining power that they are virtually adverbs, but as he gives no examples it is not easy to tell when he is being interpreted as saying more than he meant. At the least, he is showing his awareness not only of the unsatisfactory delimitation of the categories adverb and conjunction, but also of some of the reasons for its being unsatisfactory.

The renaissance grammarians have nothing to add. Some keep to the modest classification of Donatus; others, like Linacre and Lily, produce lists of up to twenty types.

5. ACCIDENTS

Even a summary of the tradition provides constant reminders that our inherited grammatical categories were shaped before a distinction had been made between formal and semantic criteria. The parts of speech were distinguished, defined and classified primarily in terms of meaning. The formal characteristics of words were treated as features which it was necessary to isolate and classify, but they were not treated as defining characteristics of word-classes. Mood and conjugation, for example, are the only characteristics which are ascribed to just one part of speech. Voice is treated by Dionysius as a characteristic of some nouns as well as of verbs; person is regularly ascribed to pronouns as well as to verbs; tense is ascribed to verbs and to participles; case to nouns, pronouns and participles. Gender and case were obvious characteristics of noun, pronoun, participle and article; *species*[1] and *figura*[2] were features of all kinds of words.

Such characteristics were known as accidents (παρεπόμενα, literally 'accompaniments'; *accidentia*). They ranged from purely formal ones (such as the distinction between simple and compound structure) to meaning itself, which was by some grammarians treated as an accident of words (the interjection especially) which seemed to have no formal or structural features. Some of the characteristics, such as the indication of case, comparison, number, tense, voice and mood, were expressed by means of formal changes in the word itself. Others, such as the expression of person, were inherent in some words (the personal pronouns, for example) but expressed through formal change in others (for example, verbs). Similarly gender was inherent in substantives but expressed through formal change in the adjective. Other characteristics, structural, not formal, such as the 'force' of conjunctions or the 'government' of prepositions, were of a different kind, and were not treated as accidents. Yet other characteristics, such as declension or conjugation, expressed neither what the

---

[1] The distinction between primitive and derivative forms, e.g. *mons, montanus*.
[2] The distinction between simple and compound forms, e.g. *nocens, innocens*.

words did nor what they were. They showed only that words which belonged to the same part of speech could be classified, according to their formal properties, into still smaller groups.

It can be seen that the category 'accident' included very diverse features: it is, in fact, a blanket term to cover all those features of words which have not been used in determining the parts of speech. Two systems of classification were used: one primarily, but not only, in terms of meaning, the other primarily, but not only, in terms of form. The second, that of the accidents, has not the appearance of a system, because its components are distributed under the various parts of speech. It is not until the renaissance period, with Linacre and Ramus, that grammarians begin to see that words in which there is a formal change to express, for instance, number, can be regarded, by that criterion alone, as a significant class.

Few of the grammarians say what they mean by accidents: rather, the accidents are defined ostensively. Dionysius' formula is, 'There are eight accompaniments to the verb' (παρέπεται τῷ ῥήματι ὀκτώ); then follows the enumeration. The corresponding formula of Donatus and Priscian is, 'Verbo accidunt septem...', but *accidentia* are not otherwise defined. Quintilian is unusual in describing the accidents of a part of speech as those features (especially of the verb) in which mistakes are made, namely voice, tense, person and mood.[1]

COMPARISON

Dionysius Thrax did not regard comparison as an accident of the noun. He treats comparative and superlative forms as kinds of derivative noun, and derivatives and primitives are the two forms of the accidental property *species*. Donatus makes comparison an accident of the noun and adverb, but Priscian does not, and later practice varied in the same way. Most grammarians follow Donatus in giving three degrees of comparison:

Positive	(*positivus* or *absolutus*)
Comparative	(*comparativus*)
Superlative	(*superlativus*)

Charisius, however, a later contemporary of Donatus, writes as if the normal practice was to make two degrees, but that some gram-

[1] Quintilian, I. v. 41.

marians include the positive.[1] Priscian, in his discussion of comparison at the beginning of Bk III, refers by name to comparative and superlative forms which he defines as those which have the meaning of, respectively, *magis* and *valde*, but he does not describe them as degrees of comparison. The tone of his discussion strongly suggests that he would not regard the positive as a degree. Servius refers to the dispute whether 'comparative' is the right term. It is held that *doctior*, for instance, 'non comparet sed praeferat'. Servius' own reply is that all preference implies comparison.[2]

The minority view, current throughout the tradition, that it was improper to say there were three degrees of comparison is an indication that the writer is to some extent aware of the importance of the formal features of language. It is not, therefore, surprising that Martin, Siger and Thomas of Erfurt, in whose grammars formal considerations are entirely subordinated to logical ones, should accept apparently without question the analysis into three degrees.

During the renaissance period the most influential proponent of the minority view was Ramus, but the most emphatic was Sanctius, who carried the argument beyond the formal criteria (that adjectives consistently vary, in the way that *rounder* and *roundest* are variations of *round*) and took it back into the field of logic: 'The perverse opinion of grammarians is so widely spread around that by now practically no engines can overthrow it: everyone is now persuaded that there are three degrees of comparison.'[3] This, he continues, is wrong; only comparatives can compare, and there is accordingly only one degree (if there are said to be any) of comparison: 'There is only a certain amplification of quality, and no comparison, in what is called the superlative—than which no worse name could have been invented.' This is perhaps the first appearance of a subtle but inadequate point of view. Once grammatical (in this case formal) criteria are abandoned it is undoubtedly valid to distinguish the comparative and superlative as categories of quite different kinds: the former logical, the latter rhetorical. But this applies only when

[1] Charisius, Bk I (K. I. 112): 'Comparationum sunt ordines duo, secundus et tertius. Dividuntur singuli in tres gradus...'

[2] Servius, *Comment. in Donatum* (K. IV. 407).

[3] Sanctius, Bk II. chap. 11. ad init.: 'Perversa grammaticorum opinio ita late pervagata est, ut iam fere nullis machinis labefactari queat; iam enim persuasum est omnibus tres esse gradus in comparatione...nulla est comparatio, sed quaedam amplificatio qualitatis in superlativo, ut vocant; nam hoc nullum aliud pejus nomen potuit inveniri.'

the superlative (of *rich*, for example) is taken in the intensifying sense of *very rich*. If *richest* is taken to mean 'more rich than any other' it is logically distinct from *richer*. *Richest* makes a comparison, but it is applicable to only one item in a series, the last. *Richer* is applicable to any item except the first.

The dispute about the number of degrees of comparison is continued in the English grammars also.

NUMBER

Singular (ἐνικός, *singularis*)
Plural (πληθυντικός, *pluralis*)
Dual (δυικός, *dualis*)
Common (*communis*)

The formal expression of number (ἀριθμός, *numerus*) is recognised by Aristotle, though he uses no distinctive terms for singular and plural.[1] Chrysippus is said[2] to have written a work about singular and plural constructions, and later Stoics made explicit the distinction between natural and grammatical number. Donatus tried to preserve for Latin the Greek category of dual number, which he applied to expressions such as '*hi ambo, hi duo*',[3] and he also suggested a common number for words like *nubes* and *res* whose nominatives are the same in singular and plural.[4] Priscian, however, rightly rejected the dual as a valid category for Latin, and limited the numbers to singular and plural. Donatus and he made number an accident of the noun, pronoun, verb and participle, and this became standard practice.

GENDER

According to Aristotle, Protagoras was the first to classify names according to gender, using the terms ἄρρην (male), θῆλυς (female) and σκεῦος (inanimate thing).[5] Aristotle himself uses also the term μεταξύ (what is between male and female and therefore neither) and makes nearly explicit the distinction between gender and sex.[6] This was established by the Stoics, and it was probably they who

---

[1] Aristotle, *Rhet.* 1407 b.   [2] Diogenes Laertius, VII. 192.
[3] Donatus, *Ars Grammatica*, II. 6 (K. IV. 376).
[4] Donatus, loc. cit.   [5] Aristotle, *Rhet.* 1407 b.
[6] Aristotle, *Soph. El.* 166 b; *Poet.* 1458 a.

replaced Aristotle's μεταξύ by οὐδέτερον, the term later translated as *neuter*.

Dionysius includes gender among the accidents of the noun, specifying masculine (ἀρσενικόν), feminine (θηλυκόν) and neuter. But, he says, some people add two others: common (κοινόν) and epicene (ἐπίκοινον).[1] He gives no definition either of gender itself or of the individual terms, but 'common' is applied always to words whose gender varies according to the sex of the creature they refer to (Dionysius' example is ἵππος, horse). 'Epicene' is applied to words whose gender is stable but may refer to creatures of either sex (Dionysius gives χελίδων—the swallow).

Donatus and Priscian explicitly recognise the distinction between gender and sex. They agree that masculine and feminine[2] are the two principal genders, 'quae sola novit ratio naturae'.[3] Donatus enumerates only masculine, feminine, neuter and common, but proceeds to elaborate his classification, distinguishing between words which may be either of two genders (*commune*—'common of two'), as *sacerdos*, or of three genders, as *felix*.[4] He further adds 'epicene' (*epicoenon, subcommune, promiscuum*) as *aquila*, and 'doubtful' (*dubium*), i.e. those words, such as *radix*, which are '*incerti generis inter masculinum et femininum*'. This classification was followed by many writers of grammars, both Latin and English, until well into the second half of the nineteenth century, if not later. Donatus—and here he was not followed—proceeds to categorise words, such as *Centaurus*, the name of a ship, which are masculine 'in sound' but feminine in meaning (because *navis* is feminine) and *poema*, which is feminine in sound but neuter in meaning (*intellectu*).

There does not seem to have been any following, either, for the unusual treatment of the genders by Thomas of Erfurt. He associates with the genders of nouns the ideas of action and passion usually associated with the verb. Gender, he says, is 'modus significandi activus, quo mediante, nomen proprietatem agentis, vel patientis, vel utrumque significat'.[5] Masculine and feminine are associated with active and passive, common with both. But the idea is not pursued. He offers, in fact, an alternative definition of common gender—'*quod nec*

---

[1] Dionysius Thrax, p. 24.

[2] P. B. R. Forbes, 'Greek Pioneers in Philology and Grammar', *Class. Rev.* 47. 1933. 108: 'Before the second century A.D. the Latins used not *masculinum* and *femininum*, but *virile* and *muliebre*.'   [3] Priscian, v. i (K. II. 141).

[4] Donatus, *Ars Grammatica*, II. 4 (K. IV. 375).   [5] TE, p. 53.

differt a masculino, nec a foeminino'—which he says he prefers; his reference to the neuter, apart from its modal terminology, is quite conventional, and epicene and doubtful take their customary place.[1]

The fullest system of genders, current throughout the tradition, comprised seven categories. The examples are Lily's, and all come, except for the first, directly or indirectly from Donatus: 'Genus est sexus discretio. Et sunt genera numero septem.'[2]

> Masculine
> Feminine
> Neuter
> Common of two (e.g. *hic, haec parens*)
> Common of three (e.g. *hic, haec, hoc felix*)
> Epicene (*his passer*, for male or female bird)
> Doubtful (*hic* or *haec dies*)

This was the system used by Perottus, Despauter and Lily; others kept to five genders, omitting *common of three* and *doubtful*.

INFLECTION

Πτῶσις is used by Aristotle for modification of the form of any kind of word, but especially of the noun and verb. The Stoics restricted it to the inflections of the noun, thereby introducing the first conception of case.

CASE

Dionysius Thrax, and later grammarians, count case (πτῶσις, *casus*) among the accidents of the noun. Dionysius enumerates five cases: nominative, genitive, dative, accusative, vocative.

Nominative (ὀρθή, *casus rectus; casus nominandi*—Varro; *nominativus*). As the term ὀρθή implies, 'the word itself' was not originally considered a case. Cases were 'fallings away' from an 'upright' norm. It soon became inconvenient to have 'the word itself' outside the system of inflections, and the 'upright' norm was aligned with other forms of the word. Thus, as the metaphor of 'falling away' (which has not been explained) weakened, the paradox of *casus rectus* became acceptable and the 'upright' form was regarded as a case.

Genitive (γενική, *genetivus; casus patricius*—Varro).

---

[1] TE, p. 54.   [2] Lily, *Brev. Inst.* 1567, sig. A vi.

Accidents

Dative (δοτική, *dativus; casus dandi*—Varro).

Accusative (αἰτιατική; *accusativus*—Varro; *incusativus*—Charisius). The term *accusativus* is usually regarded as a mistranslation of αἰτιατική, and attributed to Varro. ᾿Αιτιατική had two senses: 'related to blame' and 'related to causation'. The senses have something in common, but it is improbable that Varro was not aware of them both. Even if *accusativus* was not an actual mistranslation it was a bad choice, and led to some far-fetched and inaccurate descriptions of the function of the case.

Vocative (κλητική, *vocativus; vocandi*—Varro). The Stoics had established the first four of Dionysius' cases, but it is not known whether they included the vocative in their classification. It is possible that their fifth was the adverb, and that the vocative was regarded as a noun-form in its own right.[1]

Ablative (*ablativus; casus sextus*—Varro).

Seventh case. A seventh case was suggested by Quintilian,[2] discussed by Charisius, Sacerdos, Diomedes and Donatus, and rejected by Priscian.[3] This case was to be identical in form with the ablative, from which it would draw certain uses not depending on a preposition.

Eighth case. Robins[4] quotes Servius as referring to the view that there should be an eighth case which would withdraw from the dative those uses which could also be expressed by a preposition governing the accusative, for example *it clamor caelo; subeunt muro*.

The system of six cases was practically unquestioned throughout the tradition and need not be pursued further here.

VOICE

Dionysius Thrax ascribes to the noun, but not among its accidents (because it is not a formal property) a quality called 'disposition' (διάθεσις), the same as that ascribed to verbs and eventually called 'voice': 'There are two dispositions of the noun, action and being acted upon: action, as in *judge*, "he who performs the action of judging"; being acted upon, as in *judged*, "receiving the action of judging"'.[5] These are Dionysius' only examples, so it is not possible

[1] Robins, p. 33. [2] Quintilian, I. iv. 26.
[3] Priscian, v. 79, 80 (K. II. 190).
[4] Robins, p. 60 (Servius, *Comment in artem Donati*, K. IV. 433).
[5] Dionysius Thrax, p. 46: 'τοῦ δ'ὀνόματος διαθέσεις εἰσὶ δύο, ἐνέργεια καὶ πάθος, ἐνέργεια μὲν ὡς κριτής ὁ κρίνων, πάθος δὲ ὡς κριτός ὁ κρινόμενος.'

to tell whether he is thinking only of the narrow distinction he illustrates, which was already provided for by the participle, or whether he is thinking also of a distinction such as that between 'murderer' and 'victim'. The category does not appear in the Latin grammars.

Sandys[1] says that Plato 'recognises' the distinction between active and passive, and refers to the *Sophist* (219b) and *Philebus* (26e). It is difficult to see how either passage adumbrates, even remotely, these grammatical categories. 'Disposition' (διάθεσις) was treated by Dionysius as an accident of the verb, but active and passive forms are more often treated as kinds of verbs and are described under that heading here.[2] This classification is continued by Donatus and Priscian who, though they include disposition as an accident of the verb, call it *genus*. It is called by other writers also *significatio*, and *adfectus*, and *species*.[3] The full classification had been developed by the time of Priscian, and medieval and renaissance grammarians either repeated it or made selections from it. Whether *genus* was made an accident of the verb or not mattered very little: the classification into active, passive, neuter, common and deponent was generally accepted. In Lily's grammar, for example, 'kind' is treated as an accident, in Linacre's it is not.

MOOD

The traditional moods first appear in Dionysius Thrax. As they were usually defined in terms of the speaker's intentions, and not in formal terms, wide variations were possible. Some grammarians treated as moods what others classed as 'kinds' of verbs, and yet others as 'forms' of verbs. Dionysius makes mood (ἔγκλισις) an accident of the verb but does not define it.[4] Donatus makes mood only part of the accident *qualitas*. He gives the same categories as Dionysius but no definition.[5] Priscian says moods '...*sunt diversae inclinationes animi, varios eius affectus demonstrantes*', and gives the same list as Dionysius:[6]

> *Indicative* (ὁριστική, *indicativus; finitivus; definitivus; pronunciativus*)
> *Imperative* (προστακτική, *imperativus*)
> *Optative* (εὐκτική, *optativus*) e.g. *utinam legerem*

---

[1] Sandys, i. 10.   [2] Above, p. 94.
[3] Sacerdos, i (K. vi. 429). There is a note of pardonable exasperation in Sacerdos' reference to these variations in terminology.
[4] Dionysius Thrax, p. 47.   [5] Donatus, *Ars Grammatica*, ii. 12 (K. iv. 381).
[6] Priscian, viii. 63 (K. ii. 421).

Subjunctive (ὑποτακτική, *subiunctivus; coniunctivus*—Donatus; *dubitativus*)

Infinitive (ἀπαρέμφατος, *infinitus*)

Martianus Capella gives these five moods as the established ones, but adds another five which may be included at pleasure. These are (he gives no examples):

promissivus (i.e. future indicative forms)
impersonalia
hortativus
percunctativus (i.e. interrogative)
conjunctivus[1] (i.e. as distinct from the subjunctive)

The term 'conjunctive' was restricted to verb forms like *legerem* used after words like *ut* or *cum*; 'subjunctive' was applied to the same forms if they were attached to the sentence, not by means of a conjunction but by their position alone.

Donatus had considered, but rejected, the first two of these: other writers suggested more. Quintilian says there may be six or eight moods[2] and among those suggested were the gerund, and a concessive mood, e.g. *legerim*.[3]

Those medieval grammarians who discuss the moods keep to the customary five; sometimes impersonal forms are admitted as a sixth. The most significant addition in the renaissance period is the innovation, apparently by Linacre, of the category and term 'potential': 'The potential mode signyfyeth a thyng as mayyng or owyng to be doone. And his sygnes in englysshe be these. *may, might, wold* or *shuld*, and hit hath V tens in every verbe of lyke voyce to the subiunctyve mode.'[4] He later explains in *De Emendata Structura*, that he is seeking to combine into a single category the Latin (and English) equivalents of two conditional uses of ἄν: 'Potentialem vocamus, quem Graeci per ἄν coniunctionem et verbum duplicis modi, alias indicativi, alias optativi, explicant, quo minus illis modum unum statuere licuit.'[5] The potential was not included in the enumeration of the moods in the English part of Lily's grammar in 1527, where they are given as:

Indicative: 'sheweth a reason trewe or false by the waye of axynge or tellynge'.

---

[1] Martianus Capella, § 310. [2] Quintilian, I. v. 41.
[3] Quintilian I. 64 n.
[4] Linacre, *Progymnasmata*, sig. C iii (quoted by Funke, *Frühzeit*, p. 90).
[5] Linacre, *De Emendata Structura*, fol. 13 verso.

Imperative: 'biddeth or commandeth.'
Optative: 'willeth or desyreth' (the signs are *would, should*).
Conjunctive: 'joyneth and conteyneth sentences togyder'.
Infinitive: 'whan whith an other verbe I declare my doynge'.[1]

By 1567, at the latest, the potential had been added as a sixth mood. The other moods remained unchanged, except that the conjunctive was called the subjunctive, and defined in such a way as to show that the old distinction between the two terms was entirely lost: 'The Subiunctive mode hath evermore some Coniunction ioyned with him...and it is called the Subiunctive mode, bicause it dependeth of an other verbe in the same sentence...'[2]

TENSE

The tenses in Greek and Latin, and the relations between the tense-systems of the two languages, are too complex to summarise, but it is worth bringing out one point which is independent of the differences between the two languages: how difficult it is to relate a simple awareness of time to the network of significations carried by the tenses of verbs. In Greek, Latin and English the first consideration of tense is easy: there must be at any rate three tenses, to express past, present and future. The English grammarians kept returning to this point, but it was not a stable position. If they looked backward to the classical languages they saw an array of tenses which suggested authoritatively that English should be as well equipped. If they looked at English with an empirical eye, strictly distinguishing tense (a feature of words) from time (a feature of consciousness) they were led to conclude that English had not even three tenses, only two: present (*I love*) and past (*I loved*). But this seemed an absurd conclusion. If there were three times how could there be fewer than three tenses? It was at this point, where the formal differences between Latin and English are most obvious, that English grammarians most easily broke away from the tradition, commanding as its authority was. But the difficulties of time and tense had been just as apparent in the early stages of the tradition. It was only the weight of custom which came to obscure them.

According to Diogenes Laertius the tenses were first distinguished

---

[1] Lily, 1527, p. 26.　　　　[2] Lily, *Shorte Intro.* 1567, sig. B ii verso.

by Protagoras.[1] The distinction is suggested by Plato[2] in so far as it is implicit in any consideration of time present, past and future, and more explicitly by Aristotle,[3] but he also is thinking of different kinds of time, and not of varying forms of the verb. The Stoics recognised that the verb could express other features besides time. Using the distinction between completed (συντελικός) and uncompleted (παρατατικός) action, they clearly distinguished two forms of the present and two of the past. They do not seem to have regarded the future and aorist as tenses on the same footing as these four, but our information is inadequate.[4]

Dionysius Thrax does not define tense. He starts with the statement that there are three tenses (χρόνοι):

Present ἐνεστώς
Past παρεληλυθώς
Future μέλλων

He then subdivides the past into four, making six tenses altogether:[5]

Imperfect παρατατικός
Perfect παρακειμενός
Pluperfect ὑπερσυντελικός
Aorist ἀόριστος

Priscian defines tense as 'an accident of the verb designed for the expression of diversity of action',[6] but he discusses it later as the expression of both time and completeness of action.[7] This suggestion of part of the modern conception of aspect is very tentative and makes no advance on the Stoics. Donatus and Priscian follow the classification of Dionysuis Thrax; like him they begin with three tenses, subdividing the past into three (as Latin has no aorist), making five in all:

Praesens *or* instans
Futurum
Praeteritum imperfectum
Praeteritum perfectum
Praeteritum plusquamperfectum

---

[1] Diogenes Laertius, ix. 52: 'μέρη χρόνου διώρισε'.
[2] Plato, *Parm.*, 151 e, 156 a; *Soph.* 262 d.　　[3] Aristotle, *Int.* 16 b.
[4] Robins, pp. 35–6; Steinthal, I. 307 f.　　[5] Dionysius Thrax, p. 53.
[6] Priscian, viii. 38 (K. ii. 404): 'Tempus accidit verbo ad diversi actus significationem accommodatum'.　　[7] Priscian, op. cit. p. 406.

Priscian discusses, and rejects, the division of the future into

> Future simple (*futurum infinitum*)
>
> Future perfect (*futurum exactum*—Varro; *paulo post futurum; futurum atticum*)

This had been suggested by Varro,[1] who thus helped to form our familiar arrangement into six tenses, as well as suggesting a novel system of his own. Donatus and Priscian, however, considered the future perfect as a future subjunctive.[2]

The medieval grammarians keep close to Priscian. The names of the tenses may vary: Alcuin, for example, calls the perfect the *praeteritum paulo ante* and the pluperfect the *praeteritum multo ante*,[3] but the classification is the same. It is here that the merely verbal nature of some of the speculative grammarians' definitions is especially apparent. Siger says that tense is a mode '...designans circa rem modum essendi praesentialitatis vel praeteritionis vel futuritionis'[4] and Thomas of Erfurt calls it 'Modus significandi accidentalis verbi, quo mediante verbum, citra rem, modum temporis consignificat.'[5]

The treatment of tense in the renaissance grammars is so varied that it is possible here only to quote enough to illustrate the variety and the instability of the categories which made it possible.

Linacre keeps to the classification of Priscian but he also quotes the more systematic treatment of Grocyn, who had revived Varro's scheme, based on the distinction between perfect and imperfect forms, that is on the distinction between complete and incomplete action. The distinction proved awkward when applied to the future, though later grammarians did not hesitate to call *scripsero* a perfect tense. Grocyn's system was as follows:[6]

Present imperfect	*scribo*
Present perfect	*scripsi*
Future imperfect	*scribam*
Futurum exactum	*scripsero*
Preter imperfect	*scribebam*
Preter perfect	*scripseram*

Lily's English accidence keeps to the customary arrangement of Donatus and Priscian,[7] but the Latin accidence does treat the

---

[1] Varro, IX. 96.   [2] Priscian, VIII. 55 (K. II. 416); Steinthal, II. 289.
[3] Alcuin, col. 875.   [4] Siger, p. 112.   [5] TE, p. 111.
[6] Linacre, *De Emendata Structura*, fol. 10 recto.   [7] Lily, 1527, p. 27.

futurum exactum as a possible, if subordinate, category.[1] An additional tremor is given to the classification by treating what had originally been alternative and incompatible classifications of the form *scripsero* (on the one hand *futurum exactum*, an indicative tense, and on the other the future subjunctive) as alternatives within the same system of classification: '*Quod quidem exactum futurum etiam in subiunctivo modo reperitur.*'[2] This meant that there was both an 'exact future' and a future subjunctive, which were identical in form.

Ramus, after establishing the three primary categories of present, preterite and future, also bases his full classification of the tenses on the distinction between completed and uncompleted action. He treats subjunctive and imperative forms as separate tenses, thereby making a system of twelve.[3]

Imperfect (*infecta*) tenses:

First present	*amo*	Second present	*amem*
First preterite	*amabam*	Second preterite	*amarem*
First future	*amabo*	Second future	*ama*

Perfect tenses:

First preterite	*amavi*	Second preterite	*amaverim*
First pluperfect	*amaveram*	Second pluperfect	*amavissem*
First future	*amavero*	Second future	*amaverim*

Sanctius follows Ramus, except that he is prepared to risk an unsymmetrical classification.[4] He combines Ramus' four future tenses (two imperfect and two perfect) into one group of three, including what we call the imperative:

First future	*amabo*
Second future	*amavero*
Third future	*ama, amato*

This removes the necessity for classifying the form *amaverim* twice over. It is similarly typical of Sanctius' robust sense that, after saying, as was customary, that there are three tenses 'in nature', he accompanies his account of the eleven tenses he says there are in fact with the blunt statement of a necessary linguistic truth: 'The distinctions (between tenses) are made by us.'[5] Sanctius differs from

---

[1] Lily, *Brev. Inst.* 1567, sig. C v recto.
[2] Lily, loc. cit.
[3] Ramus, 1560, Bk II. chap. I.
[4] Sanctius, Bk I. chap. 13. 155.
[5] ibid. : 'Differentias facimus.'

Ramus also in his use of the criterion of completeness. He does not apply the distinction between perfect and imperfect forms to all the tenses, only to the pair *amabam/amarem* (imperfect) and to *amavi/amaverim* (perfect).[1]

PERSON

Unless consideration of person (πρόσωπον, *persona*) is strictly confined to its formal expression complex questions arise of great difficulty and considerable unreality. These principally concern the relation between words and things; between the way in which a speaker thinks and the form taken by his words. It is easy to regard the first person as more than a grammatical category: it seems to contain the speaker's conception of himself as being distinct from other people. Accordingly, the speaker's name, so closely involved in his awareness of his own identity, would seem to 'have' something of this quality of person. Again, the movement of the verb in *He sees me* can be regarded not only as (in some sense) an action, but also as a movement of person. The coiling utterance of the speaker moves round person after person. It starts from the speaker, an 'I'; it embraces another person, a 'he'; it returns to the speaker. The verb is related on the one hand to the 'he', on the other to the 'me'; it somehow mediates the change of person.

Difficult questions of this kind arose within the tradition. Apollonius, for example, in the second century B.C., discusses at length why there cannot be more than three persons,[2] and Roger Bacon, followed by later speculative writers, discusses whether a verb can in fact be impersonal.[3] Because the formal aspects of language were not clearly distinguished from others it was accepted without question that person was the same category when related to nouns as it was when related to pronouns and, again, to verbs. In verbs person is a formal feature: the difference between *amas* and *amat* is caused solely by their expressing different persons. But in nouns person has no formal expression at all. In pronouns person is not a formal *feature*, but what words like *ego* primarily express: it is more nearly true to say that person is their meaning. With all three parts of speech something different is meant by person. The term kept much of its human reference and never fully became a neutral technical

---

[1] Sanctius, loc. cit.   [2] Apollonius Dyscolus, *De Pronomine*, i. i. 17–22.
[3] R. Bacon, *Summa Gramatica*, p 78.

Accidents

term: its metaphor was still active. The different sense of 'person' when applied to the noun was recognised in the traditional system of accidents: person, in Dionysius Thrax, Donatus, Priscian and Lily, is an accident of the pronoun and of the verb, but not of the noun. Nevertheless it was frequently stated that all nouns were of the third person,[1] which is to admit a relationship of some kind between person and the noun. Priscian is careful to explain both why *Priscianus nominor* is correct,[2] in spite of the first person of the verb, and why *Priscianus scribo* is inadmissible.[3]

Out of this complexity the ordinary grammarian, writing a text-book, chose the plain statement of Donatus: '*Personae verbis accidunt tres, prima, secunda, tertia. Prima est quae dicit,* lego, *secunda cui dicitur,* legis, *tertia de qua dicitur,* legit.'[4] This, together with the view that all nouns are of the third person, and that impersonal verbs are misnamed, being really of the third person, made up the basic teaching of the tradition on this difficult topic.

[1] e.g. Priscian, XVII. 72 (K. III. 150).
[2] Priscian, VIII. 101 (K. II. 448).   [3] Priscian, XVII. 75 (K. III. 151).
[4] Donatus, *Ars Grammatica*, II. 12 (K. IV. 384).

6. SYNTAX

Earliest treatment. Dionysius does not mention syntax (σύνταξις) as a separate part of his grammar, nor does he pay much attention to the relations between words. His classification of words and grammatical elements does not, however, exclude illustrations of how they are used.

Chrysippus, in the third century B.C., is said to have written a syntax—'περὶ τῆς συντάξεως τῶν λεγομένων'[1]—and there exist fragments of one by Theon of Alexandria in the first century A.D.; but we do not know what these writers meant by syntax. Its basic sense of 'combination, arrangement' permitted a treatment which could be primarily stylistic, and not necessarily concerned with strictly grammatical relations.

By the second century A.D. Apollonius Dyscolus had written his subtle but obscure syntax: the earliest to have survived and probably the fullest to have been written. It is a descriptive examination of certain aspects of Greek usage, and most of it is relevant only to Greek. Syntax itself is not defined, and the work is not consistently concerned with the relations between words. Very few syntactical categories are named, for the most part those which Dionysius had already used in his description of the parts of speech.

As Varro's books on syntax are lost Priscian is the only writer (among the seven early Latin grammarians considered here) to discuss it. The last two books of his *Institutiones*, Bks xvii and xviii (*Priscianus Minor*) are 'de ordinatione sive constructione dictionum, quam Graeci σύνταξιν vocant'.[2]

Priscian discusses syntax almost entirely in terms of person and case. Of the 515 sections into which these two books have been divided just over half are given to verbs and the cases they govern; a quarter are given to pronouns, with intermittent discussion of the use of the other parts of speech. Of the remaining quarter, the greater part is given to a description of the uses of the cases, particularly of the noun, and to the rules of concord.

---

[1] Diogenes Laertius, vii. 192.   [2] Priscian, xvii. 1 (K. iii. 108).

Syntax

The earlier grammarians of the medieval period, Bede, Alcuin, Ælfric, do not discuss syntax: in so far as they are writing elementary books they follow Donatus (who gives no syntax) rather than Priscian. Increasing interest in logic seems to have led to increasing interest in Priscian and in syntax. The speculative grammarians gave particular attention to it, but Alexander and Eberhard at the end of the twelfth century, authors of two popular, long-lived textbooks, uninfluenced by speculative tendencies, discuss syntax[1] at some length. The accounts of syntax given by Alexander and Thomas of Erfurt are described here as representative of the two main points of view within the tradition at this time, and an illustration is given from Roger Bacon of the blend of logical and linguistic analysis which is characteristic of the earlier, and less 'speculative', modistae.

Alexander: '*transitio*'. Alexander, following Priscian, writes[2] as if his basic concept is the distinction between transitive and intransitive; it is only at the end that he introduces what is in fact the prior notion, that of *transitio* itself. *Transitio* is either of actions or of persons. Alexander's previous discussion was all about the former; the latter he refers to in these words:

> Quando non transit actus, nec passio cuiquam
> infertur, nunquam transit constructio plena:

and the example he gives of *transitio* of persons is *filius Alphaei*. *Transitio* is, according to this, the force which binds substantive to substantive, and substantive to verb. If it is operative within both the sentence and the phrase it may rightly be considered the primary force of syntax.

When Alexander says that all syntax is either transitive or intransitive he is thinking only of '*constructio plena*', in which there is *transitio actuum*, that is, expressions containing a finite verb. Transitive construction he defines as that in which the two elements (*partes*) in the sentence refer to different things, or to things which seem to be different. This may occur in two ways, either in simple form (itself of two kinds) or in retransitive form. This makes three kinds of transitive construction:

(i) Simple: (*a*) when the parts of the sentence refer to things which are actually different from each other, e.g. *Hic socium superat.*

---

[1] Eberhard calls it *diasyntastica* but does not define it (chap. 27. 246).

[2] Alexander of Villedieu: all the lines quoted or referred to lie between lines 1369 and 1389 (Reichling, pp. 187–8). The analysis is based on Reichling.

(ii) Simple: (*b*) when the parts of the sentence refer to things only as if they were different, e.g. *Marcum Tullius orat* (when Marcus and Tullius both refer to the same person, Cicero).

(iii) Retransitive (his only explanation of the term is 'quae retransit'), e.g. *Exorat Marcum Cicero, quod diligat ipsum.*

Priscian had explained retransitive as 'quando ab ipsa in aliam fit transitio personam et ab illa in eam retransitio',[1] and among his many examples are, rogat me servus ut miserear sui;[2] ille vocat me ad se.[3] The distinctive feature of a retransitive sentence is that it contains two parts, the second of which contains a pronoun referring to one thing in the previous part. Retransitive, in Priscian's use, is a wider category than reciprocal and reflexive. Priscian calls *video memet* retransitive; Alexander would call it reciprocal.

Alexander classifies intransitive constructions on the same pattern:

(i) Simple: (*a*) when the parts of the sentence refer to things which are actually the same, e.g. *Tullius est Marcus.*

(ii) Simple: (*b*) when the parts of the sentence refer to things only as if they were the same, e.g. *Bos est leo.*

(iii) Reciprocal (*reciproca*): e.g. *Nos diligimus nos.*

Apart from his distinction between the two kinds of simple construction there is nothing in Alexander's discussion which is not already, and more subtly, in Priscian. The principal difference in Alexander's treatment of *transitio* is that he conceives it as a relation between things as they exist in the world, whereas Priscian sees it as a relation between words. This is to oversimplify both points of view, but the difference is of this kind; it can be brought out by saying of *Tullius est Marcus* that Priscian considers the words *Tullius* and *Marcus* to be of the same grammatical person, whereas Alexander says that Tullius and Marcus are the same man.

Thomas of Erfurt: 'dependentia'. Thomas of Erfurt's account of syntax is elaborate but interesting. It represents one of the most important themes which failed to establish themselves within the tradition: the help, if only by analogy, that logic can give to an understanding of certain linguistic relationships.

Thomas defines syntax (*constructio*) as: 'the union of syntactical

---

[1] Priscian, XVII. 133 (K. III. 175).   [2] ibid.
[3] Priscian, XVII. 125 (K. III. 171).

elements, brought about by the mind by means of the modes of signification, and invented for the purpose of expressing an idea'.[1] There are four principles which govern syntactical relations:[2]

(i) *the material principle* is the syntactical element, the unit (*constructibile*), whether it is word or phrase or sentence. 'Syntax is brought about by the dependence of one element on another.'[3] But such a relation necessarily involves two elements and, Thomas seems to imply, two only. For example, in *Socrates percutit Platonem*[4] there is not just one construction: *percutit* depends on *Socrates*, and *Platonem* depends on *percutit*.

(ii) *the formal principle*, therefore, is the union of syntactical elements (*unio constructibilium*).

(iii) *the efficient principle* is of two kinds: (*a*) intrinsic; that is, the modus significandi which governs dependence; (*b*) extrinsic; that is, the mind (*intellectus*) which is causing all this to happen.

(iv) *the final principle* is 'the expression of a complex idea':[5] what the act of speech is intended to achieve.

Thomas goes on to discuss the difference between transitive and intransitive construction—the first distinction, he says, which all grammarians make in their treatment of syntax. His explanation is difficult to follow. The central concept is that of *dependentia*. 'An element is dependent (*dependens*) when, because of some mode of signification, it only seeks or demands; an element is terminal when, because of some mode of signification, it only gives or concedes.'[6] The two elements of a construction are distinguished in terms of *dependentia*: 'In every construction the first element is that which *dependet ad* a following inflected word; and that is the second which *dependet ad* a preceding subject.'[7] The difficulty concerns the interpretation of *dependet ad*. It could mean 'depends on', but the relation is clearly conceived as being effective in two complementary directions. It expresses an active relation for which 'depends on' and 'seeks

[1] TE, p. 148: '...constructibilium unio, ex modis significandi, et intellectu causata, ad exprimendum mentis conceptum compositum finaliter adinventa.'
[2] TE, pp. 144 f.
[3] ibid.: 'Constructio causatur ex dependentia unius constructibilis ad alterum.'
[4] TE, p. 145. [5] TE, p. 146: 'expressio mentis conceptus compositi'.
[6] TE, p. 151: 'Illud...constructibile est dependens, quod ratione alicuius modi significandi tantum petit vel exigit; illud vero constructibile est terminans, quod ratione alicuius modi significandi tantum dat, vel concedit.'
[7] TE, p. 150: 'Illud est in omni constructione constructibile primum, quod post se dependet ad obliquum; illud vero secundum, quod ante se dependet ad suppositum.'

or demands' are appropriate for only one direction or the other; perhaps 'goes with' is adequate for any use of *dependet ad* which is not stressing the direction.

Thomas gives various examples of intransitive construction. In *Sortes currit*[1] he calls *currit* the second element and *Sortes* the first, and says that the second *dependet ad primum*. Here 'depends on' would be appropriate. Another example is *Sortes legit bene*. Here he calls *bene* the second element and *legit* the first, on which it *dependet*.[2] Such a sentence can presumably be regarded in two ways. *Sortes* and *legit* may be taken as a pair between which there exists a syntactical relation; in which case *Sortes* is the first element and *legit* the second, as in *Socrates currit*. But *legit* and *bene* may be similarly regarded, in which case *legit* is the first element and *bene* the second. In the first case *Sortes* 'goes with' *legit* and *legit* 'goes with' its preceding subject *Sortes*. In the second *legit* goes with *bene* and *bene* with *legit*.

Transitive construction is defined as that in which the second element does not go with the first:

If, however, an element goes with the second when the second does not go with the first but with something different from the first, then the construction is transitive. Transitive construction is therefore that in which the first element (by means of its modes of signification) seeks the second and the second (because of its dependent position, if it is dependent) is receding from the first. (TE, p. 152.)[3]

Thomas gives as an example of an element which is not dependent *percutio Socratem*, in which the second element '*dependentiam non habet, sed solum prius constructibilis dependentiam terminat*'.

Thomas does not give enough illustrations for the reader to be able to check every step in his demonstration. His main distinctions seem to be between four types of sentence:

(i) sentences such as *Socrates currit*, where the construction (not the verb) is intransitive because the second element has a positive relation towards the first.

---

[1] TE, p. 152.

[2] ibid.: 'Constructio intransitiva est constructio in qua secundum constructibile, per suos modos significandi, dependet ad primum...hoc adverbium "bene", quod est secundum constructibile in ista constructione, dependet ad verbum, quod est primum constructibile.'

[3] 'Si autem primum constructibile dependet ad secundum, secundo non dependente ad primum, sed aliud a primo diversum, sic est transitiva. Constructio ergo transitiva est in qua primum constructibile, per suos modos significandi, dependet ad secundum, secundo per eius dependentiam a primo recedente, si dependens fuerit.'

Syntax

(ii) sentences such as *Socrates legit bene,* where there are more than two elements and the construction is intransitive because *bene* goes with the previous element *legit.* But *legit* has a positive relation ('seeks') towards *Socrates,* as did *currit:* it does not seek an element different from the first.

(iii) sentences such as *Socrates percutit Platonem,* where there are more than two elements, and the construction is transitive because *percutit,* the second element, does not 'seek' *Socrates,* the first element, in the way which *currit* did, but seeks 'something different from the first element'; that is, it seeks *Platonem,* which seeks *percutit* as *percutit* seeks it.

(iv) sentences such as *percutio Socratem,* in which the construction is transitive because the second element, in this case *Socratem,* has no positive relation towards the first element *percutio* but merely 'terminates the positive relation which *percutio* has towards it'.

Thomas's analysis is subtle and apparently novel, but it strikes us as unnecessarily complex because he makes it always in terms of two elements, even when common sense and logic would seem to agree that there were three. This means that the first element will be sometimes the subject and sometimes the verb, according to whether the sentence contains two words or three. The effect of this complexity, on the modern reader at least, is to make it very difficult to follow Thomas's description of the categories transitive and intransitive without a prior knowledge of and constant reference to, the categories themselves.

Both transitive and intransitive construction can be of actions or of persons.[1]

(*a*) *of actions*: e.g. *lege librum.* This construction is subdivided into four forms according to the four cases which may follow a verb (*misereor Sortis,* etc.). These four forms are known as *constructio transitiva actus signati* ('...of an action designated'). A fifth form, *constructio transitiva actus exerciti* ('...of an action performed') is illustrated only by the expression *O Thoma!* There are corresponding intransitive forms, e.g. *a Socrate legitur; Socratis interest.*

(*b*) *of persons*: transitive examples are *filius Sortis* (Socrates' son). This type is similarly divided into four, according to the four cases in which the second of two related nouns may be: *similis Sorti; albus faciem; celere pedibus.*

[1] TE, pp. 168–70.

Intransitive examples are: *Socrates albus currit bene*,[1] and constructions with the relative pronoun.

Construction is further classified as being explicit (*secundum sensum*) or implicit (*secundum intellectum*).[2] For example, *lego* is implicit, because the 'full' form could be *ego lego*, where every possible word is expressed. A similar feeling of guilt, that there is perhaps something not absolutely correct about a sentence which could be expressed in a greater number of words, is a persistent trait throughout the development of English grammar.

There is a (much needed) recognition by Thomas that his elaborate analysis of language is ultimately relevant only to communication between speaker and hearer. It is interesting that he judges the success of a communication not only by its accuracy (its correspondence to the speaker's ideas) but by its power to satisfy the hearer:

> The mark of a complete construction is to produce complete sense in the mind of the hearer...But this completeness of sense in the hearer's mind is not necessarily precise, but has degrees of completeness, greater or less, according to which the construction is said to be more, or less, complete. For a construction is the more complete the more satisfaction it gives to the mind of the hearer, and that which satisfies him less is less complete. (TE.)[3]

Roger Bacon: substantive and verb. As the most interesting part of the speculative grammarians' work is their treatment of syntax it is worth referring briefly to a passage in Roger Bacon's *Summa Gramatica* which will illustrate the presumptive subtlety and the manifest obscurity which characterise much of his grammar. It will not be possible to follow with certainty an argument of this kind (and there are many) until more texts have been printed, especially of Peter Helias, and key terms have been studied in a greater number of contexts. Because of our uncertainty about the meaning of several

---

[1] This illustration suggests not only that the name *Socrates* has been entirely dissociated from the philosopher, but also that the framing of linguistic examples is governed, for the speculative grammarians, primarily by logical rather than grammatical criteria. The meaning of the terms matters little.

[2] TE, p. 173.

[3] Quoted by Mullally, p. xcvi n.: 'Signum perfectionis constructionis est, generare perfectum sensum in animo auditoris...Sed haec perfectio sensus in animo auditoris non est punctualis, sed habet gradum perfectionis secundum magis, et minus: et secundum hoc constructio dicitur magis, et minus perfecta. Nam ea magis perfecta est, quae magis quietat animum auditoris; et quae minus quietat, minus perfecta erit.'

terms a summary of Bacon's argument is itself far from clear.[1] He is examining the syntactical relation between substantive and verb and, incidentally, between substantive and adjective. He is concerned particularly with the intransitive relation. Intransitive construction is made through identity of person. But the term 'person' is ambiguous: it may mean grammatical person, or it may mean the real subject. As grammatical person it may have two meanings; it may mean simply the grammatical person, or it may mean the real subject of the grammatical person. When it means the real subject 'person' is ambiguous: it may mean what is signified by noun and verb (which is impossible, because their significations differ) or it may mean just the real subject.

One can ask whether there is any construction between noun and verb.

Either the construction is transitive (which is not possible, because it is clear that there is no transition of action or of person) or it is intransitive. But the latter does not seem to be true either, for an intransitive construction is made through identity of person. Since *person* is ambiguous this identity must be either of the person who is the real subject or of 'person' as a grammatical property.

This identity cannot be found in grammatical 'person' because then whenever there was such identity of 'person' there would be an intransitive construction. For example, when I say 'I see me' (*video me*) there is identity of grammatical 'person' between verb and pronoun, for both are first person. Similarly, if we were to say 'Socrates' hood' (*Capa Sortis*) each word is in the third person, whence it would follow that the construction was intransitive, which it is not. Again, there is between noun and verb no identity of the person which is the real subject of the grammatical 'person', because in the verb this is the thing signified by the verb, its real meaning, and in the noun it is the thing signified by the noun. But the things signified by the noun and by the verb are plainly different, as when we say 'A man is running' (*homo currit*). And so there is no identity of person in either of the above senses, and therefore the construction is not intransitive.

It may be said that what is required is identity of the person which is the real subject. But such 'person' is ambiguous. It can mean what is signified by the noun and what is signified by the verb. Identity of this kind cannot be required.

The other meaning is the real subject underlying the thing signified by the noun and verb, i.e. that for which the thing signified is acting as subject. If, for example, I say 'a man is running' (*homo currit*) and 'a man' is acting as subject for Socrates [the real subject] then Socrates is that

---

[1] In the translation of this passage, and for its elucidation, still far from complete, I am heavily indebted to Mr S. J. Tester.

person whose identity is required in such a construction. But that person sometimes *is* the thing signified by the noun, when, that is, a sentence is about the thing signified by the noun, or when a term is acting as subject for just such a thing-signified, as when I say 'man is a species' (*homo est species*). This happens in such a case because the subject and the thing signified are the same. So, that for which a nominative acts as subject is necessarily the person mentioned in an intransitive construction: by being added to the other [i.e. to the verb] it is one and the same [person]. Similarly between adjective and substantive, as when we say 'white man' (*homo albus*), because the same real subject underlies the thing signified by both words.[1]

An argument of this style (whatever its exact meaning) implies a conception of grammar which the tradition as a whole has not accepted. Today we are familiar with the application to language of psychological and logical concepts, but we still need to find out how far analysis in these terms is a useful component of grammar, in one sense of that term: the sense in which it means 'the study of one's own language in use'.

Correctness. The grammarians of the renaissance period enlarge on Priscian's definition of syntax, but, with the exception of Ramus, add to it only the idea of correctness: syntax is the *proper* ordering of words.

[1] Roger Bacon, *Summa Gramatica*, pp. 11–12: 'Deinde potest queri si est construccio inter nomen et verbum. Aut ergo transitiva; hoc esse non potest, quia nec est transicio actuum nec personarum, ut patet; aut intransitiva. Set quod hoc non sit verum videtur: quia construccio intransitiva fit per ydemptitatem persone: cum ergo persona duplex est, aut persona que est suppositum aut persona que est personalis proprietas. Non persona que est personalis proprietas, quia tunc ubicumque esset ydemptitas talis persone esset intransitiva construccio, igitur cum sic dico "video me" inter verbum et pronomen est ydemptitas persone que est personalis proprietas, cum utrumque sit prime persone. Similiter si diceretur "capa Sortis", utrumque est tercie persone, quare esset intransitiva construccio, quod falsum est. Nec est inter nomen et verbum ydemptitas persone que est suppositum respectu proprietatis personalis, quia suppositum respectu personalis proprietatis in verbo est significatum sive res verbi, suppositum respectu personalis proprietatis in nomine est significatum nominis. Set significatum nominis et verbi sunt simpliciter diversa, ut cum dicitur "homo currit", quare neutro modo est hic ydemptitas persone, ut videtur, igitur non est construccio intransitiva.'

Et dicendum est quod exigitur ydemptitas persone que est suppositum. Set persona talis duplex est, una que est significatum nominis et verbi, et istius ydemptitas non potest exigi. Alia est suppositum deferens significatum nominis et verbi, scilicet illud pro quo supponit, ut si dicam 'homo currit', si supponat pro Sorte, Sor est illa persona cujus ydemptitas exigitur in construccione tali. Ista tamen persona aliquando est significatum nominis, cum scilicet fit sermo de significato ejus sive cum terminus supponat pro tali significato, ut cum dico 'homo est species'. Set hoc accidit quia ibi est idem suppositum et significatum; illud igitur pro quo supponit nominativus necessario est persona de qua mencio est in construccione intransitiva; illud enim unum et idem est per comparacionem ad alium. Et similiter est inter adjectivum et substantivum, ut si dicatur 'homo albus', quia idem suppositum defert significatum utrumque, et sic est in omnibus.

[Constructio] debita dispositio partium orationis in ipsa oratione. (Perottus, sig. e 5.)

[Constructio] debita et comunis ordinatio partium orationis. (Despauter, *Commentarii grammatici*, Paris, 1537, p. 404.)[1]

[Syntaxis] debita partium orationis inter se compositio connexioque, iuxta rectam Grammatices rationem. Ea vero est, qua veterum probatissimi, tum in scribendo, tum in loquendo sunt usi. (Lily, *Brev. Inst.* 1567, sig. E ii.)

Linacre, whom Lily's grammar probably quotes, emphasises conformity with the best classical usage, and also the rhetorical distinction, stressed again during the second half of the eighteenth century, between 'just' and 'figurative' syntax: 'Est igitur constructio debita partium orationis inter se compositio, sicuti recta grammatices ratio exigit. Porro recta grammatices ratio ea est, qua veterum probatissimi plurimum, cum loquendo tum scribendo sunt usi'.[2] There are, Linacre says, two kinds of syntax, 'straightforward' and 'figurative':

One kind, in which nothing is omitted, nothing redundant, nothing out of place, nothing metaphorical: this is not improperly called 'straightforward'. The other kind is the opposite to this: something is omitted, or redundant, or out of place, or metaphorical. Nevertheless there are examples of this kind, which can be called 'figurative', from the finest men who have written in the Roman tongue. (DES, Bk iii. sig. N 2.)[3]

Ramus, in a single phrase, adds a necessary reminder that the rules of syntax are derived from the functioning of words—*ex proprietatibus*—and are not arbitrary: [Syntaxis] structuram et compositionem vocum inter se ex earum proprietatibus instituit'.[4]

Agreement and government. The relations between words which came to be known as agreement (or concord) and government (or regimen) do not seem to have acquired generally accepted names during the period of the tradition. While it would be absurd to suggest that the relations were not perceived as such, the varying ways in which they are referred to, often in the same paragraph, imply that within the

---

[1] Quoted by Reichling, p. 87 n.
[2] Linacre, *De Emendata Structura*, 1524, sig. N i verso (Bk ii ad fin.).
[3] 'Alterum, cui nec deest quippiam, nec redundat, nec loco suo abest, nec immutatur, quod non immerito Iustum appellatur. Alterum contra, cui deest aliquid, vel redundat, vel loco suo abest, vel immutatur, non tamen sine summorum in Romana lingua virorum exemplo, quod figuratum dici potest.'
[4] Ramus, Bk iii. chap. 1.

The Tradition

tradition they were less sharply distinguished as syntactical categories than they were by later grammarians.

Apollonius discusses verbs and prepositions which govern the accusative, genitive and dative, but he does not adopt a fixed terminology. In three adjacent sections of the Syntax, for example, he speaks of verbs 'demanding' (ἀπαιτεῖ) the genitive;[1] 'striving towards' (συντείνουσιν) the accusative;[2] 'being carried towards' (φέρεται) the accusative.[3]

Equivalent terms are used by Priscian, who is often translating Apollonius. Some verbs *'obliquos desiderant casus nominum'*;[4] others *'egent obliquorum casuum adiunctione'*;[5] elsewhere *'obliqui casus pronominum omni modo ad verba feruntur'*;[6] Priscian's most usual term is 'join with'. Active verbs *'quae et transitiva sunt in homines, sine dubio accusativo adiunguntur'*;[7] again *'verba transitiva...variis solent casibus coniungi'*.[8] His usage is as varied with other parts of speech. He refers to *'nominibus...exigentibus obliquos'*[9] to prepositions 'of' the ablative *(casus ablativi)*[10] and to those which *'casui ablativo serviunt'*.[11] The nearest approach he makes to a term for agreement is *consequentia*: words agreeing in gender, number and case are understood *'ad convenientes...consequentias'*; when they are used correctly it is with *'aptam coniunctionem'*.[12]

Thomas of Erfurt makes agreement (*congruitas*) depend on *conformitas*,[13] meaning, apparently, that *congruitas* is a grammatical relation, between words, and *conformitas* a metaphysical one, between modes of signification. He also distinguishes between *congruitas* and *proprietas*: 'proprietas vel improprietas sermonis causatur ex convenientia vel repugnantia significatorum specialium.' His illustration is more informative than his definition. *Cappa nigra* (black cloak) is both congruous (grammatically) and proper (logically); *cappa categorica*, however, though congruous is improper.[14] Otherwise his grammatical treatment of government and agreement adds little to Priscian.

By the time of Lily's grammar the category *concord* is established in

---

[1] Apollonius Dyscolus, Syntax, Bk III. § 158 (S & U, II. 405).
[2] ibid. § 159 (S & U, ibid.).
[3] ibid. § 164 (S & U, II. 410). Egger (p. 237) makes Apollonius' failure to distinguish between agreement and government one of the main omissions of the Syntax.
[4] Priscian, XVII. 83 (K. III. 154.)   [5] ibid.   [6] ibid.
[7] Priscian, XVIII. 127 (K. III. 267).   [8] Priscian, XVIII. 8 (K. III. 212).
[9] Priscian, XVIII. 5 (K. III. 212).   [10] Priscian, XIV. 42 (K. III. 47).
[11] Priscian, XIV. 39 (K. III. 44).   [12] Priscian, XVII. 153 (K. III. 182).
[13] TE, p. 174.   [14] TE, p. 175.

Syntax

its authoritative form: 'In Latine speache there be three Concordes.'[1] These are (i) agreement between nominative and its verb; (ii) between substantive and adjective; (iii) between the relative and its antecedent. These concords had been specified, by Perottus, at least as early as 1468, but not in the exclusive form which later became customary.

Government is not so clearly established as a named category. The early renaissance grammarians and Lily use much the same variety of terms as Priscian had done. Lily's usual term is *regunt*, but he does not use the noun *regimen*. Some verbs '*dativum requirunt*';[2] the verb substantive in certain instances '*genitivum postulat*';[3] all verbs used acquisitively '*adsciscunt dativum*';[4] other verbs '*exigunt accusativum*'[5] or *desiderant accusativum*[6] or '*habent accusativum*';[7] some impersonal verbs '*in dativum feruntur*'.[8] Several of these terms are used also of the preposition, which in addition '*accusativo iungitur*';[9] some interjections '*accusativo adhaerent*'.[10] In Lily's English syntax the term usually employed with verbs is 'have', though 'govern' is sometimes used; for other parts of speech the usual term is 'require' (a given case).

Ramus makes agreement and government the two parts of syntax and distinguishes between them in these words: 'Est autem Syntaxis convenientia aut rectio: Convenientia, est syntaxis e mutua proprietatum communione, rectio est syntaxis qua vox vi sua vocem aliam certo casu regit.'[11]

Subject, Predicate, Object. Aristotle's distinction between the logical subject (τὸ ὑποκείμενον) and the logical predicate (τὸ κατηγορούμενον), though more technical than the distinction between ὄνομα and ῥῆμα, may be considered also to have had its origin in speech and discussion. The logical terms have never wholly lost their association with language, though ὄνομα and ῥῆμα soon lost their association with dialectic.

Apollonius still uses τὸ ὑποκείμενον to mean 'the thing referred to',[12] which may be indicated by the grammatical subject or by the grammatical object: these are not distinguished by name, nor is our category of complement. The predicate (κατηγόρημα) continued to

---

[1] Lily, *Shorte Intro.* 1567, sig. C iv.
[2] *Brev. Inst.*, 1567, sig. E viii.
[3] ibid. sig. E vii.
[4] ibid. sig. E vii verso.
[5] ibid. sig. F i.
[6] ibid. sig. E vii verso.
[7] *Brev. Inst.* 1567, sig. F i.
[8] ibid. sig. F v.
[9] ibid. sig. F viii verso.
[10] ibid. sig. G i.
[11] Ramus, Bk III. chap. 1.
[12] Apollonius Dyscolus, *Syntax*, Bk I. § 120 (S & U, II. 101).

be regarded primarily from a logical point of view or, as in Diogenes Laertius' interpretation of Apollodorus, from a point of view both logical and linguistic: '...what is said of something'.[1] But Diogenes gives another and more nearly grammatical description of the predicate: '...an incomplete expression which had to be joined on to a nominative case in order to yield a judgment'.[2] Apollonius, also quoting the Stoic point of view, says κατηγόρημα was used for a verb-form other than the infinitive, i.e. for a finite verb.[3]

In Priscian the categories are no more clearly formed. Where we would use the terms 'subject' or 'object' he uses 'nominative' or 'accusative' or 'oblique case'. The structure of a sentence can be discussed in terms of the formal properties of words because Latin and Greek are strongly inflected: there is no need for a separate structural category like 'subject', and it was only the later renewal of logical studies which forced attention on structure. How useful, how legitimate, a logical view of linguistic structure is remains a very live issue today.

Priscian does in one passage[4] suggest a distinction between the logical subject (*suppositum*) and the grammatical subject. He is explaining why interrogative sentences can begin with a number of different nouns and adverbs, whereas the interrogative function might have been confined to one interrogative noun or pronoun and one interrogative adverb. His explanation is that the interrogative *quis*, for example, permits an answer merely in terms of substance, whereas we wish to know about other qualities. When we are asking about substance we ask a question beginning with *quis* because we do not know the person, even if the action is apparent. The answers we receive, accordingly, contain common or proper nouns, acting as subjects in the nominative case (*subiectiones nominativae*): 'Nam substantiam alicuius suppositi quaerentes dicimus "quis movetur?" "quis ambulat?"'...cum manifestus sit actus, id est motus vel ambulatio...persona vero agens incerta; ideo subiectiones nominativae fiunt appellativorum vel propriorum.'[5]

[1] Diogenes Laertius, VII. 64: Ἔστι δὲ τὸ κατηγόρημα τὸ κατά τινος ἀγορευόμενον.'
[2] ibid.: 'λεκτὸν ἐλλιπὲς συντακτὸν ὀρθῇ πτώσει πρὸς ἀξιώματος γένεσιν.'
[3] Apollonius Dyscolus, *Synt.* I. § 50 (S & U, II. 43).
[4] Priscian, XVII. 23 (K. III. 122).
[5] Apollonius had used the same argument, but made the pronoun equivalent only to the proper noun. If the question is 'Who is Tryphon?' the answer is the pronoun *he*. If the question is 'Who is he?' the answer is the proper noun *Tryphon*. (*Synt.*, Bk I. § 120; S & U, II. 101.)

Priscian does not use the term *subiectio* elsewhere, but he here seems to be consciously distinguishing it from the term *suppositum*, the ordinary translation of ὑποκείμενον, and *subiectio* is here certainly appropriate to the later sense of (grammatical) subject, which was derived from *subiectum*.

Occam, in his analysis of the different uses of the term *subiectum*, describes one which is 'in relation to predication, because it [*subiectum*] is that part of a proposition which precedes the copula'.[1] Occam is not here making any distinction between *subiectum* and *suppositum*, nor is he writing with anything but logic in mind, but it is easy to see how *subiectum*, associated with a logical category which coincided with one element in the grammatical structure of the sentence, should eventually serve as the name for that element also. But to put it this way is to allow the accident of historical development too prominent a place. The essential fact is that logic and grammar have a common origin in the study of linguistic structure, and 'subject', a basic structural category, is one of the terms which could longest remain undifferentiated.

The distinction between logical and grammatical subject is, as it were, waiting in the wings during the whole of the medieval period. It cannot be said to have been unformulated, but it was not so clearly made that separate terms were generally felt to be necessary, and the grammarians as a whole showed little need for the category of subject at all. *Suppositum* and *subiectum* seem to have been used as equivalent terms by Roger Bacon, and *suppositum* was used in the sense of grammatical subject even by Lily, as when he speaks of the adjective agreeing *cum supposito verbi*.[2]

Predicate was more exclusively a category of logic. Thomas of Erfurt provides a rare instance of its use in a specifically grammatical context. He is describing one of the conditions necessary for an utterance to be considered complete, and he refers to '*constructio... habens suppositum et appositum*'.[3] But though the context is grammatical the reference of the terms is still logical. Thomas is not thinking primarily of words. Occam, in the passage just quoted, speaks of the predicate as 'that part of a proposition which follows the copula',[4] but the grammatical correspondence is here not so close:

---

[1] Occam, *Summa totius logicae*, chap. 30, quoted by Prantl, III. 368: 'Dicitur subiectum per praedicationem, quod est pars propositionis praecedens copulam.'

[2] Lily, *Brev. Inst.* 1567, sig. E vi, verso.   [3] TE, p. 182.

[4] Occam, in Prantl, loc. cit.: illa pars, quae sequitur [copulam], dicitur praedicatum'.

so many different kinds of words and expressions could follow the copula that the bare categories *appositum* or *praedicatum* were of little use in grammar. Predicate remains a manifest, if often unrecognised, importation from logic. It is not mentioned in Lily.

Apposition. Throughout the tradition the term is used only incidentally, and in a more general sense than is now customary. Any juxtaposition of two elements could be called apposition. Priscian treats it as a grammatical category; Peter of Spain uses it as a logical category, a type of restriction or modification 'produced by the more particular being in apposition to the more general', as in *animal, homo, currit*.[1] Roger Bacon defines apposition in logical terms within a grammatical context. A construction such as the example given by Peter he calls *appositio immediata*: 'the direct and intransitive conjunction of words referring to the same logical subject'.[2] In Lily's grammar apposition is treated both as a rhetorical category, among the figures of speech, and as part of the syntax of substantives. As a figure of speech it is defined as 'the direct or indirect conjunction of two substantives in the same case, one of which is explained by the other'.[3]

'Understood'. Grammarians within the tradition, and the English grammarians who followed it, were very ready to take account of words which might have been, but in fact were not, spoken. Contemporary school grammars are still full of explanations in which some lapse from an arbitrary standard of correctness is regularised by the influence of words 'understood'. Those who require of a sentence that it should both 'express a complete thought' and contain a subject and predicate can evade the dilemma of the one-word sentence only by postulating a subject which is understood. 'Jump!' is accordingly said to be 'really' 'Jump (you)!'. The word *you* is 'understood'. Or is it the word *John* which is understood? Or the words *you tiresome little brat*? Who can tell?

The condition of being understood, or unexpressed, which is not,

---

[1] Peter of Spain, *Summulae Logicales*, Tractatus VII, ed. and transl. J. P. Mullally, Notre Dame, Indiana 1945, pp. 46–7: '...fit per inferius nomini superiori appositum'.

[2] Roger Bacon, *Summa Gramatica*, pp. 43–4: 'Sinthesis scilicet sive apposicio inmediata est diccionum ad idem suppositum pertinencium inmediata et intransitiva conjunccio.'

[3] Lily, *Brev. Inst.* 1567, sig. G i verso: 'duorum substantivorum eiusdem casus, quorum altero declaratur alterum, continuata sive immediata coniunctio'.

of course, necessarily unreal or irrelevant to analysis, appears early in the tradition. Apollonius uses, but does not name, the category. He says that the answer *This man*—οὗτος—to the questions *Who hit you?* or *Who is called Ajax?* 'has as its verb the same verb as the question'.[1]

Priscian also uses the category incidentally. He calls such words *subaudita*. After saying, for example, that verbs can have a complete meaning without an accompanying adverb, but that an adverb cannot, without an accompanying verb or particle, he continues: 'Although adverbs can be used alone it is necessary to relate them either to verbs already used by the speaker—as when someone asks me, "Is pride good?" and I reply "No."—or to verbs spoken in ellipsis, as if I should say to someone who was reciting, "Bene, diserte or eloquenter", for the words "you speak" would be understood (*subauditur*) in each case.'[2]

The category received no systematic treatment: there is no indication within the tradition that it was questioned or discussed. It is used most often in connection with the sentence or with sentence equivalents, but also with most types of construction. Lily, for example, says that in *Quo mihi commisso non licet esse piam* and similar instances '*subaudiuntur accusativi ante verba infinita*'[3] (i.e. . . . *me esse piam*). Again, with less justice, he says that in *Abest ab urbe quingentis millibus passuum* '*subintelligitur "spacium" vel "spacio"*'.[4]

Usage, analogy. 'Usage', which we are nowadays forcing to accept the status of a technical term, is an idea too closely allied to common sense and everyday life to make a sudden and notable appearance in history. Plato refers in the Theaetetus[5] to the ordinary use—συνήθεια—of nouns and verbs, and the idea is implicit throughout much of the Cratylus. What we regard as one question was by the ancient world treated as two. A distinction was made between correctness (*whether* a particular form or use of words was correct) and the principle by which correctness was to be judged (*why* a particular form or use of words was correct). To us, who take a historical view of the development of language, whatever is, is right: judgments of 'correctness' are not usually linguistic judgments;

---

[1] Apollonius Dyscolus, *Synt.* III. § 8: 'κοινὸν ἔχει παραλαμβανόμενον τὸ ῥῆμα.'
[2] Priscian, xv. 4 (K. III. 62).   [3] Lily, *Brev. Inst.* 1567, sig. E vii.
[4] Lily, ibid. sig. F iv.   [5] Plato, *Theaetetus*, 168 b.

they are judgments based on social, conventional or aesthetic criteria. This does not make them invalid. Whether a particular usage was correct or not was, throughout the period of the tradition, a question which belonged to rhetoric rather than to grammar. In so far as the grammarians discussed it, they borrowed the rhetorical categories of barbarism and solecism. Why a particular usage was correct was the central issue in the controversy over the principles of analogy and anomaly. This controversy, which reached its height in the second century B.C. but was still active in the second century A.D., used, directly and indirectly, concepts which are still important for English grammar. The terms in which the controversy was conducted, and the assumptions on which it was based, are frequently obscure.

Both parties recognised:

(*a*) the diversity of grammatical forms in Greek;

(*b*) that some forms nevertheless resembled others;

(*c*) the need for some principle by which to judge what grammatical form to use;

(*d*) that Greek grammatical forms had not always been the same.

The Alexandrian grammarians, who supported the principle of analogy, meant by it that a classification of grammatical forms (chiefly into declensions and conjugations) on the basis of similarity, was desirable because it created order and system. If contemporary usage gave no strong guide as to what was the correct form of a word the question should be decided on the basis of analogy. But usage could be so strong that it prevailed over what was desirable for the purpose of tidy classification. The power of usage and the advantages of classification were thus to some extent in conflict.

The Stoic grammarians of Pergamum, who supported the principle of anomaly, meant by it irregularity of grammatical forms, which they regarded not only as a present feature of everyday speech, but as a right one, because the natural state of words reflected in an obscure way (onomatopoeic in principle) a reality which lay behind them.

It is clear to us now that a better understanding of usage, and of how language changes, would have removed the grounds of controversy. Diodorus of Megara seems to have been more perceptive than most of his contemporaries. In order to emphasise the conventional nature of language he called his slaves by the names of Greek particles, e.g., ἀλλὰ μήν.[1] Sextus Empiricus, in the second century A.D., is equally emphatic, but he argues the point, in a way which is worth reproducing in order to establish the antiquity of the view that language is essentially based on convention. In usage, Sextus says,

> one ought to follow the many rather than the one...It remains to hold fast by the common usage of all men (τῇ πάντων συνηθείᾳ προσέχειν.) And if so, there is no need of analogy, but of observing how most men converse and what they adopt as good Greek or avoid as not good. However, good Greek exists either by nature (φύσει) or by convention (θέσει). But it does not exist by nature, since then the same phrase would never have seemed good Greek to some and not good Greek to others; and if it exists by convention and human enactment, the man who speaks good Greek is he who is most practised and versed in common usage. (*Adv. Math.* I. 188–90; Bury's transl.)

The anomalists respected usage; the analogists had in the last resort to obey it and eventually, with Quintilian, admitted that analogy did in fact derive from, and depend on, usage (*consuetudo*).[2]

Analogy and anomaly are not discussed by any of the later grammarians, except Charisius, who has a short section on analogy in Bk I, taken from Romanus.[3] Isidore says analogy is '*similium conparatio sive proportio*'. Words may have eight features in common, and if any feature is different in two words that is a case of anomaly, '*id est extra regulam*'. The example he gives is the traditional pair of genitives *lupi* and *leporis*, which differ, though their nominatives *lupus* and *lepus* resemble each other.[4]

It is easy to see how analogy could come, in the eighteenth-century English grammars, to mean the same as etymology: variations in the form of words which basically resemble each other.

CONCLUSION

Between the grammars of Dionysius Thrax and Francisco Sanchez or Sanctius there lie seventeen centuries. Of the sixty-six works which have been used in this summary of the tradition at least one appeared during each of these centuries. It is not surprising, there-

---

[1] Ammonius on Aristotle, *Int.* p. 32.
[2] Quintilian, I. vi. 16.
[3] Charisius, I. xvii (K. I. 116 f.).
[4] Isidore, I. xxviii.

fore, that the tradition should show both continuity and fluctuation, stability and instability. But what the summary shows, more clearly perhaps than can be seen in the detailed histories, which cover only parts of the period, is the narrow and sometimes merely verbal basis of the stability, and the height and depth of the fluctuations.[1]

The continuity is most obvious in the names of the parts of speech. Dionysius, in the second century B.C., gives Greek an article, noun, pronoun, verb, participle, adverb, conjunction and preposition; Priscian, six hundred years later, follows Dionysius, except that he adds the interjection and excludes the article; Lily, after a further nine hundred years, gives exactly the same parts of speech as Priscian. But there is a more fundamental continuity than this, one virtually unquestioned. By the time of Dionysius the foundations of a descriptive procedure had been laid. Words were treated in three ways: they were analysed into their constituents—syllables and letters, vowels and consonants—more by eye than by ear; they were grouped into classes (parts of speech) sometimes according to their meaning and sometimes according to their form; these word-classes were subdivided by meaning, as in Priscian's thirty kinds of adverb (p. 102). It was assumed that grammatical analysis was concerned primarily, if not solely, with the word. So strong is this part of the tradition that we are still apt to ask, 'On what other assumption could grammatical analysis have been conducted?' But the grammatical tradition is accompanied by, and partly contains, two other procedures: the classification of kinds of discourse, which was part of rhetoric, and the analysis of discourse, which was part of logic. Grammar, rhetoric and logic were established and distinct disciplines long before they were called the trivium, and it is this consolidation into distinct named disciplines which largely explains the tendency to restrict grammar to the study of the word. Even syntax was narrowly concerned with the relations between single words—with agreement and government. The structure of larger units and of the sentence was partly the concern of logic and partly (in relation to emphasis and other aspects of mood and tone expressed, for example, through word-order) the concern of rhetoric.

The distinction between logic, rhetoric and grammar springs from, amongst other sources, certain assumptions about the nature of language and how it is used; but the distinction, once formed,

---

[1] The page references in the rest of this chapter are all to the present work.

made it more difficult to change and extend these assumptions. That there was some pressure to extend and co-ordinate the linguistic presuppositions of logic, rhetoric and grammar is suggested by the development of the term *grammar* (pp. 24–34) compared with the development of the contents of the books called grammars. Within the tradition *grammar* is usually defined in terms far wider than the contents of the books would justify. In most definitions grammar is said to cover almost the whole range of literary, and to overlap with many rhetorical, skills; whereas even those books in which it is so defined normally restrict their contents to the analysis and classification of words. The important exceptions are Apollonius and Priscian. The latter's great work includes, in its fullness, abundant literary material and some attention to the logical relationships expressed by verb, conjunction and preposition, as well as to their government.

The continuity of the grammatical tradition is apparent, generally, in its preoccupation with the word: specifically, in the formal analysis and classification of words (chap. 4), in the system of parts of speech, and in the treatment of the participle (p. 75). But everywhere the fluctuations are as evident as the continuity. Quintilian, Donatus and Priscian all say there could be other parts of speech and other systems (pp. 49–50); Bacon virtually excludes the conjunction and preposition, Ramus the preposition and interjection, Sanctius the pronoun and interjection. Sanctius, moreover, expressly comments on the instability of the traditional system of parts of speech (p. 52). Noun and verb are the two most stable categories, after the participle, but the verb is defined according to widely varying criteria (p. 60) and the noun, by combining within itself both substantive and adjective, contains a radical instability during the whole period of the tradition. Continuity and fluctuation are both illustrated by the definitions of the noun (pp. 53 f.). As early as the second century B.C. the noun is said to name a person or thing, and the distinction between common and proper nouns may go back to the same time; it certainly dates from Donatus. But thereafter the choice of criteria varies. The scholastic grammarians wrestle with meaning, in terms of substance and quality, and ignore form. Most of the renaissance grammarians rely on formal criteria, hardly at all on meaning; but Lily, in the English accidence, frames his definitions solely in terms of meaning. Other parts of speech reveal, behind a constant name, as great an instability. The conjunction, at first sight a plain and unadventurous part of speech, provokes difficult questions far wider than the classification of words, and no agreed definition is achieved within the tradition (pp. 61–4). The close relation between preposition and adverb is commented on by Diomedes at the end of the fourth century A.D., and leads Ramus, in the sixteenth century, to include prepositions among adverbs (pp. 65–6). The general instability of the adverb is discussed by Donatus (p. 73) and its particularly uncertain relationship with the conjunction is mentioned by two other fourth-century writers (p. 104). The difficulty of the pronoun (pp. 68–72) is notorious: it drives even Priscian, in the last resort, to merely ostensive definition (p. 101). But it is a mistake to regard the difficulty as unique. The pronoun is difficult because a number of radically diverse functions, incompletely perceived, are combined into one category whose bounds have to be set by a single definition. This, in a less acute form, is the hampering condition in which most of the parts of speech grew to maturity.

The continuity of the tradition, in fact, does not lie in the *nature* of its grammatical categories, but in their *names*. It lies in the procedures, especially definition and classification, more than in their products. It lies in the assumptions about language, and especially about the word, on which these procedures are based. The continuity is, in many important respects, an illusion, but this does not justify any disparagement of the early grammarians. The illusion is ours. We have tended to lose sight of the fluctuations, and to regard the tradition as more rigid, more unquestioning, than it was. With no historical or comparative studies to guide them, the early grammarians would have needed, in order to remodel their categories, an impossible imaginative effort. The fluctuations, the inconsistencies, the perceptive comments, the aridities of modal system-building, the trivial lists, are all part of a slow struggle, which still continues. The tradition which has been so briefly examined here is only superficially static. Behind the inherited masks lie human features, many of them composed and satisfied, many restless, active and chafing.

The restlessness expresses itself in many ways, some of which anticipate comparatively modern views. Dionysius conceives grammar as a unified literary and linguistic study (p. 25) and Diomedes wishes to keep it closely related to language in use (p. 26). Dionysius is already using syntactic criteria in the definition of, at least, the preposition and the article. Apollonius wants a name for the pronoun which will show that its functions are more complex than merely 'standing instead of a noun' (p. 69). Varro proposes an entirely new classification of words, based on their formal differences (p. 48). That grammatical analysis involves a consideration of the act of communication which embodies the expression to be analysed is recognised by a commentator on Dionysius (p. 25), by Peter Helias (p. 58), by Martin of Dacia (p. 32) and by Thomas of Erfurt (pp. 125, 128). The speculative grammarians see that the idea of relation is fundamental to all linguistic analysis; they describe in a new way the structure not only of substantival phrases but of the sentence itself, and by the application of logic to language open up a fresh approach to syntax (pp. 33, 95, 124 f.). Linacre distinguishes, with unique but uncertain emphasis, formal criteria from those of meaning (pp. 55–6), a distinction as much needed as it was rare. Perottus and later renaissance grammarians, including Lily, use syntactic criteria for defining even declinable parts of speech, the significance of which does not seem to have been recognised in modern times, even though the criteria were taken over and extended in the English grammars (p. 89). These moments of insight and unrest are as truly part of the tradition as are the six Latin cases. And there are even some who thought the six cases should be eight (p. 113).

PART TWO

THE ENGLISH CATEGORIES

7. THE TERM 'GRAMMAR'

There are many Persons that have had seven or eight Years'
Education in our common Schools, that are not able to write
twenty lines together with any tolerable Proprety.

DANIEL TURNER, 1739

PRESENT UNCERTAINTIES

The varying uses of the term *grammar* within the tradition were
discussed in chapter 2. Even at the present day the term has no
generally agreed reference. Its use tends in some circumstances to
obscure important differences, in others to separate aspects of linguistic study which should be closely related. This is especially true
in school, where the teaching of French grammar and the teaching
of English grammar, for example, are normally regarded as parallel,
if not identical, processes. But the common term *grammar* is concealing the fundamental difference between studying the structure of a
language which the student has used from infancy, and studying the
forms and structure of an unknown language as part of the process of
learning to use it. In using our own language we need to give conscious attention to its structure only when the smooth and uncon-
sidered processes of expression and interpretation falter; when we are
pulled up for a moment, uncertain about the meaning of a word we
read; when we cast about for the right expression; when we halt in
order to work out how one part of a sentence is related to another.
The schoolboy, however, starting a foreign language, has to learn
the actual words; he has to learn how to express plurality; he has to
learn rules of word order. His situation is very different from that in
which he is using his own language. Yet in school grammar is so
strongly felt to be one undifferentiated study that grammars for
English-speaking children of eleven or twelve sometimes include
rules for the formation of a normal plural,[1] as if an English child who

---

[1] For example: *Nelson's English Grammar Practice*, n.d., p. 134; D. B. Lickes, *The English
Language*, Bk 1. 1950. 27; A. E. Darbyshire, *Time for English*, London 1956, Bk 1. 127;
J. H. Jagger, *A Handbook of English Grammar*, London 1960, p. 149.

could call out, 'There's a squirrel!' might perhaps not know how to express himself if there were two squirrels.

The difference between grammar for a vernacular and grammar for a foreign language is, however indirectly, recognised by the variety of studies included in many contemporary school grammars or in the grammatical parts of general English textbooks. There may be sections on the use of synonyms, on word-history and derivation, on punctuation, on spelling, on figures of speech (foreign, frigid and awkward), on the conventions of letter-writing, on common fallacies. These appear as part of English, but not of foreign, grammars. But they appear in the English textbooks not because any close consideration has been given to what is meant by the term *grammar*, but as a result of the piecemeal and tentative way in which, during the last three centuries, English studies have adopted some of the orderly procedures of rhetoric. There is no agreement nowadays on how far such studies belong to grammar. Some teachers would consider that the order, in which they are listed above corresponds with an inverse order of relevance; but different teachers would draw the line at different points.

This variety of subject matter points to a sense of the term *grammar* which is equivalent to 'the study of language in use'. Yet it is just here that this traditionally broad conception of grammar proves inadequate for contemporary teaching. During the last sixty years linguistic ideas have been introduced which are essential for any discussion of 'language in use' but are not part of the traditional content of grammar, even at its widest. Any sense of *grammar* which ignores, for example, the function of intonation and pitch in indicating meaning, the importance of context and situation in analysing the structure of an utterance, the use of 'formulae', empty words and other unanalysable units, is failing to add new knowledge to old, and thereby separating aspects of language which should be studied together.

The laboured development of English studies has resulted in two contrasting views of English grammar, each of which is inadequate. The narrow view, which restricts the application of the term to morphology and syntax, is inadequate because it ignores the conditions and opportunities which are peculiar to the 'teaching' of a vernacular. The wider view, in which grammar is equated with the study of language in use, continues the work of the most perceptive grammarians of the tradition, but is inadequate today because it is restricted to the traditional subject matter shared by grammar and rhetoric and ignores many of the simplest and most accepted ideas of modern linguistics.

What is needed is a fresh synthesis of linguistic, rhetorical and logical categories, designed for the sole purpose of helping English-speaking students of English to achieve the most delicate control they can over the processes both of expression and of interpretation. Such a synthesis would be in some ways a return to one of the earliest conceptions of grammar: the study of letters, the unified study of language and literature.

SENSES OF 'GRAMMAR' WITHIN THE ENGLISH TRADITION

The term *grammar*, even within the English tradition alone, has so many shades of meaning that it must be clarified first. This clarification can come from four main sources:

   (i)   the varying types of book called 'grammar'
   (ii) the divisions of grammar, either enumerated, or implied by the principal contents of the books
   (iii) formal definitions of grammar
   (iv) the subsidiary contents of the books.

Four types of grammar-book have to be distinguished before it is possible to say even what English grammars are known to have been in existence at a given time. This is still true when the preliminary decision has been taken as to what constitutes a grammar. In the present context a grammar is considered to be any book which contains at least an enumeration, and some description, of the parts of speech. This minimum definition may seem too obvious to be worth making, but there are some works calling themselves grammars which do not comply with it. The first is '*A New Spelling Dictionary of the English Language. . . to which is prefixed, a short English Grammar, which must prove extremely useful to foreigners as well as to natives, who have not received the advantage of a school-education. . .*' For Francis Newbery (n.d.).[1] The second is a similar work, *The Royal Spelling Dictionary of*

---

[1] The complexity of Newbery's publications is formidable. A copy of this edition is in the British Museum (cat. no. 12981.de.10) where its date is estimated as 1780. Welsh, p. 200, says it is 'an entirely different work from *Newbery's New Spelling Dictionary*', but suggests no date.

the English Language, 1765, by the Rev. Thomas Green. The title-page of the first edition does not mention it, but an 'English Grammar', comprising similar material to that in Newbery's dictionary, occupies the first thirty pages. In the second edition, 1775, the grammar is largely unchanged and is referred to on the title-page as 'a short English Grammar'. A third work is George Fisher's *The Instructor, or Young Man's Best Companion*, c. 1740, to which was added, after 1755 and certainly by the 29th edition, 1805, an 'English Grammar' of about forty pages.[1] The 'grammars' in these works comprise merely the alphabet, sounds of individual letters, diphthongs, stops, the division of syllables, quantity and accent, notes of reference (e.g. the asterisk) and other marks. There is no mention of the parts of speech or of syntax.

In addition to grammars directed solely towards English three types of grammar-book need to be distinguished:

(*a*) those directed solely to Latin

(*b*) those directed to a basic grammar, viable in both Latin and English

(*c*) those which, in varying degrees, are directed towards universal grammar.

Evidence from Latin grammars. These would not need to be mentioned if it were not that it can be difficult to identify, and hence to exclude, them. The difficulty is sometimes caused by ambiguity in the term *English*, more often by ambiguity in the term *grammar*.

The ambiguity of *English* can be illustrated from several works. *An English Grammar...* by R.R., 1641, is in fact a Latin grammar. As the sub-title says, it is 'A plain exposition of Lilie's Grammar in English'. The word *English* is used in the main title to mean not 'of English' but 'in English'. It is so used also in Joshua Poole's *The English Accidence*, 1646,[2] in Edward Burles' *Grammatica Burlesa, or a new English Grammar*, 1652, and in earlier works such as the *Longe Parvula, or Englishe Rules*, 1509, and John Stockwood's *Plaine and Easie laying open of the meaning and understanding of the rules of construction in the English Accidence*, 1590. This work of Stockwood's is listed by Wells[3] among his English grammars and, more surprisingly, by Foster Watson,[4] but it is nevertheless, like the others mentioned here,

---

[1] Information privately from Professor Arvid Gabrielson.
[2] But *The English Accidence*, 1733, is an English grammar.
[3] Wells, 1878.   [4] Foster Watson, 1903, p. 181.

entirely concerned with Latin. This natural use of the term *English* is, even in theory, ambiguous only after the time when grammars of English had begun to appear, as it is in the sub-title to Entick's *Speculum Latinum,* 1728, which runs: *Latin made easy to Scholars by an English Grammar only.* Normally the ambiguity is resolved, as here, by the context.[1]

The ambiguity of the term *grammar* is equally natural, but longer lasting. *Grammar* had meant Latin grammar for so long that well after the time when in general discussion it might have been understood as basic or universal grammar it continued, in the titles of Latin textbooks, to be used without qualification to mean Latin grammar. It had been quite natural for the English form of Lily's grammar, in the middle stage of its development, to acquire, at least as early as 1549, the title *A Short Introduction to Grammar.* A century later, when five grammars of English had appeared and at least eight had been written, it was natural that Charles Hoole in 1651, and Richard Lloyd in 1653, should both call their textbooks *The Latin Grammar.* Nevertheless, quite apart from the countless editions of Lily (with titles such as *The Royal Grammar,* or *The Royal Grammar Reformed*) at least ten other purely Latin grammars appeared between 1655 and 1700 continuing in their titles the unqualified use of the term *grammar.*[2] But by 1700 a grammar need not be a Latin grammar; twenty-one explicitly English grammars had been published by then. During the eighteen century Latin grammars using the unqualified term in their titles are less common. Examples are:

R. Sabourn, *An Epitome of Grammar,* 1733

Thomas Martin, *An Explanation of Accidence and Grammar,* 1754

A Short Grammar, or Rudiments of the Latin Tongue. By a Clergyman who hath taught Grammar for twenty years past, 1759.

It is not possible to show with any precision the period during which

[1] It was only towards the end of the seventeenth century that it became generally acceptable to teach elementary Latin from a grammar written in English, not in Latin. Accordingly this sense of *English* is frequent in the titles of Latin textbooks, over a long period. Among eighteenth-century examples are: *A New English Introduction to the Latin Tongue,* 1735; *An English Essay on the Syntax of the Latin Tongue,* 1772; T. Richard, *An English Introduction to the Latin Tongue,* 4th edn 1805. In 1714 Thomas Sheridan can still say of his *Easy Introduction of Grammar in English:* 'I have compil'd the following English Grammar for the attainment of the Latin Tongue' (p. iii).

[2] e.g. A. B., *The Rudiments of Grammar,* 1678; John Twells, *Grammatica Reformata: or a general examination of the Art of Grammar,* 1683; Obadiah Walker, *Some Instruction in the Art of Grammar,* 1691; *A Complete System of Grammar* (T.C. III. 97, Nov. 1698).

it became actually misleading to use *grammar* to mean only Latin grammar. That there was a change our own use of the term makes clear; that the change could operate gradually and at different levels is shown by our expression *grammar school*, which continues an even earlier use of the term. A late limit to the period may be suggested by the fact that in 1758 Lily's grammar was adopted by Eton not as *The Eton Grammar* (which would have been possible in 1700, probable in 1658 and natural in 1600) but as *The Eton Latin Grammar*. The beginning of the period should be sought during the last quarter of the seventeenth century, but the overlapping senses of the term *grammar* make the interpretation of evidence very difficult.

If by 1700 *grammar* no longer suggested primarily Latin, but also general or universal, grammar, and if by the middle of the eighteenth century the term was, so to speak, in equipoise, it seems that by the end of the eighteenth century even the title of a book (in which there is little or no context to determine the application of a term) could use *grammar*, unqualified, to mean English grammar. Lindley Murray's *Introduction to Grammar*, prefixed to his *English Grammar* of 1795, though in the spirit of earlier discussions of universal grammar, refers almost entirely to the vernacular, and about the same time appeared Lady Fenn's *The Mother's Grammar* and *The Child's Grammar*. In 1818 James Wilkins' *Grammatical Questions*, a purely English grammar, rounds off the development of this use of the unqualified term *grammar* by echoing the anonymous *Certaine Grammar Questions*, a purely Latin grammar published about 1602.

Evidence from basic grammars. What is here called a basic grammar was not particularised or named at the time. It represents a brief and partial merging of English and Latin grammars under several influences:

(i) the purely practical desire of schoolmasters to teach Latin *in* English;

(ii) growing interest in the concept of universal grammar, which looked first for similarities between English and the classical languages. This prompted:

(iii) the purely practical desire of schoolmasters to teach Latin grammar *through* English, so that they could use the similarities to simplify explanation and to save time in teaching both Latin and other foreign languages;

(iv) a growing realisation that by adopting certain methods of teaching Latin the schoolmaster could increase his pupils' control over English itself.

Textbooks implying a grammar basic to English and Latin must be distinguished both from Latin grammars written in English and from bilingual grammars. Many seventeenth-century Latin grammars, especially in their early sections, seem at times to be treating the two languages in close combination: ' *To* or *To be*, is a sign of a Verb, if the word be not the Name of a thing, as *amare*, to love.'[1] But these are only incidental aids in the opening pages, and the grammars soon move over into Latin entirely. The bilingual grammars also[2] were intended to teach Latin in English; the basic grammar aimed at teaching Latin not only in English, but through and with English.

Ælfric's grammar, *c.* AD 1000, is a forerunner of both types of book in so far as it is a Latin grammar written in English and expressing some concern for English. The book is a selection from Priscian, translated into English, but Ælfric explicitly says that it should be a help to his young pupils in their study of both Latin and English:

Ego Aelfricus, ut minus sapiens, has excerptiones de Prisciano minore vel maiore vobis puerulis tenellis ad vestram linguam transferre studui, quatinus perlectis octo partibus Donati in isto libello potestis utramque linguam, videlicet latinam et anglicam, vestrae teneritudini inserere interim, usque quo ad perfectiora perveniatis studia... (ed. Zupitza, p. 1).

The categories in Ælfric's grammar are those of the Latin grammar, illustrated by Latin examples. But he gives an English translation of all the examples and occasionally mentions their relevance to English, as in his concluding paragraph about the parts of speech: 'There is no doubt that the whole Latin language is covered by these eight parts, and English agrees with all the parts, as we have briefly explained.'[3] Ælfric was providing a Latin grammar in English, but he did not look on the study of English as an aid towards learning Latin. He points out some differences between the two languages, but his treatment of English is at most parallel with, and usually subordinate to, his treatment of Latin. If he suggests any relationship

---

[1] I.B., *An Epitome of Grammar Principles*, 1668, p. 1.

[2] e.g. Charles Hoole, *The Latin Grammar*, 1651; James Shirley, *Grammatica Anglo-Latina*, 1651; Richard Hogarth, *Grammar Disputations/Disputationes Grammaticales*, 1712.

[3] Ælfric, p. 11: 'Witodlice on ðisum eahta daelum is eal ledenspraec belocen, and ðaet englisc geðwaerlaecð to eallum ðaem daelum, swaswa we nu sceortlice trahtnodon.'

between the two languages it is that learning Latin will be helpful for the use of English.

A broader form of the same point of view is expressed early in the seventeenth century by John Brinsley, whose *Ludus Literarius*, 1612, is a discussion between two schoolmasters about (amongst many topics) the relation between Latin and English. Spoudeus, the despondent master, complains that his young pupils cannot learn to read English before they start Latin, and that later he cannot spare time from their Latin in order to give them more practice with their English: 'I have sometimes beene so abashed and ashamed, that I have not knowne what to say, when some being a little discontented, or taking occasion to quarrell about paying my stipend, have cast this in my teeth, that their children have been under me sixe or seven yeeres, and yet have not learned to reade English well.'[1] Philoponus, who is cheerful because he has been successful, reassures Spoudeus that English is important, but can be practised simultaneously with the Latin: 'There is no care had in respect, to traine up schollers so, as they may be able to expresse their minds purely and readily in our owne tongue, and to increase in the practice of it, as well as in the Latine or Greeke; whereas our chiefe indevour should be for it, and that for these reasons.'[2] Philoponus' main reason is commonplace enough now, but it has a forthright ring, worthy of the first explicit statement of the case for English teaching: 'Because that language which all sorts and conditions of men amongst us are to have most use of, both in speech and writing, is our owne native tongue.'[3] Brinsley, through Philoponus, recommends for the teaching of English several practices which are independent of Latin: daily 'writing English heedily';[4] writing letters in English; summarising sermons. But what is relevant here is the importance he attaches to the combination of Latin with English, especially through reading the English form of Lily's grammar, and through Ascham's system of grammatical translation, whereby the Latin is put into English and that English later translated, unseen, back into Latin and compared with the original. This, says Philoponus, putting forward the thirteenth of his twenty-one advantages of the method, will

helpe to proceed as well in our English tongue as in the Latine, for reading, and writing true orthography; to attaine variety and copy of English

---

[1] Brinsley, *Ludus Literarius*, 2nd edn. 1627, ed. Campagnac, p. 14.
[2] op. cit. p. 22.   [3] ibid.   [4] op. cit. p. 23.

words, to expresse their mindes easily, and utter any matter belonging to their Authors. And so in time, to come to propriety, choise, and purity, a swell in our English as in the Latine. (Brinsley, *Ludus Literarius*, p. 107.)

Something of the spirit in which Brinsley was writing is found in the first textbook to attempt a basic grammar: John Hewes' *A Perfect Survey of the English Tongue, taken according to the use and analogie of the Latine. And serveth for the more plaine exposition of the Grammaticall Rules and Precepts, collected by Lillie, and for the more certaine Translation of the English tongue into Latine...* 1624. As this title makes clear, the work is primarily a Latin textbook. It is addressed 'To all Teachers of the Art of Grammar in the Latine tongue.' But one cause of difficulty in learning Latin—among 'the younger sort'—is a lack of 'right knowledge or censure of their owne Mother tongue, in regard it holdeth a great difference in it selfe from the dialect of the Latines'.[1] Hewes has therefore made, he says,

an exact Survey (as the time hath yeelded me) of the *English* Tongue, as the same may for the use of all the parts of Speech in Composition best conduce or accord with the *Latines*; and so have I made as *a posteriori* the English tongue for those that are English, the first groundworke to the Latine. (1624, sig. B 2.)

In the first sections of the book, accordingly, Hewes considers the parts of speech and some rules of syntax in English and with English examples. This is only a slight extension of the practice in Lily's English accidence, but the difference is significant. Lily, for example, says of the adjective: 'A Noune Adjective is that can not stand by himselfe, but requireth to be joyned with an other word: as Bonus, *Good*.'[2] Hewes makes no reference, at this stage, to the Latin: 'All wordes joyned or which may joyne with *man* or *thing*, are Adjectives.'[3] Hewes is deliberately focusing attention on the English usage, fixing that before going on to the Latin. Lily is just translating his Latin examples. It is this difference in approach which is characteristic of the basic grammars. They are, even if only in part and indirectly, grammars of English. There is, however, no evidence that Hewes thought of himself as promoting the study of English for its own sake. He is aware that it is a different kind of study from that of Latin, and he has 'enjoyned' his pupils 'to looke into it'.[4] But all is for the Latin.

[1] Hewes, 1624, sig. A 4 verso.
[2] *Shorte Intro.* 1567, sig. A v.
[3] Hewes, 1624, sig. B 3 verso.
[4] Hewes, 1624, sig. Q 4 verso.

The English Categories

The humble status of English in Hewes' book can be seen in his examples of enallage, that is, the use of one grammatical form where another would, more strictly, be expected. Hewes gives first the English expressions:

> Christ *is come* into the world to dye for sinners
> Christ *is risen* againe from Death
> Christ *is not* yet *returned* to judge the world

The 'proper' form of these expressions, namely 'Christ *hath* come... *hath* risen... *hath* not returned' he lists under the heading, 'Words changed by the English, but heere bettered to the manner of the Latines.'[1] In the second edition, 1632, however, this judgment is omitted and the heading reduced merely to, 'The Lat. say.' The implied argument is: *Christ is come* would be translated by a Latin perfect; the 'proper' English perfect is expressed by *have*; therefore *Christ hath come* is better than *Christ is come*. Hewes' second example, *Christ is risen*, which permits a deponent verb, destroys the argument. *Ortus est* exactly corresponds to *is risen*, and in one later English grammar forms such as *is risen* and *am come* are in fact called deponent verbs.[2]

Joshua Poole's *The English Accidence*, 1646, has a similar intention: it is 'a short, plaine, and easie way, for the more speedy attaining to the Latine tongue, by the help of the English'. Its grammatical categories are more firmly and consistently applied to English than are those in *A Perfect Survey*, though this consistency is often possible only because so many of the traditional definitions are expressed in terms of meaning, which could apply to either language. If a verb is a word 'signifying *to doe, to be done*, or *to be*' this is as true for English as it is for Latin (and as inadequate). Where formal criteria cannot be ignored, as with case and gender, Poole makes English follow Latin in having six cases, seven genders, and verbs of promising which govern the dative. He is quite explicit about his attitude to English:

> The reason inducing me to this little worke, was, that I have often observed how Children have been puzled and confounded, by being set to the construing, parsing, and making of Latine, before they had the least knowledge of their Mother Tongue, or were able at all therein to distinguish the parts of Speech... My drift and scope therefore, is, to have a childe so well verst in his Mothers tongue, before he meddle with Latine,

---

[1] ibid. sig. R 3.   [2] Fogg, 1792; see below, p. 384.

156

that when he comes to the construing of a Latine Authour, he shall from the signification of his words in construing, be in some good measure able to tell distinctly what part of Speech every word is, though he be not able to parse, varie, or give any other account of one word in his lesson; and when he is put to translation, or making of Latine, he shall know from his English, both what part of Speech every word is, and what Syntaxis, or ordering it should have in Latine, though in the meane time hee never heard of one Latine word. (1646, sig. A 2 verso.)

This is teaching Latin not only in, but through, English.

The close connection between the two languages, in Poole's system, can be seen also in a rule which he added to the second edition, 1655. If his pupils have difficulty in translating an English phrase into Latin they are to 'turn it into some other English of the like sense', so that 'I should be loath to do so to you' becomes easier to translate when it is expressed as 'I would not willingly do so to you'. Having explained this rule Poole takes it still further, in a postscript: 'For the better making use of this last Rule...it were not amisse, as soon as a child is capable, to exercise him in turning an English argument into another English of the same sense, by varying the phrase.'[1] One can see here English teaching in the very process of evolving out of the teaching of Latin.

The attention given to English in its own right, which is characteristic of these basic grammars and justifies their inclusion in this study, marks also an important work which is not here regarded as a grammar, William Walker's *A Treatise of English Particles*, 1655. In this work an analysis is given of the different uses of English words such as *like, let, long, be, become,* together with the articles and the most common adverbs, prepositions and conjunctions. The following senses of *like,* for example, are distinguished:

1. Like, importing resemblance...in one thing to another, is made by *par, similis,* or *aequus.*
2. Like, denoting to approve...is made by a Verb...*probo, gaudeo*...&c.
3. Like, importing likelihood, or probability of some success...is made by *verisimile, probabile,* or *credibile est.*
4. ...to signifie after the guise, garb, manner, fashion...He was brought up like a Gentleman: *Libere eductus, liberaliter eductus est.*
5. Like, coming together with any of these Particles, *as, such, manner, sort,* &c. is made by *Quemadmodum, sicut*...&c. (1673, chap. 46.)

[1] Poole (1646), 1655, p. 61.

The analysis is made as an aid to translating English into Latin and therefore takes into account only those uses of the English word which have varying equivalents in Latin. Distinctions which are made in English but not in Latin are thus irrelevant, and to that extent Latin controls (legitimately for Walker's purpose) the kind of analysis to which the English word is subjected. The Treatise was both imitated and reprinted many times: an eleventh edition was issued in 1695, and there were at least three editions during the eighteenth century, the latest in 1720. It was probably the most influential of all those works which by an imaginative approach to Latin teaching focused attention on the study of English and on the comparison of its structure with that of Latin.

The works of Mark Lewis are a good illustration not only of basic grammar itself but of its natural tendency to develop into universal grammar. Unfortunately, not only was Lewis unsystematic in his writing, but his grammars have survived in an incomplete form which makes it difficult to trace the development of his thought. In the *Institutio*, about 1670, he describes the book (apparently first published about twenty years earlier) as 'this middle way of an Introductory Grammar to the English, Latin and Greek'.[1] In the preface, though he is thinking primarily of the classical languages, he puts his argument in general terms:

The most facil way of introducing any in a *Tongue unknown*, is to shew what Grammar it hath beyond, or short of his *Mother tongue*; following that Maxime, to proceed *a noto ad ignotum*...A demonstration of this you have in the following Scheme; supposing an English Man be to learn Latin. (sig. A 1 verso.)

and later:

The Regularitie of the *English-tongue* appears from this assertion almost Universally true: Whatever Tongue hath less Grammar than the English, is not intelligible; whatever hath more, is superfluous...Thus we may compute what Grammar any language hath for *necessity* (as in the *English*:) what for ornament (as in the *Latin* and *Greek*). (ibid.)[2]

After a general description of the Parts of Speech the grammar is not consistently based on English. The section on pronouns begins, 'There be fifteen Pronouns' and enumerates fifteen Latin ones,

---

[1] Lewis, *Institutio*, 1670, p. 35.

[2] This much-quoted opinion is repeated by Lewis in his *Essay*, 1674. p. 3 (of the fresh pagination after p. (22)) and in his *Vestibulum Technicum*, 1675, sig. A 3 verso.

including *meus* and *tuus*. Then follows a list of twenty-two English words, not entirely corresponding with the Latin. Later, the section on Adjectives gives Latin examples classified as having one, two or three terminations, and does not mention the English. The verbs, however, are introduced in English paradigms, to which the Latin is afterwards added. By the time he reaches rules for gender, the principal parts and the syntax Lewis, as his plan requires, drops the English framework altogether.

In what may be the earlier form of the *Essay*, Lewis sometimes widens, without clarifying, his use of the term *grammar* so that it no longer applies primarily to English and the classical languages but suggests universal grammar:

Grammar in the Notion and Theorie of it, is one of the most difficult of the Liberal Sciences: Though it be natural to Speak, yet it is accidental to use this or that Tongue; Languages were made, and daily suffer Alterations, rather by chance, than any Art or Contrivance...Doubtless the Doctrine of Grammar is too subtile for Children; because it is communicated by Logical Definitions in the Etymologie, and by the signification of words in the Syntax, neither of which Children can reach, who cannot use Abstraction. (1670?, p. 1.)

In the 1674 version of the *Essay* Lewis talks at one time purely of Latin, at another of language in general. '...the question, I offer to be examined, is the *Hypothesis*, Whether the Grammar of the Latin ought not to be accommodated to the English?'[1]

Accordingly he prefixes to the purely Latin grammars outlined in the *Essay* an English grammar, of which he says, 'The end of this discourse is, to make the English Tongue a foundation to the Latin, or any other Language we are to learn; From this we must raise ourselves to them; and into this, when they are analysed, we must resolve them. The universal neglect of this one little thing is the great *remora* to Children.'[2] 'This one little thing' is in effect universal grammar, though Lewis never seems to have expressed the idea by which its advocates defined it: that there was a structure which all languages had in common. Lewis is almost solely concerned with English and Latin.

An intention similar to Lewis's seems to be implied by the title-page of William Clare's *A Compleat System of Grammar English and Latin*, 1690, which continues: 'Wherein that most excellent art is

---

[1] Lewis, *Essay*, 1674, p. (21).   [2] op. cit. p. 5.

plainly, fully and distinctly taught, and practically manag'd thro' every part thereof. In a method...by the use whereof the learner may attain to the perfect knowledge of the Latin tongue in less than one quarter of the time usually spent therein...' The book takes the form of question and answer between Martin and John; the English text is in the left-hand column, the Latin in the right. The definitions of the parts of speech, and many of the examples, suggest that Clare was considering their application to English, but he makes no mention of this among the nineteen features of the book which he lists in his preface, and the first feature shows that his extension of the term *grammar* to include English and Latin simultaneously was not thought out enough to affect the design of the book. He writes:

It will be sufficient for the Youth to learn *memoriter* the Latine only, the chiefest Design of the Version [i.e. the English in the opposite column] is to illustrate them thro' the dark and as yet unknown paths of a strange Language, and therefore the Examples to each Rule are to be considered in the Latin Collum, the two Languages not alway runing parallel. (Clare, 1690, sig. A 3.)

Frequently, one would think, the English must have obscured rather than illuminated the relation between the two languages. Clare's warning to his pupils to concentrate on the Latin is very necessary: they would find the following exchange distinctly puzzling:

M. Doth ti sound every where like si when a vowel follows?
J. No, for it keeps its own proper sound in Greek words made Latine, as, *Government* (op. cit., p. 6.)

It is only from the Latin that they would see that the word serving as an example of this rule is in fact *politia*.

Clare's work is not so much a basic grammar as a bilingual Latin grammar superficially influenced by basic grammars such as Lewis's.

A work published in 1696, six years after Clare's, is explicitly attempting what Clare intended, if at all, only indirectly: 'The True Method of Learning the Latin Tongue by the English, and of obtaining the more perfect knowledge of the English by the Latin; containing a grammar for both the languages in a short, sure, and easie way.' This grammar keeps the two languages in orderly relation to each other. They are treated as having the same parts of speech and are taken together, in general terms, as far as they can travel without friction. Then come 'Remarks concerning the English

Parts of Speech, shewing in what Particulars they differ from the Latin; whereby it may also be discovered, that the English Tongue is much more easie to learn than the Latin.'[1] But the author believes the difference between the languages to be one of form only. Like all his contemporaries he cannot see how important, for English alone, is, for example, word order. After saying that the English adverb and conjunction 'are of the same Nature with those of the Latin', he continues: 'Likewise the English Syntaxis is sufficiently denoted, and made easie in that of the Latin.'[2]

In the partnership between Latin and English represented by these basic grammars one is often reminded how very junior was the status of the junior partner.

By the end of the seventeenth century their limited and transitional approach had served its purpose; the idea of universal grammar had become familiar and was soon to be popular. Nevertheless the basic approach is still found in one or two works.

It is difficult to know what were the intentions of Thomas Sheridan in his *An Easy Introduction of Grammar in English*, 1714. His chief concern is with Latin, but he is aware that it is not learnt in the same way as English is learnt. He is wanting to help the introduction to a foreign language of 'these Boys, who without any Pains, become insensibly perfect in their Mother-Tongue',[3] and he has therefore 'Compil'd the following English Grammar for the attainment of the Latin Tongue'.[4] In so far as he is hoping to teach Latin *through* English he is continuing the practice of the basic grammars, but the grammar itself keeps closely to the form and language of Lily; it is only the frequency of his illustrations in English, and a kind of studied generality in his definitions, which might justify one in regarding it as more than a purely Latin grammar written in English.

The transition from basic to universal grammar can be seen in Daniel Duncan's preface to *A New English Grammar*, 1731. He describes his original plan for the book, in which '...whatever should be common to both Languages, English and Latin, should be in the English Grammar...Which Method...would make to Boys the rational Part of Grammar (thus abstracted from the Notion of any dead or foreign Language) much easier to learn.'[5] John

---

[1] *True Method*, 1696, p. 80. [2] op. cit. p. 84. [3] Sheridan, 1714, p. i.
[4] op. cit. p. iii. [5] Duncan, 1731, p. vii.

The English Categories

Entick's *Speculum Latinum*, or *Latin made easy to Scholars by an English Grammar only*, 1728, is designed to teach Latin, but carries the principle of learning Latin grammar through English so far that it becomes in effect a grammar of English distorted towards Latin. The difficulties into which the author's method leads him can be illustrated from his chapter on the Genitive:

> *Master*: Don't Verbals of rejoycing, grieving, forgiving, remembring, &c. govern a Genitive Case after them?
> *Scholar*: Yes, most commonly, if the Noun following, hath the Sign, of, before it, and the Verbs be not Actives.
> *M.* Don't some Adverbs govern a Genitive Case?
> *S.* Yes; Adverbs of Time, Place, and Quantity.
> *M.* Give an Example.
> *S. The Day before Wednesday*; here, *the day before*, is an Adverb of Time, and *Wednesday* is the Genitive Case following it. (Entick, 1728, p. 33.)

Speculum Latinum is, in effect, a basic grammar. The title-page speaks of the book being 'composed on Natural Principles', and in his preface Entick tells how it was his lot 'to be perplexed with a very *dull boy*, whose understanding I endeavoured to enable by Means of the...[traditional]...*Grammars*, but *in vain*...which caused the compiling of this *natural Order of Grammar*, and it had its desired Effect, instructing the Youth *in three Months space*'.[1]

A late example of what is in effect a basic grammar is seen in Alexander Adam's *The Principles of Latin and English Grammar*, 1772. Adam acknowledges the idea of universal grammar—'the Principles of Grammar in all languages are much the same'[2]—but restricts his treatment to English and Latin on the grounds that 'in order...to teach Latin Grammar with success, we should always join with it a particular attention to the rudiments of English. This is the design of the following attempt.'[3] He discusses the two languages together, temporarily dropping one or the other when he meets categories which do not appear in both, but he has no more success than his predecessors in making one language illuminate the other.

Evidence from universal grammars. The view that certain grammatical categories were common to all the languages of the world was given authoritative and influential support by the Port Royal grammar of 1660, and it is convenient to treat that date as the starting-point for

---

[1] Entick, 1728, title page, verso. [2] Adam, 1772, p. i.
[3] op. cit. p. v.

what became, during the first half of the eighteenth century, a commonplace opinion even in the ordinary school grammars of English. But it was not a new idea. It had been an important part of the speculative grammarians' treatment of language,[1] and was a natural extension for anyone to make who was familiar with the broad categories common to Latin, Greek and Hebrew.

Three seventeenth-century writers who supported or propounded the idea of universal grammar were considered to be, in this respect, continuing the medieval tradition, especially of Duns Scotus,[2] with whom Bishop Wilkins links them. They are Francis Bacon, Campanella[3] and Caramuel.[4] Bacon had made a distinction between literary grammar and philosophical grammar.[5] The former was the ordinary study of a language, which aimed at accuracy, speed and elegance. The latter 'aliquatenus Philosophiae ministrat'; it was concerned not with the relations which words bore to each other, but the relation they bore to reality and to reason, without, however, going so far as to trespass in the province of logic. The most noble kind of grammar 'would deal with the different characteristics of languages, showing in respect of each characteristic which language was best equipped and which was deficient'.[6] Campanella and Caramuel were both referred to by Wilkins, and later by Horne Tooke, as having written speculative grammars. Campanella's formed part of his *Philosophiae Rationalis*, 1638.[7] He makes the same distinction as Bacon, but calls the two kinds of grammar *civilis* and *philosophica*. Philosophical grammar, he says, 'non agnoscit aetatem linguae, sed rationalitatem; amplectiturque vocabula bona omnium temporum'.[8] Caramuel's *Grammatica Audax* was published in his *Precursor Logicus* (2 parts, 1654 and 1655). He refers disparagingly to Campanella but approvingly of Duns Scotus.[9]

---

[1] Above, p. 30.

[2] Whose grammar is now attributed to Thomas of Erfurt. See above, p. 15.

[3] Tommaso Campanella, 1568–1639.

[4] Juan Caramuel Lobkowitz, 1606–82.

[5] Francis Bacon, *De Augmentis Scientiarum*, 1623, Bk. VI, chap. I.

[6] op. cit. pp. 654–5: 'Illa demum, ut arbitramur, foret nobilissima Grammaticae species, si quis in linguis plurimis tam eruditis quam vulgaribus eximie doctus, de variis linguarum proprietatibus tractaret; in quibus quaeque excellat, in quibus deficiat, ostendens...Non abs re igitur fuerit Grammaticam Philosophantem a Simplici et Literaria distinguere, et Desideratam ponere.'

[7] *Philosophiae rationalis partes quinque, videlicet: grammatica, dialectica, rhetorica, poetica, historiographia*, Paris 1638.

[8] Quoted by Horne Tooke (1786), 1829, I. 6.   [9] ibid.

That the term *grammar* could be generalised, in an English context, before the end of the sixteenth century is clear from the distinction made by Mulcaster in *The First Part of the Elementarie*, 1582. In the Epistle Dedicatory he uses *grammar* to mean 'the study of Latin': 'I did promis an Elementarie, that is, the hole matter, which children are to learn...from their first beginning to go to anie school, untill theie passe to grammer'.[1] But in chapter 10 he is writing in general terms:

> By cours of natur and use of antiquitie, grammer travelleth first to have the naturall tung of ech cuntrie fined to that best, and most certain direction, which the ordinarie custom of that cuntrie which useth the tung, can lead hir unto...Secondlie grammer, as it hath bene used sence, seketh to help us to the knowledge of foren language, as the Latin, the Italian, and such other tungs, which at this daie is the principall use thereof.[2]

This passage from Mulcaster, written four years before the appearance of the first English grammar, is of great importance, both historically and absolutely. It is the explicit recognition of a truth which the early grammarians could not keep in their minds and our twentieth-century school grammarians might never have met: that the grammatical study of a vernacular is a different task from the grammatical study of a foreign language. How much more perceptive Mulcaster is than Bacon, who says of 'the art of grammar' that 'the use in a mother tongue is small, in a foreign tongue more'.[3] Although Mulcaster is using the term *grammar* (in a sense which could be applied to any individual language) to mean something between 'the study of structure' and 'the study of style' he does not speak in terms of universal grammar. This idea appears more clearly, but not yet explicitly, in Alexander Gill's *Logonomia Anglica*, 1619. *Logonomia*, of which *grammatica* is only that part dealing with the letters of the alphabet, is defined as: 'comprehensio regularum quibus sermo ignotus facilius addisci potest: ea ex Latini usu observata Latina est, ex Anglici Anglica est, &c.'.[4] Gill supposes a set of rules which govern the structure of any language. His own grammar discusses these rules only in their application to English, but his term *logonomia* directs attention to the idea of universal grammar.

---

[1] Mulcaster, *The First Part of the Elementarie*, 1582, sig. A 4 recto.
[2] op. cit. p. 55.
[3] Francis Bacon, *The Advancement of Learning*, 1605, Bk II. XVI. 4.
[4] Gill, 1619. p. 1.

John Wallis acknowledged an obligation to Gill's grammar, and claimed that the Port Royal grammar was in part an imitation of his own.'[1] Nevertheless there is in Wallis no reference to universal grammar. In one part of his preface one might suppose that he is referring to 'language in itself': he says that, as a remedy for the confused condition of English from the point of view of both teacher and taught, 'quicquid est operis ultro suscepi, ut linguam in se facillimam brevibus praeceptis tradam'.[2] But the context makes it certain that here also he is referring not to 'language in itself' but to 'the English language in itself'. Wallis has much to say about the formation of speech sounds which would apply to other languages, and there is a breadth in his discussion of English grammar which is entirely in the spirit of Gill, but Wallis has too sound an understanding of the particularity of English—which was, in fact, the point he was most concerned to establish—to have given much hospitality to the idea of universal grammar. It is the Latinists who most easily believe that there are grammatical categories common to all languages. In so far as Latin was an international language it already possessed an element of universality; the vernaculars resembled Latin, if they were not actually derived from it; only a slight adjustment was necessary in order to make Latin the type and model of all languages.

Jeremiah Wharton's *The English Grammar*, 1654, is primarily a grammar for English, though its title-page professes it to be 'more especially profitable for Scholars, immediately before their entrance into the Rudiments of the Latine-tongue'. In his preface Wharton makes the most explicit reference in any grammar before 1660 to the assumption governing the idea of universal grammar. He says that his book will prepare for learning 'any other grammatized Language; because the rules in *this*, for the most part may bee applied unto *that*'.[3] His book does not illustrate this theory, nor does he refer to it again, and there is no evidence that he attaches much importance to it. Although Wharton's grammar is not as purely derivative as Poldauf makes out[4] it is probable that in this reference to universal

---

[1] Wallis, *Opera Mathematica*, III, 1699. In the preface he refers to his own grammar 'quam post imitatus videtur Gallorum nescioquis, in sua (quam vocant) *Grammaire Universelle*'. And in the preface to the fifth edition of the grammar itself (included in the same volume) he refers to its new method 'quam, post haec primum edita, imitati videntur Gallorum aliqui in sua *Grammaire Universelle*: quae Latine post edita, *Grammatica Universalis* dicitur; methodo meae multum conformis'.
[2] Wallis, 1653, sig. A 7 verso.
[3] Wharton, 1654, preface.   [4] Poldauf, 1948, p. 75.

grammar he is only making explicit what is implied by Gill and Mulcaster, two of his acknowledged sources.

During the twenty years before the appearance of the Port Royal grammar some English writers had been led into a more specific consideration of universal grammar by their pursuit of an international, universal language. The attempt to frame such a language necessarily involved the choice of fundamental (universal) grammatical categories.

Francis Lodowyck, in *A Common Writing*, 1647, and more fully in *The Ground Work . . . for the framing of a new perfect Language and universal or common writing*, 1652,[1] classified all words under three very general headings, with numerous 'distinctions'.[2] Cave Beck, in *The Universal Character*, 1657, proposed a system of seven parts of speech[3] which was intended to be of universal application, but he takes its universality for granted and does not discuss universal grammar as such. George Dalgarno, in his *Ars Signorum*, 1661, written apparently without reference to the Port Royal grammar and on an even more severely logical basis, proposed another system[4] constructed (in words which he applied to the formation of names but aptly characterise his whole endeavour) '*per Regulas quasdam Generales et certas, secundum Analogiam Logico-Grammaticam*'.[5] The attempt to form a universal language reached its culmination and most influential expression in Bishop Wilkins' *An Essay towards a Real Character and a Philosophical Language*, 1668, in which the influence of Port Royal is clearly apparent.[6]

The Port Royal grammar is a systematic attempt to write a universal grammar. The title clearly sets out its authors' intentions:

Grammaire générale et raisonnée. Contenant les fondemens de l'art de parler; expliquez d'une manière claire & naturelle; les raisons de ce qui est commun à toutes les langues, & des principales différences qui s'y rencontrent; et plusieurs remarques nouvelles sur la Langue Françoise.

Its authors are returning to the central position from which the unity of the trivium and the best of the speculative grammars were conceived: a position in which the object of study is not so much grammar (though the study is always conducted in the name of grammar) as the way in which language is used. Such a central pursuit was a

---

[1] For the full titles of these works see Appendix VI.
[2] For Lodowyck's classification see below, p. 240.
[3] See below, p. 219. [4] See below, p. 241.
[5] Dalgarno, 1661, p. 11. [6] See below, p. 247.

study of the material of language, and therefore of grammar in the narrow sense; it was also a study of the purposes for which men use language, and therefore drew on rhetoric (that branch of learning in which the psychology of language was first developed); it was a study of the structure of certain forms of thought, and hence of the utterances in which that thought is shaped, and therefore drew on logic. The gentlemen of Port Royal produced a grammar and a logic[1] as separate works, but the two books are closely connected. The work which is sometimes referred to as the Port Royal rhetoric is not in fact a product of Port Royal. *De l'art de Parler* was published anonymously in Paris in 1675. An English translation appeared in 1676 as *The Art of Speaking: written in French by Messieurs du Port Royal...rendred into English*,[2] but it is not known whether the attribution to Port Royal was made in good faith or not. *De l'Art de Parler* was in fact written by Bernard Lamy, whose authorship was acknowledged in the third edition, 1688, in which the title was changed to *La Rhétorique, ou l'Art de Parler*.[3] Lamy's rhetoric contains much grammatical material, because 'to signifie the difference of our Thoughts, we have need of Words of different Orders'.[4] According to the Port Royal authors the art of logic 'consiste dans les réflexions que les hommes ont faites sur les quatres principales operations de leur esprit, *concevoir, juger, raisonner, & ordonner*'.[5] The grammar is based on an analysis of the first two of these operations: '*Concevoir*, n'est autre chose qu'un simple regard de nostre esprit sur les choses, soit d'une manière purement intellectuelle; comme quand je connois l'estre, la durée...soit, avec des images corporelles, comme quand je m'imagine un quarré, un rond...*Juger*, c'est affirmer qu'une chose que nous concevons, est telle, ou n'est pas telle.'[6] Judgment forms propositions, composed of subject, attribute and copula. Subject and attribute 'appartiennent proprement à la première opération de l'esprit, parce que c'est ce que nous concevons, & ce qui est l'objet de nostre pensée'.[7] The copula belongs to the second operation, judgment, 'qu'on peut dire estre proprement l'action de nostre esprit, & la manière dont nous pensons'. The primary analysis, of both thought and language, is therefore into two categories: what we

---

[1] *La Logique, ou l'art de penser*, 1662.   [2] 2nd edn 1696; 3rd edn 1708.
[3] W. S. Howell, *Logic and Rhetoric in England, 1500–1700*, pp. 378–9.
[4] *The Art of Speaking*, 1676. Pt I. chap. 3. 8.
[5] *La Logique*, 2nd edn 1664, p. 39.
[6] *Grammaire générale*, 1660, Pt 2. chap. 1. 27–8.   [7] op. cit. p. 29.

think about, and how we think about it. The authors' last step is to fit into this scheme the traditional parts of speech. To the objects of our thought and to the manner of our thinking we must add:

les conjonctions, disjonctions, & autres semblables opérations de nostre esprit; & tous les autres mouvemens de nostre âme; comme les désirs, le commandement, l'interrogation, &c...il faut aussi la plus générale distinction des mots, soit que les uns signifient les objets des pensées, & les autres la forme & la manière de nos pensées, quoy que souvent ils ne la signifient pas seule, mais avec l'objet...

Les mots de la première sorte sont ceux que l'on a appellez *noms*, *articles*, *pronoms*, *participes*, *prépositions*, & *adverbes*. Ceux de la seconde, sont les *verbes*, les *conjonctions*, & les *interjections*. Qui sont tous tirez par une suitte nécessaire de la manière naturelle en laquelle nous exprimons nos pensées.[1]

The Port Royal grammar as a whole is only the traditional grammar of Latin generalised enough to accommodate French, with some reference to other modern languages. Any universality it possesses is achieved not by a consideration of language alone but by the cautious reunion of language with logic. Logic, freed from the metaphysical superstructure which had often encumbered its application to language in the Middle Ages, now appears as a firm support. The idea of relation, for example, is again, in the Port Royal grammar, applied in analysing the functions of case, preposition, and verb; the function of the verb is again, and more fully, described as expressing affirmation.[2]

It is this return to logic which is the most important feature of the Port Royal grammar. Unfortunately it was just this feature which English grammarians largely ignored. The Port Royal grammar discusses 'les *raisons* de ce qui est commun à toutes les langues'; it is a 'grammaire générale et *raisonnée*'. The scholars of Port Royal were feeling their way towards the question which had exercised many medieval grammarians and logicians: How is the structure of language related to the structure of 'reality'? An attempt to formulate universal grammar was both a way of asking the question and a way of recording the answer, but universal grammar itself was important principally as a means towards shaping a philosophy of language. The Port Royal grammar was viewed rather differently by English grammarians. Whether because it appeared when interest

---

[1] ibid.
[2] *Grammaire générale*, 1660. Pt 2. chap. 12. 89–91. Cf. Hunt, I. 217 n.

in a universal language was strong, or because its ideas were perhaps more often received from Wilkins' *Essay* than from the grammar itself, it was influential in spreading not an interest in the working of language but a familiarity with the idea that there were some (usually unspecified) features which all languages had in common. The emphasis of Port Royal had been on *raisonnée*; in England it was on *générale*. What few of the English grammarians seemed to realise was that any principles which were in fact common to all languages must (within the modes of thought accessible at that time) be approached through logic, and unless universal grammar led towards a philosophy of language it was a dead end. It may nowadays be wise always to keep logic and language apart (the question is still active) but at the end of the seventeenth century, when the categories of rhetoric were stiff and stereotyped and the comparative study of languages was virtually untried, there was no alternative generalising system which could be applied to language. The English grammarians made little use of logic, and consequently, once enthusiasm for a universal language had waned, the idea of universal grammar was often left only as an interesting parenthesis in textbooks which it had influenced not at all. Bishop Lowth put into words what many seem to have felt (and subsequently expressed in the words he had chosen for them): 'Universal Grammar cannot be taught abstractedly: it must be done with reference to some language already known.'[1] Lowth was quite right, and references to universal grammar become fewer towards the end of the century. Nevertheless, an opportunity had been missed by all but a few: the opportunity to vitalise the study of grammar by considering, with its implications, the view: 'Que la connoissance de ce qui se passe dans nostre esprit, est necessaire pour comprendre les fondemens de la Grammaire; & que c'est de là que dépend la diversité des mots qui composent le discours.'[2] The opportunity could have been taken most ably by John Wilkins, but he was concerned with constructing a universal language. In Part Three of his *Essay*, 'Concerning Natural Grammar', he has finished 'the regular enumeration and description of such things and notions, as are to be known, and to which names are to be assigned, which may be stiled Universal Philosophy'.[3] He comes now to the 'Organical Part', the 'necessary helps' for forming these 'simple

---

[1] Lowth, 1762, p. xi.   [2] *Grammaire générale*, 1660, Pt 2. chap. 1. 26.
[3] Wilkins, 1668, p. 297.

notions into Complex Propositions and Discourses, which may be stiled Grammar, containing the Art of Words or Discourse'. He continues, echoing Port Royal:

Grammar may be distinguished into two kinds; 1. *Natural, and General*; 2. *Instituted* and *Particular*. *Natural* Grammar (which may likewise be stiled Philosophical, Rational and Universal) should contain all such Grounds and Rules as do naturally and necessarily belong to the Philosophy of letters and speech in the *General*. *Instituted* and *Particular* Grammar, doth deliver the Rules which are proper and peculiar to any one Language in Particular; as about the Inflexion of Words, and the Government of case, &c.

Natural Grammar, he says, 'hath been treated of but by few', and after naming some writers (including Duns Scotus, whom he believed to be the author of the speculative grammar now attributed to Thomas of Erfurt) who have either discussed or mentioned it, he continues: '...But all these Authors in some measure (though some more than others) were so far prejudiced by the common Theory of the languages they were acquainted with, that they did not sufficiently abstract their rules according to Nature.'[1]

Dalgarno illustrates the arrival of fresh terminology either straight from the Port Royal grammar, or from Wilkins. In *Didascalocophus*, 1680, a book on the teaching of the deaf and dumb, he refers to his earlier *Ars Signorum*, 1661, in terms which he did not use in the book itself: *Ars Signorum*, he says, 'according to the commonly received distribution of Arts, is nothing else but a Rational Grammar'.[2]

Between 1690 and 1790 there were about a dozen attempts in English to formulate a universal grammar. By Wilkins' criterion they all failed. Inevitably their authors were 'prejudiced by the common Theory of the languages they were acquainted with', and the grammars are remarkable not for their categories (which are noticed later, in the appropriate chapters) but for the points of view from which they are written. The authors are aware that the similarities they see among different languages must be important. The schoolmasters among them wish to teach first the grammar common to a number of languages so as to save time in teaching each particular language. Those who are not schoolmasters search for this common grammar for the sake of the light it will throw on the nature of language itself, or because they still hope for a universal

---

[1] ibid.   [2] p. 116 of Maitland Club reprint.

language, or because they believe that in English is to be found the first, and therefore, universal, language ever spoken by men.

The earliest attempt after Wilkins is perhaps the outline grammar included in Richard Blome's *Gentleman's Recreation*, 1686. Blome makes no reference to his own opinions. It would be possible to argue from the generality of his description that he was thinking of universal grammar, but it could also be argued, from the predominance of Latin illustrations, that he was writing in the spirit of the basic grammars. The grammar is a summary, not a textbook, and includes illustrations from English and French.

The first unambiguous attempt, after Wilkins, to write a universal grammar is found in A. Lane's *A Rational and Speedy Method of attaining to the Latin Tongue*, 1695. The book is arranged in two parts: the second part is a grammar of Latin, while the first contains 'such Precepts as are common to all Languages'.[1] Lane is basing his account of these 'precepts' so closely upon English that most of Part One is incorporated verbatim into his specifically English grammar, *A Key to the Art of Letters*, 1700. Nevertheless, Part One is not just a basic grammar; it is, in a muddled and indirect way, a genuine attempt at a universal grammar. This is apparent particularly in Lane's treatment of the parts of speech, where he appears, perhaps misleadingly, to have been an innovator. Although he does not mention the fact, he is the first English grammarian to put forward the fourfold classification into substantive, adjective, verb and particle which was the distinctive feature of the reforming 'English' approach to grammar, in deliberate opposition to the traditional Latin system.

The English grammar produced in 1711 by Charles Gildon and John Brightland claims also, in its title, to be 'giving the Grounds and Reason of Grammar in General', and in the preface the authors say, 'Since the Rational Grounds of Grammar, may be thought Useful, we have added them in the Notes'.[2] These notes form what the authors call also 'a General Grammar...which may improve some, who think themselves perhaps better Grammarians, than they really are, by letting them into the Reasons of Things, which is as Pleasant as Useful'.[3] This general grammar is mostly derivative. The notes to parts one and two (Letters and Syllables) are mostly

---

[1] Lane, 1695, title-page.   [2] G–B, 1711, sig. A 6.
[3] ibid.

translated from Wallis,[1] and the notes to part three (Words) are translated from the Port Royal grammar. As the authors themselves say disingenuously, 'There was no Spelling Book, or Grammar in English, Latin, French, &c. that we have not consulted.'[2]

In 1726 J. T. Philipps prefixed a universal grammar to an edition of a Latin grammar originally composed (in three different forms, between 1651 and 1660) by James Shirley. The whole publication Philipps called *An Essay towards an Universal and Rational Grammar; together with Rules for Learning Latin, in English Verse.* The title of the essay is an indirect—and on the title-page of a different issue, also dated 1726, there is an explicit—reference to the Port Royal grammar, but the work is indistinguishable from a basic grammar. In the second edition, 1731, the title is reduced to *A Rational Grammar; with easy rules in English to learn Latin*, but the Essay itself is little changed.

Benjamin Martin prefixed to his *Lingua Britannica Reformata*, 1749, which is an English dictionary, the most thoughtful consideration of universal grammar since Wilkins, though on quite different lines and poorly organised. Martin called the work, which has a separate title-page, dated 1748, *Institutions of Language; containing a Physico-Grammatical Essay on the Propriety and Rationale of the English Tongue.* He is concerned more with speech than with grammar, more with linguistic change than with logic: 'no language as depending on arbitrary use and custom, can ever be permanently the same, but will always be in a mutable and fluctuating state'. The language of Shakespeare, like that of Chaucer and Spenser, 'is now grown old and obsolete; read by very few, and understood by antiquarians only'.[3] Martin does not use the term *universal grammar*, though the categories he describes profess to be those common to 'the Original Mother Tongues, the Hebrew, Greek, Latin and Teutonic; with their respective Idioms'.[4]

By far the most penetrating of all the works written in the name of Universal Grammar is James Harris's *Hermes*, 1751, of which the subtitle is: *A philosophical Enquiry concerning Universal Grammar.* It is, in fact, an enquiry concerning language. The enquiry is conducted according to:

---

[1] The amount taken, with only one acknowledgment, from Wallis has been measured by M. Lehnert, 'Die Abhängigkeit frühneuenglischer grammatikern', *Engl. Studien*, LXXII 1937. 196 f. [2] G–B, 1711, preface, sig. A 6 verso.
[3] Martin, 1748, p. 111. [4] op. cit. title.

two Methods of Analysis very different in their kind, and which lead to a variety of very different Speculations[1]...We may either behold Speech, as divided into its constituent Parts, as a Statue may be divided into its several Limbs; or else, as resolved into its Matter and Form, as the same Statue may be resolved into its Marble and Figure. These different Analysings or Resolutions constitute what we call Philosophical, or Universal Grammar.[2]...that Grammar, which without regarding the several Idioms of particular Languages, only respects those Principles, that are essential to them all.[3]

Harris begins his analysis of speech with a study of the sentence, showing thereby a clearer understanding of language than was to be found in any English grammar before his day. He establishes two fundamental types of sentence: those of assertion and those of volition. He then considers the traditional parts of speech, rejects many of them, and sets up his own. This provides the main substance of the book. When he has completed the first method of analysis he turns to the second: 'Language, taken in the most comprehensive view, implies certain Sounds, having certain Meanings; and...of these two Principles, the Sound is as the Matter, common (like other Matter) to many different things; the Meaning as that peculiar and characteristic Form, by which the Nature or Essence of Language becomes complete.'[4] He proceeds to develop at length the argument 'that Words must of necessity be Symbols' and consequently that 'all Language is founded in Compact, and not in Nature'.[5] He is attracted by, but rejects, the view that 'Language (is) a kind of Picture of the Universe'.[6] The most important function of words is to symbolise general ideas,[7] but they must also be able to indicate particulars, which they do by two means: by proper names, and by 'definitives', which include what a modern logician would call quantifiers—words like the articles, *all, each, many, first, that, some*.[8] Harris then moves on to discuss the nature of general ideas, holding, against Locke, that they can exist prior to sensation. The purely philosophical part of the book is less clearly argued, and less satisfactory, than the earlier discussion of language which, though equally based on Greek, and especially Aristotelian, thought, is balanced by the findings of a sensitive introspection into the process of using language.

---

[1] Harris, 1751, p. 7.   [2] op. cit. p. 2.   [3] op. cit. p. 11.
[4] op. cit. p. 315.   [5] op. cit. p. 337.   [6] op. cit. p. 330.
[7] op. cit. pp. 341 f.   [8] op. cit. pp. 346 f.

The English Categories

In 1756 appeared the first two parts of Anselm Bayly's *An Introduction literary and philosophical to Languages; especially to the English, Latin, Greek and Hebrew; exhibiting at one view their Grammar, Rationale, Analogy and Idiom*.[1] Bayly, as his title implies, thought that he was meeting Francis Bacon's request for 'a rational grammar',[2] and should I not, he continues, 'deserve the praise of completing his so excellent plan for its supply'.[3] Bayly followed Bacon in distinguishing between literary grammar, 'employed simply about tongues themselves in order to their being more expeditiously learned', and philosophical grammar, 'in some sort subservient to philosophy, setting forth the various properties of languages, and shewing wherein each of them excelleth and falleth short'.[4]

In 1772 Bayly issued the grammar in a form designed solely for English. In the preface he refers to his intentions in writing the original version of 1756, in which:

the grammars were placed in one view comparatively and concisely for the study of men, rather than plainly and amply for the instruction of youth. [In the present, 1772, version]...as in the first scheme, the English is made the principal, as it were, the conductor into one grand edifice, whose foundation is sought for and laid in nature; this grand edifice is language in general, and particular languages, which differ only in idioms, its several apartments. (Bayly, 1772, p. vi.)

In fact Bayly's work is a short comparative grammar of the three classical languages. He has great difficulty in keeping them in line with English, and he frequently has to discuss one or other of the languages by itself, as when neuter gender and the declension of nouns can be given only in Latin and Greek, dual forms only in Greek and Hebrew, invariable adjectives only in English, and the agreement of the verb with the gender of its nominative only in Hebrew. The only categories to which he refers in really general terms are his primary parts of speech.[5] The *Introduction* is more literary than philosophical. It keeps close to the facts of actual languages, and it is just this virtue which frustrates Bayly's principal purpose.

Joseph Priestley's lectures, published in 1762, the year after his school grammar, are 'on the theory of Language, and Universal Grammar'. They come within the scope of the present discussion

---

[1] For the complete work, which appeared in 1758, see Appendix VI.
[2] See above, p. 163.
[3] Bayly (1756), 1758, preface.
[4] ibid.
[5] See below, p. 265.

because they deal with the parts of speech and with syntax, admittedly from a genetic rather than from an analytical point of view. Priestley's title is interesting as showing the juxtaposition, and suggesting the resemblance, if not the equivalence, of the new terminology to the old. 'The theory of language' was what 'universal grammar' had in fact become. Priestley describes the aim of the lectures as: 'to point out the several powers and modes of expression that sounds and characters are capable of, to trace their connexion with, or relation to the ideas they represent; and to shew the actual variety of the external expressions of the same mental conceptions which different languages exhibit'.[1] He also still hopes, though clearly with some doubts, for 'what some ingenious persons in the republick of letters have conjectured may be one of the last and greatest achievements of the human genius, viz. a philosophical and universal language'.[2] The grammatical categories which Priestley discusses in the lectures differ little from those he uses in his English grammar. What the lectures are most noticeable for, and what distinguishes them from earlier formulations of universal grammar, is Priestley's readiness to speculate in psychological terms about the origin and development of language. He discusses the parts of speech, for example, not with any regard to their logical relationship to each other, but in the order in which he thinks they may have come into existence.[3]

William Ward's *Essay on Grammar*, 1765, is a work of great interest. In spite of its length, and in spite of Ward's prolix and repetitive style, it is a book of character and originality. Ward is obscure not only through pedantry but because he is wrestling directly with difficult questions. The *Essay* comprises 'two treatises. The one Speculative, being an attempt to investigate proper Principles. The other practical, containing definitions and Rules deduced from the Principles.'[4]

It is the province of speculative grammar to consider, both language in general, and likewise each language in particular, so as to discover the principles upon which the application proceeds: not pretending to account

[1] Priestley, 1762, p. 7.   [2] op. cit. p. 8.
[3] Priestley, 1762, Lecture IV, 'Of the General Distribution of Words into Classes'.
[4] W. Ward, 1765, title. The terms 'speculative' and 'practical' are used together, in just this way, by Mark Lewis a century before.: 'The Speculative Part of Grammar ought to be left to riper years, and the Practical Part may be made very short and easie...' (*Essay*, 1670?, p. 1.)

for each particular mode of expression; but for the properties of construction which are observed in all languages, and for the peculiar turn and genius of any language that is to be especially explained. (1765, p. 261.)

Elsewhere he describes the 'principal intention of rational or speculative grammar' in more psychological terms. It is: 'to explain the proceeding of the mind in forming the conceptions annexed to words, and in applying these conceptions by the means of words, so as to communicate the perceptions, thoughts, and purposes of one man to another'.[1] Ward is, throughout, much influenced by Hartley. His debt to Locke is as great, and more frequently acknowledged. In the shortened version of Ward's *Essay*, which appeared in 1767 as *A Grammar of the English Language, in two treatises*, Ward describes his subject from yet another direction, referring the reader to the seventh and eighth chapters of Bk III of Locke's *Essay*. Ward says: 'The Theory of Grammar is the Theory of those Abstractions on which, and on their converse Operations, all our Reasoning depends.'[2] Ward hardly ever uses the term *universal grammar*.[3] His preference for *speculative* accords with the increasing interest, during the second half of the century, in language itself.

It would be impossible to give any short account of Ward's line of thought without making both his methods and his conclusions seem clearer than they are. He is, however, particularly concerned with four topics:

(i) the formation of concepts

(ii) the expression in language of the relations between concepts, and especially the distinction between:

(iii) co-ordinate relationships (in which *A* and *B* are distinct but at the same time related) and:

(iv) subordinating, or 'coalescing', relationships.

Time and again he approaches, from varying directions, 'the several kinds of connexions of the conceptions of the mind of man as denoted by words'. He continues:

It is clear that these connexions do not arise immediately from the nature of external things, but from the kinds of conceptions which the mind forms of things; because qualities, states, and relations, which cannot

---

[1] W. Ward, 1765, p. 9.   [2] W. Ward, 1767, p. xx.
[3] A consideration of stress, he says on one occasion 'has little relation to universal grammar' (1765, p. 8).

exist separately, are denoted by separate words. Therefore the conceptions denoted by several words must be capable of uniting into one conception. (1765, p. 252.)

Ward then attempts to illustrate the variety of ways in which logical relations are expressed in language. He discusses the difference in the functions of *be* and of *and* in 'Mr N *being* a widower' and 'Mr N *and* Mrs B', and he then tries to establish a basic 'mode of communication, to which, or to its converse by the passive verb, all the remaining modes may be reduced'.[1] This basic mode is of the form 'substantive: :transitive verb: :substantive'. The exercise in reduction which he thus prescribes for himself forces him to put forward many inadequate equivalences, such as that 'a roomy house' is the same as 'a house having rooms'.

It is not in his treatment of the traditional categories (which will be noticed later) that the main interest of Ward's work now lies, but in the references he makes to matters which have become important to us. He sees clearly the importance in any analysis of language of the concept of relation—'the connective part of the signification of words...which...is the part of language that requires explanation the most'.[2] He applies it to the verb,[3] to the cases, and to prepositions.[4] He sees the importance of a study of language in its spoken form:

Those who profess to teach any language, would do well to carry their researches still farther concerning the nature of human speech; because such researches, if prudently made, will enable them in many instances, to give those whom they teach, general views of the reasons of construction, which is the only sure way of fixing the art of grammar in their minds, so as to enable them to know when they may safely depart from the ordinary rules. (1765, p. xii.)

He takes the primacy of the spoken word, in advocating which he was scarcely an innovator, a step further into what was, perhaps, the most explicit statement yet made of the importance, in linguistic analysis, of the context of situation: what Ward calls 'the demonstrative circumstances':

The hearer is conceived to know the meaning of every single word which the speaker makes use of, before the word is mentioned; and therefore no single word, if considered in itself, gives the hearer any new information. But the demonstrative circumstances attending the act of mentioning a

[1] 1765, p. 254.
[2] 1765, p. 2.
[3] e.g. op. cit. p. 59.
[4] e.g. op. cit. p. 71.

single definitive verb,[1] may so far aid the signification of the verb, as to give new information to the hearer.

If a speaker should point to a house, and say 'that tree', the expression would contain a manifest falshood: or if anyone should cry out 'fire!' when nothing was in danger by fire, the person who cried out would be conceived to be a liar. For the act of pointing...and the tone of voice... amount to declarations, by the established customs observed in the use of language. (1765, pp. 263–5.)

Ward's work deserves fuller consideration than can be given it here. He was aware of its originality (which is rightly stressed by Poldauf)[2] but it is misleading to see Ward's 'special position among the grammarians of this period' just in the fact that 'he was the only one who knew how to link the descriptive grammatical problems with English grammar'.[3] There is more in the *Essay* than this, but Poldauf, apparently, had access only to the first fifty pages of the *Essay* and to Ward's summary of it in the grammar of 1767.

Rowland Jones was another original. He meant by universal grammar what might rather be called 'archetypal' grammar. In *The Circles of Gomer*,[4] 1771, he developed the English form of universal grammar which he had earlier sketched in *Hieroglyfic*, 1768. The essay, to which he gives the title, 'An Universal English Grammar', is, in its categories, an ordinary, rather thin, grammar of English. Its universality is described by Jones in the following passage:

In other languages...the nominal or literary characters as well as their sounds, like those of arithmetic, algebra, geometry, astronomy and music, seem to be arbitrarily applied, but in English they signify and are applied as real characters, representations, and expressions of nature by their symbolical figures and forms, and arithmetical proportion of sounds or divisions and multiplications of lines or musical chords agreeable to the Circles of Gomer; for Gomer supposed the world to be a large circle composed of many homogeneous lesser circles, systems, or combination of elements, sides, surfaces, figures, forms and parts. And such as will deliberately examine the foregoing definitions and grammar of the English language, will find it to be an exact copy or description of the circles or systems of Gomer. Hence also its greater pretensions to universality. (1771, pp. 31–2.)

It would seem from Jones's account that the smaller the linguistic unit the more highly charged it is with symbolic values. Of the letters *i* and *t* he says:

[4] i.e. a finite verb.   [2] Poldauf. 1948, p. 140.   [3] ibid.
[4] Gomer = Mercury, Hermes Trismegistus, and others.

178

The letter *i* is the element of fire and all its qualities, which by its rays, dots and lines penetrates bodies, and causes the flow and spring of things and also light, and it signifies man, as a lighted candle, and an upright, springing or living line and also length, the pronoun *i* and the first person singular or man...The *t* hieroglyphically represents man's legs and thighs close together with the toes outwards, the water place of man and a river flowing into the sea. (1771, pp. 3–4.)

The syllables *id, di; idd, ddi* 'signify the divisions of fire, as light, sight, colours, discernment, the human intellects, spiritual qualities and privatives thereof'.[1] Actual words, however, as they appear in his account of the parts of speech, are treated according to more conventionally linguistic, if less colourful, criteria.

The first edition of the *Encyclopaedia Britannica*, 1771, fully recognised the concept of universal grammar:

Grammar considered as a *Science*, views language in itself: neglecting particular modifications, or the analogy which *words* may bear to *each other*, it examines the analogy and relation between *words* and *things*; distinguishes between those particulars which are *essential* to language, and those which are only *accidental*; and thus furnishes a certain standard, by which different languages may be compared, and their several excellencies or defects pointed out. This is what is called PHILOSOPHIC or UNIVERSAL Grammar. (*Enc. Brit.* (A), 1771, p. 728.)

The first two editions of the *Encyclopaedia Britannica* kept closely to the views and terminology of Harris. The article in the third and fourth editions is by a different author, who repudiates much of Harris. He shows a greater interest than the writer of the 1771 article had shown in the origin of language; he lays greater stress on the arbitrary nature of words, and rejects entirely Harris's view that some kinds of words have no meaning in themselves. Nevertheless he still accepts the idea of universal grammar: 'We trust...that the principles which we shall establish will be found to apply *universally*; and that our inquiry, though *principally* illustrated from the *English* language, will be an inquiry into *philosophical* or *universal* grammar.'[2]

An Universal Grammar, 1775, by Richard Wynne, and Charles Coote's *Elements of the Grammar of the English Language*, 1788, are both designed for an elementary level. Wynne wrote his grammar for a young daughter who wanted to learn French and Italian but knew no Latin. The book is, in fact, a grammar of English in which Wynne has 'endeavoured...to explain the technical terms used by Gram-

---

[1] 1771, p. 5. 　　　　　　　　　[2] *Enc. Brit.* (B), 1797, p. 38.

marians, in as plain and concise a manner as I could, without applying them to any particular language ancient or modern',[1] except (he does not add) English. Coote's grammar is intended 'for capacities even of the junior classes of scholars'. But he quotes Locke to support his view that 'a proper acquaintance with grammar, particularly with that branch which is denominated universal grammar, cannot but be of great service in investigating the philosophy of the human mind, and the nature and limits of our understanding'.[2] Coote's outline of universal grammar is given in a short introduction to the English grammar. He does not believe that universal grammar by itself is enough: 'though the essential rules of grammar are the same in all languages, there are various modifications, as well as idiomatic forms of construction, which it would be absurd to transfer indiscriminately from one tongue to another.'[3] In these 'introductory observations, illustrating the fundamental principles of universal grammar' the system of parts of speech is taken from *Hermes*, but Coote shows also the current interest in the development of language, and makes the first of his observations refer to man's natural desire to communicate. This was scarcely a truism in the 1780s, but even in the 1970s language is sometimes discussed by people who have apparently forgotten its use in communication.

The last attempt during the eighteenth century to formulate a universal grammar is by James Beattie. His *Dissertations Moral and Critical*, 1783, contained an essay on *The Theory of Language*, which was issued separately under that title, with few changes, in 1788. The *Theory of Language* is in two parts: the first discusses 'the origin and general nature of speech', the second is 'of universal grammar', which Beattie defines in the following words: 'Those things, that all languages have in common, or that are necessary to every language, are treated of in a science, which some have called Universal or Philosophical Grammar.[4] Beattie tries to keep to what he considers fundamental categories: '[We shall] unfold the principles of Universal Grammar, by tracing out those powers, forms, or contrivances, which, being essential to language, must be found in every system of human speech that deserves the name.'[5] This leads him to postulate three basic parts of speech:

---

¹ Wynne, 1775, p. xi.   ² Coote, 1788, p. ii.
³ op. cit. p. v.
⁴ Beattie, 1783, Pt I. chap. 6 (*Dissertations*, p. 307.)
  op. cit. Pt II. Introduction (*Dissertations*, p. 322).

Now, as human thoughts discover themselves by language, and as the thoughts of men in one age and nation are similar to those in another, is it not probable, that there may be in all human languages some general points of resemblance, in structure at least, if not in sound? Since, for example, all men in all ages must have had occasion to speak of acting, and of being acted upon, of good and of bad qualities, and of the various objects of outward sense, must there not in every language be verbs, and adjectives, and nouns? (Pt I. chap. 6; *Dissertations*, p. 306.)

But in Pt II he extends the 'universal' parts of speech to nine or ten,[1] and his subsequent treatment of universal grammar, like that of his predecessors, is in fact a grammar of English, with frequent reference, and occasional concessions, to Latin, Greek and Hebrew.

Two writers inverted the customary expectation. Instead of writing a universal grammar and hoping that it would serve for English, and as a basis for learning the grammars of foreign languages, Elphinston wrote an elaborate work on English, which he hoped would 'lay the foundation of Universal Grammar'.[2] Similarly, an anonymous grammarian, J.G., in his closing *Address to Teachers* presumes 'that this Introduction may have its use among young Gentlemen and Ladies, even while they are acquiring the principles of Universal Grammar from the Latin and Greek, the French and Italian languages'.[3] Such open acknowledgment of the inductive process by which all the universal grammars were in fact devised is not made by any of their authors.

The writers just discussed, who tried, from varying points of view, actually to sketch a general or universal grammar, failed because they could not detach themselves from English. The more they went into details the more apparent was their failure; but if they discussed only broad fundamental categories (as did the wisest of them) they talked not about universal grammar but about language.[4]

About twenty-five other eighteenth-century grammarians, who are keeping professedly to a 'particular' grammar of English, never-

---

[1] op. cit. Pt II, Introduction (*Dissertations*, p. 322).

[2] Elphinston, 1765, II. 478.

[3] J. G. 1796, p. 116.

[4] What should have been the final word about universal grammar was spoken by George Campbell: 'In every region of the globe we may soon discover, that people feel and argue in much the same manner, but the speech of one nation is quite unintelligible to another. The art of the logician is accordingly, in some sense, universal; the art of the grammarian is always particular and local...In propriety there cannot be such a thing as universal grammar, unless there were such a thing as an universal language.' *Philosophy of Rhetoric*, 1776, Bk I. chap. 4 (from the 11th edn, 1841).

theless make a passing reference to universal grammar, usually to acknowledge its status. It is not surprising that they have little to say about it, and are usually rather vague. The most frequent comment is that all the languages of the world are the same, in some respect. The most definite statement in a grammar is that first made in the third London edition of Anne Fisher's grammar, 1753,[1] that the parts of speech are the same in all languages, and the same statement is made by other writers, besides the grammarians. Thomas Wilson, in *The Many Advantages of a Good Language*, 1724, had been recklessly specific: 'As all the Parts of Speech, Genders, Numbers, Persons, Tenses, Comparisons, Concords, Governments, and Transitions, are naturally the same in all Nations; all the essential Parts of Grammar are the same also in all Languages.'[2] Wilson was, presumably, confusing grammatical and natural categories, and meant much what Ephraim Chambers wrote in the *Cyclopaedia*, 1728: 'Grammar is the same in all Languages, as to its general Principles, and Notions which it borrows from Philosophy to explain the Order and Manner wherein we express our Ideas by Words.'[3]

This belief in universal grammar, often in a vague and weakened form, was widely held, and persisted. Similar views are expressed by John Stirling in *A Short View of Latin Grammar*, 1737;[4] J. Jones, in *A Step towards an English Education*, 1740;[5] S. Butler, *An Essay upon Education*, c. 1750;[6] James Buchanan, *A Plan of an English Grammar School Education*, 1770;[7] by Blair, in the ninth of his *Lectures on Rhetoric and Belles Lettres*, 1783.

Among other writers as well as among the grammarians the most popular way of referring to the postulated universal elements is to call them General Principles, after Chambers, but it is Lowth's way of putting it which was widely copied: 'Grammar in general, or Universal Grammar, explains the Principles which are common to all languages.'[8] This appears verbatim in H. Ward,[9] Ussher[10] and Bicknell,[11] and little changed in Hodgson[12] and Rothwell.[13]

Perhaps the most forceful expression of belief in universal grammar is quoted by W. C. Hazlitt from 'Dr Duncan of the Ciceronian Academy at Pimlico', who said to a father who wanted his son to

---

[1] Fisher (1750), 1753, preface, p. i.   [2] p. 30
[3] s.v. *Grammar*.   [4] preface.   [5] p. 27.
[6] p. 76.   [7] p. 127.   [8] Lowth, 1762, p. 1.
[9] H. Ward, 1771, p. 1.   [10] Ussher, 1785, p. 1.   [11] Bicknell, 1790, p. 1.
[12] Hodgson, 1770, p. vi.   [13] Rothwell, 1787, p. vii.

learn English grammar instead of Latin grammar, 'Sir, Grammar is Grammar all the world over'.[1]

Lowth's warning that universal grammar could not be taught has already been quoted. He could be more severe. In a note added, in the second edition, to his discussion of the moods of the verb he says tartly, 'Whatever other Metaphysical Modes there may be in the theory of Universal Grammar, there are in English no other Grammatical Modes than those above described.[2] Lowth is exactly indicating the weakness of the search for universal grammar. Because it could not be based on the facts of a particular language, that is on linguistic facts, it had to be based on what were considered psychological facts: on the ways in which the human mind conceived experience. And in the enumeration of those ways there could be neither certainty nor finality. Horne Tooke sarcastically remarked about enquirers into philosophical grammar: 'From the thick darkness in which they have left it, I imagine it to be one of the most difficult speculations.'[3] But the sarcasm has misfired. The words can now carry their plainest sense. We are still in the dark about the nature of language—it is a very 'difficult speculation'—and we have given up investigating its origin. But we can now see that the pursuit of universal grammar was important.[4] It was one of the interests which stimulated the development of historical and comparative linguistic studies, and by showing that universality was not to be found among the natural languages it forced men to see that universality was an imposed, artificial concept, which could be realised (for different purposes) only by different, and long-established techniques: on the one hand by an artificial language, and on the other by logic.[5]

[1] W. C. Hazlitt, *Schools, School-Books and Schoolmasters*, 1888. p. 219.
[2] Lowth, 2nd ed, 1763. p. 50 n.
[3] Horne Tooke (1786), 1829, I. 10.
[4] More important, perhaps, than we realise. A crisp comment by the author of *A Posing-Book for Scholars*, 1688, p. 7, reminds us how narrow the horizon could be: 'Some Ignorantly imagine that Grammar belongs only to the Latin Tongue, but that's a mistake.'
[5] The idea of universal grammar had lost much of its power by the end of the century, but it was still alive. In Jolly B. Florian's *Essay on an Analytical Course of Studies*, 1796, 'general and particular grammar' are suggested for the eighth year (ages 15–16), and Samuel Catlow's Literary and Commercial Seminary in Mansfield taught 'General Grammar, combined in the accurate study of the English, Latin and French Tongues' (*Mon. Rev.*, n.s. xxvii. November 1798. 327.) Two anonymous works add their support during the following decades: *Enclytica, or the principles of universal grammar*, 1814, and *Universal Grammar Illustrated*, 1835.

The English Categories

Evidence from the divisions of grammar. There had developed within the tradition two ways of displaying the constituent parts of grammar. The older, first explicit in the work of Peter Helias in the middle of the twelfth century, was in terms of material:[1] the constituents are letters, syllables, words and sentences. The alternative way was in terms of processes: orthography, etymology, syntax and prosody. Both medieval and renaissance grammarians tended to favour the former if their inclinations were logical rather than literary, the latter if they were literary rather than logical. Consequently prosody has a firmer place in the second.

The English grammarians, following Lily, favoured the literary division, but modified it according to their differing purposes and conceptions of grammar. In such a well-established and uncontroversial part of the tradition great uniformity might be expected. But as an analysis of all the available grammars does not show such uniformity it may be of interest to give some details.

It is first necessary to say briefly what the customary terms meant within the English tradition.

Orthography meant the study of the letters of the alphabet, which were enumerated, and classified as consonants, vowels, diphthongs, and often into more refined categories still. The sounds which each letter could represent were usually described. Letters compose syllables, syllables compose words; the structure of a word was therefore shown by the syllables into which it could be divided. Spelling was conceived as the division of a word into syllables, according to rules, and not simply as the enumeration of its letters: 'To Spell is to Name all the Letters of a Word, divide them into distinct Syllables, and then join them together in order to read or Pronounce them aright.'[2]

Orthoepy meant the study of pronunciation. The pronunciation of single letters was an almost invariable part of orthography, so orthoepy was made a separate division of grammar only by those who wished to give it particular attention.

Prosody retained during the whole of the period its traditional two senses of pronunciation and versification. For Gill, in 1619, it is '*de Accentu, & Metro*'.[3] Joseph Aickin puts it more fully: '...the last part of Grammar: and it Teacheth the true pronunciation of words

---

[1] See above, pp. 35–6. [2] Douglas, *c.* 1720, no. 587b fol. 39 recto.
[3] Gill, 1619, p. 128.

either in Prose or Verse, as to their accents and quantitie or time. So that Prosody is twofold, one teacheth the true accents of words: and the other the manner of making Verses.'[1] Strictly, the pronunciation of letters and syllables belonged to orthography and the pronunciation of words to prosody, but the distinction was quite unreal, and constantly ignored. From about 1760, with the multiplication of elementary textbooks which needed to discuss pronunciation but could ignore versification, the two are more often separated, with a corresponding increase in jargon: 'Prosody comprizes Orthoepy, or the Rules of Pronunciation; and Orthometry, or the Laws of Versification.'[2]

Etymology and Syntax were the basic divisions of grammar. *Etymology* carried two principal senses: 'word-variation' (including 'word-formation') and 'word-provenance'. The former was by far the more common, and *etymology* was the usual name for that division of grammar which described the parts of speech. When the provenance of words became a more frequent topic in the grammars some writers used *analogy* for word-variation and *etymology*, or more often *derivation*, for word-provenance. The use of these terms can be roughly tabulated:

Provenance of words	*etymology*: commonly till 1700, seldom thereafter.
	derivation: commonly after 1700.
Variation of words (principally inflection)	*etymology*: throughout
	analogy: sometimes before 1750; often thereafter.
Formation of words (principally suffixes and compounds)	*etymology*: throughout
	derivation: sometimes, between 1700 and 1750
	analogy: sometimes, throughout

Seven different divisions of grammar are found. They are described here in descending order of fullness.

(i) *Orthography, Orthoepy, Etymology, Syntax, Prosody.* This division is found only in William Sewell's *English Grammar Methodized*, 1789.

(ii) *Orthography, Etymology, Syntax, Prosody.* This fourfold division appeared first in the Middle Ages and was adopted by Lily, but

---

[1] Aickin, 1693, p. 25.   [2] C. Johnson, 6th edn 1779, p. 1.

not by the majority of the renaissance grammarians.[1] It appears in rather more than forty per cent of the English grammars. The only comment is by Dr Johnson, who takes a stand here against the vernacular terminology, which had been fashionable for about twenty years:

In this division and order of the parts of grammar I follow the common grammarians, without inquiring whether a fitter distribution might not be found. Experience has long shown this method to be so distinct as to obviate confusion, and so comprehensive as to prevent any inconvenient omissions. I likewise use the terms already received, and already understood, though perhaps others more proper might sometimes be invented. (Dr. S. Johnson, 1755, *ad init.*)

(iii) *Orthography, Etymology, Syntax; Letters, Syllables, Words, Sentences.* These divisions, which differ from (ii) in excluding prosody (though a very few authors add orthoepy) are found in rather more than a quarter of the grammars. The division into Letters, Syllables, Words and Sentences is significant in two ways: it picks up again the division made by Peter Helias, and it forms part of the reforming movement to establish an English, rather than a Latin, approach to grammar. This vernacular division of the parts of grammar, which was current also in Latin textbooks,[2] appears first in A. Lane's *A Key to the Art of Letters*, 1700, where it is introduced without comment. It was popular for its simplicity, and is found in 29 grammars, but not many writers discuss it. Daniel Turner, 1739, refers to it warmly: 'I have made Choice of this Division, because I tho't it the most natural and easy, and comprehending all that can be said on the Subject of Grammar.'[3] Joshua Story and Henry Bullen provide something of a reply to Dr Johnson:

Many people whom custom hath prejudiced in favour of the old grammatical division, viz, orthography, etymology &c. will perhaps be displeased at seeing it discontinued. It may not therefore be improper to observe, that the division of the subject of grammar into letters, syllables, words and sentences is much more intelligible, and natural than the old method. Indeed, it is somewhat surprising that grammarians should have followed the old method so long. (Story, 1778, p. vi.)

Bullen, at the end of the century, is a Latinist in his general treatment of English grammar, but he also adopts the vernacular division because the names are simple:

[1] Above, pp. 36–7. [2] e.g. *A Posing-Book for Scholars*, 1688, p. 7.
[3] D. Turner, 1739, p. 1.

The term 'grammar'

The unnecessary distinctions of the parts of Grammar, by Orthoepy, Orthography, Etymology, and other still harder names, are purposely avoided, both because their subjects are partly the province of the spelling-book, and because the English ear has a natural aversion from such high and valorous words, of great but unmeaning sound. (Story, 1797, p. 113.)[1]

This fourfold division into Letters, Syllables, Words and Sentences is increased by Hugh Jones, 1724, who, uniquely, adds a fifth— 'Discourses or Speeches'.[2]

(iv) *Etymology and Syntax.* Orthography and prosody are excluded. This division, which is adopted in nearly twenty per cent of the English grammars, had been favoured by the speculative grammarians, whose concern with structure, whether logical or metaphysical, led them to exclude the literary features of grammar. Ramus had also made an explicit division of grammar into these two parts only; but his classification is misleading. Ramus, and his English followers Greaves, Jonson and Evelyn (who was directly following Jonson) included within Etymology just that consideration of letters and syllables which was the customary content of Orthography. When Jonson says, after Ramus, 'Prosodie, and Orthography, are not parts of Grammar, but diffus'd, like the blood, and spirits through the whole',[3] he must, in order to avoid contradiction, be taken to mean by prosody only versification, and by orthography only the division of syllables. But the remark then loses all point. It is letters and their sounds which pervade the whole body of grammar, not the arbitrary processes of spelling and versification.

(v) *Orthography and Etymology; Letters, Syllables, Words.* Syntax and Prosody are excluded. In the small group of nine grammars, all but one from the seventeenth century, which adopt this division, syntax is excluded in order to keep the grammar at an elementary level, or because English is thought to have little syntax.

(vi) *Orthography, Orthoepy.* Samuel Edwards, 1765, who alone uses this division, is quite explicit, but uses *orthography* oddly to include Letters, Syllables, Words and Sentences.

(vii) *Etymology* alone. The few works which adopt this view of

---

[1] Bullen is more merciful to his pupils than a Bristol Schoolmaster, J.G., whose ear had no such aversion. In the previous year J.G. had published a 'Sketch of Grammar for Children under Seven Years old'. This sketch includes a list of words to pronounce, amongst which are to be found *schirrous, ochimy, metempsychosis, hypocondriacal, catachrestical, cachexy,* and *logomachy.* (J.G. 1796, pp. 30 f.)

[2] H. Jones, 1724, p. 2.   [3] Jonson, 1640, Bk I. chap. I.

grammar all appear in the second half of the eighteenth century. They are elementary works from which syntax has been excluded because it is too difficult, prosody because it is irrelevant, and orthography because there are already enough spelling-books. The tone of several of them can be represented by Mrs Eves' *The Grammatical Play-Thing, or, Winter Evening's Recreation, for Young Ladies from four to twelve years old*, 1800.[1] The plaything is a board and a set of cards, with which games are played, using the grammatical material in the book. The work is introduced by a dialogue between Mrs Friendly and her young pupils, in which the necessity for studying grammar is meant to be made plain. The dialogue is notable, however, for the decisiveness with which Mrs Friendly is routed:

> *Mrs. Friendly.* Dont be alarmed, my dear, I will help you a little at first. In this book you will find the grammar rules appropriated to the game; which I have selected from some of our best grammarians for that purpose.
> *Miss Henrietta.* I am much obliged to you, ma'am, but I am sure I shall never understand grammar; nor do I see any use in it.
> *Mrs Friendly.* You am an very clever young lady, and I loves good childs. Do you like to hear me speak so?
> *Miss Henrietta.* Ha, ha, ha, nobody ever speaks so.
> *Mrs Friendly.* Yes, my dear, there are even greater grammatical blunders made than these, and the only reason that you speak better is, that you associate with people who are well educated.
> *Miss Henrietta.* Then having this advantage, I need not give myself the trouble of studying what is so very disagreeable to me. (Eves, 1800, pp. x–xi.)

To this Mrs Friendly can make only a very evasive reply.

Two grammarians repudiate the traditional practice of making any 'divisions' of grammar, but on different grounds from those of Sanctius, quoted earlier.[2] Thomas Merriman is quite explicit: 'I have purposely omitted dividing of Grammar into four Parts; viz. Orthography, Prosody, Etymology, and Syntax. For as to the first, it is so various, and the Rules admit of so many Exceptions, and are many Times even uncertain, that the Learned themselves are frequently divided in their Opinions.' Pronunciation, he says, is better learnt by practice than by precept, and prosody is:

> more properly confin'd to Poetry, and should succeed a sufficient Progress in Grammar. Instead therefore of beginning with the Division

---

[1] cf. Abbé Gaultier's *Jeu de grammaire*, 2nd edn London 1794. [2] Above, p. 37.

abovemention'd, giving the proper Definitions to each Part, and exemplifying the same with all the necessary Variety...I have...having given a Definition of Speech proceeded to an Explanation of all its component Parts, in the rising Gradation in which they occur. (Merriman, 1750, p. vii.)

Charles Wiseman, 1764, does not question the validity of the divisions so much as their usefulness. His grammar contains the traditional material of the categories belonging to Division (ii), but he does not name or discuss the categories, because his grammar 'is designed not to gratify vain speculation, but to be converted into practical utility...it would have been needless...to croud the page, as others have done, with a multiplicity of notes collected from the Ancients, relative to the definitions, divisions and subdivisions of Grammar.'[1]

Evidence from definitions. The summary of the tradition given in Part I showed that at first 'grammar' referred to almost the whole range of literary and linguistic skills; that the tendency (very irregular in its development) was for the term to be restricted to linguistic studies, but that it always remained open enough to include, when desired, some consideration of literature and even of logic. It was also traditional practice to give a formal definition of grammar, though some writers, notably Donatus and Priscian, did not. These definitions are more uniform than the contents of the books, and from early times (at least as early as Diomedes in the fourth century A.D.) a conventional formula was frequently offered as a definition, or as part of a definition: 'the art of speaking and writing correctly'.

Among the English grammarians a third offer no definition of grammar. Presumably they take it for granted, or think the formula too trivial to be worth their pupils' time. If they had disagreed with the conventional definition, or with the usefulness of definitions in general, they would have said so.[2] Of those writers who do offer a definition over two-thirds use the formula. In the words of the first of them to do so, grammar is 'the Art of writing and speaking wel',[3] or, as it was often put in the following century, 'with propriety'.

Up till about 1740 as many writers give definitions as do not. During the rest of the century, over any period of twenty years, those who give definitions are at least twice as numerous as those who do not. It is impossible to suggest any firm reason for this change, but it

---

[1] Wiseman, 1764, p. xiii. [2] For those who did, see below, pp. 281 f.
[3] Butler, 1633, p. 1.

is perhaps related to the increasing number of purely derivative and mediocre grammars, for the compilers of which a (borrowed) definition could be an attractive substitute for original thought. But the scholarly and critical writers do not necessarily dispense with definitions: Dr Johnson, Priestley and Lowth all use the conventional formula, as do able schoolmasters like Alexander Adam, James Wood and John Shaw.

Interest lies chiefly in those writers who depart from the conventional definition. Some of them give other long-standing definitions also drawn from the tradition, as:

'Grammar is the Art of Letters.' (Howell, 1662, p. 2; *Right Spelling*, 1704, p. 31.)

'...the art of Words or Discourse.' (Wilkins, 1668, p. 297.)

'...the Doctrine of Words or Speech in General.' (Hammond, *c.* 1760, sig. A 5.)

'To know how many sorts of words there are; their names, and the meaning of those names; their variations, and use: This science is called Grammar.' (Bridel, 1797, p. 5.)

Some define grammar in terms of its components: '...teaches Persons, the true and proper Use of Letters, Syllables, Words and Sentences'.[1] One anonymous work puts an unusual emphasis on formal and structural criteria: 'Unless the Grammarian fix the Meaning and Use of Words (which is reasonably expected from every Dictionary) he has nothing left him belonging to the Language, but the Inflections, which are extremely few; and the Order in which Words are placed in a Sentence.'[2]

The three most important departures from the conventional formula are those which give particular emphasis (*a*) to communication, (*b*) to rule, (*c*) to relation.

The conventional reference to 'speaking and writing' is of course a reference to expression. In a number of grammars, however, this reference is first emphasised, and then taken further so as to include communication. This development becomes noticeable at the beginning of the eighteenth century: 'Grammar teacheth how to express our Minds by words.'[3] Fifty years later definitions in terms of communication begin:

---

[1] Dyche and Pardon, 1735, sig. A 4; verbatim in Wise, 1754, p. 1, and to the same effect in Marriott, 1780, sig. a 1.

[2] *A Vocabulary, or Pocket Dictionary*, 1765, sig. a 1.

[3] *Right Spelling Very Much Improved*, 1704, p. 25.

the Art of disposing...Words properly, in a Sentence, to express any Thought...and make it intelligible to another Person. (Martin, 1754, p. xvii.)

the art of applying [articulate] sounds and letters consistently for the purpose of communicating the thoughts of one man to another. (W. Ward, 1765, p. 3.)

With this last may be compared its author's comment in his preface: 'Words are connected together with no other intention but to affirm or to deny; and therefore the principal part of the business of a speculative grammarian is to shew how this intention is accomplished.'[1] Characteristic of the less scholarly works is George Brown's *The New English Letter-Writer*, *c*. 1779, which opens with the refreshing, if inelegant, sentence: 'Grammar is the art of one human creature speaking to another, so as to be understood.'[2]

It may seem unimportant that a dozen grammars, almost all in the second half of the eighteenth century, include in their definitions such emphasis on communication, but to view 'the art of grammar' as broadly 'the art of communication' was to introduce a live, organic and disturbing element into the customary treatment of grammar. The study of verbal communication is the study of language in use and alive, and it is to this study that grammar has intermittently aspired: in the early days of the Greek tradition and in the hands of the speculative grammarians. It is this study which is needed in our schools today. These definitions, sometimes from quite minor works, show that during the third quarter of the eighteenth century the developing interest in language was affecting (however slightly) the highly conventional conception of grammar at the elementary level.

The emphasis on rules appears first in Alexander Gill's *Logonomia Anglica*, 1619. Gill's definition of *Logonomia*, as '*comprehensio regularum*'[3] was quoted earlier, on page 164. Gill is referring to the learning of a foreign language. It is not until 1754 that a similar definition is applied to English as a vernacular, in the peculiar style of Daniel Farro:

Q. What is the simple and absolute meaning of Grammar?
A. Grammar is both a Science and an Art, consisting in the System of a

---

[1] W. Ward, 1765, p. v.   [2] G. Brown, [1779?], p. 17.
[3] Gill, 1619, p. 1.

regular Digestion of Rules and Observations, which properly and absolutely appertain to each Part of a Language or Speech as is intended to
be taught. (Farro, 1754, p. 1.)[1]

References to 'observation' carry two senses of *observe*, 'to notice'
and 'to comment'. The latter is always the dominant sense: 'observations' are comments. But both senses are active, because you comment on what you notice. It would, however, be misleading to treat
references to 'observation' as more than very faint anticipations of
descriptive grammar.

'Observation' does not appear again in this context until Priestley
makes the same point, not in his definition of grammar, for which he
adopts the conventional formula, but in his lectures published the
following year: 'To improve upon a language, observations must be
made upon the manner in which words are actually used in it. A
methodical enumeration of the rules and laws of its construction is
the Grammar of it.'[2] Priestley is followed by three other grammarians
in similar words,[3] and four or five others emphasise rules without
reference to observation:

the art of using words according to certain established rules. (Devis, 1775,
p. 1.)[4]

the art which regulates languages. (*A Comprehensive View of English
Grammar*, 1794, p. 6.)

The third noticeable emphasis, on relation, was prompted by
Richard Johnson, the forceful Master of the Free School in Nottingham. In his *Grammatical Commentaries*, 1706, Johnson attacked Lily,
and most other Latin grammars, on a number of grounds, including
the traditional definition of grammar: *recte loquendi* is ambiguous,
because it includes choosing the right word, i.e. 'not to say *Hand* for
Foot', which is no part of grammar. Johnson's own definition is:
'Grammar is the Art of Expressing the Relations of Things in
Construction, with due Accent in Speaking, and Orthography in
writing, according to the Custom of those, whose Language we
learn.'[5] Johnson's emphasis on relation was deliberate, and he

---

[1] It is not only Farro's syntax which lacks grace. He can hardly have won many hearts
with the remark in the dedication of his grammar 'to the Public' that, 'This grammar
contains a Method so easy, that every Female Teacher in the British Dominions may open
an English Grammar School, and render themselves much more useful to the Public.'
[2] Priestley, 1762, pp. 182–3.
[3] Perry, 1774, p. 1; Ussher, 1785, p. 1, followed almost verbatim by Marshall, 1790,
p. 137.   [4] Followed verbatim by Nicholson, 1793, p. 5.
[5] Richard Johnson, *Grammatical Commentaries*, 1706, p. 3.

thought it important. He repeats it in *Noctes Nottinghamicae, or Objections against the Syntax of the Common Grammar* where, in the 'Preface to the School-Masters', he says: 'There are *Thousands* of Ways of expressing the *Relations* of *Things* (the only Business of *Grammar*) which that in Use among us gives no Direction for; and *great Numbers* of Conceptions, which that teaches us to express *no Way whatsoever.*'[1] It is not clear when Johnson is talking about relations between things, about relations between words, or about relations between words and things; the sense shifts:

the Relation of Words one to another, in Sentences, has no other Significa-tion, than what I intend by it, namely, of Cause, Effect, Means, End, Manner, Instrument, Object, Adjunct, and the like; which are Names given by Logicians to those Relations, under which the Mind compre-hends things, and therefore the most proper to discover them by, or speak of them to others. And if this be too hard for Children, then Grammar is too hard; for there neither is, nor can be, any grammar without them. (Richard Johnson, *Grammatical Commentaries*, 1706, p. 4.)

Few of the English grammarians share Johnson's view. William Ward is much influenced by it, but other grammars quote Johnson's definition without allowing it to affect their general approach. The author of *An Easy Introduction to the English Language*, published in 1745 by John Newbery as the second volume in his collection *The Circle of the Sciences*, gives first the traditional definition of grammar, and then continues: 'Or it may be defin'd more accurately, but less intelligibly, to be The Art of expressing the Relation of Words in Construction, with due Quantity in Speaking, and Spelling in Writing, according to the Custom of those whose Language we learn.'[2] Here Richard Johnson's '...the Relation of Things in Construction' is significantly changed to '...the Relation of Words...'—another sign that this anonymous author was no unthinking hack. This amended definition is repeated by Buchanan[3] and by John Bell;[4] Johnson's original definition is repeated by Anne Fisher.[5] John Burn makes the same point as Johnson, in his own words,[6] and Martin Trinder amends it concisely: '...the art of expressing rightly the relation of words to one another in sentences'.[7]

The philosophical approach of James Harris and William Ward

[1] Richard Johnson, *Noctes Nottinghamicae*, 1718, p. i.
[2] *Easy Introduction to the English Language*, 1745, p. 2. [3] Buchanan, 1762, p. 1.
[4] Bell, 1769, p. 19. [5] Fisher, 1750, p. 1. [6] Burn, 1766, p. vii.
[7] Trinder, 1781, p. 1.

has already been quoted. Horne Tooke had an equally broad view of grammar but did not have such confidence in philosophy. Though *The Diversions of Purley* is, like *Hermes*, more a book about language than a systematic grammar, Horne Tooke is more of a grammarian than Harris or Ward in that he concentrates his attention on words. At his best he is inductive, whereas Harris and Ward tend to work from philosophical or psychological concepts, which are treated as if they were *a priori* but have an unacknowledged origin in the authors' own language. In Horne Tooke's opinion the traditional view of grammar was quite misconceived. In the past 'all has been dispute, diversity, and darkness. Insomuch that many of the most learned and judicious Grammarians, disgusted with absurdity and contradictions, have prudently contented themselves with remarking the differences of words, and have left the causes of language to shift for themselves.'[1] In the conversation which frames the argument of *The Diversions of Purley* Horne Tooke deliberately exploits the ambiguities of the term *grammar*: though grammar is 'usually among the first things taught it is always one of the last understood'.[2] The wide sense in which he wishes to use the term becomes apparent: Grammar is 'absolutely necessary in the search after philosophical truth'.[3] Yet the only grammars which his interlocutor can offer him are those of Ben Jonson, Lowth or Harris. Horne Tooke rejects these, and when pressed reveals the full depth of meaning he is attaching to the term *grammar*. 'I very early found it, or thought I found it, impossible to make many steps in the search after truth and the nature of human understanding, of good and evil, of right and wrong, without well considering the nature of language.'[4] But the starting-point for his inquiry is not to be in philosophy. 'Hermes, you know, put out the eyes of Argus: and I suspect that he has likewise blinded philosophy...If therefore Philosophy herself has been misled by Language, how shall she teach us to detect his tricks?'[5] Horne Tooke gives no definition of grammar, but nothing less than 'a consideration of the nature of language' would have satisfied him.

Hermes may or may not have blinded James Harris, which is what Horne Tooke means; he certainly blinded Rowland Jones, whose *Circles of Gomer* (i.e. Hermes) was referred to earlier in this chapter.[6] Jones's last attempt to persuade the world to accept his theories was

---

[1] Tooke, (1786), 1829, I. 23.   [2] op. cit. p. 4.   [3] op. cit. p. 5.
[4] op. cit. p. 12.   [5] op. cit. p. 14.   [6] Above, p. 178.

The Io-Triads; or *the Tenth Muse*, published in 1773. Ios seem to be systems, magically connected with the number ten and with 'a dark point or intelligent omega, from whence all things flow'.[1] Amongst the many strange effects produced by the Ios is a definition of grammar as, 'a system of sculpture on the country, and their sounds'.[2] Rowland Jones is distractingly quotable. His first definition of grammar, in *Hieroglyfic*, was a long-winded version of the ordinary definition, but he managed to make it memorable by suggesting, during the course of it, that ἐντελέχεια meant 'intelligent echo'.[3] Yet there is common ground between Rowland Jones and Horne Tooke, on which we also stand. Like them, we are still involved in a puzzling enquiry, 'it being', as Rowland Jones says, 'somewhat difficult to conceive how symbols, sounds, ideas, and things, naturally correspond with each other; how the few characters of our alphabet can be sufficient to express all things'.[4] How far should philosophical questions, or at least logical questions, be excluded from grammar as taught in a vernacular? If such questions are to be included should the resulting study be called grammar?

Evidence from subsidiary contents. It will have been evident already that the grammars considered in this study include works of widely varying character. This, and an even greater variation in their quality, is still apparent in their subsidiary contents.

The most frequent subsidiary section is one on punctuation, which appears first in Charles Butler's *English Grammar*, 1633. Punctuation is included in about sixty per cent of the grammars, taken over the whole period; the proportion is a little higher during the middle of the eighteenth century and rather lower during its last decade. More specifically rhetorical material, such as figures of speech and exercises in resolution and transposition, is much less frequent during the seventeenth century, increases during most of the eighteenth and declines towards the end. During the first half of the eighteenth century between fifty and sixty per cent of the grammars included rhetorical material, but during the last decade (when over 60 grammars were produced) the proportion fell to one third. During the whole of the eighteenth century a small number of grammars included passages, usually of prose, from writers chosen for their

[1] R. Jones, *The Io-Triads*, 1773, p. 8.
[2] op. cit. p. 27.
[3] R. Jones, *Hieroglyfic*, 1768, p. 11.
[4] R. Jones, *The Io-Triads*, p. 12.

devotional, moral or literary worth.[1] Such passages appear first in the second edition, 1712, of Brightland and Gildon's grammar. Much more frequent (and worth a short diversion) are the examples of bad English which were usually given as exercises for correction. Lists of solecisms had been given by Howell, 1662, and by Christopher Cooper, 1685, but these were errors of pronunciation rather than of syntax. Anne Fisher, in her grammar of 1749, incorporated some 'exercises of false English' supplied by an anonymous teacher in Carlisle in imitation of those in Nathan Bailey's *English and Latin Exercises*, 1706, and John Clarke's *New Grammar of the Latin Tongue*, 1733, where faulty Latin had to be corrected. Exercises of this kind became very popular.[2] Not only were ad hoc sentences set for correction, but passages of natural prose were distorted and defaced in the hope that their stylistic merits or their factual content would, after suitable childish manipulation, still have an improving effect. What the pupil was asked to handle might be improbable English, but simple in meaning: 'Death is all Men Fate'.[3] It might be improbable and scarcely comprehensible: 'Careless boys tears his best books; for which attentive teachers corrects them.'[4] Or it might be more full of errors than, presumably, even the writer of the grammar knew, as in an extract added (whether as a literary puzzle or for moral elevation is not made clear) to an early nineteenth-century edition of Fisher's grammar:

> The Cloud-capt Towers,
> The gorgeous Palaces,
> The solemn Temples,
> The great Globe itself,
> Yea, all which it inherits,
>   Shall dissolve:
> And, like the baseless Fabric of a Vision,
> Leave not a Wreck behind.
>
> A HYMN[5]

[1] A modern reader finds them depressing but the response of children may have been much what it would be now. In Dilworth's *A New Guide to the English Tongue*, 1740, there is a section 'Sentences in Verse', the first of which is headed 'Life is short and miserable'. Down the inner margin of the page in a copy of the nineteenth edition, 1757, a childish hand has written, 'as miss Patty got the Ball'. The reply, written underneath, appears to be, 'yes dont talk'.

[2] Many teachers were objecting to them by the end of the century, but even in 1803 the titlepage of Mark Anthony Meilan's *An Introduction to the English Language* can boast of 'an appendix containing Five Hundred Violations of Grammar'.

[3] Fisher, 2nd edn 1750, p. 129.   [4] Pape, 1790, p. 39.

[5] *Fisher's Grammar, improved*, 1806, p. 200.

Other subsidiary material is less impòrtant. Lists of words pro-
nounced or spelt alike are often included in the seventeenth-century
grammars. They appear first in Butler, and in six other grammars
before 1700. They are less common in eighteenth-century grammars,
being kept usually to the spelling books. Other features are occasionally found: lists of abbreviations, examples of handwriting, the super-
scription of letters, snatches of history and geography, and in one
case logic. These scarcely affect the general picture. All these subsidiary features throw light not so much on the term *grammar* as on
the development of grammar-books. But the two are, of course,
connected. The grammar-books became more specialised as different
aspects of English teaching, and of the so-called English subjects,
developed greater autonomy. During the seventeenth century
rhetoric had been still a distinct subject, with its own textbooks.
During the first three-quarters of the eighteenth century its independence seems to have weakened, and more rhetorical material was put
into the grammars. But towards the end of the century, under the
influence of Campbell[1] and Blair,[2] rhetoric was considered more
important, and in fresh forms it appeared in separate textbooks,
literary rather than grammatical.

CONCLUSION

The English grammars show the same tendency which appears
in the tradition. On the one hand they apply the term *grammar*
to a wide range of studies;[3] on the other they restrict it to the classification and analysis of words. It is difficult to generalise with
certainty, because the contents of the books reflect more than their
authors' conception of grammar: they reflect also a growing demand
for English teaching, and the beginning of specialisation in English
textbooks. Until we know something about the quantitative development of spelling-books, rhetorics and books of extracts we must be
cautious about following the evidence of the grammars alone.
Nevertheless this evidence would seem to justify the following
observations:

[1] George Campbell, *The Philosophy of Rhetoric*, 1776 (but written at intervals since 1750).
[2] Hugh Blair, *Lectures on Rhetoric and Belles Lettres*, 1783 (but delivered annually at
Edinburgh for twenty-four years previously).
[3] Even in 1824 Thomas Martin's 'Catalogue of English Grammars' includes Sir
Thomas Wilson's *The Arte of Rhetorique* and Locke's *Essay*.

The English Categories

(i) The treatment of English grammar during the seventeenth century was more open and flexible, especially in relation to logic, than the dominance of Latin, and especially of Lily's grammar, has hitherto led us to suppose.

(ii) By the end of the seventeenth century Lily's grammar had forced on English grammars either conformity with the Latin tradition or a (very modest) revolt against it.

(iii) During the first two-thirds of the eighteenth century the closer association, in the textbooks, of rhetoric and grammar made for a unified conception of grammar in which literary elements had a place. But the idea of universal grammar made for a psychological, analytical and less literary treatment of grammar.

(iv) Throughout the English, as in the Latin, tradition, there is a recurring tendency for discussion conducted in the name of grammar to become discussion of language.

(v) The idea that grammar is fundamentally concerned with communication appears explicitly in the English grammars at least as early as the middle of the eighteenth century, but had always been implicit in its definition as 'the art of speaking and writing well'. One feature of the whole tradition, classical and English, is that grammarians so often reproduced this broad definition at the beginning of their work and repudiated it by the narrowness of every subsequent paragraph. No doubt they interpreted 'well' more narrowly than we do, but for many writers the definition was a conventional gesture. They did not check their own work against it.

(vi) We need to remember how difficult it was for the early English grammarians to see English, as a language, as clearly as they saw Latin. They could not easily scrutinise the language in which they thought.

(vii) Until well into the eighteenth century the cultural dominance of Latin was embodied in the word *grammar*. This also has made it difficult for English to develop a grammar of its own.

(viii) We need to remember also (though this is more evident in later chapters) that the area of meaning surrounding *grammar* scarcely included the historical and developmental aspects which our use of the term takes for granted.

(ix) Although there is among the grammars greater variety than is commonly supposed, and intimations of ideas which we regard as modern, we must not underestimate the massive uniformity which is their most striking (but not their most significant) characteristic.

The development of grammars during the seventeenth and eighteenth centuries shows again, what was so plain in the tradition, that *grammar* was an elastic and ambiguous term. It could mean the study of a vernacular, or of a foreign language; it could mean 'parts of speech', with or without syntax; it could mean 'the study of language in use', at the everyday or at the literary level; it could mean the study of language itself. That grammar should have such an elastic significance is only natural: it may seem over-elaborate to document its elasticity in detail. But elasticity is something we have lost. We have allowed ourselves to accept an interpretation of *grammar* which is narrow, rigid and yet imprecise; we argue fiercely about its utility, and eye our grammatical forebears with sour respect. All the sourness, and some of the respect, is misplaced. Most of our forebears were, like ourselves, more ignorant than they need have been, and they were all necessarily more ignorant about language than we are. But they did adjust their conception of grammar to the circumstances they were in. One lesson of the tradition is that the study of language and the study of literature must illuminate each other. By keeping flexible the reference of the term *grammar* the eighteenth-century grammarians achieved a theoretical unity which in practice they almost always ignored. Our practice is better than theirs, but it is hampered by an inappropriate and inadequate linguistic theory, the chief defect of which is too narrow a conception of grammar.

James Elphinston should close this chapter. His own summary of his work, at the end of his vast *Principles of the English Language Digested: or English Grammar reduced to Analogy*, 1765, brings together almost all the themes of this widely spread discussion. His comprehensive outlook is not representative of his time, but it is one of the oldest elements in the tradition:

Thus it has been endeavoured to investigate and ascertain the ENGLISH LANGUAGE, in all its parts of *Orthoepy* and *Orthography*, *Etymology*, *Syntax*, *Prosody*; or more intelligibly, of *speaking* and *writing*, of *formation*, *construction*, and *versification*; not only to fix literal propriety, but to digest the figures of Rhetoric, as well as the language of Poetry; to communicate talent and inspire taste, by pointing what is to be avoided, and what to be imitated, by furnishing at once the precept and the power, and evincing, through the whole, every questionable assertion by Reason along with Example. Such has been the attentive execution of that Plan, which could alone fix a standard for instability, or promise permanence to a living tongue; and which by laying the foundation of UNIVERSAL GRAMMAR, anticipates the line of every Language. (Elphinston, 1765, II. 477–8.)[1]

---

[1] It was of Elphinston that Dr Johnson said, 'He has the most *inverted* understanding of any man whom I have ever known.' (*Life*, ed. Hill and Powell, III, 379.)

8. SYSTEMS OF PARTS
OF SPEECH

We have at present an infinite number of English grammars; but few of them are worth reading. They are filled with beggarly elements, mere technical terms and phrases, dry definitions, scholastic subtilties and rules attended with innumerable exceptions. The authors seem to have had no idea of applying their directions to any valuable purpose.[1]

UNCERTAINTY AND DIVERSITY OF CLASSIFICATION

The tradition offered, with specious unanimity and overwhelming authority, one system of parts of speech, with which every grammarian had been made familiar in his childhood. The earliest statement about the parts of speech in an English grammar, by William Bullokar, is emphatic, and firmly within the tradition: 'There is no one word to be uttered in our speech, but it is one of the eight parts before mentioned.'[2] Most English grammars followed the Latin in beginning with an enumeration: 'there are so-many parts of speech...' and the list followed. It would seem a simple matter to identify the system of classification used by each grammarian, and to record the variety of systems used by them all. But there are difficulties.

Inconsistency. The very weight of the tradition created difficulty. It crushed, without concealing, the ambiguities and uncertainties of its own classification. The result was inconsistency in the writer. Jonson enumerates the traditional eight parts and adds the article as a ninth, but discusses it among the pronouns;[3] he is obliged to say that interjections are 'in right' adverbs,[4] that pronouns are 'irregular nouns'[5] and that prepositions are a kind of adverb.[6] The grammarian

---

[1] *Crit. Rev.* 32, October 1771, referring to M. A. Meilan's *A Grammar of the English Language.*
[2] Bullokar, 1586, p. 339.
[3] Jonson, 1640, Bk 2, chap. 3.
[4] op. cit. Bk 1. chap. 21.
[5] op. cit. Bk 1. chap. 15.
[6] op. cit. Bk 1. chap. 21.

who obediently listed the participle among his parts of speech on the same footing as, and therefore distinct from, the verb and the adjective, could nevertheless maintain that it partook of the nature of both. He might, even so, include the participle in the conjugation of his verbs without referring to it in his discussion of the adjective. According to the evidence of what he does, he seems to be classifying the participle not as a separate part of speech but as a form of the verb. The articles did not form a part of speech in the Latin tradition, but clearly have a significant function in English. Some writers who do not include them in their preliminary enumeration, nevertheless discuss them as if they had the same status as parts of speech. Similarly, some writers who include in their enumeration the noun, but not the adjective—which traditionally must mean that the substantive and adjective are to be regarded as subordinate categories within the noun—nevertheless treat them in the body of the grammar just as if they were primary categories. Amongst those grammarians who advocate a fourfold system of parts of speech there are several who call the fourth category the particle but discuss its four constituents (the adverb, preposition, conjunction and interjection) exactly as if they were primary parts of speech under the Latin system. In such cases as these it is often difficult to know when a classification implied by the arrangement of material has become actual and should take precedence over an explicit, but nominal, enumeration. It has seemed wise to follow one consistent practice rather than to attempt in each case a judgment about the author's intentions for which there is often insufficient evidence. Precedence is therefore given to the author's formal enumeration, but other classifications clearly implied by his practice are also recorded.

Incompleteness. A second difficulty lies in the fact that not all the grammarians enumerate their parts of speech. This may be because they are taking the traditional system for granted: even so it makes it difficult to know how they regard, at the very least, the adjective, article, participle and interjection. It may be, however, that some writers refrain from enumeration because they are aware that the tradition leads them into inconsistency, and they see, more or less clearly, that one way to mitigate this inconsistency is not to postulate a definite number of mutually exclusive word-classes. If this were the unformulated view of any writer it would be misrepresentation for us to infer from the arrangement of his material any system of parts of speech. He might more truly be said to be implying the rejection of the whole concept of 'system'. This is particularly true of Wallis, whose important and influential grammar was first published in 1653.

Wallis is writing in Latin, and assumes in his reader a knowledge of Latin grammar. He also assumes that English and Latin have many technical terms in common:

Nollem exspectetis ut singula artis vocabula, quae Grammaticae Anglicanae cum aliarum linguarum Grammaticis sunt communia, sigillatim explicarem; ut Quid sit Nomen, Pronomen, Verbum, Participium, &c. Quid Substantivum, Adjectivum, Simplex, Compositum, Primitivum... Quid Genus, Casus, Numerus...aliaque similia. Esset plane supervacaneus labor; cum nemo sit, Latinae linguae non prorsus ignarus, qui isthaec ignorare possit. (Wallis, 1653, p. 68.)

On the other hand his grammar is important just because it is the first to point out that the classical languages cannot necessarily be taken as a pattern for English: 'Neque tamen exspectetis vellem, ut in hac lingua nostra omnia Latinorum linguae penitus respondeant. Est enim tum in hac tum in modernis fere omnibus, a Graecae Latinaeque linguae syntaxi immanis discrepantia.'[1] It is significant that it is a difference in syntax which Wallis stresses, not only here but in his preface; he nowhere suggests that there is need in English for a different system of parts of speech. It is at this point that care is necessary. There is no doubt that Wallis is cautiously seeking to give English a grammar in its own right. His attitude towards the classification of words will be a significant part of his attitude towards English grammar. As he does not enumerate his parts of speech it is in the arrangement of his material that evidence must be found for that attitude, which will lie somewhere among a group of three possibilities: (i) accepting the Latin system; (ii) inclining towards some fresh system; (iii) inclining towards the rejection of any system.

Some parts of speech Wallis treats in separate chapters: the substantive, article, adjective, pronoun and verb. But this is not in itself conclusive evidence, as he gives a chapter each to incomplete and to complete auxiliary verbs, and to the comparison of adjectives. He also says that pronouns are really nouns,[2] and that articles are really adjectives;[3] but comments of this kind are made by many

---

[1] Wallis, 1653, p. 68.   [2] op. cit. p. 86.
[3] op. cit. p. 71. Here Horne Tooke scribbled in the margin of his copy, 'Wallis not aware of the nature of adjectives'.

writers: they are more a sign of strain in the system than of indecision in the writer. But if we take account of Wallis's admitted conservatism—'(nolo) praeter necessitatem quidpiam innovare'[1]—it is safe to say that he is accepting those of the traditional parts of speech to which he has given separate chapters. He treats the preposition, also, in a separate chapter, immediately following that on the articles, because the preposition is so closely associated with the noun. But we cannot safely assume that the preposition is treated as a primary part, because he also discusses it, together with the adverb, conjunction and interjection, in the last of his chapters on the classification of words. To treat these four parts in one chapter suggests very strongly that Wallis is grouping them together as particles, which Gill had done more than thirty years earlier. But Wallis nowhere uses the term. His comment on these parts of speech is emphatic enough, but can be taken as support either for grouping them into one category, or for rejecting such categorisation altogether. Wallis says:

Si quis tamen harum aliquot voces [i.e. conjunctions] potius Adverbia esse dicat; aut etiam ex Adverbiis aliquot ad Conjunctionum classem referre malit: non tanti est ut hac de re quis contendat, cum, et apud Latinos, eadem non raro vox nunc pro Adverbio, nunc pro Conjunctione censenda est. Neque forsan aliquod grave detrimentum pateremur, si tam Adverbia quam Conjunctiones et Interjectiones, ad eandem classem redigerentur. Est quidem nonnihil discriminis, sed leviusculum. (1653, p. 110.)

This passage is typical of Wallis. It shows a natural deference to the authority of Latin, together with a relaxed, pragmatic attitude towards classification such as is found in few grammarians before the nineteenth century. In so far as Wallis is grouping these four parts of speech together he is anticipating a fourfold system—a consciously reforming system—which appears at the end of the century. If Wallis is, however tentatively, suggesting the futility of any system using the traditional parts of speech he is anticipating a comparatively modern judgment. Wallis was an acute enough critic to have formed such a view, but the tone of his work as a whole suggests that he would have found distasteful any such radical assault on tradition. That he was, however, 'inclining towards some fresh system' there seems to be no doubt at all.

Evidence from the arrangement of material is seldom as ambiguous

---

[1] op. cit. Preface, sig. A 8.

as in the case of Wallis, and is sometimes quite certain. Butler, 1633, though not enumerating his parts of speech, makes their rank clear. Of his third chapter, *Of Words*, the second section is headed *Of a Noun*; of this second section the three subsections are headed *Of a Noun Substantive*, *Of a Noun Adjective*, *Of a Pronoun*. Then follows the third section of the chapter, headed *Of a Verb*. In this instance noun and verb are clearly to be treated as primary parts of speech, and the pronoun as a secondary one. Sometimes there is no evidence at all. Thomas Cooke, 1775?, has four parts of speech: names, adjectives, verbs, particles. He discusses the use of the articles, which he calls by that name, but he nowhere says how he would classify them. There would be precedent for including them within any of his categories, except the verb, or for excluding them altogether.

Not every writer advocates just one system. Smetham, 1774, includes three distinct grammars in one book. The first is a grammar designed for English alone; the second is a versified form of the first; the third is a grammar designed for those going on to learn Latin. The first two of these use the same system of parts of speech, but the third has a different one. Wynne, 1775, gives the traditional eightfold classification first, but expresses a cautious preference for a fourfold one.[1] Groombridge says that words are divided 'by grammarians' into nine classes, but are divided 'naturally' into three.[2] James Douglas, *c.* 1720, proposes, at different times, four different classifications. Lister Metcalfe and J. Haywood take the opportunity of a new edition of their grammars to change the classification of the parts of speech.[3]

A writer will occasionally contradict himself so completely that no simple change of opinion is enough to explain the inconsistency. Mark Lewis, whose grammatical writings have survived in a fragmentary state, enumerates the traditional eight parts of speech: noun, pronoun, verb, participle, adverb, conjunction, preposition, interjection.[4] In the *Essay*, 1674, he says on page one that the six parts of speech, substantive, adjective, preposition, adverb, verb and conjunction 'will serve well enough for us to express our thoughts by fully and distinctly', but on page six he returns to the eightfold classification. It is probable that his first classification in the *Essay*

---

[1] See below, system 52. p. 271.   [2] Groombridge, 1797, p. 19.
[3] See below, Systems 18 and 10, pp. 234 and 225.
[4] Lewis, *Institutio*, 1670, sig. A 2.

was intended primarily for English, or at least for universal grammar, and that the second was intended for Latin. But in another edition of the *Essay*, of unknown date, he advocates a different system of six primary parts: in this case the noun, pronoun, verb, participle, adverb and conjunction. He further complicates this system by saying that it is really fivefold, because it is not worth while to distinguish between adverb and conjunction: 'it matters not much which the Child calls it'.[1] In 1675 he is recommending, in the *Vestibulum*, a still smaller number of primary parts: 'I conceive less than five parts of Speech are sufficient for us to express our thoughts by in any Language in the world.'[2] Nevertheless he immediately enumerates exactly five parts: substantive, adjective, verb, preposition and conjunction, and soon afterwards[3] he is referring to the adverb as if it was a part of speech of the same rank as those he has just mentioned.

Violent contradictions in other grammars are usually caused by hasty compilation or pilfering from different writers following incompatible systems.

Primary and secondary parts of speech. In describing the systems it is necessary to distinguish between primary and secondary parts of speech. This is seldom because the writers are following a fully considered theory of language. On the contrary, most of them take for granted the traditional eight or ten parts and form their systems by grouping the familiar parts in varying combinations variously emphasised. By a primary part of speech is here meant one which is included in a writer's enumeration; by a secondary part of speech one which is included within a primary category, either by name or by reference to its traditional content. If there is no enumeration there is usually some internal evidence to show whether any parts of speech are being put into a subordinate position. The noun, for example, is always a primary part of speech, whether it is used in the Latin sense (comprising substantive and adjective as secondaries) or as a synonym for substantive. The substantive and adjective are sometimes regarded as secondary parts and sometimes as primaries. The interjection is occasionally included within the adverb, either by name, as by Maittaire,[4] who calls *lo* and *behold* interjections but says

---

[1] Lewis, *Essay*, 1670, p. 4. An echo of Wallis?   [2] Lewis, *Vestibulum*, 1675, sig. A 4.
[3] op. cit. sig. A 5.   [4] Maittaire, 1712, p. 103.

they must be classed as adverbs, following the practice of the Greeks, or by implication, as by Butler,[1] who does not use the term *interjection* but includes *lo* and *behold* among the examples of his primary category of adverb.

Variations in arrangement. This illustrates another difficulty. By classifying among the adverbs the *content* of the traditional category of interjection, but without using that term, Butler implies a repudiation of the category itself. In this he appears to differ significantly from Maittaire, who accepts and names the category but puts it in a subordinate position. The difference is not as real as it seems. Butler classes among the adverbs also those words 'that join sentences and their parts, together', and his examples include *but, and,* and *or.* In the margin, however, he prints the heading 'Conjunction'. His treatment of the content of the two categories, interjection and conjunction, is the same, except for this marginal heading. It would be reading too much into his text to say that he repudiates the category of interjection, in any status, but accepts that of conjunction in a secondary one. The Latin grammarians had made the interjection into too definite a category for an English grammarian to intend that his return to the Greek classification should in itself be interpreted as a repudiation of the whole conception of the interjection as a category. If Butler had meant such a positive attack on the Latin tradition he would have had to make it more explicit. His classification, therefore, can safely be treated as equivalent to Maittaire's. But scrutiny of this kind is necessary because incipient dissatisfaction with the tradition is expressed far more through variations in arrangement and classification than through direct discussion.

Some writers, as Gildon and Brightland,[2] and Loughton,[3] who include the interjection within the category of adverb, include the adverb within their primary category of particle. In such cases the interjection is here referred to as a tertiary category.

Variations in terminology. There is considerable variation in the names given to the different parts of speech. *Adnoun* and *quality*, for example, are sometimes used as synonyms for *adjective*, *affirmation* for verb, and *relative* for pronoun. So that it will be easier to compare the systems the names of the parts of speech have, in the summary tables, been

---

[1] Butler, 1633, p. 53.   [2] G–B, 1711, p. 119.   [3] Loughton, 1734, p. 99.

made as uniform as possible, and in agreement with the tradition. Only two categories need comment: *noun* here always means the primary category including substantive and adjective; *pronoun*, the category whose content is least clearly defined, refers, as a basic minimum, to the personal pronouns. The terminology actually used by individual writers is described in the chapters on the separate parts of speech.

The force of the tradition is so great that even genuinely new categories, such as Kirkby's *adjunctive*, are usually expressed in terms of the traditional parts. Kirkby himself describes the adjunctive as being 'either an Adjective properly so called [which he has previously defined] or a Verb'.[1] Harris has a similar primary category, the *attributive*, which is a carefully thought-out innovation, not just a conflation of existing categories; but even he makes it permissible, for the present comparison, to express the category in traditional terms. After defining attributives as 'all those principal Words that denote Attributes, considered as Attributes' he says in a note that they include 'what Grammarians called Adjectives, Verbs, and Participles, inasmuch as all of them equally denote the Attributes of Substance'.[2] It is clear, though, that he regards this description of the new category in terms of the old as a concession to a timid reader, for he says, in introducing his four primary categories, 'If any of these Names seem new and unusual, we may introduce others more usual, by calling...the Attributives, *Verbs*',[3] which is so rough an approximation that it omits the adjectival function altogether.

We are accustomed in English and Latin to a system of eight parts of speech. Most people are aware that some variation of this number was possible within the tradition, but the diversity of systems among the English grammarians is surprising. Of the 259 relevant grammars some classify the parts of speech in alternative systems, so that there are in all 275 classifications. These classifications fall into no fewer than 56 different systems.

Diversity of systems. It is the purpose of the present chapter to display and document both this diversity of classification and the instability of the parts of speech, of which it is in part a consequence. But first it must be asked how real the diversity is. Is it perhaps just a product of the method used to describe the systems, significant of an

---

[1] Kirkby, 1746, p. 57.   [2] Harris, 1751, p. 87.   [3] op. cit. p. 31.

over-refinement of analysis rather than of any genuinely linguistic condition? The diversity exists; it can be dismissed only if it is thought to express merely trivial variations on the solid basis of the accepted ten parts of speech. But a distinction needs to be made. It is a matter of very little importance, in relation to his life's work, that John Wesley in 1748 classifies the parts of speech in a system used by only one other writer of a grammar, Cave Beck, 1657, who was probably unknown to him. It is not nearly so trivial a question to ask how it was possible for a well-educated man in the middle of the eighteenth century to be an apparently unconscious innovator in such a longstanding matter as the parts of speech. The short answer is that the range of possible variation was so great that any given combination might chance to be unique. But it is surely very odd for so much variation to be possible within a discipline which is commonly supposed to be governed by a centuries-old tradition.

Instability of categories. The diversity is caused not only by the number of unstable parts of speech but also by the degree of their instability. It is not that there are peripheral variations round a firmly agreed centre. The only possible centre is the combination of verb and sub-stantive (and Dalgarno would not accept even that—see System 26). But the substantive is in an ill-defined and unstable relation with the adjective, the pronoun and the article; the verb is in an unstable relation with the participle and the adjective. The preposition is one of the most stable parts of speech, because its function is precise (or can be so regarded if attention is fixed on the expression of spatial relations) but even it is sometimes included within the adverb, within the verb, as part of the substantive, and within the particle, and is itself made to include the articles. The article is associated with, or included in, the substantive, the adjective, the pronoun, the preposi-tion, as well as being treated as a particle and as a primary part of speech. These are not trivial differences if the validity of the categories is assumed: as it usually was by the writers.

The grammars are neither numerous nor homogeneous enough for statistical treatment to be appropriate. But their number is too large to be handled except in tabular form. Two sets of tables, accordingly, are given in Appendix I and Appendix II.[1]

Appendix I shows the number and variety of ways in which the

[1] See below, pp. 521 ff.

parts of speech were grouped into systems. It shows the components of each system, the number of grammars in which it was adopted, and the dates of the first editions of the earliest and latest grammars in which each system appears. As the dates are in any case only a rough guide to the development of the systems the fact that some terminal dates are only approximate is not indicated in the tables but appears in the account of the appropriate system. The systems are arranged in four groups and in chronological order within each group.

The systems

(i) *Latin systems.* The first of these Latin systems is the traditional system as found in Lily, and the nineteen others are minor variations of it. The variations are often unwitting, and do not suggest any desire to modify the system substantially, far less to reform it. They are latinate and conservative.

(ii) *Modified systems before* 1700. These vary greatly. They range from Greaves' (No. 21), which might be counted a Latin system (if its modifications are not considered substantial) to the deliberate innovations of Dalgarno and Wilkins (Nos. 26 and 27). These systems all (except No. 29) precede the appearance of the following distinctive group of modified systems:

(iii) *Vernacular systems.* These are deliberate modifications of the Latin systems, which they profess to reform. They agree in proposing four primary parts of speech (substantive, adjective, verb, particle) though they vary in their distribution of the secondary parts. They are here called 'vernacular' systems because they are closely associated with the reforming movement which sought to give English a grammar in its own right.[1]

(iv) *Modified systems after* 1700. These modifications appeared after the introduction of the vernacular systems of the previous group but did not use their distinctive fourfold classification. They range from thoughtful attempts at reform to the constructions of ignorance and eccentricity. The relation between primary and secondary parts of speech is shown in three ways: (i) 'including' (incl.) is a relation between two customary parts of speech. When, for example, the substantive is said to include the pronoun this means that words like *he* and *they* are to be considered as a kind of substantive; (ii) 'com-

---

[1] See below, chap. 17.

prising' (compr.) is a relation between a descriptive or ad hoc part of speech and several customary ones. The particle, for example, comprises a number of parts such as the preposition and conjunction; (iii) 'with' expresses the relation between article and substantive. The article is said to be 'with' the substantive when it is being treated as a 'sign of a case' or a vaguely logical appendage, and is often being excluded from the enumerated parts of speech.[1]

Appendix II is designed to show the instability of most parts of speech. Each part of speech is shown in the different forms it takes, that is, according to its different constituents and according to whether it is classed as a primary or as a secondary part. The number of grammars is listed in which each part of speech is used in each of its forms. Two alternative systems suggested in the same grammar have been treated separately, as have different works by the same author, even if they use the same system, which they some-times do not. The works of Mark Lewis and Mrs Lovechild (*c.* 1798) are exceptions. Three of Lewis's, the *Institutio* and the two versions of the *Essay* (which propose different systems) represent him, and three out of Mrs Lovechild's four (one of which refers to an alterna-tive system) give her sufficient weight. The various totals are not significant except as being 'large' or 'small'. The totals in the two sets of tables do not always correspond, because in some grammars there is no evidence for the classification of some parts of speech, and in some of the alternative systems no information is given about the secondary parts.

Other information can be found in the tables. For example, in order to know in how many grammars the interjection is treated as an adverb, see *Interjection* in Appendix II, where (*c*) and (*e*) record the number of grammars and give cross-references to the different primary categories within which the adverb is classified when itself including the interjection. But the main purpose of the tables is to present the detailed evidence for believing that practically all the parts of speech, on the testimony of those who used them, were much more unstable than has been realised. This instability is more than a matter of definition. It is a radical instability: not only does it seem

---

[1] e.g. 'The *Article* stands *with* a *Noun*,
And shows us its extent;
A, is indefinite; *A* Town;
The, *definite*; *The* Rent.'
(Williams, 1780?, p. 5.)

hard to draw boundaries between the different categories, it seems almost impossible.

In this chapter each system is examined in turn. The grammars which adopt it are listed (this makes austere reading, but the information is essential for any consideration of development) and the writers' comments on their classifications are discussed. Appendix III[1] shows which system each author supports, and which authors support more than one system.

Novel categories. The fifty-six systems contain many categories bearing traditional names which are nevertheless unique combinations of secondary parts of speech. Charles Butler, for example, is the only grammarian to include both interjection and conjunction within the primary category of adverb (System 23). Such innovations, and other combinations which are unusual but not unique, are described here (as they were conceived by their authors) in terms of the traditional categories; they are the evidence which shows how unstable these categories were. There are, however, other parts of speech which are offered as more explicit novelties; they are named, not after one of the traditional categories, but in some new way. Even though they are formed, in fact, by the combination or conflation of traditional categories they represent an attempt to break away from the tradition and are worth listing as evidence not only of instability among the categories but also of dissatisfaction among the writers. These novel categories are described in the account of the authors' systems of parts of speech:[2]

Word of Action. Compr. substantive and verb (Lodowyck, 1652; System 24).

Word of Help. Compr. adverb, pronoun, preposition, conjunction and interjection (ibid.).

Substitutive particle. Compr. pronoun and interjection (Wilkins, 1668; System 27).

Connexive particle. Compr. preposition and article (ibid.).

'Other' particles. Compr. some adverbs and the conjunction (ibid.).

Sign or *particle.* Compr. article, interjection, auxiliary verb, preposition, some adverbs, etc. (*True Method*, 1696; System 30).

Noun Epithet. A secondary part, compr. adjective and participle (Hugh Jones, 1724; System 42).

[1] See below, pp. 536 ff.   [2] See below, pp. 214 f.

Adnoun. Compr. adjective, pronoun and participle (Saxon, 1737; System 37).

Adjunctive. Compr. adjective (incl. article) and verb (incl. participle) (Kirkby, 1746; *Practice* 1750?; System 43).

Attributive. Compr. verb. adjective, participle, adverb (incl. interjection) (Harris, 1751; System 44).

Definitive. Compr. articles and words like *this, any, some, other, all* (Harris; 'Mica', 1793; Systems 44 and 54).

Conjunctive. Compr. conjunction and preposition (ibid.).

Sub-quality; Comparative. Compr. (i) words which limit adjectives; (ii) words which limit adverbs (Meilan, 1771? System 50).

Manner. The use of this term is vague. The only statement which proves that it sometimes denoted an actual category is made by Gildon:

Chap. VIII. *Of the Manner of Words.* A Manner of a Word is a Part of Speech...that signifies the Manner, Circumstance, or Connection of Words, and are join'd to other Parts of Speech. It is known by this; that it admits not in good Sense, either the Signs of the several States of Names, as, *of, to*...nor the Personal Names...Tho' this be in my Opinion a sufficient Mark, to discover this Part of Speech; yet since others, have divided them into three Branches...I shall follow their Example. (G–B, 1711, p. 117.)

The three branches are adverbs, prepositions and conjunctions, so *manner* is here equivalent to *particle*. *Manner* had been used by Lodowyck in two examples to refer to *hastily* and *much*,[1] but it is not clear how widely he was using the term: it may be equivalent only to *adverb*. Mark Lewis had used *manner* almost as the name of a category, less wide than Gildon's: 'Adjectives are the manners of Substantives, and stand before them...Adverbs are the manners of Verbs...and are sometimes joyned to Adjectives, as the manners of those manners.'[2] Lewis would seem to be wishing to treat adjective and adverb as one category, whereas Gildon is thinking more of the adverb than of the adjective, and is extending the term *manner* so as to include those parts of speech usually associated with the adverb as particles. A source for Lewis's practice is perhaps the Port Royal grammar, in which those nouns are said to be adjectives 'qui signifient des substances, lors que par leur manière de signifier, ils

---

[1] Lodowyck, 1652, p. 15.
[2] Lewis, *Essay*, 1674, p. 1. OED records none of these uses.

The English Categories

doivent estre joints à d'autres noms dans le discours'.[1] Gildon also says, 'Qualities [i.e. adjectives] are the Manners of...Things, as *good, bad, round*',[2] but, as in the Port Royal grammar, which he is following, this is a philosophical rather than a grammatical statement.

LATIN SYSTEMS

SYSTEM I

NOUN (article with substantive)		ADVERB
PRONOUN		CONJUNCTION
VERB		PREPOSITION
PARTICIPLE		INTERJECTION

Bullokar	1586	*English Scholar*	1706	Fenning	1761
Hume	*c.* 1617	*Compleat*		J. Johnson	1762
Poole	1646	Sheridan	1714	Manson	1762
Wharton	1654	Harland (3rd edn)	1719	*Universal Dictionary*	1763
Newton	1669	Entick	1728	Bayley	1764
Lewis	1670	Owen	1732	Wiseman	1764
Lye	1671	Stirling	1735	Joel	1770
Lewis	1674	Dilworth	1740	Metcalfe (2nd edn)	1771
Newton	1677	Jas. Corbet	1743	Clarke	1772
Miege	1688	Merriman	1750	Smetham (*b*)	1774
Clare	1690	Bailey	1755	Wynne	1775
Aickin	1693	*Complete Letter*	1755	*English Grammar*	1776
R. Brown	1700	*Writer*		James Smith (3rd edn)	1778

This system, together with No. 5, is the 'purest' of the Latin systems. It is the one used by Lily, and represents the direct application of Latin to English. The article is attached to the noun (in ways which are discussed in chapter 11) without any attempt to incorporate it into the parts of speech: it is regarded as a tiresome particle about which there is little to be said.

Incomplete classification. Hume does not enumerate his parts of speech, nor discuss them all. The noun, verb, adverb and conjunction are treated as if they were primaries, the article as an attachment of the noun. The pronoun seems to be a primary, but may be treated as the article. Hume is more interested in his main division of words into personal (the noun and verb) and impersonal than in any further classification. It is probable that when he uses the names of other

---

[1] *Grammaire générale*, 1660, Bk 2. chap. 2. p. 31.   [2] G–B, 1711, p. 88.

parts of speech he is thinking of the Latin system in its commonest form.

In the group of identical grammars published in the 1760s (Fenning, Bayley, *Universal Dictionary* and J. Johnson) there is no evidence as to how the article is classified.

Alternative classifications. Mark Lewis, in the 1674 version of the *Essay*, enumerates six parts of speech in the 'English', that is the general, grammar, for which see System 6. The present system is used in his grammar for Latin, beginning on p. 6 of the *Essay*. Miege or his reviser, in an undated edition, recognises the claims of a reduced system, for which see System 22. Wynne, nearly a century later, expresses doubts about a Latin system and a cautious preference for a fourfold one (System 52). In Smetham, 1774, and the *English Grammar*, 1776, the present system is itself the alternative one, in a grammar intended specially for pupils who are going to learn Latin.

Grammarians' comments. Most writers take the system for granted. Up till about 1730, when there had appeared only four or five grammars following a vernacular system, such comment as there is refers to the precedent of Latin: 'Note, that I divided the Parts thus, on the account of the Method we use in teaching Latin, &c.'[1] Several writers slip in a reference even more casually: 'In English, as in Latin, there are Eight Parts of Speech.'[2]

> Master: How many Parts of Speech...are there in English?
> Scholar: Eight, just as many as in the Latin. (Entick, 1728, p. 1.)

After the middle of the century this was too disputed an opinion for a grammarian to offer it casually; Wiseman is the last to do so.[3] Other writers feel obliged to be defensive, either aggressively as Merriman, or in the mood of tolerant conservatism expressed by Dr Johnson and by Blair. Merriman's comments are worth quoting as one of the few judgments made by a grammarian about the rival approaches. He comments with severity on the reforming fourfold system and defends the traditional classification:

Some Grammarians have...rejected the usual Number of the Parts of Speech, and reduced them to fewer: While others, refusing both the

---

[1] R. Brown, 1700, added by the 3rd edn 1707.
[2] *English Scholar Compleat*, 1706, p. 1.   [3] Wiseman, 1764, p. 96.

Number and their Names, have introduced an entire new Plan. We shall not spend much Time, however, in enquiring into the Merits of either, but chiefly confine ourselves to those Reasons we have to offer for following the more received Method.

Most Grammarians have divided Speech into eight Parts; and those who have reduced them to four, have made a Sub-division of the last, which they call Particles, exactly agreeing with *Adverb, Preposition,* and *Conjunction.* But if this Sub-division was necessary, the other Division might well have remain'd, for any thing that appears to the contrary...The invincible Desire of introducing some new Model of Grammar, and of adapting it to the English Tongue, induced several Writers to lay aside the old Form, and to substitute a new Division of the Parts of Speech, and also new Names. But should it be granted that the old Form would admit of some Amendment, yet 'twere to be wished that those Gentlemen who undertook to make it had confined themselves to what was necessary, without introducing an entire new System. (Merriman, 1750, p. iii.)

Blair's lectures, first published in 1783, had been given at Edinburgh for twenty-four years. It is probable that his views on the parts of speech go back to the fifties and are contemporary with those of Merriman. Blair speaks as if the classification and terminology were being questioned, which was more true in 1750 than in 1780:

The common grammatical division of Speech into eight parts; nouns, pronouns, verbs, participles, adverbs, prepositions, interjections, and conjunctions; is not very logical, as might easily be shown; as it comprehends, under the general term of nouns, both substantives and adjectives, which are parts of Speech generically and essentially distinct; while it makes a separate part of speech of participles, which are no other than verbal adjectives. However, as these are the terms to which our ears have been most familiarised, and, as an exact logical division is of no great consequence to our present purpose, it will be better to make use of these known terms than of any other. (*Lectures on Rhetoric and Belles Lettres* (1783), 4th edn 1790, Lecture VIII, *Structure of Language.*)

SYSTEM 2

NOUN	ADVERB
PRONOUN	CONJUNCTION
ARTICLE	PREPOSITION
VERB (incl. participle)	INTERJECTION

Tomkis	1612	Spence	1775
J. Smith	1674	*A Short English Grammar*	1794
T. M.	1774	*Essay*	1800

This system differs from No. 1 in making the article a primary part of speech and including the participle within the verb.

There is no evidence for Tomkis's or Spence's classification of the interjection. Smith enumerates his parts of speech indirectly, by saying that he is concerned only with the article, noun, pronoun and verb; 'As for Adverbs, Conjunction [*sic*] Prepositions, and Interjections, it is enough to know their meaning, and that you may learn by proper Dictionaries.'[1] T.M. enumerates his parts of speech[2] without referring to the participle, which he elsewhere describes as 'one of the variations of a verb, which in effect is equal to an adjective'.[3] If this statement is taken as adequate evidence that T.M. included the participle within the adjective yet another, and unique, Latin system must be formed.

SYSTEM 3

NOUN (article with substantive, which incl. pronoun)	ADVERB
	CONJUNCTION
VERB	PREPOSITION
PARTICIPLE	INTERJECTION

Hewes 1624

It seems unlikely that Hewes, who is writing 'according to the use and analogie of the Latine', should make a system of his own. But no economy of classification can justifiably neglect the evidence he provides. He enumerates his parts of speech as: noun, verb, participle (declined); adverb, conjunction, preposition and interjection (undeclined).[4] He refers frequently to words which in Latin grammar would be pronouns, usually calling them 'persons' or 'relatives'. Even though Hewes seems to be following Sanctius and Ramus in refusing to give the pronoun the status of a part of speech he treats the *words* as a kind of noun.

System 4 (overleaf) differs from No. 1 in making the article a primary part of speech.

Alternative classifications. For Jonson's inconsistencies, which Evelyn in part follows, see above, p. 201, and for Adam's glance at an alternative threefold system see No. 22. Haywood enumerates his

---

[1] J. Smith, 1674, sig. A 3 recto.   [2] T.M., 1774, p. 63.
[3] op. cit. p. 41.   [4] Hewes, 1624, sig. B 3 verso.

SYSTEM 4	
NOUN	ADVERB
PRONOUN	CONJUNCTION
ARTICLE	PREPOSITION
VERB	INTERJECTION
PARTICIPLE	

Jonson	1640	W. Ward	1765	Marriott	1780
Evelyn	c. 1650	W. Ward	1767	John Corbet	1784
Howell	1662	Cooke	1771?	*Key to Spelling*	1788
Douglas	c. 1720	Du Bois	1771?	*Outlines*	1791
English Accidence	1733	Fenning	1771	Dearle	1792
New English	1736	Adam	1772	Huntley	1793
Accidence		Barlow	1772?	Haywood	1800
Fenning	1756	Bettesworth	1778		

parts of speech according to this system, but discusses substantive and adjective in sections whose headings and layout make them seem of equal status with the primary parts. It is not surprising that in his second edition, 1805, he makes substantive and adjective primaries. He also then takes the opportunity to include the participle explicitly within the verb. His revised classification is therefore that of System 10. Later editions of Cooke follow systems 35 and 41. For Douglas see also Systems 9, 10 and 22.

Grammarians' comments. The author of the *New English Accidence*, 1736, is apologetic for a venial deviation: 'I confess I have at the beginning added a Part of Speech more than is in the Latin Grammar; namely the Article.'[1] William Ward rejects new systems and new terms:

Some writers on grammar have divided words into more or fewer sorts than are here set down, and have given other names to the several sorts. But no real benefit ensues from such a proceeding; and therefore it is mere trifling, or worse, to put the learner to the trouble of learning a new grammatical language, when the old received terms of the art will answer the same end. (W. Ward, 1765, p. 320.)

This may be a natural attitude for a schoolmaster but it is curmudgeonly from the author of *An Essay on Grammar*, which puts its reader to a great deal of trouble. In both his works Ward explicitly says the article is a distinct part of speech,[2] but he does not really know what to do with it. In 1765 he discusses it merely as an attach-

---

[1] *New Eng. Acc.* 1736, preface.   [2] W. Ward, 1765, p. 2; 1767, p. 18.

ment of the noun,[1] and in 1767 he treats it with the pronouns, amongst which it 'may very properly be considered as belonging'.[2] Dearle rather smugly rejects innovation: 'Some authors have extended them [the parts of speech] to ten; some fix them at eight; and some comprise them under three classes, viz. Noun, Verb, and Adverb. But I go on to make the matter as plain as possible.'[3]

SYSTEM 5

NOUN (article with substantive)	ADVERB (incl. interjection)
PRONOUN	CONJUNCTION
VERB	PREPOSITION
PARTICIPLE	

Beck 1657 Wesley 1748

This system differs from No. 1 only in treating the interjection as a kind of adverb, as the Greeks had done.[4] There is no reason to suppose that Wesley's classification is in any way derived from Cave Beck.[5]

SYSTEM 6

SUBSTANTIVE (incl. pronoun)	ADVERB
ADJECTIVE	CONJUNCTION
VERB	PREPOSITION (incl. article)

Lewis, *Essay* 1670

Amongst Lewis's contradictions, already mentioned at the beginning of this chapter, the reference to this system is too explicit to be ignored. He excludes the participle and the interjection from the parts of speech because they are 'contracted sentences'. He includes the signs of the cases (and hence by implication, and in accordance with his practice elsewhere, the articles) among the prepositions. After referring, in a few words for each, to verb, substantive, preposition, adjective, adverb and conjunction, Lewis says, 'These six parts of Speech will serve well enough for us to express our thoughts by, fully and distinctly.'[6] The only category to which he does not refer is the pronoun; the secondary position which that must presumably hold is within the substantive.

---

[1] idem, 1765, p. 320.
[3] Dearle, 1792, p. 142.
[5] Above, p. 209.

[2] idem, 1767, p. 39.
[4] Above, p. 73.
[6] Lewis, *Essay*, 1674, p. 1.

This version of Lewis's *Essay* is perhaps the earliest work in which substantive and adjective are clearly separated as primary parts of speech. Clara Parker puts the separation too late when she says that Lowth's grammar, 1762, is 'the first of those retaining the traditional terms which separate the noun from the adjective',[1] and the more generally held view that Richard Johnson, in the *Grammatical Commentaries*, 1706, was the first to make the separation is not strictly accurate. Johnson was perhaps the first to defend it, but not the first to make it. If the separation is only implied by Wallis it is explicit in Lewis. If it is only implied by Dr Johnson it is explicit in Priestley, 1761. But the century between Wallis and Priestley is significant: it took all that time for the Latinists to see that the English adjective was a distinct part of speech. On the other hand the separate status of the adjective was characteristic of the vernacular systems, the first of which appeared in 1695.

Lewis is working his way through to the idea that English requires a separate system of categories from Latin. In this respect he is a bridge between the traditional systems and the vernacular systems. But his ideas are too fragmentary to be more than indications of an attitude: one wishes to accept the invitation he offers to 'those, that desire to see more of this Subject' who 'may be further satisfied by the Author, upon any Thursday at three of the Clock in the Afternoon, at the Tun and Bolt in Fleet-street'.[2]

SYSTEM 7

NOUN (adjective incl. article)	ADVERB
PRONOUN	CONJUNCTION
VERB	PREPOSITION
PARTICIPLE	INTERJECTION

W. Turner	1710	G. Wilson	1759	Buchanan	1767
Greenwood	1711	(2nd edn)		Sewell	1789
Duncan	1731	Buchanan	1762	Marshall	c. 1790
Barker	1733?	*British Letter*	1765?	Stapleton	1797
Greenwood	1737	*Writer*			
Buchanan	1753				

This system differs from No. 1 in treating the article as an adjective, not as the sign of a case or of a substantive.

[1] Parker, 1930, p. 234. [2] Lewis, *Rules*, 1675, p. 8.

Latin systems

Uncertain classification. Buchanan and Marshall illustrate the kind of uncertainty which often accompanies the classification of the article. Although Buchanan enumerates his parts of speech according to this system he treats substantive and adjective virtually as primaries, and though he says emphatically that the article is really an adjective he discusses it in the section on the substantive, not in that on the adjective. Marshall's first reference to the article immediately follows his discussion of substantives,[1] which suggests that he is treating it in the Latin style as the sign of a case and therefore as an attachment of the substantive. His second reference, however, in the syntax, is to make agreement between article and substantive the first of his three kinds of concord.[2] This makes sense only if the article is being treated as an adjective, and I have assumed that this is his view. William Turner treats only *an* as an adjective; *the* he treats as a pronoun.[3]

Comment. Buchanan defends the traditional system on traditional grounds:

As to the Parts of Speech, I have retained the Terms of the old Grammarians, as has been agreed on by the Learned in general, knowing it to be of much greater Ease to Boys that are to learn Latin, who, having but simple Ideas of Words, would easily be confounded by any unnecessary Alteration; and the Parts of Speech being the same in all Languages. (Buchanan, 1753, p. xii.)

Sewell is more aware that there is little agreement about the parts of speech: 'Scarce two Authors who write on the Subject of Grammar agree together, as to the Number of the Parts of Speech; some reckon five, some eight, some nine, and some ten.'[4] Nevertheless he is no advocate of reform:

The Grammatical Terms and Divisions have been long since generally adopted; and herein, I conceive, Gentlemen who write on the Subject of Grammar mistake their Point. Instead of more plainly methodizing the Parts of Grammar already received...Grammarians seem intent on introducing Innovations, and advancing Notions that tend rather to obscure the Science, than to render it more instructively plain to young Capacities.[5]

---

[1] Marshall, *c.* 1790, p. 150.
[2] op. cit. p. 156.
[3] W. Turner, p. 7.
[4] Sewell, 1789, pp. v–vi.
[5] ibid.

SYSTEM 8

NOUN	PARTICIPLE
PRONOUN	ADVERB (incl. interjection)
ARTICLE	CONJUNCTION
VERB	PREPOSITION

Maittaire   1712

This system differs from No. 4 only in the treatment of the interjection. Maittaire was a strict classicist and insisted on treating the
interjection as an adverb. His incidental comments are a reminder
that the classical tradition is not to be identified with the Latin
systems: it contains precedents for a reduced system.[1] Of the parts
of speech Maittaire says: 'In relation to what they are the signs of,
they are all chiefly reduced to two: Nouns, the signs of Things, and
Verbs and signs of Motions.'[2] And on the next page he brackets
together the adverb, conjunction and preposition as particles, which
term he uses throughout the grammar as a cross-category.

    System 9 (see facing page). Ash's is the first published grammar to
advocate this system, but it was anticipated by James Douglas's first
draft of his grammar, written after 1711. Douglas epitomises the uncertainty of so many grammarians about the parts of speech. In his first
draft he said, 'There are Ten different Sorts of Words in the English
Tongue, commonly called so many Parts of Speech' (System 9).[3]
Later he included the participle within the verb and corrected the
manuscript to read: 'English men make use of nine different Sorts
of Words, commonly called Parts of Speech' (System 10).[4] And in a
later manuscript he put the adjective back into the noun and wrote:
'There are Eight different Sorts of Words, called Parts of Speech'
(System 4).[5] For his further reduction of the parts or speech to three,
see System 22.

Uncertain classification. Trusler deliberately offers an incomplete
classification: 'The only words necessary to be known grammatically,
are Nouns, Pronouns, Adjectives, Verbs, Adverbs, and Participles...
These are the different parts of speech, I would wish my pupil to be

---

[1] cf. pp. 48 and 52 above.   [2] Maittaire, 1712, p. 22.
[3] Douglas, *c* 1720?, MS. No. 585. fol. 1 recto.
[4] ibid.   [5] idem, MS. No. 587 a. fol. 49 recto.

SYSTEM 9

SUBSTANTIVE	PARTICIPLE
ADJECTIVE	ADVERB
PRONOUN	CONJUNCTION
ARTICLE	PREPOSITION
VERB	INTERJECTION

Douglas	*c.* 1720?	Rothwell	1787	Lynch	1796
Ash	1760	*Rudiments*	1788	John Carter	1797
Art of Teaching in	*c.* 1770	Francis	1790	(5th edn)	
Sport		Pape	1790	Bullen	1797
Hodgson	1770	Trusler	1790?	*Encyclopedia*	1797
Tutor	1772	J. Wilson	1792	*Britannica* (B)	1797
Ash	1775	*Lily's Accidence*	1793	Kitson	1798
Devis	1775	*Improved*		Lovechild, *MG*	1798?
Harrison	1777	Nicholson	1793	Lovechild, *PY*	1798
E. Owen	1777	*Easy S.S.I.*	1794	and *PE*	
H. Ward	1777	*Short Grammatical*	1795	Lovechild, *CG*	1799
Wood	1777	*Introduction*		Bowen	1799
Merchant Maiden	1779	Crakelt/Entick	1795	Gardiner	1799
Williams	1780?	Rhodes	1795	Mayne	1799
Oliphant	1781	*Rudiments*	1795	*Pupils Friend*	1799
Trinder	1781	T. Wright,	1795?	(3rd edn)	
Beattie	1783	*Miscellany*		Eves	1800
Ireland	1784	T. Wright,	1795?	*Short and Easy*	1800
Knowles	1785	*Grammar*		*Rules*	
Harrold	1787	Coar	1796	Meilan	1803
(3rd edn)		Mrs Edwards	1796		
A. Murray	1787	J. G.	1796		
(2nd edn)					

acquainted with.'[1] He 'aims not at teaching his pupil what words are particles, what prepositions, and so on; but merely to avoid false concords and incorrect language'.[2] Trusler is not offering a new system; for pedagogical purposes he stops short of what he would regard as the full system, here taken to be that in which all the categories he refers to are treated as primaries.

The only other uncertainty occurs in the grammar of John Williams (before 1780) the explicitness of whose classification is handicapped by his writing in verse.

Alternative classifications. Harrison, 1777, does not comment on the classification, but by his sixth edition, 1794, he is explicitly including the article within the adjective (No. 19). Wood, 1777, supports

[1] Trusler, 1790?, pp. 1–2.   [2] op. cit. preface.

Harris's classification also (No. 44); H. Ward supports a fourfold classification (System 36); Bullen, 1797, sketches a threefold system (No. 55) which he dare not adopt, and Mrs Lovechild, in the preface to *Parsing Lessons for Young Children*, published the following year, quotes him approvingly. Meilan, 1803, describes the system he uses as 'the usual method of dividing English words', but continues by suggesting the 'much more just division'[1] which he had used in his earlier grammar (System 49).

Grammarians' comments. Wilson, the editor of Fisher's grammar, which first appeared in 1749 with a fourfold classification (No. 36), changed to this system 'for the sake of those...who learn the English Grammar either before or after any other, and to save them the trouble of getting a new set of Terms'.[2] Rhodes, 1795, makes about all grammarians the point which Merriman and Fogg make about the reforming, vernacular, systems in particular: 'Whether they say there are four parts of speech, or seven or eight, or nine, all, in general, make use of ten parts of speech in their explanation.'[3] The author of *Short and Easy Rules*, however, implied support for a reduced system by his recommendation that 'young pupils ought not to be required to distinguish beyond the first five parts of speech—but be allowed to sink the rest under the general appellation of particles'.[4] Henry Bullen is not happy with this tenfold system, which in fact he adopts:

If any Grammarian should feel disconcerted at hearing that there are ten parts of speech, let him remember that I write for children, not for critics. Properly speaking, perhaps, there are but three, the Substantive, the Adjective, and the Verb; but if we exclude all the other names, what account are we to give of them which would be intelligible to young minds? It is therefore thought preferable to multiply terms a little, than to take advantage of a simplicity which would be altogether obscure. (Bullen, 1797, p. 115.)

He recognises, but does not discuss, the weakness of the categories themselves:

In parsing English it is not to be expected that every word should upon all occasions preserve its proper title; there is a certain blending of the parts of speech by which each sort of words is connected with the rest...

---

[1] Meilan, 1803, p. 3.   [2] J. Wilson, 1792, p. v.
[3] Rhodes, 1795, p. 7.   [4] *Short and Easy Rules*, 1800, p. 27.

yet the young Grammarian had better be taught to call these equivocal words by the name of that part of speech to which they are most nearly allied by natural resemblance. (Bullen, 1797, p. 133.)

The writer in the third edition of the *Britannica* abuses Harris's system (No. 44), which had been adopted in the first two editions of the encyclopaedia, and then proclaims in hearty tones his support for this system of ten parts:

The division of words into those which are significant of themselves, and those which are significant by relation, is absolute nonsense, and has been productive of much error and much mystery in some of the most celebrated treatises on grammar. It is indeed probable, that any attempt to establish a different classification of the parts of speech from that which is commonly received, will be found of little utility either in practice or in speculation. As far as the former is concerned, the vulgar division seems sufficiently commodious; for every man who knows any thing, knows when he uses a noun and when a verb. With respect to the latter, not to mention that all the grammarians from Aristotle to Horne Tooke, have differed on the subject, it should seem to be of more importance, after having ascertained with precision the nature of each species of words, to determine in what circumstances they *differ* than in what they agree. (*Enc. Brit.* (B), 1797, p. 38.)

SYSTEM 10

SUBSTANTIVE	ADVERB
ADJECTIVE	CONJUNCTION
PRONOUN	PREPOSITION
ARTICLE	INTERJECTION
VERB (incl. participle)	

Douglas	*c.* 1720	M'Ilquham	1781	Barrie	1794
Dr S. Johnson	1755	Fell	1784	*Compr. View*	1794
Lowth	1762	*Elementary Principles*	1785	G. Wright	1794
Burn	1766	Ussher	1785	Alderson	1795
Houghton	1766	Bentick	1786	L. Murray	1795
W. R.	1768	*Short and Easy*	1786	Postlethwaite	1795
Raine	1771	*Introduction*		Fogg	1796
Crocker	1772	Coote	1788	Gentleman	1797
Johnston	1772	*Newbery's New*	1788	(2nd edn)	
Perry	1774	*Spelling Dictionary*		Groombridge	1797
Perry	1775	Seally	1788	Hewlett	1798
Perry	1776	Bicknell	1790	(4th edn)	
Remarks	1776	Taylor	1791	Mercy	1799
Stubbs	1777	Fogg	1792	Angus	1800
Shaw	1778	Hornsey	1793	Haywood	1805
Story	1778	Scott	1793	(2dn edn)	
G. Brown	1779?	*Short Intro.*	1793		

This system differs from No. 9 only by including the participle within the verb.

Uncertain classification. Dr Johnson does not enumerate the parts of speech, nor discuss them all. It is hard to say how significant this omission is. His treatment of the article suggests strongly that he regards it as a part of speech like the others; his treatment of substantive and adjective suggests that he regards them as distinct parts of speech, but it is consistent with the older practice of 'the common Grammarians' whom Johnson says he is following. Johnson may be adopting Wallis's indifference to the niceties of classification; or he may be taking for granted the Latin classification of System 1, which Bailey, who was following Johnson closely, certainly adopts. However Johnson's procedure is regarded, it seems to show that by the middle of the century System 1, even in the hands of a Latinist, was sufficiently weakened to become, in fact, a different kind of system. Alderson does not enumerate his parts of speech either, but they can be inferred from the syntax rules he proposes. W. R. Seally and G. Wright provide no evidence for their classification of the participle; such silence usually means that it is included within the verb, rather than within the adjective as in System 17.

Alternative classifications. There are many references to other classifications. For Douglas see also Systems 4 and 9. Coote quotes with approval Harris's ranking of the noun and verb as 'essential' and of the other parts as 'accidental' (System 44). Scott is here publishing separately a grammar he had earlier prefixed to two of his dictionaries, where it had contained a different classification of the parts of speech (System 19). Haywood also changes his classification: in the first edition, 1800, he had used System 4. Groombridge refers to this system as that of 'the grammarians', which he opposes to the 'natural' one of System 56. Blanch Mercy uses this system without comment in her first volume, but in volume two, the teacher's book, she explains that she has not used the tenfold classification (System 9) because it is impossible for the learner to understand the participle without first knowing what a verb is. There is accordingly no point in separating the two categories in the early stages.[1]

[1] Mercy, 1799, II. 12.

Grammarians' comments. Lowth writes in the same spirit as Johnson that 'The common Divisions have been complied with, as far as truth and reason would permit.'[1] Fell says, quite wrongly, 'English Grammarians have generally considered the Language as consisting of nine parts of speech.'[2] In fact less than a fifth of his predecessors had done so. He expresses strong doubt as to whether he should count the adverb, conjunction and interjection as parts of speech. 'The adverb', he says, 'can never be strictly and justly considered as a distinct part of speech; for there is not an adverb, which may not be found either among the nouns, pronouns, adjectives, verbs, participles or prepositions.'[3]

Lindley Murray and Blanch Mercy (who may be echoing Murray) both take an attitude towards classification which is as sensible and pragmatic as it is infuriatingly illogical. In his second edition, 1796, Murray adds a comment on the various systems used by different grammarians, and says he is following 'those authors who appear to have given...the most natural and intelligible distribution'.[4] Between 1797 and 1802 he added a reference to Horne Tooke's view:

that adverbs, prepositions, and conjunctions, are corruptions or abbreviations of other parts of speech. But as this system is not yet fully admitted... [it is best to keep to the traditional system]...It is of small moment, by what names and classification we distinguish these words, provided their meaning and use are well understood. (L. Murray (1795), 1802, p. 110.)

Blanch Mercy refers to the difficulty of classification:

It is often very immaterial (when the distinction is not absolutely essential to grammar) by what name we call a word, provided the nature and use of it be comprehended; and, as it has been seen, the same word is frequently employed in different forms; not that the radical sense of it can possibly undergo any material change; but because, in English particularly, we name words rather from their actual form or signification in a sentence, than from their primitive or radical import—this I hint, to prevent an useless solicitude about the appellation of a word of little importance. (Mercy, 1799, II, 34.)

Fogg's tart comment on the reforming grammarians is an indication that their influence was still active, although only two grammars with a 'vernacular' classification of the parts of speech had been published in the previous fifteen years:

---

[1] Lowth, 1762, p. xiv. [2] Fell, 1784, p. 2. [3] op. cit. p. 67.
[4] L. Murray (1795), 1796, p. 29.

Those frugal writers who start with informing us that there are only four parts of speech, while their enumeration contains double the necessary number, do still make them nine by their subdivisions...Their terms also, while they appear to be popular words, bear a technical sense. Who, but an innovating grammarian, ever called *I* a name, or *twenty* a quality? (Fogg, 1796, p. 209.)

SYSTEM 11

SUBSTANTIVE	ADVERB
ADJECTIVE (incl. article and participle)	CONJUNCTION
PRONOUN	PREPOSITION
VERB	INTERJECTION

Collyer 1735   Bridel 1797

In enumerating his parts Collyer says that he has followed 'as near as possible the common Latin Grammar, yet could not entirely fall in with it, especially as to the Adjective coming under the Class of Nouns'.[1] He feels that the number of the parts of speech ought to be eight, and includes the participle within the adjective to offset the extra part he has made by separating adjective and substantive. The articles, he says, are 'commonly reckoned as no part of speech', but he considers them 'real Qualities'.[2] He considers, and rejects, the practice of 'some modern Grammarians' in having only four parts, but he gives, and often uses, the 'modern' names for the parts of speech.

Bridel's classification is quite explicit. He lists the eight primary parts, and says of the adjective: 'We consider as adjectives all the words contained in the following list', which comprises articles, adjectives 'strictly so called', participles and gerunds.[3]

SYSTEM 12

SUBSTANTIVE (incl. pronoun substantive)	ADVERB
ADJECTIVE (incl. pronoun adj. and participle)	CONJUNCTION
	PREPOSITION
VERB	INTERJECTION

Daniel Turner 1739

[1] Collyer, 1735, p. 3.   [2] op. cit. p. 37.   [3] Bridel, 1797, p. 20.

There is no evidence for Turner's classification of the article, but the rest of his system is considered and defended. After enumerating his seven primaries he says that the parts of speech are normally reckoned eight, but 'the substantive and adjective seem to me to be as distinct parts of speech as the verb and adverb; and the pronoun is either substantive or adjective; the participle a peculiar sort of adjective'.[1] For his regretful decision not to adopt a fourfold system see System 38.

SYSTEM 13

NOUN	ADVERB
PRONOUN (incl. article)	CONJUNCTION
VERB	PREPOSITION
PARTICIPLE	INTERJECTION

Henson   1760?   *Real English Grammar*   1764

Henson was a conventional, if slightly muddled, Latinist, and shows no sign of being a deliberate innovator. But it is important to recognise the evidence that he introduced a new classification. The more unaware he was that his system was unusual the more evident it is that the categories he was using were unstable. He enumerates the parts of speech according to System 1. In his discussion of the six cases of substantives he says, 'The Nominative and Accusative are known by their Places; the other by their Signs.'[2] This shows that he did not regard the articles (as did most of those writers proposing System 1) as the signs of the nominative and accusative. He does, however, use the articles as one of the defining characteristics of the substantive: 'A Substantive is a Word...having before it, *a, an,* or *the*.'[3] If at this point Henson had made his principal reference to the articles he would clearly have been regarding them as attachments of the substantive (however vaguely conceived). But he puts his principal reference to the articles in the middle of his section about the pronoun: pronoun adjectives include relatives, among which is *that*.[4] Immediately following comes his account of *the* and *a*, and then a reproduction of Wallis's tabular arrangement of the personal and possessive pronouns. The conclusion seems inescapable that Henson regarded *a* and *the* primarily as 'pronoun adjectives'.

[1] D. Turner, 1739, p. 12.
[2] Henson, 1760?, p. 5.
[3] op. cit. p. 4; cf. pp. 291 f. below.
[4] op. cit. p. 9; cf. pp. 354 below.

The author of *A Real English Grammar* was one of those trying to give English a grammar of its own, but he accepted the idea of universal grammar sufficiently to believe 'that the definitions, and the nature of the dependence of the several parts of Speech on each other, may be learned in any Language'.[1] His classification is therefore conservative:

In the elemental principles, I have followed the antient method, and have set down eight parts of Speech; tho' I am clearly of opinion, that the Substantive may, with great propriety, be considered in English as different from the Adjective...Some have set down nine parts of Speech, and made *The* and *A* the first, and called them Articles; but they so strictly agree with the definition of the Pronouns, that I have rejected this part, and ranged them in that Class, with whose definition they agree. (pp. x–xi.)

The author comments also on what are here called the vernacular systems: 'Others have set down only four parts, but they have been obliged to give separate definitions of those they lumped together, which cannot instruct the Learner more than if they followed the old way, and for that reason I have not imitated them.'[2]

SYSTEM 14

SUBSTANTIVE (incl. pronoun substantive)	ADVERB (incl. interjection)
ADJECTIVE (incl. pronoun adjective; article; participle)	CONJUNCTION
VERB	PREPOSITION

The Young Mathematician's Logic   1760

Here again an author, apparently without knowing it, puts forward a system which is unique. No single characteristic is unique: the pronoun substantive and pronoun adjective had been divided in one earlier grammar; the interjection had been included within the adverb in three earlier grammars; the article had been treated as an adjective in six earlier grammars and the participle in two. This combination of characteristics happened to be unique, but it is not a careless or uncertain classification. The author is aware of an alternative, which he rejects because his classification is based on the categories of logic: 'Some modern philosophers divide the parts

---

[1] *Real English Grammar*, 1764, p. iv.   [2] op. cit. pp. x–xi.

of speech into four; and they subdivide the fourth part into three more parts.'[1]

The form of the fourfold classification which he illustrates, without supporting, is that of System 33, first used by Gildon and Brightland in 1711.

SYSTEM 15

SUBSTANTIVE	ADVERB
ADJECTIVE (incl. article)	CONJUNCTION
PRONOUN	PREPOSITION
VERB (incl. participle)	INTERJECTION

Priestley	1761	Elphinston	1765	Binns	1788
Priestley	1762	*A Vocabulary*	1765	Salmon	1798

Uncertain classification. In Elphinston's grammar and in *A Vocabulary* there is no clear evidence of where the author places the article. The arrangement of the work suggests this classification. Elphinston does not enumerate his parts of speech, a significant omission in such a detailed work, and consistent with his view that 'the parts of ours, as of all other speech, are doubtless transmutable into each other'.[2] Priestley discusses the articles in his chapter on the substantive, because they are so closely connected with it, but says they should 'in universal grammar'[3] and 'strictly speaking'[4] be considered as adjectives.

Alternative classifications. Nicholas Salmon would like to treat adjective and adverb as a single part of speech, but the need to learn foreign languages makes this impracticable.[5] The resulting category he would call *Definitive*, which is Harris's term for words like *an, the, this, any*. Harris has a category which comprises the adjective and the adverb but he calls it *Attributive*. See System 44.

Grammarians' comments. Priestley says of his classification:

I do this in compliance with the practice of most Grammarians; and because, if any number, in a thing so arbitrary, must be fixed upon, this seems to be as comprehensive and distinct as any. All the innovation I

---

[1] *Young Mathematician's Logic*, 1760, p. 27.   [2] Elphinston, 1765, I. 371.
[3] Priestley, 1761, p. 6.   [4] Priestley (1761), 2nd edn 1768, p. 145.
[5] Salmon, 1798, p. 6.

231

have made hath been to throw out the Participle, and substitute the Adjective, as more evidently a distinct part of speech. (Priestley (1761), 2nd edn 1768, p. 3.)[1]

The comment shows clearly the assumption that there ought to be a certain number of parts of speech. Priestley sees that the number is arbitrary and the assumption questionable, but even he is not radical enough to take the next step. He speaks, apparently without irony, of 'throwing out' the participle, as if the membership of a society was over-subscribed.

The fourth of Priestley's lectures on the theory of language is on 'The general Distribution of Words into Classes', but he is more concerned to discuss the psychological justification for, and genesis of, the existing classes than to criticise them on logical grounds. He summarises his views in these words:

All the words of which the languages of men consist are either the names of things and qualities (the ideas of which exist in the mind) or words adapted to denote the relations they bear to one another; or lastly, a compendium for other words, with or without their relations. The names of things or qualities are termed Substantives and Adjectives: the substitutes of these are Pronouns. Their coincidence or agreement is expressed by Verbs: The relations of words by Prepositions, and of sentences by Conjunctions. And Adverbs are contracted forms of speech, which may be analized into words belonging to other classes. (Priestley, 1762, pp. 65–6.)

His discussion groups together 'those which are substitutes for other words':[2] the conjunction, pronoun, adverb and interjection, but he makes no suggestion that they should be considered as one grammatical category.

In a work published thirty years later Elphinston refers to 'the seven parts of human speech, which some would dilate to above a dozen, so might as well to a hundred; and others would gladly reduce, if not to fewer, to three'.[3] He specifies the three as noun, verb, and particle, which are the primary categories of four systems: Nos. 22, 42, 46 and 48.

System 16 (see facing page). Anne Fisher's is a blend of the vernacular and of the Latin systems. In her earlier work she had adopted a vernacular system of four primary parts (System 36). Here she keeps to eight parts, but calls substantives *names*, adjectives *qualities* and, as

---

[1] But the wording of 1761 is almost identical. [2] Priestley, 1762, p. 60.
[3] Elphinston, *Fifty Years Correspondence*, viii. 1794. 143. The reformed spelling which Elphinston uses has here been de-reformed.

SYSTEM 16

SUBSTANTIVE (incl. pronoun)	ADVERB
ADJECTIVE (incl. article)	CONJUNCTION
VERB	PREPOSITION
PARTICIPLE	INTERJECTION

Bell   1769   Fisher (3rd edn)   1774

in the vernacular system, treats the pronoun as a name and the article as an adjective. In making the participle a primary, however, she is breaking completely with the vernacular approach. She does not discuss her classification in this work nor give any reason for adopting one which is followed by only one other writer.

John Bell's only comment on the parts of speech is that they are the same in all languages. He does not show that he is aware that his classification, which is quite specific, is at all unusual.

SYSTEM 17

SUBSTANTIVE	ADVERB
ADJECTIVE (incl. participle)	CONJUNCTION
PRONOUN	PREPOSITION
ARTICLE	INTERJECTION
VERB	

Rowland Jones   1768   Rowland Jones   1771

In *Hieroglyfic*, 1768, Jones does not enumerate his parts of speech, but the arrangement is fairly clear. In *The Circles of Gomer*, 1771, he enumerates them reluctantly, on the grounds that language is now so far advanced that there is little to be gained from going back to the primitive 'radicals of places, of which those of things are genuine copies'[1]—whatever that means. His combination of the participle with the adjective is clearly implied in 1768,[2] and explicit in 1771, when he applies the same definition to both parts of speech.[3] This makes him by chance the sole proponent of a system, unless Seally, W. R., and others adopting System 10, who say nothing about the participle, should be placed here.

[1] R. Jones, 1771, p. 8.   [2] R. Jones, 1768, p. 32.
[3] idem 1771, p. 9.

SYSTEM 18

SUBSTANTIVE (with article)	ADVERB
ADJECTIVE	CONJUNCTION
PRONOUN	PREPOSITION
VERB	INTERJECTION
PARTICIPLE	

Metcalfe (3rd edn)　　1777　　Sedger　　1798

In this edition Metcalfe treats substantive and adjective as primaries; in the previous edition they had been secondaries. The change is explicit, but made without comment. (See System 1.)

Sedger's is in places a naïve work, but it is unusual in bringing independent thought to several parts of grammar, including the classification of words. In one passage Sedger more or less explicitly repudiates any definite classification of words into kinds. Discussing words like *learning, eating, drinking* he says that whether they ' be taken as original names of actions or proceeding out of verbs from what are called participles, cannot be of material consequence to the learner. There are more ways than one of conceiving operations of arithmetic, and why may there not be different ways of conveying grammar.'[1] The whole tone of the book is in sympathy with this relaxed and uncategorical spirit. Sedger makes no enumeration of the parts of speech. The nearest he comes to one is in a 'Summary Chart'.[2] The headings of the chart agree in content, but not in arrangement, with the material in the grammar, which follows the present ninefold system. Immediately after the chart Sedger says: 'The noun is the first part of speech. The verbs are drawn from nouns of habit or progression, to put language in motion. And the rest are words collected about nouns and verbs, for the sake of definition and connection, and to afford ease and neatness of expression.' This would seem to suggest a threefold classification into Noun, Verb and Particle, but Sedger's section on the noun makes it clear that he is here expressing a view about the *development* of the parts of speech rather than about their present classification.

The material of the grammar is arranged so that the section on the substantive is followed by sections on its accompaniments—the

[1] Sedger, 1798, p. 32. 　　　　　　　[2] op. cit. p. 88.

articles, prepositions ('local articles of nouns'), adjectives ('a kind of qualifying definites to nouns') and pronouns. The article is expressly said to be 'a kind of appendage' to the noun, but the other parts are treated as primaries. The participle is given prominence in his discussion, under the noun, of forms in -*ing*.

The chart reinforces the separate status of the participle, whose distinctive heading is 'Gradations from Noun to Verb', but it treats the Conjunction and Preposition together ('abstracted from nouns and verbs'). The personal and relative pronouns are given separate headings but there is no discussion in the text of such a division.

The absence of enumeration in Sedger's grammar is probably evidence that he may be counted among the very few writers of school grammars to see that any classification of words according to the traditional categories was unsatisfactory. Sedger was not the man to succeed in breaking new ground, but it was a lively action even to question the old.

SYSTEM 19

SUBSTANTIVE	ADVERB
ADJECTIVE (incl. article)	CONJUNCTION
PRONOUN	PREPOSITION
VERB	INTERJECTION
PARTICIPLE	

Scott   1786   Scott   1789   Harrison (6th edn)   1794

These two grammars of William Scott's are those attached to his dictionary and to his lessons in elocution. In the grammar he published separately in 1793 he adopts System 10. In his first edition Harrison had treated the article as a primary (System 9), but by 1794, if not earlier, he explicitly included it within the adjective.

SYSTEM 20

NOUN (incl. interjection; adjective incl. article)	ADVERB
PRONOUN	CONJUNCTION
VERB (incl. participle)	PREPOSITION

Dalton   1801

Dalton discusses in some detail his reasons for 'having deviated considerably from the path of my predecessors in Grammatical science',[1] but his remarks apply more to the constitution of the different categories than to their arrangement in a system.

In his enumeration of his primary parts he explains that he is regarding the interjection as an 'interjective noun'.[2] He is not happy about his classification of the articles, quoting Horne Tooke as saying that they 'trench closely upon' the pronouns.[3] He also quotes from Tooke the traditional view that 'the Parts of Speech essentially *necessary* to communicate our thoughts are, the Noun and the Verb'.[4]

MODIFIED SYSTEMS BEFORE 1700

SYSTEM 21

NOUN (adjective incl. article)	ADVERB (incl. preposition and interjection)
PRONOUN	CONJUNCTION
VERB (incl. participle)	

Greaves   1594

Greaves does not enumerate his parts of speech. He must be taken as treating the substantive and adjective as secondary parts of the noun, in view of his definite statement: 'Vox numeri est nomen aut verbum. Nomen est Substantivum, aut Adjectivum.' But his arrangement also suggests that he regards them as primaries. He discusses them in separate chapters, headed *De Substantivo* and *De Adjectivo*, not, as was the usual Latin practice, in one chapter or section headed *De Nomine*. On the other hand, their syntax is discussed in one chapter, *De syntaxi nominis*.

There is no doubt about his treatment of the other parts. The participle is clearly included within the verb, and of the adverb he says, 'Huc referuntur etiam quae volgo praepositiones appellantur ...huc etiam Interiectiones.'

If Greaves is tending to separate substantive and adjective he is, like Wallis sixty years later, anticipating a practice which was not followed, except apparently in some moods by Lewis, until Lane in 1695 first used the fourfold vernacular system (No. 31).

[1] Dalton, 1801, p. i.
[3] op. cit. p. ii.
[2] op. cit. p. 7.
[4] op. cit. p. 5.

SYSTEM 22

NOUN (incl. pronoun)
VERB (incl. participle)
PARTICLE (compr. adverb; conjunction;
preposition; interjection; article)

Gill   1619   Douglas   *c.* 1720?

Gill's is a firm, explicit classification into three primary parts:
'Partes orationis sunt tres: nomen; verbum; consignificativa dictio,
ubi sunt Articulus, Adverbia, Praepositiones...'[1] and in a later
chapter he adds to these last the conjunction and interjection.[2] This
is basically the threefold classification of Sanctius,[3] but Gill
distributes the secondary parts in a different way.

James Douglas proposed, in different drafts of his grammar,
systems of ten, nine and eight parts of speech (Nos. 4, 9 and 10). He
remained constant, however, to the view that: 'All the Parts of
Speech may be reduc'd to three, viz. Noun, Verb and Particle.'[4]
Douglas is unusual in specifying his arrangement of secondary parts
and in making it quite clear that he did consider them subordinate
to, and included within, his primary categories. Beside the sentence
just quoted an addition to the manuscript reads:

(beside 'Noun'):   'adnoun and pronoun'
(beside 'Verb'):   'participle' (later deleted)
(beside 'Particle'):   'article, adverb, preposition, conjunction,
                   interjection'[5]

In a later manuscript the same reduced system is proposed with the
comment, 'The Noun comprehends the Pronoun...The Particle
includes article, adverb (etc.)'[6]

The primary parts of this system are put forward by several later
writers as the basis for an alternative classification. The suggestions,
which are not developed in any detail, seem to be independent of
Gill and of each other. No subtle thread of influence is needed to
explain their intermittent appearance: the primacy of the noun
and verb is one of the oldest parts of the tradition, as is the distinction

---

[1] Gill, 1619, p. 36.   [2] op. cit. p. 67.
[3] See above, p. 53.   [4] Douglas, *c.* 1720?, MS. 585. fol. 2 recto.
[5] ibid.   [6] MS. 587a. fol. 49 verso; Bundle 1.7. fol. 1 recto.

between variable and invariable words. This system is a combination of both views. Gill was original among the English grammarians in making it the explicit basis of his classification, but by the early part of the eighteenth century, when the fourfold system was established, the further reduction of the primary parts from four to three was a step which anyone might have suggested.

In an undated and anonymous edition of Miege's *English Grammar* (1688)—for which see System 1—issued about 1689 as *A Compleat Guide to the English Tongue*, Miege or his reviser adds not only the traditional comment that the noun and verb are the 'most considerable' of the parts of speech, but the further remark that 'Pronouns and Participles are in their Nature half nouns. And what are Adverbs, Conjunctions, Prepositions, and Interjections, but Accessories to Nouns and Verbs, and as it were their Attendants?'[1] This is very close to Gill's classification.

J. T. Philipps, whose English grammar of 1726 advocates System 34, gives explicit support to this system, No. 21, in an earlier work, partly original, partly compilation, on teaching languages.[2] He objects that 'Substantive, Adjective, Genitive, Accusative, &c and the like Grammatical Terms...preposterously suppose the Child to be already a Logician, a Metaphysician, and very well accustomed to abstracted Notions.'[3] The teaching of such terms 'indisposes the Mind to enquire after the Nature and Causes of Things, and disposes it credulously to swallow Mill-Stones with passive Obedience, and implict Faith'.[4] Philipps shows his pupils:

that all the Words in any Language may be reduc'd to three Classes or kinds; namely, Words denoting the Names of Things, or Qualities explaining their Nature. 2dly, Words signifying any Action or Suffering. And lastly, Words which are employ'd in joining other Words and Sentences together; and in expressing the Circumstances of Things, and the manner how any Thing or Person acteth or suffereth; and sometimes to express the Passion of the Mind...Now, if any one will stiffly contend for the Number *Eight*, and that the Latin Speech must be divided exactly into so many Parts; I must confess, I have nothing to offer in favour of my Division here proposed, but that 'tis very natural for a Beginner, and

[1] Miege [1689?], p. 7. Miege's 'attendants' are perhaps echoed by Anselm Bayly. See System 46.
[2] J. T. Philipps, *A Compendious Way of teaching Ancient and Modern Languages, formerly practised by the learned Tanaquil Faber...and now, with little Alteration, successfully executed in London*, 2nd edn London 1723.
[3] op. cit. p. 52.　　　　　　　　　　　[4] ibid.

sufficient for a Youth, whose Memory must not be over-charged with many Divisions and Subdivisions at his first setting out. (J. T. Philipps, 2nd ed. 1723, pp. 58–9.)

Alexander Adam, in *The Principles of Latin and English Grammar*, refers to a threefold system in the merest aside: that all words may be divided into Substantives, Attributives, and Connectives.[1] But he does not say whether, for example, he follows Harris in regarding the verb as an attributive or whether he would regard it as a connective.

This threefold system received support towards the end of the eighteenth century from the Abbé Gaultier, whose grammars were influential in this country partly through their influence on Lady Fenn and partly because Gaultier himself came as a refugee to England and opened a school in London for émigré children. In his *Leçons de grammaire*, 1787, Gaultier defends this system of parts of speech: 'Quelques personnes, qui ne connoissent que des Méthodes peu philosophiques, ont paru ne pas approuver la division en trois parties essentielles du Discours. Cependant l'Auteur n'a fait que suivre le sentiment de plusieurs Grammairiens célèbres. Il paroit même que cette division n'appartient pas aux modernes...'; but, he goes on, quoting a fellow scholar, it was used by 'les plus fameux philosophes, les plus grands Orateurs & les Grammariens les plus célèbres de l'Antiquité'.[2] Like other writers striving to make an effective elementary grammar Gaultier bought all the grammars on the market. But they all told him that there were ten parts of speech, and their definitions were useless because they assumed knowledge which his pupils lacked.[3] So he had to evolve his own system, which agrees exactly with Gill's, except that Gaultier treats the article as a noun adjective.[4]

SYSTEM 23

NOUN (article with substantive; pronoun)	ADVERB (incl. conjunction and interjection)
VERB (incl. participle)	PREPOSITION

Butler   1633

[1] Adam, 1772, p. 4. For Adam's own system see No. 4 above.
[2] L. E. C. Gaultier, *Leçons de Grammaire*, 1787, p. xiv.
[3] op. cit. pp. 3–4. For Gaultier's influence on methods of analysis and précis see below, pp. 486 f.   [4] op. cit. p. 42.

The basis of Butler's primary classification is the distinction between declined and undeclined words: 'A Word is either with number and case, as Noun and Verb; or without, as Preposition and Adverb.'[1] The evidence for his secondary classification is clear but indirect. Section two of chapter three is headed *Of a Noun*, and its three subsections are headed *Of a Noun Substantive, Of a Noun Adjective, Of a Pronoun*. Section three is given to the verb. Section four is headed *Of Words without Number*, and contains two subsections. The first subsection is headed *Of a Preposition*, the second *Of an Adverb*. Butler's examples of adverbs include *lo!* and *behold!*, as well as words 'that join sentences, and their parts, together', marked by the marginal heading *Conjunction*.

SYSTEM 24

| WORDS OF ACTION | WORDS OF HELP |
| WORDS OF QUALITY | |

Lodowyck   1652

Lodowyck is discussing the structure of 'a new perfect language' rather than that of English, but it is difficult to separate his remarks about language in general (and hence about English) from his description of his own particular proposals. All words, he says, belong to one of three kinds:

Words of action: 'such as are distinguished by the word (Verb), or by circumlocution, words signifying with time'.

Words of quality: 'such as express any circumstance of a thing, or that which distinguisheth one substance from another, as *hot, cold, dry, sharp*'.

Words of help: 'such as express time, place, person, &c., as *now, then, where, who* &c.'[2] ... (They) 'are according to Grammar nominated, Pronouns, Adverbs, Prepositions, Interjections and Conjunctions'.[3]

Lodowyck's earlier book, *A Common Writing*, 1647, of which *The Ground-Work* is a development, is less explicit about the classification of words. It seems to imply a division into only two parts: verbs

---

[1] Butler, 1633, p. 32.   [2] Lodowyck, 1652, pp. 4–5.
[3] op. cit. p. 12.

(signifying action) and words which signify no action, namely 'Nounes Substantives: Pronounes; Nounes Adjectives; Adverb, Preposition, Interjection and Conjunction'.[1] Lodowyck does not seem at all clear about his classification: in *A Common Writing* he implies that the substantive does not signify action, but in *The Ground-Work* it does. Words of action, he argues, are in their primitives (that is, in their roots) 'indefinite to Verb or Noune', in the same way as the Latin root *am* appears in the nouns *amor* and *amicus* as well as in the verb *amo*.[2]

SYSTEM 25

SUBSTANTIVE	ADVERB	
ADJECTIVE	CONJUNCTION	perhaps as
PRONOUN	PREPOSITION	particle
ARTICLE	INTERJECTION	
VERB (incl. participle)		

Wallis   1653

Wallis's classification has been discussed earlier in this chapter. See above, pp. 203 ff.

SYSTEM 26

THE NOUN AS THE ONLY PRIMARY PART OF SPEECH

Dalgarno   1661

To say that there is only one primary part of speech reduces almost to absurdity the whole concept of word-classes, but Dalgarno is serious and explicit: 'There is only one principal part of speech; there can be said to be as many minor parts as there are grammatical flexions and variations, of which the number can be greater or less according as one decides to use many or few auxiliary particles in the structure of speech.'[3] In fact he goes even further than this. He is not just saying that the noun is the only primary part; he is saying that the secondary parts, the particles, are all in origin nouns. He came to

---

[1] Lodowyck, 1647, sig. A 3.   [2] Lodowyck, 1652, p. 5.
[3] Dalgarno, 1661, p. 65: '...unica tantum fit Pars orationis principalis; tot dici possunt minus principales, quot Grammaticae Flexiones, et variationes; quarum numerus potest esse vel major, vel minor, prout quis statuat pluribus vel paucioribus Particulis Auxiliaribus, in structura Orationis uti.'

see: 'that there was no particle which was not derived from the name of some predicament, and that all the particles were really cases or modes of nominal ideas'.[1] For the most part, however, he tends to ignore this part of his theory and to speak as if he were using two categories, the primary one of noun and the secondary one of particle.

Dalgarno is trying to make an international language, expressed in a logical and systematic symbolism devised from the letters of the alphabet. The symbolism is to be logical because it is based on a selection of fundamental general ideas arranged, as it were, by genus and species according to a selection of the qualities belonging to each idea. It is to be systematic because one letter of the alphabet will signify only one category. The only arbitrary elements are the signs *ei* and *s*, inserted where necessary in order to make pronounceable the clusters of vowels and consonants formed by the rules governing the symbolism. For example, the form F—M signifies 'food and clothing'; FL—M signifies 'food'; FLAM signifies 'bread', FLIM 'butter', and FLOM 'cheese'. The radical idea 'good' is signified by SIM; SIMAM means 'very good', SIMAN 'fairly good', SIMAF 'not good enough', SIMAB 'better', SIMAD 'equally good', SIMAG 'less good', SIMAP 'best'.

Dalgarno attaches considerable importance to the fact that his symbolism can be spoken; 'I admit no difference whatever between any symbolism (*characterem*) which can be thought up for the purpose of communication and a language...Whatever can be represented by visual shapes (*figuris*) can by the same skill be represented by sounds.'[2]

He is led therefore to two preliminary tasks of classification: to establish his fundamental categories—'Summa Genera Rerum'— and the simple sounds which are to represent them. The number of his fundamental categories is limited by the number of simple sounds, which he considers to be seven. He sees the relation between these two tasks, that between the sign and the thing signified, as an expression of the unity of, on the one hand, Metaphysics and Logic, and on the other, Grammar: 'Since we may represent things themselves by signs it is fully in accordance with reason that the Art of

---

[1] Dalgarno, 1661, p. 74: '...nullam esse Particulam quae non derivetur a Nomine aliquo Praedicamentali, et omnes Particulas esse vero Casus, seu Modos Notionum Nominalium'.

[2] op. cit. p. 35.

Signs should follow the Art of Things. Just as I deem Metaphysics and Logic to constitute only one branch of knowledge, so Grammar differs from these only as the sign differs from the thing signified.'[1] He is able to form this opinion because his clearly conceived primary purpose is to facilitate communication. Communication is the unifying idea which makes his incidental discussion of language so much more acute than is the 'universal character and philosophical language' which he invents. In his preface he warns the reader who judges his book: 'Be careful not to separate what must not be separated, that is, the logical and grammatical parts. So that you may form a fairer opinion of the book remember from the first what is its final goal—ease of communication.'[2] To see logic and grammar as closely related aspects of communication is an unfashionable view nowadays, though there is a sense in which it offers great help to the teacher of English. Dalgarno is dealing with matters which are still of concern to us, but it is not easy to know what he himself felt to be the implications of what he says here. To some extent he is only repeating the point of view inherent in the trivium: that communication can be analysed in linguistic terms (as grammar), in psychological terms, as a structure expressing the speaker's intentions and emphasis (rhetoric), and in terms of its structure as a piece of reasoning (logic). But the unity of the trivium had been destroyed long before the middle of the seventeenth century. Its three related areas had been intensively worked over and elaborately partitioned; the majority of those who cultivated them no longer raised their eyes from the ground. Though logic had gradually ceased to be taught in the schools there had been little change in the teacher's approach to grammar and rhetoric. If the three branches had been taught as a unity the postponement of one of them till the university stage of education would have modified the teaching of the other two in the schools. Dalgarno is saying something novel, even if it is not new. He is restating a view which our own times also need to reconsider.

Once he had established his fundamental categories and their signs he had to evolve a method of varying the signs to correspond

---

[1] op cit. p. 37: 'Cum enim Signa a nobis pro Rebus ipsis supponantur, omnino rationi consentaneum est, ut Ars Signorum Artem Rerum sequatur. Et sicut judico Metaphysicum et Logicam unicam tantum constituere Artem, sic Grammatica non aliter vel plus differt ab his, quam Signum a Signato.'

[2] op. cit. p. 7: 'Cave...ne inter judicandum, non separanda separes, id est, partem Logicam et Grammaticam; sed ut sententiam aequius feras, finem ultimum (communicationis facilitatem) primo respice.'

with the range of qualities belonging to each fundamental category. These variations correspond to the inflections of a natural language and lead him into a discussion of the parts of speech:

Grammarians teach that there are eight parts of speech; logicians say, more truly, that there are only two. I, following the freedom to philosophise which I have taken to myself, recognise only one primary part of speech properly so called, that is the Noun. What are commonly regarded as the other parts of speech should be reckoned among the inflections and cases of the noun. (op. cit. p. 63.)[1]

He proceeds to justify this view at some length. His first step is to state that 'every entity must necessarily have a place in the list of predicaments; but the idea expressed by each of the predicaments is a noun'.[2] He does not bother to express the next step in his argument, assuming that his reader will at once remember that among the Predicaments are Actio ('the manner of doing') and Passio. Dalgarno continues, 'From which it follows that the Verb [which he, of course, takes to express doing or suffering] no less than the other parts enumerated by grammarians, is only a case or inflexion of the noun.'[3] He assumes that if he can make good this last step in the case of the verb *to be* it will be true of all verbs. He has, therefore, to prove that the substantive verb, which is the copula in every proposition, is not 'derived from Being'. He admits a sense of the verb *to be* which is 'derived from Being', but says this is quite distinct from the use of the verb as the copula.[4]

He takes the two propositions *Homo est ens* and *Homo est*. If it is admitted that the first is a legitimate proposition he has made his point: *ens* expresses being, *est* does not (for if it did *ens* would be redundant). If it is objected that *ens* is redundant, and that *Homo est* means exactly the same as *Homo est ens* he replies that either *Homo est* is not a legitimate proposition (because a proposition must contain subject, copula and predicate) or, if it is legitimate, then *est* must be expanded into two terms, i.e. *est ens*, so as to express fully the copula and predicate. In which case he makes his point in the same way as before.

---

[1] 'Ego vero...unicam tantum Orationis partem, Primariam, et proprie sic dictam agnosco; Nomen scil. Caeteras vero vulgo sic habitas, esse inter Flexiones, et Casus hujus, numerandas.'

[2] op. cit. p. 64: 'Omne Ens quodcunque necessario primo locum habet in linea praedicamentali; omnis autem Notio praedicamentalis est Nomen.'   [3] ibid.

[4] ibid: 'Non nego posse derivari verbum ab Ente...verum hoc verbum longe aliud est a verbo Substantivo.'

This is not much of an argument, as the conlusion is identical with his preliminary distinction between the two uses of *be*.

His second argument is more interesting. It is, he says, generally agreed that the verb is nothing more than the formal part of a proposition, that is, the sign of a mental act of judgment. Judgment is twofold, agreement or disagreement; hence there are two forms of the verb *be*, affirmative and negative, which 'are modifications of the ideas of affirmation and denial and, according to the rules governing the Predicaments, must be conceived as names, that is as nouns'.[1]

Dalgarno then reinforces his emphasis on the copulative function of the verb by separating from it the expression of time, which is purely contingent. It is therefore, he says, quite correct to regard, as some people do, yes (*ita*) and no (*non*) as proper logical verbs: they are signs of an act of judgment. They have also a copulative function. *Homo est lapis* and *Homo ita lapis* are logically equivalent. He then proceeds to separate the idea of negation from the copulative function of the verb. His illustration is brief. In the negative proposition *Homo non est lapis* the *non* implies an assertion—is equivalent logically to *non est*; the *est* is therefore redundant. From this Dalgarno concludes that 'negation is never expressed by means of simple terms'.[2] By this he presumably means that the negative verb substantive of the earlier part of his argument has not the primary status of the affirmative verb, because it can always be resolved into two parts: an assertion and a negation—'a Mental Act, separating one thing from another'.

Neither of Dalgarno's arguments is fully worked out. They both seek to establish two main points: (*a*) that the copulative function of the verb *to be*, and therefore of other verbs, is basic, and distinct from the verb's other possible functions—to signify existence, affirmation or time; (*b*) that this pure copulative function is fundamentally an aspect of naming. The weakness of his contention is evident enough to us. In so far as it is true it is both trivial and useless. It is trivial, in that any relation *can* be regarded as in some sense expressing a name, if only because its function can be named. His contention is useless because in so far as a relation *is* being considered only as expressing a name it is prevented from fulfilling its only task—to relate. Putting it crudely, if the copula is regarded only as a form

---

[1] ibid.: '...sunt casus Notionum *affirmare*, et *negare*, quae secundum leges praedicamentales primo concipienda sunt Nominaliter.'

[2] op. cit. p. 65. 'Insuper ex dictis infero, nullam esse Negationem in terminis simplicibus; omnibus enim Negatio est Actus Mentis, separans aliquid ab aliquo.'

245

of the name *junction* it cannot *join. Subject*: *relation*: *predicate* is not a schema for a proposition; *subject*: *is related to*: *predicate* is.

He refers briefly to the particle, which term covers 'the notions commonly called, by grammarians, conjunction, preposition and interjection...The modifications expressed by the adverb, however, are different from these, signifying a mode of action.'[1] He does not develop this point, and shows little interest in the particles.

Dalgarno's attitude is most clearly revealed in an interesting passage which follows his discussion of the verb. He condemns, in austerely intellectualist terms, the concepts of 'ornatus' and 'elegantia', which in the natural languages are, absurdly, governed by rules. In his own 'philosophical' language 'speech is a logical analysis of our conceptions'.[2] The naïve speaker of an artificial or of a natural language does not need to be a logician, but he suffers the handicap of being unable to examine his own use of language.

For before men have been instructed in the precepts of logic they speak mostly like parrots. They have inherited certain traditional formulae; if they are no longer free to use them, they fall dumb. If the English countryman is not allowed to use expressions like *he must be born with*; *put out the candle*; he will stand silent...His mind can make no logical analysis of these complex ideas; and certainly many aspects of things and many combinations of ideas are very difficult to express logically... It is in fact the height of logical subtlety to be able to express the mind's sensations accurately in this [i.e. Dalgarno's] language. (op. cit. p. 67.)[3]

Only the good logician can speak elegantly.

Dalgarno is not unique in seriously maintaining that there is only one part of speech. At the end of the eighteenth century Captain Thomas Gunter Browne attempted 'to shew that there is in reality but one sort of word, and that there is no distinction originally between the noun and the verb'.[4] Browne based his view on the number of words (*head* is one of his examples) which can be used both as noun and as verb: 'In our mother tongue...almost every word,

---

[1] op. cit. p. 78.

[2] op. cit. p. 67: '...ita, ut sermo sit Analysis Logica Conceptuum nostrorum.'

[3] 'Homines enim, priusquam praeceptis Logicis imbuantur, loquuntur in multis more psittacorum: Formulas quasdam traditione acceperunt, quibus utendi libertate sublata, obmutescent. Si enim inhiberetur Rusticus Anglus uti his phrasibus, *he must be born with*; *put out the candle*; mutus stabit...Logicam vero Analysin horum complexorum conceptuum perficere in mente nequit: Et quidem nonnulli sunt respectus Rerum, et concursus Notionum, quos Logice exprimere est perdifficile: Imo fastigium est acuminis Logici, posse bene Animi sensa hac Lingua exprimere.'

[4] Thomas Gunter Browne, *Hermes Unmasked*; *or the art of speech founded on the association of words and ideas*, 1795, p. 3.

truly English, is both noun and verb.'[1] His argument is derived from an incomplete understanding of Horne Tooke and Hartley, both of whom he praises, and it has a decorative wildness reminiscent of Monboddo. Browne's point, learnt from Horne Tooke, is that an originally small, primitive vocabulary is enlarged by the process of metaphorical extension:

Thus it appears, that the same word will do the office of a noun in one sentence, and of a verb in another; that is, when it is used to express the full and complete idea of a thing altogether, it is then said (by grammarians) to be a noun; but when it is used to express, and to transfer to another word, some particular properties or actions only of the thing; then they would call it a verb, or an adjective, or an abstract word of some sort—I, for my part, call it a metaphor, when used in this abstract manner. (T. G. Browne, 1795, p. 29.)

The most general statement that Browne makes shows also the extent of his confusion between word and thing: 'Any object, of any sort, may serve to make any part of speech of any kind.'[2] Apart from his refreshing breeziness Captain Browne's advocacy of this system carries no weight.

Less substantial is Mark Anthony Meilan's brief comment in favour of having only one part of speech, a conflation of noun and verb, for which see System 50, below. Meilan's implied argument is the same as Browne's, and may derive from him.

SYSTEM 27

Integral

NOUN (adjective incl. participle)
VERB (with derived adverb)[3]

Grammatical particle

COPULA
SUBSTITUTIVE PARTICLE (pronoun; interjection)
CONNEXIVE PARTICLE (preposition; article)
OTHER PARTICLES (underived adverb; conjunction)

Cross-categories

SUBJECT AND PREDICATE
ABSTRACT AND CONCRETE FORMS
TRANSCENDENTAL PARTICLES

Wilkins   1668

[1] op. cit. p. 40.   [2] op. cit. p. 55.
[3] e.g. words formed like *wisely*, contrasted with words like *now, yes*.

Wilkins was acquainted with Dalgarno's work and had the same intention: to construct an international language. He is trying to do this by means of a system of symbols which will do for the whole range of ideas what the numeral figures do for numbers: 'not signifie words, but things and notions, and consequently...be legible by any Nation in their own Tongue'.[1]

He is not writing a grammar, but his system involves an analysis of the concept of language and an examination of the terminology of grammar: 'For the farther compleating this Work, I found it necessary to take into consideration, the framing of such a Natural Grammar, as might be suited to the Philosophy of Speech.'[2]

It is convenient to describe his grammatical categories as a whole because they do not follow the tradition closely enough to be amenable to the topical treatment here applied to other grammars.

Wilkins' two broadest categories are *Integrals* and *Particles*: 'By Integrals, or Principal words, I mean such as signifie some entire thing or notion: whether the Ens or Thing it self, or the Essence of a thing, as Nouns Neuters, whether concrete or abstract; or the Doing or Suffering of a thing, as Nouns Active or Passive; or the manner and affection of it, as Derived Adverbs.'[3] Integrals can be considered either 'according to their natures'—that is, in terms of meaning—or 'according to their Place and Order in a proposition'—that is, syntactically or logically.

Considered semantically integrals may be:

Absolute, a category including concrete and abstract;
Relative to the Names of Things, i.e. substantive or adjective;
Relative to the Actions and Passions of Things, i.e. as verb or derived adverb.

Considered according to their place and order, integrals may be *Subject* or *Predicate.*

Particles are either *Grammatical* or *Transcendental*: 'Those are stiled Grammatical, which supposing words to retain their primary sense, do serve for the circumstantiating of them, either by union, abbreviation, inflexion, or some other way for the qualifying of their significations or constructions.'[4] They indicate, that is, mainly syntactic relationships.

[1] Wilkins, 1668, p. 13.
[3] op. cit. p. 298.
[2] op. cit. Epistle to the Reader.
[4] op. cit. p. 304.

Grammatical particles can be considered as *Essential* or *Non-essential*. The essential grammatical particle is the copula. There are three types of non-essential particles: *Substitutive* particles are the pronoun and the interjection, which are used 'in the room either of some Integral word, or of some sentence or complex part of it'.[1] *Connexive* or *declarative* particles are the preposition and the article, which are 'proper to Substantives, being usually prefixed before them'.[2] The third type, *particles common to other words*, comprises the underived adverb and the conjunction.

Transcendental particles 'circumstantiate words in respect of some Metaphysical notion; either by enlarging the acception of them to some more general signification, than doth belong to the restrained sense of their places: or denoting a relation to some other Predicament or Genus, under which they are not originally placed'.[3]

They express semantic relations lying outside the traditional categories of grammar. The transcendental particles are not distinctive words. They are uses of words. Wilkins proposes a number of symbols, 'transcendental marks', which would indicate, for example, the extended or metaphorical use of a word. Thus *element*, accompanied by one kind of transcendental mark, would mean *rudiment; crooked* would mean *perverse*. Another mark would indicate that a word was being used to express habitual action: *rejoicing* (i.e. a single act of rejoicing) with this mark would mean *cheerfulness, worshipping* would mean *devotion*. Another kind of mark would express the idea of artist or craftsman, corresponding to the final syllables of the words mathema*tician* or geome*trician*.[4]

A word accompanied by a transcendental mark would be a transcendental particle.

In effect Wilkins is accepting the traditional parts of speech with some modification and rearrangement, and adding five categories in three groups which function, in relation to the other primary groups, as cross-categories. These are:

Subject and predicate: syntactical categories
Abstract and concrete: semantic categories
Transcendental particle; a rhetorical category.

The nine groups given at the beginning of this system are the nearest to a set of primary categories which Wilkins' treatment

---

[1] op. cit. p. 46. [2] ibid. [3] op. cit. p. 318.
[4] op. cit. p. 338.

permits. He mixes semantic, syntactic and rhetorical criteria in an attempt to bring all aspects of the use of language within his scheme. The attempt to crowd very diverse elements into the two classes of integral and particle strains the framework, but the scheme as a whole, just because its starting point lies outside the technical and narrow conception of grammar, implies (it can scarcely be said to do more) the kind of unified treatment of language-in-use which seems to be a persistent, though obscure, feature of both the classical and the English tradition.

One or two features of Wilkins' classification can best be commented on here.

Verb. He would like to isolate from the verb its assertive function. This he considers can always be expressed by means of the copula, which he makes the equivalent of a separate part of speech: 'That part of speech, which by our Common Grammarians is stiled a Verb...ought to have no distinct place among Integrals in a Philosophical Grammar; because it is really no other than an Adjective, and the Copula *sum* fixed to it or conteined in it; so *caleo* ...is the same with *sum calidus.*'[1]

Concrete and abstract. Every radical idea, he says, is theoretically capable of being expressed in the form of a substantive, an adjective and an adverb, and each of these three can have a concrete or abstract form. His examples can best be shown in tabular form.[2]

	Substantive	Adjective	Adverb
Concrete	light	light	lightly
	heat	hot	hotly
Abstract	lightness	luciditative	luciditatively
	hotness	caloritative	caloritatively

Neuter, active, passive. Each substantive, adjective and adverb should have not only a concrete and an abstract form, but a neuter, an active, and a passive one. The concrete and abstract forms given above are all neuter. The active and passive equivalents would be, for *light*:

---

[1] op. cit. p. 303 (from the Port Royal grammar).   [2] ibid.

	Active	Passive
Concrete		
substantive	Enlightening	Enlightened
adjective	Enlightening	Enlightened
adverb	Illuminatingly	Illuminatedly
Abstract		
substantive	Illuminativity	Illuminability
adjective	Illuminative	Illuminable
adverb	Illuminatatively (*sic*)	Illuminably[1]

Wilkins admits that he has had to coin many new words 'according to common analogy', but it is only 'the imperfections of Languages' which make this necessary. He does not explain why the concrete substantive and adjective have the same form. It can hardly be a mere failure of ingenuity.

Adverb. He distinguishes in the adverb one function which is descriptive (the derived adverb) and a loose combination of functions which are, broadly, conjunctive (the underived adverb). The underived adverb Wilkins does not consider, to form, strictly, a proper category. Some are derived from Pronouns, *As, So, From, This, That*[2] or else they are Modes of Verbs, *Yea, Nay, Perhaps, Truly,* or else they are Conjunctions, *Rather, Than*; and some of them may be periphrastically expressed by Radicals. So that according to the true Philosophy of speech, I cannot conceive this kind of words to be properly a distinct part of speech, as they are commonly called. But until they can be distributed into their proper places, I have so far complied with the Grammars of instituted Languages, as to place them here together. (Wilkins, 1668, p. 312.)

SYSTEM 28

NOUN (article, preposition and pronoun   CONJUNCTION
with substantive; adjective incl.
participle)
VERB   INTERJECTION
ADVERB

Cooper   1685

[1] ibid.
[2] This is obscure. One is tempted to read '...*As, So,* from *This, That*', but it would still not be clear how *As* was 'derived from' *This*. There is a possible parallel between, e.g. '...*this* I have told him' and '...*as* I have told him', which might permit a kind of 'derivation'.

The English Categories

It is difficult to say how Cooper ranks his parts of speech. He is strongly influenced by Wilkins, and begins his chapter *De partibus orationis* with a classification of all words as either integrals or particles, though his definitions are not so metaphysical as Wilkins's: 'Dictiones quae principales constituunt sententiae partes, *integrales* vocantur; quae circumstantias, sensum modificantes, *particulae* nuncupantur. Integrales vel nomina sunt vel verba'. (Cooper, 1685, p. 86.) This would be decisive if it were not that Cooper never again uses or refers to this classification. It is, in effect, only an incidental description, though its position and tone seem to give it a more significant status. Whatever classification Cooper uses, this is not it. As he makes no other general statement about the classification of words, though clearly assuming that they are to be classified, evidence for his point of view must be sought in the arrangement of his material.

The chapter on the parts of speech is almost entirely taken up with a discussion of the kinds of noun substantive and noun adjective. A short section at the end gives examples of the formation of verbs (e.g. *blacken* from *black*) and a final section of seven lines does the same for the adverb. At the end of the section he says, 'The other parts of speech are reviewed by name in their respective places.' There is no doubt about their names; it is their places which depart from the tradition.

Cooper's second chapter, *De Substantivorum Accidentibus*, lists four accidents: articles, numbers, genders and prepositions. The first numbered section is headed *De Articulis a et the*; the second section is headed *De Pronominibus*. Genders, numbers and prepositions make up the other three sections. This is an inconsistency which cannot be resolved. The pronoun is not enumerated as an accident of the substantive, but is treated as one. There is no evidence, here or elsewhere, that Cooper is treating the pronoun within an enlarged category of article. It can only be supposed that he forgot to list it among the accidents at the beginning of the chapter. His third chapter deals with the accidents or adjectives; his fourth with the verb; the next three with the adverb, conjunction and interjection in turn.

We are left, therefore, with a sytem which puts into a primary status the noun (with an unusual variety of attachments), the verb, adverb, conjunction and interjection. The participle is included within the adjective. The effect is a reduced system; how far that was Cooper's primary intention it is impossible to say.

SYSTEM 29

NOUN (incl. pronoun; adjective incl. article)	ADVERB (incl. interjection and preposition)
VERB (incl. participle)	CONJUNCTION

Blome   1686

This system, which is quite explicit, seems to be influenced by the idea of universal grammar. It is proposed without comment and without any apparent awareness that it is unique.

SYSTEM 30

SUBSTANTIVE (incl. pronoun substantive)	ADVERB
	CONJUNCTION
ADJECTIVE (incl. pronoun adjective)	PARTICLE (compr. article; interjection; auxiliary
VERB (incl. participle)	verb; preposition; some adverbs, etc.)

The True Method of Learning the Latin Tongue by the English   1696

This basic grammar contains a deliberate and explicit reclassification of the parts of speech. It respectfully rejects 'the Parts of Speech set down, as Ancient Use hath directed', but 'for the sake of the terms in general vogue, the scholar is not to be ignorant of them'. 'Then', the author continues...

all the Parts of Latin and English Speech are fitly comprized under six Heads; where also the English Particles, which are not contained under any of the former...are properly contained under the Head of Signum (Sign)...In Speech are usually reckoned these Eight Parts following... Which terms are to be used as being most known: But the Parts of Latin and English Speech may be fitly reduced to six Heads, and distinguisht according to their Properties in this Natural Order.

Sign	Signum	Verb	Verbum
Noun	Nomen	Adverb	Adverbium
Adnoun	Adnomen	Conjunction	Conjunctio.[1]

[1] *True Method*, 1696, sig. A 2 recto; p. 1.

The particle or sign is here a genuine part of speech and not a merely synthesising label. Although the author refers by name to the article, interjection, preposition and auxiliary verb he is quite clear about their common function as *signs*—of cases, of tenses, of passions, even (as with *more* and *most*) as signs of an adjective. The author rejects the pronoun as a primary part on the grounds that 'it was through inadvertency of the Ancient Grammarians, that this was made a distinct Part of Speech, they not considering the Nature of an Ellipsis'.[1]

VERNACULAR SYSTEMS

SYSTEM 31

SUBSTANTIVE (incl. 1st and 2nd person pronouns)	VERB (incl. participle)
ADJECTIVE (incl. 3rd person pronouns and article)	PARTICLE (compr. adverb; conjunction; preposition)

Lane 1695   Lane 1700

Lane's odd classification of the personal pronouns is quite explicit. In his section on the noun (i.e. the substantive) he gives a separate paragraph to the declension of each of the 'personal substantives' *I/we* and *thou/you*,[2] and in the section on the adjective he describes how 'the Adjectives, *he, she, it,* are...declined'.[3]

Lane is the first English grammarian to propose this fourfold system, which he does in philosophical terms: 'There are but four kinds of Words, because there are but four kinds of things to be signified by Words: for whatever is in the whole Universe, is either a thing, or the manner of a thing; the action of a thing, or the manner or an action.'[4] What are here called vernacular systems are those using these four primary categories. They vary in the distribution of the secondary parts of speech (Lane excludes the interjection altogether) but their fourfold basis is firm and distinctive. It does not seem to have, nor does Lane claim for it, any single source, although it is most immediately under the influence of the Port Royal grammar of 1660. Its basis (apparent in the quotation from Lane given here) is the fundamental distinction between noun and verb which goes back to Aristotle and is part of the logical tradition; the separa-

---

[1] op. cit. sig. A 2 verso.
[3] op. cit. p. 33.
[2] Lane, 1700, p. 28.
[4] Lane, 1695, p. 1, and 1700, p. 20.

tion of substantive and adjective had been pending throughout the second half of the seventeenth century;[1] the particle is also within the logical tradition, had been explicit in Sanctius and Gill and, especially after the appearance in 1655 of William Walker's *A Treatise of English Particles*, had been used in some Latin grammars as a descriptive term for the 'undeclined' parts of speech.

SYSTEM 32

SUBSTANTIVE (with article; VERB (incl. participle)
incl. pronoun) PARTICLE (compr. adverb;
ADJECTIVE conjunction; preposition)

Right Spelling 1704

The author does not enumerate all his parts of speech, but his primary categories are clear: '...all Things may be comprehended under four sorts of words, viz. Substantives, or the things themselves; Adjectives, their Quality; Verbs, their Actions or Sufferings, and Particles, their Circumstances'.[2] He has not really understood the system, however, because he says later: 'Both Substantives and Adjectives are called Nouns'.[3] If he makes adjective and substantive separate primary parts he cannot admit a category of noun. Only three particles are referred to,[4] and as the author is frequently following Lane, and quotes him on the particles, it is reasonable to suppose that, like Lane, he rejects the interjection.

SYSTEM 33

SUBSTANTIVE (incl. pronoun) VERB
ADJECTIVE (incl. article and PARTICLE (compr. adverb,
participle) incl. interjection; conjunction; preposition)

Gildon and	1711	*New English*	1746	Farro	1754
Brightland		*Grammar*		Entick	1765
Loughton	1734	*English Grammar*	1750?	Farro	1776

In addition to this form of the fourfold classification Gildon and Brightland refer to a twofold division of words, into those 'which signifie the Objects of our Thoughts'—in the Latin terminology

[1] cf. above, p. 220.   [2] *Right Spelling*, 1704, sig. a 1 verso.
[3] op. cit. p. 32.   [4] ibid.

substantives, adjectives, pronouns, participles, adverbs and prepositions—and those 'which signifie the Manner'[1]—verbs, conjunctions
and interjections. They use this twofold classification only, and not
then consistently, to determine the order in which they discuss their
four primary parts. According to the twofold classification the
preposition and adverb should be treated with the substantive and
adjective. In fact they treat them within the fourth category of
particle. In their second edition, 1712, the chapter on the adjective
is much enlarged, and the inclusion of the article and participle is
made more specific.

In *A New English Grammar* there is no clear evidence for the
classification of the interjection until the second edition, 1760, where
it is explicitly included within the adverb. The author of *An English
Grammar* calls his four parts of speech, *name, quality, verb* and *particle*.
He gives an unusual reason for his treatment of the interjection:
'Some particles express a sudden passion of the soul; these are what
the grammarians call interjections, but they are more properly
stiled adverbs, for tho' they are indeed used alone, they must relate
to other words in sense.'[2] This system is quoted by the author of
The Young Mathematician's Logic, 1760, as that of 'some modern
philosophers',[3] but he does not himself support it.

SYSTEM 34

SUBSTANTIVE (incl. pronoun)	VERB
ADJECTIVE (incl. article and participle)	PARTICLE (compr. adverb, conjunction, preposition)

Philipps   1726

This system differs from No. 33 only in excluding interjections
altogether because they are 'only Signs of some sudden Passion'.[4]
Earlier Philipps had advocated a system of three primary parts of
speech, for which see p. 238 above. Now he says that the four
primary parts of this system comprise 'the four principal kinds of
Words [which] are sufficient to express all the Ideas of Things, and
the Judgements we make upon them, and render them intelligible to
others'.[5]

[1] Almost verbatim from Port Royal; cf. *Grammaire générale*, 1660, p. 30.
[2] *English Grammar*, 1750, p. 50.   [3] See above, p. 230.
[4] Philipps, 1726, p. iv.   [5] op. cit. p. xvii.

SYSTEM 35

SUBSTANTIVE (with article;   PARTICLE (compr. adverb;
  incl. pronoun)   conjunction; preposition;
ADJECTIVE   interjection)
VERB (incl. participle)

Dyche & Pardon	1735	Wise	1754	Bayly	1771
Martin	1748	*Spelling Dictionary*	1755	C. Johnson	1779
Pocket Dictionary	1753	Hammond	1760?	(6th edn)	
Gough	1754	Mr S. Johnson	1758	Cooke	1775?

Uncertain classification. In many of these grammars the treatment of the article has to be inferred from the arrangement. Martin, Hammond and Cooke say little about it. Gough's classification is obscure. He refers to the articles by name and discusses their use in a footnote to his chapter on the substantive; he does not refer to them in his chapter on the adjective. In the praxis added to the edition of 1792 they are referred to as particles, with a cross-reference to the footnote already mentioned.[1] It is probable that they are to be regarded as attachments to the substantive. In almost all these grammars the status of the participle is uncertain. The evidence of arrangement, and the normal practice, by those who wish it to be regarded as an adjective, of saying so, justify the present classification. One advantage of a fourfold system was that it permitted an evasion, through silence, of awkward decisions about the participle.

Alternative classification. In 1754 Martin, writing more specifically for English alone, adopted System 45. For an earlier edition of Cooke see System 4 and for a later one System 39. Anselm Bayly seems to be adopting this system by inadvertence; for his alternative classification see System 46.

Grammarians' comments. Dyche explicitly rejects a division into eight parts of speech in favour of one into four:

neither shall I divide the Language into eight Parts or Distinctions, as is generally done; but into four only, that being sufficient for my present Purpose, which is only to give a generall Hint how Grammar may be as effectually applied to the English Tongue as to any others. Nor shall I enter into all the Niceties that may be stated relating to these four Parts,

---

[1] Gough, 6th edn 1792, p. 182.

intending here only a general Direction to know the Coherence between and Dependence of one Part of a Discourse or Speech on another. (Dyche and Pardon, 1735, sig. A 4.)

There is a lot to be said for offering 'a general hint' rather than fine analysis in an elementary grammar, but Dyche leaves a great many obvious questions unanswered.

Gough offers a gently philosophical reason for his use of a fourfold classification:

We have Occasion to make use of several Sorts of Words; some to denote our bare Ideas of Objects, others the Modes, Qualities or Properties, which the Mind perceives in the Objects of our Ideas; some to denote Action, &c. and some to denote the Manner of Action: Whence those who write of Grammar say there are several Parts of Speech, which are generally reckoned Eight, but it may be sufficient for our Purpose to say there are four parts of Speech; Name; Adjective; Verb; Particle. (Gough, 1754, p. 40.)

The author of *A Pocket Dictionary* is one of the comparatively few advocates of a reduced system who attempt a justification for the particle. Of its four constituents he says: '...though of different natures [they] ought to be reduced to one class, since they always retain their form, and are subject to none of the variations of the other parts of speech'.[1] He is converting into a specific part of speech the classical category of indeclinables. This, and the attachment of the article to the substantive, a feature of the Latin systems, is a reminder that not all the grammarians adopting what is here called a vernacular system agreed in every respect with the reformers who provided its impetus.

SYSTEM 36

SUBSTANTIVE (incl. pronoun)	PARTICLE (compr. adverb;
ADJECTIVE (incl. article)	conjunction; preposition;
VERB (incl. participle)	interjection)

Lowe	1737	*New and Improved*	1771	John Carter	1773
Lowe	1755	*Spelling Dictionary*		Smetham	1774
Fisher	1750	*Court Letter Writer*	1773	H. Ward	1777

Uncertain classification. The grammar in the *New and Improved Spelling Dictionary* is a feeble work. The author adopts the fourfold classification, but calls the fourth category *article*. This is presumably a

[1] *A Pocket Dictionary*, 1753, p. 10.

mistake for *particle*, as he places *an* and *the*, which he calls *articles*, among the adjectives. He does not treat the adverb, conjunction, preposition and interjection in any way together nor use the term *particle* elsewhere. Carter and Ward leave uncertain the classification of the article, and Smetham and Ward that of the participle. The grammar in *The Court Letter Writer* is confused in its treatment of the interjection. It says first that there are three kinds of particle: adverb, conjunction and preposition. Later it says that the interjection is 'a particle that betokens a sudden passion of the mind'.[1]

Alternative classifications. Anne Fisher, in her general English textbook *The New English Tutor*, 1774, included a grammar using System 16, and Wilson, in his revision and modification of Fisher's 1750 grammar, changed the classification to that of System 9. Ward uses No. 9 also, but offers this one as an alternative: 'The Author presumes (and believes it will not be denied by proper Judges) that the preceding ten Parts of Speech, may with Propriety be reduced to four only...Supposing this Reducement approved, the kinds of Words to be treated of, are Substantives, Adjectives, Verbs and Particles.'[2] He makes it clear that he would treat the pronoun within the substantive. Smetham's alternative classification, for future Latin scholars, is System 1.

Grammarians' comments. Lowe describes the subdivision of the particle into its four constituents as the practice of 'grammarians',[3] which illustrates the continuing overtone by which grammar still implied Latin grammar, and also the generally accepted view that the use of the category *particle* was one sign of a vernacular system. Fisher discusses the four constituents of the particle separately and by name, but their common nature is described, and their classification in one category justified by implication, in the following passage:

Concerning all those Particles, i.e. an Adverb, Conjunction, Preposition, and Interjection, this, in general, may be observed, that they are very often used interchangeably, the one for the other, according to the Tenor and Exigency of the Sentence or Expression; the same Word being now an Adverb, then a Conjunction, sometimes a Preposition, at others an Interjection, as is obvious to the Eye of every observant Reader. (Fisher, 1750,p. 106.)

[1] *Court Letter Writer*, 1773, pp. 26 and 30.   [2] H. Ward, 1777, p. 35 n.
[3] Lowe, 1737, p. 8.

SYSTEM 37

| SUBSTANTIVE (with article) | VERB |
| ADNOUN (compr. adjective; pronoun; participle) | PARTICLE (compr. adverb; conjunction; preposition; interjection) |

Saxon (2nd edn)   1737

This odd classification is quite explicit. Saxon calls the substantive a noun, but there is no doubt that the adjective is considered not as a part of the noun but as the first of the three kinds of adnoun. Saxon recognises that pronoun, participle, adverb, conjunction, preposition and interjection are 'commonly called...distinct Parts of Speech',[1] but he makes no other comment about his classification.

SYSTEM 38

| SUBSTANTIVE (incl. pronoun substantive) | VERB |
| ADJECTIVE (incl. pronoun adjective and participle) | PARTICLE (compr. adverb; conjunction; preposition; interjection) |

Daniel Turner   1739   *An Easy Introduction* 1745   J.J., *Prittle Prattle*   1752

Turner uses System 12 but says, regretfully: 'I had divided [words] into four, viz. Noun, Adjective, Verb, Particle; but as the word *particle* signifies a little part, I thought it did not well agree with some adverbs, such as *unquestionably*, and therefore have preferred the above sevenfold division.'[2] This alternative suggestion of Turner's is the same as System 39, except for the position of the article. Turner does not mention *a* and *the*, nor the term *article*, but there is no reason at all to suppose that he would have included it within the preposition, as Barclay does in System 39. Systems 38 and 39 must therefore be kept distinct. Much of the material in *An Easy Introduction* resembles the *Pocket Dictionary*, 1753, and the *Spelling Dictionary*, 1755 (System 35) but here the article and participle are explicitly, though with some hesitation, included within the adjective.

The author of *Prittle Prattle* is 'not about to write an English Grammar'[3] and his classification is not very detailed. He makes no reference to the article or to the classification of *an* and *the*; otherwise

---

[1] Saxon, 1737, pp. 34–5.   [2] D. Turner, 1739, p. 12.   [3] J.J. 1752, p. 27.

he is clear enough, and clearly based, directly or indirectly, on the Port Royal grammar:

The Latin and Greek Grammars do both mention eight Parts of Speech; but in English they are all comprehended in four: for the four last Parts of Speech in the Latin Grammar, are comprehended in English under the Name of Particle: And as to the Pronoun and Participle, I shall have no Occasion to take Notice of, for they are all either Substantives or Adjectives. So there are but four Sorts of Words or Parts of Speech in English, for whatsoever is in the World is either a Thing, or the Manner or Quality of a Thing; the Action of Things or the Manner or Circumstance of Action. (J. J., 1752, p. 8.)

In other respects the grammar is Latinate, offering six cases for the personal pronouns and three genders for adjectives.

SYSTEM 39

SUBSTANTIVE (incl. pronoun
  substantive)
ADJECTIVE (incl. pronoun
  adjective and participle)

VERB
PARTICLE (compr. adverb;
  conjunction; preposition,
  incl. article; interjection)

Bellamy   1760   Barclay   1774

This is the fourfold system for which these virtually identical grammars express a strong preference over the Latin system (No. 1) which they in fact use. Bellamy and Barclay say that eight parts of speech are given 'by most Grammarians', but 'for Brevity's sake, may with propriety enough, be reduced... to these four only'.[1] Of the adverb, conjunction, preposition and interjection they say: 'they are too inconsiderable... to deserve such a distinct Separation or Division, they may all very naturally and properly be included under the general Term of Particles'.[2] The two articles are explicitly included within the preposition.[3]

SYSTEM 40

SUBSTANTIVE (incl. pronoun)
ADJECTIVE (incl. participle
  and article)

VERB
PARTICLE (compr. adverb;
  conjunction; preposition;
  interjection)

S. Edwards   1765

[1] Bellamy, 1760, p. xxxii; Barclay, 1774, p. xxi.   [2] ibid.
[3] Bellamy, p. xl; Barclay, p. xxvii.

Edwards is interesting as the only schoolmaster grammarian to see that some of the categories traditional in 'Etymology' could be regarded as different ways of classifying the same range of words: 'There are several Classes of Words; viz. 1. Possessive, demonstrative, relative and interrogative. 2. The Parts of Speech. 3. Primitive, derivative and compound.'[1] His classification is the same as that of System 33, except that he treats the interjection as a distinct particle from the adverb. He also has doubts about the articles. They 'seem too inconsiderable to make a distinct Part of Speech', so he allows them to be 'a kind of Adjective'.[2]

SYSTEM 41

SUBSTANTIVE (with article)   VERB
ADJECTIVE   PARTICLE (compr. adverb;
                                conjunction; preposition;
                                interjection; pronoun)

Cooke   1790?   Fordyce   1790?

These two grammars, which are very similar, treat the article in the section on the substantive but do not discuss its classification. There is no evidence to show whether the participle is to be put with the adjective or with the verb.

MODIFIED SYSTEMS AFTER 1700

SYSTEM 42

NOUN (incl. pronoun and participle)
VERB
PARTICIPLE (compr. article; adverb; conjunction; interjection; preposition)

Hugh Jones   1724

This is Gill's system (No. 22) except for the position of the participle, which Gill included within the verb. Jones is definite and clear: 'There are three Kinds of English Words or Parts of our Speech. 1. Nouns; 2. Verbs; 3. Particles.'[3] He classifies each subsidiary part of

---

[1] Edwards, 1765, p. 39.   [2] op. cit. pp. 41 and 44.
[3] H. Jones, 1724, p. 22.

speech and has special terms for some. The substantive is also called the *Noun Essential*, the adjective and the participle together form the *Noun Epithet*; pronouns are called *Nouns Adjutant*. His other innovations are recorded in chapter 12, pp. 390 and 391 below.

SYSTEM 43

SUBSTANTIVE (incl. pronoun)
ADJUNCTIVE (compr. adjective, incl. article; verb, incl. participle)
PARTICLE (compr. adverb; conjunction; preposition; interjection)

Kirkby 1746 *Practice* *c.* 1750?

Kirkby is quite explicit in describing this system: 'All Words may be reduced into three Kinds or Classes; viz. Substantives, Adjunctives and Particles.'[1] The Substantive comprises Names and Alternatives; these last are the personal pronouns together with *who*. The Adjunctive is defined as '...a Word which being joined with a Substantive expresses it under some Quality, Action or Condition: and this again is either an Adjective properly so called, or a Verb; according as the Substantive to which it belongs is a Name, or an Alternative'.[2] He defends the category later:

I think it must appear to anyone, who duly considers; that the Words, which Latin Grammarians call Verbs, are as truly Adjectives or Adjunctives to such Alternatives or Persons, as what we usually call Adjectives are to such Names: And what is understood by each is equally inconceivable, but as it exists in what we mean by its Substantive. (Kirkby, 1746, pp. 86–7.)

The Particle is said to comprise only the adverb, conjunction and preposition,[3] but the interjection is later treated as a part of speech, with these three,[4] and must presumably be included.

There are many difficulties in this system, including the fact that Kirkby does not in any full sense use it. He keeps to its terminology, but treats names, adjectives, verbs, adverbs and prepositions in separate chapters, headed with these names. But the threefold classification is not an incidental description: it is prominently placed at the beginning of the book. He seems to have been writing of it but not thinking in it.

[1] Kirby, 1746, p. 55.   [2] Kirkby, 1746, p. 57.
[3] op. cit. p. 58.   [4] op. cit. p. 114.

The English Categories

The Practice of Speaking and Writing English is likely to have been written after Kirkby's book. What Kirkby calls the adjunctive is called in *The Practice* the adjective,[1] but Kirkby, in the passage quoted above, had referred to verbs as 'Adjectives or Adjunctives' to pronouns. Both Kirkby and the anonymous writer call an adjective joined to a substantive 'the Adjective properly so called'.[2] *The Practice* treats the constituents of the particle in exactly the same way as Kirkby.

SYSTEM 44

SUBSTANTIVE (incl. pronoun) ATTRIBUTIVE (compr. verb; adjective; participle; adverb, incl. interjection)	DEFINITIVE (compr. article, etc.) CONJUNCTIVE (compr. conjunction and preposition)

Harris 1751	W. R. 1768	*Encyclopedia Britannica* (A)	1771

Harris describes substantives and attributives as 'Principals' because 'they still preserve a Meaning' when 'they stand separate and detached'.[3] Definitives and conjunctives he calls 'Accessories' because they have meaning only 'when in company, or associated';[4] these are the syncategoremata of Priscian and later logicians.[5]

The verb, participle and adjective are attributives of the first order. The verb expresses (i) an attribute, (ii) time, (iii) an assertion. The participle expresses only (i) and (ii), and the adjective only (i).[6] The adverb is an attributive of the second order, denoting an attribute of attributes.[7]

Definitives include the articles 'properly so called', and also 'pro-nominal articles' such as *this, any, all, no*.[8]

W. R. seems to accept Harris's system, which he describes fully,[9] but he finally adopts System 10. In the first two editions of the *Britannica* Harris's categories and terminology are taken over completely, although he himself is not named. For the third and fourth editions see System 9.

---

[1] *Practice, c.* 1750?, p. 47.
[2] op. cit. p. 48.
[3] Harris, 1751, p. 26.
[4] ibid.
[5] See above, p. 49.
[6] Harris, 1751, Bk 1, chap. 10.
[7] op. cit. Bk 1, chap. 11.
[8] op. cit. Bk 2, chap. 1.
[9] W.R. 1768, p. 139.

SYSTEM 45

NOUN (incl pronoun) ADVERB
VERB (incl. participle) PARTICLE (compr. conjunction;
        preposition, incl. article; inter-
        jection)

Martin 1754

The only comment Martin makes on this classification, which is quite explicit, is to doubt whether the adverb is really a part of speech: 'This Article of Adverb is, I think, too inconsiderable, to make a distinct Part of Speech; they might very well be classed under the Head of Adjective Nouns.'[1]

This is a radically different system from the one he advocated in 1748 (No. 35).

SYSTEM 46

NOUN (incl. pronoun, PARTICLE (adverb; conjunction;
 which incl. article) preposition; interjection)
VERB (incl. participle)

Bayly 1756 Bayly 1772

The first of Anselm Bayly's four works, *An Introduction literary and philosophical to Languages,* is trying to treat simultaneously four different languages—English, Latin, Greek and Hebrew. His attitude towards classification is unusually restrained; he comments that words can be divided into eleven, nine, eight, five, four, three or even two classes. To some extent this attitude is forced upon him by the necessity of handling so many languages together, but his support for a threefold system seems to be based on genuinely linguistic grounds as well as on expediency:

Words are the Substitutes of Things, their Actions and Relations... We have two principal Parts of Speech, Noun and Verb; which are the Foundation of all Discourse...There are other Words, which though not of absolute Necessity to the constituting a Sentence, yet serve to connect, carry on and form Discourse; being, as it were, Attendants on

[1] Martin, 1754, p. 113.

Nouns and Verbs, explaining their several Circumstances, Degrees, Relations.

These lesser Parts of Speech might be comprehended under one general Term, instead of these four modern; namely, *Adverb, Conjunction, Preposition, Interjection*: The Hebrew Grammarians give them a Name, which we may express by the Word *Particle*.

Thus there are three Parts of Speech, *Noun, Verb, Particle*. (Bayly, 1756, pp. 19–21.)

Bayly regarded his *Plain and Complete Grammar of the English Language*, 1772, as another edition of the *Introduction*, 1756,[1] and the grammar in *A Practical Treatise on Singing and Playing*, 1771, as 'a mere sketch.[2] He shows no sign of deliberately changing his classification of the parts of speech, but his practice is not consistent. In 1756 he had said there were three parts of speech; in 1771 he says there are four— Substantive, Adjective, Verb, Particle.[3] The *Practical Treatise* of 1771 must therefore be regarded as adopting System 35, q.v. In 1772 Bayly does not enumerate his parts of speech, but the arrangement of the material and his frequent references to the *Introduction* of 1756 suggest that he is again following a threefold classification and keeping substantive and adjective in one category. The important fact is that a major variation of this kind could occur without any comment from the author; the important implication is that Bayly was not clear in his mind about the distinction between substantive and adjective; the reason for this general failure is that grammarians were relying on meaning to distinguish categories which were more appropriately distinguished by logical or structural criteria.

SYSTEM 47

SUBSTANTIVE (incl. pronoun substantive)	ADVERB
ADJECTIVE (incl. pronoun adjective)	PARTICLE (compr. conjunction; preposition; interjection; article)
VERB (incl. participle)	

Wells   1760

This unique fivefold classification, from a writing-master in Cheltenham, is quite specific (except for some slight uncertainty about

---

[1] Bayly, 1772, pp. vi and x.   [2] Bayly, 1771, p. 2.
[3] op. cit. p. 13.

the placing of the article) but undiscussed. The author gives no indication that he is knowingly following, or departing from, any precedent.

SYSTEM 48

NOUN (substantive incl. pronoun; adjective incl. participle)	PARTICLE (compr. adverb; conjunction; preposition incl. article; interjection)
VERB	

Swaine and Sims   1761

The classification is firm: 'Words contained in our Tongue may be rightly and properly referred to three general Heads or Classes, viz. Nouns, Verbs, Particles.'[1] This is one of only five grammars to include the article within the preposition, but it is done without hesitation. The term *article* is not used; all that is said is, 'Prepositions are *a, an, the, of, for, from, by*...&c.'[2]

SYSTEM 49

SUBSTANTIVE	VERB (incl. participle)
ADJECTIVE	PARTICLE (compr. article; adverb; conjunction; preposition; interjection)
PRONOUN	

Hallifax (5th edn)   1765?   *Only True Guide*   1779

This system differs from the vernacular ones only in making the pronoun a distinct part of speech and in its treatment of the article. Hallifax uses the traditional terms, except that he mentions *quality* and *affirmation* as alternatives for *adjective* and *verb*. In the *Only True Guide* the 'English' terms are used: *name, quality,* and *substitute* for *pronoun*. Hallifax, or his printer, is confused by particles, participles and articles. On p. ix *an, the, from, with* are called articles; on p. xvii *from* and *with* are included, as prepositions, among the particles; on p. xvii the participle (which is in fact treated within the verb) is given as one of the particles, presumably by a misprint for *article*. The general intention seems clear.

---

[1] Swaine and Sims, 1761, p. iv.   [2] op. cit. p. xv.

SYSTEM 50

SUBSTANTIVE (incl. pronoun substantive)	ADVERB (words limiting only the verb)
VERB (incl. some participles)	COMPARATIVE (words which limit (i) adjectives, (ii) adverbs)
ADJECTIVE (incl. some participles; article; pronoun adjective)	PARTICLE (compr. conjunction; preposition; interjection)

Meilan   1771?

Although this is a fairly elementary work Meilan bases his classification on first principles:

What is the first step towards Etymology? To ascertain the different kinds of words. How is this to be effected? By considering how many kinds of thoughts the mind is capable of forming; words being only symbols of those thoughts...There are five different kinds of thoughts; namely, those of things; qualities of things; actions and qualities of actions, which last, as well as the qualities of things, may have their qualities likewise... besides these, there must be certain sounds which have no existence in nature, but like the tools of an artist, that are necessary in the execution of his designs, serve to connect word with word. (Meilan, 1771?, pp. 39–40.)

These six parts of speech he would call *name, nominal quality, action, actional quality, sub-quality,* and *non-entity,* but 'not utterly to leave the beaten track' he uses *noun, adnoun, verb, adverb, comparative* and *particle.*[1] His term *comparative* indicates a new category. He sees the adverb as having three functions: to express the quality of a verb, of an adjective, or of another adverb:

This obscurity is here prevented, by the introduction of a comparative, which has indeed a twofold office, but then it is branched out into two distinct species, being called *adnominal,* when it is connected with an adnoun, and *adverbial,* when joined with an adverb: by this division, the service of an adverb is limited to that of defining the quality, mode or circumstance of a verb, to which purpose only, its name shews it is applied. (op. cit. p. vii.)

In his later work, *An Introduction to the English Language,* 1803, Meilan uses System 9, but suggests System 50 as 'a much more just division'. For *comparative,* however, his previous term for words limiting adjectives and adverbs, he now uses the term *sub-quality,*

---

[1] Meilan, 1771?, pp. 39–40.

though he says little about it. He is describing the origin of language, and how 'the savage in the wilderness' gradually evolved different kinds of words:

As qualities may have *their* qualities, these last *theirs* also, and so downward through an infinite descent, he will proceed to introduce another part of speech, such as may designate sub-qualities. 'Sub-qualities', we say, and nothing lower; for to sink beneath the second state, might be considered too minute. For these sub-qualities, he must provide another general name, which may be that, already mentioned, of sub-qualities; but branched into two heads,as it sets forth the qualities of adnouns and of adverbs. (Meilan, 1803, pp. 3 and 5.)

Meilan refers, seriously, to the possibility of maintaining (as only Dalgarno and Captain Browne had so far done)[1] that there is only one part of speech in English. He quotes Horne Tooke as saying that by means of the noun and verb 'we may communicate whatever is communicated by the aid of all the ten'.[2] Meilan thinks: 'Mr T. might have gone further, and asserted that *one* part of speech will do for such a purpose, as is obvious in our mother tongue, when almost every real English word is both a noun and a verb: videlicet, *A hand, we hand. A fire, ye fire.*'[3] His implied argument is much the same as Captain Browne's, and may be derived from it.

SYSTEM 51

SUBSTANTIVE (incl. pronoun and article)
VERB (incl. participle; adjective; adverb; conjunction; preposition; interjection)

Monboddo   1774   Horne Tooke   1786

Horne Tooke and Monboddo advocate the same system of primary parts, for different reasons. The secondary parts shown above are Monboddo's; Tooke does not recognise secondary parts of speech. Monboddo is thinking in terms of logic, Tooke in terms of his own highly personal theory of abbreviation. Monboddo admits that the common division into eight parts

may serve the purpose of ordinary grammar [but] it will not be sufficient for a philosophical inquiry, such as this, into the nature of language, which requires that every thing of speech should be considered relatively to the nature of the things expressed by it. And therefore I prefer that division

[1] Above, p. 246.   [2] Meilan, 1803, p. 4.   [3] ibid.

of the parts of speech that has been given both by Plato and Aristotle, into noun and verb; and I will endeavour to shew, that all the other parts of speech above mentioned, may be fitly referred to one or other of these two. (Monboddo, 1774, pp. 28–9.)

He takes as the basis for his classification the distinction between substance and accident: 'The verb...I understand to denote every accident of any kind belonging to substance; whatever, in short, can be predicated of any substance as a property or accident, whether it be quality, quantity, action, or suffering, relation, or connection with anything else.'[1] He attaches particular importance to *action* and *passion*...

so far as they relate to the mind of the speaker...because all speech whatever, besides what it may express concerning the nature of things, does of necessity express some energy, passion, disposition, or, as I would chuse to call it by one word, *affection*, of the mind of the speaker...We may therefore say, that every word expresses substance, or accident, or the affections of the mind of the speaker. The first is what I call a noun, the other two are verbs...When the substance is expressed separately, it makes, what is commonly called, a substantive noun; when the accident is expressed separately, it is a preposition, adjective, or conjunction, which, according to my notion, are to be ranked under the verb; and if any affection of the mind of the speaker be separately expressed, it is either an interjection, or a species of verb known by the name of the substantive verb. (op. cit. pp. 31–3.)

Horne Tooke maintains that only two sorts of words—the substantive and the verb—are 'necessary for the communication of our thoughts', and that the other kinds of words we use are only abbreviations of these. When asked how many parts of speech he prescribes his reply is:

That shall be as you please. Either Two, or Twenty, or more. In the strict sense of the term, no doubt both the necessary Words and the Abbreviations are all of them Parts of Speech; because they are all useful in Language, and each has a different manner of signification. But I think it of great consequence both to knowledge and to Languages, to keep the words employed for the different purposes of speech, as distinct as possible. And therefore I am inclined to allow that rank only to the necessary words. (Horne Tooke (1786), 1829, I. 46.)

System 52 (see facing page) may derive just from a slip of the pen. Wynne uses, and has just enumerated, the Latin parts (System 1). He then adds a footnote: 'Some divide it [a language] only into four parts, and perhaps with more propriety and

[1] Monboddo, 1774, p. 30.

.SYSTEM 52

NOUN	VERB
PRONOUN	PARTICLE (compr. adverb; conjunction; preposition; interjection)

Wynne   1775

simplicity.'[1] He then enumerates the four primary parts of System 52 but refers to no secondary ones, except those within the particle. The resulting system is not one used or mentioned in any other English grammar, and though 'some' may be referring only to himself it is also possible that Wynne intended *adjective* for *pronoun*. He would then have been indicating a vernacular system and allying himself with a substantial number of grammarians, to whom 'some' could fairly refer.

SYSTEM 53

NOUN (incl. pronoun)	VERB (incl. participle)
ARTICLE	PARTICLE (compr. adverb; conjunction; preposition; interjection)

Cook   1793

Cook sees English as requiring a different system from other languages: 'Words...are commonly divided into nine Classes...viz. Article, Noun, Pronoun, Verb, Participle, Adverb, Preposition, Interjection, Conjunction; but in the English Language are reduced to the four [above].'[2] But he is not confident: 'An Adjective is not a Noun, but a Quality; yet may as properly be called a Noun in our Language as in any other.'[3]

SYSTEM 54

ARTICLE	ADJUNCT
NAME	RELATION
DEFINITIVE	CONJUNCTION
SUBSTITUTE	INTERJECTION
QUALITY	NUMBER
EXISTENCE	

'Mica'   1793

[1] Wynne, 1775, p. 4.   [2] Cook, 1793, p. 126.   [3] ibid.

This anonymous writer suggests what it is not entirely accurate to call a system of parts of speech: he seems to be trying to break away from the customary idea of definite word-classes. He says that he is attempting a fresh approach to English 'instead of...cutting and carving, twisting and bending, the parts of one language to fit them to the size, form, and structure of another'.[1] His short description uses eleven categories, most of which are equivalent to a part of speech.

The article, conjunction and interjection appear, by those names. Six other categories are named by the ideas they express: name, substitute, quality, existence, relation and number. The writer implies that these would be the names of word-classes as well, but his proposal is not clear on this point. *Substitute* and *existence* are certainly the names of word-classes, because for *substitute* he suggests the alternative 'relative term', and of *existence* he says, 'The next class here denominated *existence*, has hitherto defied the powers, and disdained the restraint of definition.'[2] The writer implies that *quality* refers also to a word-class, and the only examples he gives of *relation* are the words *of*, *to* and *with*. *Number*, on the other hand, can hardly be regarded as a category of the same kind. If his categories refer to word-classes, number is out of place; if they refer to ideas the expression of which modifies the form or use of words, then there are many more besides number. *Adjuncts* are described in terms usually applied to the adverb, including the view that 'they are only abbreviations'. *Definitive* seems to mean here much what it meant with Harris—a combination of the articles and the demonstratives. But 'Mica' uses *definitive* as a cross-category: some definitives are articles, some are not; some definitives can be used as names, others cannot. He gives no adequate illustrations, and one can only assume that while following Harris in stressing the logical function of words such as *this*, *any*, *some*, he is unwilling (because they can also function as substantives), to commit them to a single word-class.

The final result is a compromise between Harris's emphasis on logic and the mixed criteria of the traditional systems. 'Mica's' sketch is important as an attempt to establish a system of grammatical categories purely for English, but it remains only a sketch.

System 55 (see facing page), is offered, without further detail, as an alternative to the tenfold Latin system (No. 9). Bullen's

[1] 'Mica', 1793, p. 227.　　　　　　　　[2] op. cit. p. 230.

SYSTEM 55

SUBSTANTIVE   VERB

ADJECTIVE

Bullen   1797   Lovechild *Parsing Lessons for Elder Pupils*   1798

comments, which express uncertainty over the whole question of word-classes, are quoted above, p. 224. Lady Fenn, the author of Mrs Lovechild's *Parsing Lessons for Elder Pupils*, 1798, quotes,[1] but does not adopt, Bullen's system as an alternative to System 9.

SYSTEM 56

NOUN (incl. pronoun; article)   ADVERB
VERB (incl. participle; conjunction;
preposition; interjection)

Groombridge   1797

He says that words are divided 'by grammarians' into the nine parts of System 10 (which he himself uses), but are divided 'naturally' into the three parts of this alternative system, about which he says just enough to show that he is in a thorough muddle. He divides the primary category of noun into substantive and adjective; the substantive 'consists of', article, adjective and pronoun:

Q. How does that appear?
A. A noun includes its property...and is limited by its article: and a pronoun has relation to its noun, for which it stands. (Groombridge, 1797, p. 20.)

He then says that the verb includes prepositions, conjunctions and interjections.

Q. How is that evident?
A. The preposition implies action, and has reference to a verb, as well as to nouns and pronouns; to which it is either expressed or understood. The conjunction denotes action...the interjection signifies emotion or passion, which implies action. (op. cit. p. 21.)

[1] Lovechild, PE, 1798, p. viii.

273

CONCLUSION

Two questions were asked earlier in this chapter: how real is the instability of many of these parts of speech, and how real the diversity of the systems? The variations shown in the tables are real enough. The question is rather whether we are justified in calling what they signify 'instability'. We need to remember the historical background. Nine out of the ten common parts of speech went back, as a system, nearly two thousand years to Dionysius Thrax, and had been in continuous use, and to some extent under continuous consideration, ever since. They had originally developed, and had almost without exception subsequently been used, as a comprehensive set of word-classes: all words could be put into one of them. Even within the tradition, however, these classes had not been mutually exclusive. It was possible, as the summary of the tradition has shown, to discuss whether the interjection 'was' an adverb and whether the pronoun 'was' a noun. Grammarians were, in our eyes, inconsistent in their use of word-classes. Their belief that the classes were comprehensive could be justified only if the classes were mutually exclusive. If some words could be considered as belonging to two or more classes there was always the possibility that the characteristics which permitted this alternative classification were the criteria by which a new class should be determined. Until this question had been answered it was not possible to say how many word-classes there were. That these uncertainties were not understood by the early grammarians is another consequence of the fact that they had not yet distinguished between formal, structural and syntactic criteria. When a system of classification is backed by such longstanding and continuous consideration it is reasonable to assume that it will have become as stable as it can. Any considerable variations can fairly be regarded as evidence of instability. The English grammarians were less conscious than we are of the range of diversity. There are many reasons for this. Variations are often expressed only in single grammars, sometimes of largely local distribution. Only the scholarly writers, who are in a minority, consult more grammars than the few from which they are actually borrowing. But fundamentally the reason is that the writers have a different view of grammatical categories. They see 'the participle' as a category, unquestioned. Its content is verb-forms in -*ing* and -(*e*)*d*, but these are not the reality;

274

the reality is a traditional category *participle*. Their question is 'What is a participle?'. It could not yet be, 'How, and for what purposes, shall we classify such-and-such a linguistic feature?'. It followed, therefore that 'where to put' the participle could be, for the writer, a fairly unimportant matter. This suggests one answer to the question 'How real is this diversity of systems?'. To the schoolmaster in the middle of the eighteenth century it is not very real: in his eyes we are fussing about mere matters of arrangement. But to us, still entangled in the tradition and suspicious of its prestige, the diversity is real, because it is proof that the impressive solidity of this tradition is a sham; that our predecessors, too, suffered from a rigid and inappropriate schematic system. The diversity of systems is evidence of the grammarians' discomfort, which expressed itself in the only way it could: by shifting the elements in the scheme uneasily round and round.

Another possible source of misapprehension could invalidate our judgment about the systems. A merely arithmetical survey of the grammars treats the subtle grammar of John Wallis, who was a mathematical scholar and an influential founding member of the Royal Society, on an equality with the *Short Compendium*, 1796, by Mrs M. C. Edwards of Brentford Butts. May not counting heads in this way give unimportant variations a misleading significance? Certainly, of the 56 systems described above 28 are advocated, or accepted, by only one author. But it is not normally the hack or the ignorant writing-master who proposes the unique variant. There are six Latin systems which are accepted by only one author, but none of the writers could be said to be making an innovation through ignorance, and only one, possibly, through inadvertence. John Hewes, who proposes System 3, in which the pronoun seems to be included within the substantive, may have made a slip in his enumeration, but this is a facile explanation for his variant, and there is no evidence to support it. Hewes was certainly not so ignorant that he misused his terms. Mark Lewis, whose *Essay* of 1674 suggests system 6, seems to have been breezy and unsystematic, but his various efforts to classify the parts of speech show, in spite of their inconsistency, that he was deliberately trying to modify the customary Latin system. Maittaire's grammar, 1712, the sole proponent of System 8, is the work of a good classical scholar. It advocates a system which is unique only because Maittaire returns to the Greek

practice of classifying the interjection within the adverb. Daniel
Turner is the only advocate of System 12. His grammar is a concise,
elementary work but in no way suggests that its author, a dissenting
minister in Abingdon, was ignorant or careless. The fact that Isaac
Watts 'took an Hour's survey' of it is perhaps a reassurance, but
proves nothing. Turner is quite explicit about his system, which is a
minor, but deliberate, variant. John Henson, System 13, was master
of a Nottingham grammar school and a university man. He cannot
have classified the articles among the pronouns out of ignorance.
Rowland Jones, System 17, had a mind set on higher things, perhaps,
than the conventions of grammatical classification, but there is no
reason at all to suppose that his inclusion of the participle within the
adjective was other than deliberate. It had been so classified in
seventeen grammars before his. It is only the number of unstable, and
hence variable, parts of speech which permits the chance uniqueness
of his system. The same is true of the author of *The Young
Mathematician's Logic*, 1760. The last unique classification within the
Latin systems is that of John Dalton, 1801, System 20, whose
inclusion of the interjection within the noun is part of his deliberate
deviation 'from the path of my predecessors'.

The unique systems need to be regarded: they are not the work
of hacks. The hacks wrote grammars, but they copied them from
other people. The only unique classifications which might fairly be
regarded as the result of unimportant ignorance are those of
System 56 (proposed by H. Groombridge, 'Lecturer in Elocution,
Geography, &c.', which is conceived in a philosophical strain which
the author clearly cannot control), System 32 and System 47.

Not all parts of speech are equally unstable. As the tables show, the
variations are caused by three or four in particular. Within the 20
Latin systems, if No. 1 is taken as the norm, the 19 others vary from
it fifteen times in respect of the article, eleven times in respect of the
adjective, nine times in respect of the participle, six times in respect
of the interjection and five times in respect of the pronoun. Most of
these variations are trivial but real, and their cumulative effect is
significant. It matters little enough whether a particular writer
treats the adjective and the substantive as primary parts or as
secondaries. What does matter is that these were among the
numerous alternatives which faced every writer of an English grammar within our period.

Systems of parts of speech

Of the 275 classifications put forward in 259 grammars, seventy-four per cent belong to the Latin group of systems and fifteen per cent to the vernacular group. Practically all the systems which are proposed by individuals, outside the Latin and the vernacular systems, tend to favour a reduced system of parts,[1] often three or four in number. It is therefore possible to view almost all systems in only two groups: the Latin systems and the reduced systems. Only five grammars propose systems which are clear departures from the Latin but do not significantly reduce the number of parts of speech. It is then possible to see during what period reduced systems were most popular.

Up till 1730 the number of new grammars issued in each decade was too small to provide adequate evidence. During the decade 1681–90 four new grammars were issued, two with Latin systems and two with reduced systems; during the decade 1691–1700 two out of the five new grammars had a reduced system; during 1701–10 one out of three, and during 1711–20 two out of seven had reduced systems. Between 1721 and 1730 there were still only three new grammars, but two of them had reduced systems. The following table shows, for each subsequent decade, the number of new grammars (sometimes proposing alternative systems, which are treated as if they were separate grammars) and the proportion which propose a reduced system.

Decade	No. of new grammars	Percentage of new grammars which propose reduced systems
1731–40	15	33
1741–50	10	70
1751–60	22	62
1761–70	31	19
1771–80	55	27
1781–90	32	9
1791–1800	64	6

The popularity of reduced systems, shown here as lying broadly within the fifth and sixth decades of the eighteenth century, can be more precisely said to last from 1734, with the appearance of

---

[1] An exception would have been the grammar proposed by Sir Thomas Urquhart, in which there were to be twelve parts of speech (*Logopandecteison*, 1653, p. 18).

William Loughton's *A Practical Grammar of the English Tongue,* to 1761, the year of James Swaine's and Joseph Sims's *Cryptography.* During those twenty-seven years sixty per cent of the new grammars advocated a reduced system. In 1761 Priestley's influential grammar appeared; in 1762 the even more influential grammar of Lowth, together with Buchanan's *The British Grammar.* All three put forward Latin systems, and the reduced systems became steadily less popular.

There are three noticeable features of the Latin group: (1) The most frequently used system is not that of the Latin grammars, No. 1, but the tenfold system, No. 9. (ii) This tenfold system did not appear in print until 1760. (iii) When the tenfold system did appear it completely ousted System 1, which was used only thirteen times after 1760 and not again after 1778. The popular alternative to the tenfold system was that of System 10, which differed from it only by treating the participle within the verb and not as a primary part of speech. It is this treatment of the participle, both in Latin and in English, which has prevailed.

The grammars contain too little evidence for us to be sure about the reasons for these changes, but they strongly suggest that it was what are here called the secondary parts of speech that seemed to the teachers a source of difficulty. To make all ten components of the system of equal status was the novel feature of James Douglas's first draft (which he later altered) and of Dr John Ash's *Grammatical Institutes,* 1760, in which the tenfold system was first published, and it seems likely that this feature was welcomed as a helpful simplification. Ash had written originally for his five-year-old daughter, and had printed the grammar for the use of schoolmaster friends. When Lowth's grammar (itself called *A Short Introduction to English Grammar*) appeared in 1762 Ryland offered Ash's work as an introduction to Lowth's because it was so much more simple. This emphasis on simplicity coincides with the increase during the last decades of the eighteenth century in the number of elementary grammars. It would also explain the decay of the English systems, which were commonly considered to conceal a nine- or tenfold system beneath the appearance of a fourfold system. It was just this sort of complication which the teacher of young children wished to avoid.

One prominent feature of the vernacular systems is their use of the particle as a primary category. This classification has its precedents among the English grammarians in Wilkins, Lodowyck and Gill and perhaps in Wallis. Among the Latin grammarians of the renaissance it was advocated by Sanctius, 1587,[1] and it is implicit throughout the logical tradition, which regarded the noun and verb as the only significant kinds of words. Another feature of the vernacular systems, although not so distinctive, is the inclusion of the pronoun within the substantive. This also had been advocated by Gill and by Sanctius, and was part of the logical rather than the grammatical tradition.[2] It seems likely that Ramus's division of words into two primary classes, those with number and those without, was one influence behind the advocates of all reduced systems. That Ramus's system could lead into a fourfold one can be seen from a passage in an anonymous Latin grammar published about 1602:

Q. Can there bee no fewer than eight termes which doe conteine in them all sorts of wordes?

R. Yes it were more easie to say there are but 4, a Nowne & a Verbe, an Adverbe & a Conjunction.

Q. How so?

R. Because a Pronowne & a Participle may very wel be referred to a Nowne, & a Preposition and Interjection may well be referred to an Adverbe.

Q. What were the first differences among wordes if there were but foure partes of speech?

R. This. Some be wordes that have number in them, as a Nowne, & a Verbe. Some be wordes that have no number in them as an adverbe and a conjunction.[3]

The significance of these vernacular systems is discussed in chapter 16. The interest of those advocating other variations lies in their individual proposals. They have little in common except, generally, a desire to reduce the number of parts. Wallis, 1653, is the most conventional. He makes no explicit innovation, but by keeping strictly and simply to the facts of the language he manages to pass by those intricacies of classification which had usually been thought an important part of a grammarian's task. His grammar supports the customary classification if one chooses to interpret it that way, or a reduced system if that is preferred. It is understandable that Wallis

---

[1] See above, p. 53.

[2] For Roger Bacon's use of this Classification see above, p. 51.

[3] *Certaine Grammar Questions for the Exercise of young Schollers in the learning of the Accidence* [1602?], sig. B2 verso. The same grouping into these four parts of speech is suggested by Samuel Shaw, *Grammatica Anglo-Romana*, 1687, p. 3 n.

was freely used both by Brightland and Gildon in 1711, who adopted a reduced system, No. 33, and by Greenwood, who produced in the same year a conventional grammar adopting System 7. Modified systems are frequent in the seventeenth century, partly through interest in an international language, partly because there was as yet no alternative to the Latin systems and any potential reformer had to strike out for himself. Of the eighteenth-century modified systems that of Harris is by far the most robust and influential. Horne Tooke makes more noise, but is less interested in the formation of word-classes. His main concern is with his trenchant derivations and occasional abuse of Harris. Most of the other advocates of unique systems are accidental innovators, like Wells (System 47) or simplifiers like Wynne (System 52) and Bullen (55), or concerned with universal grammar, like Martin, 1754 (45) and Bayly (46).

Something of a puzzle is System 43, proposed by John Kirkby (1746) and the unknown author of the manuscript *The Practice of Speaking and Writing English*, to which Kirkby's work is closely related. Kirkby's grammar is, he says, designed to prepare for Latin, but he proposes a system found only in *The Practice of Speaking and Writing English* and unlike the Latin. It is basically the threefold system of Sanctius and Gill, but unlike theirs it combines the adjective and verb into a single primary part. No English grammarian had yet suggested this combination, though Harris was to do so five years later.

In face of these fifty-six systems what conclusions can legitimately be drawn? They have already been suggested:

(i) that this diversity *could* occur within an established tradition shows that the components of the systems, the parts of speech, were imprecise, inadequate and unstable;

(ii) that such great diversity *did* occur shows that the grammarians were dissatisfied—much more than we have realised—with the tradition they had inherited.

(iii) the vernacular systems point to the existence of a conscious movement of reform. This is discussed in chapter 17.

9. NOUN, SUBSTANTIVE
AND ADJECTIVE

DEFINITIONS

It was the practice of almost all the grammarians to introduce each part of speech by a general statement: 'A noun is. . .'. These general statements have the air of definitions, but are seldom referred to by that, or by any, name. It will be convenient to call them definitions, but too much must not be expected from them. Except in the hands of writers who were consciously breaking with tradition and were anxious to make their categories clearly understood the general statements were largely conventional. The grammarians sometimes offer examples which are inconsistent with their general statements; sometimes the general statements are too wide, or too narrow, for the examples. They are not, in fact, to be regarded as definitions in any sense which we should find satisfactory. They were not intended primarily to clarify and delimit a concept. They would be more accurately called descriptions: what they say about a part of speech is true, but not all the truth; it is true of that part of speech, but not necessarily of that part of speech only. In the same way that a system of parts of speech was customary, so it was customary to offer a general statement, short enough to be learnt by heart. Many of these definitions were virtually traditional formulae, appearing verbatim in grammar after grammar, and the subsequent treatment of the part of speech was not always closely integrated with the definition. Nevertheless they provide useful information about the grammarians' conception of the categories.

The inadequacy of definitions was not discussed as often as it should have been. Mark Lewis, as a good follower of Comenius, is admirably forceful and still worth attending to when he stresses that children do not *learn* by means of a definition:

Doubtless the Doctrine of Grammar is too subtile for Children; because it is communicated by Logical Definitions in the Etymologie, and by the signification of words in the Syntax, neither of which Children can reach, who cannot use Abstractions...These things [the functions of the parts of speech] are ordinarily represented to Children by second Notions. 'A Noun is the Name of a Thing, seen, felt, heard or understood. A Substantive stands by it self and requires not another word to shew its signification. An Adjective cannot stand by it self, but requires another word to shew its signification.' How unintelligible these Logical Definitions are to Children, those know that have been toyled with them...Consider whether it is not unintelligible to say, 'A Verb signifies doing, suffering, or being': The Notion of Action and Passion are out of a Childs reach...Do you think a Boy would judge, that *have sate* is a Verb, because it signifies doing? (Lewis, *Essay*, 1670, pp. 1 and 3.)

In a later edition of the *Essay* he again attacks the Etymology in Lily's grammar

because the Rules to know the parts of speech (one great cornerstone of Grammar) are logical definitions, reflecting the English tongue no more, than they do Welsh or Dutch. They are unintelligible to Children...I would fain see that Master which dares to stand by these Descriptions, as useful to Children; or that will undertake to justifie them against such visible marks, as may be laid down by Particles in the English Tongue, to to know the parts of speech by. (Lewis, *Essay*, 1674, p. 18.)

By the last sentence he seems to mean that a definition is a less effective means of learning than is attention to syntactic criteria—the 'visible marks': that children learn what a noun is by looking for the presence of an article rather than by learning a definition in terms of naming. Lewis may mean, however, that the definitions are incompatible with syntactic criteria; it is not just a matter of a more effective teaching technique but of a truer account of the function of the part of speech.

James Greenwood also questions whether definitions can do what is expected of them:

Definition [is] only the Explaining one Word by another that is more familiar...Languages are not always so made according to Rules of Logick, that every Term can have its Signification, exactly or clearly expressed by two others: I have therefore rather endeavour'd after a Description of what the Terms mean, than after a strict Definition of them. (Greenwood, 1711, p. 42.)

Even Michael Maittaire, whose method was based on 'Definition and Division...calling in often the help not only of Logick but even of Metaphysick to discuss these minute Principles of Speech', says he finds it 'very difficult...to give a just Idea of Things in the Definition of knotty and dry Grammatical Terms'.[1]

The difficulty is not mentioned again in an English grammar until the end of the eighteenth century, when it is crisply put by Henry Bullen: 'It is a much easier matter to write definitions for metaphysicians than for schoolboys.'[2] and an anonymous author exclaims more passionately: 'It is next to impossible to make the definition of verbs even tolerably clear to children.'[3] The practical experience of some schoolmasters that grammatical definitions were ineffective was supported by Thomas Reid: 'The definitions given by Aristotle of a noun, of a verb, and of speech, will hardly bear examination. It is easy in practice to distinguish the various parts or speech; but very difficult, if at all possible, to give accurate definitions of them.'[4]

The noun was always an unreal category in English. The formal bond between substantive and adjective which existed in Latin and Greek was lacking in English, and from the very beginning of the English tradition the substantival function of the noun dominated the adjectival to such an extent that the noun, sometimes in its definition and frequently in the body of the grammar, was practically equated with the substantive. For this reason it is impossible altogether to separate the definition of the substantive from that of the noun.

The commonest definitions of the noun, as distinct from the substantive, follow one or other of these patterns:

A Noun is a word that signifies a person or thing, as *an author, a book, learned, gilded*. It is either a Substantive, or an Adjective. (Wharton, 1654, p. 32.)

A Noun denotes the Thing, or its Quality. (Stirling, 1735, Sig. A 1.)

The duration of the primary category noun can be seen in the tables in Appendix One. The change by which the term came increasingly to be applied to the substantive is discussed in the section on terminology at the end of this chapter.

Criteria. The most important feature of the definitions of many parts of speech is the use made of different kinds of criteria: formal, syntactic and semantic.[5] The definitions are therefore examined in relation to their criteria: first the noun and substantive, then the adjective, each in relation to the three types of criterion.

[1] Maittaire, 1712, p. viii. [2] Bullen, 1797, p. 112.
[3] *Short Eng. Grammar*, 1794, p. 15.
[4] Reid, *An Analysis of Aristotle's Logic* (1773), 1812, II. v.
[5] These terms are defined in the introduction, above.

NOUN AND SUBSTANTIVE: SEMANTIC CRITERIA

There are ten recurring elements in the definitions:

(i)   *Naming*: this is by far the most frequent, but it is not used by all writers. Those who do not describe the noun or substantive in terms of naming do so in terms of other relations, variously described, between words and things. These other relations are, in order of frequency:

(ii)   *Other relations*: (*a*) expressing, (*b*) signifying, (*c*) denoting, (*d*) conveying, (*e*) declaring, (*f*) regarding. The things which words may name, express or signify are variously referred to. By far the commonest is the open term:

(iii)   *Thing* or *the thing itself*. Next most frequent is the pair:[1]

(iv)   *What is perceived* (by the senses) or is 'real', and:

(v)   *What is conceived* (by the understanding) or is 'imaginary'.

Frequent also is the familiar:

(vi)   *Person, place or thing.*

The remainder are less common:

(vii)   *A person or thing.*

(viii)   *A substance,* or 'the absolute Being of a thing', or 'things which subsist'.

(ix)   *What can be spoken of.*

(x)   *An idea or image.*

A few representative definitions will illustrate these types:

The name of a thing is a Noun (i and iii) (Lowe, 1737, p. 4.)

The substantive...denotes the thing it self or its qualitie. (ii and iii) (Aickin, 1693, p. 3.)

Nouns Substantive...are words whereby things, whether sensible or intelligible, are express'd. (ii, iii, iv, v) (*Pocket Dict.* 1753, p. 7.)

Substantives express the names of things or substances, whether real or imaginary...Anything that can be apprehended by the senses...is a substantive. (i–v, viii) (Wood, 1777, p. 6.)

The confusion shown in this last quotation, between word and object, between symbol and thing symbolised, is frequent. Other examples are: 'A Noun Substantive is the Thing itself',[2] and—an

---

[1] Especially in the form given it by Lily; above, p. 55.
[2] G. Wilson, 2nd edn 1759, p. 5.

Noun, substantive and adjective

extreme instance—'All things are nouns: you are surrounded with nouns.'[1]

Noun or Substantive is the Name of any Person, Place, or Thing. (i, vi) (Ash, 1760, p. 8.)[2]

Noun Substantives are Words that express Things themselves, that convey a certain Idea to the Mind. (ii, iii, x) (*Easy Introduction*, 1745, p. 59.)

Substantives express a Thing, of which we think or talk. (ii, iii, ix) (J. Williams, before 1780?, p. 5.)

In only a few grammars have the categories noun or substantive received fresh thought. Mark Lewis, at one stage, suggested an entirely novel sense for the terms *substantive* and *adjective*:

All Sentences are ordinarily composed of six Parts of Speech: Noun, Pronoun, Verb, Adverb, Conjunction, Praeposition. I would chuse to call the three first by these Names, viz. Substantives, Adjectives, Verbs. By a Substantive, I mean, a Noun Substantive and a Pronoun Substantive. By an Adjective, I mean, a Noun Adjective and a Pronoun Adjective. (Lewis, *Essay*, 1670?, p. 11.)

This anticipates the practice, common in the next century, of eliminating the pronoun as a primary part of speech. Lewis describes the process more clearly than do those who actually carry it out, but his own practice is less clear. In the *Institutio* he certainly makes the pronoun a primary part of speech.[3]

John Dalton offers a considered definition, in which *noun* is firmly used in its old sense. He is one of the few grammarians who are consistent enough to say, for example, 'the nouns *blue, hard, sweet*, &c. are the simple names of particular ideas'.[4] His full definition runs: 'A Noun is the simple or complex, the particular or general sign or name of one or more ideas or affections.'[5] The substantive he defines partly as implying 'matter or substance' but mainly in syntactic terms, which are discussed later in this chapter.

William Ward deters the modern reader by his elaborate academicism. Nevertheless his work is of interest, because he is retaining traditional categories but attempting to redefine them in the light of his own introspections into the working of language. He accepts the traditional category of noun, divided into substantive and

---

[1] *Art of Teaching in Sport, c.* 1770. p. 40.
[2] This is the first appearance of this formula in the definition of the substantive. It had been used in the definition of the proper noun in 1700. See below, p. 298.
[3] Lewis, *Institutio*, 1670, sig. A 2.   [4] Dalton, 1801, p. 6.
[5] ibid.

adjective, and gives an elaborate description of the criteria on which he bases it. One of his key terms is *object*:

> I shall use the word *object* in a sense somewhat more extensive than that in which it is commonly applied... [by it] is meant... not only whatsoever produces an image in the eye... but likewise whatsoever produces any sensation, or gives occasion to any internal conception, such as that the mind can employ its discursive powers upon that conception only. (W. Ward, 1765, p. 11.)

A second key term is *principle of existence*. Nouns express a *constant* principle of existence, verbs an *occasional* one. An occasional principle of existence is one 'considered as beginning, continuing, ending, being renewed, destroyed, and again repeated'.[1] A constant principle is one not so considered:

> As the conceptions denoted by nouns represent objects so exceedingly various; and the conceptions denoted by verbs likewise denote states of being so exceedingly various, it is difficult to discover any property which is not found in any verb, so general as to extend to all nouns; and to discover a property which is not found in any noun, so general as to extend to all verbs. Yet the constant and peculiar principle of existence, upon which the definition of the noun... is founded, and the inconstant and occasional principle of existence on which the definition of the verb is founded, are such properties as effectually distinguish the conception denoted by any noun, whether substantive or adjective, from the conception denoted by any verb in any of its forms (participles not excepted). (W. Ward, 1765, p. 13.)

This constant principle of existence may or may not 'be taken notice of'. When it is taken notice of there is formed 'the conception denoted by a substantive'. Ward recognises the weakness of his 'principle of separate existence' and guards himself against excessive realism:

> Very many objects denoted by substantives have really no separate principle of existence in themselves; as for instance, all the virtues, vices, arts, sciences... and in general all objects, the conceptions whereof are usually called abstract ideas. But the mind considers these objects as if each of them had a peculiar constant principle of existence in itself; and this the mind does merely for its own convenience. (op. cit. p. 14.)

In the grammar Ward expresses the difference between verb and noun in terms of number (another aspect of time); 'Every State that is denoted by a Verb, may be counted by the Numbers of Repetition,

[1] W. Ward, 1767, p. 41.

once, twice, thrice, &c ... as *such a thing was once, twice, thrice, so and so.*'[1]
And of the noun:

The Object or Circumstance denoted by a Noun is not subject to the
Numbers of Repetition *once, twice, thrice,* &c. Thus you cannot consistently
say *a Man once-twice-thrice*; or *Action once-twice-thrice.* Therefore *a Man* and
Action are Nouns: For they denote Objects not considered as beginning,
ending, and again renewed...nor can you consistently say *a virtuous Man*
or *a virtuous Action, once-twice-thrice,* therefore the Word *virtuous* is a Noun,
denoting a coalescent Circumstance. (W. Ward, 1767, p. 18.)

Coalescence is another of Ward's key terms. A 'coalescent Circumstance' is described as 'such as unites with an Object, without
increasing the number of the Object'.[2] Coalescence seems to be
equivalent to 'putting one concept into a subordinate relation with
another'.

It is now possible to approach Ward's definitions: 'Nouns are the
names of objects, as the conceptions thereof are distinguished in the
mind by constant marks or characters, which are conceived to be
evidences of a constant principle of existence peculiar to each object,
whether such principle is to be taken notice of or not.'[3] Nouns, that
is, all imply a separate principle of existence; to take notice of this
principle is to express the concept as a substantive; not to take notice
of it is to express it in 'coalescent' form: as an adjective. Ward's
definition of the substantive, however, raises great difficulty: 'Noun
Substantives either denote Objects, as distinguished by fixed or
habitual Marks or Characters; or coalescent Circumstances, to be
derived from these Objects.'[4] This seems to be inconsistent with all
he has so far said. A coalescent circumstance cannot be a substantive.
When he says, in the passage already quoted, '*virtuous* is a Noun,
denoting a coalescent Circumstance', he must mean noun adjective;
otherwise the point of his repeated contrast between object and
circumstance is lost, together with the subordination implied in
coalescence. Ward gives practically no illustrations of his exposition,
but it seems clear that if a coalescent circumstance is to unite with
its object without increasing the number of the object it must function
as in *garden hose* (one object) rather than *garden and hose* (two objects).

Ward's definition of the adjective virtually repeats what has
already been said in connection with the noun: 'Noun adjectives are

[1] W. Ward, 1767, p. 41.   [2] W. Ward, 1767, p. 18.
[3] W. Ward, 1765, p. 12.   [4] W. Ward, 1767, p. 19.

the names of abstract conceptions, similar to those which are denoted by substantives; only these adjective names give express notice, that no principle of separate existence is to be attended to, in whatsoever is denoted by any of them.'[1] To ask how the adjective gives 'express notice' would be to introduce all those structural considerations which Ward entirely ignores. The exasperating characteristic of Ward's *Essay* is that inside the network of abstractions one senses original thought and a fundamentally empirical approach, but every attempt to fix this impression in words is frustrated by the density of explanation through which one has to penetrate. His intriguing perversity can be illustrated in a discussion, more lucid than much of his writing, which has some relevance to the present chapter. He is discussing the substantival and adjectival expressions of the same concept:

The conception denoted by a noun adjective cannot be separately ascertained in the intellect, and laid up in the memory as so ascertained. For if it were considered under such ascertainment, it would become the conception of an abstract object, to which the mind gives a separate principle of existence... The conceptions denoted by the adjectives *woody, fertile*... if considered as separately ascertained in the intellect, become the abstract conceptions which are denoted by the substantives *woodiness, fertility*... Hence it is clear, that every adjective expresses a conception, which in itself is capable of representing an abstract object. But the grammatic form of the adjective gives notice, that the conception is never to be so considered, when it is expressed by its adjective name. All adjectives express abstract conceptions: even such adjectives as are derived from substantives which are the names of real beings. As for instance, the conceptions denoted by *manly, brutish, earthy* are not the same with those denoted by the substantives *man, brute, earth*, but with those denoted by *manliness, brutishness, earthiness*... It is true, that many adjectives have no abstract substantives corresponding with them, because such have not been found necessary in language. But the conceptions denoted by such adjectives are abstract conceptions... Thus the adjectives *Trojan, Sicilian, Miltonic*, do not denote the same conceptions which the substantives *Troy, Sicily, Milton* denote; but abstract conceptions formed from the objects denoted by *Troy, Sicily, Milton*, although these conceptions have no substantive names. (W. Ward, 1765, p.14.)

This is ingenious but false, because it neglects the fact that all names, even proper names, are in a sense abstract: *Milton* is the name of an idea.

The valuable part of Ward's discussion of the substantive and

---

[1] idem, 1765, p. 113.

adjective is the strong emphasis he puts on the view, inherent in the traditional category of noun, that the adjective is a linguistic device for expressing a relation between two concepts.

SUBSTANTIVE: SYNTACTIC CRITERIA

In Colet's Latin accidence, written about 1510 and incorporated into Lily's Latin grammar, the substantive is defined in syntactic terms: '...standeth by hym selfe, and loketh not for an other worde to be joyned with hym.'[1] This is not a satisfactory definition of the substantive, because it could be applied also to imperative verbs, to the interjection and to many adverbs. It served, however, to distinguish the two secondary categories within the noun: the substantive could stand alone, the adjective could not. This distinction was taken over into the English grammars, frequently with the words *man* and *thing* as tests. If a word could have *man* or *thing* after it, it was an adjective; if it could not, it was a substantive:

A Noun-substantive is a perfect word of itself without any word to be joined with it. (Bullokar, 1586, p. 340.)

Gildon and Brightland refer to independence both of meaning and structure:

Names, (as the Word imports), express the things themselves, and convey some certain Idea, or Image to the Mind, that wants not any other Word to make it the Object of the Understanding: for when we say a *Man*, a *Horse*...*Sweetness*, *Happiness*, and the like, who ever hears it, apprehends what we mean. And since *Names* express the *Things* themselves, you cannot put the Word *Thing* after them, without Nonsense, as you cannot say the *Man thing*, the *Horse thing*, &c. (G–B, 1711, pp. 72–3.)

To this definition they add, in a footnote, several paragraphs translated from the Port Royal grammar, in which the distinction between substantive and adjective is put in a more narrowly logical form. The distinction is developed in three stages. First, it is made in the customary way according to the thing signified: the substantive signifies substance, the adjective signifies qualities. But more importance is attached to the second distinction, which can cut across the first: the difference in the 'Manner of signifying':

Even those Words, which signifie Substances, are call'd *Adjectives*, when by their Manner of signifying, they may be join'd to other *Names* in

---

[1] Lily, 1527, p. 12.

Discourse: As the *Warriour God, the Bowyer King,* and the like, which tho' they are called Names put together by Apposition, degenerate here plainly into the Signification of Qualities, belonging to the *Names*; and are therefore *Names* degenerated into *Qualities,* or *Substantives,* into *Adjectives.* (G–B, 1711, pp. 72–3.)[1]

The third stage is to account for this incongruity in the manner of signification by distinguishing between 'distinct signification' and 'confused signification' or 'connotation'. *Red* signifies *redness* distinctly, but the subject of that redness confusedly. Gildon does not apply the Port Royal explanation to his own illustration, but presumably *warrior* in 'warrior God' is to be regarded as an adjective because its signification is no longer 'confused' but, by juxtaposition with *God,* is made distinct. This connotation is regarded as something which can be added to words and taken away from them:

As, therefore, that Connotation makes the Adjective, or Quality, so when that is taken away from Words, which Signify Accidents; they become Substantives or Names: as from *Colour'd, Colour*; from *Red, Redness*...On the contrary, when you add to Words signifying Substances, that Connotation, or confus'd Signification of a Thing, to which the Substances have a Relation, makes them Adjectives, or Qualities, as *Man, Manly, Mankind,* &c. (G–B, 1711, p. 74.)[2]

Abstract nouns are formed by the same process, though Gildon's translation does not bring out the full point of the Port Royal passage: 'Si l'on dépouïlle ces adjectifs formez des noms de substances, de leur connotation, on en fait de nouveaux substantifs, qu'on appelle *abstraits,* ou separez. Ainsi d'*homme,* ayant fait *humain,* d'*humain* on fait *humanité,* &c.'[3] The last stage in the Port Royal analysis, which Gildon also adopts, illustrates the awkward clash between different criteria which an inappropriate reliance on logic can cause:

But there is another sort of *Names,* which pass for *Substantives,* tho' in Reality they are Adjectives, since they signify an *accidental* Form; and besides denote a Subject, to which that Form agrees: Such are the Names of the several Offices, and Professions of Men; as *King, Philosopher, Painter, Soldier,* &c. but the Reason why these pass for Substantives, is, that they can have nothing but Man for their Subject, at least, according to the ordinary way of Speaking, and the first Imposition of Names, it is not necessary to join their Substantives with them; since they may be under-

---

[1] cf. *Grammaire générale,* 1660, p. 31.
[2] Translating *Grammaire générale,* 1660, p. 32.
[3] *Grammaire générale,* pp. 32–3; G–B, ibid.

stood without any Confusion, and they can have no Relation to any other Subject. By this means, these Words have obtain'd what is peculiar to *Substantive* [sic], viz. to Subsist by themselves in Discourse. (G–B, 1711, p. 74.)[1]

What is here described as if it were a feature of certain kinds of words is better described as a consequence of the processes of definition. A definition in terms of accident is discovered to be incompatible, in some cases, with a definition in terms of structural independence. Because *King* expresses an accidental property it should be an adjective; because it can stand alone it should be a substantive. The difficulty is evaded by saying that *King* is not really standing alone, because some word such as *man* is implied, but need not be expressed because it is the only word which could be implied. Difficulties of this kind still abound in our elementary grammars, and this would not be worth mentioning if it were not that the Port Royal grammarians seem at this point to be showing an awareness of the difference between a name and a description—a difference that was not clearly formulated until Bertrand Russell put forward his theory of incomplete symbols.

Many definitions which are framed in terms of meaning or of structural independence also say that a distinctive feature of the substantive is that it can be preceded by *a* and *the*. 'A substantive is that, which, without an Adjective, may have the Articles before it.'[2] Proper names, and words like *courage* and *grass*, which are used as often without the articles as with them, were an obvious reminder that the definition was inadequate (or, in its safely permissive form, 'may have...', no definition). This criterion, therefore, is less used than is that of independence.

Less frequent still, though a more satisfactory criterion, is the type of definition used by Bishop Wilkins: 'Every Noun which in conjunction with a Verb makes a compleat Sentence...is called a Substantive.'[3] This definition occurs in varying forms:

A Substantive is any Name or Word...of which any Thing may be denyed or affirmed. (Philipps, 1726, p. v.)

Most Substantive Nouns will make Sense with the Word *stand* after them, as, *a House stands*. (Corbet, 1743, p. 54.)

A similar test is the use of 'I speak of...' This is suggested by several writers: 'If, by prefixing the words "I speak of" before any word,

---

[1] Translating *Grammaire générale*, p. 33. [2] Butler, 1633, p. 33.
[3] Wilkins, 1668, p. 299.

the sense be complete, you may be sure that word is a noun."[1]
Martin Trinder adopts this criterion of combination with a verb, but
follows closely the criticism of the criterion of independence, first
voiced seventy years earlier by Richard Johnson, whose definition he
repeats: 'A Noun Substantive is: "the name of a thing that may so
subsist, by itself, in the understanding as to be the subject of predication."'[2] Trinder, still following Johnson, adds in a note:

The common definition of a Noun Substantive, that it requires no other
word to be joined with it to shew its signification, is also applicable to the
adjective; for the adjective signifies something by itself, and, as far as it
goes, it requires no other word to be joined with it to shew its signification.
The adjective, indeed, cannot stand by itself in discourse, but it must be
joined with a Substantive to make sense, but it, nevertheless, signifies
something though not distinctly, and particularly; and that something, so
much of it as there is, is to be known without the addition of any other
word, thus Good and Fair signify something of themselves, namely, the
denoting of those qualities to be in some Substantives. (Trinder, 1781, p. 8.)

This comment is significant because Trinder is trying to explain that
the criterion of independence ('...requires no other word to be
joined with it') was being interpreted in two ways. The interpretation which he considers false is one in terms of meaning. He says,
rightly enough, that the adjective, just as much as the substantive,
can mean something by itself. The interpretation which he accepts
is one in terms of syntax ('the adjective...cannot stand by itself in
discourse').

SUBSTANTIVE: FORMAL CRITERIA

It is not easy to say how far, if at all, considerations of case, number
and person enter into the definitions of the noun and substantive.
In the Latin grammar the initial general statement about a part of
speech was normally followed by an enumeration of its accidents.
Some accidents were often treated as defining properties of the part
of speech; some were seldom so treated; all could easily be incorporated into a general statement which was part definition, part description. When Thomas Lye describes the noun as 'the Name of a
thing without any difference of Time, or Person'[3] the reference to
time and person add nothing to the statement regarded as a defini-

[1] Rothwell, 1787, p. 63; similarly Harrison, 1777, p. 2 and Knowles, 4th edn, 1796, p. 7.
[2] Trinder, 1781, p. 8, from Richard Johnson, *Grammatical Commentaries*, 1706, pp. 6–7.
[3] Lye, 1671, p. 113 (actually 103).

tion: there are no names (unless you include the pronoun, which Lye did not) which *do* express time or person, from which other names need to be distinguished under the term *noun*. The first part of Lye's statement acts as definition, the second as description. The nearest approach, perhaps, to the inclusion of formal criteria within a definition comes towards the end of the eighteenth century, when John Knowles says of the substantive that it names a substance, makes sense by itself, and is declined.[1] But he later describes the declension of pronouns, which he treats as a separate part of speech, so here again his general statement (which is itself separate from his 'test' criterion, quoted above) must be regarded as part definition, part description. This seems the correct interpretation in other doubtful cases relating to declension. There seems no doubt that sometimes the plural form was taken as a defining characteristic of the substantive, especially by the seventeenth-century writers, and by eighteenth-century Latinists. A representative statement, more explicit than most, is Mark Lewis's:

A Noun is two-fold, Substantive and Adjective. These may be distinguished by Sense[2] thus. Substantives have usually a plural number, and stand after the Adjectives; Adjectives have not any thing to difference the plural from the singular, and stand before the Substantive; as *a little Book, little Books*: but we cannot say *littles Books*. (Lewis, *Essay, c.* 1670, p. 2.)

ADJECTIVE: SEMANTIC CRITERIA

There are three elements in the definitions of the adjective, all of which vary, one to a significant extent. The adjective is said (i) to 'express' (ii) 'a quality', sometimes (iii) of a word, sometimes of a thing. *Quality* is at all times by far the commonest name for what the adjective expresses. Most of the alternatives to *quality* are used as explanatory synonyms. The most frequent is *property*; then, between 1700 and 1760, *manner*; towards the end of the century, *nature*. Other terms, like *attribute, accident, circumstance* and, oddly, *form*, are used occasionally, the most frequent being probably *affection*, especially during the middle of the eighteenth century.

There is no agreement among the grammarians about the third element in the semantic definition: whether the quality which the adjective expresses belongs to a word or to a thing:

[1] Knowles, 1785, p. 4.
[2] *Sense* here means observation, uncomplicated by reasoning.

implieth a quality belonging to a Substantive (Butler, 1633, p. 36.)
signifies the nature and property of a thing. (Poole, 1646, p. 3.)
denote the properties of nouns. (Johnston, 1772, p. 12.)
explains the quality of things. (T.M., 1774, p. 11.)

There seems to be no pattern or development which would enable
one to predict whether a grammarian will attribute quality to the
word or to the thing. It is attributed to the word by a writer as
scholarly as Lowth,[1] and also by his unknown contemporary Mr S.
Johnson.[2] The thing rather than the word is favoured by a slight,
but not a significant, majority of grammarians. None of them discusses the question, not even the two or three who include both word
and thing. One is again forced to conclude that the difference
between words and their signification was not yet an available idea.
The status of words had yet to be understood, even though Locke
had put great emphasis on their conventional nature[3] and on that
'great abuse of words...the taking them for things'.[4]

ADJECTIVE: SYNTACTIC CRITERIA

As the purpose of introducing (syntactic) criteria into the definition
of the substantive was often to show how it differed from the adjective
it follows that the definitions of the adjective are often correlative to
those of the substantive and need not be discussed in detail. A few
representative definitions will illustrate the criteria:

(i) *Dependence*: 'Al nounes that wil join with a substantive are
called adjectives.'[5] Richard Johnson, insisting that the adjective can
make sense by itself (and therefore does not 'need a substantive to
explain its signification') offers an improved definition:

a Word added to a Substantive, to declare some Additional Accident of
the Substantive consider'd by it self, as of Quality, Property, Relation,
Action, Passion or Manner of being. I have added 'considered by it self',
because the Relations of Substantives, as consider'd in Sentences, is [sic]
declared by Prepositions, and not by Adjectives. (Richard Johnson,
Grammatical Commentaries, 1708, p. 8.)

The next quotation shows how completely Johnson's improvements
could be ignored:

[1] Lowth, 1762, p. 40.
[2] Mr S. Johnson, 1758, p. 4.
[3] Locke, *Essay*, 1690, Bk 3, chap. 2.
[4] op. cit. Bk 3, chap. 10.
[5] Hume, *c.* 1617, p. 30.

[an extreme instance] An Adjective signifies nothing by itself, and can convey no Idea to the Mind, without a Noun Substantive expressed or understood. (Buchanan, 1762, p. 91.)

express the nature, quantity, quality or form of substantives. Whatever word, not ending in -*ing*, or -*ed*, that will take the word *thing* after it, and an article before it, is an adjective. (A. Murray, 2nd edn. 1787, p. 27.)

(ii) *Use of the article.* Only a handful of writers refer to the articles in their definitions, and those who do find that they have to use them in combination with the '*thing* test'. This can be seen in the definition just quoted from Murray, and in one from *A New English Accidence*: 'Adjectives are distinguished by putting *a* or *the* before them and *thing* after them'.[1] The mere absence of an article does not indicate that a word is an adjective, in the way that the presence of an article can be regarded as the sign of a substantive.

ADJECTIVE: FORMAL CRITERIA

As with the substantive, formal characteristics are introduced into the description of the adjective rather than into its definition. A few writers say that the adjective has no gender; some say that it 'admits of comparison' (though they have to consider exceptions such as *some* and *all*, and the fact that adverbs can also be compared). A greater number of writers merely point out that the adjective does not change its form. Sometimes they say it is indeclinable, lacking case-inflection: sometimes, disregarding comparative and superlative forms, they say it is invariable. The seventeenth-century grammarians, in particular, emphasise the adjective's lack of number.

GRAMMARIANS' COMMENTS

Although the noun (comprising substantive and adjective) was sometimes made a primary part of speech up till, and after, 1800, this practice was much less common in the second half of the eighteenth century than it had been earlier. Between 1700 and 1740 the number of grammars classifying the noun as a primary is considerably greater than the number separating substantive and adjective. But between 1780 and 1800 the latter are eight times as numerous.

---

[1] *A New English Accidence*, 1736, p. 7.

The classification is frequently discussed: 'I use the words *Noun* and *Substantive* indifferently one for the other, to signify the name of a thing...the substantive and adjective seem to me as distinct parts of speech as the verb and the adverb.'[1] Lowth, whose influential grammar was issued more than twenty times between 1762 and 1800, gave judgment in emphatic terms, which are frequently quoted by other writers:

Adjectives are very improperly called *Nouns*; for they are not the *Names* of things. The Adjectives *good, white,* are applied to the Nouns *man, snow,* to express the Qualities belonging to those Subjects; but the Names of those Qualities in the Abstract (that is, considered in themselves, and without being attributed to any Subject) are *goodness, whiteness*; and these are Nouns, or Substantives. (Lowth, 1762, p. 40 n.)

In the same year Buchanan, whether independently of Lowth or not we do not know, expressed the same opinion. He discusses:

the strange Absurdity of ranging [Adjectives] with Nouns into which grammarians fell, misled by their having Terminations in the ancient languages like Nouns...Though a Man may be called *good,* and therefore *good,* in some Sense, may be said to be his Name, yet it is not equally as much his Name as Man; this last representing all that is essential to his Nature, the other only what is accidental. (Buchanan, 1762, p. 92 n.)

It is the tone of Buchanan's explanation, quite as much as the error he is attacking, which convinces us that this point of classification was a genuine difficulty (to him, at least) and not always an unexamined habit derived from Latin. Other grammarians continued to press the matter:

Adjectives are very improperly termed *nouns adjective,* by Mr Metcalfe, Mr Fenning, and several other grammarians: but...how can an *adjective* be called a *noun,* when a *noun* is the name of a thing, and an *adjective* expresses the quality of that *noun* to which it is joined? (Story, 3rd edn 1783, p. 13 n.)

In their nature, no two sorts of words can be more unlike, than the substantive and the adjective. (Beattie, 1788, p. 165.)

Many grammarians regard the adjective as a noun; but I would ask those who consider the import of the last mentioned word, with what propriety can that which does not express the *name* of a substance, but only applies the designation of a quality to the noun...be deemed a noun? (Coote, 1788, p. 13 n.)

[1] D. Turner, 1739, p. 12.

This was no doubt convincing, but the Latinists had their own view of the truth, and Alexander Adam, who was writing simultaneously for English and Latin, undertook the difficult task of agreeing with Lowth and at the same time repudiating him:

The Adjective...is only a word *added to* a substantive or noun...and should therefore be considered as a different part of speech. But as the substantive and adjective together express but one object, and in Latin are declined after the same manner, they have both been comprehended [in his own grammar] under the same general name. (Adam, 1772, p. 6.)

Some later writers of purely English grammars continue to follow the Latin practice, but the only tentative defence of it is by George Stapleton: 'Adjectives, in reality, are only the modificatives of nouns; though in one view they may be considered as nouns, viz. as they do not so much represent a quality or circumstance of the object, as the object itself, clothed with that quality or circumstance.'[1]

CLASSIFICATION WITHIN THE SUBSTANTIVE

The content of the category *substantive* was normally discussed in terms of sub-classification.

Common. The English grammarians add nothing to the traditional treatment of the common noun.[2] The standard form of their definitions was; 'A Substantive Common, is a name common to all things of the same kinde, as *a man, a land, an angel*.'[3] Some writers confuse themselves with too ambitious a use of the terms *genus* and *species*, and even Lowth's simplification of Priscian could be misunderstood. Lowth says: 'Common Names stand for kinds, containing many sorts; or sorts, containing many individuals under them; as *Animal, Man*.'[4] This is misinterpreted by John Fell[5] in such a way as to make the common noun stand for an individual: 'Common names stand both for general kinds, which contain different sorts, and also for individuals of each sort.'[6] The confusion may be to Fell's credit, for it may be a sign of independent thought. It would seem natural that

---

[1] Stapleton, 1797, p. 4.   [2] See above, pp. 83 and 87.
[3] Wharton, 1654, p. 33.   [4] Lowth, 1762, p. 22.
[5] Fell, 1784, p. 2.
[6] Beattie, writing the year before Fell, comments on the fusion of the meanings of *kind* and *sort*: 'Antiently the English noun *Kind* was the same with *Genus*, and *Sort* with *Species*: but *kind* and *sort* have long been confounded by our best writers; and we are obliged to borrow the words *genus* and *species* from the Latin.' (Beattie, 1783, p. 327 n.)

if *horse* is a common noun, an expression like *a horse*, which is singular and refers to an (unspecified) individual animal, should permit the common noun to be defined as referring also to individuals. But Fell and other writers did not sufficiently take into account the function of the article. The expression *a horse* is equivalent to 'a member of the class of horses'. It is the article which individuates; *horse* is still the name of a class.

Proper. The proper noun is still one of the categories over which grammarians and logicians quarrel, largely because they both assume that what is needed is one definition which will suit everybody, rather than a range of definitions appropriate to different purposes. The English grammarians follow the two principal approaches which are found in the tradition. Some attempt a logical definition, others what is here called a material definition: one based on the formula, 'person, place or thing'. Four variations in the treatment of the proper noun need to be noticed.

The seventeenth-century grammarians, who provide descriptions rather than definitions, refer especially to the absence of the articles: 'Nomina propria...articulos recusant nisi sit emphaseos gratia, ut the Harry of Harries.'[1] Gill adds also that proper nouns do not form a plural, but he is not defining them by these criteria, for he discusses also mass-words like *bread* and *blood*.[2] Jonson has the same wording as Tomkis: 'Proper Names...refuse Articles, but for Emphasis sake: as *The Henry of Henries*.'[3] Evelyn follows Jonson: 'Proper Names [substituted, as he wrote, for Nou...] and pronounes, but for Emphasis sake, as The Richard of Richards &c refuse Articles.'[4]

Two forms of the logical definition of the proper noun exist side by side throughout the period. The simple form of the definition is first found in Wilkins: 'Proper Nouns...belong to one.'[5] This form appears usually in words such as:

signifies the name attributed to some particular person or thing. (Clare, 1690, p. 22.)

the names appropriated to individuals: as *George, London, Thames*. (L. Murray, 1795, p. 23.)

The fuller form of the logical definition, which merely underlines what is implied by the simple form, runs to this effect: '...the name

---

[1] Tomkis, 1612, fol. 4 verso. [2] Gill, 1619, p. 36.
[3] Jonson, 1640, I. chap. 9. [4] Evelyn, *c.* 1650, fol. 95 recto. [5] Wilkins, 1668, p. 299.

given to some particular Thing to distinguish it from others of the same kind.'[1]

The fourth approach to the proper noun is apparent in Smith's *nomen proprium tam hominum quam urbium*,[2] but the first appearance of the common English formula is in 1700: '. . .the proper name of some one Individual Person, Place or Thing, whereby it may be known, and distinguished from others of the same kind: as, *William. . . December*.'[3] The only variation in this type, which is popular, but less used than the more purely logical type, is in the extent of the enumeration: '. . .Names of Men, Women, Cities, Towns, Rivers, pick'd out from the rest, by names peculiarly proper to them.'[4]

This material approach, which these examples show to be combined also with a logical approach, is implied very often by the examples which follow the more purely logical definitions. These examples are almost always the names of people or geographical features. Discussion of them has made the logical and material approaches seem more distinct than in fact they are. There is no reason to suppose that those who gave a logical definition would have repudiated its material form. It is more likely that they considered the greater generality of the logical form more suited to a definition than was the particularity of the material form, where enumeration of constituents might be continued indefinitely.

Abstract and Concrete. Throughout the tradition, certainly since Donatus,[5] various attempts had been made to include within the classification of the noun a distinction corresponding to that between 'material' and 'immaterial'. The distinction was unhelpful linguistically, because it in no way affected the functioning of words, and philosophically it was either trivial or too difficult to be relevant to the grammarian, however widely his interests were conceived. Less than forty of the English grammarians make use of these categories, and most of them refer only to abstract nouns.

Wilkins uses the terms *abstract* and *concrete* in his vast attempt to make a 'distinct expression of all things and notions that fall under discourse'.[6] He does not define either term, but illustrates them by examples. Concrete substantives are *heat* and *light* (that is, the names

[1] Barker, 1733, p. 3.   [2] J. Smith, 1674, p. 223.
[3] Brown, 1700, p. 90.   [4] Collyer, 1735, p. 7.
[5] See p. 86 above.   [6] Wilkins, 1668, Epistle Dedicatory.

of the physical sensations); *hotness* (*caloritas*) and *lightness* (*luciditas*)[1]
are abstract substantives. Cooper, who here follows Wilkins closely,
defines the categories in traditional terms: 'Id, quod significat ens
vel rem ipsam, denominetur *concretum*; id quod essentiam significat,
abstractum.'[2] To Wilkins' examples, which he repeats, Cooper adds
love, as concrete, and *amity* as abstract. Although Cooper is writing
an ordinary English grammar he is, like Wilkins, more concerned at
this point with philosophical than with grammatical categories:
'Divisio nominum in *concrete* et *abstracta*, maxime nostram meretur
disquisitionem.'[3] But his purpose is '. . . ut intima eorum natura magis
illucescat'. Joseph Aickin seems to have borrowed Cooper's examples,
and through him some of Wilkins' coinings: 'Substantives and Adjectives are divided into, *Concretes*, and *Abstracts*: as, *heat, hot; heating,
heated;. . . amity, amorous. . . hotness, calefactive.*'[4] The term *concrete* is
little used in the English grammars before 1800, and then, as by
Dr Johnson,[5] as an incidental descriptive term rather than as the
name of a distinct category. James Douglas is unusual in making
concrete ('belongs to any substance') an explicit class of substantives.[6] Lane is the last of the seventeenth-century grammarians to
classify the substantive according to these criteria, and the last before
Harris, 1751, to provide a correlative term for *abstract*: 'A Substantive is a Word that signifies a thing whether Corporeal or Incorporeal; as *God, Man, Reason, Wisdom*. . .A Corporeal thing is that
which can be perceived by the Senses. . .An Incorporeal. . .thing
is that which [can be perceived] only by the Understanding. . .as
Justice, Knowledge.'[7] *Abstract* Lane restricts to substantives formed
from an adjective, as by the addition of *-ness*, which 'signifies a
Quality, as Abstracted or separated from any Subject'.[8] This
restricted use of the term corresponds to Greaves' *substantiva qualitatis*,[9]
which are those formed from adjectives. It is found also in later
grammars.[10] Other writers say that abstract nouns 'relate to the

---

[1] Wilkins, 1668, p. 303. Wilkins wrote in English. The Latin terms he gives to explain,
or make good the lack of, English terms are a measure of the inadequacy (in his view) of
English, and also of the artificiality (in our view) of his approach. But he was primarily
concerned with an artificial language.

[2] Cooper, 1685, p. 87.   [3] ibid.

[4] Aickin, 1693, p. 3.

[5] Dr S. Johnson, 1755, section 'Of Derivation'.

[6] Douglas, *c.* 1720, MS No. 585, fol. 18 recto.

[7] Lane, 1700, p. 20.

[8] Lane, 1700, p. 62.   [9] Greaves, 1594, p. 11.

[10] e.g. Dr Johnson, 1755; Gough, 1754; Wiseman, 1764; Bayly, 1772.

powers of the soul only',[1] or 'can only be known by the operations of the mind',[2] or 'denote the essence of the thing',[3] or 'belong to qualities, passions, etc.'[4] or 'are only perceptible by the more refined operations of the mind'.[5] Abstraction is regarded more as a beautiful condition than as a process. The most thoughtful account that any grammarian gives of it is in Beattie's chapter on Nouns:

> Now the things we speak of either have a real existence, as man, tree, house, hatchet; or have had a real existence, as Babylon, Eden, Cesar; or are spoken of as if they had existed, or did exist, as Jupiter, Fairy, Lilliput; or are conceived by the mind as having at least the capacity of being characterised by qualities, as virtue, beauty, motion, swiftness. These last are called Abstract Nouns; and the understanding forms them, by abstracting, or separating, from any natural or artificial substance, either real, or imaginary, certain qualities, and making those qualities the subject of meditation or discourse: as—the eagle *flies*—its *flight* is swift;...Voltaire was *witty*—his *wit* was indecent. (Beattie, 1783, p. 323.)

Natural and Artificial. Of some influence, but no grammatical importance, was James Harris's threefold classification of substantives into *natural*, *artificial* and *abstract*.[6] He speaks at first of substance, not substantives, but his argument assumes that 'Words [follow] the nature and genius of Things', and those who borrowed from him interpreted him in this way. His examples explain his terms: *telescope* is artificial; *vegetable* is natural; *temperature* is abstract. This classification is followed or referred to by Buchanan, 1762;[7] Burn, 1766;[8] *Encyclopaedia Britannica* (A), 1771;[9] M'Ilquham, 1781;[10] Lynch, 1796;[11] and by Meilan, 1803.[12] Lynch, who classifies substantives also as generic, specific and individual, is one of the very few writers before 1800 who will occasionally treat a phrase as a single part of speech: as examples of an abstract individual substantive he gives *falcon's flight* and *hound's course*.[13]

Collective. The collective noun had long been a recognised category and appears regularly in the English grammars. It is referred to in

[1] Crocker, 1772, p. 9.
[2] Wood, 1777, p. 6.
[3] Shaw, 1778, p. 85.
[4] Devis, added by 5th edn 1786, p. 9.
[5] Devis, 8th edn 1795, p. 8.
[6] Harris, 1751, Bk I. chap. 4.
[7] Buchanan, 1762, p. 75 n.
[8] Burn, 1766, p. 21.
[9] *Enc. Brit.* (A), 1771, 2. 729.
[10] McIlquham, 1781, p. 32.
[11] Lynch, 1796, p. 8.
[12] Meilan, 1803, p. 9.
[13] Lynch, p. 9.

the syntax more often than in the etymology, and for this reason, perhaps, it is mentioned in only about a dozen grammars before 1770. After that, when the treatment of syntax was more thorough and usage was discussed in detail, it appears in practically every grammar: advice had to be given on whether to use a singular or a plural verb with words like *crowd*. For the same reasons definitions are few. The category is self-explanatory, as is its usual name, *noun of multitude*:

signifies many, as if they were one. (Entick, 1728, p. 6.)
Names which have the Ending of Singulars and Meaning of Plurals are called Collectives: as *an Army, Brace, Company*. (Kirkby, 1746, p. 65.)

Other classifications.[1] The variety of word-forms which can be pressed to serve under the noun is too great to record completely. Most of the categories are traditional: Entick's 'partitive' (*some*), Wiseman's 'distributive', Miege's 'interrogative' and Blanch Mercy's 'verbal'. Some classifications relate solely to word-formation, such as diminutives, augmentatives, derivatives and Wilkins's 'substantives of the person' (i.e. forms in *-er* and *-or*). Others, like the 'relative noun' (i.e. words like *husband*) of Miege and Maittaire, recall the excesses of earlier list-addicts.

Wilkins is interesting for reintroducing,[2] though not into a conventional grammar, the idea that nouns have voice. One of the ways in which he classifies substantives is as active, passive and neuter. Active substantives 'signifie...the Doing of a thing'. They express 'the same notion which in Greek and Latin is expressed by the Infinitive Mode'.[3] His example is the much overworked *heating* (*calefactio*). Nouns substantive passive 'signifie...the Suffering of a thing',[4] e.g. *being heated, calefactibility*.[5] Cooper adds *loveliness* (*amabilitas*), where the Latin is a necessary pointer to the relevant sense of the English word. Wilkins's neuter substantive is identical with the concrete substantive already described.[6]

Mass-words were recognised as having particular features, but were seldom treated as a distinct category. Bullokar seems to have anticipated Jespersen, but his reference is ambiguous. In discussing plural forms he says: '*People, folk, swine, cattle, fowl, deer*, are used in

---

[1] For the personal noun see below, p. 347.   [2] Above, p. 113.
[3] Wilkins, 1668, p. 300.   [4] op. cit. p. 298.   [5] op. cit. p. 303.
[6] See above, p. 299.

both numbers, and most collectives and massatives, and some ending in *x*, or *z*, form the plural by adding *en*, as of *ox, oxen*: or *hose, hoses* and *hosen*.'[1] If 'collectives and massatives' refers back to the illustrations just given Bullokar is not referring to our mass-words or uncountables; if collectives and massatives are different from the illustrations he presumably does mean our mass-words. The traditional name for the category is introduced by a few writers of English grammars: the 'specific' noun.[2] The earliest English grammar in which this name appears seems to be the grammar prefixed to Daniel Fenning's *The Royal English Dictionary*, 1761, a very ordinary grammar which is not likely to be original: 'A specific name is that which signifies a whole species or kind, and may be distinguished, in our language, both from its having no plural, and likewise from its never being used in the singular with *a* before it.'[3] Fenning's examples of specific nouns are *gold* and *flesh; man*, in *man is mortal* is a noun 'used specifically'. Words of this type are, of course, frequently discussed in connection with the plural, or with the use of the articles, but Fenning (and the three authors who reproduce him) together with Marriott[4] and Fell,[5] is one of the very few who revive the old name for them. Ussher, 1785, misleadingly refers to them as 'collective terms', in addition to his collective nouns.[6] James Douglas is unusual in reviving for English that class of substantives 'whose sound seems to resemble the Thing for which they are design'd, as Clank, Crash'. These he calls 'fictitious nouns'.[7]

Barely relevant here, but altogether delightful, is a marginal note in Christopher Cooper's chapter on compound words, especially substantives and adjectives, which suggests an alternative classification for *clank* and *crash*. Cooper says that *gruff, whirl* and *twinch* are examples of 'compound monosyllables'; *gruff* is compounded from *grave* and *rough; whirl* from *wheel* and *hurl; twinch* from *twitch* and *pinch*.[8] Dr Johnson also, in the section of his grammar headed 'Derivation', takes up this suggestion and offers *scroll* (*scrip* and *roll*),

---

[1] Bullokar, 1586, p. 345.
[2] See above, p. 84.
[3] Fenning, 1761, p. 8, as also in the identical grammars: J. Johnson, 1763; *Universal Dictionary*, 1763; Bayley, 1764.
[4] Marriott, 1780, sig. b 1.
[5] Fell, 1784, p. 3.
[6] Ussher, 1785, p. 5.
[7] Douglas, c. 1720. MS. No. 587 a. fol. 69 verso. Cf. Priscian's *factitium*, above, p. 83.
[8] Cooper, 1685, p. 148.

prance (*proud* and *dance*) and others. Lewis Carroll was the first to apply the term *portmanteau* to such words, but he did not invent the category.

Lily's grammar had enumerated over twenty kinds of noun adjective, almost all of them in Donatus or Priscian, and it would have been possible to add as many again from the resources of the tradition.[1] As the English equivalents of these words lacked the formal resemblance to each other which had kept *meus, alius, unus, bonus, Marcus* and *hodiernus* in the same broad word-class many categories hitherto regarded as adjectival were treated in English under the pronoun or were dropped altogether.

Minor categories. One or two seventeenth-century grammarians try to preserve within the adjective the distinction between proper and common which had always been attached more firmly to the substantive: 'The Noune Adjective Proper is derived from a noune substantive Proper, as *English.*'[2] Lye makes the same distinction and uses the same example, with *great* and *rich* as common adjectives.[3] Proper adjectives may be real enough, but the common adjective is even less real than the common substantive, and the distinction did not flourish. Some late-eighteenth-century grammarians refer to 'common' adjectives, as *good* and *white*,[4] but neither proper nor common adjectives form a continuing category.

More frequent are various kinds of derivative adjective formed from substantives. The fullest classification is given by Lane:[5] *material* (golden); *of fullness* (those ending in *-ful, -y,-ous*); *of emptiness* (those ending in *-less*); *of likeness* (manly); *diminutives*; *ordinals*; *possessive* (described below, p. 307). Material adjectives are mentioned by other seventeenth-century grammarians,[6] and P. W. Fogg at the end of the eighteenth century refers to but does not adopt the category.[7]

A few writers refer to concrete and abstract adjectives. Wallis refers to 'Concreta Adjectiva' such as *white* and *great*;[8] Wilkins,

---

[1] cf. pp. 83 f. above.
[3] Lye, 1671, p. 113 (actually 103).
[4] Coote, 1788, p. 76; Bridel, 1797, p. 20.
[6] e.g. Wallis, 1653, p. 84; Cooper, 1685, p. 114.
[7] Fogg, 1796, p. 212.
[2] Poole, 1646, p. 3.
[5] Lane, 1700, p. 66.
[8] Wallis, 1653, p. 118.

Cooper and Aickin apply to adjectives the quasi-logical classification they applied to substantives: *concrete* (hot) and *abstract* (caloritative).[1] The term *concrete* is not frequent. Dr Johnson is unusual in referring to *white* and *skilful* as 'concrete adjectives' from which abstract substantives are formed. Wilkins and Cooper also repeat their classification into *active* (heating), *passive* (heated) and *neuter* (hot) adjectives.[2]

Most other subdivisions of the adjective are closely bound up with the pronoun. When the early-eighteenth-century grammarians had to classify words like *my* and *this* many of them seem to have lost control of the system they were supposed to be expounding. The chaos created by their incompatible classifications is discussed in the next chapter. They were suffering, as every grammarian suffers, from the internal maladjustment of the category *pronoun*, which contains words of such a wide range of function that any attempt to classify them in traditional ways forces the grammarian either to destroy the category by truly displaying its diversity, or to make his classification worthless by keeping together what should really be separated.

A few grammars contain quirks in the classification of the adjective which are of interest only in showing how much variation could be introduced into established and familiar categories. Such are Bell, 1769; Fell, 1784; Coote, 1788; Fogg, 1792 (who comes to his senses in 1796 when he adds, 'I see little or no necessity for subdivision')[3] and Postlethwaite, 1795. Three representatives will suffice: Nicholas Salmon, who is illuminatingly muddled; Mrs Eves, who is unthinkingly original; and John Dalton, who is wrestling.

Salmon briefly classifies adjectives under two heads: *special* and *numerical*. 'An Adjective may be either *special* or *numerical*; that is, an Adjective either particularizes a Noun so as to *determine its species*, or else it fixes its *quantity* or *number*. An Adjective may also *particularize a Pronoun*.'[4] He does not develop this classification, nor use it in his own examples. Elsewhere he thinks in more conventional terms. The following passage shows not only the categories he actually uses but the mixing of formal and semantic criteria which is the main source of the confusion surrounding the adjective and pronoun. He is (as usual) discussing lines from *Edwin and Emma*:

> Nor let the pride of great ones scorn
> This charmer of the plains.

[1] Wilkins, 1668, p. 303.
[3] Fogg, 1796, p. 212.
[2] ibid.
[4] Salmon, 1798, p. 1.

'*Ones*', he says,

might be supposed to be a Pronoun, because it seems to stand of itself instead of a Noun...such as *folks, men, persons,* &c. but it is there a *Substantive Adjective* used in the plural (the sign *s* is seldom allowed in English to Substantive Adjectives, but we find it in *ones, others, betters, inferiors, superiors*)...because *one* is an Adjective when a Noun comes along with it, and a Substantive Adjective when the Noun is left understood...When the Noun is left understood after an Adjective, this Adjective, though it retains its power or influence in regard to the particularizing of objects, ought rather to be considered as a Noun in Grammar: but as such Noun presents the idea of an Adjective, and tacitly of a Noun or Substantive, I would then call it a Substantive Adjective. (Salmon, 1798, pp. 24–6.)

Other examples of substantive adjectives are *mine, his, hers. My* and *his* Salmon calls possessive adjectives, and *this, that* Pronominal Demonstrative Adjectives. The feature which he is discussing is real enough: the interesting thing about his discussion is that the category of substantive adjective, which ought to be a suicidal paradox, leaves the traditional parts of speech shaken, perhaps, but undamaged. One sees what he means. It remains to be decided whether this invulnerability is to the credit of the system or not.

Mrs Eves is not likely to be original, but her threefold classification of the adjective does not seem to occur in any earlier English grammar:

Of quality: e.g. an *elegant* lady
Of form: e.g. a *long* table
Of number: e.g. *three* peacocks[1]

One wonders whether Mrs Eves would have classified *slender* in 'a *slender* lady' as an adjective of quality or of form?

Dalton sees more clearly, perhaps, than any of his predecessors that two of the traditional functions of the adjective are significantly different, and he makes, accordingly, a distinction between logical and attributive adjectives.[2] Harris had made the same distinction as part of his return to Aristotle, but had been misled by the post-Aristotelian practice of regarding the copula as the fundamental verb into treating the verb, together with the adjective, as basically the expression of an attribute. This is to depart too far from the formal data of language to be an acceptable analysis grammatically. Dalton's two kinds of adjective are: *Definitives* or *Articles* 'which are applied to *general* terms to limit their signification'; *Qualities*

---

[1] Eves, 1800, p. 14.   [2] Dalton, 1801, p. 15.

Noun, substantive and adjective

'...applied to complex general terms [i.e. common nouns];[1] they signify certain ideas which are to be added to or subtracted from the collection denoted by the general term.' His examples of definitives are grouped into those of number and those of time or place. 'Number' is stretched to include *neither, none, other, or,* and 'time' to include *early* and *soon.* 'Other definitives' are *the, this, same, like, such, as, so, which.* Dalton seems to be trying to do what logicians have more clearly achieved through the notion of quantification; but his definitives perform a number of quite different logical functions.

By far the most interesting and influential categories within the adjectives are two created, it would seem, by Wallis, 'possessive' and 'respective': 'Duo sunt Adjectivorum genera, a Substantivis immediate descendentia, quae semper Substantivis suis praeponuntur. Eademque omnium fere Praepositionum vices supplent.'[2]

Wallis's possessive adjectives. Wallis's 'Adjectiva Possessiva' are substantives or substantive phrases in possessive form. His examples, which specifically draw attention to the group genitive, are: '*Mans nature, mens nature, Virgils poems, the Kings Court, the King-of-Spain's Court*......toti nempe illi aggregato *the King of Spain,* tanquam uni Substantivo, postponitur litera formativa *s*.'[3] Most of his examples are printed without the apostrophe, but Wallis admits that it may be added. Wallis's idea, but not the category, is found four years later in Dalgarno:

Nomen Adjectivum et Genitivus casus, per strictam Analysin Logicam, eandem constituunt Notionem, seu Nominis Radicalis Flexionem, et ei superaddunt respectum pertinentiae...[e.g., 'a man *of might'*]...Sic vicissim quaedam Linguae Genitivum casum propriissime sic dictum a Grammaticis, adjective exprimunt; ut, Anglice, *God's house, John's Father* ...*his foot*...In omnibus quibus, Flexio Adjectiva, seu Genitivus Casus, significat Relationem pertinentiae, possessionis, seu habitionis. (Dalgarno, 1661, pp. 70–1.)

Dalgarno is making the same point as Wallis, but seems to be writing independently of him. Wallis is thinking of the relation between substantive and adjective, Dalgarno of case.

The category of possessive adjective, in Wallis's sense, is adopted by eighteen later grammarians, and is mentioned by others. As this category has not hitherto been noticed the grammars in which it occurs are listed here:

[1] See above, p. 285. [2] Wallis, 1653, p. 80. [3] ibid.

The English Categories

(i)   Newton, 1669 (p. 19). He follows Wallis exactly.

(ii)   Lye, 1671, (p. 116, misprinted for 106). He follows Wallis in substance and keeps the term *possessive*.

(iii)   Lewis, *Essay* 1674 (p. 32). He is the first to pull back a little from the freedom which Wallis was offering: 'The Adjective possessive is made of any Substantive which is the Genitive case; as, *The House of my Father, my Father's house.*' In the *Vestibulum*, 1675, he puts it more strongly: the genitive case 'in truth is nothing but an Adjective elegantly expressed'.[1]

(iv)   *True Method* 1696 (p. 81). 'Note, That the Adjective possessive is formed by adding 's...to the Noun.'

(v)   Lane, 1700 (pp. 66–7). 'A possessive Adjective is nothing else but the Genitive of the Possessor under the form of an Adjective.' Among his examples is 'the *house Door* for the *houses Door*'.

(vi)   Loughton, 1734 (p. 61).

(vii)   Fisher, 1750 (p. 75.)

Both writers disapprove of the term *possessive*, though they adopt the category, which they prefer to call just a genitive case. But they are quite sure that it is an adjective.

(viii)   Dilworth, 1740 (p. 118). He follows Wallis in substance and keeps the term *possessive*.

(ix)   *Easy Introduction*, 1745 (p. 72). The author gives *man's nature* and *Dryden's works* as examples of 'possessive qualities'.

(x)   Kirkby, 1746 (p. 73). He completely misunderstands the nature of the genitive and of the category he is adopting: 'The Plurals of Names make Adjectives Possessive by putting an Apostrophe before *s* or *es*; as *A Lion's Courage* for *the Courage of a Lion*'.

(xi)   *The Practice of Speaking and Writing English* (p. 89) contains Kirkby's error in almost the same words.

(xii)   Farro, 1754 (p. 230). He calls the category 'possessive quality words'.

(xiii)   S. Edwards, 1765 (p. 45). 'Common and proper Nouns become possessive Adjectives by annexing an *s* and Comma; as *God's Grace, John's Horse.*'

(xiv)   Smetham, 1774 (p. 81). He oddly converts the usual description of the category, which he calls a case, the only one in English, 'which answers to the Latin genitive case; and is formed of

[1] Lewis, *Vestibulum*, 1675, sig. A 3 verso. James Anderson, in *The Bee*, No. 89. x. 1792. 276, inverts this argument and says that the first element in *gun-barrel* is a genitive.

what Grammarians term possessive qualities: that is, when a noun...
seems to be changed into a quality; as, *the King's Palace'*.

(xv)   Cooke, 1775? (p. 15). As No. ix, above.

(xvi)   Gentleman, 1797 (p. 29). He does not use *possessive* but
accepts the category: In 'Man's life is short' *Man's* 'is equivalent
to an Adjective'.

(xvii)   *Elementary Principles* 1798 (p. 55) as No. xvi, above.

(xviii) Salmon, 1798 (pp. 13–14). He draws all his illustrations
from *Edwin and Emma*, in one stanza of which he discusses the phrase
beneath a mother's eye. Of *mother's* he says, 'It is virtually a compound
Adjective in regard to *the eye*'. It is equivalent to '"beneath the eye
of a mother", wherein *of a mother* is virtually the equivalent of the
Adjective *maternal*'.

Dr Johnson, Alexander Adam and P. W. Fogg also refer to Wallis's
category but do not wish to adopt it.[1]

Wallis's respective adjectives. The second of Wallis's subdivisions is, as
he himself says, 'nihil aliud quam ipsa vox Substantiva Adjective
posita; & quidem non raro sequenti voci per Hyphen conjungitur,
quasi fieret vox composita'.[2] These adjectives he calls '*respectiva*'
('quoniam aptius non occurrit vocabulum') and gives as examples:
*a sea-fish, river-fish, Turky-voyage, sea-voyage, a wine-vessell, home-made,
self-love, self-murder, man-slaughter, a gold-ring*. They may be attached
not only to substantives but to adjectives, as in *a sun-shiny day*. But in
such cases two kinds of analysis are possible, of which he prefers the
second: the respective adjective *sun*, in *sun-shiny*, may be said to
become an adverb (*in Adverbium degenerare*); or it may be said to have
coalesced first with the substantive so as to form a compound noun
sun-shine, and thence to have formed the adjective *sun-shiny*. It is
noticeable, and unusual, not only that Wallis sees that forms such as
sea-fish and *sun-shiny* can be analysed in different ways but that he
does not feel it necessary to say that only one way is right. He suggests
treating the first element as a respective adjective, but if anyone prefers
to treat the whole form as a compound he is free to do so, provided
he treats in the same way forms like *quare* and *huiusmodi*, which some
people deny to be compounds on the ground that both elements in
the word are inflected.

[1] Dr Johnson, 1755, *Grammar*, under *Noun Substantive*; Adam, 1772, p. 8; Fogg, 1796
p. 212.   [2] Wallis, 1653, p. 82.

It seems likely that this category of Wallis's is a development of Gill's *substantiva sterilia*: words like *sea* in *sea-water*, so called because they do not produce any formal change to indicate their adjectival function.[1]

This new category, the respective adjective, was adopted in fifty-five grammars, but in only five of them was the term *respective* taken over from Wallis's Latin. In addition another seven grammars refer to the category by Wallis's term but prefer his suggestion that such forms should be treated as compound nouns.

The grammars in which Wallis's category is adopted together with the name he gave it are:

(i)   Newton, 1669 (p. 19). He follows Wallis exactly.

(ii) Cooper, 1685 (p. 115). He follows Wallis closely.

(iii) *Easy Introduction* 1745 (p. 73). ⎫ In these grammars *sea* in

(iv) Farro, 1754 (p. 230). ⎬ *sea-fish* is called a 'respective

(v) Farro, 1776 (p. 55). ⎭ quality'.

Mark Lewis uses Wallis's category, and his example *sea-fish*, but calls such words *relative* adjectives;[2] John Fell and Alexander Bicknell prefer to call them *characteristic* adjectives.[3]

The fifty grammarians who adopt the category without naming it or referring to (perhaps without having heard of) Wallis, do not vary much in their treatment of it. The first of them is Thomas Lye, who translates Wallis directly: 'Some Adjectives are only Substantives put adjectively; as, a *Water-snake*'.[4] Similarly the author of *The True Method*: 'When two Nouns are joyn'd together by an Hyphen, as if they were but one Compound Noun, then the former of them is taken Adjectively...as, a *Sea-fish*.'[5] The hesitation as to whether the word is to be called a noun or an adjective is apparent in Buchanan: 'There are a sort of Words deemed Adjectives that derive themselves immediately from Nouns, or rather they are nothing else but Nouns put for, or after the manner of Adjectives, and joined to the following Word by a Hyphen; thus, *Sea-Horse*...*Gold-ring, Self-love*.'[6]

During the rest of the century the emphasis shifts, a little, but significantly. Wallis had clearly seen and clearly said that so far as its function was concerned the first element, whether hyphenated or

---

[1] Gill, 1619, p. 70.   [2] Lewis, *Essay*, 1674, p. 32.

[3] Fell, 1784, p. 16; Bicknell, 1790, p. 43.

[4] Lye, 1671, p. 116, misprinted for 106.   [5] *True Method*, 1696, p. 81.

[6] Buchanan, 1762, p. 91.

not, *was* an adjective. Only a few of his successors would venture quite so far: they spoke increasingly as if the word *was* a substantive pushed somehow out of its proper role into that of the adjective: Raine says that: 'Two Substantives linked together by a Mark of Conjunction [i.e. a hyphen] agree with each other in Case, the former supplying the Place of an Adjective; as...Sea-swallow.'[1] But the tendency is by no means invariable. Devis talks of the substantive becoming an adjective and taking its place (*sea-water*);[2] Metcalfe talks of 'two names compounded into one, the former takes to itself the nature of an Adjective, as *sea-fish...gold-ring*'.[3] Lindley Murray, whose judicious compilation exactly suited the expectation of his times, seems to reproduce the practice of most grammarians at the end of the century: 'Sometimes the substantive becomes a kind of adjective, and has another substantive joined to it by a hyphen: as, *A sea-fish*.'[4] The fifty-five grammars in which the respective adjective is accepted as a category are evenly distributed throughout most of the period. Between 1770 and 1789, however, the category is particularly popular, and appears in twenty-two grammars. Sixteen other grammars show Wallis's influence, either by referring to respective adjectives by name or by using one of his illustrations, but the writers prefer his alternative suggestion that *sea-fish*, for example, should be regarded, not as a substantive preceded by a respective adjective, but as a single unit—a compound noun. The earliest of these grammars is Gildon and Brightland's second edition, 1712. They had seemed to accept the adjectival category in their first edition, 1711, though not using the term *respective*: 'When two Names are put together in Composition, the first is of the Nature of a Quality'.[5] In 1712, however, though they introduce the term *respective*, they now say that such forms are better treated as compound names.[6]

The word *sea-fish*, which is the first of Wallis's examples of his new category, the respective adjective, is so distinctive, and so memorable, that it acts rather like a radioactive tracer. It shows where Wallis's influence has reached, usually at several removes, and it is worth pursuing shortly as an indication of the amount of borrowing which the accepted conventions at this level of authorship entirely permitted.

---

[1] Raine, 1771, p. 125; similarly Story, 1778, p. 49, and Postlethwaite, 1795, p. 162. Story dropped the category in his 5th edn 1793.
[2] Devis, 5th edn 1786, p. 33.   [3] Metcalfe, 2nd edn 1771, p. 26.
[4] L. Murray, 1795, p. 140.   [5] G–B, 1711, p. 90.
[6] idem, 1712, p. 76.

The English Categories

If Wallis's respective adjective was suggested by Gill's *substantiva sterilia*[1] *sea-fish* may well be an echo of Gill's example *sea-water*. And *sea-water* had earlier been used by Thomas Tomkis, in his unpublished grammar of 1612, as an example of a noun used as an adjective.[2] But it is the forward history of *sea-fish* which ramifies. It appears as an example, in this context, in thirty-two grammars, the latest of which is Jane Gardiner's, 1799. In another nineteen one or other of the two elements of *sea-fish* appears: particularly in *sea-water* and *sea-horse*, sometimes *sea-crab*, *sea-swallow*, *sea-man*, *river-fish* (another of Wallis's examples) or *shell-fish*. In eight other grammars the selected example is Wallis's *gold-ring*, varied in some to *gold-watch*. Even examples which contain neither element of *sea-fish* tend to follow its aquatic tone: *water-spider*, *water-snake*. Of Wallis's other examples *self-love* is often quoted, *Turkey-voyage*, *self-murder*, *man-slaughter*, and *wine-vessel* very seldom, and *home-made*, surprisingly, not at all. This pursuit of *sea-fish* is not quite as trivial as it may seem. It does provide a crude measure of how derivative parts of these early grammars could be. Such a measure is not easy to find. It is only some distinctive element, new to the tradition but appearing early in the English grammars, which could serve as a tracer. Any more refined measure would require a detailed textual study of quite ludicrously inappropriate complexity.

William Turner's grammatical adjectives. William Turner discusses, and brings under a rule, a puzzling feature of some early grammars, which must often have been dismissed as a misprint. He treats as a particular kind of adjective (which he does not name) those accompanying the names of the parts of speech:

Adjectives that are Terms of Grammar sometimes take *s* in the Plural Number; and are then set after the Substantive; as, *Nouns Adjectives*, *Verbs Passives*, &c. Or else are put alone without the Substantive; as, *Substantives*, *Adjectives*, &c. for *Nouns Substantive*, *Nouns Adjective*. So likewise *others* for *other Men* or *things*. (W. Turner, 1710, p. 9.)

His last example seems a hasty afterthought, as it is scarcely parallel to the first examples and spoils the special application of the rule to grammatical terms. Whether or not Turner's explanation is correct— that the independent form, with its plural substantives, contaminated the dependent form—the feature he describes is not unknown. He

---

[1] Above, p. 310. [2] Tomkis, 1612, fol. 13 verso.

himself refers in the same section to *Nouns Adjectives*,[1] and other instances are:

1567 'Verbes transitives...'[2]

'...certaine nounes Adjectives of an other manner of declining.'[3]

1586 'Verbes-Neuters-Un-Perfect[4]...Nouns Adjectives.'[5]

1647 'Nounes Substantives...Nounes Adjectives'.[6]

1655 '*A, an* are Signs of Nouns Substantives common.'[7]

1668 'Nouns Neuters...'[8]

1677 'Comparison belongeth only to Nouns Adjectives.'[9]

1690 'Nouns Substantives common.'[10]

1724 'Nouns Epithets are Names added to the Substantives.'[11]

1724 'Nouns Adjutants...are commonly called Pronouns.'[12]

1735 'Nouns Substantives, Nouns Adjectives and Verbs.'[13]

1750? 'Nouns adjectives.'[14]

1755 'Nouns Substantives.'[15]

1761 'Nouns Substantives are those Names, which denote the Things themselves...Nouns Adjectives are those Names which express the Properties...of Things.'[16]

1773 'Of Qualities, or Nouns-adjectives.'[17]

1774 'Names (which have commonly been called nouns, or nouns substantives).'[18]

This harsh subjugation of English to Latin is not referred to by any other grammarian and seems to have escaped comment in modern times.

TERMINOLOGY

Accident. J. T. Philipps refers in one place to 'the adjective or accident', but this is only a passing description.[19]

Added Word. This common explanatory phrase is given more formal

---

[1] W. Turner, 1710, p. 9.
[2] Lily, *Shorte Intro.*, 1567, sig. D i verso.
[3] op. cit. sig. A viii verso.
[4] Bullokar, 1586, p. 353.
[5] op. cit. p. 371.
[6] Lodowyck, 1647, sig. A 3.
[7] W. Walker, *A Treatise of English Particles*, (1655) 1679, p. 1.
[8] Wilkins, 1668, p. 298.
[9] Newton, 1677, p. 9.
[10] Clare, 1690, p. 135.
[11] Hugh Jones, 1724, p. 28.
[12] op. cit. p. 30.
[13] Dyche, 1735, sig. A 2.
[14] *English Grammar*, 1750?, p. 11.
[15] Dr S. Johnson, 1755, in the section of his grammar headed 'Etymology'.
[16] Swaine and Sims, 1761, p. iv.
[17] *Court Letter Writer*, 1773, p. 14.
[18] Smetham, 1774, p. 72.
[19] Philipps, 1736, p. xi.

status by Samuel Edwards, who heads one chapter 'Of the Adjective, or added Word'.[1]

Adjective. Used at all times, and with slowly increasing frequency, for *noun adjective*. *Adjective noun* is used regularly in *The English Accidence*, 1733, and interchangeably with *noun adjective* in *The Westminster Spelling Book*, 1793.[2]

Adname. Gildon and Brightland refer to both *adname* and *adnoun* as alternatives to their term *quality*, which they use for the adjective.[3] *Adname* seems to have been used as a vernacular alternative for *adnoun*. Goldsmith, in the preface to Wiseman's grammar, mentions *adname* as one example of the vernacular terminology which he thought uncommon and uninfluential:

The mere English reader frequently hears of the terms Noun Adjective, Verb or Adverb, and can probably tell what they mean from their frequent occurrence; but as for their modern substitutes, such as Name, Forename, Adname, and such like, he is quite at a loss to know their meaning, and requires as much information to lead him into their etymology as was requisite in the Latin terms themselves, but with this disadvantage, that he may never meet with these again; whereas the Latin terms may probably occur in the next book he has recourse to. (Wiseman, 1764, p. ix.)

Similarly, the author of *The Young Mathematician's Logic*, 1760, refers to the 'adjective or adname' as one of the parts of speech favoured by 'some modern philosophers'.[4]

Adnoun. Few grammarians use the term regularly.[5] The first English grammar in which it appears is Cave Beck's *The Universal Character*. 1657, in which it is referred to as an alternative name for *adverb*.[6] The first English grammar in which *adnoun* is used for the adjective is *The True Method*, 1696, in which it is the normal term. It appears also in a Latin grammar of the previous year,[7] whose author uses the term as if it was still something of a novelty: he refers to 'Adjectives or Adnouns... The Adjective (under the more expres-

---

[1] S. Edwards, 1765, p, 43.

[2] J. Cook, *The Westminster Spelling Book*, 2. 1793. 126 f.

[3] G–B, 1711, p. 72 n.   [4] *The Young Mathematician's Logic*, 1760, p. 27.

[5] e.g. Douglas, *c* 1720; Lowe, 1737; Scott, 1786 and in his later works. Lowe is unusually thorough: in a specimen page of French grammar published in his *Occasional Critique*, No. 4. 1736. 22, he refers even to 'a participial adnoun'.

[6] Beck, 1657, p. 26. See below, p. 451; for *adnomen* as a term for the preposition see p. 460 below.

[7] The earliest instance in OED is from Chambers's *Cyclopaedia*, 1753. No reference is made to its use for the adverb.

sive name of *Adnoun*) . . .'[1] An English grammar of 1700 also refers to *adnoun* as if it were not an entirely familiar term: 'A Noun Adjective. . . must have another word joyn'd to it, whose manner, kind, or quality it sheweth, (and therefore it may properly be term'd an Adnoun).'[2] Gildon and Brightland, in the note from which a quotation has already been made,[3] refer to *adnoun* and *adname* as alternatives to quality, and Solomon Lowe combines both terms by saying, 'the quality of a noun is an Adnoun'.[4] *Adnoun* was a favourite term of Lowe's. Besides the examples already quoted he had used it in an earlier work for two categories: in Latin grammar, for the adjective, pronoun and participle taken together,[5] and in French grammar for the adjective and pronoun taken together.[6] Between 1737 and 1770 *adnoun* appears in only one work, where it is used only once.[7] It appears again substantially in Mark Anthony Meilan's *A Grammar of the English Language*, where it is the usual term: 'The word adjective, may therefore with great propriety be changed into that of adnoun.'[8] In his later version of the grammar Meilan used *adjective* in the text but retained in a footnote his belief that the properties of things required a 'general name, which may be that of qualities, or adjectives, or adnouns, which last name is more adapted to their office'.[9] *Adnoun* appears next in T.M.'s *Grammarian's Vade-Mecum*, 1774, where it is given as an alternative for *adjective*. *Adnoun* is similarly referred to in ten later grammars before the end of the century. Beattie comments on the term and seeks to find a use for it:

Adjectives are sometimes called *Adnouns*; which would seem not altogether improper, because they are joined to nouns; but it is not accurate, because it does not distinguish the adjective from the participle and verb, which are also joined to nouns. . . If adjectives may ever with propriety be called *Adnouns*, it seems to be, when they are necessary to give the full signification of a noun. Thus the *golden eagle* is no more than the *name* of one species of the aquiline tribe. (Beattie, 1783, p. 351.)

[1] *The Royal Grammar Reformed*, 1695, sig. A 3.
[2] Brown, 1700, p. 93.
[3] Above, p. 314. The only instance of *adname* in OED is from Chambers's *Cyclopaedia*, 1753.
[4] Lowe, 1737, p. 4.
[5] Lowe, ΚΟΙΝΑ ΚΑΙΝΩΣ, *An Appendix to Grammar*, 1719, p. (3).
[6] op. cit. p. 36.   [7] Wiseman, 1764, p. 96.
[8] Meilan, 1771?, preface, p. v.
[9] Meilan, 1803, I. 5.

Postlethwaite picks up this suggestion, but does not develop it. All he does is to make a few token alterations in Beattie's wording, and by his very self-consciousness turns customary appropriation into manifest plagiarism: 'Adjectives, however, are sometimes called *Adnouns*; and, when they are necessary to shew the full Meaning of a Substantive, this Term does not seem improper: As, the *Humming-Bird*; which is but the Name of one Species of the feathered Tribe.'[1] By the end of the century reforming terminology, though seldom used, is still familiar enough for a writer to introduce one part of speech as the 'adjective, adnoun, adname, quality or attribute'.[2]

Appellative. The traditional term *appellative* is linked with the common noun as an exact synonym in about twenty-five grammars, spread over the whole period. In all but three or four *common* is the term actually used and *appellative* is the alternative.

Epithet. Anselm Bayly says that adjectives are also called *epithets*,[3] but the term remained a rhetorical, not a grammatical one. Hugh Jones' use of *epithet* for the combination of adjective and participle is described above, p. 263.

Essential (noun). *Noun essential* is Hugh Jones' term for the substantive. See above, p. 263.

General (noun). Gildon and Brightland, following the Port Royal grammar ('noms généraux ou appellatifs') refer to *general* or *appellative* nouns,[4] and a few writers follow their example.

Individual (noun) .Used for *proper* by Patrick Lynch.[5]

Manner. For the use of this term by Mark Lewis and Gildon see above, p. 213.

Name. The use of *Name* for the noun substantive is frequent in the term *proper name*, even in the seventeenth century,[6] and is characteristic of most of the vernacular group of grammarians, though others refer to it as an alternative term. As a general term in regular use it appears first in Lane, 1700, and in Gildon and Brightland, 1711, who defend it aggressively:

The Words that signify the simple Objects of our Thoughts, are in all Languages, but English, call'd *Names*; but our first Formers of Grammar, either out of Affectation, or Folly corrupted the Latin Word *Nomen*, into

---

[1] Postlethwaite, 1795, p. 69.
[2] Lynch, 1796, p. 26.
[3] Bayly, 1771, p. 13.
[4] G–B, 1711, p. 75.
[5] Lynch, 1796, p. 9.
[6] p. 298, above.

the Barbarous sound *Noun*, as it is call'd in the Vulgar Grammars. And thus the Grammarians have made a Division of Names, calling the Name of a Thing or Substance, a *Noun Substantive*, and that, which signifies the Manner or Quality, a *Noun Adjective*. But these additional Terms of *Substantive*, and *Adjective*, seem to me superfluous, and burthensom to the Minds of the young Learners, without any manner of Benefit to the Understanding; for the different Natures of the two Words, is fully express'd by the Terms *Names*, and *Qualities*, and it is vain to do that by many, which may be done by few. (G–B, 1711, p. 72 n.)

This use of *name* for *noun* is referred to, or followed, not always consistently, in about forty grammars distributed more or less evenly throughout the eighteenth century. It was always the usage of a minority. Those grammarians who were adopting a vernacular system often said that Names were 'called Nouns Substantive in Latin Grammar'.[1] Otherwise the comments are to the effect that Names 'have commonly been called nouns, or nouns substantives';[2] or 'Name, Noun and Substantive mean the same Thing';[3] or *name* 'is but a familiar term for' substantive.[4] James Wood, 1777, admits that he would have used *name* and other self-explanatory terms if it had not been for the need to comply with 'all our best English dictionary-makers',[5] and most grammarians show a similar respect for authority. Nevertheless, what Lindley Murray calls 'this spirit of innovation' was sufficiently powerful for him to add, after the third edition of 1797 and by 1809, a stiffly disparaging comment on terms such as *name* and *substitute* (for the pronoun) and to repeat Dr Johnson's conservative remarks about terminology,[6] already quoted.

Nominal quality. For Meilan's use of this term for what he regularly calls *adnoun* see above, p. 268.

Noun. So long as the noun was generally regarded as a primary category, of which substantive and adjective were secondary divisions, there was little variation in terminology. Very occasionally *noun* by itself was used for *noun substantive* or *noun adjective*. John Newton, for example, heads one of his chapters 'Of the Comparison of Nouns'.[7] *Noun* begins to be used regularly for the substantive early in the eighteenth century. The two terms are both used by Douglas, perhaps as early as 1711, and by Philipps, 1726; but

[1] *A New English Grammar*, 1746, p. 41.
[2] Smetham, 1774, p. 72, quoted above, p. 313.
[3] Williams, 1780?, p. 5.   [4] Fogg, 1796, p. 210.
[5] Wood, 1777, p. 3.   [6] L. Murray, 1809, p. 64.   [7] Newton, 1669, p. 21.

Solomon Lowe, 1737, is the first English grammarian to use *noun* as the only term for the substantive. Up till 1760 about one writer in five uses *noun* as an alternative to *substantive*; thereafter the practice grows more common until by the end of the century at least three-quarters of the grammarians refer regularly to 'the Noun or Substantive'. Comparatively few, however, use *noun* as the only term.[1]

Personal. Benjamin Martin uses *personal noun* for *proper noun*.[2]

Primary (noun). Monboddo's preference for *secondary noun* and *primary noun* for common and proper nouns was not shared by anyone else.[3]

Qualifier. Sometimes used by Elphinston for *adjective*.[4]

Quality. Less common than the use of *name* for *noun* was that of *quality* for *adjective*. It appears first in Gildon and Brightland, as the regular term, but does not seem to be derived, as are the names of their other primary parts of speech, from the Port Royal grammar. But no such definite source need be looked for. Once it was felt desirable to have 'English' names for the parts of speech *quality* was an obvious choice: traditionally the function of the adjective was 'to express the quality' of the noun. *Quality* is used in eight other grammars before 1755, but in no more than twenty-five during the rest of the century. It seems to have been a live enough term for Lister Metcalfe to have added it to the third edition of his grammar, in 1777,[5] but after this date it seldom appears. Cooke's *Universal Letter Writer*, which first appeared about 1770, had always used *quality*, but an edition published about 1790 gives the term a misleadingly popular status by referring to 'Qualities, or as they were heretofore called Adjectives'.[6] In fact Daniel Pape, 1790, is the last grammarian to use the term regularly and almost the last to use it at all. This means more than it may seem to do at first: it is always necessary to remember that at least sixty new English grammars were published during the last decade of the eighteenth century.

---

[1] Those at the end of the century include Bridel, 1797; J.G., 1796; the author of *Short and Easy Rules*, 1800. When P. W. Fogg, 1796, who uses 'substantive, or name', says that 'the more antient word *noun*...is nearly obsolete' (p. 210) he seems to be referring to the term, and not to the primary category. If this is so he is clearly wrong. Anderson, four years earlier, comments that now people 'indifferently say *noun* or *substantive*' (x. 242).

[2] Martin, 1748, p. 27.   [3] Monboddo, 1774, pp. 37 and 38.

[4] Elphinston, 1765, II. 184, 186.

[5] Metcalfe, 3rd edn 1777, p. 21.   [6] Cooke, 1790?, p. 19.

Secondary (noun). See above, *primary*.

Substantive. See above, *noun*. *Substantive* was more often used alone than was *adjective*. The substantive was more easily regarded as a name. It was the dominant member of the partnership and attracted to itself the term *noun*, which it eventually monopolised. By 1700 we find Lane writing, 'A Substantive is also called a Noun, or a Noun-substantive, or a Name'.[1] For the rest of the period each grammarian makes his choice from among these four terms.

To-noun. A review of George Sampson's *An Essay towards the ascertaining of English Grammar*, 1790, quotes from it some 'English' terms, which include *To-noun*, presumably Sampson's name for the adjective.[2] But no copy of the grammar has yet been traced, and Sampson's terms are not self-explanatory. If *To-Noun* is the adjective, and *For-Noun* the pronoun, *To-Verb* is presumably the adverb. But what is *For-Verb*? Perhaps, the preposition. The other two of the six terms quoted are *Marker* and *Partaker*. The latter is presumably the participle, and *Marker* the article.

OED gives no instances of the following terms in the senses recorded above: *accident, manner, marker, noun-essential, partaker, personal, quality, to-noun, to-verb*. The only instance given by OED of *name* meaning *noun* is from George Buchanan's *Opinion anent the reformation of the Universitie of St. Andros*, 1563–7.

[1] Lane, 1700, p. 21.   [2] *Mon. Rev.* n.s. 7. January 1792, p. 94.

10. THE PRONOUN

DEFINITIONS

The complexity of the functions which the tradition grouped under the label *pronoun* is not revealed by the definition customary in the English grammars: in fact, the definition is almost completely dissociated from many of the functions. It is, perhaps, this very complexity which has caused the customary definition to be repeated, unchanged even in its wording, by scores of grammarians. When a category is too complex to handle easily the writer falls back on what is customarily said about it.

More than eighty per cent of the definitions are based on the statement that a pronoun is used 'instead of a noun', and more than half of these definitions continue: '...in order to avoid its too frequent repetition'. Both elements in this definition are traditional. 'Standing for a noun' is the literal meaning of *pronoun* in English, Latin and Greek, and was the basis of Dionysius Thrax's definition in the second century B.C.[1] 'Avoiding repetition' was put forward as a reason, at the latest, by Isidore in the seventh century A.D.[2] English practice differs from the tradition in the hardening and narrowing of its definition. Comparatively few English grammarians in the eighteenth century indicate any of the other functions of the pronoun. During the last quarter of the century, for instance, eighty-five writers offer formal definitions of the pronoun, but in only eight of these is there the least trace of an idea other than 'standing for a noun' and 'avoiding repetition'. The definitions offered in seventeenth-century grammars, and those in the first half of the eighteenth century, contain a wider range of ideas. All the traditional approaches to the pronoun are represented, but such great emphasis is not put on its standing for the noun: this latter idea is not included in any definition until Thomas Lye, in 1671, writes: 'A Pronoun is a word put for a Noun, and supplying its stead.'[3] This is not to say that

---

[1] Above, p. 69.　　　　　　　　　　　　　　　[2] ibid.
[3] Lye, 1671, p. 118 (actually 108).

earlier English grammarians would have repudiated this criterion. They sometimes refer to it in passing, as Howell remarks that pronouns are 'so called because they stand somtimes for Nouns'.[1] What is important is that seventeenth-century grammarians did not make 'standing for a noun' the only criterion, and that even a compiler like Howell could guard his generalisation with a 'sometimes', which a comparable writer in the late eighteenth century would not have done.

The earliest definition in an English grammar, that of William Bullokar, is taken from the later form of Lily's English accidence.[2] 'A Pronoun is a part of speech much like a noun, & used in Shewing or Rehearsing.'[3] If a pronoun is used instead of a noun it seems inconsistent, or at least confusing, to say that it is 'like' a noun, or is 'a noun imperfect',[4] or an 'irregular noun'.[5] The pronoun's affinity with the noun can be described in two ways. In syntactic terms both noun and pronoun can act as subject and object; in formal terms they can both express number and case, but not tense. A definition in terms of meaning, on the other hand, will stress the difference between pronoun and noun: it is only the most unthinking writer who maintains that the pronoun *names*. Charles Butler suggests both syntactic and formal criteria in his explanation of why the pronoun is an 'imperfect' noun: 'A Pronoun is a Noun, because it is a word of number, without difference of time: and imperfect, that cannot have *a* before it; because it is not the name of a thing.'[6] The attempt to keep the pronoun in close *formal* association with the noun does not last far into the eighteenth century. The definitions increasingly stress the substitutive function of the pronouns. Only a few isolated grammarians hark back to its affinity with the noun, and they do not understand the formal and syntactic criteria which were thought to justify it. Thomas Joel, for instance, says loosely that the pronoun 'is used in all Respects as a Noun',[7] and Daniel Pape is even vaguer: pronouns 'bear the nature of names'.[8] At least the stereotyped

---

[1] Howell, 1662, p. 48.
[2] Lily, *Shorte Intro.* 1567, sig. A viii verso; cf. above, p. 72.
[3] Bullokar, 1586, p. 351. [4] Butler, 1633, p. 39.
[5] Jonson 1640, p. 513; Wallis, 1653, p. 83. The author of *The True Method*, 1696, p. 82, gives Wallis's table of pronouns under the heading, 'A Table of the English Irregular Nouns and Adnouns [i.e. adjectives], termed Pronouns', but is consistent enough to exclude the pronoun from his parts of speech.
[6] Butler, loc. cit.
[7] Joel, 1770, p. 17. [8] Pape, 1790, p. 18.

customary definition which Pape's contemporaries were using prevented them from teaching such a fundamental error.

The two remaining elements in Bullokar's definition are of greater interest. What is meant by 'shewing' and 'rehearsing' is best seen in a fuller version of the same definition which appeared in 1706. The pronoun is 'much like to a Noun, and is used in shewing some Person or thing present to the Sight or Mind; or in rehearsing a thing spoken of before'.[1] Similarly, with a slight shift, Thomas Sheridan in 1714: 'A Pronoun is a Word set before a Noun, either to Shew it, or put in it's Place, when the repeating of the Noun wou'd be Ungrateful.'[2] The distinction between 'shewing' and 'rehearsing' is an attempt to bring into the definition of the pronoun a distinction between those of its functions which are substitutive and those which are not. A speaker does not use the word *I* as a substitute for his own name; still less does he use *you* as a substitute for the name of the person he is addressing. In normal, unemphatic, face-to-face conversation the speaker will use *you* even when he knows the name of the person he is speaking to. This aspect of the pronoun, though indicated in some of the earlier definitions, seems to have been first discussed in relation to English (nominally universal) grammar by John Wilkins, who is using Scaliger:

Pronouns...represent things either 1. *Immediately* and in kind, without respect to the names of those things. So when it is said, I exhort thee or him: The Pronoun I represent[s] to our thoughts the person speaking, suppose *John*; and the words thee, him, the person spoken to or of, suppose *William* or *Thomas*. 2. *Mediately*...for Brevities sake, at the repeating of the mention of a thing lately before spoken of. (Wilkins, 1668, p. 305.)

John Kirkby, 1746, uses different terms for the same distinction. Pronouns he calls 'alternative substantives', which 'are of two Sorts; First, Direct, which have no Respect to any other Substantive: Secondly, Relative, which have'.[3] The distinction is barely preserved in an unpublished grammar, closely related to Kirkby's, where pronouns are classified as either Absolute (for which the MS in one place substitutes 'Irrelative') or Relative,[4] and it is uncertainly touched on also by James Harris who linked it to the customary explanation (derived from Priscian) as to why there were three persons.

[1] *English Scholar Compleat*, 1706, p. 5. [2] Sheridan, 1714, p. 56.
[3] Kirkby, 1746, p. 79. [4] *Practice*, 1750?, p. 49.

The pronoun

James Harris. Harris is worth quoting at length partly because he was reintroducing that consideration of the total situation in which words are used which had been the common element in dialectic and rhetoric among the Greeks, and had been one of the most valuable achievements of the medieval speculative grammarians,[1] and partly because none of the eighteenth-century English grammarians took the analysis of the pronoun any further. Harris begins by seeming to make the same point as Wilkins, and then to contradict it:

Now as all Conversation passes between *Particulars* or *Individuals*, these will often happen to be reciprocally Objects...*till that instant unacquainted with each other.* What then is to be done? How shall the Speaker address the other, when he knows not his Name? or how explain himself by his own Name, of which the other is wholly ignorant? Nouns, as they have been described, cannot answer the purpose. The first expedient upon this occasion seems to have been Δεῖξις, that is, *Pointing*, or *Indication by the Finger or Hand*, some traces of which are still to be observed, as a part of that Action, which naturally attends our speaking. But the Authors of Language were not content with this. They invented a race of *Words to supply this Pointing*; which Words, *as they always stood for Substantives or Nouns*, were characterized by the Name of...*Pronouns*. (Harris, 1751, pp. 64–5.)

By his insistence on the significance of gesture, and by his recognition that 'nouns...cannot answer the purpose' Harris seems to realise that the pronoun is sometimes equivalent to, and not a substitute for, a noun. But he immediately says that the pronoun is *always* a substitute for a noun.

He then takes up and develops Priscian's account of person:

Suppose the Parties conversing to be wholly unacquainted, neither Name nor Countenance on either side known, and the Subject of Conversation to be *the Speaker himself.* Here, to supply the place of Pointing by a Word of *equal* Power, they[2] furnished the Speaker with the *Pronoun*, I...Again, suppose the Subject of the Conversation to be *the Party addrest.* Here for similar reasons they invented the *Pronoun*, Thou...Lastly, suppose the Subject of Conversation neither the Speaker, nor the Party addrest, but *some Third Object, different from both.* Here they provided another *Pronoun*, He, She, or It. (Harris, 1751, pp. 65–6.)

In a footnote he commends, with justice, his alteration of the traditional account:

[1] cf. E. Egger, *Apollonius Dyscole*, 1854, p. 140: 'L'Anglais Harris a eu, peut-être seul au XVIIIᵉ siècle, le mérite, de remonter sur chaque question, soit directement, soit par l'intermédiaire de Priscien, jusqu'au théories des grammairiens grecs.'

[2] 'they', viz. 'the Authors of Language'.

This account of *Persons* is far preferable to the common one, which makes the First the *Speaker*, the second, the Party *address*; and the Third, the *Subject*. For tho' the First and Second be as commonly described...yet till they become *subjects of the discourse*, they have no existence. Again as to the Third Person's being the *subject*, this is a character, which it *shares in common* with both the other Persons, and which can never therefore be called a peculiarity of its own. (op. cit. p. 67 n.)

What Harris is correcting in the traditional account is a confusion between word and thing. The first (grammatical) person is not a (human) person, but a word, a 'subject of discourse'. He continues, on the same lines, to explain why pronouns of the first and second person make no distinction of gender, but that the third person, in English, has the distinct forms *he, she* and *it*.

Hence too we see the reason why *a single Pronoun* to each Person, an *I* to the *First*, and a *Thou* to the *Second*, are abundantly sufficient to all the purposes of Speech. But it is not so with respect to the *Third* Person. The various relations of the various Objects exhibited by this (I mean relations of near and distant, present and absent, same and different, definite and indefinite, &c.) made it necessary that there here should not be one, but *many* Pronouns, such as *He, This, That, Other, Any, Some*, &c. (op. cit. pp. 71–2.)

This account of Harris's, together with Lily's definition, points to four aspects of the pronoun:

(i) The distinction usually expressed as the difference between substantival and adjectival forms (e.g. between *we* and *our*). This is discussed later in the chapter.

(ii) The function of the pronoun to refer to things without naming them.

(iii) The concept of person and the pronoun's power to express it.

(iv) The difference between pronouns of the third person and those of the first and second.

Few writers after Harris mention these matters and those who do, especially William Ward, 1765, Monboddo, 1774, Beattie, 1783, and Dalton, 1801, follow Harris closely and add little to him. Priestley's penetrative common sense fails him here, and he dismisses pronouns as 'nothing more than commodious substitutes for nouns...not entitled to a distinct class among the different kinds of words...only the universal irregularity of their inflexions makes it necessary to give them a distinct consideration.'[1] The two most important facts about

---

[1] Priestley, 1762, p. 87.

the pronoun which had so far been formulated were both negative: that its function was not to name; that it was not necessarily a substitute for a noun. The only definition in a school grammar which makes these facts clearly accessible is Alexander Adam's: 'Pronouns...serve to point out objects, whose names we either do not know, or do not want to mention.'[1] Few present-day school grammars provide anything as useful as that.

The expression of person is a regular, but infrequent criterion. In a definition it appears first in John Newton: 'A part of Speech, much like to a Noun, implying a Person, and not admitting the sign *a* or *the*, before it.'[2] But the criterion of person is implicit in the frequent use of *person* and *personal name* for *pronoun*, which dates from Gill, 1619, and is in regular use until the 1770s. Maittaire uses it with some subtlety: '...implies and supplies a Noun understood or before mentioned, with the additional character of a Person'.[3] This combines at least three of the pronoun's functions: being the syntactic equivalent of a noun; being an actual substitute for a noun; expressing person. Other grammarians who wish to stress the expression of person usually refer to no other function:

An Alternative is that which belongs to all Beings interchangeably, when taken as a Person. (Kirkby, 1746, p. 56.)

As Proper Names of Men, Women, or Children, denote Persons; so those which we make Use of to denote the three-fold Distinctions of Persons are in a peculiar Manner expressed, and called...Pronouns. (Bellamy, 1760, p. xxxiii.)

James Wood puts it more narrowly: pronouns 'serve for the purpose of determining the persons of verbs',[4] and Charles Coote is insistent, in much the same words, that the pronoun 'indicates the person' of the noun.[5] After Coote no one bases his definition on the expression of person.

An attempt is sometimes made in the classification of the pronouns to continue the Latin practice of making a difference between pronouns of the third person and those of the first and second.[6] This point is not made in any of the definitions, but Beattie, after following Harris closely, expands his explanation here:

The pronouns of the first and second person differ also in another respect from those of the third. *I* and *Thou*, *We* and *Ye*, *Us* and *You*, *Me* and *Thee*,

[1] Adam, 1772, p. 53.   [2] Newton, 1669, p. 25; 1677, p. 10.
[3] Maittaire, 1712, p. 49.   [4] Wood, 1772, p .15.
[5] Coote, 1788, p. 40.   [6] See below, p. 328.

point out the persons whose names they stand for, and are therefore understood even when nothing previous has been said. But *He, She, It,* &c. are terms of universal application; and cannot be understood, unless they are referred to something that went before, or is to come after, in the discourse. If I say, 'I am hungry', or, 'Thou art good', the person signified by the pronoun is known to be no other than myself the speaker, or him or her to whom I address myself; and this is equally known, whether I have said anything previous or not. But If I begin a subject by saying, '*He* is wise, *She* is fair, I want *them*', I am not understood, till I say expressly, what the persons or the things are, to which I allude.' (Beattie, 1783, p. 343.)

This distinction is only another aspect of the more fundamental difference between pronouns which are closely related to a verbal antecedent and those whose reference is directly to a part of the situation in which they are used.

The last feature of the definitions, one not mentioned by Harris, is a relic of the older view that the essential function of the pronoun is to indicate 'substance without quality', that is, bare individuality.[1] This view is suggested by William Ward's spacious description of pronouns as: 'Names of objects of certain species, distinguished by characteristics of so extensive a nature, as to comprehend all objects whatsoever as individuals thereof.'[2] Peter Walkden Fogg gives a similar, if distorted, echo from the past: 'The pronoun...recalls the idea of substances [*sic*] not absolutely but relatively. Their real meaning is to be traced to the general and abstract notions of person, being and thing.'[3]

Enumeration. Throughout the period a few grammarians adopt the traditional method of enumerating what they find it difficult to define. This ostensive approach would be more helpful if the writers agreed about what constituted a pronoun: but they enumerate partly because there is so little agreement.

Bullokar speaks with confidence: 'There be XVI Pronouns, to wit, *I, thou, he, she, it, this, that, same, self, my or mine, thy or thine, his, her, their, our, your...*'[4] This already suggests that there are eighteen, but he continues: '...To these may be added *who, which* (and *that* for *which*) relatives before shewed in a noun.' John Newton enumerates twelve pronouns; Lewis enumerates fifteen in Latin and twenty-two in English; Clare gives nineteen, to both Latin and English.

---

[1] See above, p. 70. [2] W. Ward, 1765, p. 125.
[3] Fogg, 1796, p. 211. [4] Bullokar, 1586, p. 351.

Maittaire also is firm: 'The Pronouns are these: *I, thou, self, he, that, my, our, thy, your, his, their, own,*'[1] All others, he says, are adjectives. John Wesley says there are thirteen pronouns; Dr Johnson does not say how many there are, but in fact lists thirty-two, which Nathan Bailey repeats verbatim. Fogg, 1792, says there are 'about 49 pronouns'. The author of *A Short English Grammar*, 1794, says there are twenty-nine, which he lists; he counts *your* and *yours* as two pronouns but *my* and *mine* as one, and adds also *own* and *self* 'used in composition'.[2] Roger Kitson includes practically everything and produces a list of fifty.[3]

The short lists are short partly because, as with Newton's and Wesley's, they exclude *we, you* and *they* as being merely the plurals of *I, thou,* and *he,* and *she* and *it* as being merely the other genders of *he.* With this exception the lists agree in including our personal, possessive and demonstrative pronouns (though Maittaire excludes *this*). Beyond that there is no agreement.

The grammarians classify and name the types of pronoun in so many different ways that it is wise to describe first their treatment of certain word-classes, and only then to discuss the sometimes conflicting names attached to them. These word-classes will be referred to by abbreviations:

    (i) *I, thou, he,* etc., our personal pronouns (ITH)
    (ii) *My, mine; her, hers; our, ours,* etc.   (MM)
    (iii) *This* and *that*   (TT)
    (iv) *Who* and *which*   (WW)
    (v) Pronoun substantives (PS) and pronoun adjectives (PA) are used sometimes as cross-categories, sometimes as autonomous ones. The content of the categories varies widely, but the essential difference between PS and PA corresponds to the syntactic difference between *I* and *my.*

It is probably at this point that a quantitative survey of the pronoun ceases to be profitable. The grammarians differ widely in their treatment of this difficult part of speech, and many of them make only a tentative gesture towards it. Many words (*what* is a frequent instance) are not mentioned and sometimes seem, misleadingly, to be excluded altogether. Many classifications are too vague to be used in any comparative way. The classification of some of the principal

---

[1] Maittaire, 1712, p. 49.   [2] *A Short English Grammar*, 1794, p. 11.
[3] Kitson, 1798, p. 12.

word-classes is here described in some detail, but no attempt is made
to give a comprehensive account of the treatment of the pronoun.

Particular classifications are debated by many grammarians, but
classification within the category as a whole is discussed hardly at all.
R. Harrison is the only grammarian explicitly to question the value
of the established classes, though the actual changes he makes are
made by others. He writes in his preface:

Little originality is to be expected in a work of this nature. In what relates
to Pronouns, however, I have chosen to depart from the common plan,
having noticed under this class, those only that have the nature of Substantives. The usual distribution of them into *possessive, relative, demonstrative*, and *distributive*, seems unnecessary at least, if not without foundation. *My, thy, our*, and the like, are with more propriety termed Adjectives
derived from Pronouns. The words *this, that, each, the same*. &c. are rather
to be called Adjectives, whose Substantives are frequently understood.
They are no more entitled to the appellation of Pronouns, than *the good,
the wise*, Adjectives of Number, and many others which it would be thought
absurd to rank under this class. (Harrison, 1777, p. iv.)

I, THOU, HE, ETC. (ITH)

Bullokar, 1586, makes a distinction between pronouns of the first
and second person and those of the third. *I, thou* are treated as one
category, whereas *he, she, it* are joined with *who, which* and *that* to form
the class of relatives. This follows the practice of Lily's grammar[1] and is explained by the literal sense of the term *relative*:
'rehearsing a thing spoken of before', which is closer to the sense of
demonstrative than is our use of *relative*. In this sense *he, she, it* are
relative: they imply a previous reference in word or gesture. The
Latin classification was strongly influenced by the fact that *ille* and
is, where the 'relative' (i.e. demonstrative) function is most apparent,
were also used as third personal pronouns. The use of this classification in English was always felt to be a Latinism, and is not common.
After Bullokar only twelve grammarians adopt it, of whom six wrote
before 1715. The later instances are quite untypical.

I and Thou, distinguished from He. A similar separation is made in a few
grammars where *I, thou* are classed as personal pronouns but *he*, etc.

[1] See above, p. 101.

as adjectives. The first English grammar in which this classification appears is Lane's, 1700, in which *I, thou* are called 'personal substantives'[1] and *he, she, it*, adjectives,[2] declined in four cases. Lane gives no explanation, but the classification is obviously an attempt to make the English third personal pronouns play the same part as the Latin *is, ea, id* and *ille, illa, illud*, which can act both as pronouns and adjectives. There is no such resemblance between the Latin and English categories, and this attempt to force English into the Latin pattern had few supporters. In James Greenwood's grammar the attempt is even more obviously absurd. Greenwood enumerates pronoun substantives as: *I, thou, we, ye, you, they, who,...*[3] and pronoun adjectives as *he, she, it, my, mine, thy, thine...what*. He puts pronouns of all three persons among the pronoun substantives, yet *he, she, it* appear among the pronoun adjectives. Well may the author of *A New English Accidence*, 'a school-master in the country' who is basing his work on Greenwood, confess himself as a loss:

I leave it to the Grammarians to dispute whether *He, She* and *It*, are Substantives or Adjectives: Mr Turner in his Grammar for the English Tongue, pag. 11 says they are Substantives; but Mr Greenwood in his Essay towards a Practical English Grammar, pag. 123, places them among the Adjectives, tho' he confesses that *He* and *She* are most frequently used as Substantives. (*New English Accidence*, 1736, p. 24 n.)

This may be carrying open-mindedness a little far, but the author's respect for Greenwood was not unreasonable. Greenwood was then sur-master at St Paul's, and the grammar was well thought of.

The last grammarian to adopt this practice, in the year after Greenwood, was Michael Maittaire, an enthusiastic classicist. Maittaire, also dividing the pronouns into substantive and adjective, says: 'Two are Substantives, *I, thou*: the rest are Adjectives, except *Self*, which is sometimes one, sometimes t'other...The Adjectives Primitive are *he, that, own*.'[4] The vestiges of this classification are apparent (if it is not sheer error) in the group of identical grammars: Fenning, 1761; J. Johnson, 1763; *Universal Dictionary*, 1763; Bayley, 1764. Here *he, she* and *it* are classified among the adjective pronouns, although *he* and *she* have already been included among the substantive pronouns.

[1] Lane, 1700, p. 28. [2] op. cit. p. 33.
[3] Greenwood, 1711, p. 107. [4] Maittaire, 1712, pp. 49–50.

ITH treated with this and that. Just as *ille* and *is* could be called either relative or demonstrative so ITH were sometimes put with TT among the demonstrative pronouns. This is the practice of only four English grammarians: Greaves, 1594; Tomkis, 1612;[1] Brown, 1700; Saxon, 1737. Saxon's definition of a demonstrative pronoun as one that 'points out or shews the Noun itself'[2] tries to justify this classification, but to treat *I* and *thou* as demonstrative pronouns alongside *he, she, it* obscured the real difference between the first two persons and the third, a difference which the definitions and classifications of the pronoun, taken together, show to have been a constant, if unobtrusive, part of the English tradition. It is not surprising that the combination of ITH with TT did not prosper.

ITH as a single category. This is the normal classification within the English tradition, whether the pronoun is made a primary or a secondary part of speech. Personal pronouns are those 'quae immediate denotant rem ipsam quae non referuntur ad nomen',[3] or in formal terms, 'Personal Pronouns only alter their state',[4] that is, have case-inflection. Gill, 1619, calls pronouns in general *personalia* and has no separate name for ITH. Later writers who also call pronouns *persons* or *personals* use these terms to name both the part of speech as a whole and its principal, eponymous, sub-class—ITH. The classification is not at all tidy. Many writers discuss person, and enumerate demonstrative, possessive and relative pronouns, but make no mention of ITH, which they are presumably taking for granted. It is difficult, therefore, to see whether there is any development in the use of the category. In the period up to 1740 it appears in just half of those grammars which classify the pronoun; after 1740 it appears in practically all, though between 1770 and 1775 there is a sharp and unexplained increase in the number of grammars in which no classification of ITH is attempted. It is safe to say that once ITH had escaped from the shadow of *is* and *ille* their status as a separate category was virtually unquestioned.

ITH among pronouns substantive. The only variation from the normal practice of classing ITH as personal pronouns was either to identify

---

[1] Tomkis calls *I, thou, he* and *she* 'demonstrativa' (fol. 7 verso) but does not mention *this* and *that*; it is hardly possible that he did not regard *this* and *that* as demonstratives also.

[2] Saxon, 1737, p. 47.   [3] Cooper, 1685, p. 103.   [4] *Right Spelling*, 1704, p. 32.

them with PS (which was merely to change the name) or to include them within PS when that category was more widely conceived. PS are discussed in the next section. The purpose, and the effect, of these variations was to emphasise the syntactic criteria by which ITH could be regarded as a distinct class of pronoun. ITH could function syntactically as substantives: they could be the subject or object of a sentence, or be governed by a preposition. But person was always the dominant criterion, as is shown by the fact that *who*, which shares some of the syntactic characteristics of ITH, was often included among the substantive pronouns but never among the personal pronouns.

Pronoun substantive (PS). This is usually a cross-category, correlative with pronoun adjective. In many grammars words which are classified as personal or demonstrative or relative pronouns are also called, on syntactic grounds, pronoun substantives. As Joshua Poole says, they 'belong not to another word in speaking'.[1] They are referred to by Bullokar, and appear explicitly in Greaves, who says, '*I, thou; Hee, Shee* substantiva censentur, reliqua vero pro adjectivis habenda sunt'.[2] Here PS are identified with the personal pronouns, but this was not the usual practice until the middle of the eighteenth century. At first PS were broadly conceived, as by Mark Lewis:

I, me, we, us, thou, thee, ye, you, he, she, it, him, her, they, them, self, who, whom, what, mine, thine (if you will allow the words) *hisen, ourn, yourn*: These are Substantives, they are the things themselves as much, if not more than Noun Substantives. They have all accidents which Noun Substantives have. They have Gender by the Signification; that is, they are of the same Gender with the thing, whereof they are spoken.' (Lewis, 1674, pp. 9–10.)

More often PS comprised just ITH and *who* (as in Stirling, 1735); sometimes *self* was added also (as by W. Turner, 1710, Douglas, *c.* 1720[3] and Bettesworth, 1778); sometimes *this* (Wells, 1760). After about 1770 it was uncommon for PS to include anything but the personal pronouns. The general view was expressed by a heading such as, 'Personal Pronouns, called Substantives',[4] or by the statement, 'Personal Pronouns are Substantives, all other Pronouns

[1] Poole, 1646, p. 6.
[2] Greaves, 1594, p. 12.
[3] Douglas, *c.* 1720, Bundle 1.7 fol. 91 verso.
[4] Wiseman, 1764, p. 140.

are Adjectives',[1] or, in a more cautious, and more frequent, form, 'Personal Pronouns have the Nature of Substantives'.[2] This distinction between substantive and adjective pronouns is made by more than eighty grammarians. It occurs throughout the period, especially during the 1770s and 1780s. Priestley is alone in attaching so much importance to it that he would be inclined to abolish the category of pronoun and class ITH among the substantives and the rest among the adjectives, if it were not that 'there is something particular in their inflexion'.[3] It is interesting that it is the formal and not the logical difference between pronoun and substantive which he considers important.

Some classifications need particular mention: A few grammarians,[4] throughout the period, use formal criteria to distinguish ITH, and call them *primitive*, as opposed to MM, which they call *derivative*. Collyer, 1735, who calls pronouns 'representatives', calls PS *representatives of names*, as opposed to MM, which are *representatives of personal properties*.[5] Harris, 1751, though he is thinking in different terms, has a near equivalent to PS in his prepositive pronouns, those which 'are capable of introducing or leading a Sentence, without having reference to anything previous'.[6] The correlative category to *prepositive* is *subjunctive*, comprising *who*, *which* and *that*, and it is this which shows that Harris is not thinking of substantival and adjectival forms of the pronoun, but of independence of reference. The subjunctive pronoun 'serves to subjoin one to some other, which is previous'.[7] *Subjunctive* is, in fact, Harris's term for *relative*. He writes as if prepositive pronouns were to be identified with ITH,[8] but this cannot be so, because he admits that *any*, *some*, *other*, *this* can be pronouns,[9] and he says explicitly that 'Pronouns are either Prepositive, or Subjunctive'.[10] The details of Harris's classification are not worked out.

James Wood, 1777, adopts Harris's category *prepositive* but restricts it to ITH, and makes the correlative category the customary pronoun adjective. The *Encyclopaedia Britannica* (A), 1771, and Stapleton, 1797, follow Harris exactly.

Alexander Murray, 1786, brings together several of these classifi-

---

[1] Knowles, 1785, p. 6. [2] Barlow, 1772, p. 8. [3] Priestley, 1761, p. 8 n.
[4] viz. Greaves, 1594; Gill, 1619; Duncan, 1731; Ash, (1760) 1768; Postlethwaite, 1795.
[5] Collyer, 1735, p. 20. [6] Harris, 1751, p. 77. [7] op. cit. p. 80.
[8] op. cit. p. 77. [9] op. cit. p. 72. [10] op. cit. p. 85.

cations of ITH: he himself calls them *personal* pronouns, but, he says, 'Some grammarians call these pronouns *substantives*, some *prepositive*— and others call them *demonstrative*.'[1] But by Murray's time the class of personal pronouns was established, under that name, in almost every grammar that appeared.[2]

My, mine, her, hers, etc. (MM). These forms, which (understandably) caused the grammarians much difficulty, are classified in four different ways:

    (i)   as possessive pronouns;
    (ii) as the possessive case of personal pronouns;
    (iii) as pronoun adjectives, treated sometimes among the pronouns and sometimes among the adjectives;
    (iv) as possessive adjectives.

The pronoun and the adjective, in terms of their customary definitions, were mutually exclusive (it is difficult to see how a word could both stand instead of a noun and express its quality). Nor was there in the tradition any synthesising category through which some accommodation might have been attempted, in the way that the participle combined features of both verb and adjective. A third source of uncertainty was the difference between Latin and English: the Latin possessives were, formally, indisputable adjectives; some of the English ones lack a formal criterion. In English, therefore, syntactic characteristics had to be taken more into account. The syntactic difference between conjoint (*our*) and absolute (*ours*) forms was clear, but confusion was still possible where the absolute forms *mine* and *thine* were used as conjoint forms before a vowel, and particularly with *his*, which was both conjoint and absolute. It is not surprising that MM are classified in ways which overlap and contradict

---

[1] Murray, 1786, p. 12 (printed 22).

[2] The ingenuity of James Anderson is worth recording. It was applied not to the classification of the personal pronouns but to making them more precise. He proposed an arrangement of thirteen genders for plural forms of the third person—including a 'matrimonial' gender for 'males and females known to be such, though not meant to be separated', and an 'imperfect' gender to be used in addressing eunuchs. The ambiguity of *he* also bothered him. He suggested extra forms: *hei* (with *heim* and *hei's*) for the person mentioned second, and *heo* (with *heom*, *heo's*) for the third: 'John presents his compliments to James, begs that *hei* will be so kind as to call upon George, and bring *hom* with *heim*, tomorrow to dinner, when *he* will expect *hom*...' (xi. 123, 198, 199 f.). Anderson should be remembered perhaps even more for his view that a lexicographer should be so little bound by the authority of mere usage that it is better for him to make up all the illustrations himself (vii. 278).

each other; that desperate remedies are tried and astonishing statements made; that it is hard to know what is standard practice at any time or what development there is within the period. The *Encyclopaedia Britannica* (A) expresses the difficulty in moderate language. Of possessive pronouns and adjectives it says: 'These two classes of words are so nearly allied to one another, that it is difficult to ascertain, in all cases, the precise boundary between them.'[1]

MM as possessive pronouns. This is the most frequent classification, adopted by about half the grammarians who classify the pronoun at all. It is not an exclusive classification. More than a third of those who adopt it classify MM also as PA. Some call *my* a possessive pronoun but *mine* the possessive case of the personal pronoun. The classification of MM as possessive pronouns is more frequent before 1740 and after 1775 than it is during the middle of the century, but no quantitative comparison can mean very much. The figures suggest, very roughly, that the grammarians, when required to say whether MM were primarily pronominal or primarily adjectival, at first chose the former; that in the middle of the century their emphasis moved slightly towards the adjective, and that during the last few decades they were more prepared to say that MM were both pronominal and adjectival.

MM as the possessive case of personal pronouns. Wallis, in 1653, had arranged the personal pronouns in a tabular form[2] which was reproduced by fifteen eighteenth-century grammarians. He does not refer to these forms as cases. *I* and *me* are primitive pronouns 'in statu recto' and 'in statu obliquo' respectively; *my* and *mine* are 'eorum possessiva'. The personal pronouns have only two forms; the possessives are adjectives, although 'peculiari plerumque modo formata'.[3] Some writers who reproduced Wallis's table seem to have treated the possessive forms almost as cases, and Priestley certainly considered doing so: 'Pronouns possessive...might not improperly have been called the genitive cases of their corresponding personal pronouns, were it not that their formation is not analogous to that of the genitive cases of other words.'[4] Lowth, however, seems to have been the first English grammarian to call *mine* (but not *my*, which he

---

[1] *Enc. Brit.* (A), 1771, II. 733   [2] Wallis, 1653, p. 88.
[3] ibid. p. 86.   [4] Priestley, 2nd edn 1768, p. 86.

called a pronominal adjective) the possessive case of *I*.[1] Earlier grammarians who had attributed a possessive or genitive case to the personal pronouns had used *of me*, etc. But Lowth does not write as if he thought he was making an innovation. Lowth was followed by Ash, in Ryland's version,[2] and by at least twenty other grammarians, including Lindley Murray, before the end of the century. Joshua Story, 1778, was one of a small group who followed Lowth in treating *mine* as a possessive case, but Story kept *my* as a possessive pronoun. Edward Owen, 1777, and more than a dozen later grammarians, treat both *my* and *mine* as a possessive case. This is to do what Wallis would not because MM were adjectives and what Priestley would not because they lacked the formal qualification of a possessive case, that is a final *s*.

Lindley Murray states, but scarcely argues, the view that *mine*, etc. are the possessive case:

The possessives...like other parts of grammar, may indeed have some properties peculiar to themselves; and may not, in their present form, be readily accommodated to every circumstance belonging to the possessive cases of nouns: but they should not, on this slight pretence, be dispossessed of the right and privilege, which, from time immemorial, they have enjoyed. (Murray, (1795), 2 vol. edn 1809, I. 93.)[3]

Lindley Murray's tone is typical of what it is not unfair to call a pre-linguistic age: the traditional category is so real that its function cannot be examined impartially. His appeal to 'time immemorial' (if it is more than rhetoric) is one of the infrequent historical references made by a grammarian, and it is not clear, even so, that he realises that *mine*, etc. did form the possessive case in Old English. The absence of any historical knowledge of the language is particularly apparent in Nicholas Salmon's long discussion of the possessives. Salmon (always inept) argues that English has no possessive case, in substantive or pronoun. The 's is a corruption of 'that German adjective *es*' which is equivalent, he says, to 'the'. In 'whose house do you prefer?' *whose* is equivalent to '*whom es* house'. *Whom* 'contracts' to *who*, and the inversion of *es* turns *who es* into *whose*.[4]

[1] Lowth, 1762, p. 34.

[2] Ash orginally treated MM as separate pronouns (1760, p. 16). They were made a possessive case by 1768, presumably by Ryland, following Lowth.

[3] This passage was added after 1802.

[4] Salmon, 1798, pp. 42–6. We dare not feel too superior to Salmon. The historical explanation, in a modern elementary grammar, of the genitive of *dog* concludes: 'Later

The grammarians were struggling among their incomplete and conflicting perceptions of formal and syntactic characteristics. They lacked the historical knowledge which would have given them one firm criterion by which to judge the status of MM and other possessive forms, and they were precluded by the rigidity of the parts of speech from making possessives a synthetic category like the participle. Form and meaning seemed to show that MM were pronouns; their function showed that they were adjectives. The variety of classification is caused by oscillation between these two truths.

MM as possessive adjectives. Many grammarians do not make it clear whether they regard MM primarily as pronouns or as adjectives, so the distinction between a classification as pronoun adjective and one as possessive adjective is largely artificial. Nevertheless more than thirty grammarians, especially those adopting a vernacular system of parts of speech, say uncompromisingly that MM are adjectives and often (the stricter test) discuss them among other adjectives and not among the pronouns. The earliest writer to put MM firmly among the adjectives is Lane, 1700, followed by Gildon and Brightland, 1711, and by Loughton, 1734. The practice is regular, if not frequent, until about 1775, when it stops, except for Bridel (before 1790) and Bicknell, 1790. Three seventeenth-century grammarians, Charles Butler, 1633, and Wharton and Smith (who were quoting Butler, as Dr Johnson did on this point) say that MM are adjectives, but they discuss them among the pronouns. Butler is quite explicit: from ITH 'are derived Possessives: which (like other Adjectives) have no case: as My, thy...'.[1] A frequent form of words[2] is that MM 'have the nature of adjectives', and Bicknell, who deals with MM in his chapter on the pronouns, says nevertheless that they are 'wholly of the nature of adjectives'.[3]

John Dalton equates 'adjective pronouns' and MM. After enumerating MM he says:

They are all possessive; and it may be observed, that the possessive case of the substantives, and the nominative and accusative case of the adjec-

---

the *e* in the ending was omitted...The word *dog-es* was then written *dog's*, and the word *dogs-es* became *dogs's*. As the two s sounds coming together were difficult to pronounce... the last s was omitted .'J. G. Altham, *First Steps in English Grammar*, 1934, pp. 64–5.

[1] Butler, 1633, p. 40.

[2] e.g. Priestley, 1762, p. 90; Barlow, 1772, p. 8; *Short English Grammar*, 1794, p. 13.

[3] Bicknell, 1790, p. 35.

tives, are the same both in form and signification. However, as some of the forms in the genitive case are not regular, that is, not made by the addition of 's, it seems better to call them all adjectives, rather than to make nominal distinctions where the signification admits of no distinction. (Dalton, 1801, p. 31.)

He then gives, and defends what he considers to be the declension of both substantive and adjective pronouns, as in the following table:

	Substantive		Adjective	
Nom.	*Gen.*	*Acc.*	*Nom. & Acc.*	*Gen.*
I	my/mine	me	my/mine	—
We	our	us	our	ours

This illustrates clearly the involved condition of this part of the grammatical system, especially when it is linked to a consideration of case. Even a man as clear-sighted as Dalton, and anxious to approach grammar in an empirical and reforming spirit, does not yet see that the central question is the distinction between form and function. Dalton is as near to seeing it as are any of his predecessors: he sees that *my* is 'the same both in form and signification' whether it is 'in' the nominative, accusative or genitive case, but it is not yet possible for him to take the next step and use function as the criterion within which form and meaning can both play their part without conflict.

MM as pronouns adjective. Although comparatively few grammarians unhesitatingly call MM adjectives the desire to recognise their adjectival function is strong throughout the whole period. This was normally done by including them within the pronoun, or pronominal adjectives, even if they had already been classified in other ways. Rather more than half the grammars after 1760 do this, but the classification is less frequent in the seventeenth and first part of the eighteenth centuries, when it is used in about a third of those grammars which categorise the pronoun. The pronoun adjective appears at the beginning of the English tradition as a category already taken for granted.[1]

Pronoun Adjective (PA). PA are more varied than PS, though less often enumerated. PA are all the pronouns which are not PS. Besides MM

---

[1] See Greaves, 1594, quoted above, p. 331.

the most usual are *this, that,* and *who.* Lewis, 1674, adds *which* and *what*; W. Turner, 1710, adds *same, some* and *own*; Wells, 1760, adds *all, very, much, each, no* and *enough*; Raine, 1771, adds *other*; Crocker, 1772, adds *either, one* and *none*; Wood, 1777, adds *such*; Ussher, 1785, adds *whether* and forms in *-ever.* Reciprocal pronouns, in *-self,* if they are not made a separate category, are classified sometimes among PS and sometimes among PA. Very little is said about PA. A perceptive comment such as Adam's is rare: 'A pronominal adjective differs from a common adjective in this, that it does not express quality.'[1]

My and *Mine,* etc. Throughout the period practically every grammarian points to the difference between *my, our,* etc. and *mine, ours,* etc. *My* is used 'when a substantive follows'; *mine* when the substantive does not follow, because it is understood. After 1762, when Lowth made *mine,* rather than *of me,* the genitive case of *I,* the distinction between *my* and *mine* enters the classification of MM, with which it had hitherto been parallel but independent. The distinction is not often named. Tomkis, 1712, calls *my,* etc. 'possessiva praepositiva' and *mine,* etc. 'possessiva subiunctiva',[2] but the more common term for the latter is *absolute.*

The necessary task of trying to bring some order into the confused classification of MM has made it seem as though the grammarians pictured, more or less clearly, a number of different classifications, among which they had to choose. Of some grammarians this is certainly true, but most of them offered a confused classification because they did not see even the full variety of choice which was open to them, and because they were looking backwards at traditional categories and not at the facts of the language which they professed to be describing. 'Looking at the facts of a language' is a modern idea, suggesting an attitude of scientific enquiry; it formed no part of the outlook of a classical scholar like Harris, one of the subtlest eighteenth-century grammarians, nor of an antiquarian radical like Horne Tooke. The two grammarians who most nearly 'look at the facts of language' are the scientists Priestley and Dalton, and their empirical approach is the product of their relatively amateur status as well as of an enquiring turn of mind.

In order to balance the misleading tidiness of the foregoing analysis

[1] Adam, 1772, p. 54.   [2] Tomkis, 1612, fol. 7. verso.

a few comments follow from representative grammarians, which may quickly restore the possessives to their original obscurity:

Aickin, 1693, classifies pronouns as personal, demonstrative and relative, but he enumerates *my*, *mine*, etc. and *this*, *that*, as 'possessives'.[1]

Brown, 1700: 'Those Pronouns that are declined with Substantives, are used exactly as Adjectives; they themselves being such.'[2]

Collyer, 1735, calls MM 'representatives of personal properties' and says that most grammarians call them adjectives: 'they may frequently pass well enough for such', but they do not agree in number with names, as do adjectives, 'therefore I rather think they come nearest to Truth, who call them Pronouns of the Genitive Case in the form of Adjectives...which solves an Objection, that would otherwise lye against them in English, of their being neither Pronouns nor Adjectives'.[3]

Farro, 1754, rolls into one term as many aspects of MM as he can by calling them 'personal possessive quality words'.[4]

Bell, 1769, first classifies *mine, thine, his, yours, theirs, its*, etc. as 'possessive pronouns'.[5] He then proceeds to treat some of these, including *my, this, his* and *its*, as 'improper...non-nominal...non-appellative, non-nominative pronouns';[6] but later he includes *my, his* and *its* among 'possessive qualities'.[7]

Wood, 1777, argues that MM cannot, 'though they are by most grammarians', be called PA because 'were they really adjectives, they must either express the quality of their agreeing substantive, or limit its extent'. Moreover, he continues, adjectives agree in number with their substantives (a persistent Latinism) but in '*my books*' *my* is singular and *books* is plural; therefore *my* cannot be an adjective.[8]

Elementary Principles, 1798: 'Pronouns Possessive (which may also be called personal pronouns of the genitive case) are *my*...[and] wholly of the nature of adjectives.'[9]

Marshall, 1790: 'The possessive pronouns *my*, *thy*...are neither so absolutely Pronouns, nor so completely Possessive, as *Mine*,

---

[1] Aickin, 1693, p. 10.   [2] Brown, 1700, p. 96.   [3] Collyer, 1735, pp. 28–9.
[4] Farro, 1754, p. 230.   [5] Bell, 1769, p. 194.   [6] op. cit. p. 195.
[7] op. cit. p. 203.   [8] Wood, 1777, p. 18.
[9] *El. Principles*, 1798, p. 19. Not in the edition of 1785.

Thine...because they always require the Substantive they belong to, to be expressed...[they are] more properly called Pronominal Adjectives, for they are really Adjectives.'[1]

Gardiner, 1799: She gives the declension of the possessive pronoun *my* as follows:

Nom.	my
Gen.	of my, mine
Dat.	to my
Abl.	from, by, with, in my[2]

Evidence of this kind is not offered in mockery of quite unpretentious schoolmasters and schoolmistresses: teachers today have similar difficulties. These largely unknown eighteenth-century grammarians are being required to provide evidence not of their own incompetence but of the unsatisfactory nature of the grammatical tradition of which they, and we, are the too patient inheritors.

THIS AND THAT (TT)

The uncertainties in the classification of TT are much the same as those already described for MM: especially whether to call them adjectives or pronouns. The most frequent practice is to call TT demonstrative pronouns, but they are unreservedly classified as adjectives by a substantial minority of grammarians: more than half as many as call them pronouns. TT are also classified among PA: by those who call them pronouns, by those who call them adjectives, and by those who classify them in no other way. The grammarians' treatment of TT is very similar to their treatment of *mine*, in that those who wish them to be adjectives say that in their independent use ('I did *that*; I have brought *mine*') a substantive is always understood, and those who wish them to be pronouns say they are absolute. The adjectival functions of TT are more strongly stressed than those of MM, probably because there is no formal difference which distinguishes the conjoint and absolute uses of *this* and *that* as there is to distinguish *mine*, etc. from *my*, etc.

At all times there were emphatic proponents of any classification. In 1633 Butler says, 'Pronouns Demonstrative are three: *this, that, the same*';[3] in 1653 Wallis says of *this, that* and *the same*: 'nulla ratione

---

[1] Marshall, 1790, p. 152. [2] Gardiner, 1799, p. 17.
[3] Butler, 1633, p. 41.

dicenda puto Pronomina, sed plane nomina Adjectiva'.[1] Maittaire, 1712, says TT are pronouns;[2] Greenwood, 1711, says they are not;[3] Dr Johnson and Lindley Murray call them pronouns; Mr S. Johnson, 1758, and John Dalton call them adjectives. Those grammarians who clearly show their awareness of the dual role of TT are no more helpful, because they too assume that a given word *is*, inherently, one part of speech. So when Buchanan first classifies TT as demonstrative pronouns, then adds a footnote to say they are 'not Pronouns but Adjectives', and finally concludes that they 'are more properly Articles than any Thing else' he is merely floundering.[4] Such signs of strain are not uncommon; 'Demonstrative and distributive pronouns are real adjectives;[5] 'all these Pronouns are Adjectives';[6] '*this, that, which*...are adjectives, though commonly reckoned to be pronouns'.[7]

The relative use of *that* is sometimes attributed also to *this*, and leads to some overlapping of categories. Entick, 1728, has a composite type of pronoun, 'demonstrative and relative', which includes *this, that, which* and *the same*, but his account of it is confused. He illustrates it by *which* in 'This is the Study *which* I follow', saying it is demonstrative and relative because it 'also rehearses what was spoken of before', that is, *this*.[8] Entick is presumably trying to combine the relative and a pronominal antecedent into one category. Bell, 1769, is more successful in linking the two categories: he uses the term *absolute* for pronouns which 'shew the relation or reference between the noun and the...pronoun; as, *this, these, that, those, who...which ...what*'.[9] Alexander Murray, though he at first calls TT demonstrative pronouns, later includes them, together with *which*, among relative pronouns, of which he gives as an example '*this* is virtue'.[10] Similarly John Sedger includes TT among his relative pronouns.[11]

WHO AND WHICH (WW)

The distinction between the relative and interrogative functions of *who* and *which* is clearly recognised, but once again the assumption that these word-forms belong 'really' to only one part of speech

[1] Wallis, 1653, p. 89.   [2] Maittaire, 1712, p. 49.
[3] Greenwood, 1711, p. 107.   [4] Buchanan, 1762, p. 97.
[5] Fenning, 1771, p. 106.   [6] W. Ward, 1767, p. 37.
[7] Barlow, 1772, p. 9.   [8] Entick, 1728, p. 13.
[9] Bell, 1769, p. 195.   [10] A. Murray, 1786, p. 14 (printed 24).
[11] Sedger, 1798, p. 27.

makes their classification unnecessarily complicated and inconsistent. The usual treatment can be seen early in the English tradition: of WW, which he calls 'relative pronouns', Poole says, 'but if a question be asked by any of these, then are they called Interrogatives'.[1] The relative function is generally considered more fundamental than the interrogative, and none of the writers show any awareness that historically the forms *who* and *which* were interrogative before they were relative:

Relativum *which*...usurpatur etiam interrogative; ut in aliis linguis fieri solet. (Wallis, 1653, p. 89.)

Who, which...are also called Interrogative pronouns, when they are used in asking questions; but even then they still retain their relative quality. (Burn, 1766, p. 29.)

Pronouns Relative...are much used in interrogatories or questions. (Sedger, 1798, p. 26.)

A few writers give the interrogative and relative functions equal status: 'The Interrogative and Relative Pronouns mutually pass into each other.'[2] This, Buchanan explains, is because the interrogative pronoun has something of a relative character: 'The Relative has Reference to a Subject which is antecedent, definite and known; the Interrogative has Reference to a Subject which is subsequent, indefinite, and unknown, and which is expressed and ascertained in the Answer.'[3] This point is stressed by later writers. Lindley Murray, who quotes Buchanan verbatim, underlines it: [Relative Pronouns] 'are too nearly related [to Interrogative Pronouns] both in nature and form, to render such a division proper. They do not, in fact, lose the character of relatives when they become interrogatives.'[4] Daniel Farro proposes a similar mutuality among interrogatives, demonstratives and relatives. He treats them all as adjectives ('quality words') and his chapter headed 'Of Demonstrative, Interrogative and Relative Quality Words' is an attempt to show that they can all be regarded as relatives:

Q. Have not the modern British Tongue the Term *Relative Quality Words* to accord and agree with the Term *Relative* in other Languages?

A. There is no such Term admitted. Nevertheless, there are abundance of Expressions require it; we expressing ourselves very often in relative or rehearsal Expressions.

---

[1] Poole, 1646, p. 7.
[2] Buchanan, 1762, p. 99.
[3] Buchanan, 1762, loc. cit.
[4] L. Murray (1795), 1809, I. 96.

Q. How are relative or rehearsal Expressions supplied with relative or rehearsal Quality-Words?

A. By borrowing the two Demonstratives, and two of the Interrogatives, and adjoining to their Company the Word *same*, as appears in the following List:

$$\left.\begin{array}{l}\text{This} \\ \text{That}\end{array}\right\}\left.\begin{array}{l}\text{who \&c.} \\ \text{which}\end{array}\right\}\text{same}$$

Q. How do you explain, or make these to appear relative or rehearsal Quality-Words, seeing they are demonstrative and interrogative Quality Words before shewn?

A. Very easily, by the following Examples.

1. The Stick, &c. you cut, &c. is *This* or *That*.
2. That is the Pen, &c. *which* I made.
3. I am the Man *who* made it, &c.
6. That Fellow is the *same* I saw picking a Pocket.
7. That Thing, is indeed the very *same* (meaning Thing) with, or to, mine. (Farro, 1754, pp. 236–7.)

These examples, Farro says, explain 'that the foregoing borrowed relative or rehearsal Quality Words do each of them…save the Repetition of the foregoing Name'.

This is not a very convincing analysis, but Farro's main point is one implied by all these interacting classifications: that the traditional categories are not the only, nor perhaps the most satisfactory, framework in which to display the variety of 'pronominal' functions. More words are 'relative' than the pronouns so named in the tradition. Other grammarians show that they have a similar classification in mind. Sometimes it is only a confused awareness that demonstratives are linked with relatives through the common word-form *that*, and that relatives are linked with interrogatives through the common word-forms *who* and *which*. Sometimes it is an explicit statement, like Abraham Crocker's: 'Relatives…are either Interrogatives or Demonstratives.'[1] It is sometimes difficult to know whether a confused analysis is caused by mere muddleheadedness or by a tentative groping towards an alternative. In some cases the grammar as a whole suggests that the former is the more likely, but many variations are not to be scorned quickly. G. N. Ussher's *Elements of English Grammar*, 1785, for example, is a sensible, eclectic work, intended for 'young beginners'. As it is meant especially for 'young ladies' it must dispense with 'all abstract terms'. With what deliberation were the young ladies offered the statement: 'In interrogative

[1] Crocker, 1772, p. 16.

343

forms of speech...the antecedent is often understood: as, *Whom* did you speak to? *Whom* is a relative agreeing with its antecedent *person* understood.'[1] Rowland Jones, on the other hand, classifies relatives in an eccentric way for which there is nothing to be said. It does not seem to support either of his professed topics—the facts of language in general, or the concealed symbolism of English. His tabular arrangement is not entirely clear, but it seems certain that he grouped the relative pronouns according to the person to which he thought they belonged:

		Relative Pronoun
Singular	1st Person	one, any, none
	2nd Person	this, each, every, either
	3rd Person	that, some, another, such
Plural	1st Person	who, whose, whom
	2nd Person	which
	3rd Person	what, those, others (R. Jones, 1771, p. 10.)

This is, at the very least, an unhelpfully wide conception of mutality.

WW are unreservedly called adjectives by only a few of the grammarians, usually those (the deliberate advocates of a vernacular system) who make the adjective a primary, but the pronoun only a secondary, part of speech.[2] The distinction between PS and PA breaks down at this point: *who* may (strangely) be classified as PA (as by Poole, 1646; Dilworth, 1740; Stapleton, 1797) or as PS (as by Lewis, 1674; W. Turner, 1711; Pape, 1790). *Which* is almost always treated as PA until the end of the eighteenth century, when Pape and Dalton put it among the substantives. That *who* could ever be regarded as an adjective is an indication of how difficult many grammarians found it to use the simple facts of usage: they seem often to have been blinded by preconceived ideas of what a word ought to *be* (usually according to the precedent of Latin),[3] so that they could not see what it *did*. The function of a word was not yet an idea which could be used readily. John Kirkby, for instance, whose grammar was written with independent, if rather laboured, thought, finds it necessary to explain why he calls *which* an adjective and *who* a pronoun:

---

[1] Ussher, 1785, p. 20.   [2] e.g. G–B, 1711; Entick, 1765.
[3] cf. *Certaine Grammar Questions*, c. 1602,   sig. E 1 verso: 'There is a dout amongst the Grammarians of qui, for some say it is a nowne, and some say it is a pronowne'.

The pronoun

If it be asked why the Word *Who* was not ranked before with the general Adjectives *what, which*: since this both interrogates and refers, the same Way concerning all intelligent beings of whatever Denomination; as *which* does both to the same and to all other Beings. I answer that *Who* can be joined to no Name as an Adjective, as *which* can. For Instance, we can say *which Person*... but we can not say *who Person*. (Kirkby, 1746, pp. 79–80.)

This is undoubtedly an appeal to usage; but in this case the reference to usage is almost as surprising, in its laboriousness, as the neglect of usage quoted earlier. Kirkby's explanation does not seem to be designed solely for the pupil. It is in a footnote, and in a tone which implies an adult reader.

Questions of usage are outside the scope of this work, but Priestley's discussion of the difference between the relatives *who* and *which* is worth quoting here as a reminder that even the bones of grammar are very close to the sensitive flesh: 'We can hardly consider children as persons, because that term gives us the idea of reason, and reflection; and therefore, the application of the personal relative *who*, in this case seems to be harsh. *A child who.*'[1]

Other functions of WW are recognised by some grammarians throughout the period. Bullokar calls WW and *what* 'indefinite', as do Adam, 1772, and Perry, 1774—they are 'easily distinguished from relative and interrogative'. Kirkby calls *who* indefinite, also, and Elphinston, 1765, includes *which* and *what* among his indefinite pronouns.

OTHER WORDS

A similar uncertainty of classification is shown in the treatment of other words. They are usually discussed among the pronouns because they 'are' pronouns; they are classed among pronoun adjectives because they 'are' adjectives. This oscillation between pronoun and adjective persists to the end of the period, and beyond. Mark Meilan, for example, in the later version of his grammar, after classifying pronouns in three groups: primitive (viz. ITH), relative (*who* or *that*), and possessive (*my* etc.) continues: 'Besides these Pronouns, many grammars reckon other words as Pronouns, such as *what, whether, same, this, that, other, any, some, one, none, each, every, either, neither*: but though these may all seem Pronouns, it is only in appearance, since the definition of an adjective belongs to every one of

[1] Priestley, (1761) 1768, p. 98.

345

them.'[1] The words which Meilan lists, and the inherited categories *distributive, definite, indefinite* and *reciprocal*, are more stable than some of those already discussed, but variations still occur, more often because the author is ignorant than because he is thoughtful.

The grammarians' treatment of *some* shows the greatest variation. According to the way in which it is being used *some* may be considered definite or indefinite: 'He can't tell me how many eggs were broken; all he can say is that *some* were.' Or, 'It doesn't matter exactly how many eggs were broken; what matters is that *some* were.' We would consider that the degree of definiteness depends on the context, rather than on the use solely of the word *some*, but variation there admittedly is. Accordingly Miege, 1688; Maittaire, 1712; Bell, 1769; Lindley Murray, 1795, and many more are justified in calling *some* 'indefinite', while Lowth and the many grammarians who follow him are justified in classing it among the 'definitives'. Alexander Murray says that *some, any, whoever, none, one, other* are indefinite 'when they express nothing distinct or determined, but definitive when they ascertain those names to which they either refer, or are joined',[2] and Alexander Barrie similarly includes *some, any, one,* and *other* among both definite and indefinite pronouns.[3] Other writers treat *some* in still other ways: as demonstrative (Devis, 1775), partitive (Hodgson, 1770); distributive (Fell, 1784), and merely as a pronoun adjective (W. Turner, 1710 and many others throughout the whole period). A particular sign of desperation is the classification in the *Encyclopaedia Britannica* (A), 1771, of *some, any, all* and TT as 'improper pronouns', so called because they often are not pronouns at all.[4] They are later, along with *other* and *none*, said to be 'pronomial articles'.[5]

The treatment of other pronouns is less often given in any detail. It adds nothing to the picture which has already been offered of the category as a whole, and need not be pursued here.

[1] Meilan, *An Introduction to the English Language*, 1803, I, 39.
[2] A. Murray, 1786, p. 14 (printed 24).   [3] Barrie, 1794, p. 283.
[4] *Enc. Brit.* (A), 1771, 2. 733.   [5] op. cit. p. 742.

TERMINOLOGY

(*Noun*) *Adjutant*. Hugh Jones' regular term for the pronoun, adopted by no one else.[1]

Adnoun. Bellamy, 1760, refers to '*Pronouns*, or, as they are termed by some, *Adnouns*', and Barclay, 1774, repeats this verbatim. This is puzzling. *Adnoun* was often used for the adjective,[2] and exceptionally for the adverb and preposition,[3] but this is its only association with the pronoun.

Alternative. This is Kirkby's term for the pronoun, which no one adopted.[4]

Deputy name. James Douglas in one place refers to 'Pronouns or Deputy Names', but neither he nor others use it as a regular term for the category.

For-noun. Apparently George Sampson's term for a pronoun.[5]

Person. Hewes, 1624, and Wise, 1754, refer to the personal pronouns as 'persons' but do not use the term regularly. Hewes, for example, discusses constructions in which 'the Substantive, Person or Relative' either precedes the verb or has no verb at all.[6] *Person* is the term regularly used by the author of the unpublished *The Practice of Speaking and Writing English*, who is consistent enough to write: 'The Relative and Interrogative Person is only one Word', and to discuss the syntax of 'A Person or Name following a Preposition'.[7]

Personal. Poole, 1646, applies this term only to pronoun substantives, 'which are also called Personals'.[8] Daniel Turner, in 1739, followed verbatim by Samuel Edwards, 1765, uses it still as a conscious ellipsis: 'The *Personal*, or *pronoun*, is used instead of the proper'.[9] It is similarly used in *The Pocket Dictionary*, 1753 ('Personals are the only nouns that are expressed differently, when placed before or after a verb');[10] and by C. Johnson, 1779. Meilan in his first grammar, speaks regularly of 'personals' and occasionally of 'personal nouns'; in both cases he means the whole category of pronoun: '*Pronoun*...I call this part of speech a

[1] H. Jones, 1724, pp. 30 and 39.   [2] See above, p. 314.
[3] See below, pp. 451 and 460.   [4] See above, p. 322.
[5] Sampson, 1790, from *Mon. Rev.*, n.s. 7. January 1792. 94. See above, p. 319.
[6] Hewes, 1624, sig. C 2 verso and sig. C 3 recto.
[7] *Practice*, 1750?, especially chap. VII and pp. 145–7.
[8] Poole, 1646, p. 6.   [9] D. Turner, 1739. p. 13; S. Edwards, 1765, p. 40.
[10] *Pocket Dictionary*, 1753, p. 8.

personal noun, and deny, that the English language has any more than four personals; namely *I, thou, he* and *who*.'[1] William Francis, in 1790, talks of 'Pronouns or Personals'[2] and Thomas Huntley, in 1793, refers to *my, thy, his*, etc., which he has previously called *pronoun adjectives*, as 'personals', but it is not clear in how general a sense he is using the term.[3] The term *personal* is also a feature of some grammars with vernacular systems, in which the noun is divided into common, proper and personal.

Personal name; Nomen personale. Gill and Wallis, who are writing in Latin, use *nomen personale*. Similarly Thomas Granger, in his Latin grammar *Syntagma Grammaticum*, 1616, refers to the 'Noune personall...called a pronoune'.[4] *Personal name* was the regular term among those reforming grammarians who used a vernacular terminology,[5] but it was not quite as common as is suggested by Thomas Smetham's remark that personal names were 'heretofore called pronouns'.

Personal substantive. Used for the pronoun by Lane, 1695 and 1700, and by Farro, 1776.

Proname. Two writers speak as if the term was used by others, but it is not in regular use in any English grammar. Gildon refers to 'certain words...call'd *Pronames*, or *Personal Names*, or vulgarly *Pronouns*';[6] and Carter mentions '*Relative Names*...also called *Pronouns* or *Pronames*'.[7] Elphinston occasionally uses *proname*, but does not discuss it at all.[8]

Relative (name). Martin, 1748, and Fisher, 1750, both speak of 'relative names or pronouns', and Hammond says 'relative Names [are] call'd by the Latins Pronouns'.[9] Seven later grammarians mention the term, sometimes restricting it to the personal pronouns, but none uses it regularly.

Representative. The term first appears in Collyer, 1735, who uses it as an explicit alternative for *pronoun*.[10] Lowth uses it only in describing the pronoun: '...a word standing instead of a Noun, as its Substitute or Representative',[11] but some of the grammarians who follow

---

[1] Meilan, 1771?, preface, p. iv. [2] Francis, 1790, p. 46.
[3] Huntley, 1793, p. 14. [4] sig. G 2 recto.
[5] e.g. G–B, 1711; Loughton, 1734; *Easy Intro.* 1745; *New Eng.Grammar*, 1746; Farro, 1754; Gough, 1754; Mr S. Johnson, 1758; Entick, 1764; *New & Impr. Sp. Dict.* 1771; Smetham, 1774; Cooke, 1774.
[6] G–B, 1711, p. 76 n. [7] Carter, 1773, p. 57 n.
[8] Elphinston, 1765, 2. 173, 184. [9] Hammond, *c.* 1760, sig. A 5 verso.
[10] Collyer, 1735, p. 20. [11] Lowth, 1762, p. 31.

Lowth use it more nearly as an equivalent for *pronoun*, as in: 'Pronouns or relatives or representatives of nouns.'[1]

Substantive of the secondary order. This is Harris's general descriptive term for pronouns,[2] taken over by Beattie as *noun secondary*[3] but not regularly used by either.

Substitute. Lindley Murray, quoted above, p. 317, speaks as if *substitute* was used as a synonym for *pronoun*. If it was, it was very rare. The only grammar in which *substitute* is regularly, but not consistently, used for *pronoun* is *The Only True Guide*, 1779. Murray may be thinking also of Lowth's descriptive reference just quoted or of 'Mica's' use of *substitute*, or *relative term*, as the name of those words which are substitutes for names.[4]

Other variations can be briefly mentioned:

Other terms for TT

Demonstrative is the standard term, which seldom varies.

Definitive. About a dozen grammarians follow Lowth, 1762, in classifying TT as, or among, definitives.

Definite. Introduced by Ryland into the 1768 edition of Ash's grammar, and adopted by a few writers.

Emphatic. An alternative term of Ash's.

Exhibitive. A variation of Elphinston's.

Indicative. First used by Benjamin Martin, 1754, and adopted by three or four others.

Other terms for WW

Relative is the standard term.

Connective. Suggested by Wood, 1777.

Conjunctive. Suggested by Salmon, 1798.

Subjunctive. A Greek term (ὑποτακτικός) favoured by Harris, 1751, and suggested also by Stapleton, 1797.

Other terms for MM

Peculiar. Used by H. Jones, 1724.[5]

[1] Wood, 1777, p. 3; repeated by A. Murray, 1786, p. 12 (printed 22).
[2] Harris, 1751, title to chap. 5 of Bk 1.   [3] Beattie, 1783, p. 337.
[4] 'Mica', 1793, p. 229; cf. above, p. 272.
[5] Of the above terms the following are not recorded, in this sense, in OED: *adjutant, adnoun, alternative, conjunctive, connective, definite, deputy, emphatic, exhibitive, for-noun, indicative, peculiar, person, personal, proname, representative, substitute.* For *relative* OED quotes one instance from 1677 in which *he* is called a relative, but the dictionary does not recognise that *relative* here means *pronoun*.

11. THE ARTICLE

As the grammarians found no clear precedent in Latin, and as few of them took notice of Greek, their treatment of the words *a, an, the* is at first uncertain and varied. Four types of classification are used: (i) the articles may be linked firmly with words like *of, by, with, to* as 'signs of cases'; (ii) they may be treated in various ways as attachments to the substantive, but distinct from the signs of cases; (iii) they may be included within another part of speech; (iv) they may themselves be treated as a primary part of speech.

As signs of cases. Those grammarians who wished English to have cases comparable with the Latin system were able to say that English cases were indicated not by case-endings on the noun but by 'signs' put before it. *Of* was the sign of the genitive, *to* of the dative, *by, with,* and *from* of the ablative. The nominative and accusative lacked such obvious signs, and it was tempting, to the tidy-minded, to push the articles into the position of signs, on the ground that they also preceded the noun. Two cases lacked signs; there were two articles; the accommodation was inviting. But not even the most determined Latinist could altogether shut his eyes to the plain facts of everyday speech, and most of those who include the articles among the signs of cases show some hesitation. One of the frankest of them is Jeremiah Wharton. He gives the declension of *book* as follows:

Nom.	a book
Gen.	of a book
Dat.	to a book
Acc.	the book
Voc.	o book
Abl.	in a book

To which he adds, in a tone of some desperation: 'Note that *a* is not alwaies a sign of the Nominative case, or *the* of the Accusative, but that usually it is so, and there is no better way to distinguish them in

350

declining.'[1] John Entick and Mr S. Johnson are among the few who express no such uneasiness. Entick includes *a* and *the* among the signs of cases, and describes 'declining a Noun by Case' as 'repeating the Noun with its Article, and with the several Changes of the Article',[2] thus equating *article* and *sign of a case*. Similarly Mr S. Johnson says, 'Instead of Cases...we have only the Articles, *a, an, the, of, to, by, from, with*, &c.'[3] More often the question of case is sidestepped, in various ways. Thomas Lye, for example, uses *case* to mean only inflected forms of the noun, which encourages him to say that English nouns have no cases. So, he continues: 'The English, instead of changing the terminations-or-endings of Nouns Substantive, prefix-or-set before them Articles, viz. A, An, The.'[4] John Newton also says that English nouns have no cases: 'All other distinctions [than the plural] are made by these Articles and Prepositions; *a, of, to, the*...'[5] Dyche, 1735, avoids the term *case*: 'Instead of the various Terminations and Declensions of the Latins, &c. the English use *a* or *the, of, to, by, from* or *with*, &c, to distinguish the several Circumstances of the Subject.'[6] John Clarke makes a compromise in terms of 'real' cases, that is, ones made by inflection: 'As there is but one real Case in our Tongue, viz. the Genitive... we are obliged to have Recourse to Articles to decline our Nouns.'[7] He then gives the declension of *man* just as Wharton had declined *book*, in, presumably, one real case and five quasi-cases. Like Wharton he makes *a* the sign of the nominative and *the* the sign of the accusative.[8] Most other grammarians just list the English cases with their signs, distinguishing nominative and accusative by *a* and *the* respectively or, as Philipps,[9] making *a* the sign of both nominative and accusative, which are then identical. Others distinguish nominative and accusative not by allotting a different article to each but by introducing syntactic criteria also:

Nom.   A, the; this goeth before the Verb
Voc.   O
Acc.   A, the; this follows the Verb.[10]

[1] Wharton, 1654, p. 35.   [2] Entick, 1728, p. 2.   [3] Mr S. Johnson, 1758, p. 4.
[4] Lye, 1671, p. 104 (printed 114).   [5] Newton, 1677, p. 9.
[6] Dyche & Pardon 1735, sig. b 2 verso.   [7] Clarke, 1791, p. 75.
[8] This arrangement appears first in Hume, *c.* 1617, p. 29, and as late as 1776, in the English grammar (designed as an introduction to Latin) which was added to the edition in this year of *Grammar and Rhetoric*, the combination of vols. I and III of *The Circle of the Sciences*.   [9] Philipps, 1726, p. ix.
[10] Lewis, *Institutio*, 1670, sig. A 2; also Sheridan, 1714, p. 5.

More than thirty grammars, nearly all published before 1760, treat the articles, explicitly or indirectly, among signs of cases. The last purely English grammar to do so is Barclay's, in 1774. Smetham, 1774, and the anonymous grammarian of 1776, already referred to, confine this classification to a second, alternative English grammar intended for pupils going on to learn Latin.

As attachments to substantives. Many grammarians who did not wish to call the articles signs of cases nevertheless wished to stress their relation to the substantive. It was often considered a defining characteristic of the substantive that it could be preceded by an article, so it was only natural to use the converse relationship in an attempt to clarify the status of the article. The attempt took three forms: (*a*) to call the article the 'sign of a substantive', as distinct from the sign of a case;[1] (*b*) to call it an accident of the substantive; (*c*) to describe the article's relation to the substantive in terms of its function, and not to attempt a statement of what the article was. These three approaches cannot be entirely separated, either in themselves or in the work of most grammarians, but occasional examples are found of 'pure' forms of each:

(*a*) Articles are: Signs of Nouns Substantives common, every of which may have one of these Particles before it in the Nominative case singular. (W. Walker, *A Treatise of English Particles* (1655), 1679, chaps. 1 and 79.)

(*b*) There belong to a noun...Articles, Numbers, Genders, and Prepositions. (Aickin, 1693, 2nd part of the *Eng. Grammar*, p. 3.)

(*c*) Q. How are these Particles (*A, An, The*) used?

A. *A* is set before a Consonant, *An*, before a Vowel, which extend the Signification of a Noun to any one particular, and so to all, one by one of its kind, but *The* restrains it [to] some known and special Thing, and thereby rendering a Substantive Common, equivalent to a Proper. (Brown, 1700, p. 90.)

Sometimes the sign of the substantive is only narrowly distinguished from the sign of the case. Mark Lewis, for example, when he says, '*A, the, an*, are no particular signes: because they are common to all Cases',[2] is thereby treating the articles as signs of the substantive. Merriman, similarly, does not make it clear how far he distinguishes

---

[1] Addison complains in *The Spectator*, No. 135, that 'some of our Poets have been so indiscreet as to imitate Hudibras's Doggrel Expressions in their Serious Compositions, by throwing out the Signs of the Substantives, which are essential to the English Language'.

[2] Lewis, *Essay*, 1674, p. 7.

articles and signs of cases: 'Nouns have different Significations according to the Articles or Signs prefixed to them; this answers to what in Latin is called Declension.'[1] He certainly treats the article as part of the declension of the noun, but there would be no point in naming the article at all unless he distinguished it to some extent from the signs of the cases.

John Stirling's grammar, 1735, illustrates the tangle of categories which could surround the article, even when it is expressly distinguished from the signs of the cases. Stirling's enumeration of his eight parts of speech does not include the article. He then says: 'All Words (Signs excepted) are reduced to these eight Classes...Every Word ...is either an Article, or a Sign of a Part of Speech, or a Part of Speech itself.'[2] His second category, 'sign of a part of speech' is in fact divided into two: 'signs of cases' (e.g. *of*) and 'signs of verbs' (e.g. *may, would*).[3] *A, an, the* are listed as signs of the nominative and accusative in his tables of the declension of substantives,[4] but he also says: '*A, an, the*, are not Signs of Cases, but Articles...the Genitive, Dative, and Ablative only have Signs.'[5] Here again the distinction between an article and a sign of a case is very fine, but Stirling stresses it, without clarifying it. The article, already linked with the noun and preposition, and linked elsewhere with the pronoun and adjective, is here linked (through the cross-category *sign*) with the verb.

Only a few seventeenth-century grammarians[6] treat the articles, along with gender and number, as accidental features of the substantive. But during the second half of the eighteenth century some writers, who wish to keep the article closely associated with the substantive but consider, presumably, both accident and sign of a case to be categories inappropriate for English, link the articles loosely to the substantive, being careful, it would seem, not to specify the nature of the attachment. Such writers are Gough, 1758; Wiseman, 1764; Carter, 1773; Wynne, 1775, *Short and Easy Introduction* 1786. James Smith, who does not make the article a primary part of speech, is quite explicit: 'Note, *a, an*, and *the* are not signs of cases, but articles.'[7] John Sedger calls the articles 'a kind of appendages to nouns',[8] and Monboddo, going even further, thinks that

---

[1] Merriman, 1750, p. 4.   [2] Stirling, 1735, sig. A 3 verso.
[3] op. cit. sig. B 2.   [4] op. cit. sig. A 4.   [5] op. cit. sig. A 2.
[6] viz. Cooper, 1685, p. 101; Miege, 1688, p. 29; Aickin, 1693, quoted above, p. 352.
[7] James Smith, 3rd. edn 1778, p. 11.   [8] Sedger, 1798, p. 9.

because the article is used *with* the noun it can be regarded as *within* the category noun: 'I rank it, as well as the pronoun, under the noun; because it cannot be without the noun, and is truly a modification of the noun.'[1] This second type of classification, in which the article is treated as a sign, accident or attachment of the substantive, is used in about thirty-five grammars, at least half of which date from before 1740.

Within another part of speech. In over sixty grammars the articles are included within one of four different parts of speech: the adjective, pronoun, preposition and particle. By far the most frequent classification is within the adjective, usually on the strength of the demonstrative tone of *the*. Yet W. Turner, 1710, the only grammarian to classify the two articles as different parts of speech, makes *an* an adjective and *the* a pronoun. The articles are first put among the adjectives by Greaves, 1594, and this classification continues throughout the whole period, being most common between 1700 and 1760. Some grammarians comment on it, but by assertion rather than explanation:

Some have been inclined to make the Articles a particular Part of Speech; but since it is evident that they are of the Nature of Adjectives, they may be called so. (Barker, 1733, p. 6.)

[the articles]...commonly reckoned as no part of Speech, but Signs of Names, are real Qualities. (Collyer, 1735, p. 37.)

Priestley says that some grammarians make the article a primary part of speech, but he implies that it is unnecessary: 'Grammarians who make articles a part of speech distinct from adjectives define them to be *words which fix or limit the signification of nouns*, which is true of all adjectives whatever.'[2] The articles are included among the pronouns only by Ben Jonson, by Evelyn (who seems to be following Jonson), by Anselm Bayly, 1756 and 1772, and by John Henson, *c.* 1760, none of whom comments on the classification.

The link between article and preposition was suggested by John Wilkins, 1668, who includes them both within his category of 'connexive or declarative particles', on the grounds that they are '...proper to substantives; being usually prefixed before them, either that whose office it is to join integral with integral on the same side

---

[1] Monboddo, 1774, p. 73.   [2] Priestley, 1762, p. 54.

of the Copula [the preposition], or that which serves for the more full
and distinct expression of Substantives [the article]'.[1] Wilkins, who is
writing in 'universal' terms, does not, in combining preposition and
article, obscure the difference between them. The two other writers
who link them make the article a kind of preposition. Benjamin
Martin is clearly thinking of signs of cases when he defines the prepositions (and hence the articles) as being 'prefixed to Nouns to
indicate the Case, or particular State or Relation in which they are
used and related to each other'.[2] But he misconceives the function
of the article, as does James Barclay, 1774, who agrees with Martin
almost word for word.[3]

The article is included within the particle for varying reasons. For
Gill, 1619, the particle is a large category containing all those parts
of speech which do not express number. For William Walker,
particle is a term so wide that it means virtually 'small word' and
includes even the verb *to be*. In *The True Method*, 1696, the article is
similarly included, together with auxiliary verbs, prepositions and
others.[4] In Wells, 1760, the classification is no more than suggested.
He specifies as components of the particle the conjunction, preposition and interjection; it is only in a footnote to the same
paragraph that he refers to the articles, leaving their exact status
uncertain.[5]

As a primary part of speech. Here also the example of Lowth was
decisive. Before the appearance of his grammar in 1762 nine grammarians (less than ten per cent) had made the article a primary part
of speech. The seventeenth-century grammarians Tomkis, Jonson,
Evelyn and Howell had been hesitant. Jonson and Evelyn, followed
by Howell, say that the article is a ninth part of speech, but they
discuss it among the pronouns: 'In our English speech we number the
same parts with the Latines...only we add a ninth, which is the
Article.'[6] The first English grammarians unambiguously to make the
article a primary part of speech are Michael Maittaire, 1712, and
James Douglas, whose first draft was perhaps written soon after 1711.
Between the appearance of Lowth's grammar, in 1762, and 1801
more than three-quarters of the grammars make the article a primary

---

[1] Wilkins, 1668, p. 46.　　　　　[2] Martin, 1754, p. 114.
[3] Barclay, 1774, p. xxvii.　　　　[4] See System 30, above, p. 253.
[5] Wells, 1760, p. 12.　　　　　　[6] Jonson, 1640, p. 505.

　　　　　　　　　　　　　　　　　　　　12-2

part of speech; by the 1790s this practice is almost universal. It was, of course, the obvious cure for the uncertainty which so many grammarians had felt about the classification of the article.

The grammarians never say that it is difficult to define the article, but their practice admits it. The few definitions they give slide quickly into a description of how the articles are used. One reason for the absence of definition might be a feeling that only words with the full status of a part of speech are worth defining, but it is more likely that definitions are not offered because none are found in the tradition: creating a definition is more difficult than adopting, adapting and passing one on.

Two types of general statement are common. The articles are said to be words 'set before a Substantive for the more particular expressing of it',[1] and they are described as 'certain Kinds of Limitations prefixed to our Nouns'.[2] But such statements are uninformative. The more specific characteristics of the articles are described by the early grammarians, especially John Wallis, with greater penetration, and with stricter attention to purely linguistic facts, than is given to more traditional parts of speech, whose Latin analogues filled the grammarians' minds with preconceptions, and misconceptions, about what English words should be. As the articles were not part of the tradition the English grammarians were obliged to look for themselves at the facts of usage. The characteristics most frequently discussed need only be illustrated from the earliest grammar to state them clearly; little was added during the whole period, except by James Harris, to the lead given by Wallis in 1653. Features common to both articles are here described first; then each article is discussed separately.

Declension. It is difficult for us to believe that any writer of a grammar (not to say a grammarian) could seriously offer a declension of the English articles. That a few writers did so is powerful evidence of how difficult, in fact, it could be to look at the plain facts of one's own language. Tomkis, 1612, declines the singular of *the* as follows:

---

[1] *Complete Letter Writer*, 1755, p. 20.   [2] Bellamy, 1760, p. xxxii.

The article

Nom.	The
Gen.	Of the
Dat.	To the
Acc.	The
Voc.	O the
Abl.	From, etc. the (Tomkis, 1612, fol. 5.)

A is declined in the same way. The plural of *the* 'a singulari non differt', but *a* 'caret omnino plurali'. The articles are also declined by Smith, 1674; Entick, 1728; and Wiseman, 1764, but these writers differ from Tomkis in saying that there is no vocative.

Not used before proper nouns and pronouns. This is one of the characteristics which most writers mention. 'Nomina propria et pronomina articulos recusant nisi sit emphaseos gratia, ut the Harry of Harries, Henricus Henricorum, the onelie hee or shee of the towne, unicus ille vel unica illa urbis.'[1] This is almost exactly the same in Jonson: 'Proper Names, and Pronouns refuse Articles, but for Emphasis sake: as The Henry of Henries. The only Hee of the Towne.'[2] Evelyn makes slight changes: 'Proper Names and pronounes, but [i.e. 'except'] for Emphasis sake, as The Richard of Richards &c refuse Articles.'[3] Gill, in 1619, had illustrated the same 'exceptional' use of the articles with proper nouns but had made no special reference to emphasis. His examples are: 'He is a Gil, id est, unus est, cuius nomen est Gil...the Grahams, i. universa Grimaeorum familia.'[4]

Not used before a general term. Gill's explanation for the absence of the article in a sentence like 'Virtue alone makes men happy' (his example) is to say that words like *virtue* 'do not need' an article: 'Substantiva solitaria, id est, sine ulla ad aliud relatione posita, articulos negligunt.'[5] Both Wallis and Cooper see clearly the significance of this absence of the article, but, more than Gill, they treat 'generality' as a feature of the noun (so that articles are not used with nouns of this sort) rather than as a consequence of the absence of the article (so that nouns become general when the article is withheld): 'Neuter horum articulorum praefigitur voci generali generaliter significanti (utpote cuius significatio particularibus actu non applicatur).'[6] Cooper includes here also mass-words: '...voces quae significant res homogeneas, quae dividi non possunt in distinctas

---

[1] Tomkis, 1612, fol. 4 verso.   [2] Jonson, 1640, p. 506.
[3] Evelyn, *c.* 1650, fol. 95.   [4] Gill, 1619, p. 73.
[5] ibid.   [6] Wallis, 1653, p. 72.

357

partes et differentes...ut...diversa genera herbarum, frugum...
virtutum, vitiorum'.[1]

Not used with 'some', etc. Wallis's explanation is ingenious, if incomplete:
words like *any, some, this* resemble *one* in containing within themselves
the function of the articles, which are therefore unnecessary. The
articles are not used: '...ubi aliud aliquod adjectivum adest quod
hos articulos virtualiter contineat (redundarent enim) ut...*one
man...some man...any man...this world*'.[2]

Before adjectives. The articles are used before adjectives only when a
following substantive is understood. During the eighteenth century
this is one of the most frequent comments about the articles. Dilworth, though not the earliest, is typical:

Q. Do the Adjectives admit of any Article before them?
A. They do; but it is by Virtue of some Substantive expressed or understood. (Dilworth, 1740, p. 100.)

The converse, that an adjective may be used as a substantive if the
article precedes it, is to be preferred in that it attributes power to a
word that is present rather than to one which is absent, but this
account is rarely put forward. It appears first in Tomkis, who gives
as an instance of enallage (the use of one part of speech for another)
'Adjectivum pro substantivo, addendo articulum, ut *take the good
and wave* [sic] *the badd*'.[3]

'The' individuates. This is the most frequently mentioned function of
the definite article:

Articulus finitus vim habet ut incerta et infinita declaret et definiat.
(Tomkis, 1612, fol. 4 verso.)

The notat Particularium unius pluriumve...Determinationem, (Wallis,
1653, p. 72.)

individuum denotat terminationem. (Cooper, 1685, p. 101.)

restrains [the signification of a Noun] to some known and Special Thing,
and thereby rendering a Substantive Common, equivalent to a Proper.
(Brown, 1700, p. 90.)[4]

The last comment is interesting and unusual in its support for a
logical definition of the proper noun.

---

[1] Cooper, 1685, p. 102.
[2] Wallis, loc. cit.
[3] Tomkis, 1612, fol. 13 verso.
[4] Harris, 1751, p. 222, makes the same point.

'*The*' *has a demonstrative function.* '...est articulus Demonstrativus, idemque significat ac *that* illud, sed minus emphatice'.[1] Horne Tooke underlined in his copy of Wallis's grammar the words *minus emphatice* and put two exclamation marks in the margin, because he considered it either an understatement or too obvious to mention. But Wallis was writing with scarcely any historical knowledge of the language, and in terms of logic it was a perceptive remark. Maittaire, in 1712, attempts a historical explanation. He reinforces his emphasis on the demonstrative function of *the* by suggesting that *the* derives from the first element in *this* in the same way as the French *il* is the first element in *ille*, and *le* the last.[2]

'*The*' *implies previous reference.* This use of the definite article, which cannot be discussed without reference to a context within which the article is used, is early referred to. Cooper says *the* is used

quando loquimur de re vel persona, quam lector vel auditor scit vel scire supponatur, quia eminens est, vel antedicta; ut *the king.* (Cooper, 1685, p. 102.)

The mostly supposes a thing mentioned before. (Mattaire, 1712, p. 34.)

The suggestion of 'eminence', which is discussed also by Harris,[3] is only another way of regarding the individuating function of the definite article, which is apparent both in logically proper names like *the chair* ('Please bring *a chair*...Would you put *the chair* here.') and in descriptions such as *the King of England.* Harris is also the first grammarian to make the implication of previous reference the essential function of the definite article:

A respects our primary Perception, and denotes Individuals as unknown; *the* respects our secondary Perception, and denotes Individuals as known. To explain by an example—I see an object pass by, which I never saw till now. What do I say? 'There goes *a* Beggar with *a* long Beard.' The Man departs, and returns a Week after. What do I say then? 'There goes *the* Beggar with *the* long Beard.' The Article only is changed, the rest remains unaltered. (Harris, 1751, p. 215.)

This quotable passage was much used by later grammarians.

'*A, an*' *equivalent to* '*one*'. '*A*...idem omnino significat ac *one*, unus, sed minus emphatice.'[4] Wallis here speaks only of equivalence of mean-

---

[1] Wallis, 1653, p. 72.
[2] Maittaire, 1712, p. 34.
[3] Harris, 1751, Bk 2, chap. 1.
[4] Wallis, 1653, p. 71.

ing. He refers to *a*, not to *an*, and does not show that he is aware of any formal connection between *an* and *one*.

'A, an' make the following noun indefinite. This is the correlative of the individuating function of *the*.

extends the Signification of a Noun to any one particular, and so to all, one by one of its kind. (Brown, 1700, p. 90.)

used in a vague sense to point out one single thing of the kind, in other respects indeterminate. (L. Murray (1795), 1802, Pt I. chap. 2.)

'A, an' imply first reference. A, an imply that the noun to which they are attached has not been previously mentioned, or is not clearly identified: correlative to *the* for previous reference. '*A* [supposes] something new...it of itself neither shews, nor determines it'.[1]

Absence of 'a, an'. Both Wallis and Harris note that plural forms without an article express indefiniteness in the same way as *a, an* do in the singular: 'Si vero pluribus particularibus (sive speciebus sive individuis) vox generalior applicetur, illud numero Plurali innuitur...sic *men* homines, de individuis dici manifestum est; & *vertues* virtutes, de virtutis vel speciebus vel individuis.'[2] Harris, after referring to the Greek ἄνθρωπος ἔπεσεν, *a man fell*, in which the place of the indefinite article is taken 'by a negation of their Article ὁ' (the definite article), continues:

Even in English, where the Article *A* cannot be used, as in plurals, its force is exprest by the same Negation. *Those are THE Men*, means those are Individuals, of which we possess some previous Knowledge. *Those are Men*, the Article apart, means no more than that they are so many vague and uncertain Individuals, just as the Phrase, *A Man*, in the singular, implies one of the same number. (Harris, 1751, pp. 217–18.).

Horne Tooke derided Harris's use of 'negation'.[3] The term is not well chosen, but Harris is one of the first English writers to point out that the absence of a linguistic element (which is, in a sense, a negative condition) can have a positive significance.

Lowth's synthesis. Besides Wallis and Harris, the most influential writer about the article was Bishop Lowth, whose definition and description were quoted frequently. Some of Lowth's short section

---

[1] Maittaire, 1712, p. 34.   [2] Wallis, 1653, p. 71.
[3] Tooke (1786), 1829, I. 112, 274.

on the article is reproduced here, partly because it was so widely copied, partly so as to bring together in a single representative account most of the elements which have been separated from each other in the foregoing analysis.

The Article is a word prefixed to substantives, to point them out, and to shew how far their signification extends...

A is used in a vague sense to point out one single thing of the kind, in other respects indeterminate: *the* determines what particular thing is meant.

A substantive without any article to limit it is taken in its widest sense: thus *man* means all mankind; as

'The proper study of mankind is man:' POPE

where *mankind* and *man* may change places without making any alteration in the sense. *A man* means some one or other of that kind, indefinitely; *the man* means, definitely, that particular man, who is spoken of: the former therefore is called the Indefinite, the latter the Definite, Article...

It is of the nature of both the Articles to determine or limit the thing spoken of: *a* determines it to be one single thing of the kind, leaving it still uncertain which; *the* determines which it is, or of many which they are. The first therefore can only be joined to Substantives in the singular number; the last may also be joined to plurals. (Lowth, 1762, pp. 15–19.)

Lowth chooses two 'exceptions' to comment on: the use of *a* before *few* and *many* when these precede plural nouns (*a few men, a great many men*) and in expressions such as *a hundred, a thousand*; and the use of the definite article before comparative adverbs (*the more I examine it, the better I like it*). He himself in later editions, and many later grammarians, assiduously pursued 'irregularities' of usage, but these are not here under consideration.

One of the most sensible comments about the articles, and one which gives fair warning of 'irregularity', is quoted by Charles Wiseman, who cannot usually be entrusted with the last word about any category: 'The English Articles are but few...and such as will presently discover any stranger[1] in the world from a natural Englishman'.

TERMINOLOGY

definite, indefinite. These terms appear, in an English grammar, for the first time in one of the most derivative works in the canon— James Howell's, 1662.[2] They must have been in use before then,[3]

---

[1] i.e. 'distinguish any foreigner'.   [2] Howell, 1662, p. 42.
[3] OED quotes nothing earlier than Chambers' *Cyclopaedia*, 1727.

but they were not common until well into the eighteenth century. Tomkis had used *finitus* and *infinitus* or *vagus*,[1] Jonson[2] and Evelyn *finite* and *infinite* (though Evelyn writes it *finie*)[3] and Wallis had well called them *articulus demonstrativus* and *articulus numeralis*.[4]

emphatical. Stubbs calls *the* 'the emphatical Article' on the only occasion when he refers to it.[5]

demonstrative. Samuel Edwards calls *the* the demonstrative article, following Wallis, who had called it *articulus demonstrativus*.[6]

general. In *A Short Introduction to Grammar*, 1793, *a* and *an* are called 'general or indefinite Articles'.[7]

specific. Duncan calls *some* the 'specific' article, because it 'denotes a Parcel of the whole kind'.[8]

[1] Tomkis, 1612, fol. 4 verso.   [2] Jonson, 1640, Bk I, chap. 9.
[3] Evelyn, *c.* 1650, fol. 95 recto.   [4] Wallis, 1653, pp. 71 and 72.
[5] Stubbs, 1777, p. 3.   [6] S. Edwards, 1765, p. 45; Wallis, 1653, loc. cit.
[7] *Short Introduction*, 1793, p. 4.   [8] Duncan, 1731, p. 3.

12. THE VERB

The tradition contained three principal approaches towards a definition of the verb: one in terms of form and two in terms of meaning. Dionysius Thrax had framed his definition almost entirely according to formal criteria: the verb had no case-inflections but had tense, number and person. This remained the basis of most later definitions. Dionysius had referred also to the 'active or passive force' of the verb, which became more explicitly a criterion of meaning in Donatus, who said the verb signified doing, suffering, or neither. A second semantic criterion entered the tradition, apparently with Peter Helias in the twelfth century, when the importance of the verb in logical propositions focused attention on its assertive function. A fourth approach, using syntactic criteria, is apparent in some of Lily's explanatory descriptions but does not enter into any definition within the tradition.[1]

Mixed criteria. Among the English grammars definitions relying solely on formal criteria are found only in the small group of works, early in the seventeenth century, which follow Ramus closely: Greaves, Butler and Jonson: 'a word of number, which hath both Tyme, and Person'.[2] Bullokar and Cooper add mood, which, on the model of Latin, they count as an accident of the English verb; Hume adds mood and excludes number. Frequently the reference to the accidents of the verb moves naturally into a reference to the ideas represented by them: '...signifies being, doing or suffering; with relation to Time, Place, Number, and Person'.[3] The blending of formal and semantic criteria is here complete, because the expression of place, though loosely associated with time, has no formal expression in the verb: it is, in fact, difficult to see why it forms part of the definition. Such mixed definitions are rare after 1750: they

---

[1] See above, pp. 56–7.   [2] Jonson, 1640, Bk 1. chap. 16.
[3] Merriman, 1750, p. 11.

appear in about half a dozen grammars, the latest of which is Beattie's: '...a word, necessary in every sentence, signifying the affirmation of some attribute, together with the designation of time, number and person'.[1] Beattie admits that this definition is more suited to ancient than to modern languages. His reason—that the modern languages rely so much on auxiliaries—shows that he is thinking in terms of formal characteristics: time, number and person are properly 'designated' by changes in the form of the verb. In his very full discussion of alternative definitions he rejects both those which rely solely on meaning and those which rely solely on form. The traditional formula '...signifies to be, to do, or to suffer' he rejects because it does not distinguish the verb from the participle; the formal '...a declinable word with time and person' he rejects because it overlooks the assertive function of the verb. Pickbourn goes one step beyond the mixed definition and says, in effect, that no definition is satisfactory. He considers Beattie's definition adequate for the finite verb, and Lowth's—'a word which signifies to be, to do, or to suffer'[2]—adequate as a general definition for all languages, except that it does not distinguish verbs from verbal nouns. Pickbourn sees that assertion is the fundamental idea in any satisfactory definition, but he does not wish, or is not able, to unite formal and semantic criteria in a single definition:

> If *affirmation* be essential to verbs, I think it possible for a tolerably copious language to be formed with only *one verb* in it; for infinitives, participles, adjectives, &c. may be so united to nouns by the *copula*...as to express almost any idea which we can have occasion to communicate. But if the circumstances of time, person, and number, be essential to verbs, I question whether there may not be languages in the world without a single *verb* in them. (Pickbourn, 1789, pp. 165–6.)

Semantic criteria. The earliest English grammar to offer a definition purely in terms of meaning is Joshua Poole's basic grammar, *The English Accidence*, 1646, where all he says of the verb is that it signifies 'to doe, to be done, or to be'.[3] This is by far the commonest criterion in the English tradition, and in about seventy-five grammars it comprises the whole definition, either in these words or in the corresponding form, '...signifies the Action, Passion, or Being of a thing'.[4] Two variations can be noted. Those grammarians who deny

---

[1] Beattie, 1783, p. 373.   [2] Lowth, 1762, p. 44.
[3] Poole, 1646, p. 9.   [4] Lane, 1700, p. 37.

that English has a passive modify the definition accordingly: '...signifies the Acting, or Being, of a Person, Place, or Thing'.[1] These grammarians are discussed later in this chapter. The second variation is more puzzling. Three grammars, apparently unrelated, include the expression of *possession* among the defining characteristics of the verb:

betokens Existence...Action...or Possession, as to have, to injoy. (Miege, 1688, p. 4.)

that which being joined to an Alternative [i.e. a pronoun]...signifies it to be in some State, to do, or to have something; as *I live, thou readest, he hath*. (Kirkby, 1746, p. 57.)

a word whereby something or other is represented as Existing, Possessing, Acting, or being Acted upon, at some particular Time, Past, Present, or Future; and this in various manners. (White, 1761, p. 1.)

There is no reason why possession, any more than place, should be treated as a defining characteristic. A possible explanation is that because the auxiliaries *do* and *be* were considered to express the defining characteristics 'action' and 'existence' it was felt that the auxiliary *have* should be given the same status. This would be reasonable: if mood, which in English is expressed almost entirely through auxiliaries, is regarded as an accident of the verb there is no objection to treating as accidents also those aspects of the verb which are expressed by the other auxiliaries. The line of thought which could readily lead to such a result is apparent in a much later grammarian, John Sedger, who is something of an original. The point he is most concerned to make is that verbs are derived from nouns. As he justly remarks, 'much ingenuity has been employed in the contrivance of the English Language'. He is arguing that the ideas expressed by the auxiliary verbs are more uniform, and require less formal variation, than the ideas expressed by principal verbs:

From the consideration that such beings, as *possession, existence or being, liberty, necessity, will, power*, &c., which do not admit of particular heads or divisions, and having a sameness at all times in themselves, we take the helping verbs *have* for *having* or *possession, am* or *be* for *being* or *existence*; *may* for *liberty*; *must* for *necessity*, &c.

the particular names or divisions of *action, passion, rest*...or rather the beings of which these are names, have many beginnings, and continue and end many times, and, therefore, require affirmations or verbs to express mode, time, number, and person, more at large than helping verbs do.

---

[1] Ash, 1760, p. 16.

Verbs in general seem to be contrived modifications of the names of some beings, to express ourselves about other nouns...*I wrote the book*, What is *wrote* but a modification of writing, to say something more particularly about the writer and the book? (Sedger, 1798, pp. 30–1.)

Entangled in Sedger's confusions is this same view, that *possession*, along with others, is an 'auxiliary' idea, belonging to the verb. The relation between formal and semantic criteria, and the difficulties of definition, which are clearly apparent in this intrusion of *possession* into the definition of the verb, are more fully discussed later in this chapter.

There is little variation in those parts of the definitions which refer to doing, being and suffering. This threefold criterion was at least fifteen hundred years old; it had become a conventional formula which the ordinary schoolmaster-grammarian did not question. The few writers who depart from it do not make it any more useful. Bridel, for example, in an attempt to classify forms like *it rains* (which he says express neither action nor being nor being acted upon) adds to the traditional triad a fourth criterion, *happening*.[1] Haywood seems to be trying to move the emphasis of the traditional definition away from the expression of action towards the expression of intention: '...a word by which the action of the body, or some other effect of the mind are signified'.[2] Modest this may be, but the weight of the tradition was such that even this unhelpful generality is a resonant innovation: so much so that Haywood dropped it in the second edition.

Affirmation. Much more interesting is the gradual introduction into the definitions of the idea of assertion, or, as it was almost always called, 'affirmation'. Assertion is, historically, a logical rather than a grammatical category, although it is implicit in the grammatical category of finite verb, and it was only among the scholastic grammarians that it received much attention. It played no part in the English definitions until Gildon and Brightland introduced it from the Port Royal grammar of 1660, where the verb is defined as: 'un mot dont le principal usage est de signifier l'affirmation'.[3] Gildon's first reference to affirmation is tentative: 'A Word [i.e. a verb] is join'd to a Name, to express its Being, doing, or suffering, or which affirms something of the Name, with the several Circumstances

---

[1] Bridel, 1797, p. 6.   [2] Haywood, 1800, p. 12.
[3] *Grammaire générale*, 1660, p. 90.

of Person, Number, Time, and Manner.'[1] In the second edition, a year later, affirmation is not only made the first criterion in the definition but is used as the name of the part of speech itself: 'An Affirmation is a Part of Speech...which affirms some Attribute, which [sic, presumably for *with*] the Designation of Time, Number and Person, expressing being, doing or suffering, or the want of them, or the like.'[2] The word *affirmation* was seized on by many grammarians, especially those adopting a vernacular system of parts of speech,[3] but even those who followed Gildon in using it instead of the term *verb* did not pursue its implications, and an opportunity was lost for restoring one of the useful links between logic and grammar. The next writer to refer to affirmation in his definition of the verb is J. T. Philipps, in 1726, who gives several alternative definitions, one of which is: '...a Word made use of when we affirm one Thing of another'.[4] Loughton uses the same definition as Philipps,[5] and later writers use equivalent forms such as '...serves to express what we affirm of any Subject,'[6] and, very commonly, 'a Word used when we affirm one Thing of another'.[7] James Harris, who goes back, as he thinks, to Aristotle, in classing adjective, verb and participle together as *attributives*, keeps to the logical tradition not only in making assertion the feature of the verb which distinguishes it from both adjective and participle, but in treating all verbs as capable of being resolved (actually or notionally) into the copula followed by an attribute:

When we say, *Cicero eloquent, Cicero wise*, these are imperfect Sentences, though they denote a Substance and an Attribute. The reason is, that they want an *Assertion*, to shew that such Attribute appertains to such Substance. We must therefore call in the help of an Assertion elsewhere, an *is* or a *was* to complete the Sentence, saying *Cicero is wise, Cicero was eloquent*. On the contrary, when we say, *Cicero writeth, Cicereth walketh*, in instances like these there is no such occasion, because the Words *writeth* and *walketh* imply in their own Form not an Attribute only, but an Assertion likewise. Hence it is they may be resolved, the one into *is* and *writing*, the other into *is* and *walking*.

Now all those Attributives, which have this complex Power of denoting both an Attribute and an Assertion, make that Species of Words, which Grammarians call Verbs. (Harris, 1751, Bk I, chap. 6.)

---

[1] G–B, 1711, p. 97.
[2] idem, 1712, p. 86.
[3] See below, p. 392.
[4] Philipps, 1726, p. xii.
[5] Loughton, 1734, p. 75.
[6] Saxon, 1737, p. 52.
[7] *Easy Introduction*, 1745, p. 82.

Harris is followed very closely by the writer of the article on *Grammar* in the first two editions of the *Encyclopaedia Britannica*, who accepts his statement that it is the process of assertion which 'energizes' the verb, and discusses it with even greater emphasis.[1] Monboddo, in 1774, had also been influenced by Harris, here as elsewhere, but had subordinated the idea of energy to that of accident. Monboddo made only two primary parts of speech: substantive and verb. The latter included every kind of word which could be thought of as expressing an attribute—adjective, adverb, conjunction, preposition and interjection, and its definition had been correspondingly wide: '. . . a word principally significant of accident, of the energy of the mind of the speaker relative to that accident, of the substance to which the accident belongs, and it is consignificant of time'.[2] Monboddo's discussion of the verb, which in fact treats it in its customary sense, is much more valuable than this definition would suggest. By *energy* it is clear that he means the speaker's intention, which he explicitly says can be expressed as assertion, wish or command. He in fact forestalls Lindley Murray's criticism, quoted later in this chapter, by himself criticising on two grounds the common definition of the verb as a word of action: (*a*) it omits reference to the speaker's energy; (*b*) it mentions, if at all, only affirmation, and omits command and wish.[3]

William Ward and Lindley Murray are the only grammarians actually to dispute the criterion of affirmation. Ward describes first the three 'characters or offices' of the verb: the *verb objective* (i.e. the infinitive and the verbal noun), the *verb coalescent* (the participle) and the *verb definitive* (finite forms of the verb). Then he continues: 'It has been laid down as a principle in grammar, of late years, that the essence of the verb consists in affirmation, and that affirmation is a particular act of the judgment, which the mind passes upon the object which is the subject of such act of judgment.'[4] Ward rejects this view on the grounds that a speaker makes an act of judgment whenever he expresses any relationship between the things he is talking about. Judgment therefore cannot be a criterion by which to distinguish one part of speech from another, and as affirmation is a form of judgment it also is no criterion. Ward admits that the hearer need not judge until he hears the definitive verb, but he seems not to

[1] *Enc. Brit.* (A), 1771, pp. 735 f.
[3] Monboddo, 1774, p. 122.
[2] Monboddo, 1774, p. 124.
[4] W. Ward, 1765, p. 168.

think that this spoils his argument. Ward's own definition of the verb, most concisely given in the grammar of 1767, is based ultimately on the expression of recurrence. He is combining the idea of action with the idea of time, but he does not clarify the category at all:

Verbs denote *states of being*, considered as *beginning, continuing, ending, being renewed, destroyed,* and *again repeated,* so as to suit any Occasion. Every State that is denoted by a Verb, may be counted by the Numbers of Repetition, *once, twice, thrice,* &c....And any Object that is represented in the State denoted by a Verb, may be considered as in that State, *once, twice, thrice,* &c. as *such a thing was once, twice, thrice, so and so*...Thus *action once, twice, thrice*; or *an active man once, twice, thrice,* are absurd Expressions: But *to act, acting, once, twice, thrice,* are consistent Expressions: Therefore *action* and *active* are Nouns; but *to act* and *acting* are Verbs. (W. Ward, 1767, pp. 41–2.)

Lindley Murray's protest was pointed and justifiable but interpreted *assertion* more strictly than most writers had done:

There are...some grammarians, who consider *assertion* as the essence of the verb: but, as the participle and the infinitive, if retained, would prove insuperable objections to their scheme, they have, without hesitation, denied the former a place in the verb, and declared the latter to be only an abstract noun. This appears to be going rather too far, in support of a system. It seems to be incumbent on these grammarians, to reject also the imperative mood. (L. Murray (1795), 8th edn 1802, p. 55 n.)[1]

In a later edition Murray supposes a critic to object that *depart instantly* is equivalent to *I desire that you depart instantly* and is therefore an assertion. To this Murray replies that the only part which is now an assertion is *I desire*; he puts the whole matter into a sentence which is so clear-sighted and, for its day, so profound that one doubts whether the words were originally his: 'The position is not tenable, that Equivalence in sense implies similarity in grammatical structure.'[2] Those words, appearing in the most popular textbook of several decades, should have ended the old uncertainties about meaning and form. But the system to which they were attached was strong. It had contained other damaging truths for a long time, and had survived.

Apart from these instances the assertive function of the verb is

---

[1] This passage does not appear in any of the first three editions.
[2] Murray (1795), two-vol. edn 1809, I. 106.

often stressed but little described or discussed. There is however a small number of grammars in which the logical function of the verb is more fully recognised in the definition even if it is not developed in the discussion of the category as a whole. The most surprising of these, and the only English grammar which defines the verb solely in relational terms, is John Newton's *School Pastime*, 1669: 'A Verb is a Word or Part of Speech, that joyneth the Signification of other Words together'.[1] Duncan, whose definition seems to be the product of independent thought, combines the ideas of affirmation and relation: 'A Verb is a Word, that expresses the Judgment we bear of the Agreement or Disagreement between one thing and another, or between a Thing and a Quality.'[2]

Later grammars draw attention to the relational aspect of the verb by including a reference to the 'attribute' which is affirmed by it, that is to the predicate:

A verb is

that part of speech, by which one thing is attributed to another, as to its subject. (J. Ward, 1758, p. 81.)

a part of speech that implies predication, or by which something is applied to another as to its subject...The common definition of a Verb, that it signifies to do, to suffer, to be, is not sufficiently accurate; for there are many Verbs which signify neither to do, to suffer, nor to be; as, *It behoveth*, &c. (Trinder, 1781, p. 37.)

Assertion...or predication, is certainly the very essence of the verb, as being that part of its office, *and that part only*, which cannot be discharged by other kinds of words...The office of the verb...seems to be merely this, 'To join together the subject and predicate of a proposition': its powers are analogous to those of the sign + in Algebra. (*Enc. Brit.* (B), 1797, p. 56.)

The analogy which the last writer makes between the verb and the plus sign in algebra, though not unique, is extremely rare.[3] It is an anticipation of the cross-fertilization of logic and language which was not explicitly attempted by any mathematician before Boole, in 1853, and is still regarded with suspicion by most students of language.

[1] Newton, 1669, p. 28. The definition is also given in his *English Academy*, 1677. p. 12. Compare the anonymous *An English Introduction to the Latine Tongue*, 1683, p. 19: 'A Verb is a word, that joyneth the signification of the rest together.'

[2] Duncan, 1731, p. 16.

[3] Sedger, 1798, p. 36, makes a comparison between the auxiliary verbs, 'used to represent words of importance' (as *have* 'is a kind of substitute for *possession*') and the symbols of algebra, which are used to represent numbers. Cf. William Ward, below, p. 458.

The verb

Syntactic criteria. The syntactic element in the definition of the verb, faintly suggested in Gildon's definition,[1] where the verb 'is join'd to a Name', first appears explicitly in Sheridan: '...a Word that cannot Signify any thing without a Noun'.[2] It was not a novelty then, for it is the correlative of the syntactic definition of the substantive as a word that makes complete sense with a verb, and this had been used at least as early as 1688. The commonest form of this type of definition is that which appears first in a comment by Douglas, apart from his formal definition,[3] and next in James Corbet, 1743: 'Every Word is a Verb that will make sense with the personal pronouns... before it'.[4] This and its various equivalents occur in more than thirty grammars before the end of the century.

Other patterns are used for the syntactic test. Kirkby uses the infinitive *to*, in a mixed definition: 'Every Word is a Verb, which, by putting it after the Particle *to*, can have no other Signification than to express indefinitely the simple Act, effective Quality, or changeable State of some Being'.[5] P. W. Fogg, trying to make allowances for the strong verbs and those descended from mutated presents, whose nature he does not understand, uses a purely syntactic test: 'Any word is a verb, that will fill up either of the following blanks, used in the same sense. But sometimes *-est, -eth,* or *-ed* is to be taken from it first, and sometimes a change is to be made equal to leaving out *ed,* as *bind* for *bound, think* for *thought.* "I am—ing; it is —ing"'.[6] Beattie admits that such definitions are valid as far as they go, and quotes approvingly, 'A verb is a word, which forms, when joined to a noun, a complete sentence.' Nevertheless he rejects the definition because it 'does not sufficiently express [the verb's] character as proceeding from an operation of the mind'.[7] The ordinary schoolmaster, however, clearly found syntactic definitions useful, and would agree with H. Ward: 'For a general Rule to direct a Learner how to distinguish Verbs...I know of none better than this, viz. Place some personal Pronoun before them, and if they be good Sense, they will be Verbs: as, *I read, Thou writest, They cipher.*'[8] The definitions in these early grammars were not at the time considered as falling into the four types described here. Those

[1] Above, p. 366.
[2] Sheridan, 1714, p. 60.
[3] Douglas, *c.* 1720?, Bundle 1.7. fol. 107 recto.
[4] Jas. Corbet, 1743, p. 63.
[5] Kirkby, 1746, p. 81.
[6] Fogg, 1792, p. 89.
[7] Beattie, 1783, p. 378 (= 1788, p. 206).
[8] H. Ward, 1777, p. 45 n.

framed according to syntactic criteria were felt to be different from the others, and were often put forward as alternative, and more pedagogical, definitions; but criteria of form and meaning were regularly combined in the same definition without any recognition of their difference. In Latin the connection between meaning and form was always close. All active verbs, except *sum*, ended in -o; all passive verbs ended in -or. 'Active' meant primarily 'ending in -o'; it was a formal , not a semantic, criterion. *Action* applied to all active verbs; *passion* applied to all passive verbs; *existence* applied to *sum*; apart from the deponents there were no other verbs. When this convention was applied to English it lost its firm basis in form. Action, passion and existence could be regarded as purely semantic categories and there was no longer any reason why they should not be joined by other meanings which the verb could express. That this in fact happened only to a limited extent was due to the force of the conventional definitions. A definition was felt to be important because it gave the writer a feeling of intellectual power and provided the plain pedagogical task with elevations, whose peaks rose even to philosophical heights. It was important also because of current assumptions about the nature of learning—assumptions which it was the great achievement of Comenius to challenge.[1] Most teachers believed that their pupils were dependent, in the early stages, on learning a definition by heart. These textbook definitions are of two kinds, inclusive and partial. The inclusive definition lists all the properties, and only those properties, which are peculiar to the category; the partial definition is framed in terms of only one or two properties, chosen in relation to a particular purpose. The inclusive definition tries to express the whole truth; the partial definition expresses nothing but the truth.

CLASSIFICATION

The verb is subjected to less explicit classification than any part of speech except the preposition. Bellamy's hotch-potch of 'kinds' of verb—active, passive, neuter, substantive, auxiliary, regular, irregular, impersonal—is odd.[2] The ideas of doing and suffering,

[1] One of Comenius' English admirers was Mark Lewis, whose rhetorical question, already quoted, still has force: 'Do you think a Boy would judge, that *have sate* is a Verb, because it signifies doing?' (Lewis, *Essay*, 1670?, p. 3.) See above, p. 281.

[2] Bellamy, 1760, p. xxxvii.

on which the usual definition was built, were naturally used to distinguish active and passive verbs. Whether actives and passives were treated as *kinds* or as *forms* of verb matters little. The area of uncertainty, and hence of greatest interest to us, was that surrounding the idea of *being* and the neuter verb. Of interest also is the range and confusion of criteria used in discussing the verb. The early grammarians' treatment of the neuter verb shows with particular clarity the consequences (affecting almost every category discussed in this work) of their lack of the fundamental distinction between formal and semantic criteria.

A few writers see that the criteria need scrutiny and, exceptionally, that there are different kinds of criteria. Ben Jonson, followed by Evelyn, says merely 'A Verbe is divided two manner of wayes. First, in respect of persons, it is called *personall* or *impersonall*...Secondly, in consideration of the times, we terme it *active*, or *neuter*.'[1] Maittaire is one of the few who make explicit a distinction which must have been obvious enough to any thoughtful writer but could usefully have been made many times: 'What...the Grammarians call Action and Passion in Verbs, is not to be taken in the same strict sense with that of the Philosophers; for else a Verb Active must needs often be reckon'd a Passive; as *I suffer wrong*.'[2] John Ward, in *Four Essays upon the English Language*, alone follows Linacre in distinguishing three kinds of criterion: 'with respect to their signification' verbs are active passive or neuter; 'with respect to their construction' they are transitive or intransitive; 'with respect to their formation' they are regular or irregular, perfect or imperfect.[3] There could not be more explicit recognition of the three criteria, formal, semantic and syntactic. Linacre, in 1524, and Ward, in 1758, saw clearly, in at least one context, what the early grammarians most needed in order to improve their methods of classification. It was not just lack of linguistic knowledge which held the grammarians back: Linacre and Ward show that some of the knowledge was there. It was the accumulated weight of the tradition which made it enormously difficult to recognise new knowledge and to use it. It is surprising that the verb, which received individual attention more than any other part of speech, should not have provoked more writers into a

[1] Jonson, 1640, Bk I. chap. 16; also Evelyn, fol. 95 verso.
[2] Maittaire, 1712, p. 62. Lodowyck, 1652, had commented (p. 4) that verbs like *suffer* were really passive, but he said it did not matter.
[3] J. Ward, 1758, pp. 81–2; cf. Linacre, quoted above, p. 96.

discussion of the relation between meaning and form; Bell[1] and Meilan[2] are the only ones who follow John Ward. But those—White, Pickbourn and Warren Hastings—who wrote specially about the verb, were preoccupied with the classification of moods and tenses; others either did not classify the verb at all (as Wallis) or, pre-occupied with Latin and Greek, did not question the transfer to English of the basically formal categories *active* and *passive*. Many English grammarians questioned whether English had a passive: the way in which they entangled themselves in the question is further evidence that the distinction between meaning and form was not readily available to them.

Active verbs. Among the English grammars there are few significant departures from the traditional definition in terms of 'doing' or 'action'. In 1586 Bullokar wrote: 'It is called a Verb-active when it signifieth *to do*: as, *I love*.'[3] In 1880 Mrs Eves began her definition of the verb in the same way: 'A Verb active denotes the doing of an action...'[4] One development during the two hundred years is that she continues, '...and therefore supposes an agent or person who acts, and an object acted upon'. The active verb had come to be identified, by many writers, with the transitive verb. The earliest English grammarian to express this identity is Joseph Aickin, in 1693: 'The verb Transative [*sic*] or the verb active, or adjective active, have always the Oblique or Accusative word after it.'[5] Less ambiguous is James Greenwood, in 1711: 'A Verb Active, is a Verb that signifies so to act, as that the Action passes over on some other thing: As, *to read a Book*.'[6] This equation of active and transitive occurs explicitly in about forty grammars, evenly distributed over the last sixty years of the eighteenth century, and it is assumed in many more. The popular wording, approved by Lindley Murray, was, '...expresses an action, and necessarily implies an agent, and an object acted upon'.[7]

On another view, however, *active* and *transitive* were different categories: a verb was active if it expressed action, whether or not that action was 'carried over' to an object. This was (and is) the weakened English equivalent of the traditional criterion—weakened

[1] Bell, 1769, pp. 209 and 211.
[2] Meilan, *An Introduction to the English Language*, 1803, I. 57–8.
[3] Bullokar, 1586, p. 353.   [4] Eves, 1800, p. 28.   [5] Aickin, 1693, p. 17.
[6] Greenwood, 1711, p. 153.   [7] L. Murray, 1795, p. 38.

because it lacked any formal reinforcement. *Video* was active not primarily because seeing is an action (a slippery question to discuss) but because it ended in -o. *I see* is active only because it is held to express 'doing' rather than 'suffering' (which ought to be an equally slippery question). Maittaire has already been quoted[1] as pointing out the consequent difficulty with the verb *I suffer*: a difficulty which can be resolved only by abandoning the criterion of meaning and using instead formal or structural criteria. Occasional attempts to do this are described later, but the difficulty was evaded by most of the few writers who perceived it by supposing, with Maittaire, two senses of the terms *active* and *passive*.

A few grammarians who do not equate active and transitive say that transitive and intransitive verbs are 'active verbs distinguished in respect of their objects'.[2] A transitive active verb 'admits Various Objects'; an intransitive active verb 'admits of one Accusative and that of its own Signification, as, *I live a life...I go a journey*'.[3] This is, in effect, to abolish the category of intransitive verb, which is how Collyer, 1735, interprets the classification, which he mentions with approval.[4] It is more common, especially towards the end of the century, to make active verbs include both transitive and intransitive, which are treated as separate categories. This practice is followed by S. Edwards, 1765; Shaw, 1778; Huntley, 1793; Bullen, 1797; *Encyclopaedia Britannica* (B), 1797; Salmon, 1798, and Dalton, 1801.

One of the many small signs that Lane was an independent and thoughtful grammarian is his introduction into the definition of the active verb of a useful syntactic criterion: 'Every Verb that admits the Auxiliaries *do*, or *did*, before it in good Sense, is a Verb Active.'[5] Surprisingly, only one other grammarian, Maittaire, uses this criterion in his treatment of the active verb.[6]

Some of the earlier grammarians, Bullokar, Jonson and Evelyn, follow the practice, which goes back to Priscian, of defining the active verb in terms of the passive: a verb is active if it has a passive participle which can be joined to it with the verb *be*.[7]

---

[1] p. 373 above.
[2] Lane, 1700, p. 39.
[3] ibid, cf. Douglas, c. 1720?, MS. No. 587a. fol. 288 recto.
[4] Collyer, 1735, p. 69.
[5] Lane, 1700, p. 38.
[6] Maittaire, 1712, p. 62.
[7] Bullokar, 1586, p. 353; Jonson, 1640, Bk I. chap. 16; Evelyn, fol. 95 verso.

Passive verbs. In spite of the common definition, according to which it is one function of the verb to express 'suffering', and in spite of the generally accepted classification of verbs into active, passive and neuter, there is intermittent agreement throughout the whole period that English has no passive verbs, only a passive voice. Because formal and semantic criteria were not clearly distinguished many grammarians are superficially inconsistent. *The Complete Letter Writer,* 1755, merely puts into one paragraph what dozens of grammarians said on separate pages: 'those [verbs] that signify Suffering are called Verbs passive. But we have in our Tongue no Verbs passive.'[1] The assumption had always been that only inflected forms could truly be called passive. In 1594 Greaves had written of the passive verbs in English: 'Nullam certam flexionem admittunt, sed qualiscunque sit, constat ex perfecto participio, et verbo *am*.'[2] But the first explicit repudiation of the passive is Gildon's, from the Port Royal grammar: 'The vulgar Tongues of Europe have no Passive.'[3] By 1735 Collyer is saying ,'Most English Grammarians are pretty unanimous in their opinions that we have no passive Verbs.'[4] The argument which Collyer quotes, however, carries less weight than the customary one. He supposes that the grounds for denying passive verbs to English are: that a simple sentence can contain only one verb and one nominative; therefore if in *I am loved* 'am' is a verb (which it clearly is) then *loved* must be a participle and not a verb; if *loved* is not a verb it cannot, *a fortiori*, be a passive verb. This argument was still powerful enough in 1783 to convert Joshua Story. In his first edition, 1778, Story had fully supported the passive as one of the three kinds of verb. By his third edition, at the latest, he expressly repudiates the category, using Collyer's argument.[5] This small eddy round the status of the passive verb clearly illustrates some of the difficulties which hampered the work of the early grammarians: confusion between the nature of a linguistic feature (about which there was no disagreement) and how it was to be classified; confusion between form and meaning; a narrowness which treated inflection as an intrinsically superior way of expressing a change of function (Joel, for example, speaks of 'two or more words' being used 'to supply

---

[1] *Complete Letter Writer,* 1755, p. 24; verbatim in G. Wilson, 2nd edn 1759, p. 12.
[2] Greaves, 1594, p. 16.
[3] G–B, 1711, p. 106; *Grammaire générale,* Bk II, chap. 17. Cf. Priestley, 1762, p. 97: 'This modification of verbs...is universally wanting in the modern European tongues.'
[4] Collyer, 1735, p. 70.   [5] Story (1778), 1783, p. 16.

the want of passive verbs'[1] and even Priestley says, 'Paucity of inflexion is the greatest defect in our language.');[2] a rigidity which treated the single word as the only significant unit (*am* and *loved* cannot 'be' a verb). As Ash puts it later, 'In Parsing, every Word should be considered as a distinct Part of Speech; for though two or more Words may be united to form a Mode, or a Tense, or a Comparison; yet it seems quite improper to unite two or more Words to make a Noun, a Verb, an Adjective, &c.'[3]

There are about fifty grammars in which passive verbs, but not, of course, the passive voice, are repudiated directly or indirectly. The number is of interest only as evidence that the question of 'kinds of verbs' was felt throughout this period to be one needing discussion. It is ignored by most of the more scholarly writers; two exceptions are John Ward[4] and the writer in the first edition of the *Encyclopaedia Britannica*. The latter for once diverges from Harris, in a paragraph which is worth quoting as the authoritative dismissal of the passive verb:

Verbs have been distinguished into the three classes of *active, passive* and *neuter*. These, however, might with more propriety be divided into two classes, which might be called verbs *transitive*, and *not transitive*; the first class including all those verbs which are usually called *active*, with the passives belonging to them; for it is evident, that these passives are not verbs themselves, but a variation only of a verb; and the second class including those verbs commonly called neuter. (*Enc. Brit.* (A), 1771, p. 738.)

Dispute about the passive concerned three points of view. In terms of common-sense 'meaning', by which hitting someone is a different thing from being hit by him, there were two categories, active and passive. On a more sophisticated consideration of action, but still conceiving it largely in physical terms, rose the view that action entailed the receipt of action, active entailed passive, and there was therefore 'really' only one category. From a narrowly formal point of view, that of inflection, English could be thought to have virtually no passive form. The active was therefore the only significant category. The dispute seems trivial to us, but the early grammarians were accustomed to thinking about language in labelled categories, and found it difficult to look without preconceptions at the moving parts of linguistic machinery and record what they saw.

[1] Joel, 1770, p. 19.
[2] Priestley (1761), 1768, p. 123.
[3] Ash, (1760) 1771, p. 36.
[4] J. Ward, 1758, p. 82.

Transitive verbs. Transitive verbs, as distinct from active verbs, are mentioned by comparatively few of the English grammarians, and then more commonly in the syntax than in their classification of the verb. They are conceived always as verbs in which there is a transfer of action, not, as by Priscian and by most of the scholastic grammarians, a transfer of person.[1] Action 'passes into another Subject'[2] or 'passes upon some external object'.[3] An occasional writer, thinking more of Latin than of English, says a transitive verb has an accusative after it.[4] Anselm Bayly, writing more like a lawyer than a grammarian, narrows the meaning of *transitive* when he is discussing several languages simultaneously. He gives as an example of a transitive verb 'He *made* the horse move' and defines it as one which expresses 'the inducing, procuring, employing, deputing, empowering, any way causing another to do an Action'.[5] But when he comes to write only of English Bayly adopts the customary definition.[6]

Two writers make comments which are worth attention. William Ward, in fact, makes a very full analysis of the transitive verb, too full, and too involved, to be described adequately here.[7] Ward is one of those who are anxious to take the reader beyond the schoolroom idea of 'action'. He points out that 'a verb in the active voice very frequently denotes a state which implies no real action [e.g. *to resemble, to equal*]...and a verb in the passive voice, frequently denotes a state which implies no real suffering; as, *to be lost*'.[8] He treats the transitive/active and passive verbs under the wider heading of relations. He stresses, for example, the equivalence of *John holding James* and *James held by John*, which can be represented by the same picture: 'We are at liberty to consider either John or James as the capital object concerned in the appearance; and...if we consider John as such object, the state, *holding James*, is a dependent circumstance of the complex object, expressed by *John holding James* [and vice versa].[9] Ward goes on to press the equivalence of 'a man *of learning*', 'a *learned* man' and 'a man *having learning*', explicitly saying that *of* and the transitive verb are both expressing the same kind of relation, though the latter expresses it 'more exactly'. Never-

[1] See above, p. 95.
[2] Philipps, 1726, p. xii.
[3] J. Ward, 1758, p. 82.
[4] Stirling, 1735, sig. A 3 verso.
[5] Bayly (1756), 1758, p. 74.
[6] idem. 1772, p. 36.
[7] W. Ward, 1765, pp. 58–65.
[8] op. cit. p. 58.
[9] op. cit. p. 62.

theless, just at the point when one is most excited Ward breaks off and abandons what has hitherto been one of his key concepts, relation, for the psychological language he likes so much: 'This sign, *of*, is...neither the mark of relation in general, nor of one particular sort of relation; but is the mark of a certain sort of operation of the mind itself.'[1] Ward's analysis of language is based on the idea of 'states of being'. How uneasily they combine with his logical ideas can be seen in his generalising summary of the extremely interesting discussion which arises out of his account of the transitive verb:

The objects, between which every particular kind of relation can exist, are each of them in a certain state of being, in consequence of such relation; so that to consider two objects as the terms between which a certain relation exists, is, in effect, to consider one of the objects as in a state of being, with which the state of being, in which the other object is, has the same kind of correspondence as that is which occasions the relation. (W. Ward, 1765, p. 62.)

The second comment on the transitive verb comes from Charles Coote, who uses one of Ward's illustrations and may owe something to him. Coote also is worried by the inadequacy of the traditional definition. He quotes the usual reference to action which 'passes over to and has an effect on, some object', and registers his dissatisfaction in a note:

Some words that do not agree with this definition, are nevertheless ranked among verbs active or transitive; as, *to equal*, *to succeed*, &c. We say, *his son equals him in learning*; in which sentence, *him* is governed by the verb, as if the circumstance implied by it had an effect on the object expressed by the pronoun; whereas we only intimate the actual state of the person alluded to, with respect to the equality between him and another, without referring to any action or effect as operating upon the latter. (Coote, 1788, p. 83.)

Intransitive verb. In the treatment of the intransitive verb there is no significant variation from the two traditional approaches, semantic and syntactic;[2] the former is the more frequent but the syntactic criterion is surprisingly often used. Action 'remains in the Agent... terminates in its own Subject...does not pass in a Subject, different from him who acts...terminates in the Person acting'. Ash's version, quoted already, was adopted widely; so was Lowth's less satisfactory way of putting it: a verb is neuter (i.e. intransitive)

[1] op. cit. p. 65. [2] Above, pp. 94 f.

'when the Agent and the Object acted upon coincide'[1]. The essential point of the category surely is that there is *no* Object, and can therefore be no coincidence. Less frequent is another form of the semantic criterion, that the intransitive verb 'makes complete sense of itself', or, as W. Johnston puts it,[2] has a signification which is 'generally immanent'. The syntactic criterion is always the same: that an intransitive verb cannot have a noun or pronoun after it. This appears by 1695,[3] and in at least thirty grammars between then and 1800.

Middle verbs. Maittaire calls them *Meed* verbs, and gives *go* and *enter* as examples, on the strength of those forms like *I am gone, I am entered the town*, which troubled so many of the grammarians. But he expresses considerable uncertainty about the validity of the category.[4] In its commonest form the category was encouraged, though not firmly proposed, by James Harris. His scheme of tenses—for universal, as well as English, grammar—had included middle forms for present, past and future: *I am writing, I was writing, I shall be writing.*[5] By *middle* Harris does not mean here 'between active and passive' (though elsewhere he refers to middle verbs in this sense)[6] but 'between intention and completion', that is, between his inceptive and completive forms. These middle forms are our progressive forms of the verb. Harris does not attribute to English either a middle voice or middle verbs. This was first done by James White, who called our progressive forms 'the Second Active or Middle'.[7] William Ward, who says he is following 'a grammatic treatise, published not long ago, concerning this part of speech'[8]—presumably White's—makes a middle voice not only of the progressive forms but of expressions (which Dr Johnson had called 'vicious') like *the house is building*: 'The verb in this voice, whether considered in its signification, or in its grammatic forms, partakes of the nature, both of the active, and passive verb.'[9] It can be seen from James Wood's description in 1777 how this idea of a middle verb or voice (he calls it both) is based on the misconception that *am* for example, in *I am loving*, has some passive force, because it appears also in, and is,

[1] Lowth, 1762, p. 45.
[2] W. Johnson, 1772, p. 29.
[3] Lane, 1695, p. 12.
[4] Maittaire, 1712, pp. 83–4.
[5] p. 412 below.
[6] Harris, 1751, Bk 1, chap. 9.
[7] White, 1761, p. 23.
[8] W. Ward, 1765, p. 181.
[9] op. cit. p. 182.

apparently, primarily associated with, expressions like *I am loved, I am being loved*. Of middle verbs Wood says:

Though the signs of the tense be passive, they yet admit of an active signification...Some grammarians may perhaps object to this voice on account of its novelty, but...they cannot bring one argument in favour of the passive voice; but what will make equally for this, and without such distinction the difficulty that would otherwise arise in disposing of the active participle when it follows the verb *am*, would be insuperable. (Wood, 1777, p. 27.)

This treatment of the progressive forms is continued by Martin Trinder,[1] M'Ilquham,[2] and Rothwell,[3] who cautiously quotes it from 'some grammarians'. Ussher and others who follow Harris exactly here make the progressive forms merely 'the definite form of conjugation'.[4] Unless its origin is in some earlier Latin grammar it seems as though this treatment of the progressive forms as a middle voice springs from a misunderstanding of Harris's much subtler treatment of them as a kind of tense.

Neuter verbs. The tradition had always contained a category *neuter verb*, although grammarians differed in the use they made of it. For some, neuter verbs were 'neither' active nor passive; for others they were 'neither' transitive nor intransitive. But as the categories *active* and *transitive* were constantly merging into each other there was, even in Latin, little use for the category *neuter*, and in English there was less. The time that it took for the category to be dropped from the English grammars witnesses not only to the strength of the tradition but also to the power of a name: because there existed a category labelled *neuter verb* neuter verbs had to be found. The typical examples, in English as in Latin, were *I walk* and *I live*. These were not exactly active (if active entailed passive) because they could not be passive. How then could they be described? They were neuter verbs, but what was a neuter verb? The question, which called out all the (frequently groping) ingenuity of which the English grammarians were capable, was given, by the most economical reckoning, six kinds of answer.

[1] Trinder, 1781, pp. 38 and 56.
[2] M'Ilquham (1781), 1789, p. 64. The category does not appear in the first edition.
[3] Rothwell, 1787, p. 79.   [4] Ussher, 1785, p. 41.

NEUTER VERBS DESCRIBED

No passive participle. The formal criterion that neuter verbs have no passive participle is offered by only six grammarians in all: Bullokar, Jonson, Evelyn, and Howell before 1670, John Ash in 1771, and J.G., who is following Ash, in 1796. Jonson's examples are *pertaine, live, die*.[1] Howell, who is trying to follow Jonson, does not understand him, and instead of saying that a verb is neuter when its passive participle cannot 'be joyned with the Verbe *am*', says merely, 'the Neuter verb is where *am* cannot be added, as *I live, I weep*', without mentioning the participle at all.[2] John Ash, by his fifth edition, 1771, had attempted a fuller explanation in formal terms. His difficulty suggests a probable reason why so few grammarians used this criterion: they were uncertain about the status of a word like *moved*. Because it was used in the passive, which *moving* never was, it was often called the passive participle, to distinguish it from the active participle *moving*. It seemed the same in *he has moved* and *he has been moved*; if it was a passive participle in the latter might it not be one also in the former? If so, could one safely say that in, for example, *he has fallen* there was no passive participle? Ash's explanation runs:

> Verbs intransitive, which have no Object, can have no passive Participle; some of them have a participial Form joined to the neuter Verb, as, 'The Man is *fallen*'. But as *fallen*...has no Reference to any Agent or compulsive Cause different from the Subject of the Verb, so it cannot with any Propriety be denominated a passive Participle: And notwithstanding its Form, it differs very little, if any Thing, from a common Adjective. (Ash (1760), 5th edn 1771, p. 52.)

In this passage Ash is using *neuter verb* to refer only to the verb *to be*, as distinct from intransitive verbs in general. In other places, although grudgingly, he uses *neuter* as a synonym for *intransitive*, and his uncertainty about terminology does not affect the point he is making here. What is significant is that the attempt to describe the nature of neuter verbs in purely formal terms, which had proved possible in Latin (apart from the deponent verbs) was soon seen by the English grammarians to be of little help.

Ambiguous relation to the passive. Three closely related views show the neuter verb as having an ambiguous relation with the passive. They

---

[1] Jonson, 1640, Bk 1, chap. 16.   [2] Howell, 1662, p. 56.

have in common a wish to explain expressions like *I am come* (the type which Dr Johnson called neuter passives, with which Ash had been struggling) and, less justifiably, *I am sick*. According to the first view neuter verbs comprise those which are active without being passive and those which are passive without being active. According to the second view neuter verbs include some which can be both active and passive. According to the third view neuter verbs are virtually passive verbs which express motion. The first view appears in Poole's basic grammar of 1646 and in eight later grammars, three of which are (on this point) identical. According to Poole a neuter verb '...either signifies like an Active, and cannot bee turned into a Passive, as, *to winke, to kneele*; or else...like a Passive, and cannot be turned into an Active: as, *to be sick*'.[1] The later grammars give various examples of Poole's active neuters (which are just intransitive verbs) but his example of the passive neuter *to be sick*, a Latinism, is repeated by all of them except Duncan, 1731 (*I am gone*); Clarke, 1773 (*be warm*); and Shaw, 1778 (*be glad*). It is difficult to see how the last example, especially, could ever be mistaken for a passive verb.

The second view is latent in many references to the neuter verb. W. Turner, for instance, in 1710, says, 'The signification of Verbs Absolute is in a manner Passive...[e.g.] *The wood burns* (for *is burn'd*); *I am griev'd* (for *I grieve*).'[2] James Harris makes the view more explicit in a passing reference to 'that species of Verbs, which grammarians have thought fit to call *Verbs Neuter*, as if indeed they were void both of Action and Passion, when perhaps (like Verbs middle) they may be rather said *to imply both*'.[3] The same view was expressed later by, among others, James Gough: 'Some Verbs Neuter are indifferently expressed, actively or passively; as, *I am grieved*, or *I grieve*.'[4] John Shaw, 1788, made the same point, with *to rise, to be risen* as examples.[5]

The third view derives from Lowth: 'The Neuter Verb is varied like the Active; but, having somewhat of the Nature of the Passive, admits in many instances of the Passive form, retaining still the Neuter signification; chiefly in such Verbs as signify some sort of

---

[1] Poole, 1646, p.9. Cf. Douglas, *c*. 1720, Bundle 1. 7. fol. 168 verso: 'Neutro-passive... Of this Sort are all Adnouns that are form'd into Verbs by the Help of the Substantive Verb *to be* as an Auxiliary as To be Pale, To be Sick.'
[2] W. Turner, 1710, p. 26. Similarly in Barker, 1733, p. 11; G. Wilson, 1756, p. 13.
[3] Harris, 1751, p. 177.   [4] Gough, 1754, p. 55.
[5] Shaw, 1778, p. 67.

motion, or change of place or condition: as, *I am come; I was gone; I am grown; I was fallen.*[1] Cooke takes this further with a reference to 'some Verbs called Neuter, but properly speaking, they are really passive, as *I am rejoiced*, for *I rejoice*'.[2] Shaw inverts the argument: instead of saying that *I am come* is a neuter verb but 'really' passive he calls it a passive verb which 'still retains its neuter signification'.[3] But he agrees with the others in attributing this characteristic to verbs of motion. Three others follow Lowth more or less closely, and Fogg tidies the situation up by bringing these verbs under a rule and labelling them: 'Neuter verbs...signifying motion or change of condition, and perhaps a few others, change the auxiliary *have* for *be*, when they may be said to be in the *deponent* state...[e.g.] *who are ascended from the successful trade of their ancestors...I was now returned.*'[4]

Neither active nor passive. The view that neuter verbs are neither active nor passive assumes that active and passive are correlative categories. If a verb cannot, because of its meaning, be put into the passive it cannot properly be called active: it is neither active nor passive. The first English grammar in which this view is expressed is the universal grammar in Lane's *A Rational and Speedy Method*, 1695, where it is the first of the three criteria he uses to distinguish the neuter verb. It appears in about twenty-five later grammars, evenly distributed over the century, but never as the sole criterion. It was important because it recognised the inadequacy of action as the defining characteristic of the verb and gave a place for verbs in which 'the event is properly neither Action nor Passion, but rather something between both: as, *I am; I walk; I sleep*'.[5]

The same as intransitive verbs. The general and ultimate conclusion, expressed in various ways, was that neuter verbs are the same as intransitive verbs. It had been frequently stated within the tradition, and was implied by Cooper,[6] but the identification is first made explicit by Richard Brown: 'This Verb [the neuter] is also term'd Intransitive, because it confines it's [*sic*] signification on one particular Object, which is imply'd in the Verb itself: as *I live* (the Life),

[1] Lowth, 1762, pp. 61–2.
[2] Cooke, 1771?, p. 15; similarly Du Bois, 1771?, p. xxii.
[3] Shaw, 1778, p. 68.   [4] Fogg, 1792, p. 161.
[5] Lowth, 1762, p. 45.   [6] Cooper, 1685, p. 132.

I run (the Race) &c.'[1] The term *intransitive* is not always used, but
the neuter verb is defined in corresponding terms: 'All the Bustle
some Grammarians have made about Verbs Neuter, is dispatch'd
in these four Lines...that when the Action of the Affirmation does
not extend or relate to any other Person or Thing, but terminates in
the Subject, there is no Name requir'd after it; as, *I grieve.*'[2] Merriman is more discriminating than most grammarians in trying to
separate neuter verbs which signify action from those which do not.
He therefore uses two criteria, the first of which is discussed later in
this chapter: '[The neuter verb] shews some State, Manner, Quality,
Situation, &c. as *to be, to sit.* But if Action be signified, such Action
terminates in its own Subject, without having Relation to any other;
as, *to speak, to walk.*'[3]

Some objections were raised against the practice of identifying
neuter and intransitive verbs. James Buchanan, in *The British
Grammar*, 1762, writes:

I have, according to the accurate Ruddiman, given a different account of
Neuter Verbs, from that commonly received by Grammarians, who
comprize under them all intransitive Verbs, though their Signification
be ever so much Active...With what Propriety...can a Master teach
that *to walk, to run*...&c. are Active Verbs, and at the same time that they
are Verbs Neuter? That is, they are Active Verbs, but they are not Active
Verbs: or they are Active Verbs, but neither Active nor Passive Verbs.
How wise the Scholar will become! (Buchanan, 1762, p. 137 n.)

Lowth wished to maintain a logical difference between intransitive
and neuter, while agreeing that there was no grammatical difference:
'The distinction between Verbs absolutely Neuter, as *to sleep*, and
Verbs Active Intransitive, as *to walk*, though founded in nature and
truth, is of little use in Grammar...[the construction of both is the
same]...Grammar is not so much concerned with their real, as with
their Grammatical, properties.'[4] The last protest is by John Ash,
who, by the fifth edition of his grammar, added a mild objection,
but did not discuss the question: 'Verbs intransitive, or such as do
not pass over or convey their Force to any Object: as, *sleep*...are
commonly, though perhaps not very properly, called *neuter* Verbs.'[5]

---

[1] R. Brown, 1700, p. 97. [2] G–B, 2nd edn 1712, p. 114.
[3] Merriman, 1750, p. 11. He is followed by the author of *The Young Mathematician's
Logic*, 1760, p. 31, and by others.
[4] Lowth (1762), 1767, p. 47 n. This passage does not appear in the first edition.
[5] Ash (1760), 5th edn 1771, p. 18.

The different criteria used in defining neuter/intransitive verbs are described in the next section of this chapter.

Can be followed by a nominative. The criterion that neuter verbs can have a nominative after them would practically restrict neuter verbs to the verb *to be*, which seems to be the intention of Lane, 1695, the author of *The Only True Guide*, 1779, and Philipps, who are the only grammarians to put it forward. They do not say whether they regard it as a defining characteristic.

Express being. That neuter verbs express being is, in various forms, the second most frequent criterion, appearing in nearly seventy grammars after 1669; it is especially popular between 1775 and 1800. John Newton first states the view, by implication. His description of the passive suggests that he regards the neuter and substantive verbs as being identical: 'A Verb Passive, is the same throughout all Moods and Tenses, with a Verb Neuter, the Preterimperfect Tense of the Active Voice being added thereunto.' [e.g. *I am loved*][1] J. Smith, in his *Grammatica Quadrilinguis*, states the view explicitly: 'Verbum neutrum...essentiam explicat personae vel rei, ut, *I am.*'[2] The expression of 'being' is a regular, and sometimes the only, criterion of the neuter verb thereafter. Several refinements on the idea of *being* were fashionable. John Ward, in 1758, introduced the expression 'denotes either the existence of a thing or the manner of its existence'.[3] This wording, which was often used, was intended to cover verbs like *sit* and *sleep* (Ward's examples) which expressed more than mere being. Other popular variations were 'state or being', first used by Greenwood, 1712; 'condition or habit', introduced by Dr Johnson in 1755, and an oddly specific but widely adopted expression which must have been suggested by the traditional examples of a neuter verb, *to sit*, and *to stand*: the expression seems to have been used first by William Turner, in 1710: '*To be* must be understood here to mean not only bare Existence, but also to be in some Posture or Circumstance, or some way or other Affected; as *to sit...to want ...to fear.*'[4] In the same spirit, though no one else adopted it, was Henson's phrase, '[the neuter verb] signifies Inaction or Being: as, *I sit, I am*'.[5] One voice was raised in disagreement. William Ward,

[1] Newton, 1677, p. 14; similarly in Newton, 1669, chap. 6.
[2] J. Smith, 1674, p. 232.　　　　[3] J. Ward, 1758, p. 81.
[4] W. Turner, 1710, p. 13.　　　　[5] Henson, 1756, p. 10.

while admitting that *to be* was a neuter verb would not grant that it was the type and pattern of all neuter verbs. 'Verbs intransitive, or neuter, as they are sometimes called' he defined characteristically as: '...Verbs in which it is not easy to distinguish the state as it is in exertion, from the state as it is in the reception of the effect produced by such exertion...verbs which denote neither action nor suffering, or states which are intermediate between both [e.g. *to grow, wither, rest, exist*].' He then explains the peculiar status of *be.*

The verb *to be* is manifestly a verb neuter; but it differs from all other verbs in this very considerable circumstance, viz, that it admits of every noun substantive to depend upon it in immediate apposition: whilst by such apposition, a connexion is denoted between the state signified by it, and the object signified by the substance on which it depends; yet no new state is considered as in the substantive. (W. Ward, 1765, pp. 176–7.)

By this Ward presumably means (the illustration is not his) that in, for example, *John walks* the verb *walks* adds something to the idea conveyed by *John*; John is in the 'new state' of walking. But in *John is*, the verb adds nothing, because John must already *be* in a state of existence; the verb *to be* can add no 'new state' to an already existing subject. Ward complicates his explanation of a simple point by speaking at one moment as if *John* 'depended on' *walked*, and at the next as if *walked* depended on *John*, and by referring simultaneously to the two words as being in apposition, which should mean that neither depends on the other.

SUMMARY

It is difficult not to feel suffocated by the cloud of trivial detail which is stirred up when a category such as the neuter verb is examined at all closely. But a detailed examination does bring out very clearly certain facts: that most of the early grammarians thought they were discussing a firmly established category; that they nevertheless treated it in a great variety of ways (far greater than they themselves realised); that the category was radically unstable.

The treatment of active, passive and neuter verbs can be summarised as follows:

Active verbs:

    (i) 'express doing' (commonly throughout)

    (ii) are identical with transitive verbs (first in 1693; frequently after 1750)

        13-2

(iii) include both transitive and intransitive verbs (first in 1700; commonly at end of eighteenth century)

(iv) are those which can be made passive (seventeenth century).

Passive verbs:

(i) are a kind of verb which expresses 'suffering' (commonly throughout)

(ii) are a way of using the active verb, properly called *passive* (commonly throughout)

(iii) are a way of using the active verb, not properly called *passive*, which term should apply only to inflected forms (frequently throughout)

From (ii) it may, and from (iii) it must, follow that English 'has no passive verbs'.

Neuter verbs:

(i) are those which have no passive participle (seventeenth century)

(ii) are those which:

(*a*) are active without being passive, and vice versa (mostly after 1750)

(*b*) include some which are both active and passive (mostly after 1750)

(*c*) are passive verbs of motion (after 1762)

(iii) are those which are neither active nor passive (fairly common after 1695)

(iv) are the same as intransitive verbs (usual after 1688)

(v) can have a nominative after them (three times only)

(vi) express 'being' (frequent after 1669)

TERMINOLOGY

Other kinds of verb are noted briefly:

Absolute verb. (*a*) a traditional term used in the seventeenth century by Wallis and Butler, and in the eighteenth by Anne Fisher, J.J. and others, for those verbs which are not auxiliary (cf. *Principal*; *Proper*). (*b*) a traditional term for neuter or intransitive, used in the English grammars at least as early as 1710[1] and in eleven later grammars.

---

[1] W. Turner, 1710, p. 26.

Adjective verb. This peculiar use of the term *verb adjective*, which normally refers to the participle, seems to originate with Maittaire, who calls all verbs except *be* 'adjective' because they can, in logic, be analysed into *be* and a participle. *Hears = is hearing*, and therefore 'contains' a participle, that is, an adjective. The term is also used in thise sense in *The English Accidence*, 1733, where the Adjective Verb is described as: 'that which, together with the signification of being, has a peculiar signification of its own; as, *I love*, that is, *I am loving*'.[1] The term appears only once again, in 1736.[2]

Auxiliary Verb. Used throughout the period. During the seventeenth and early eighteenth centuries the commonest term for this category is *sign of the tense* (cf. *Helping*; *Neuter-unperfect*; *Supplement*; *Suppletive*).

Choicative verb. One of Bullokar's characteristic categories. His example is *to have-liefer*.[3]

Common verb. Occasionally used for *active*[4] and for verbs which can be either transitive or intransitive,[5] or for those which can be either active or passive (e.g. *I am grieved* for *I grieve; I am come* for *I come*).[6]

Compound or concrete verb. Rowland Jones uses *compound* or *concrete* for verbs other than *be*, which he calls *simple*, q.v. It is his only classification of verbs. His compound verbs, like Harris's attributives, include adjectives and participles or: '...the qualities and attributes of the subject of a proposition, as man *thinks* or *think is*; sometimes only the subject, as... *sum*; and frequently the subject, affirmation and attribute, as *walketh*, "man is upon action"'.[7] This is only an extreme example of the general confusion about criteria. Jones considers *thinks* to be not only logically but even formally equivalent to *is thinking*. Elsewhere he analyses *walketh* into *w-al-ak-eth*, where the four formal constituents of the word correspond respectively to 'a man, upon, action, is.' Similarly *talketh* (*ta-al-ak-eth*) is analysed as 'the tongue upon action is'.[8]

Deponent Verb. Fogg's use of the term for forms such as *I was returned* has been mentioned already.[9]

---

[1] *English Accidence*, 1733, p. 72.   [2] R. Brown (1700), 11th edn 1736, p. 90.
[3] Bullokar, 1586, p. 353.   [4] Collyer, 1735, p. 50.
[5] Kirkby, 1746, p. 82; *Practice*, p. 53; Bell, 1769, p. 210.
[6] Douglas, c. 1720, Bundle 1.7. fol. 169 verso.
[7] R. Jones, 1768, p. 39.   [8] idem., *The Philosophy of Words*, 1769, p. 6.
[9] Above, p. 384.

Essential verb. Be is frequently called 'the essential verb'. The term first appears in Greenwood[1] and is used by twelve later grammarians, mostly in the middle of the eighteenth century. It is sometimes equivalent to *neuter*. (Cf. *Verb of Existence*; *Expletive*; *Simple*; *Substantive*; *Universal*).

Verb of Existence. Harris prefers this translation of ῥῆμα ὑπαρκτικόν to the term *verb substantive*, and extends it to cover also verbs like *grow* and *become*.[2] Similarly, in 1764, 'the boy *grows* tall' and 'the fire *burns* very bright' are examples of a verb of existence.[3] (Cf. *Essential*; *Expletive*; *Verb of Existence*; *Substantive*; *Universal*.)

Expletive verb. Hugh Jones's term for *be*.[4] (Cf. *Essential*; *Verb of Existence*; *Simple*; *Substantive*; *Universal*.)

Helping verb. A very common alternative or additional term for *auxiliary*. During the second half of the eighteenth century it is used by many grammarians who did not support vernacular terminology. On one occasion the auxiliaries are called *helpers*.[5] (Cf. *Auxiliary*; *Neuter-unperfect*; *Supplement*; *Suppletive*.)

Identic verb. Duncan calls verbs which are followed by words like *myself*, *himself*, 'identick or reflected pronominal verbs'.[6] (Cf. *Reflected*; *Reflexive*.)

Impersonal verb. The traditional name for forms like *it rains*; very seldom an item of formal classification.

Implicant verb. The term is used by Kirkby and in *The Practice* for *transitive*. It is correlative in Kirkby with *absolute* and in *The Practice* with *pure*.[7] (Cf. *Pure*.)

Indefinite verb. A name for verb forms preceded by *to* which is used in only one grammar.[8]

Verb of nature. A nonce-term of Lane's for impersonal verbs, on the strength of *it rains*, etc.[9]

Neuter-unperfect verb. Bullokar's term for an auxiliary verb.[10] (Cf. *Auxiliary*; *Helping*; *Supplement*; *Suppletive*.)

Particular verb. One which is not *universal*, q.v.[11]

Personal. The traditional term for the finite forms of a verb; sometimes treated as a kind of verb.

---

[1] Greenwood, 1711, p. 113.
[2] Harris, 1751, Bk I. chap. 6: see also p. 97 above.
[3] *A Real English Grammar*, 1764, p. 42.   [4] H. Jones, 1724, p. 34.
[5] *Short & Easy Introduction*, 1786, p. 26.   [6] Duncan, 1731, p. 17.
[7] Kirkby, 1746,p. 81; *Practice*, p. 53.   [8] *Practice*, p. 72.
[9] Lane, 1700, p. 79.   [10] Bullokar, 1586, p. 353.
[11] *Practice*, p. 52.

Possessive verb. Another of Bullokar's categories; *to have* is a verb possessive.[1]

Principal verb. Several eighteenth-century grammarians[2] contrast auxiliary verbs with what are sometimes called 'principal' verbs, but more often just 'the verb itself'. (Cf. *Absolute*; *Proper.*)

Pronominal verb. One followed by compounds in *-self* or by *one another*.[3] (Cf. *Reflected*; *Reflective*; *Reciprocal.*)

Proper verb. Warren Hastings' term for verbs which are not auxiliary.[4] (Cf. *Absolute, Principal.*)

Pure verb. A term for *intransitive*, used in only one work.[5] (Cf. *Implicant.*)

Reciprocal verb. Expressions such as *we love one another* are said to contain reciprocal verbs.[6] (Cf. *Pronominal.*)

Reflected verb. An occasional term for a verb followed by compounds in *-self*.[7] (Cf. *Indentic*; *Reflective.*)

Reflective verb. An occasional term for *reflected*.[8] *Reflexive* does not seem to be used in the grammars before 1800. (Cf. *Reflected*; *Indentic.*)

Signal. Hugh Jones's term for an auxiliary verb. *Have, do, will*, etc. are *proper* signals; *can, may, should*, etc. are *improper* signals.[9]

Simple verb. Rowland Jones seems to use *simple* as yet another term for distinguishing the verb *be* from all others, which he calls *compound* or *concrete*. Simple verbs are: '...those springs or energic signs in human speech, which mark the relation and connection of the subject and attribute of a proposition, and affirm or deny the agreement or disagreement betwixt things, as, "man *is* an animal"'.[10] (Cf. *Essential*; *Verb of Existence*; *Expletive*; *Substantive.*)

Substantive verb. A traditional term for *be*, widely used. Occasionally extended to cover all neuter verbs.[11] (Cf. *Essential*; *Verb of Existence*; *Expletive*; *Simple*; *Universal.*)

Supplement. Butler's term for an auxiliary.[12] (Cf. *Auxiliary*; *Helping*; *Neuter-unperfect*; *Suppletive.*)

Suppletive verb. An alternative term for an auxiliary, used only by Butler.[13] (Cf. *Auxiliary*; *Helping*; *Neuter-unperfect*; *Supplement.*)

[1] Bullokar, loc. cit.
[2] e.g. Fisher, 1750, p. 89; Meilan, 1771?, p. 104; *Essay*, 1800, p. 8.
[3] Duncan, 1731, p. 17.   [4] Hastings, 1800?, fol. 166 verso.
[5] *Practice*, p. 53.
[6] Duncan, 1731, p. 17; Wiseman, 1764, p. 234; Bell, 1769, p. 211.
[7] Duncan, loc. cit.; Bell, loc. cit.; Bridel, 1790, p. 6.
[8] Wiseman, 1764, p. 154.   [9] H. Jones, 1724, pp. 33 and 34.
[10] R. Jones, 1768, p. 39.   [11] Adam, 1772, p. 62.   [12] Butler, 1633, p. 45.
[13] ibid.

Universal verb. Used in one grammar for *be, endure, exist.*[1] (Cf. *Essential*; *Verb of Existence*; *Simple*; *Expletive.*)

There are few alternatives to the term *verb* iself, and only the first of them is important.

Affirmation. In adopting the Port Royal grammar's emphasis on affirmation as the primary function of the verb[2] Gildon also adopted, in his second edition, 1712, the word *affirmation* as the 'English' name for the part of speech. In the first edition, 1711, he had often used *word of affirmation* in the text but *verb* also in the notes.[3] *Affirmation* became one of the terms distinctive of the vernacular group of grammarians, who considered *verb* a Latinist's term. Even so most of the vernacular group are liable to use *verb* when they are off their guard. *Affirmation* is used, or at least recognised, in thirty-one grammars before 1800. It appears in four grammars before 1746, and in the period 1746–70 it is used, sometimes in only a passing reference, in one grammar out of every four. It is less popular during the following twenty years, and in the last decade of the century it is referred to only twice. The term rouses a little comment. Charles Coote prefers *affirmation* to *verb* because it is 'a term by which the purpose of its introduction is better expressed, than by the appellation that has usually been affixed to it'.[4] Nevertheless he himself uses *verb* throughout. Alexander Murray also commends the term for being self-explanatory,[5] but uses it only on occasions. The author of the unpublished grammar, *The Practice of Speaking and Writing English,* about the middle of the eighteenth century, refers to *affirmation* as a contemporary term, but rejects it:

When a Word, taking the ending *-ing* after it, signifies the doing or having of something, or being in some State, it is called a Verb, or the Adjective of a Person. Thus *call, possess, live* are Verbs...I chuse to retain the name *Verb*...rather than, in Conformity with the late Writers of English Grammar, to give the Title of *Affirmations* to such kind of Adjunctives. The Title *Adjective*, I conceive, is much more adequate to the end for which it is brought than that of *Affirmation*. For the Word *Adjunctive*[6] always agrees with what is meant in Speech by the Verb; except when it is put indefinitely...as *to teach, to read.* But the Title *Affirmation* neither reaches that,

---

[1] *Practice*, p. 52.   [2] See above, p. 366.
[3] e.g. pp. 69, 71.   [4] Coote, 1788, p. 9.
[5] A. Murray, 1787, p. 19 (printed 29).
[6] The MS. clearly reads *adjunctive*, in a closely written correction, but the context seems to require *adjective*.

nor when the Verb is used in Bidding or asking a Question. For what Affirmation can be understood in such Expressions as these? *Do you this...* *Shall he?*...yet it is plain the Words *do...shall...*are in these last Adjectives of the Persons *You, He.*[1]

The author is using the same argument, in much the same language, as does Kirkby, but his *adjective* is Kirkby's *adjunctive*, and Kirkby's reference is to 'modern grammarians' who favour the term *affirmation.*[2] A further disapproving comment is by Benjamin Martin, who supports a different innovation, namely:

Predicate. Martin says that what in Latin is called a verb is sometimes in English called an affirmation 'with great impropriety':

I know of no word that so fully expresses the nature of these words as that of *predicate*, because whatever we affirm, deny, or declare by these words, we are properly said to predicate, which is a general word, and includes in it the agency of every other.[3]

Martin is no more successful than the rest in consistently using the term he advocates. In the *Institutions of Language*, 1748, he frequently refers to 'verb or predicate', and in *An Introduction to the English Language*, 1754, he uses *verb* only; in one place he so far forgets himself, or changes his opinion, that he uses *affirmation.*[4]

Word. The use of *word* for *verb*, not uncommon in early elementary Latin grammars, is frequent in Gildon's first edition, together with *word of affirmation*, but is dropped in later editions for *affirmation*. Daniel Bellamy, in 1760, and James Barclay, as late as 1774 (here following Bellamy verbatim) speak of 'Verbs, or Words; otherwise termed Affirmations',[5] but *word* in this sense was by then an archaism. Later examples are rare. George Brown, about 1779, says that adverbs are added 'to Verbs or words', and the context makes it almost certain that by 'words' he does not mean words other than verbs.[6] When Lynch refers in a footnote to 'a set of words denominated, by way of preeminence, VERBS or WORDS' it is likely that he is copying from an older work. He uses the term *verb* on every other occasion.[7]

Motion. B. M. Charleston says that *motion, affirmation* and *word* are frequent terms for the verb. *Motion* is certainly not frequent. No

[1] *Practice*, 1750?, pp. 52–3. [2] Kirkby, 1746, p. 86 n.
[3] Martin, 1748, p. 30. [4] idem, 1754, p. 98.
[5] Bellamy, 1760, p. xxxvii; Barclay, 1774, p. xxv.
[6] G. Brown, 1779?, p. 21. [7] Lynch, 1796, p. 5.

instance has been noted here of its use as an exact synonym for *verb*; the nearest is a reference to the 'Verb or motion of thing'.[1]

Existence. The pseudonymous 'Mica', 1793, refers to a class of words, which he calls *existence*, which seems to be identical with the verb,[2] but he is very vague, and it is not clear, for example, whether he would ever talk about such-and-such words being 'existences'

'*Time*' *as a variant of* '*tense*'. The term *tense* was anglicised on the same principle as *verb*, but earlier and more widely. The process of change can be seen in Lily. In the English accidence of 1527 *time* has not yet become a fully grammatical term: 'al verbes vary by reason of tymes, called tenses'.[3] In 1567 *time* is a synonym for *tense*: 'There be five Tenses or Times'.[4] The only seventeenth-century English grammarians who use *time* for *tense*, and then rarely, are Alexander Hume[5] and Joseph Aickin.[6] Even in the first half of the eighteenth century, when *time* was often adopted as a vernacular term very few grammarians use it throughout. Most make their first reference to the category 'tenses or times', and then continue with the customary term. Even the very few who say first 'times or tenses' usually write *tense* as often as *time*. Too few use *time* regularly for there to be any significance in its distribution.[7]

---

[1] *Right Spelling*, 1704, p. 31.
[2] See above, p. 272.
[3] Lily, 1527, p. 27.
[4] Lily, *Shorte Intro.* 1567, sig. B iii recto.
[5] Hume, *c.* 1617, p. 32.
[6] Aickin, 1693, p. 10.
[7] Of the above terms OED gives no instance of *helper* before Lindley Murray's fifth edition, 1824; no instance of *reflective* before 1843; and no instance of *time* meaning *tense* later than Alexander Hume. In the senses referred to here OED gives no instances of *absolute, adjective, affirmation, choicative, common, compound, concrete, essential, verb of existence, expletive, identic, implicant, indefinite, motion, verb of nature, possessive, predicate, pronominal, proper, pure, signal, simple, suppletive, universal, word.*

13. TENSE

SIX TYPES OF TENSE SCHEMES

The English grammarians' treatment of tense is too complex to discuss fully here. It is, however, important to show its variety and the ways in which some writers tried to break away from the authority of Latin. This chapter describes only the indicative tenses of the active, taken usually from a writer's enumeration of his tenses or from his tables of verbs. Often these two sources clash: a writer will enumerate three tenses but his tables will show five. Sometimes there will seem to be even three incompatible statements in the same paragraph: in effect, that there are two tenses, three tenses and six tenses. This occurs when different criteria are being used by a writer who does not fully understand that they are different. There are two tenses in English if by *tense* is understood one-word, finite, inflected forms (*loves*, *loved*). There are three tenses if *tense* is taken to mean 'time' (past, present, future). There are varying numbers of tenses if verb-forms composed of auxiliaries are included. Sometimes a writer says that there are only three tenses although five tenses 'are commonly used'. In all cases where a writer mentions two classifications without repudiating either both are recorded. Sometimes he is using several authorities because he is too ignorant to choose between them, but sometimes he is timidily proffering a minority view under the protective companionship of an accepted practice. Because many grammarians express more than one opinion there is much over-lapping, and the tense-schemes might be described in many ways. They are grouped here according to what seems to be the particular emphasis of each grammarian: his starting-point for the description and analysis of linguistic material which (it is sometimes hard to remember) was virtually the same for all the grammarians. The following are the starting-points which most clearly stand out from the whole range of grammars

Group I (pp. 396–402). Thirteen tense-schemes based on the Latin system as found in Lily. Those most frequently adopted are 1.1 and 1.3. Seven others are individual variants.

395

The English Categories

Group II (pp. 402–5). Two tense-schemes based on the assumption that as *tense* means 'time' there are three tenses, past, present and future.

Group III (pp. 405–7). The scheme based on the formal criterion: English has only two tenses, present and past.

Group IV (pp. 408–10). Two schemes based on the distinction between incomplete (imperfect) and complete (perfect) action.

Group V (pp. 410–19). Seven schemes based on a threefold distinction between (*a*) time as past, present and future; (*b*) time or action as definite or indefinite; (*c*) action as complete or incomplete. None of them is widely used but together they are important.

Group VI (pp. 419–21). Four individual schemes based on other criteria.

In the following tables the model verb is always given as *love* (the example most commonly used in the grammars) so that comparison may be quicker. The author's own model, if it is not *love*, is given in a footnote.

Group I. This group comprises the many tense-schemes based on the Latin system as given in Lily. The two schemes proposed by Lily are treated first; other Latin schemes are given in the order of their first appearance in English.

I.1 Lily's English accidence uses the five tenses of Donatus and Priscian:

Present	love, do love
Imperfect	loved, did love
Perfect	have loved
Pluperfect	had loved
Future	will/shall love

This scheme is used from the first by those English grammarians who are not following Ramus. Bullokar proposes it, but in a secondary form: he says first that there are 'Three times called Tenses' (Group II, below) and then makes this tense-scheme by subdividing the Preter into three.[1] The first grammarian to propose this scheme without qualification is Alexander Gill, 1619. It is by far the commonest scheme, occurring in 40 per cent of the grammars, and is in regular use throughout the period, with some decline in popularity

[1] Bullokar, 1586, p. 354. Some uses of the present, e.g. *I ride ten days hence*, and of the past, *I would I loved*, he calls 'doubtful future' and 'doubtful preter' tenses respectively. See Poldauf, p. 270.

towards the end. Scheme I.1 is often given as a refinement of II.1. In a three-tense scheme the past tense can be divided into three, making the five tenses of I.1, as was done by Bullokar. The same practice is adopted by other seventeenth-century grammarians— Hume and Butler, as well as by a few in the eighteenth century.[1] Over the whole period at least a dozen grammars offer I.1 an as equal alternative, and the same number as a subsidiary alternative, to one of the other tense-schemes, usually II.1 or I.2.

There are two variants of I.1. Daniel Duncan distinguishes a perfect definite which is identical in form with the imperfect:

I.2		
	Present	love, do love, am loving
	Imperfect	loved, did love, was loving
	Perfect definite	loved, did love, was loving
	Perfect indefinite	have loved, have been loving
	Pluperfect	had loved, had been loving
	Future	shall/will love, shall be loving, am to love

He argues that although the forms of the perfect definite and the imperfect are the same their meanings vary according to the context, and therefore they should be treated as distinct tenses: 'Tho' this Tense [the perfect definite] is formed like the last, yet it differs from it in Signification. For the former [the imperfect] has something of the present in it in relation to a Time past...whereas this implies Time as absolutely past, without any Relation to another.'[2] Francis Lodowyck, in *The Ground-Work*, 1652, one of the early books on universal language, divides the past into two instead of three. His scheme is odd, because he seems to wish to distinguish (but not to subdivide) perfect forms in the past, and not to distinguish them in the future:

I.3		
	Present	love
	Imperfect	loved
	Perfect	have loved, had loved
	Future	will/shall love, should have loved

Lily's Latin accidence also says there are five tenses, but adds the *futurum exactum* (amavero) as a sixth. This form had traditionally been regarded as a subjunctive tense, because it was usually

---

[1] e.g. Martin, 1748 and 1754; Hammond, 1760; H. Ward, 1777; *Short Grammatical Intro*. 1793.
[2] Duncan, 1731, p. 23. His model verb is *carry*.

preceded by a conjunction. English grammarians adapting the Latin tenses to English were divided on whether to make *shall have loved* an indicative or a subjunctive tense.[1] The grammars in group I.4 make it indicative:

I.4 Present   love
     Imperfect   loved
     Perfect   have loved
     Pluperfect   had loved
     1st Future   shall/will love
     2nd Future   shall/will have loved

This scheme appears first in Guy Miege's *The English Grammar*, 1688, as an expansion of a three-tense scheme, and in Richard Brown's *The English School Reformed*, 1700, as an expansion of a two-tense scheme (Brown calls *shall have loved* the Preter-future, but he is hesitant and admits 'this is usually termed the Future Subjunctive').[2] The first grammarian to offer scheme I.4 firmly is William Turner, 1710. Gildon and Brightland suggest it as an alternative to I.1, but after them it appears only eight times (in the works of only six authors) before 1780. It then becomes more popular and is put forward in 24 grammars before the end of the century, usually as a second choice until its adoption by Lindley Murray in 1795, after which it is almost always a principal tense-scheme.[3]

Greaves combines these two Latin schemes with some features adopted from Ramus: the numbering rather than the naming of the past tenses and the treatment of the imperative as a future.[4] The system is quite explicit, but no one else uses it:

I.5 Present   love[5]
     1st Preterite   loved
     2nd Preterite   have loved
     3rd Preterite   had loved
     1st Future   love (imperative)
     2nd Future   shall/will love

Greaves notes the emphatic forms with *do* and *did* but does not make them into separate tenses. Thomas Tomkis, 1612, not only treats the

---

[1] The grammars in Groups I.1, II, III and VI make the future perfect a subjunctive tense. The practice was still common at the end of the eighteenth century.

[2] R. Brown, 1700, p. 99.

[3] By the end of the century the Second Future is called the Future perfect. *The Pupil's Friend*, 1799, is unusual in keeping the old term.

[4] Funke, 1938 (Greaves), pp. xliv–xlv.   [5] His example is *hate*.

emphatic forms as distinct tenses but separates *will* and *shall*, and is the first grammarian to make *shall have loved* an indicative tense:

I.6 First Present   love
    Second Present do love
    Imperfect   did love
    Aorist   loved
    Perfect   have loved
    Pluperfect   had loved
    First Future   will love
    Second Future   shall love
    Third Future   shall have loved

None of Tomkis' examples of the third future contains *will*, but he does not, as strict consistency required, make a separate tense for *will have*. James Howell also separates *loved* and calls it perfect or aorist, from *did love*, which he calls *imperfect*, without mentioning *have loved*. Otherwise his scheme, so far as it can be made out, is that of I.1:

I.7 Present   love[1]
    Imperfect   did love
    Aorist or perfect loved
    Pluperfect   had loved
    Future   will/shall love

Cave Beck, 1657, *The Tutor*, 1772, and Martin Trinder, 1781, agree on a variant which differs from I.1 only in the separation of *will* and *shall*:

I.8 Present   love, do love
    Imperfect   loved, did love
    Perfect   have loved
    Pluperfect had loved
    1st Future   will love
    2nd future shall love

A variant of I.4, attributed by Monboddo to Theodore of Gaza, also agrees with I.6 and I.7 in giving English an aorist:

I.9 Present   love[2]
    Imperfect   did love, was loving
    Indefinite   loved
    Perfect   have loved
    Pluperfect had loved
    1st Future shall/will love
    2nd Future shall/will have loved

---

[1] His example is *desire*.   [2] Maittaire's example is *read*.

This scheme is proposed by seven grammarians, five of whom were scholarly and influential: Maittaire, 1712; James Douglas, *c.* 1720; John Ward, 1758; Wiseman, 1764; Monboddo, 1774; Stapleton, 1797; the author of the article on Grammar in the third edition of the *Encyclopaedia Britannica*, 1797. Maittaire restricts the second future to the potential mood and mentions the progressive form of the imperfect only as an alternative.

Douglas's treatment of tense, which is divided between two principal manuscripts, is unusual, although his intentions are not entirely clear. He sets out the forms of a verb in three different kinds of paradigm: (i) forms containing an auxiliary verb;[1] (ii) forms composed of the 'radical' alone or variations of it—e.g. *love, loved, loving*;[2] (iii) forms preceded by a preposition—*to love, of loving, about to love, etc.*[3] These paradigms, together with his enumeration of the tenses in another manuscript,[4] exactly correspond with this tense-scheme, I.8. Douglas and Ward give both emphatic and progressive forms for the imperfect; Wiseman, Monboddo and Stapleton give only the progressive form and mention the emphatic as an alternative. Monboddo and the writer in the *Britannica*, who calls *loved* the aorist, join the emphatic *did love* with that tense and give *was loving* as the only form for the imperfect. This, which is the most satisfactory form of the tense-scheme, is equivalent to Beattie's basic tenses without his proverbial present.[5]

John Collyer offers a variant which he supports by argument. He is an emphatic upholder of a vernacular system and rejects altogether the Latin imperfect. He quotes with approval from Richard Johnson's *Grammatical Commentaries*[6] the view that 'there is no such thing in nature as a time imperfectly past',[7] and he mentions disapprovingly the 'passing time' of Gildon and Brightland, and Greenwood's 'preter time of action not finished'. Collyer is attracted to a simple scheme of three tenses, but agrees that in it the past would be 'too generally expressed, and that something farther is necessary to signify whether an action was lately done, or had been done some time'.[8] He therefore proposes four tenses 'in their natural Order';

---

[1] Douglas, 1720?, Bundle 3.3. fols. 72 recto f.
[2] op. cit. fol. 46 verso. [3] op. cit. fol. 60 verso.
[4] Bundle 1.7. fol. 114 recto. [5] See below, p. 414.
[6] R. Johnson, *Grammatical Commentaries*, 1706, p. 280.
[7] Collyer, 1735, p. 55 n. [8] op. cit. p. 56 n.

I.10 [Pluperfect] 'Time more than perfectly passed' had loved; did love

Past	loved, have loved
Present	love, do love, am loving
Future	shall/will, may, must love; let them love

Much the same is James Gough's revised scheme, in his third edition, 1764. Gough, who had started as a trimmer in Group II, here differs in two ways from Collyer. He treats all the past forms except *had loved* as the Past Tense, which therefore comprises *loved, was loving, did love, have loved* (Collyer makes no mention of *was loving*) and he restricts the future to *shall* and *will*.

Thomas Dilworth, 1740, seems to have been misled by the term Second Future into thinking that it must refer to some time 'more than future', much as the pluperfect was often said to express time 'more than perfectly past'. Dilworth does not discuss his tense-scheme, which is an unimportant variant of I.3. It appears also in the *New and Improved Spelling Dictionary*, 1771, which does not elsewhere rely on Dilworth and in *The Court Letter Writer*, 1773. In the *New and Improved Spelling Dictionary* the Second Future is called the 'Time of long space to come', and in *The Court Letter Writer* 'the time some great while to come'. Dilworth's variant is as follows:

I.11	Present	love[1]
	Imperfect	loved, did love
	Perfect	have loved
	Pluperfect	had loved
	1st Future	shall/will love
	2nd Future	shall/will love hereafter

James White, in *The English Verb*, 1761, makes the varying sign of the tense (i.e. the auxiliary) the central feature of his classification, so that the expression of tense is closely related to the expression of mood. The basic tense-scheme he offers is that of I.4, but he separates *shall* and *will*, *shall have* and *will have*, so as to make four futures instead of two. Later grammarians praise his book but no one adopts his tense-scheme. B. M. Charleston's high praise of White's as 'by far the most interesting of the grammatical works published before or during the eighteenth century'[2] refers particularly to his remarks on usage, but seems generous in any case. White's scheme is as follows:

---

[1] Dilworth's example is *educate*.
[2] B. M. Charleston, *Studies on the Syntax of the English Verb*, Berne 1941, p. 177.

I.12 Present   love[1]
    1st Past or Historical Tense   loved
    2nd Past   have loved
    3rd Past   had loved
    1st Future or Prophetic Tense   shall love
    2nd Future   will love
    3rd Future   shall have loved
    4th Future   will have loved[2]

The progressive forms White treats as a 'Second Active or Middle Voice'.[3]

The tense-scheme used by Richard Wynne in *An Universal Grammar*, 1775, is difficult to describe and to classify because, amongst other reasons, Wynne uses in his tables two more tenses than he enumerates. Apart from the different use of *perfect* his full scheme is that of I.8 with two conditional tenses added:

I.13 Present   love
    Imperfect   did love, was loving
    Perfect or Past   loved
    Compound Perfect   have loved
    Pluperfect   had loved
    1st Future   shall/will love
    2nd Future   shall/will have loved
    Uncertain Tense   should love
    Compound Uncertain   should have loved

Wynne's Uncertain tenses, which are indicative, are distinguished from the subjunctive (in which they would often be classified by other writers) by not being preceded by a conjunction. In *I should love you though I were a king* (his example) *should love* is in the uncertain tense and *were* is a subjunctive.[4]

Group II. Here are grouped those tense-schemes whose starting-point is a division into three 'natural' times.

II.1 Present   love, etc.
    Past   loved, etc.
    Future   will/shall love, etc.

There is a close connection between many of the grammars in this group and those in Group I. Some writers mean what they say, and face the consequences of a three-tense system, distributing all the

---

[1] White's example is *have*.
[3] See above, p. 380.
[2] White, 1761, pp. 4–9, 84, 98.
[4] Wynne, 1775, pp. 33–6.

English verb-forms (or all they remember at the time) under the tense-headings Past, Present and Future. These grammarians comprise the strict group. A greater number say that there are really only three tenses, but when it comes to the distribution of verb forms in a table they find it necessary to use additional tenses. These grammarians are, in no derogatory sense, the trimmers. Both groups frequently confuse tense and time. Tense was customarily defined as 'distinction of time', an expression which permitted further confusion between things and words. 'Distinction of time' might mean divisions of time, of which there 'could' be only three: past, present and future conceived as objective and real. Or it might mean the different ways in which we refer to time. The trimmers felt themselves to be under the authority of both meanings. Sometimes, as with the Latinists, they were conscious of no inconsistency, and said easily: 'Tenses are three, Present, Preterit and Future: and Preterit threefold, Imperfect, Perfect and Pluperfect.'[1] More often the inconsistency is recognised, even if it is left unresolved. James Buchanan, answering the question 'How many Tenses or Times are there?' says that 'the most natural division' is into three, 'but the common Number of Times are [sic] five'.[2] The strict writers were obliged to treat as one past tense a number of very varied verb-forms, but none of them attempts to explain why there should be this variety if the verb-forms all belong to the same tense. Samuel Saxon says there are three tenses, present, past and future 'which (strictly speaking) are all the Times that a Person or Thing can be said to do or suffer...The Action past, (for the ease of the Learner) I have comprehended under the perfect; how far my Opinion may agree with some, I can't determine; but shall submit that to their Judgments.'[3] Saxon's perfect tense comprises *I read, did read, have read, had read, was reading, have or had been reading.* The more usual practice among the strict group is either to give no illustrations of the tenses, or to ignore the compound forms. Charles Johnson, for example, illustrates his past tense by the single form *I danced.*[4] The strict group tended to oversimplify in this way not only through ineptitude but because they were writing elementary grammars for pupils who would not be learning Latin. The authors were free to abandon the Latin tenses but they did not know how to use their freedom. It seems, also, that

---

[1] Butler, 1633, p. 42.   [2] Buchanan, 1762, p. 107.
[3] Saxon, 1737, p. 56.   [4] C. Johnson, 6th edn 1779, p. 6.

even those of them who did not actually support a vernacular system of parts of speech were influenced by vernacular prejudice: *tense* was often rejected as 'a term in Latin grammar', for which the proper English equivalent was *time*. Calling tenses *times* made it all the easier to confuse the 'real' divisions of time and the verb-forms which reflected them. The strict form of the threefold tense-scheme is essentially doctrinaire.

One trimmer deserves particular mention. Daniel Pape, in *A Key to English Grammar*, 1790, divides his loyalty not between a three-tense scheme and one of five or six, but between a three-tense scheme and one of no tenses at all. He attacks the use of both tense and case but does not take his argument very far:

I am particularly against the use of tenses in verbs, and also of cases in names in the English Language; for long experience has convinced me, that these methods are only labouring the language to no purpose, and calculated only to tease and perplex; for instance, let *should have given* be called the preter tense, would it not be equally as familiar, and intelligible, to say, *have given*, taken together, is a verb of the past time, and form it thus? Singular, *I have given*...Or to say, *of man*, is the genitive case, &c., is it not much more easy for the scholar, and will it not answer the same end, to say, *man* is a name singular, and depends upon, or is connected with the preposition *of*. (Pape, 1790, p. 22.)

Pape's suggestion, so far as it is clear, is more than the rejection of the grammatical category tense in favour of the natural category time. He seems to be proposing to transfer the classification into past, present and future from forms of the verb to kinds of verb: *will give* would not be the future form of the verb *give* but the only form of the future verb *will give*. It is hard to know which is the more surprising: the ineffectiveness of this device, or the air of novelty with which Pape puts forward the longstanding objection to using *case* for the prepositional equivalents of Latin case-endings.

Patrick Lynch, in one set of tables, advocates a tense-scheme which can be regarded as a variant within Group II. To a basic three-tense scheme he adds a conditional tense, which is in fact the subjunctive form of the verb:

II.2	Present	I love
	Past	I loved
	Conditional	I love, thou love, he love etc.
	Future	I shall love. (Lynch, 1796, pp. 51–2.)

He also gives tables to illustrate the more elaborate classification of Group V.7, which is described below, p. 418.

There are 58 grammars in Group II, of which 22 are strict. The trimmers appear fairly regularly from the beginning of the period until about 1790, after which they are less common. The strict approach does not appear until 1733, with Isaac Barker, followed by Saxon, 1737, and Anne Fisher, 1750. After 1770 it becomes less frequent.

Group III. Some writers use a formal criterion, giving two 'real' tenses. This group, also, reflects a tension between two not always clearly formulated interpretations of *tense.* Here too there are the trimmers and the strict, both of whom felt the power of the formal criterion. Those grammarians who were strict only because they were writing for an elementary level, and could ignore Latin, said merely that English had two tenses: present (*love*) and preterite (*loved*). Very few—Wallis, James Corbet, Priestley, Warren Hastings —were strict not because of their limitations but because they understood what they meant by *tense.* Wallis, restricting English tenses to two, had to classify the other verb-forms. This he did (and he should be assumed to have done it knowingly) not in terms of tense, the inconsistency into which most writers fell, but in terms of the 'rest' of the verb, those parts formed by auxiliaries: 'Nos duo tantum habemus Tempora in quovis verbo, Praesens & Praeteritum imperfectum...Quod superest, verborum aliquot auxiliarium adjumento fere totum perficitur.'[1] Priestley is the most emphatic advocate of the view that English had only two tenses. Unlike all the earlier grammarians except Wallis he sees that the fundamental question is how the term *tense* is to be interpreted:

The only natural rule for the use of technical terms to express time, &c. is to apply them to distinguish the different modifications of words; and it seems wrong to confound the account of *inflections,* either with the grammatical uses of the *combinations* of words, of the *order* in which they are placed, or of the *words which express relations,* and which are equivalent to inflections in other languages...A little reflection may, I think, suffice to convince any person, that we have no more business with *a future tense* in our language, than we have with the whole system of Latin moods and tenses; because we have no modification of our verbs to correspond with it. (Priestley (1761), added in 2nd edn 1768, pp. vii and viii.)

[1] Wallis, 1653, p. 91.

Priestley stresses the importance of the subjunctive forms (*if he love*) which he says are neglected and inconsistently used,[1] but he does not recognise them as tenses. He argues, with some hesitation, that *love*, in *if he love*, is merely the radical (infinitive) form of the verb and that the expression is elliptical, its full form being *if he should love*. Similarly *if thou loved* is an ellipsis of *if thou hadst loved*, but he admits the awkwardness of this argument in the case of verbs in which the past participle is not the same as the past tense: *if thou drew* can hardly be regarded as an elliptical form of *if thou hadst drawn*.

One distinctive feature of Priestley's treatment of tense is his attempt to classify the compound forms by two criteria: (i) according to the form of the principal verb, (ii) according to the number of auxiliary verbs used in the compound form. This leads him, in spite of his earlier statements, virtually to accept the trimmer's compromise:

The compound tenses...may be commodiously distributed into three distinct classes or orders; according as the auxiliary verbs that constitute them require the radical form, the participle present, or the participle preterite to be joined with them. They are likewise single, double, or triple, according as one, two, or three auxiliary verbs are made use of. (Priestley, 1761, p. 24.)

This gives the following scheme, in which the richness of English verb-forms overwhelms Priestley's attempt to maintain a system of two tenses.

First order	Present	shall love
	Preterite	should love
Second order	Present	am loving
	Preterite	was loving
First double compound	Present	shall be loving
	Preterite	should be loving
Second double compound	Present	have been loving
	Preterite	had been loving
Triple compound	Present	shall have been loving
	Preterite	should have been loving
Third order	Present	am loved
	Preterite	was loved
First double compound	Present	shall be loved

and similarly as in the second order (Priestley, 1761, pp. 24–6.)

When, in *A Course of Lectures on the Theory of Language and Universal Grammar*, Priestley comes to discuss tense in general he practically

[1] Priestley (1761), 1768, pp. 119–20.

admits that this cannot be done: the diversity of practice among languages is too great. He treats the customary Latin classification (Scheme I.1) as basic, but discusses it without particular reference to English.[1] He rejects the classification of Scheme IV.1 (below) because the present cannot be subdivided into perfect and imperfect, 'being properly nothing more than a point. *Scripsi* is a preterite, not a perfect.'[2] Priestley's empirical approach enabled him to see the irrelevance, for English, of many inherited grammatical categories, but it also led, as here, to misleading oversimplification.

No other writers using this tense-scheme discuss tense. Among the strict a few, notably James Corbet, 1743, and Warren Hastings, show that they understand the main implication of the classification: that the verb must be described as a structure of auxiliaries and participles and *tense* strictly reserved for the forms *love*, *loved*.

The contradiction into which less clear-minded writers fell, to become trimmers, is shown by Joseph Aickin. Although he is translating Wallis, he imports the words 'of the tenses' and completely misses the point of Wallis's restraint in *not* calling the auxiliary forms tenses: 'We have only two times, present, and preterit...and all the rest of the tenses are supplyed by auxilary Verbs.'[3] There is nothing surprising in such a contradiction. It is more surprising that there are forty-three grammars in which the formal criterion is recognised and the English verb is said, with varying degrees of consistency and conviction, to have properly only two tenses. The grammarians did not agree with Wallis that the verb, 'quae in reliquis linguis maximam sortitur difficultatem, apud Anglos levissimo negotio peragitur'.[4] They found the verb difficult, and its tenses the most difficult part of it. John Hornsey, who taught in Scarborough at the end of the eighteenth century, is typical of many in saying, with no undue air of desperation, that most grammarians propose five tenses; that it is more useful 'to a mere English scholar' to keep to nature, in which there are three; that English has strictly only two.[5]

Of the 43 grammars in Group III twenty appear between 1745 and 1770; the rest are evenly distributed over the period.

---

[1] Priestley, 1762, Lecture the Eighth.
[2] op. cit. p. 108 n.
[3] Aickin, 1693, p. 10. Wallis, quoted above, p. 405.
[4] Wallis, 1653, p. 91.   [5] Hornsey, 1793, p. 30.

Group IV. Here the criterion is the distinction between complete and incomplete action.

IV.1	Present Imperfect	love
	Present Perfect	have loved
	Past Imperfect	loved
	Past Perfect	had loved
	Future Imperfect	shall/will love
	Future Perfect	shall/will have loved

This is Varro's tense-scheme as revived by Grocyn.[1] It is important because by using as its starting-point the distinction between perfect and imperfect it avoided the division of the past into imperfect, perfect and pluperfect which was the central feature of most other schemes. Aspect (used loosely to indicate those elements in an English verb-form which express features other than time: the term was not used before 1800) is in this scheme becoming a more powerful, and time a less powerful, criterion, so that it is possible for *have loved* to be regarded as a present, and not as a past, tense. It is this feature which links the tense-scheme, historically and descriptively, with those in Group V. It is through the grammars which use, or at least mention, the tense-schemes of Groups IV and V that the line of fruitful development has lain.

This tense-scheme, though it appears in twenty-seven grammars, does not seem to have had the popularity it deserved. It is first proposed in English by James Greenwood, 1711, and by William Loughton, 1734. The anonymous *New English Accidence*, 1736, which is based on Greenwood, and Greenwood's own shorter grammar of 1737, use it, and it is mentioned as an alternative scheme by Daniel Turner, 1739; by the author of *An Easy Introduction*, 1745; by Daniel Farro, 1754; and by Nathan Bailey, 1755. Lowth's influence promoted it, unintentionally. Lowth, in 1762, does not himself use it, but it is the basis of his scheme.[2] Some grammarians who followed Lowth in other respects seem to have simplified his tense-scheme and returned it to Greenwood's form, which is proposed, usually as the only scheme, in thirteen grammars between 1762 and the end of the century.

One variation gives unusual prominence to the progressive and colloquial forms of the verb. John Williams, a Hampshire parson

---

[1] See above, p. 118, and Poldauf, p. 264, who is, however, inconsistent about its introduction into English (cf. pp. 264 and 279).

[2] See below, 413.

and admirer of James Harris, offers a tense-scheme which, in its simplicity, might be regarded as the purest example of this group:

Present Imperfect	He's going
Present Perfect	He is gone
Past Imperfect	He was going
Past Perfect	He was gone
Future Imperfect	He will be going
Future Perfect	He'll be gone![1]

Ben Jonson's treatment of the tenses cannot be called a variation of Group IV, as he differs fundamentally from Grocyn and wrote nearly a hundred years before Greenwood. But it does emphasise strongly the difference between perfect and imperfect forms and it is more closely associated with this group than with any other. Jonson's account of the English tenses is unsystematic and incomplete: as both Funke and Jonson's modern editors comment, it is incomprehensible without reference to Ramus, whom Jonson often follows word for word and on whose tense-scheme his own is obviously, but not clearly, based. In spite of Jonson's awareness of 'our common speech...upon the which all Precepts are grounded, and to which they ought to be referred'[2] his treatment of the tenses is an extreme instance of forcing English to match the Latin pattern. Jonson does not enumerate his tenses, but his Latin examples with their English forms imply the following scheme. He distinguishes sharply between tenses formed with, and those formed without, auxiliaries: 'A Verbe finite... hath three only Tymes'. These, *I love, I loved*, and *love* (imperative) he treats in Book I, the accidence, and these are the only forms he gives in his tables of verbs. To this extent Jonson is adopting a formal criterion and is in sympathy with the grammarians in Group III, but his starting-point is that of Ramus: the distinction between perfect and imperfect. Tenses using an auxiliary verb, formed 'by a Syntaxe', which are bracketed in the following table, Jonson discusses in Book II, the syntax. It is, then, possible to infer from Jonson's disconnected remarks, and from Ramus, the following tense-scheme:

IV.2

Imperfect tenses

First present	love
Second present	(may, can love)

---

[1] Williams, 1780?, p. 7. The exclamation mark is his. *The Young Mathematician's Logic*, 1760, p. 30, which is probably by Williams, has the same tense-scheme.

[2] Jonson, 1640, Bk II. chap. I.

Imperfect tenses (cont.)

Third present	(might, could love—because Ramus treats *amarem* as both a present and as a past tense)
First Preter	loved
Second Preter	(might, could love)
First Future	(shall/will love)
Second Future	love (imperative)

Perfect tenses

First Preter	(have loved)
Second Preter	(could, might have loved)
First Pluperfect	(had loved)
Second Pluperfect	(might have loved)
First Future	(shall have loved)
Second Future	(may have loved)

Funke does not infer a second future perfect from what Jonson says.[1] But Jonson is following Ramus so closely that it seems unlikely he would not also disinguish between *amavero* and *amaverim*.

Group V. A number of tense-schemes are based on a threefold distinction between time as past, present and future; time or action as definite or indefinite; action as complete or incomplete. These distinctions had all appeared, singly or in pairs, within the tradition; it is the combination of all three which marks the point at which the grammarians began to give systematic empirical attention to the forms of the English verb. This attention was not fully sharpened until the middle of the eighteenth century, but it was most remarkably anticipated by Christopher Cooper in 1685, whose treatment of tense has, among other merits, that of being the first to recognise adequately the status of the progressive forms.[2]

Cooper is explicitly repudiating the application to English of the usual Latin tense-scheme, but he has considerable difficulty in freeing himself from it, and his conclusions are not altogether clear. He begins by accepting the logician's view that all active verbs can be resolved into the copula and an adjective. He therefore first divides verb-forms into those in which the copula is expressed and those, derived from the first, in which it is understood:

[1] O. Funke, 'Ben Jonson's English Grammar', *Anglia*, LXIV 1940. 131.
[2] Poldauf, p. 90 n.

(i) *Forms in which the copula is expressed*

Present	am loving[1]
Imperfect	was loving
Preterite	have been loving
Pluperfect	had been loving
Future	shall/will be loving

(ii) *Forms in which the copula is understood*

Present	love (emphatic, do love)
Preterite	loved (emphatic, did love)
Future	shall/will love

Cooper admits that the preter may be divided—'ut accommodentur tempora latinae grammaticae'[2]—into perfect and pluperfect, but he rejects such a scheme and produces his own: 'accommodatio temporum anglice ad grammaticam latinam, in tribus gradibus praeteriti, in quibus *did* attribuitur imperfecto, *have* praeterperfecto, *had* plusquam perfecto; in obscuritatem, errorem et loquandi incongruentiam ducit'.[3] The forms in (i) he therefore rearranges into three double tenses:

V.1	Present Indefinite	am loving
	Present Definite	have been loving
	Preterite Absolute	was loving
	Preterite 'Destinatum'	had been loving
	Future Declarative	shall be loving
	Future Promissive	will be loving

He classifies other verb-forms, including some in (ii), in the same way, according to their signs:

Present Indefinite	do love
Present Definite	have loved
Preterite Absolute	did love
Preterite 'Destinatum'	had loved
Future Declarative	shall love
Future Promissive	will love

This scheme leaves what he also calls the aorist forms *I love* and *I loved* very loosely attached to his main classification, which is strongly based on the 'signs' of the tenses, and wedded to symmetry. Cooper makes the difference between *shall* and *will* the distinguishing mark between two tenses, but he can satisfy the facts of the language only by adding, after his tabular classification,[4] that the English

---

[1] His example is *prepare*. [2] Cooper, 1685, p. 124.
[3] op. cit. p. 125. [4] op. cit. p. 126.

present has in fact three forms, and he does not mention the form *loved* again after his preliminary classification. Nevertheless Cooper's is the fullest and most perceptive treatment of the English tenses before James Harris and Lowth, seventy years later.

The first grammarian after Cooper to combine the three distinctions which characterise this group of tense-schemes is James Harris, in 1751, who adds inceptive forms, thus giving a scheme of twelve tenses. Harris held that the verb *be* is 'a latent part in every other Verb',[1] but his tense-scheme is not distorted by logic. It respects the facts of the language and is more perceptive than any previously suggested. It is meant to apply universally, but is in fact based on Greek and moderated by English. Harris had a sufficiently sound understanding of the nature of language to question the universality of his own scheme: 'It is not to be expected that the above Hypothesis should be justified through all instances in every language. It fares with Tenses, as with other affections of speech; be the Language upon the whole ever so perfect, much must be left, in defiance of all analogy, to the harsh laws of mere authority and chance.'[2]

Harris has three aorist tenses 'to denote Time absolute', and nine tenses 'to denote it under its respective distinctions'.[3]

V.2

Aorist of the present	love[4]
Aorist of the past	loved
Aorist of the future	shall/will love
Inceptive present	am going to love
Middle or extended present	am loving
Completive present	have loved
Inceptive past	was beginning to love
Middle past	was loving
Completive past	had done loving
Inceptive future	shall be beginning to love
Middle future	shall be loving
Completive future	shall have done loving

Harris's inceptive tenses were usually rejected, even by those writers who followed the rest of his scheme, on the grounds that they were were indistinguishable from the future. All verb-forms were regarded as tenses and tense was felt to be fundamentally the expression of time. The expression of completion (perfective aspect) was incon-

[1] Harris, 1751, p. 90.
[2] op. cit. p. 122.
[3] op. cit. p. 121.
[4] His example is *write*.

sistently admitted as another function of tense, but aspect as a category was unrecognised: inceptive forms were not seen to be linguistic features of the same type as imperfect forms, and it was therefore not considered reasonable to allow them the same status. Harris influenced every writer in this group, but only John Dalton adopts the same tense-scheme, though with 'English' terms. Dalton does not use aorist, but treats *love* and *loved* as expressing merely the idea of time; for *inceptive* he uses 'beginning' and for *completive* 'ending'. Dalton includes *may, can, must* among the signs of the future because he admits no subjunctive mood: its 'essential character' is 'found in the conjunctive term preceding the verb'.[1] Otherwise he follows Harris exactly.[2]

Lowth uses only the three minimum characteristics of this group, which gives him a system of nine tenses: practically the same as Harris's but without the inceptive forms; the same as Group IV.1, but with the important addition of the three indefinite forms.

V.3 *Indefinite or undetermined*

Present	love
Future	shall love
Past	loved

Definite or determined

Present Imperfect	am loving
Present Perfect	have loved
Past Imperfect	was loving
Past Perfect	had loved
Future Imperfect	shall be loving
Future Perfect	shall have loved

It is surprising that few writers followed Lowth's tense-scheme. He was so influential in other ways that it seems they may have misunderstood his tenses, seeing only the tabular arrangement of the definite tenses and missing the point of his preceding reference to the indefinite tenses. If this is so it would mean that one effect of Lowth's proposal was to encourage scheme IV.1. The only grammars in which Lowth's complete tense-scheme is reproduced are those in William Perry's three works of 1774, 1775 and 1776; Joshua Story's *Introduction to English Grammar*, in which the tense-scheme was changed by the third edition, 1783, from that of IV.1 in the original edition of 1778; *A Short Introduction to Grammar*, 1793; Alexander Barrie's dictionary of 1794, and his *Tyro's Guide* about 1800.

[1] Dalton, 1801, p. 65.　　　　　　　　　　[2] op. cit. pp. 54 f.

Beattie rejects as 'a needless nicety' the view that a tense is properly one inflected word and that English has therefore only two tenses: '*I did hear* is as much a tense as *I heard*'.[1] Like Harris he is attempting an analysis of tense which will be valid for any language. He proposes eleven tenses, two of which, he says, have no equivalent in English: *scripturus sum* and *scripturus eram* (Beattie presumably rejected Harris's inceptive present and inceptive past on the grounds that *go* is not primarily an auxiliary). These eleven tenses are grouped according to whether they are (*a*) definite or indefinite, (*b*) complete or incomplete, (*c*) simple or compound. In this arrangement verb-forms can belong to more than one tense, according to the way in which they are used. Beattie's scheme thus includes Harris's awareness of aspect and Priestley's emphasis on the compound forms, to which it adds an implied reference to the importance of context:

V.4 *Definite in time*

1.	Present	love[2]
2.	Preterperfect	have loved
3.	Paulo-post-future	(*scripturus sum*)

Indefinite in time, or aorist

4.	Present	A merry heart maketh...&c.
5.	Past	loved
6.	Future	shall love

Complete in respect of action

a.	(No. 2)	
b.	(No. 5)	
7.	Plusquamperfect	had loved
8.	Future Perfect	shall have loved

Incomplete in respect of action

9.	Imperfect, or continued past	was loving
c.	(No. 6)	
d.	(No. 3)	

Compound, as uniting two or more times in one tense

e.	(No. 2)	
f.	(No. 7)	
g.	(No. 8)	
h.	(No. 3)	
10.	Past with future	(*scripturus eram*)
11.	Imperfect with future	I shall be loving

[1] Beattie, (1783), 1788 p. 216.   [2] Beattie's example is *write*.

Tense

Simple, expressive of one time
   k. (No. 1)
   l. (No. 4)
  m. (No. 5)
  n. (No. 6)
  o. (No. 9)

If it is wished, Beattie says, to reduce the number of tenses, numbers 10 and 11 may be omitted.[1]

Richard Postlethwaite follows Beattie closely, but not unthinkingly. He argues that the scheme of six tenses (IV.1) is inadequate: (i) it does not allow for the distinction between definite and indefinite time, (ii) 'the term *Past Perfect* [does not] sufficiently distinguish the Preterpluperfect from that which is simply Preterit'.[2] That is: between on the one hand *I loved* (which is 'simply preterit' and indefinite) and on the other hand *I had loved*, there is needed another complete (perfect) tense to express definite time. Postlethwaite therefore agrees with Pickbourn[3] in treating the same forms *loved/did love* as both a definite and an indefinite perfect tense. Otherwise he accepts Beattie's eleven basic tenses, though what Beattie calls Paulo-post-future (*scripturus sum*), with the implication that it is not an English tense, Postlethwaite calls *Paulo-ante-futurum*, 'I am about to write'.

V.5 *Incomplete*

1. Present definite	love, am loving
2. Present indefinite	A Friend loveth at all Times
3. Preter imperfect	was loving

Complete

4. Preterperfect definite	loved, did love
5. Preterperfect indefinite	loved, did love
6. Present perfect	have loved
7. Preterpluperfect	had loved

Incomplete

8. Future imperfect (definite)	shall/will be loving
9. Future indefinite	shall/will love

Complete

10. Future perfect	shall/will have loved

Incomplete

11. Paulo-ante-Futurum	am about to love
12. Praeteritum-cum-Futuro	was about to love

[1] Beattie, 1783, p. 409.   [2] Postlethwaite, 1795, p. 90.
[3] Below, p. 416.

As Beattie had said of his eleven tenses so Postlethwaite says that twelve 'are a very uncommon Number'.[1] Children need not learn all twelve, but if there *are* twelve distinct tenses one must say so. Postlethwaite follows Beattie in rejecting the practice of 'not allowing any Thing to be a Tense but what, in one inflected Word, expresses an Assertion with Time'.[2]

James Pickbourn's *Dissertation on the English Verb*, published in 1789, six years after Beattie and six before Postlethwaite, was prompted by the difficulty he found in explaining the English tenses to Frenchmen, and throughout he keeps the discussion closely related to both French and Latin. Pickbourn is rather scornful of his predecessors: Lowth gave him no detailed help; Priestley's grammatical writings 'appear most wretchedly mean and of no value whatever';[3] Beattie was 'a reader and a writer, but no thinker, or understander'.[4] Pickbourn's own book is original, and deservedly described by Poldauf as 'a truly great work'.[5] Pickbourn's particular contribution was to use *definite* and *indefinite* not to name two specific tenses but to refer to the way in which any tense could be used. He refers to customary practice: 'By an aoristical, or indefinite tense, is generally meant a tense which cannot be used in ascertaining the precise time of an individual action.'[6] Pickbourn, however, uses *definite* and *indefinite* to refer to both time and action: 'The same tense...may, therefore, in one connexion be definite, and in another aoristical. Whenever a verb is so circumstanced as to become *incapable*, with the assistance of adjuncts, of fixing the time of an individual action, it is indefinite, and, when it is *capable* of doing it, it is definite.'[7] He distinguishes, for example, three kinds of 'aoristical propositions': (i) those which are indefinite with respect to action and to time, as 'wisdom excels folly': (ii) those that are indefinite with respect to action, and definite with respect to time, as 'When she first appeared upon the stage she danced elegantly': (iii) those which are indefinite with respect to time, and definite with respect to action, as 'Mr Horne Tooke has published an excellent grammatical work'. The last example illustrates an opinion which, Pickbourn admits, has many opponents: that forms like *have written* are always indefinite with respect to time. English, he says, emphatic-

[1] Postlethwaite, 1795, p. 97. [2] op. cit. p. 98.
[3] Pickbourn, 1789, p. xxx. [4] op. cit. p. xxii.
[5] Poldauf, p. 294. [6] Pickbourn, 1789, p. 40. [7] op. cit. p. 44.

ally, 'has no other tense' than *I wrote* or *I did write* 'by which the
perfect action of past time can be expressed definitely', and he argues
the point at length against Harris, Lowth, Monboddo, Beattie and
Blair. Pickbourn is unusual, too, in recognising the importance, in
any account of tense which uses semantic criteria, of context. He does
not see this clearly, but the words 'so circumstanced' in the passage
just quoted are one of many indications that he was at times thinking
of the function of the whole sentence and not only of the verb.
Pickbourn's tense-scheme is as follows:

V.6 *Present Tenses*

1. love ⎫
2. do love ⎭ indefinite[1]

3. am loving ⎫
4. have been loving ⎭ definite

5. have loved indefinite

Past Tenses

1. loved ⎫
2. did love ⎭ definite or indefinite

3. was loving ⎫
4. had been loving ⎭ definite

5. had loved definite or indefinite

Future Tenses
Simple

1. shall love ⎫
2. will love ⎭ definite or indefinite

3. shall be loving ⎫ ⎧ definite as to time; incomplete
4. will be loving ⎭ ⎩ as to action

Complex

5. shall have been loving ⎫
6. will have been loving ⎭ denotes continuance

7. shall have loved ⎫
8. will have loved ⎭ denotes completion

Poldauf comments[2] justly on the attention Pickbourn pays to the
progressive forms *have been loving* and *had been loving*, but he is wrong
in saying that Pickbourn was the first grammarian to include them
in a system of tenses. Cooper, in 1685, and Priestley, in 1761, had
made them both distinct tenses.[3]

P. W. Fogg discusses the arrangement of tenses in both parts of his
Elementa Anglicana. His proposals are the same in both, but are more

---

[1] His example is *write*.   [2] Poldauf, p. 295.
[3] Cooper, 1685, p. 125; Priestley, 1761, pp. 24–6. See above, pp. 411 and 406.

clearly set out in Part Two, 1796. He proposes a scheme of twelve tenses, which differs from Pickbourn's in three ways. Fogg does not treat *do* and *did* as signs of separate tenses (Pickbourn's Present 2 and Past 2); he does not distinguish *shall* and *will*, thereby reducing Pickbourn's eight future tenses to four; he does not preserve Pickbourn's attempt to show that some forms may be definite or indefinite. In fact Fogg drops the category *definite* altogether, and attaches special importance to the progressive forms:

The continued times have been neglected by grammarians, or partially enumerated and treated as nondescripts. The other nine, invented by our countryman Grocin, and by him supposed the whole of the verb, have been missed by some through ignorance and inattention...

   The misfortune has been, that respecting time as well as other grammatical topics, the mind has been lavishly swayed by the technicals of the Latin grammar. That language, poor in itself with regard to tenses, and more miserably impoverished by the mistakes of modern teachers, has been reckoned by many to express only five various times. (Fogg, 1796, p. 221.)

Fogg's scheme is as follows:

V.7   1. Present indefinite   love[1]
          2. Past indefinite   loved
          3. Future indefinite   shall/will love
          4. Present imperfect   am loving
          5. Past imperfect   was loving
          6. Future imperfect   shall/will be loving
          7. Present perfect   have loved
          8. Past perfect   had loved
          9. Future perfect   shall/will have loved
         10. Present continued   have been loving
         11. Past continued   had been loving
         12. Future continued   shall/will have been loving[2]

This scheme of Fogg's, in a slightly different arrangement, was first put forward in the *Monthly Review* for October 1791.[3] The anonymous writer was reviewing Pickbourn's *Dissertation*, and disputing, in particular, Pickbourn's use of the term *aoristical*, without, it would seem, fully understanding it; he blames Pickbourn for not seeing that *every* tense may be definite or indefinite, and that precision of time is indicated not by tenses but by adverbs. Whereas it is just this flexibility and understanding of context which makes Pickbourn's

---

[1] His example is *walk*.   [2] op. cit. p. 219.
[3] *Mon. Rev.*, n.s. 6. October 1791, pp. 175–81.

analysis so sound. The reviewer then proceeds to offer his own tense-scheme, which, if he was not himself P. W. Fogg, P. W. Fogg adopted.

Patrick Lynch in *The Pentaglot Preceptor* uses, besides II.2, the same tense scheme as Fogg, though in a slightly different arrangement and calling 'restricted' those tenses which Fogg calls 'continued'. Lynch also acknowledges his obligation to the *Monthly Review*, but refers throughout to the issue of March 1791, and to 'Pinkbourn'.

George Wright, in *The Principles of Grammar*, 1794, uses the same scheme as Fogg, with two differences. Wright keeps Pickbourn's classification in terms of definite and indefinite (but misses the point of it, for he omits Pickbourn's alternatives; Pickbourn was classifying the *uses* of tense-forms, Wright is classifying tense-forms themselves). And Wright, presumably in error, omits any reference to the form *have loved*,[1] which his scheme would treat as a present indefinite perfect. He has therefore only eleven tenses instead of twelve.[2]

Group VI. The tense-schemes of a few grammarians are based on criteria which do not fit into any of the preceding groups, but are not without interest.

VI.1 *Logical criteria.* Wilkins is writing not only for English, but for a universal language, and he is therefore more concerned with ideal tenses. He makes two initial assumptions:

i) 'That part of speech, which by our Common Grammarians is stiled a Verb...ought to have no distinct place among Integrals in a Philosophical Grammar; because it is really no other then an Adjective, and the Copula *sum* affixed to it or contiened in it; so *Caleo*...is the same with *sum Calidus*.'[3]

(ii) The copula expresses the time of the action, and the adjective expresses 'the state of the Person or Subject'. This, as he says, is to endow both copula and adjective with tense. In fact Wilkins goes further: 'The Tenses in instituted Languages are appropriated only to Verbs, yet 'tis very plain that according to the true Philosophy of speech...as there is *Amatio*, so there should be *Amavitio* and *Amaturitio*, &c.'[4]

These assumptions enable Wilkins to establish a system of twenty-seven tenses: *I have been, I am* and *I shall be* are each followed by each

---

[1] His example is *write*. [2] G. Wright, 1794, pp. 143 f.
[3] Wilkins, 1668, p. 303. [4] op. cit. p. 316.

14-2

of the following nine predicates: *hot, having been hot, to be hot hereafter; heating, having heated, to heat hereafter; heated, having been heated, to be heated hereafter.* The tenses are given in Latin, where they are a little more comfortable, as well as in English. They derive much of their 'universality' from the flexibility of the Latin participles, but they remain logical constructions with little relevance for English.

VI.2   *The distinction betweem absolute and conditional forms.* This is in effect the starting-point of Rowland Jones's classification, but his preliminary argument and his subsequent illustrations are practically incomprehensible. In *Hieroglyfic* he maintains that:

> tho' present, past, and future, seem to be necessary expressions, according to our present mode of conception, yet they are not in reality any representation of time, but of our manner of dividing or reckoning the changes of motions or number of actions in extension, which in the eternal state of spirits, or perhaps in a vacuum, might be deemed as one intire action or the present tense. (R. Jones, 1768, pp. 40–1.)

Throughout Jones mixes philosophical and grammatical points of view. He is interested in universal grammar but, unlike Wilkins, he believes that English has more claim than any modern language to be considered universal because it is directly descended from the first and only language spoken in the world. It is not clear from Jones's tense-scheme whether he is describing the current English tenses, or whether he is, to an unspecified extent, 'universalising' them. His scheme is simple: past, present and future have each an absolute and a conditional form. But his examples mix active and passive, main and auxiliary, with such inconsistency that it is possible to indicate the scheme only in a misleadingly coherent outline:

Present Absolute	love
Present Conditional	may, ought to, love
Past Absolute	loved
Past Conditional	might, ought to, have loved
Future Absolute	shall/will love
Future Conditional	shall have loved[1]

J. Haywood, in *A Short Introduction to the English Tongue,* 1800, makes the same basic classification, though his outlook is entirely different from Jones's. Haywood does not discuss the question, directly, but he is clearly trying to fuse indicative and subjunctive

---

[1] R. Jones, 1771, p. 13.

into one mood.[1] He is not abandoning the category *mood* altogether—
he has indicative, imperative and infinitive moods—but his unique
tense-scheme suggests that he is trying to recognise subjunctive forms
without having a subjunctive mood:

VI.3

Positive Present	love
Positive Past	loved
Conditional Present	I love...he love
Conditional Past	loved
Conditional Future	shall/will love

VI.4 *The distinction between simple and compound forms.* Jane
Gardiner is the only writer who tries to make the distinction between
simple and compound forms the central feature of a tense-scheme.
Priestley and Beattie had emphasised the distinction and Postlethwaite had referred to it in terms which showed he was thinking of
Beattie. Jane Gardiner's scheme, however, not only confuses the
distinction itself but obscures more important aspects of tense. It can
hardly have helped the young ladies of York in their English studies,
but these were not the author's primary concern. She says: 'I have
ventured to differ from the Grammarians I have consulted, in the
declination of nouns and pronouns, and in the conjugation of verbs,
to make them as nearly conformable to the French grammars, as the
two languages will permit.'[2] Unless *compound* is interpreted in relation
to French verbs Jane Gardiner's tense-scheme is meaningless:[3]

Simple Tenses

Present	love, do love, am loving
Imperfect	did love, was loving
Past or Preterite	loved
Future	shall/will love

Compound Tenses

Present	am come, have loved
Imperfect Preterite	had loved
Future	shall have loved (subjunctive only)

---

[1] Haywood, 1800, p. 13: The indicative 'shews or declares a thing positively...or
conditionally: as, *if I give*. In this case it may with a degree of accuracy be termed the
conditional indicative, which is seldom or never used, unless some conjunctions precede.'

[2] Gardiner, 1799, p. iii.

[3] op. cit. pp. 27, 38–41.

CONCLUSION

The 248 relevant grammars contain 299 tense-schemes, which have been here classified in six broad groups. The first impression given by this grouping is that the schemes following the Latin system, with its variations, form by far the largest number, 149. But a second, and stronger, impression is given by the number of schemes in which the Latin system is not adopted, 150. It is important not to make too strong an opposition between Latin and non-Latin tense-schemes: all classifications were strongly influenced by Latin. Broadly speaking, those grammarians who proposed a scheme of five or more tenses were accepting the Latin system, or elaborating it; those who proposed fewer tenses were withdrawing from the Latin system and probably giving more considered, if sometimes ill-considered, thought to their proposals. But there are important exceptions to this. The non-Latin tense-schemes include those of Harris, Lowth, Beattie and Pickbourn (Nos. V.2, V.3, V.4, V.6 above) in which the number of tenses is far more than five. These schemes, however, are not just extending the Latin system. They are based on fresh criteria, carefully related to English itself (as by Lowth and Pickbourn) or to English regarded, together with Latin, as representing language in general (as by Harris and Beattie).

The 150 non-Latin schemes represent a considerable measure of dissatisfaction with the application of the traditional categories to English. The strongest dissatisfaction is expressed by those of Group II, proposing only two tenses. This is a purely English classification, for which there is no precedent in the tradition, but it simplifies too much. The eclectic approach of the 15 grammars in Group V, which draws on the expression of both time and aspect, implies dissatisfaction with the tradition and also gives constructive regard to the varied and complex elements, which make up the English verb. A middle position is occupied by the tense-schemes of Group IV. The distinction on which it is based, that between complete and incomplete action, is part of the Latin tradition, but its application to English is discriminating, especially in treating *have loved* as a present tense. These schemes are looking away from, rather than back to, Latin.

Some evidence of dissatisfaction is shown also by the variety of schemes even within Group I. Although the great majority of the schemes belong either to I.1 or to I.4 there are still eleven other types in the group, even if they are proposed by only one or two writers in each case. Although it is difficult to assess its significance the mere presence of such variety in the application of established categories suggests, at the least, some uncertainty about their value, even if it was not seen as such by the writers.

Such development as appears in the treatment of tense is slight, and rather uneven. The five-tense Latin scheme of Group I.1 is only half as frequent towards the end of the eighteenth century as it had been towards the beginning. On the other hand the six-tense scheme of Group I.4 is much more frequent after 1780 than before. The two-tense 'English' scheme of Group III is no more frequent at the end of the century than it was at the beginning, but it rose in popularity between 1745 and 1770. The most significant development lay not in any bold conversion from a 'Latin' system to an 'English' one, but in the careful empiricism of Harris, Beattie, Postlethwaite, Pickbourn, Fogg and Dalton, proponents of the individual schemes in Group V. The first and most influential of these was Harris (V.2). After him increasing attention was paid to aspect: the verb was seen to express more than time and completeness of action, the traditional elements which the schemes of Group IV had particularly emphasised. The eclectic approach of the grammarians in Group V represents the beginning of a new outlook on the verb, not yet based on anything which could be called linguistic science but reflecting the interest of the times in anthropology and in the psychology of language.

14. MOOD, CONJUGATION, IRREGULARITY

The category of mood illustrates, even more sharply than that of tense, not only how closely the English grammarians had tied themselves to the Latin tradition but the way in which the bonds restricted them and the effort it took to make their first steps towards independence.

The five basic moods go back to Dionysius Thrax; the sixth, the potential, only to Linacre. So strong is the tradition, and so weak their historical knowledge of English, that most of the grammarians pay no more attention to the 'real' English subjunctive—the formal difference between (*if*) *he love* and *he loves*—than to the optative and the potential. Here again the fundamental distinction, which it was possible for only a very few of them to see, was that between formal and semantic criteria. Even those who saw the distinction did not agree how to apply it. The author of *A Real English Grammar*, 1764, says that people are led astray into thinking there is a subjunctive in English 'by the habit of taking the termination for their guide instead of the occasion'.[1] Patrick Lynch, in 1796, on the other hand, argues that 'no more Modes should be admitted in a language than there are different inflexions of the Verb for expressing the various manners of mental affirmation'.[2]

In Greek the optative was a formally distinct mood. In Latin there was, formally, no optative: an equivalent could be found only by calling optative those subjunctive forms, usually preceded by *utinam*, which expressed a wish. The precedent had been established for treating as a mood any expression of attitude, but because it was not generally understood that this was what had happened most of the Latin and English grammarians enjoyed neither the clarity of a formal, nor the freedom of a semantic, criterion for mood. The point

---

[1] *Real English Grammar*, 1764, p. xxiv.
[2] Lynch, 1796, p. 39.

of view which the English grammarians inherited was that of Linacre, who prescribed, for Latin, a potential mood which he expressly said was identical in every tense with the subjunctive.

Because most of the English grammarians felt that they ought to keep the classical categories, but had little guidance from the inflections of the English verb, there are wide and wild differences in their treatment of, especially, the subjunctive, optative and potential. Behind the differences lies only one general agreement: that forms with *may* are not indicative. In the seventeenth century, and during the first two-thirds of the eighteenth, the most common practice is to call *may*, as well as *can*, the sign of the potential. Forms in which *may* or *can* is preceded by a conjunction are then regarded as a special case of the potential and are called subjunctive, or conjunctive. The potential is the dominant mood of the two. During the latter part of the eighteenth century the auxiliaries are gradually regarded less as signs of moods and more as verbs significant in their own right. The potential, therefore, of which *may* and *can* had been the signs, ceases to be the dominant non-indicative mood, and when it is mentioned at all is often described as a special case of the subjunctive. But this is only a general tendency: there is no steady development. Thomas Lye, for example, in 1671, makes the subjunctive the dominant mood and says that it is called optative when used in wishing and potential when preceded by *may*, *might* or *can*.[1] Mark Lewis, three years later, makes the potential the dominant, saying, 'When this Mood is subjoyned by a Conjunction, it is called the Subjunctive Mood.'[2] The general tendency is similarly contradicted at the end of the eighteenth century when Henry Bullen makes the potential dominant: 'The Subjunctive Mood appears to be merely the Potential used without its sign, and is therefore omitted.'[3] The optative withered more quickly than the potential. Its sign was an adverb of wishing, but although *O* might be considered the equivalent of εἴθε or *utinam* a construction such as *would I were*...seemed so closely allied to the subjunctive that there could be little justification for making it a separate mood.

The grammarians were floundering, understandably,[4] and the

[1] Lye, 1671, p. 120.   [2] Lewis, 1674, p. 38.   [3] Bullen, 1797, p. 46.
[4] But not enough to justify Leonard's remark, 'Before Dr Johnson issued his dictionary, the idea that English has a subjunctive mode seems not to have been suspected' (Leonard, 1929, p. 200). The English forms were recognised, but the criterion of mood was felt to be a 'sign'.

variety of their classifications expresses their uncertainty. This variety is sufficiently displayed in the tables which follow and need not be examined more closely here. It is, however, worth mentioning the desperate remedy of J. T. Philipps, in 1726, who treated Optative, Potential and Subjunctive as synonymous terms.[1]

Not all the grammarians use the category *mood*. Among the 258 relevant grammars nineteen authors exaggerate their freedom and say there are no moods in English at all, and another thirty do not mention mood. It is difficult to interpret the silence of the thirty. Some of them are writing elementary books in which they may not think it appropriate to discuss mood. Some, from their vernacular terminology, seem to share the prejudice that mood is a purely Latin category. It is a reasonable estimate that not more than half the thirty, and not more than thirty-five grammarians in all, repudiate mood in English.

The explicit repudiation of mood is first made by James Greenwood, in 1711: 'In English there are no Moods, because the Verb has no Diversity of Endings.'[2] Greenwood is followed by Loughton, 1734; Collyer, 1735; the *New English Accidence*, 1735, and he repeats the view in *The Royal English Grammar*, 1737, an abridgment of his 1711 grammar. Anne Fisher's influential grammars, first published about 1749 and 1763, and those of Daniel Fenning, 1756 and 1771, all maintain the same view. But the opinion weakens about the middle of the century, and only eight grammars after 1760 maintain it explicitly. Fenning is much less sure in 1771 than he had been in 1756. In 1771 he says that English 'properly speaking' has no moods.[3] but he nevertheless discusses five. Priestley would have liked to deny English any moods but was too honest to do so. In 1762 he goes so far as to say, 'English has none...' but continues '...except if I *be*',[4] and in both the grammar of 1761 and the Lectures of 1762 he accepts the subjunctive as a genuine mood, but with some regret. After referring to the Latin moods he says:

It is easy to see that, upon these principles, moods might have been increased almost *ad infinitum*: since the ways a sentence may be modified, or vary from a direct assertion, are innumerable: for instance, for the same reason that a *wish* constitutes a mood, an *interrogation* might constitute one, a *permission* another, and so on without end. (Priestley, 1762, p. 100.)

[1] Philipps, 1726, p. xiv.
[2] Greenwood, 1711, p. 119.
[3] Fenning, 1771, p. 38.
[4] Priestley, 1762, p. 98.

James Pickbourn hesitates in much the same way as Priestley and accepts the subjunctive, if he can be said to do so at all, with even greater reluctance: 'The English language may be said...to have as many modes as it has auxiliary verbs; for the compound expressions which they help to form, point out those modifications and circumstances of actions which in other languages are conveyed by modes.'[1] Of the subjunctive Pickbourn says: 'I have some doubts whether it has a real existence or not. What is called the subjunctive may possibly be only the infinitive, governed by an auxiliary verb understood.'[2] For example, he goes on, *though he slay me* is *though he (may) slay me*. Pickbourn admits that the form *were*, in *if he were*, 'is an obstacle to this theory, but a single exception', and as no one knows the origin of the word he is inclined to disregard it.

James Gregory, Professor of Medicine at Edinburgh, whose paper on the 'Theory of the Moods of Verbs' was read to the Royal Society of Edinburgh in 1787 but not published until 1790, is discussing mood 'universally' and does not specify any number of moods for English. He uses many suggestions from Monboddo and puts more explicitly than any one before him the distinction between formal and semantic criteria:

The moods of verbs may be considered in two very different points of view; either *with relation to any particular language* or *with relation to human thought*, which must be supposed the same in all ages and nations. For the sake of distinctness, I shall call the expression of them, by inflection or otherwise in language, *grammatical moods*; and the thoughts, or combinations of thoughts, though not always, or perhaps never expressed in the same way, I shall call *energies*, or *modifications*, or *moods of thought*.[3]

Gregory begins an enumeration of the moods of thought, such as affirming, denying, testifying, foretelling, believing, doubting, stipulating, but when he has listed thirty-five he is obliged to say that there are 'perhaps numberless' others.[4] Two points in his discussion are of particular interest. He sees that one function of modal expressions is to enable different aspects of the speaker's intention to be expressed simultaneously:

Grammatical moods of verbs, like other inflections of words, express much better than any succession of words can do, the intimate connection and

---

[1] Pickbourn, 1788, p. 156,   [2] op. cit. p. 160.
[3] James Gregory, 'Theory of the Moods of Verbs', *Transactions of The Royal Society of Edinburgh*, 2. 1790. 12.
[4] op. cit. p. 14.

relation of various thoughts, which are not successive, but simultaneous or coexistent, and which appear unnaturally disjointed, and in some measure altered, when they are expressed by a series of words denoting each of them separately and in succession. (Gregory, op. cit. p. 24.)

Later Gregory develops the analogy with mathematical, especially algebraic, symbols, which are designed for economical and simultaneous expression. More unusual still is Gregory's linking of modal expressions with gesture:

Some of the most interesting modifications of thought, I mean emotions or passions, express themselves by natural language, that is by the countenance, voice and gesture, almost as quickly as they are conceived... A grammatical language, as quick as thought, and as concise as natural language, is manifestly unattainable. But every approximation to it is valuable. All the moods of verbs, even the indicative and the simple subjunctive, are such approximations. (Gregory, op. cit. pp. 39 & 42.)

The author of the article *Grammar* in the third edition of the *Encyclopaedia Britannica* quotes Gregory with approval. He also is discussing mood universally but he seems more anxious than Gregory to take only formal criteria into account. He shows this attitude in two ways: positively, in his statement that only the indicative, imperative and subjunctive are 'real distinct modes of the verb' found in 'the most copious and varied language';[1] negatively, in his rejection of one of the customary views—that mood expresses variation in the action of the verb. He does not say explicitly that mood expresses the speaker's attitude, but he is thinking on those lines: 'Thus much, however, seems to be obvious, that those variations which are called *modes* do not imply different modifications of the action of the verb. *Amo, amem, ama*, do not signify modes of *loving*; for modes of loving are, loving much, loving little, loving long, &c.'[2] The writer in the *Britannica* makes no advance on Gregory, but he is not just reproducing him (he does not agree, for example, with Gregory that the infinitive is a mood). He stands not only with Gregory and Pickbourn but with other writers towards the end of the century—Monboddo, Campbell, Blair, Beattie—whose interest in language kept flexible their views about English grammar.

One of the sad features of our grammatical tradition is that flexible thinking of this sort has had so little influence, until recent times, on the development of English grammar. In the middle of the eighteenth

[1] *Enc. Brit.* (B), 1797, p. 66.   [2] op. cit. p. 64.

century it seemed for a short time that English might develop a grammar in its own right, not only as a language distinct from Latin but as a language *already known*, and therefore open to entirely different teaching techniques. But neither development was fulfilled; and in the schools neither has been fulfilled yet.

Some of the more thoughtful discussions of mood are briefly mentioned here; the full deployment of the category is shown in the tables which follow.

A very early statement about mood in English, that of Alexander Hume, about 1612, is distinctive for the freedom with which it interprets the term. Although Hume is not writing about universal grammar, and is not so free from the influence of Latin as Gregory and Pickbourn could be, he has something of their flexibility. Hume is unusual in not naming or classifying the moods. Although his eighth chapter is headed *Of the Moods of the Verb* it is in fact a tentative classification of utterances. Its tone is strikingly modern and its resemblance to parts of Wittgenstein's *Tractatus* is not only stylistic:

1. The mood is an affection of the verb serving the varietie of utterance.
2. We utter the being of thinges or our awn wil.
3. The being of thinges is uttered be inquyring or avouing.
4. We inquyre of that we wald knaw; as, Made God man without synne? and in this the supposit[1] of the verb followes the verb.
5. We avoue that quhilk we knaw; as, God made man without sinne; and in this the supposit precedes the verb.
6. We utter our wil be verbes signifying the form of our wil, or post-posing the supposit.
7. We wish be *wald god, god grant*...
8. We permit the will of others be letting; as, *let God aryse*...
9. We bid our inferioures, and pray our superioures, be postponing the supposit to the verb; As, goe ye and teach al nationes; Here me, my God. (Hume, *c.* 1617, pp. 30–1.)

In their first edition, 1711, Gildon and Brightland made three moods, referred to not by names but by numbers.[2] The first two corresponded to indicative and imperative; the third included expressions with *may, can, ought, should*. The notes to the same chapter, which were taken from the Port Royal grammar, give a different and not very clear arrangement of moods: the (indicative) verb itself, a subjunctive form and three forms representing three ways of expressing will: potential, optative and imperative. In the

---

[1] The grammatical subject.　　　　　　　[2] G–B, 1711, p. 102.

second and later editions the enumeration of moods in the text, but not in the notes, is omitted in favour of a more extended description of the use of the auxiliary verbs.

Dyche, 1735, used both numbers and names for his four moods, in spite of his rejection of names on the ground that potential and subjunctive differ only 'by some accidental Signs'.[1] Dyche is also the first among those who say there *are* moods in English to destroy his own assertion by adding: 'As to the Distinctions of what is commonly called *Moods*, it is undeniably certain that they may be denominated as variously, and be as numerous, as the particular Circumstances require.'[2]

James Harris, in *Hermes*, 1751, is unusual among writers on universal grammar in making a definite enumeration of moods, firmly based on meaning. He postulates first two 'powers of the soul', perception and volition: 'By the Powers of Perception, I mean the Senses and the Intellect; by the Powers of Volition, I mean, in an extended sense, not only the Will, but the several Passions and Appetites; in short, all that moves to Action, whether rational or irrational.'[3] In so far as speech 'exhibits the Soul' all sentences are related to one or other of these powers: 'Every Sentence will be either a Sentence of Assertion or a Sentence of Volition.'[4] As Harris further states that 'the Species of Modes in great measure depend on the Species of Sentences'[5] one would expect him to posit two primary moods. But he extends his analysis of the speaker's intention and proposes a set of four moods:

the Indicative or Declarative, to assert what we think certain; the Potential, for the Purposes of whatever we think Contingent; the Interrogative, when we are doubtful, to procure us Information; and the Requisitive, to assist us in the gratification of our Volitions. The Requisitive too appears under two distinct Species, either as it is Imperative to inferiors, or Precative to superiors. (Harris, 1751, p. 144.)

Harris includes the subjunctive within the potential, and uses *precative* and *optative* as synonyms. He seems later in the chapter to treat the infinitive as a mood also. In English, he says, moods are expressed entirely by auxiliary verbs: 'The English Tongue...is so poor in this respect, as to admit no Variation for Modes.'[6] If Harris had not been so persistent an admirer of Greek (Latin is 'but a

[1] Dyche, 1735, sig. b 4 recto.   [2] ibid.
[3] Harris, 1751, p. 15.   [4] op. cit. p. 17.
[5] op. cit. p. 144 n.   [6] op. cit. p. 148 n.

Species of Greek somewhat debased')[1] he would have seen that his argument led either to fewer, or to many more, moods. He is less helpful, and less influential, on the topic of mood than on any so far considered.

James Buchanan, in *The British Grammar*, 1762, breezily dismisses those who say English has no moods:

Most Writers of English Grammars implicitly follow one another in asserting, that our Tongue has no Moods, which, added to our supposed Want of Variety of Tenses...is manifestly affirming, that the English Language is nothing superior to that of the Hottentots; and that the wisest and most respectable Body of People upon the Face of the Globe, own a Language which is incapable of ascertaining their Ideas, or of exhibiting the Soul, and its various Affections. (Buchanan, 1762, p. 105 n.)

The grammarians have been led to this view, he says, by our paucity of terminations: 'But as a great Variety of Terminations are not absolutely necessary to the Existence of Moods, why is our Grammar to be modelled by that of the Latin, especially in Cases where there is not the least trace of Analogy?'[2] Buchanan's comments are interesting in several ways. His argument illustrates clearly the confusion which constantly surrounded terms like *mood* and *tense* when the distinction between meaning and form was not borne in mind: to say that English has no (formal) moods is not to say that there are certain meanings ('various affections of the soul') which it cannot express. Buchanan's first statement seems, in view of the small number of grammars (about 35 out of 240) in which English is in fact said or implied to have no moods, an extraordinary exaggeration. Buchanan was writing, however, soon after the period 1730–55, during which the vernacular approach was most influential, and his exaggeration is to some extent an indication of its strength. It is interesting too that Buchanan regards the system of moods which he himself supports—indicative, subjunctive, imperative, infinitive (No. I.7 below, and the most widely used)—as distinct from the Latin system. This agrees with the opinion of many other mid-eighteenth-century grammarians, and is confirmed in later grammars, that it was the potential and optative which were felt to be Latin, and un-English.

James White's *The English Verb*, 1761, was written, he says, because previous efforts to achieve a grammar of English 'seem to

---

[1] ibid.   [2] Buchanan, 1762, p. 106.

have been rendered ineffectual hitherto, chiefly by the prevalency of two false notions...that our Verbs have no Moods...and that our Language hath no Syntax'.[1] White is particularly concerned to counter the first of these views. In proposing his scheme of ten moods (No. II.2 below) he writes as though he is taking meaning as his sole criterion. In fact he is selecting only certain meanings. He is adding to the common scheme—indicative, subjunctive, imperative, infinitive—five moods based on the auxiliaries: potential (*can*), determinative (*would*), obligative (*should*), elective (*may*) and compulsive (*must*). White is also the first English grammarian to make the participle a mood in its own right, instead of classifying it under the infinitive. White's scheme of moods, combined with his rich system of tenses,[2] leads him into considerable difficulty, because in his detailed account of the use of the auxiliaries, which occupies half the book, he treats them sometimes as signs of tenses and sometimes as signs of moods. The resulting inconsistencies spoil his schematic structure, but his observations on usage are acute.

Lowth seems to have hesitated about the treatment of mood. He was sufficiently influenced by White to make the participle a mood, and to consider, even if he rejects, the possibility of an interrogative mood:

In Theory...the Interrogative form seems to have as good a Title to a Mode of its own, as either of the other two: but Practice has determined it otherwise...If it be true, as I have somewhere read, that the Modes of the Verbs, are more numerous in the Lapland Tongue than in any other, possibly the Laplanders may be provided with an Interrogative Mode. (Lowth, 1762, p. 115.)

But Lowth's main statement about mood, which is designed to avoid the need for a potential and an optative, is based on what are, in effect, formal or syntactic criteria:

The Mode is the Manner of representing the Action or Passion. When it is simply declared, or a question is asked concerning it, it is called the Indicative Mode; when it is bidden, it is called the Imperative; when it is subjoined as the end or design, or mentioned under a condition, a supposition, or the like, for the most part depending on some other Verb, and having a Conjunction before it, it is called the Subjunctive; when it is barely expressed without any limitation of person or number, it is called the Infinitive; and when it is expressed in a form in which it may be joined to a Noun as its quality or accident, partaking thereby of the nature of an Adjective, it is called the Participle. (op. cit. p. 46.)

[1] White, 1761, p. ix.   [2] Above, p. 402.

He later distinguishes between 'primary modes' (indicative and imperative) and 'secondary modes', those expressing possibility, liberty, will and necessity. The former are modifications of the verb itself; the latter are expressed by auxiliaries.[1] Lowth's hesitation seems to have centred on the subjunctive: whether it was a primary or a secondary mode. It is expressed usually by auxiliaries, but it has one purely formal feature (*loves: love*). Lowth's description of the secondary modes resembles Gildon and Brightland's use of the Port Royal grammar, and it is possible that his hesitation comes from his attention to their inconsistent classification of the moods.

In his second edition Lowth added a passage strengthening his emphasis on the criterion of form: 'As far as Grammar is concerned, there are no more Modes in any language, than there are forms of the Verb appropriated to the denoting of such different manners of representation...Whatever other Metaphysical Modes there may be in the theory of Universal Grammar, there are in English no other Grammatical Modes than those above described.'[2]

Haywood, 1800, and Dalton, 1801, both propose only three moods: indicative, imperative and infinitive (System I.12 below). They agree in excluding the auxiliary verbs; Dalton's argument is that the potential, for instance, is 'destitute both of distinction and consistency' because we should either have four moods for *may, can, shall, will,* or put them all into one, the indicative. It is inconsistent to make *should* and *would* the expressions of different moods and not to do the same with *shall* and *will*.[3] Haywood and Dalton deal with the form (*if*) *he love* in different ways. Haywood makes it a conditional form of the present indicative; Dalton recognises it as a subjunctive, but omits the subjunctive mood altogether 'both because it differs little from the indicative mood, and because that difference is principally from an abbreviation of construction, and of such a partial nature as not to give sufficient ground for a Modal distinction'.[4]

SYSTEMS OF MOODS

The following table shows the different systems of moods proposed between 1586 and 1801. Group I comprises systems using only the five traditional moods together with the potential, Group II those

[1] Lowth, 1762, p. 60   [2] Lowth, 2nd edn 1763, pp. 48 n. and 50 n.
[3] Dalton, 1801, p. xi.   [4] op. cit. p. x.

433

in which fresh moods are introduced. Group I are arranged according to the number of moods used, Group II chronologically. The dates are given of the first editions of the earliest and latest grammars in which each system appears.

SYSTEMS OF MOODS

Group I							Distribution	No. of grammars
1.1	Indic.	Imper.	Infin.	Opt.	Pot.	Subj.	1612–1790	13
1.2	Indic.	Imper.	Infin.	Opt.	—	Subj.	1586–1797	3
1.3	Indic.	Imper.	—	Opt.	Pot.	Subj.	1624–1774	3
1.4	Indic.	Imper.	Infin.	—	Pot.	Subj.	1710–1800	40
1.5	Indic.	Imper.	Infin.	—	Pot.	—	1619–1796	30
1.6	Indic.	Imper.	—	Opt.	—	Subj.	1774	1
1.7	Indic.	Imper.	Infin.	—	—	Subj.	1671–1800	72
1.8	Indic.	Imper.	Infin.	Opt.	—	—	1797	1
1.9	Indic.	—	Infin.	Opt.	—	Subj.	1662	1
1.10	Indic.	Imper.	—	—	—	Subj.	1695–1795	11
1.11	Indic.	Imper.	—	—	Pot.	—	1686–1711	2
1.12	Indic.	Imper.	Infin.	—	—	—	1764–1801	6
1.13	Indic.	—	—	—	—	Subj.	1712–90	2
1.14	Indic.	Imper.	—	—	—	—	1737	1

Group II								
II.1	Indic.	Imper.	Infin.	Subj.	Participle		1732–1800	8
II.2	Indic.	Imper.	Infin.	Pot.	Interrog.	Precative	1751	1
II.3	{Indic.	Imper.	Infin.	Pot.	Subj.	Participle}	1761–71	2
	{Elective	Determinative	Obligative	Compulsive}				
II.4	Indic.	Imper.	Infin.	Participle			1764	1
II.5	Indic.	Infin.	Participle	Subj.			1765–88	2
II.6	Indic.	Imper.	Infin.	Subj.	Interrog.	Participle	1771–98	2
II.7	Indic.	Imper.	Infin.	Subj.	Interrog.	Precative	1777	1
II.8	Indic.	Imper.	Infin.	Subj.	Pot.	Participle	1787	1

Total number of classifications 204
Grammars explicitly denying moods in English 19
Grammars silent about moods 35

258

To the question, 'What moods are there in English?' the grammarians respond in, at the very least, twenty-four ways: by ignoring the question; by saying that English has no moods; by proposing one or more of the above twenty-two systems. In fact the response was even more varied and uncertain than the table shows, but it would be tedious to document all the qualifications and doubts with which the systems are proposed.[1] In their handling of mood the English grammarians had much the same limited freedom as they had in

---

[1] B. M. Charleston, 1941, p. 202: 'On the whole, the treatment of moods...shows a confusion and hesitancy which is still to be observed today.'

their treatment of conjugation:[1] they inherited the category, but had in English no obvious guide as to how (and whether) it could be used. As with conjugation, any description of their treatment is interesting mainly for what it shows about the use they were able to make of their freedom. It is particularly true with regard to mood that the ideas necessary for a consistent treatment of the category were available, even if only just available, quite early in the period. Wallis had suggested, by his silence, that mood was an unsuitable, or an unimportant, category for English; Thomas Lye had used System I.7, which is based on formal and syntactic criteria, in an English grammar by 1671; Richard Johnson had firmly stated, 'There is no necessity, that the Mood should be in the Word it self',[2] and had thus emphasised the possibility, *a fortiori* for English, that any means of indicating the speaker's attitude (through adverbs, word-order or other forms of emphasis) could be called a mood. The table shows that the grammarians did use their freedom, but it shows also how slowly they used it. System I.1, the full Latin system, is used less often in each successive period; the most commonly used system, No. I.7, contains neither potential nor optative; some of the systems in Group II show a readiness to experiment with a purely semantic conception of mood. On the other hand there is no real escape from the example of Latin. System I.4, which includes both potential and subjunctive, is still flourishing at the end of the eighteenth century. Any attempt to conceive mood as the expression of the speaker's attitude would include, at the least, interrogative expressions, but in only four grammars is the category of mood extended so far. The points of development, in fact, are to be found less in the systems than in the comments, already quoted, of the more perceptive writers, who may, like Alexander Hume, also propose a system or, like Gregory, eschew one. Mood could not become a self-consistent category until the distinctions between form, syntax and meaning had been more clearly realised.

IRREGULARITY

The grammarians all noticed that some English verbs formed a past tense and a past participle in -ed or -d and that some did not. The ways in which they described this difference are too varied to be

[1] See below, p. 439. [2] R. Johnson, *Grammatical Commentaries*, 1706, p. 254.

discussed in full, but even an outline shows up yet another part of that border country between Latin and English.

It was natural that the grammarians should look to Latin for guidance in such a problem of classification. Some of them regarded conjugation as the most relevant of the traditional categories; most of them turned to the concept of irregularity. It was not then at all obvious that to group verbs in classes according to their formal differences was sounder practice than to label them merely as regular or irregular: sounder because it recognised, but did not pass judgment on, the facts of the language.

From the first it is assumed, by Bullokar and Greaves, that verbs which do not form a past tense and past participle in -(e)d are irregular. Bullokar says little more than, 'Some verbs change voice in all preter tenses: as, *to seek...*',[1] but Greaves lists about forty which are irregular in one form (*sit, sate*) and as many which are irregular in two (*get, gate, got*).[2] Thomas Tomkis expresses the rule in its converse form: 'Aoristum verborum regularium fit a themate addendo d si litera ultima fuerit vocalis, ut to love...aorist I loved, sin consonans, ed, ut to omitt, aoristum I omitted.'[3] Charles Butler gives a slightly fuller classification. He distinguishes in his list of irregular 'oblique cases' (i.e. forms in -*ed* or -*en*) those which are (i) used as a past tense only; (ii) used as a past participle only; (iii) used 'both ways'.[4] But systematic classification of irregular verbs really begins with Wallis, who distinguishes:

(i) those which contract -ed to -t
(ii) those whose past participle is in -en
(iii) those whose irregular past tense and past participle (*a*) differ, (*b*) are the same.[5]

There are many minor variations, but Wallis's classification of irregular verbs, and Gill's classification of the conjugations, are the basis of all later classifications of irregular verbs. Not every writer, however, agrees with Wallis that all contracted forms are irregular. The author of *The English Scholar Compleat*, 1706, says explicitly, 'By Regular Verbs is meant, whose Imperfect Tense ends in -ed...-d or -t.'[6]

J. Smith, in his *Grammatica Quadrilinguis*, 1674, is the first of many

---

[1] Bullokar, 1586, p. 362.   [2] Greaves, 1594, p. 14.
[3] Tomkis, 1612, fol. 8 recto.   [4] Butler, 1633, p. 48.
[5] Wallis, 1653, chap. xii.   [6] *English Scholar Compleat*, 1706, p. 11.

who treat separately those verbs which have the same form in the present and past tenses and in the past participle. This group of verbs, combined with Wallis's third class, led eventually to an attractively tidy classification, first proposed by James Douglas, in his unpublished grammar completed before 1740, and first appearing in print in John Ward's *Essays upon the English Verb*, 1758. Douglas and Ward both made four classes of verbs. They described them, not as irregular verbs, but as conjugations, and the overlapping of these two categories can be seen in the use made by later writers of this classification which, whoever originated it, was treated necessarily as Ward's. The classes were determined by the form of the verb's three 'radicals': present tense, past tense and past participle:

- (i) verbs with all three radicals the same, e.g. *read*
- (ii) verbs with first and third the same, e.g. *run*
- (iii) verbs with second and third the same, e.g. *esteem*
- (iv) verbs with all three different, e.g. *write*.[1]

Those, like James White, 1761, who took over these classes as a system of conjugations, kept them unchanged at the traditional number of four. But the majority of writers, who took them over as a classification of irregular verbs, omitted the third class, which they regarded as regular. Abraham Crocker, 1771, seems to have been the first to use Ward's classification in this way, and he was followed by ten later grammarians.

Lowth classified irregular verbs in three groups, with more regard to their formal differences: (i) some, but not all, contracted forms, especially those like *beat* (which he regarded as a contraction of *beated*) where, in fact, the same form appeared in all three positions; (ii) those with forms in -ght, many of which had the same form in two positions; (iii) those with past participle in -en, many of which had different forms in all three positions.[2] Lowth's classification is followed exactly by more than a dozen writers, but many more use one or two of his groups.

Other classifications of irregular verbs all represent attempts to describe systematically the variety of vowel change. Gildon sets up five classes on this basis:

[1] J. Ward, 1758, p. 87. Douglas originally (MSS. No. 585 and No. 587a fol. 277) proposed three conjugations. The system of four first appears in Bundle 1.7. fols. 137–8. Some connection between Douglas and Ward, who were living in London at the same time, is possible. [2] Lowth, 1762, pp. 64 f.

    (i)   verbs of the type *win/won; wind/wound*

    (ii) verbs of the type *fight/fought*

  (iii) verbs of the type *take/took; tread/trod*

  (iv) *give, bid, sit*, only

   (v) verbs of the type *draw/drew*, including *go*.[1]

These five classes were used by Dr Johnson, together with Wallis's first two.

    Joshua Story keeps close to Lowth but treats separately verbs which 'change i short into a, or u, and i long into ou' and have dropped -en in the past participle; such are *begin, bind, cling, come*.[2] Charles Coote makes a careful classification into four groups, with more regard than Story gave to the nature of the formal differences which were the symptoms of irregularity:

    (i)   verbs irregular by contraction, e.g. *bend, flee, sell, sweep*

    (ii) verbs with past participles in -n or -en

  (iii) verbs with u, ou, o before final consonant in past participle, e.g. *hang, begin, wind*

  (iv) verbs with past tense and past participle in -ght.[3]

    John Fell's rather despairing treatment has at least the merit of admitting that the customary definition of an irregular verb involved the grammarian in a much more difficult task than was generally recognised. Three of Fell's four classes adopt the usual approach, but he makes a separate class also of verbs whose past tense and past participle have a vowel less than the present, e.g. *bleed, flee*. But this is as far as he can go. His fifth class comprises a hundred and eight verbs which are 'variously irregular', including *am, buy, catch, shake, shrink*.[4]

    The most determined attempt to bring order out of irregularity is made by P. W. Fogg, who sets up twelve classes of irregular verbs, largely by distinguishing different formations in -n and -en. They show clearly the weakness of even a careful empiricism which is supported by no historical knowledge.[5] It is fair to contrast Fogg's elaborate analysis with the comment by John Collyer, also a thoughtful grammarian, in 1735, that the irregular past tense 'is formed by leaving out the e final when the Affirmation ends with it, as *hide, hid*,

---

[1] G–B, 1711, pp. 114–16.   [2] Story, 1778, p. 40.
[3] Coote, 1788, pp. 115–30.   [4] Fell, 1784, pp. 48–57.
[5] Fogg, 1792, pp. 144–5.

and sometimes by changing a Letter or two, as *spin, spun*'.[1] During the sixty years between Collyer and Fogg grammarians had been looking at verbs with enough care to make it impossible for the author even of an elementary work to dismiss their variety as a matter of 'changing a letter or two'.

The only writer who argues that all verb-forms are natural, and therefore none can be regarded as irregular, is Rowland Jones, whom it is a pleasure to quote, for once, with approval. In *The Circles of Gomer* he examines what are in effect Lowth's three classes according to the following principle: 'Instead of laying down rules for the establishment of error or forcing our language from its natural state of precision to the arbitrary modes and forms of languages with which it has but a very small connection, I shall endeavour to rescue her from such violence.'[2] It must, however, be said that the arguments by which Jones seeks to establish that there are no irregular verbs do not exemplify the linguistic purity of his intentions.

CONJUGATION

More than a hundred and thirty grammarians discuss irregular verbs; only twenty-seven, seven of them in the seventeenth century, set up conjugations. There is little coherence or development in the use of this category.

Bullokar makes three conjugations out of (*a*) active and neuter verbs; (*b*) the verb *to be*; (*c*) auxiliary verbs. But this is not a pattern which anyone follows. Tomkis, who here differs from Jonson, says there is only one conjugation: verbs with the past tense and past participle in -ed or -d; all other verbs are irregular. Conjugation and regularity are already overlapping categories, and Tomkis' view is expressed throughout the period: for example, by John Wesley, 1748, by Dr Johnson, and by William Ward, 1765.

Ben Jonson begins his scheme of conjugations with the distinction between verbs which form the past tense by adding -ed and those which form it 'by the only change of his Letters, namely of Vowels alone, or Consonants also'.[3] If it had not been for the precedent of Latin Jonson would probably have kept just to these two conjugations. He achieves four by making separate conjugations of verbs with past

---

[1] Collyer, 1735, p. 64. [2] R. Jones, 1771, p. 15.
[3] Jonson, 1640, Bk I. chap. 17.

tenses in -d or -t, and of those in which the changed vowel is a diphthong.[1]

Grammarians who kept to two conjugations include Cooper, 1685; Aickin, 1693; Entick, 1728; Elphinston, 1765. Entick seems to equate his conjugations with active and passive verbs; the others, generally speaking, make their conjugations correspond with verbs whose past participles end in -(e)d and -en.

Gill sets up his conjugations in the way which, with its variants, became the basis for the classification (according to the writer's point of view) of either conjugations or irregular verbs. He makes three conjugations:

    (i)   verbs which have no change except into -ed
    (ii) other verbs which change in one position, e.g. *run*
    (iii) other verbs which change in two positions, e.g. *speak*.[2]

Gill's first conjugation corresponds to the regular verbs of most grammarians, and his second and third conjugations to the most frequent classes of irregular verbs. His scheme closely resembles that of Douglas and John Ward, 1758;[3] Gill's first conjugation corresponds to Ward's third; his second to Ward's second; his third to Ward's fourth. Douglas and Ward differ only in making a separate conjugation of verbs, like *read*, in which there is no visible change at all.

The assumption that English must have four conjugations is vividly illustrated by James Howell, behind whose classification no criterion can be seen except, perhaps, the crudest imitation of Latin; 'There are', he says, 'in English, as in other languages, fower cadences and Conjugations of Verbs':

    (i)   those ending in *-all* or *-are* or *-ace*
    (ii) those ending in *-eare*, *-ease*, *-ead*, *-ind*, *-end*
    (iii) those ending in *-ite*, *-ight*, *-ell*, *-ink*
    (iv) those ending in *-y*, *-ire*, *-ine*.[4]

Daniel Duncan admits the artificiality of the category: 'There is in [English] scarcely any such thing as strict Conjugations...However, if we must have Conjugations as well as our Neighbours, they...will

---

[1] op. cit. chaps. 19 and 20. Evelyn's account of the conjugations resembles Jonson's very closely.
[2] Gill, 1619, pp. 47–9.   [3] See above, p. 437.
[4] Howell, 1662, pp. 56–7.

be of those Verbs where the Participle Passive ends in 1.D 2.T 3.N 4.G or K.'[1]

Samuel Saxon has the same classification, except that it is based on the past tense, and his fourth conjugation ends in 'anything else'.[2]

The fusion of the categories *conjugation* and *irregular verb* is seen very clearly in the grammars by John Bell, 1769, and Thomas Coar, 1796. Bell's third and fourth conjugations, and Coar's second and third, are identical with Lowth's second and third classes of irregular verbs: those which form the past participle in *-ght* and in *-en*.

CONCLUSION

English verbs vary so much that any adequate classification which could have been achieved before the nineteenth century must have attempted to set up classes based either on the historical development of verb-forms (a diachronic classification) or on their contemporary spelling and pronunciation (a synchronic classification). Much of the material necessary for a diachronic classification was available to the eighteenth-century grammarians, but they were only slowly acquiring a historical view of language. Those who attempted any classification were considering, almost exclusively, the contemporary forms of the verb, but here also they lacked the attitude appropriate to such an undertaking: rigorous concentration on the present without reference to other languages or to standards of correctness—an attitude which has in our own day produced marvels of austere systematisation. So also with regularity. Any concept of regularity implies a norm. This norm could have been determined either historically or according to contemporary usage. The former approach was open to the early grammarians in so far as the necessary material was available, but closed to them for lack of an adequate conception of how languages developed. Here also they were left to rely on tradition or on common sense. The evidence quoted in this section shows how little the tradition could help. Common sense at least prevented meaningless classification, and the voice of common sense may for once speak through Charles Wiseman:

There is no ascertaining how many Conjugations the English Verbs properly consist of, and those who have limited them to four, do at the

[1] Duncan, 1731, pp. 21–2.   [2] Saxon, 1737, p. 59.

441

same Time admit, that 'there are many Verbs which may be conjugated so as to belong either to the third or to the fourth Conjugation', which I apprehend is seldom, if ever, the case with other languages, and therefore if it be so in ours, it were better in my opinion not to give any account at all than to be at such an uncertainty about them, and only to distinguish our Verbs in general, as they really are, into regular and irregular. (Wiseman, 1764, p. 151.)

15. OTHER PARTS OF SPEECH

Of all the parts of speech, the conjunctions are the most
unfriendly to vivacity.   GEORGE CAMPBELL[1]

'UNDECLINED' PARTS OF SPEECH:
THEIR INSTABILITY

Both in the tradition and in the English grammars the boundaries
are not always clear between the adverb, the conjunction, the preposition and the interjection, as can be seen from Appendix II,
pp. 530–5. Most English grammarians thought there was little
difficulty about these 'undeclined' parts of speech. Horne
Tooke showed unusual perceptiveness and spirit in running away
from school at the age of ten because, amongst other reasons, 'his
master was utterly unfit to instruct *him*: for although he might
perhaps know what a noun and a verb was, yet he understood
nothing about a preposition or conjunction'.[2]

The Greek grammarians always, and later grammarians often, had
treated interjections as adverbs;[3] the difficulty of distinguishing
between adverbs and conjunctions is regularly referred to by both
Latin and English grammarians, and Charles Butler makes even
conjunctions, as well as interjections, a sub-class of adverbs.[4] These
uncertainties are expressed in the very first of the English grammars:
'The voice of an adverb joining words, clauses or sentences together
is a Conjunction: but governing any case is a preposition. And these
be the three special points to be noted, how to know these three parts
of speech asunder.'[5] Wallis's indifference about the classification of
conjunctions and adverbs has already been quoted.[6] James Greenwood translates Wallis verbatim, and others follow him: 'If any shall
reckon some of these Words as Adverbs, and some of the Adverbs as
Conjunctions, they being often used in both Senses, there will be no

---

[1] *Philosophy of Rhetoric* (1776), 1841, Bk IV. chap. 3. § 2.
[2] Alex. Stephens. *Memoirs of J. H. Tooke*, 1813, I. p. 20.
[3] Above, pp. 73 and 76.   [4] Above, p. 207.
[5] Bullokar, 1586, p. 368.   [6] Above, p. 204.

great Harm done.'[1] A similar indifference is expressed by Mark Lewis, but more recklessly:

To enumerate Adverbs and Conjunctions, as we do Pronouns and Prepositions, is tedious; to know them by their second Notion, is very difficult: Therefore I propose this Rule, which is not much above Sense. Whatsoever English word is not a Noun, Pronoun, Verb, Participle nor Preposition, is an Adverb or Conjunction: it matters not much which the Child calls it, only if the word, found under none of those five former heads, do begin a Sentence, it is a Conjunction; if it be in the middle of a Sentence, probably it is an Adverb. This is also obvious to Sense. (*Essay*, 1670?, p. 4.)[2]

Other expressions of uncertainty are frequent:

Adverbs are 'many of them put under this class of words because we do not know what else to call them'.[3]

The distinguishing of all these different kinds of particles, is not always very material. Sometimes the same word may be accounted of one kind, sometimes of another; it is frequently enough if they be known by the general denomination of particle. (*Only True Guide*, 1779, p. 13.)

The adverb can never be strictly and justly considered as a distinct part of speech; for there is not an adverb, which may not be found either among the nouns, pronouns, adjectives, verbs, participles or prepositions. (Fell, 1784, p. 67.)

Fell is here echoing Horne Tooke, who called the adverb 'that common sink and repository of all heterogeneous unknown corruptions',[4] and similar views are expressed by writers up to and beyond the end of the eighteenth century. In 1803 Mark Meilan still needs to say: 'It is necessary that the learner should be informed, what embarrassment Grammarians undergo, in ascertaining whether many words, by some considered as Conjunctions, ought to have such name, or that of adverbs.'[5]

The absence of case-inflection in English nouns made the distinction between preposition and adverb less clear than it was in Latin. Any attempt to subordinate English to Latin produced, in this instance, absurdity so gross that it could hardly be persisted in. Joshua Poole, in 1646, shows an obstinate subservience to Latin when with the preposition *de* in mind, he says that *of* in English governs

---

[1] Greenwood, 1737, p. 103, translating Wallis, 1653, p. 110.
[2] 'Second notion' is reasoning; 'obvious to sense', i.e. 'ascertainable by direct observation'.
[3] Collyer, 1735, p. 78.   [4] Tooke, (1786) 1829, I. 430.
[5] Meilan, 1803, p. 120 n.

only the ablative case.[1] But another Latiniser, John Stirling, makes the same statement even in 1735.[2] The usual way in which uncertainty about the preposition is expressed appears first in Bullokar also: 'A Preposition is of divers voices...alway governing an accusative case, otherwise it is an adverb.'[3] Statements of this kind occur regularly before 1750 and are not unknown at the end of the century. John Williams, for instance, about 1780, says that prepositions...

> Words unite
> And their Relations show.
> When they to be Connectives cease,
> They into Adverbs grow. (Williams, *c.* 1780, p. 9.)

And Barrie, in 1794, says that prepositions become adverbs when, as in *root up*, they are 'subjoined to verbs'.[4] Haywood, in 1800, calls *after* in 'Soon after [i.e. afterwards] he broke his arm' a preposition, and is forced to suppose an ellipsis: 'Soon after (this) he broke his arm', so as to provide the preposition with an object.[5] Some writers emphasise the distinction between prefixed and detached forms. Although the function of *up* in *to root up* is presumably the same as in *to uproot*, in the former it would be called an adverb and in the latter, with a rather antiquarian literalism, a preposition. Bishop Wilkins states the problem:

The difference between these two parts of speech, Prepositions and Adverbs, being so nice, that it is hard in some cases to distinguish them, upon which 'tis questioned, whether every Preposition as it compounds a Verb, do not put on the nature of an Adverb; and it seems to be so, because it modifies the Act after the same manner as Adverbs do, as in the words *Praeficio, Benefacio,* &c. (Wilkins, 1668, p. 312.)

This comment of Wilkins is only the earliest in the English grammars of a number, especially at the end of the eighteenth century, which show a hesitant willingness to treat verb and preposition as a single unit. John Sedger argues not only that the preposition may be taken with the verb but that a verb is implied in the use of every preposition:

It may be observed, that where a preposition occurs in English, the noun to which it applies, will be in the objective case; but it is not because a preposition occurs that a noun is in the objective case...It is because whenever a preposition does occur, a verb...is present or understood, or

---

[1] Poole, 1646, p. 19.
[2] Stirling, 1735, sig. C 1 verso
[3] Bullokar, 1586, p. 371.
[4] Barrie, 1794, p. 298.
[5] Haywood, 1800, p. 29.

may be taken in before the noun without destroying the sense, and the noun is in the objective case, on account of the verb, and not by reason of the preposition. (Sedger, 1798, pp. 35–6.)

He then makes the more constructive point: 'The preposition conveys an idea of the direction or mode of effect of the verb or action, in respect to the location of the *object*, and, consequently, when a preposition occurs, the noun before which it stands must be in the objective case.'[1] What Sedger recommends is implied also by Mrs Mercy[2] and put into practice by Abbé Gaultier,[3] who, in his analysis of the sentence 'Le chagrin rongeur monte sur les chars ornés de bronze', calls *monte sur* the verb.

John Kirkby, whose novel definitions tend to increase rather than to diminish confusion, blurs the distinction between preposition and adverb in a way which is emphatic but still within the tradition: 'A Preposition is an Adverb, which may also come before a Name, expressing it to have some particular Relation or Situation with Respect to another Thing.'[4] Lowth makes the same point, and extends still further the area of uncertainty: 'As the Preposition subjoined to the Verb hath the construction and nature of an Adverb, so the Adverbs *here*, *there*, *where*, with a Preposition subjoined, as *hereof*, *therewith*, *whereupon*, have the construction and nature of Pronouns.'[5] Similarly, John Dalton, following Harris,[6] seeks to blur the distinction between preposition and conjunction:

As the only distinction between conjunctions and prepositions is, that the former connect one *sentence* to another, whilst the latter connect one or more *words* to a sentence; it is no wonder if the same connective term be used for both purposes. Accordingly we have several instances of the same word being used at one time as a conjunction and at another time as a preposition; but late writers, having adopted the false notions and distinctions of language of the Greek and Latin grammarians, have endeavoured to separate the prepositions and conjunctions into distinct classes, and to keep them apart as much as possible. (Dalton, 1801, p. 84.)

John Hunter, in a paper which was read to the Royal Society of Edinburgh in 1784, argued, in effect, that some conjunctions in English, Latin and Greek were merely a special case of the preposition, and that the preposition in some instances could not usefully

---

[1] ibid.
[2] Mercy, 1799, I. 67.
[3] Below, p. 488.
[4] Kirkby, 1746, p. 104.
[5] Lowth, 1762, pp. 130–1
[6] Harris, 1751, Bk II. chap. 2.

be distinguished from the adverb. His English examples, which illustrate this part of the argument, include:

I came *after* he departed (conjunction)
I came *after* his departure (preposition)
Wisdom he has, and, *to* his wisdom, courage (preposition)
Wisdom he has, and courage *too* (adverb)

He maintained, therefore, that such distinctions in the classification of words into parts of speech were unscientific: 'The *classing disparate phaenomena*, and referring them to one common principle, is held to be *science* in *Physics*—and why should it not also be accounted *science* in *Grammar?*'[1]

It was natural that many grammarians should seek to resolve the awkwardness of these overlapping categories by amalgamating them into one, an arrangement for which the tradition contained at least two tentative precedents. The logician's view was the older of these precedents: noun and verb are the only kinds of word which have meaning on their own; the rest had meaning only in relation to other words. Although this view derived from Aristotle it was first proposed in a purely grammatical setting by Priscian, who did not, even so, use it in his primary classification of the parts of speech.[2] The medieval grammarians frequently referred to the conjunction and preposition as mere connectives and not full words, but they also treated this as a logical, and not primarily a grammatical, classification.[3] The second precedent was that of Ramus, whose primary distinction between noun (including pronoun) and verb, on the one hand, and the remaining parts of speech on the other, was based not on logic but on the formal expression of number.[4] These two precedents were blended by Sanctius, whose *Minerva*, in 1587, first made a primary grammatical category of the particle, comprising adverb, conjunction and preposition (he did not recognise the interjection as a part of speech).

The tables in Appendix II show that there are 59 English grammars in which the particle, sometimes firmly, sometimes hesitantly, is offered as a primary category. In 48 of these grammars the constituents of the particle include the adverb, conjunction, preposition and interjection. In addition to these 59 grammars there are at least

---

[1] John Hunter, 'A Grammatical Essay on the Nature, Import and Effect of certain Conjunctions', *Transactions of the Royal Society of Edinburgh*, 1784, p. 20.
[2] Above, p. 49. [3] Above, p. 51. [4] Above, p. 52.

another 15 in which several, if not all, of these parts of speech are casually described as particles without there being any attempt to combine them into a single category. The grammars in which the particle is made a primary category are not evenly distributed over the period. Nearly two-thirds of them appear between 1695 and 1760. A primary category of particle is one of the features of the reforming vernacular systems and the popularity of the category died with the movement of reform.

ADVERB

The Alexandrian influence in the tradition had restricted the category of adverb to those words which modified the verb.[1] This restriction, however, was fully effective only in the definitions. Words which could modify verbs were incidentally referred to as adverbs even when they were modifying other parts of speech. The restriction proved unhelpful, and began to weaken during the renaissance period. Nevertheless signs of it are not uncommon among the English grammars up till about 1775; it appears in *The True Method*, 1696; Clare, 1699; Saxon, 1737; Wesley, 1748; Monboddo, 1774. After 1775 it is rare but not unknown. In 1781 Martin Trinder, for example, is still protesting that 'the common definition' wrongly restricts the adverb to use with verbs,[2] and Hallifax, G. Brown and Fordyce restrict its modifying function to the verb alone. A final attempt to enforce the restriction involves John Sedger in a discussion of whether it is permissible (as he would like) to modify an adjective by another adjective, as in 'an extraordinary fine horse': 'I might be told to use the adverb *extraordinarily*; but I use *extraordinary* to heighten the quality, why then should I use an adverb?'[3] Sedger admits that existing rules forbid him to modify an adjective by another adjective. He considers it unreasonable, therefore, that they should permits him to modify an adverb by another adverb—'That man speaks remarkably hastily'. He proposes alternatives: 'He speaks remarkably hasty...remarkable hastily...in a remarkable hasty manner...which latter seems to be the proper English idiom.'[4] Sedger's difficulty was as old as Priscian: he was the prisoner of his own definition. If he wished to keep the definition, but was unwilling to tolerate even the slight inconsistency which Priscian allowed[5] (far

---

[1] Above, pp. 73–4.   [2] Trinder, 1781, p. 86.
[3] Sedger, 1798, p. 80.   [4] op. cit. p. 81.   [5] Above, p. 74.

less the gross inconsistencies which arose from the unthinking application of the definition to English) there was only one line to take: if the idiom of the language did not fit the definition the language must be changed.

When the adverb was conceived as modifying other kinds of words besides the verb there was at first, among the English grammarians, some uncertainty about its range. In the seventeenth century it was most frequently said to modify verbs and nouns (i.e. nouns adjective). A few writers, such as Greaves and Lye, said merely that it modified 'other words'. By the end of the century Richard Brown had expressed what remained the usual formula for the next hundred years: '...joyn'd to a Verb, Participle, Adjective, and sometimes to another Adverb'.[1]

It had been recognised early in the tradition that the adverb (which then included the interjection) could function as the equivalent of a longer expression,[2] but practically no attention was paid to this characteristic in the early English grammars. The most that Wallis, for example says is that some adverbs 'sunt...Periphrases, ut, *diu*, a longwhile'.[3] It was the Port Royal grammar of 1660 which made explicit the point taken up later by several English grammarians: 'Le désir que les hommes ont d'abréger le discours, est ce qui a donné lieu aux Adverbes.'[4] *Sapienter*, the authors point out, is the equivalent of *cum sapientia*. This was expanded by Lane, but with no obvious debt to Port Royal: 'There are some words that are Abbreviatures of two or three Parts of Speech, which the Grammarians call Adverbs of time and place.'[5] Gildon and Brightland, *The English Accidence*, 1733, *The Complete Letter Writer*, 1755, and five later grammars, repeat the view, and sometimes the words, of the Port Royal grammar: 'Adverbs seem originally to have been contrived to express compendiously in one Word, what must otherwise have required two or more.'[6]

Daniel Duncan states clearly the influence of Latin and is prepared to treat the adverb as a functional, and not at all a formal, category: 'Most of these compounded Adverbs are nothing else but phrasaical Expressions...which have crept into the List of Adverbs, by reason of some Latin Adverb answering to them in Signification; as

---

[1] R. Brown, 1700, p. 107.
[2] Above, pp. 73 and 137.
[3] Wallis, 1653, p. 110.
[4] *Grammaire Générale*, 1660, Bk 2. chap. 11.
[5] Lane, 1700, p. 58.
[6] *Complete Letter Writer*, 1755, p. 27.

Utinam, God grant, or I wish.'[1] He also readily treats as adverbs 'to speak *plain*...to feel *soft*...*by chance*...*on the right side*...to chop *Logick*'.[2] Priestley puts the matter more shortly; adverbs are 'contractions for other words, or rather clusters of words',[3] and in 1768 he uses the popular expression: adverbs are 'contractions of sentences, or clauses of a sentence'.[4] This way of putting it appears also in *A Vocabulary*, 1765; Barlow, 1772; Harrison, 1777; Gentleman, 1788, and Fogg, 1796. The final extension of this view of the adverb is made by Horne Tooke, whose central purpose is to prove that all words except the substantive and verb are 'the wheels of language, the wings of Mercury...abbreviations employed for the sake of dispatch'.[5]

Such was the death and apotheosis of a useful descriptive procedure. What had begun as a statement about equivalence of meaning (and therefore an aid to flexibility of interpretation and expression) ended as a theory about the origin of word-forms, hotly argued by Horne Tooke and his many followers at temperatures to which Mercury never rose.

Classification. The English grammarians added nothing (there could be nothing to add) to the detailed and unrestrained classifications of the adverb found throughout the tradition. Nor did they refine the process of classification. *The English Accidence*, 1733, lists forty-one kinds of adverb, but although the grammarians recognised, increasingly, that there are 'as many kinds of adverb as there are circumstances of an action',[6] even at the end of the eighteenth century lists of fifteen and twenty are not uncommon: Groombridge, 1797, gives nineteen; Mrs Mercy, 1799, gives twenty-two; Haywood, 1800, gives thirteen. The more usual number is between five and ten, and a representative list, given by George Stapleton in 1797, is: adverbs of time, place, number, order, quantity, affirming, denying, doubting, comparing.

Terminology. The term *adverb* seems to have been acceptable to the reformers, and there is no sustained attempt to replace it.
Added word. Gildon and Brightland sometimes use *added word* for *adverb*,[7] but they abandon the innovation after the first edition. It

---

[1] Duncan, 1731, p. 38.
[2] ibid.
[3] Priestley, 1762, p. 64.
[4] Priestley, 1768, p. 27.
[5] Horne Tooke (1786), 1829, I. 24.
[6] Bicknell, 1790, p. 79.
[7] G–B, 1711, pp. 71, 119.

appears as an alternative descriptive term in *The Young Mathe-matician's Logic*, 1760.

Adjunct. For 'Mica's' use of this term for what may be the adverb see above, p. 272.

Adnoun. Cave Beck in one place refers to *adnoun* as an alternative to *adverb*; 'An Adverb is a part of speech, joyned to Verbs or Nouns (whence some call them Adnouns)'.[1] This seems to be a con-fusion between *adnoun*, in its normal sense of *adjective*,[2] and a category (such as Mark Lewis's use of *manner*[3] and the later term *qualifier* sometimes indicated) which would combine adjective and adverb.

Manner. For Lodowyck's possible use of *manner* to refer to the adverb see above, p. 213. Collyer similarly makes it almost the name of a part of speech when he uses 'Manners of being, &c.' as a deliber-ately vernacular description to take the place of *adverb*.[4]

CONJUNCTION

The traditional uncertainty whether to define the conjunction as oining sentences only, or both words and sentences,[5] is apparent in the English grammars also. The uncertainty is temporarily resolved at the end of the eighteenth century.

Three principal definitions are used in the English tradition: the conjunction joins (*a*) words only; (*b*) sentences only; (*c*) words or sentences. In addition about twenty grammars say more vaguely that conjunctions join 'words and parts of sentences'.

There are at least half a dozen grammars, scattered throughout the period, which say that conjunctions 'join words'. Howell, for instance, says that they 'tie words together',[6] and T.M., in *The Grammarian's Vademecum*, a century later, says they 'unite words'.[7] Such definitions might be taken as including, loosely, sentences as well as single words, but the view that the conjunction joins *only* words is one of the oldest and most persistent parts of the tradition, and some English grammarians, even towards the end of the eighteenth century, still felt it necessary to protest explicitly against

---

[1] Beck, 1657, p. 26.
[2] See above, p. 314.
[3] See above, p. 213.
[4] Collyer, 1735, p. 2.
[5] Above, pp. 62–4.
[6] Howell, 1662, p. 17.
[7] T.M. 1774, p. 19.

it. Buchanan, for example, in 1762 includes in his catechetical exchanges:

Q. Does the Conjunction join Words together?
A. No.

Monboddo, followed by later writers, similarly says that though the conjunction often seems to connect words it really joins sentences.[1] Many writers, in fact, wished to confine the term to words which were joining sentences. This restriction seems to have originated with Scaliger, and to have been emphatically reinforced by Sanctius' *Minerva* in 1587.[2] James Harris tries to establish Aristotle's authority for the restriction, arguing from passages in the *Poetics* and the *Rhetoric*, but he interprets Aristotle too narrowly in both places.[3] The restriction was not quickly applied to English. Bishop Wilkins hesitated: conjunctions, according to him, 'serve for the joyning together of words, or rather of sentences'.[4] The first English grammar in which it appears is Lane's universal grammar of 1695, where the conjunction is described as 'a Particle that denotes the Connexion or joining of two Verbs, or (which is the same) of two Sentences together'.[5] The equivalent definition is given in *The True Method* of 1696 and in Lane's more strictly English grammar of 1700. The first English grammarian to support the restriction by argument is Michael Maittaire, using the illustration *Honour thy father and mother*. 'The Conjunction', he says,

supplies what one part wants, out of the other...and therefore where the Conjunction joins only two words expressed, there are really two Clauses or Sentences, whereof if but one is expressed at full, it maketh up, what in the other is wanting, and, to avoid a needless repetition of the same words, understood. (Maittaire, 1712, p. 96.)[6]

Many other writers argue on the same lines. John Collyer says that in *Marlborough and Eugene did beat the French* the word *and* 'compounds the Affirmation', so that the full form of the sentence is *Marlborough did beat the French and Eugene did beat the French.*[7] Lowth argues that: '*You, and I, and Peter, rode to London*, is one Sentence made up of these

---

[1] Monboddo, 1774, p. 178. Cf. *Comprehensive View*, 1794, p. 26.
[2] Above, p. 64.
[3] Harris, 1751, Bk 2. chap. 2 ad init.   [4] Wilkins, 1668, p. 314.
[5] Lane, 1695, p. 23.
[6] This line of reasoning would seem to require that *and* should be called a kind of pronoun.
[7] Collyer, 1735, p. 86.

three by the Conjunction *and* twice employed; *You rode to London; I rode to London; Peter rode to London.*[1] This illustration, in various forms, was used by nearly twenty later writers.[2]

Up till 1740 less than a third of the relevant grammars follow Sanctius in restricting the conjunction to use with sentences. During the next thirty years this restriction grew more popular and was adopted in about half the grammars. But its popularity suddenly waned, and of the grammars published between 1790 and 1801, only ten per cent follow Sanctius. The change cannot be attributed to any particularly influential author, though the forceful illustration in Richard Postlethwaite's *The Grammatical Art Improved* may have influenced writers at the end of the century: 'It is not indeed true, that Conjunctions *always* connect Sentences...If *A*, *B*, and *C* form a triangle, *A* is not a Triangle, *B* is not a Triangle, *C* is not a Triangle.'[3] A similar refutation of Sanctius is proposed by the writer in the third edition of the *Encyclopaedia Britannica*, who uses the example, *A man of wisdom and virtue is a perfect character.* This, he says, 'is not resolvable into two'.[4]

Classification. Like the adverb, the conjunction can be classified under as many labels as there are conjunctions. The full vigour of this traditional activity had waned by the eighteenth century. The only fresh approach was that of James Harris, who introduced a distinction between connecting sentences (as is done by *and* and *but*) and connecting meanings (which is done by *and*, not by *but*).[5] This was an attempt to circumvent the paradox of the disjunctive conjunction, which was a longstanding difficulty. Most grammarians who make any classification at all propose the two groups copulative and disjunctive; others more usefully make a threefold division into conjunctive, disjunctive and adversative, so as to cover the three common words *and*, *or* and *but*. The three most frequent labels after these are causal, conditional and illative (*therefore*). The absurdity of still further classification is brought out especially by Horne Tooke, who lists thirty-eight 'kinds' of conjunction in order to illustrate 'that farrago of useless distinctions...which explain nothing; and

---

[1] Lowth, 1762, p. 92.
[2] This kind of discussion has modern equivalents. Cf. N. Chomsky, *Syntactic Structures*, 1957, § 5.2.
[3] Postlethwaite, 1795, p. 144.   [4] *Enc. Brit.* (B), 1797, p. 78.
[5] Harris, 1751, pp. 240 f.

serve only to throw a veil over the ignorance of those who employ them'.[1]

Terminology. The only innovation comes again from Gildon and Brightland. In their first edition they use *conjunction* in the notes (which are translated from Wallis and the Port Royal grammar) and sometimes *joining word* in the text.[2] But in later editions *joining word* is dropped in favour of the non-committal phrase 'the third sort [of particle]'.[3] Collyer is the only later grammarian to use *joining word* as the name of the category and not just as an explanatory description.[4]

PREPOSITION

The most important, and the most obvious, fact about the preposition would seem to be that it expresses a relation. This fact is recognised in the tradition, principally by the speculative grammarians, but is given no prominence.[5] The function of the preposition was traditionally 'to be set before' another word; the grammarian's eye was fastened not on the preposition itself but on the word it governed. When Donatus says that a preposition 'changes, adds to or takes away from the meaning of words to which it is prefixed' he is describing as a change of meaning what is more certainly a change of form.[6] This can be illustrated more easily in English than in Latin. In *the priests were walking near the town* and *the priests were walking in the town* there is no formal change to express the 'government' of the two prepositions, as there is in *sacerdotes prope oppidum (in oppido) ambulabant.* Nor is the meaning of *town* changed. It would be truer to say that here the prepositions change the meaning of *were walking* and to say in general that the preposition 'adds to or takes away from the meaning of words *after* which it is used'. *Walk-near* and *walk-in* distinguish two kinds of walking. The early grammarians were aware of this backward reference of the preposition: it underlies their frequent comments about the similarity between preposition and adverb. But hardly any of them considered an alternative analysis, partly because the change of case kept their attention on the noun; partly because the idea of relation had seldom been applied

---

[1] Horne Tooke, (1786) 1829, I. 111.
[2] G–B, 1711, pp. 71, 118.
[3] G–B, 1712, p. 103.
[4] Collyer, 1735, p. 2.
[5] Above, pp. 65–6.
[6] ibid.

to language; partly, and principally, because the idea that there could be 'alternative analyses' was not available to them.

A modest attempt was made by William Scott, an eighteenth-century Edinburgh schoolmaster, to recognise in a definition the adjectival and adverbial function of the phrase formed by a preposition. The preposition, he says, 'always requires another part of speech after it, with which it expresses a circumstance of some word or words preceding it'.[1] Scott adds a footnote suggesting that this was an original definition: 'This definition is given rather than the common one, being fully as just, and more easily understood.' To have such a flexible view of the preposition was not, in the 1770s, an entirely trivial achievement. It may owe something to William Ward,[2] but there is no sign that Scott knew Ward's work.

Wallis had reintroduced into the description of the preposition a reference to its expression of relation: 'The Preposition, when it is put before a substantive which is "governed" shows what relation it (the substantive) has to the word—whether a verb, a noun, or some other part of speech—by which it is governed'.[3]

Among the other seventeenth-century English grammarians only Bishop Wilkins comes near to Wallis's point. Wilkins, in his discussion of universal grammar, says that 'the proper office' of the preposition is 'to joyn Integral with Integral on the same side of the Copula'.[4] Wallis and Wilkins were explicitly using logical relations in the analysis of language. It is probable that Wilkins was more directly influenced by the Port Royal grammar than by Wallis (but the Port Royal grammar itself owed much to Wallis). The Port Royal chapter on the preposition is almost wholly devoted to an analysis of the different relations (*rapports*) expressed by the French prepositions.[5] The other English grammarians meantime continued with the customary description: the preposition is 'set before other parts; either in Apposition or Composition',[6] or it 'expresses some Circumstance or other of the Noun'.[7] It is Gildon and Brightland, thanks to

---

[1] Scott 1786, p. lv; 1789, p. 406; 1793, p. 18 n.

[2] See below, p. 457.

[3] Wallis, 1653, chap. 4 (p. 73): 'Praepositio enim, Substantivo quod regitur praefixa, ostendit quem habeat illud respectum ad vocem illam (sive verbum sit, sive nomen, aliave orationis pars) a qua regitur.'

[4] Wilkins, 1668, p. 309.   [5] *Grammaire Générale*, 1660, Bk 2. chap. 10

[6] Wharton, 1654, p. 58; Newton, 1669, p. 51; Newton, 1677, p. 16; Lye, 1671, p. 134; Aickin, 1693, Pt 2, p. 5; Clare, 1690, p. 97.

[7] Miege, 1688, p. 7.

their extensive borrowings from both Wallis and Port Royal, who preserve the reference to relation. Prepositions 'are Expressions of the Relations of Names to Names'.[1] Gildon makes no attempt to relate this statement to the syntactic definition he gives later: prepositions 'may be known by making compleat Sense with a Word [i.e. a verb], or a Quality deriv'd from a Word [i.e. a participle] before it, and a Name with some of the Signs of its States after it, as, *I speak to him*, not *I speak to he*'.[2] Some grammarians give several definitions of the same part of speech in a more or less conscious effort to express its complexity. There is no sign that Gildon is taking this amount of thought. He is here a compiler, not a grammarian. James Greenwood, however, whose grammar appeared in the same year as Gildon and Brightland's, uses Wallis with more understanding. He gives two definitions of the preposition, both relying on the idea of relation, but one regarding it as a relation between words and the other as a relation between things:

a Part of Speech, which being added to any other Parts of Speech, serves to mark or signify their State or Reference to each other. (Greenwood, 1711, p. 71.)

a Word added to other Words, to shew the Respect, or Relation one Thing has to another. (op. cit. p. 72).

This alternation between word and thing persists in the treatment of the preposition throughout the period. A majority of writers say that the preposition expresses a relation between words, but there are always some who say that it expresses not only 'the circumstances of things' but also a relation between them. Soon after Greenwood the emphasis on relation becomes suddenly much more common. Of the relevant grammars written before 1740 only a quarter refer in their definitions to the expression of relation, but over the rest of the period the proportion is a little below three-quarters.

The most interesting discussions of the preposition derive from James Harris, whose definition is based on the idea of 'coalescence'. By coalescence he means the relation between adjective and substantive, between adverb and verb, between subject and verb, between verb and object. Harris sees this relation as being more than grammatical; it corresponds to relations in the real world: 'Those Parts of Speech unite of themselves in Grammar, whose original Archetypes unite of themselves in Nature.'[3] A preposition is: '...a

[1] G–B, 1711, p. 83.   [2] G–B, 1711, p. 121.   [3] Harris, 1751, p. 263.

Part of Speech, devoid itself of Signification, but so formed as to unite two Words that are significant, and that refuse to coalesce or unite of themselves'.[1] He illustrates 'this connective Power (which relates to Words only, and not Sentences)' by a heavily demonstrative sentence: *The splendid Sun genially warmeth the fertile Earth.*

But suppose [he continues] we were desirous to add other Substantives, as for instance, Air, or Beams. How would these co-incide, or under what Character could they be introduced? Not as Nominatives or Accusatives, for both those places are already filled...Not as Attributives...for Attributes by Nature they neither are, nor can be made. Here then we perceive the Rise and Use of Prepositions...Let us assume for instance a pair of these Connectives, *Thro'*, and *With*, and mark their Effect upon the Substances here mentioned. 'The splendid Sun *with* his Beams genially warmeth *thro'* the Air the fertile Earth.' The Sentence, as before, remains intire and one; the Substantives required are both introduced; and not a Word which was there before, is detruded from its proper place. (Harris, 1751, p. 265.)

Harris's difficulty is, again, caused by confusion between word and thing. One of his misconceptions lies in the statement that *air* and *beams* 'attributes by nature...neither are, *nor can be made*'. The *substance* 'beam' cannot be made a *grammatical* attribute, but the *word* 'beam' can. It is as legitimate to say *The beamy sun with his splendour* as it is to say *The splendid sun with his beams.* Nevertheless Harris is directing fresh thought to an important question: the different ways in which a language can express relations. He sees that 'coalescence' and the preposition have similar functions, but he misunderstands the nature of their difference.

William Ward, whose frequent use of the term *coalescence* recalls Harris's *Hermes*, approaches the preposition from a different point of view. He is concerned particularly with its flexibility:

It is obvious to perceive, that they are all expressions of relation, but the difficulty is to determine, how such various kinds of relations amongst objects themselves, can be expressed by one and the same preposition without confusion: and why one and the same relation may be expressed... by the help of different...prepositions. (W. Ward, 1765, p. 243.)

Ward uses as his illustrations the following three expressions:

(i)   The distance of London from York
(ii) The distance from London to York
(iii) The distance between London and York.

[1] op. cit. p. 261.

He says that the difference between these three comes from 'three different modes of estimating one and the same quantity'. He then introduces an analogy with algebra:

This is no more than comes to pass in estimating all kind of quantity, so as to express the result of the process in algebraic species: for we are usually at liberty to proceed several different ways; and yet, if the reasoning is just, we shall always come at last to an expression, which, though different in form, is in effect the same with that which is the result of any other way of proceeding, in which the reasoning is also just. (op. cit. p. 244.)

Ward is in fact saying that though the preposition is not a word without meaning, it is not a word with a clearly determined meaning. It is akin to a variable (though he does not use the term). In language as in algebra: '...a fictitious quantity is always introduced merely to assist the mind in registering the steps of the process; and this quantity is frequently placed in a fictitious state, till the results of the operation arises, in which whatsoever was fictitious is ascertained'.[1] Ward is building on the point emphasised by Harris: that most English prepositions express literally a spatial relation which is then extended to relations between abstract objects between which no such relation can hold. Ward does not follow Harris in treating this as an instance of metaphor; he sees it rather as a process of depriving the preposition of its literal, spatial reference until it has something of the emptiness of an algebraic symbol. It retains from its literal sense a vague suggestion of direction, but its meaning can be discovered only by inference from the meaning of the words it is relating:

The mind perceives, that abstract objects have connexions with each other, which require nearly the same modes of estimation which the relations of local situation do; and therefore, in language, whatsoever connexion is conceived to require the same mode of attention in order to estimate it, is denoted by one and the same sign, and the precise nature of the connexion, as it is in itself, is left to be determined by the judgment, from the nature of the conceptions which are united by the sign. (1765, p. 244.)

Ward's point is simpler than he makes it appear, but he is struggling to express what no earlier grammarian had attempted. The 'emptiness' of some words needs no explanation nowadays, but a simple illustration may show how just Ward's argument is. In each of the

---

[1] W. Ward, 1765, p. 244. For the link between algebra and language see above, p. 370 n.

following titles there is suggested a vaguely 'possessive' direction or, in Ward's terminology, mode, but the meaning of the relation can be understood (if at all) only by inference from the verbal context:

  (i)   *A Dream of Fair Women* (dreamed about)
  (ii) *The Dream of Gerontius* (dreamed by)
  (iii) *A Midsummer Night's Dream* (dreamed on)

The varied uses of the English prepositions had been a long-standing difficulty in teaching Latin and the principal concern of books such as William Walker's *Treatise of English Particles*, 1655, and its many imitations. Ward's originality lies not in drawing attention to this variety of meaning but in offering a good explanation of how the English reader in fact understands the meaning of a word which is apparently empty.

The line of thought from Harris to William Ward seems to have been taken up by Patrick Lynch, who knew Ward's work, though he refers to its definitions as generally 'superfluous, equivocal or obscure'.[1] Lynch classifies prepositions as either 'proper' (those 'which represent the different relations of body') or 'metaphysical' (those 'applied in a metaphorical sense').[2]

Few writers followed Harris in regarding the preposition as meaningless. Horne Tooke, especially, mocked him with a good argument but an illogical, though graphic, illustration: why, if prepositions have no meaning of their own, is there more than one preposition in the language, seeing that there is only one symbol for nought?[3] But Horne Tooke's own theory of language was no more helpful. It required him to explain all prepositions (along with conjunctions and other parts of speech) as corruptions of original nouns and verbs. His obsession with the origins of words blinded him to significant differences in their current use. Even his concession to the schoolmaster was made on formal grounds which are less important (for English) than the logical grounds towards which Harris and William Ward, in their different ways, were both moving. Horne Tooke scorned Harris's admiration for the classics, but his own reference to the teaching situation is more relevant to Latin than to English: 'To the pedagogue, indeed, who must not

---

[1] Lynch, 1796, pp. iv–v.   [2] op. cit. pp. 58–9.
[3] Horne Tooke (1786), 1829, I. 287.

trouble children about the corruption of words, the distinction of prepositions and conjunctions may be useful enough (on account of the cases which they govern when applied to words; and which they cannot govern when applied to sentences).'[1] The distinctive approaches of these three grammarians can be summarised from their own illustrations. Harris uses, but does not discuss, the example *Caius walketh with a staff*.[2] His previous argument commits him to saying that the preposition *with* is a particular kind of connective (one of his primary parts of speech). It has no meaning in itself but its function is to unite *walketh* and *staff*, which cannot coalesce, because *staff* is not an attribute. But his argument carries no weight. In many sentences containing a preposition coalescence is possible; in, for example, *Caius indicated with a staff* the function of *with* cannot be merely to take the place of coalescence, because in *Caius indicated the staff* coalescence has taken place 'naturally'. Harris's approach is, for him, unusually doctrinaire, but is valuable for its emphasis on the preposition's expression of relation. William Ward, in the school version of his grammar, discusses the phrase *a seat before the fire*. His conclusion is perhaps the most illuminating comment about the preposition to be found in any of the English grammars: 'The Preposition *before*, by which the Names *seat* and *fire* are connected, is a Notice to consider *the fire*, in such a Manner as to form a Conception from it which will unite with *Seat* into *one objective Conception*.'[3] Lastly, Horne Tooke, referring to the expression *A house with a party-wall*,[4] is committed to asserting that *with* has intrinsic meaning; that it is a corruption of an original imperative of a Gothic verb wiðan, *to join*; 'that Etymology will give us in all languages, what Philosophy has attempted in vain'.[5]

Terminology. There are few variants:

Adnomen. Christopher Cooper, writing in Latin in 1685, refers to but does not use, the term *adnomen* for prepositions 'quia substantivorum circumstantias limitant'.[6] Horne Tooke quotes the seventeenth-century grammarian Campanella as using the same term,[7] but the English *adnoun* referred normally to the adjective, and exceptionally to the pronoun and adverb.[8]

[1] Horne Tooke (1786), 1829, I, 308. [2] Harris, 1751, p. 267.
[3] W. Ward, 1767, p. 79. [4] op. cit. p. 301. [5] op. cit. p. 299.
[6] Cooper, 1685, p. 109. [7] Horne Tooke (1786), 1829, I. 276 n.
[8] See above, pp. 314 and 451.

Fore placed word. Gildon and Brightland introduced this anglicism in 1711, but dropped it the next year and in later editions.[1] A few supporters of an 'English' terminology tried to keep it going.

Forename. Goldsmith, in his preface to Wiseman's grammar, quoted on p. 314 above, objects to the term *forename*, which presumably means 'preposition' but does not in fact occur in any English grammar.

For-verb. For George Sampson's term, which may mean the preposition, see above, p. 319.

Relation. For 'Mica's' use of *relation* for what may be (or include) the preposition see above, p. 272.

INTERJECTION

The English grammarians continue most of the traditional ways of treating the interjection, and add little to them. Only two radical changes are suggested, and these are scarcely discussed. Groombridge, in 1797, tries to treat them as verbs,[2] and John Dalton, under the influence of Horne Tooke, treats them, without explanation, as a kind of noun.[3] The potentially fruitful analysis which Roger Bacon had applied to the interjection is not found in English.[4] It had dropped out of the tradition which, in rejecting the super-subtleties of scholasticism, lost the benefit also of Bacon's acute linguistic insight. Bacon necessarily expressed his thought about languages in the predominantly logical mode of his day, which was often inappropriate. If he had been less conditioned to logic his analysis could have taken more account of those intentional and expressive aspects of language of which he seems at times tantalisingly, but incompletely, aware.

Very few grammarians deny altogether that the interjection is a part of speech. The most explicit is Lane: 'Those Voices call'd Interjections are not properly words, because they do not signify by the *custom* of any Language, but are Natural Expressions or Signs of the Passions of the mind, and are the same in all Languages, as, *ah, o, oh, ha, he,* &c.'[5] Many more writers disparage interjections, even if they allow them the status of a secondary part of speech. Inter-

---

[1] G–B, 1711, pp. 71, 118, etc. [2] See above, p. 273.
[3] See above, p. 236. [4] See above, pp. 78 f.
[5] Lane, 1700, p. 60. Others adopting the same view are Mark Lewis (in some moods, cf. *Essay*, 1674), *Right Spelling*, 1704, and perhaps Philipps, 1726.

jections are '...that brutal Language, whereby they [the brutes] give hints to one another of anything good or bad';[1] they are 'broken or imperfect words';[2] they are 'no more than an imperfect sound, occasion'd by some suddain motion of our Passions'.[3] Anne Fisher, in 1750, tries to answer a similar objection in Chambers' *Cyclopedia* that interjections are 'mere natural Signs of the Motions ...of the Mind, expressed by these inarticulate Sounds, several whereof the Brutes have in common with us'. Her reply is: 'But as there are Passions, and must be represented in Writing and Discourse, the Interjection has a good Foundation in Nature, and is a Necessary Part of Speech.'[4]

When the interjection was defended it was often on these lines. The interjection was one of the means by which the speaker conveyed his attitude and tone. This modal aspect of language is not so much unrecognised during this period, as undeveloped. Rowland Jones's comment is more perceptive than most: 'Tho' interjections are supposed to add nothing to the sentence, they certainly express the sorts and degrees of energy with which the whole is affirmed.'[5] Another defence is on grounds of fair play: 'Hard indeed has been the Usage of this Class of Words...it is quite unreasonable...to consider these symbols of sensation as no Sort of Words.'[6]

John Fell recognises the variety of interpretation to which interjections are open. He is bothered not by their status (they are parts of speech if they are articulate) but by their use. They are generally thought to be 'clear and obvious', yet 'they are more difficult to be understood than any other part of grammar; so many and so various are the tones and gestures which ought to accompany their application...Grammar may teach a person to read the ideas of Locke; but in its present state, it will never enable him to reach the conceptions of Shakespeare.'[7] The difficulty which is most discussed in the grammars is, in fact, another aspect of the one-word sentence. Even when it was agreed to exclude merely animal ejaculations there was still left the question whether an admitted word, say 'Horror!', was to be called an interjection or a noun. If it was accepted as an interjection how was a line to be drawn between 'Horror!' and 'O Horror!'; between 'O Horror!' and 'O, it is horrible!'? William

---

[1] Lewis, *Essay*, 1674, p. 17.   [2] *Vocabulary*, 1765, sig. b 2 recto.
[3] Sheridan, 1714, p. 129.
[4] Fisher, 2nd edn 1750, pp. 105–6, echoed by Buchanan, 1762, p. 154 n.
[5] R. Jones, 1768, p. 45.   [6] Postlethwaite, 1795, p. 147.   [7] Fell, 1784, p. 74.

Bullokar, in 1586, had classified as interjections expressions such as
'O abominable act!' and 'Away with him!',[1] but few writers were
as broad-minded, or as confused, as this. They saw that there was a
difference between the rhetorical category 'exclamation' and the
grammatical category 'interjection'. To accept the single word
'Horror!' as the exclamatory use of a noun was easy, but the word
'*O*' did not clearly 'belong' to some other part of speech, as *horror*
did. Yet it was difficult to deny *O* its status as a familiar word (its
accent was certainly human). Words of this kind seemed to form a
legitimate class and to justify the continuance of the interjection's
humble post. The uncertainty lasts right through the period. At the
end of the eighteenth century the author of the article on *Grammar*,
rewritten for the third edition of the *Encyclopaedia Britannica* in 1797,
expresses a violent antipathy both to interjections as such and to their
being given the status of parts of speech. He is disagreeing with
Beattie's view that 'Strange!' should be counted an interjection.
It is, he says, still as adjective:

Every one sees, that the exclamation is equivalent to, That is strange, or,
That is a strange story. Real interjections are never employed to convey
truth of any kind. They are not to be found amongst laws, in books of
civil institutions, in history, or in any treatise of useful arts or sciences;
but in rhetoric and poetry, in novels, plays, and romances, where in
English, so far from giving pathos to the style, they have generally an
effect that is disgusting or ridiculous. (*Enc. Brit.* (B), 1797, p. 90, also
numbered 98.)

Other writers, less extreme, sought a compromise in that process of
'becoming' which has bedevilled the whole history and present
teaching of English grammar: 'The Passions are sometimes expressed
by other Words, which by that means, become Interjections, as...
A Mischief on him.'[2]

The standard practice among the English grammarians is to
describe the interjection (in the standard phrase, derived immediately from Linacre but at least as old as the fourth century A.D.) as
'a passion of the mind'. This phrase, or its near equivalents such as
'a sudden emotion (or affection) of the mind', is used by almost every
grammarian throughout the period. So universal is it that when seven
writers during a period of twelve years (between 1762 and 1774) say
'soul' rather than 'mind' the effect is disproportionately startling:

[1] Bullokar, 1586, p. 373.   [2] Raine, 1771, p. 95.

what shift of opinion can be implied by so emphatic a breach of convention? And why do only three grammarians during the rest of the century follow it?

More interesting is the view that the interjection, like the adverb, is a sentence-equivalent. This view appears first in John Wilkins' *Essay towards a Real Character*, in which he calls interjections 'those Substitutive Particles, which serve to supply the room of some sentence or complex part of it'.[1] Mark Lewis calls the interjection 'a contracted sentence',[2] and this is repeated in six grammars during the first half of the eighteenth century. During the rest of the century it is proposed in only two grammars. In the *British Letter Writer*, 1765, interjections are referred to as a 'compendious Way of expressing a whole Sentence in one Word',[3] and Charles Coote repeats another expression of Lewis's, calling the interjection 'a virtual sentence'.[4] This way of regarding the interjection is not found in the tradition, although it obviously resembles the Greek view, in which interjections were classed with those adverbs which acted as sentence modifiers. Its nearer origin is uncertain. Lewis does not write as if he is putting forward a new idea of his own. It may derive from the Port Royal emphasis on 'le désir que les hommes ont d'abréger le discours',[5] though this applied, in the Port Royal grammar, to the adverb and not to the interjection, which is treated in the traditional way. The so-called Port Royal rhetoric, *L'Art de Parler*, 1675, says also, in its discussion of tense, that 'the desire to abbreviate our discourse, is natural to all men',[6] and the logical outlook of Port Royal certainly favoured this emphasis on equivalence of function (*Alas* is equivalent to *I am distressed*).

Classification. The futility of classifying interjections had been recognised by Alcuin,[7] if not earlier, but the point needed to be made again from time to time, as (rather gloomily) by Samuel Saxon: 'There are as many Interjections as there are Disorders in the Soul.'[8] Judging by their illustrations the early grammarians seem to have

[1] Wilkins, 1668, p. 308.   [2] Lewis, *Essay*, 1674, p. 17.
[3] *British Letter-Writer*, 1765, p. 12.
[4] Coote, 1788, p. 39; Lewis, *Institutio*, 1670, sig. B i verso.
[5] *Grammaire générale*, 1660, Bk 2. chap. 11.
[6] *The Art of Speaking: written in French by Messieurs de Port Royal...Rendered into English*, London, 1676, p. 24.
[7] See above, p. 78.   [8] Saxon, 1737, p. 77.

assumed that English interjections more frequently express un-
pleasant than pleasant feelings. George Brown goes further in saying
that the interjection 'implies a strong expression, arising from some
affliction in life'.[1] Perhaps the question has not yet been investigated.
One of William Ward's minor achievements was to suggest at least
two new classes of interjection: 'Incitement to Dogs' and 'Injunction
to remit Speed',[2] but the only classification which achieved any
popularity was Bishop Wilkins' tour de force. He divided interjections into three classes: (i) solitary, (ii) passive, (iii) social and
active.[3] Each class was subdivided, but it was the principal division
which caught the fancy of eight or nine later grammarians. Even
greater popularity was achieved by *Pish!* and *Pshaw!* as examples
of the expression of sudden passion. *Pish!* is first suggested (in the
grammars) about 1650[4] and *Pshaw!* about 1720.[5]

[1] G. Brown, 1779?, p. 22.   [2] W. Ward, 1767, p. 81.
[3] Wilkins, 1668, p. 308.
[4] Evelyn, fol. 96 verso gives Pish! and Faugh! as expressions of disdain.
[5] Douglas, *c.* 1720, No. 587 *a.* fol. 361 verso.

16. SYNTACTICAL CATEGORIES

Logic had begun to lead the speculative grammarians along a new path towards psychology. Earlier thought about the psychology of language had been directed towards, and expressed through, the technical terms of rhetoric. Rhetoric was the art of persuasion, primarily concerned with the relation between the speaker and his audience. The speculative grammarians turned their attention more towards the relation between the speaker and his words. They saw that the grammatical relations between words considered as parts of speech were not the fundamental relations of language, but the machinery. The speculative grammarians were beginning to ask how it was that, in order to produce an act of communication, the speaker's intentions could give power to this machinery and be at the same time, as it were, processed by it. They attached great importance to transitivity, by which they meant more than the relation between a verb and its object, because they recognised the dynamic nature of language: that words cannot function without the power given them by the speaker's intention. Transitivity was a relation between constituents of an utterance, not just between members of different word-classes. The speculative grammarians' most significant extension of the grammatical tradition was their enlargement of the concept of syntax: they were less interested in whether a verb or a preposition governed a particular case than in what was meant by saying that it 'governed' a case at all. By virtue of what power did it govern? This new approach to syntax, for all its patterned artificially, was, at its best, a linguistic enquiry. But it is perhaps only by hindsight that it can be seen as such. The renaissance grammarians ignored it, and the English tradition shows no trace of it. The set definition of syntax remains virtually unchanged throughout the whole period: 'the right placing or joyning Words together in a Sentence'.[1] But, as is constantly appearing in

[1] Greenwood, 1711, p. 35.

this study, the treatment of actual syntactical categories is much more varied than the uniformity of the definitions would suggest.

It was not immediately apparent to the English grammarians that English had any syntax to speak of: 'As English hath few and short rules for declining of words, so it hath few rules for joining words in sentence or in construction.'[1] The grammarians' natural assumption was that syntactical relations were expressed only through inflection; a largely uninflected language therefore was one largely without syntax. John Wallis neither discusses nor describes English syntax. He insists that English is different from Latin: 'In English things are entirely different from Latin. There is no reason therefore why we should bring in (more than is absolutely necessary and basic to English itself) an artificial and obviously unsuitable mass of cases, genders, moods and tenses of this sort.'[2] If Wallis does not discuss syntax he at least refrains from saying that English has none. Others were not so careful: 'Here should follow the Rules of Concord, and Construction: but because there is little, or no variation in the parts of the English tongue: they are altogether needless.'[3] James Howell, whose whole approach is rather slovenly, absolves himself from the need to discuss syntax (which Jonson, whom he otherwise follows, had tackled) by the opposite argument—the amount of variation in English. '[English] having such varieties of incertitudes, changes and Idioms, it cannot be in the compas of the human brain to compile an exact regular Syntaxis thereof.'[4]

The author of the *English Scholar Compleat* argues that an English syntax would be impossible, and if possible, would be dull:

If it be expected from me that I should now proceed to the Regular Construction of these Parts of Speech, which is Grammar; I must tell thee before-hand, I shall make but blind Work of it (as others have done before me) it being as impossible to do such a thing well, as it is impertinent to undertake it at all, from the Nature of our English Tongue, which wants Variation in its declinable Parts of Speech; so that...I should have told thee a great many things thou knowest already; and others thou hadst as good be asleep as read, or would be for Opium to make thee sleep, they are so dull and dry; instead of pleasing, profiting, or diverting thy Mind.

---

[1] Bullokar, 1586, p. 374.
[2] Wallis, 1653, preface, sig. A 8: 'Apud nos igitur, ubi res omnino secus se habet quam apud Latinos, cur hujusmodi Casuum, Generum, Modorum, Temporumque fictam et ineptam plane congeriem introducamus citra omnem necessitatem, aut in ipsa lingua fundamentum, nulla ratio suadet.'
[3] Wharton, 1654, p. 60.   [4] Howell, 1662, p. 80.

In short, to make a Grammar in a Language whose declinable Parts of Speech are without suitable Variations, is, in my Opinion, like exercising a Company of Faggot-Sticks, that have no Motion. (*English Scholar Compleat*, 1706, p. 26.)

Uncertainty about criteria led to paradox; if a syntax for English was not impossible it was easy: 'the Syntax...in the English Tongue is absolved in three easie Rules, and all the rest depends on the Preposition'.[1] This view, supported by Dr Johnson, was expressed at intervals throughout the eighteenth century. In 1761 James White is still combating the 'false notion...that our Language has no Syntax',[2] but during the last decades of the century nobody says that English lacks syntax and few say that its syntax is simple.

A rough quantitative measure confirms the general impression that syntax was given steadily increasing attention. Up till 1740 about 60 per cent of the grammars include sections on syntax; between 1740 and 1770 the proportion is about 70 per cent, and between 1770 and 1800, even in spite of the growing number of elementary works, the proportion rises to about 85 per cent.

This increased attention is not altogether to the credit of the grammarians. It can also be regarded as a falling away from the position hesitantly taken by the seventeenth-century grammarians, or at least as a failure (however understandable) to use an opportunity. Several seventeenth-century writers had seen that Latin syntax was inappropriate; but they did not know what to do for English. The eighteenth-century grammarians had the opportunity, and the prompting, to think afresh about syntax. But even the reforming grammarians could make no real use of the opening, and for lack of any other a Latinate syntax became even commoner than before.

ANALYSIS

Because the distinction between parts of speech and parts of an utterance had not yet been clarified the early English grammarians continued the traditional conception of syntax as primarily the relations (agreement and government) between parts of speech.[3] Parsing corresponded to the division of grammar usually called etymology: it consisted in saying to what part of speech each word

[1] Aickin, 1693, sig. A 3 verso. [2] See above, p. 432.
[3] See above, pp. 131 f.

belonged, and was a familiar practice taken over from Latin teaching. But there could as yet be no distinct analytical procedure related to syntax. Before 1800 there are no exercises requiring the schoolboy to divide a sentence even into subject and predicate, and the routines of clause analysis are unknown. Nevertheless it is possible to see how the early grammarians did in fact describe the structure of an utterance before they had any established categories in which to do so; to trace the gradual application of logical terms to grammatical material; and to see at the very end of the eighteenth century the development, out of sentence analysis, of the first suggestion of both précis and clause analysis.

Four procedures need to be distinguished: (i) the classification of single words as parts of speech; (ii) the full description of each word in its context, (iii) the rearrangement of the words of an utterance into their 'natural 'order and fullest possible form; (iv) the correction of 'false English'.

Parsing and construing. Throughout the period the first two procedures are usually combined under the name *parsing*, but they have other names also. In Latin[1] and sometimes in English,[2] they are called *analysis*; frequently, after Lowth, 1762, they are called *grammatical resolution*; exceptionally they are called *construing*.[3] More often construing, which is seldom used in the English grammars, refers only to the second of these procedures, a weakened form of the technique traditional in teaching Greek and Latin. John Burn, for example, gives 'Exercises upon all the preceding Rules, to be written out, corrected, parsed, and construed by the Learner.'[4]

One illustration will show both kinds of parsing in their characteristic form, scarcely differentiated:

The Application of the foregoing Grammar is best learnt by verbal Instructions: A short Specimen of the Author's Method follows.

When the Grammar Boys are standing in a Line before the Master, they take Sentences to Pieces in the following Manner.

Example. The Boy that answers most Questions best shall stand uppermost.

Q. What Part of Speech is each Word in this Sentence?

A. *The* an Article, *Boy* a Substantive... [etc.].

---

[1] e.g. Greaves, 1594, p. 30.

[2] e.g. Lewis, *Rules*, 1675, p. 1; Story, 1778, p. vii; Harrold, before 1787, p. 96.

[3] e.g. T.M. 1774, p. 19: 'Construe or Parse...'.   [4] Burn, 1766, p. 142.

When each word has been labelled the questions start again:

> *Q.* Which is the Nominative Word to the Verb *stand?*
> *A. Boy*: For, if it be asked, who shall stand uppermost, the Answer is, the Boy that answers most Questions.
> ...*Q.* [of the verb] What Mode, Time, Number and Person?
> *A.* Indicative Mode, future Time, third Person, Singular Number. (Wells, 1760, pp. 24–5.)

An explicit distinction was made between the two kinds of parsing by Lindley Murray, in the two-volume edition of his grammar, exercises and key, which first appeared in 1808. Murray calls them Etymological Parsing and Syntactical Parsing, but a short example of the latter will show how far it is still based on the parts of speech. Murray's syntactical parsing of *To err is human* is as follows:

> *To err*, is the infinitive mood, and the nominative case to the verb 'is'. *Is* is an irregular verb neuter, indicative mood, present tense, and the third person singular, agreeing with its nominative case 'to err', according to Note 1, under RULE the first. *Human* is an adjective, and belongs to its substantive 'nature' understood, according to RULE VIII which says... etc. (L. Murray, 2-vol. edn, 2nd edn 1809, p. 325.)[1]

Until the last decade of the eighteenth century the grammars do not normally contain exercises for the pupils to do on their own. Parsing was learnt by memorising a model, often in question-and-answer form. Hence the term *praxis*, which strictly meant a worked example on which the pupil could *practise*, and not, as the term was sometimes used, a parsing problem for him to solve. Such worked examples were sometimes described as 'the parts of speech exemplified'[2] or 'delineated',[3] but the term *praxis* was common till about 1780, when it was increasingly displaced by 'Parsing Examples'.

The third procedure, which took various forms and was given various names, appears in the first of the English grammars, although in a very naïve form. The following passage has to be 'resolved':

> On an earth-bank near meadow-ground,
>   I saw a horse-comb lie,
> Which I brought into a horse-mill,
>   that a stone-wall stood nigh.

---

[1] Rule VIII says: 'Every adjective...belongs to a substantive, expressed or understood.'
[2] Fisher, 2nd edn 1750, p. 113; Fenning, 1771, p. 118; *Rudiments of Constructive Etymology*, 1795, p. 53.
[3] Bettesworth, 1778, p. 34.

This becomes:

On a bank of earth or earthen bank, near ground for meadow, I saw a comb for a horse lie, which I brought into a mill with horse, that stood nigh a stonen wall, or wall of stone...(Bullokar, 1586, p. 380.)

This procedure was at first called *resolution*, as distinct from *grammatical resolution*. At its best it could develop into an exercise in judging equivalence of meaning, and hence could be valuable in unifying linguistic and literary studies. It was seldom as crude as Bullokar's example. During the eighteenth century the procedure was extended, on the whole harmfully: 'Resolution in any Language, is the unfolding of a Sentence, and placing all the Parts of it, whether expressed or understood, in their proper and natural Order, that the true meaning of it may appear.'[1] The potential harm lay in the terms *proper* and *natural*. The process by which words were put *out* of their 'proper' order was called *Transposition*: '...the placing of Words in a Sentence...out of their natural Order, to render their Sound more harmonious and agreeable to the Ear'.[2]

Closely linked with transposition was *ellipsis*. There developed, accordingly, within the wider process of resolution, narrow and pedestrian practices described by one grammarian as 'to regulate the Transpositions, supply the Ellipses, and remark the Tropes and Figures'.[3] These procedures, in combination, provided the normal techniques for teaching analysis and interpretation:

Q. Since the Composition of Sentences are often intricate and obscure, how may the sense and meaning of them be best found?

A. The best way to find the true sense and meaning of any Sentence, is to reduce transpos'd words to the Natural Order, to supply supprest words, and to change substituted words into the words for which they are substituted, and lastly to distinguish ambiguous words. (Lane, 1700, pp. 108–9.)

A frequent victim was Milton: 'The clearest and best writers in Prose have the fewest Transpositions in their Discourses, and in Poetry they are never used but when the Nature and Harmony of the Verse require it; as, of Man's first Disobedience...The Order is thus: Heavenly Muse, sing of Man's first Disobedience...'[4] The opening of *Paradise Lost* was continually used for demonstrations of this kind, largely under the influence of James Buchanan, whose

---

[1] Buchanan, 1767, p. xix.   [2] Fisher, p. 122.
[3] D. Turner, 1739, sig. A 3 verso.   [4] Fisher, op. cit. p. 123.

471

The First Six Books of Paradise Lost rendered into Grammatical Construction, 1773, was a massive exercise in resolution. But there was not the agreement one would expect on what the 'natural' order of the words was. John Clarke, for example, disagrees with Anne Fisher. He quotes the first six lines of *Paradise Lost* and comments: 'These Lines should have begun with, Sing, Heavenly Muse, of Man's first Disobedience. &c. But the Nature of the Poem, the Harmony of the Numbers, and Turn of the Versification, seem to require the Transposition; it is in this Place therefore properly used.'[1] Milton is found not guilty, but only at the last moment. The initial smear sticks: poetry is an unnatural practice. Transposition could seem to be austerely grammatical, as when Elphinston enumerates the 120 possible variations in the order of the words, 'The donor makes duly the donation to the donee',[2] but the commoner exercise is illustrated by the following, in which 'transposed' and elliptical writing has to be 'resolved':

Examples of Transposition and Ellipsis together

1. Do you, Father, take in your Hand the sacred Symbols, and the Gods of our Country: For me just come from War, so fierce and recent Bloodshed, to touch them would be a Profanation, till I have purified myself in the living Stream.

This becomes, after manipulation:

Father, do you take in your Hand the sacred Symbols, and Father, do you take in your Hand the Gods of our Country: For it would be a Profanation for me to touch them, who am just come from War, and who am just come from so fierce and from so recent a Bloodshed, till I have purified myself in the living Stream. (Buchanan, 1762, pp. 217–18.)

Some of these exercises may, with careful teaching, have focused the pupils' attention on the structure of sentences without leading them to suppose that it was necessarily 'better' to express every word that could be expressed in one arbitrarily 'natural' order. But the general effect must have been that 'Of Poetry turned into Prose'—the heading of an appendix to the 3rd edn, 1777, of Lister Metcalfe's *Rudiments of the English Tongue*, in which the customary lines of Milton are transposed.

False English. The fourth procedure is of importance in the history of English teaching, but is relevant here only because it could, but

---

[1] Clarke, 1772?, p. 82.   [2] Elphinston, 1765, vol. 2. p. 201.

by no means always did, require a measure of analysis. 'Exercises in false English' or '...false Syntax' became fashionable after their introduction as a novelty in Anne Fisher's grammar of 1749.[1] During the rest of the century they appeared in almost every English grammar and even in separate textbooks. Most of them were, at the best, trivial, and at the worst so far-fetched that they can only have suggested mistakes which no one would have made who was capable of profiting from the exercises. Discussion of 'A clergyman is one whom the libertine will always fear, but never openly affront him',[2] will raise real questions of structure, but there is no such value in 'The celebrated Eronout Mr Lunardi his arrived in these Town and purpose about the middle of these Month to take a ariel Excurshon.'[3]

These different procedures–simple parsing, construing, resolution, regulating transpositions, supplying and correcting false English— had gross and obvious defects. But they all, except parsing, had one classroom virtue: they kept some sort of relation between grammatical analysis and the study of style. They belong as much to the rhetorical as to the grammatical tradition, and for the teacher's purposes this could be a source of strength.

CLAUSE

The only units for which there were more or less unambiguous names were the word and the sentence. Our ancestors were as confused about the sentence as we are, but they achieved some consistency through not realising that they were confused. A few of them did discuss, unsystematically, the relations between units which were neither words nor sentences.

The term *clause* is not uncommon, but still has its traditionally wide meaning of *expression*:[4] it does not necessarily imply either subordination or the presence of a finite verb. The italicised parts of the following expressions are all 'clauses':

God, *creating the World*, made man.[5]
God created man in his image, *to be Lord of the Creatures*.[6]
The boys playing truant made the horse run.[7]

---

[1] See above, p. 196. [2] Meilan, 1803, II. 42.
[3] [John Carter], *Exercises, instructive and entertaining, in False English* (1787), 6th edn Leeds 1797, p. 73.
[4] See above, p. 43. [5] Lewis, *Rules*, 1675, p. 1.
[6] ibid. [7] D. Turner, 1739, p. 23.

To rise betimes in the Morning, is the most wholsom Thing in the World.[1]
There is a Man here.[2]
Hallowed be Thy Name.[3]
A man generous *to his enemies.*[4]
He who *ye pretend*, reigns in Heaven.[5]
Alexander, *in three battles*, conquered Darius.[6]

Conjunctions are often said to join 'the clauses of a Sentence',[7] but here also the term means no more than *parts*. An illustration from Lindley Murray, added to the 2nd edition of his grammar, is a clear warning against too modern an interpretation of *clause*: '"Thou seest a man, *and* he is called Peter" is a sentence consisting of two distinct clauses, united by the copulative *and*: but "the man *whom* thou seest is called Peter" is a sentence of one clause, and not less comprehensive than the other.'[8]

The existence of what we call subordinate clauses was, of course, recognised in the English, as in the Latin, tradition. But they were scarcely given any distinct status, and their structure was described in different ways. A distinction was sometimes made between main and subordinate *verbs*, as by Maittaire, who refers to two kinds of verb: '...the one is the main Verb of every Sentence, the other is the Verb of such clauses as are joined to and attending upon the main one, whether expressed or understood'.[9]

The first of the very few references in the English grammars to subordinate clauses as a category is surprisingly early, in the 1674 version of Mark Lewis's *Essay*: 'We have Infinitive Moods, Gerunds, Supines, Participles, Apposition, Vocative Cases, and Interjections. These are all contracted Sentences...They are depending clauses: Their dependency is ellipted.'[10] Later, referring to a favourite quotation from Sallust—'Man's excellency consists in his Soul, and in his Body. His Soul commands, and his Body obeys'—Lewis says, 'The latter Periods are exegetical to the former: yet are not depending Clauses'.[11] Lewis recognises, that is, not only that the function of the subordinate clause is to amplify and explain ('exegetical') but that the relation between one clause and another can be expressed by

[1] Dilworth, 1740, p. 122.
[2] *Practice*, 1750?, p. 157.
[3] Farro [1776?], p. 134.
[4] Priestley (1761), 1768, p. 41.
[5] Knowles, 4th edn 1796, p. 53.
[6] *Short & Easy Intro.* 1786, p. 48.
[7] Clare, 1690, p. 96; Trinder, 1781, p. 91.
[8] L. Murray, (1795) 1796, p. 92.
[9] Maittaire, 1712, p. 138.
[10] Lewis, *Essay*, 1674, p. 1.
[11] op. cit. p. 2.

juxtaposition as well as by co-ordinating or subordinating connectives. He develops this point more fully in a later work.

Lewis's treatment of subordination and the relation between sentences is unique. For all his elliptical inconsistency he is a genuine pioneer and worth quoting at length. The chief points he is making in the following passages from his *Plain and Short Rules for Pointing Periods* are (i) there is subordination of meaning (viz. when the subordinating connectives are 'understood') as well as, and distinguishable from, subordination of structure; (ii) a 'comparatively principal' verb is one in which there is subordination of meaning but not of structure, (iii) this subordination of meaning can be shown by 'resolving' the sentences so that the connectives become explicit and the clauses become subordinate structurally:

A Proposition, Theme, or Matter treated of is either Simple; (As *God created the World...*) or it is Compounded, in which there is a principal Verb, expressed, or suppressed, and another Verb, or Verbs depending upon it, to explain, enlarge, restrain, divide, or confirm the principal Proposition laid down, to which these depending Verbs are united by some Conjunction, expressed or understood. (Lewis, *Rules*, 1675, p. 2.)

Postscript. I should have spoken more distinctly to a principal Verb: upon which the whole process depends. A principal Verb is twofold: absolutely principal; or comparatively. A verb absolutely principal expresses the state, or motion of a Subject; or affects an Object not treated of in a former Period. its Clause shall begin with a Great Letter, and shall have a Periodus Supina before it. as, *God created the World. Man rules over the Creatures. The Sun shines in the Firmament.* A verb comparatively principal expresses the state, or motion of a Subject; or affects an Object immediately spoken of before, i.e. relates to the same matter, as the former Period doth. yet it is a principal verb: because it is no member of a Period: neither is it tacked on by a Conjunction to a former Clause. it doth indeed relate to a former Period: for Periods may have the same respect to Periods as Clauses have to Clauses. neither is it absolutely principal: because it will easily resolve into a depending verb. This Period shall begin with a small Letter, and shall have a Periodus pendens before it: because the sense yet hangs. As that of Salust. *Mans excellency consists in his Soul, and Body. The Soul commands, the Body obeys. In this we are like to God, in that to Beasts.* It resolves thus. *Our excellency consists, either in our Souls, by which we we command like God; or Bodies, with which we work like Bruits.* (Lewis, op. cit. Postscript.)

Most frequently units which we would call subordinate clauses appear as undifferentiated examples of a compound sentence, but what we would call a relative clause is in fact distinguished, some-

475

times by that name: Lane, Greenwood and many others refer to 'relative sentences'. Their attention is directed much more to the relative pronoun and its antecedent than to the function of the clause itself. Edwards defines an 'independent clause' as one which 'may be dropped without disturbing the rest of the Sentence', and gives as an example 'Paul, *who was once a Persecutor*, was a great Apostle'.[1] Few writers[2] explicitly say that the clause acts like an adjective, although exercises in transposition and contraction make the point indirectly, and Priestley, in his discussion of the relative, stresses the equivalence of the two sentences *God who is invisible made the world which is visible* and *The invisible God made the visible world*.[3] The fluidity of the category can be seen in the odd example given by James Gough, who treats the sentence *Stories, that are very common, are generally irksome* as an instance of what he calls *interposition*, the putting of one sentence ('that are very common') inside another.[4] Gough has the usual things to say about the relative pronoun, but the relative clause is not, for him, a standard category.

What we would call a noun clause is occasionally referred to, but has no distinctive name. One of the earliest references is Lane's:

A whole Sentence is often taken as one aggregate Substantive of the Neuter Gender, and third Person singular; and then it may be the Nominative Case before a Verb, or the Accusative after it, a Substantive to an Adjective, or an Antecedent to a Relative: as for Example, *He who is vertuous is content with his Condition, which is the true property of Riches.* (Lane, 1700, p. 78.)

Lane's explanation is clearer than his example, for he seems to take *He who is vertuous* as a complete sentence, but he continues: '...When a declarative or final Sentence is the Nominative Case, it usually comes after the Verb, and then the Adjective *it* comes before the Verb; as for example, *It grieves me much that thou art idle*, or *that thou art idle grieves me much*.'[5] The more usual reference to these clauses is of the type, 'Sometimes a whole phrase or sentence will serve as the nominative case to a verb.'[6]

Examples of a clause as object of a verb are rare. William Ward, in a section of his school grammar headed 'Of whole Sentences used as Substantives' gives the example, 'I know *that my Redeemer liveth*' as

[1] S. Edwards, 1765, p. 70.   [2] W. Ward is one: 1765, pp. 136 f.
[3] Priestley, 1762, p. 147.   [4] Gough, 1754, p. 108.
[5] Lane, 1700, p. 78.   [6] Coote, 1788, p. 200.

'a kind of Accusative'.[1] Sometimes clauses introduced by *that* are given as illustrations of the use of a 'declarative' conjunction,[2] and this also is the usual treatment of what we would call adverbial clauses: they provide examples of the use of different kinds of conjunction. The grammarians' attention is, again, fixed on the word rather than on the larger unit: on the conjunctions *as*, *if*, and *because* rather than on the clauses they introduce. Gildon and Brightland give *As I went to School, I met my Master* to illustrate the use of conjunctions 'to shew the Relation of one Notion to another', but without any reference to subordination.[3] Similarly Harris, who classifies conjunctions with ardour and freshness, gives 'You will live happily, if you live honestly' as an instance of a suppositive conjunction connecting two sentences: and 'You live happily, because you live honestly' as an instance of a causal conjunction, not of an adverbial clause.[4] It is only the larger grammars or the more thoughtful grammarians who give even this attention to the subordinate clause. In most books it is not mentioned, even indirectly. It is a pity that John Stirling did not, apparently, write the fuller version of his grammar, in which he was going to 'endeavour to resolve the greatest Difficulty of the English,'viz. When a compleat sentence is used in a great Variety of Instances for one particular Word only in Syntax.'[5] This sounds like a study of clauses.

William Ward, an even more strenuous linguistic wrestler than Mark Lewis, and perhaps necessarily long-winded, tried, in terms which were entirely original, to analyse the nature of subordination. Ward's arguments are always difficult to follow, because he gives so few illustrations. Those which follow are derived from the only one he gives—'that a peace is concluded is now past doubt'. His analysis is in terms of syntactical 'degrees'. A complete sentence is of the highest degree: 'A peace is concluded.' The sentence can be made into a noun-equivalent by prefixing *that*; it is then of a second, lower, degree: 'that *a peace is concluded* is now past doubt'. The sentence can be put in a third degree by prefixing a relative: 'We welcome the peace *which is concluded.*' Here the relative clause is subordinate to the substantive, which is itself a part of the whole sentence.

The conception denoted by words in the form of a compleat sentence may be considered merely as that of an object denoted by a noun substantive;

[1] W. Ward, 1767, p. 116. [2] Lane, 1700, p. 96.
[3] G–B, 1711, p. 121. [4] Harris, 1751, p. 244.
[5] Stirling, 1735, sig. B 4 verso.

477

and it is frequently convenient to consider the conception, as that of such an object. But when this is done, some notice must be given of it; for without such notice, the grammatic form in which the words are drawn up, would lead the hearer or reader to consider them, as a separate expression, of compleat truth or falshood. This notice is usually given in English by prefixing the particle *that* to a sentence, when the meaning of it is to be considered as of the same nature, or order, with the conception denoted by a noun substantive in some case.

Thus a sentence of compleat truth or falshood is reduced one degree lower, viz. to a level with the expression of a mere object of the intellect, as denoted by a noun substantive. But it is of the utmost convenience in language to reduce a compleat sentence lower still, viz. to a level with the expression of a conception denoted by a noun adjective, or dependent participle; and the relative pronouns are introduced into language to give notice when a speaker or writer is proceeding in this manner. (W. Ward, 1765, pp. 135–6.)

Analysis of this kind is rare among the grammarians. Ward lacked Priestley's commonsense, but he thought more deeply about language than any eighteenth-century grammarian except Harris, Beattie and the anonymous grammarian of *Encyclopaedia Britannica* (A). Ward writes appallingly, but he makes an elegant writer such as Campbell seem almost superficial.

The next significant stage in the development of clause-analysis is described at the end of this chapter in the account of the Abbé Gaultier's grammatical works.[1]

SENTENCE

During the whole of the period there is one dominant approach to the sentence, a continuation of the traditional definition[2] in terms of completeness of meaning. But whereas *oratio perfecta* had been an elastic term, extended to units much larger than the sentence, and to imperatives and other one-word units, in the English grammars the sentence is regularly required to contain at least two, and often three, words, and any utterance containing more than one finite verb is normally distinguished as a compound sentence. The modern situation has been reached, in which everyone can use the term *sentence*, in a particular context, satisfactorily, but varying contexts require varying criteria, and varying criteria make any fixed definition unsatisfactory.

[1] See below, p. 486.　　　　　　　　　[2] Above, pp. 38 f.

Lily had ignored the sentence, presumably regarding it as a rhetorical or logical, not as a grammatical, category. Perhaps for this reason there is little mention of it in the seventeenth-century grammars. It is not formally defined until about 1669, when John Newton calls it 'a number of Words, joyned together in perfect Sense'.[1] The requirement of substantive and verb is added by Lewis about the same time: 'Every Sentence consists of a Substantive, called the Nominative Case and a Verb, with their dependents. These are the two Legs upon which a Sentence doth stand.'[2]

The requirement that there should be more than two legs is made in *The True Method*, 1696, but immediately modified:

Every Sentence consists of two Nouns, or a Noun, and Adnoun, and a Verb, at the least, either exprest, or which may be supplied; though for abridgement of Speech, or Elegancy sake, either the Noun or Adnoun, or both may sometimes be supprest; so that sometimes two words, sometimes but one, is put to express the whole Sentence; as, *I love, ego amo*, or *Amo* alone. (*True Method*, 1696, p. 57.)

The requirement of, in our terms, subject, verb and object or complement, is surprising but not uncommon. It springs, perhaps, from the feeling, often expressed, that every intransitive verb has *one*, cognate, object: *I run* entails the object *race; I love*, the object *loved one*. This requirement of three words is made in about ten grammars, the last of which, that in John Entick's *New Spelling Dictionary*, appeared in 1765 (and by the edition of 1784 the requirement had been changed to two words, noun and verb). Although it is often inconsistent with their definitions some of the grammarians recognise (as does the author of *The True Method*), usually in an aside from their discussion of the adverb, that a speaker can 'express his whole intention, on some occasions, by a single word which is not a verb'.[3] The commonest examples of such words are *yes* and *no*, but Beattie says that every kind of word except the article and the conjunction can function in this way.[4] Ward is unusual in treating as sentences examples such as *My kingdom for a horse*[5] which most grammarians would have regarded as eminently elliptical.

There is so little variation in these definitions of the sentence, based on meaning, that two examples will cover the whole period, one

[1] Newton, 1669, p. 67; 1677, p. 18. [2] Lewis, *Essay*, 1670?, p. 11.
[3] W. Ward, 1765, p. 266. [4] Beattie, 1783, p. 365.
[5] W. Ward, loc. cit.

frequently reproduced in the first half of the eighteenth century and the other in the second:

A sentence comprehends at least three [often changed to two] Words, by which some Sentiment or thought of the Mind is express'd. (G–B, 1711, p. 141.)

an assemblage of words, expressed in proper form, ranged in proper order, and concurring to make a complete sense. (Lowth, 1762, p. 95.)

The only other approach to the sentence differs in its terminology rather than in its aim. Instead of naming the essential constituents as parts of speech (noun and verb) it names them as parts of a logical structure, the proposition. The conscious introduction of logical terms is illustrated more fully in the next section of this chapter, which deals with *subject* and *object*. The effect can be seen in a few (less than ten) definitions of the sentence, most of which belong to the period 1700–60. The earliest statement is one of the fullest:

A Proposition is a perfect Sentence, or Speech wherein something is affirmed, or denied of another...All that comes before the principal Verb, in sense and Construction, that is, the Substantive in the N. Case with all its appendants, is called the Subject; all that follows it is called the Predicate; the Verb is the Copula...which may also be considered as part of the Predicate, which when not exprest, it virtually includes. (*True Method*, 1696, p. 57.)

This would be commonplace in an elementary logic. In a grammar it was a novelty, as Lane makes clear five years later:

I hope the Learned will forgive me, if I be forc'd to make use of some terms not usual in Grammar, as *Subject, Predicate, Object*, and such like, which I have not used out of vanity, but of necessity, either to prevent Circumlocutions in terms of Art, or to avoid terms which are vagous or common to several Arts. If I have borrowed these Terms from Logick, I am perswaded that Aristotle borrowed them first from Grammar, which was in being long before his Logic, which I think (with submission to better Judgments) to be nothing else but Grammar, except his superadded invention of Syllogisms, and some other things of less use, which he ingrafted upon the Stock of Grammar. And in my weak opinion the Art of thinking and speaking are not two, but one Art; for Grammar first teaches us how to conceive of things in the order of Nature, and then how to express our Conceptions by speaking or writing. (Lane, 1700, p. xvii.)

Lane's own definition of the sentence is of the logical type, though he adds that a verb and 'nominative of the subject' are essential: '...a construction of words wherein something is said of another, as *man is Mortal*'.[1]

---

[1] Lane, 1700, p. 74.

As Lane implies, the distinction between the two types of definition is only one of emphasis. By defining the sentence as an assertion the grammarian is accepting the logician's formalisation of a commonplace, necessary way of describing human thought and speech. On this point logic was no help, and the grammarians were wise to disregard it. A logical definition of this kind must exclude questions, commands and exclamations, and such a definition is too narrow for the grammarian to use.

SUBJECT AND OBJECT

The terms *subject* and *object* had long histories in logic and philosophy before they were applied to grammar. Although *subject* came into the English grammars at the end of the seventeenth century it remained primarily a logical term until well into the eighteenth century.[1] The metaphysical contexts of both *subject* and *object* scarcely affected the grammars, but *object* was also a term of wide non-technical reference: some of its more general uses were equivalent to the loose use, in some contexts, of *subject*. This was one possible ground for confusion. Another was the persistent confusion between word and thing: between the performer of an action and that part of a sentence which referred to the performer. The main ambiguity rests in *subject* (which is used to refer to words and to things, even when they are the 'recipients' of action) and in *agent* and *object* which mean sometimes the thing and sometimes the word.

In discussing subject and object the grammarians sometimes (usually in connection with active and passive verbs) refer directly and unambiguously to things: 'There can be no Action without an Agent, nor Passion without a Patient.'[2] Here *agent* and *patient* are material categories; the agent is the initiator of action and the patient is the recipient. Such unambiguous references are not common. More often the reader is uncertain (because the writer is) how far the terms refer to things and to material relations; how far to words and to grammatical relations: '[the active verb] expresses an Action, and therefore supposes an Agent, and an Object acted upon... [the passive verb] expresses a Passion, or a Suffering, or the receiving of an Action, and necessarily implies an Object acted upon, and an Agent by which it is acted upon.'[3] *Agent* and *object* here, though

[1] See above, pp. 133 f. [2] Lane, 1700, p. 77. [3] Carter, 5th edn 1797, p. 18.

perhaps also indicating the parts of a sentence, have a primary reference to the material categories. But when Alexander Hume says 'the active verb adheres to the person of the agent' and 'the passive verb...to the person of the patient'[1] how far do the words *agent* and *patient* refer to people and how far to words? It is difficult to say.

The transfer of the terms to words can be seen in an early sentence analysis by Francis Lodowyck. In the sentence 'John loveth Mary' he calls the word *John* 'the Noun Agent or Relative' (he does not explain this use of *relative*) and *Mary* 'the Noun Patient'.[2] The passive form of a similar sentence he analyses as follows (the layout is his):

| *Thomas* | *is loved* | *much* | *of Father his*[3] |
| Noun Patient | verb | manner | the agent |

Although *noun patient* refers to the word *Thomas* it is still substantially a material category. It relates more to the world of things, to the receipt of action, than to the *grammatical* relation between subject-word and verb. *Agent*, applied to *Father*, has an even stronger material reference. What in fact distinguishes the material use of *agent* and *patient* (or *object*) is that the two latter terms may be applied to the grammatical subject of the sentence, and that *agent* may be applied to the word preceded by a passive verb and a preposition. These material categories are quite frequent. Joshua Story, in 1778, gives independently almost the same example as Lodowyck, 'Thomas is loved by me'. Story says, 'the object *Thomas* goes before [the verb] and is followed by the agent with the preposition'.[4] Story defines *object* as 'the person acted upon'—a material category; yet he uses the term to indicate the word which is the grammatical subject of the sentence. Similar examples, from the end of the eighteenth century, are *Mary is praised by William*, where *Mary* is referred to as the object,[5] and *Her gown is torn by a nail*, where '*nail* is the agent, and the *gown* the object of that agent'.[6] The same jostling of material and grammatical categories is apparent in the common description of an intransitive verb as one in which 'the agent and the object acted upon coincide, and the action...does not pass over to any other object: as, *I am, I sleep*'.[7] The 'coincidence' cannot be one of words; it is, presumably,

[1] Hume, *c.* 1617, p. 32.   [2] Lodowyck, 1652, p. 14.
[3] op. cit. p. 15.   [4] Story, 1778, p. 16.
[5] *Short & Easy Intro.* 1786, p. 20.   [6] Mayne, 1799, p. 41.
[7] Story, 1778, p. 14.

the coincidence of two roles. It was only because they did not consider closely the nature of the coincidence that the grammarians were able to put forward such an explanation.

The term *patient* was never popular, and had virtually dropped out by 1775. The commoner name for the material category correlative with *agent* was *object*, as in the previous quotation from Story. But as *object* was also a common name for the grammatical category most instances of its use (apart from this passive construction) are ambiguous. Another, and surprisingly frequent, correlative term for the material category *patient* is *subject*. It appears first in Greenwood: '[The Neuter Verb] can have no Noun after it, to denote the Subject of Action.'[1]

This form of words was taken over by Buchanan, 1762, and by *The New and Improved Spelling Dictionary*, 1771. Abraham Crocker goes so far as to say that the neuter verb 'has no subject to fall on'[2] and two or three later grammarians use the term in the same way.

This use of *subject* for a material category is not just a quirk of Greenwood's. *Subject* is used as a synonym for *object* explicitly by M'Ilquham: 'Accusative is the subject, or object, on which the action implied in an active verb, terminates.'[3] The same use appears in the third edition of the *Britannica*, in the discussion of the active verb, in which 'action passes from some agent to some subject... the action of *lego* refers to some external object as well as to the agent'.[4] John Dalton, in 1801, similarly says that a verb is called transitive 'when the action affects another subject besides the agent'.[5] That *subject*, even in a material sense, could be used for what we would call the object shows how loosely the term was still attached to the syntactical category at that time generally called *nominative*.[6]

The grammatical subject of a sentence was called either the *nominative* or the *subject*. The former was used particularly by the Latinists, but also, however inconsistently, by many who denied that English nouns had cases: 'From these instances [i.e. pronouns] and in conformity with the practice of the ancient languages, it is usual to call the noun or pronoun preceding the verb its nominative case, and that which follows, its accusative case.'[7]

---

[1] Greenwood, 1711, p. 153. [2] Crocker, 1772, p. 17.
[3] M'Ilquham, 5th edn 1797, p. 43. [4] *Enc. Brit.* (B), 1797, p. 70.
[5] Dalton, 1801, p. 34.
[6] Other instances occur in *A Real English Grammar*, 1764, p. 42; *The British Letter-Writer*, 1765?, p. 11; Fordyce, 1790?, p. 20. [7] *Comprehensive View*, 1794, p. 28.

For a long time *subject* was treated as a term imported from logic. Wilkins is the first to use it in an English grammatical work: 'The word *Subject* I use, as the Logicians do, for all that which goes before the Copula; which [i.e. the subject] if it consist of only one word, then it is the same which the Grammarians call the Nominative case.'[1] Christopher Cooper, writing nearly twenty years later, says similarly, 'Substantivum, de quo aliquid affirmatur aut negatur... a grammaticis nuncupatur *casus nominativus*, a logicis *subjectum*.'[2] Comments to the same effect in *The True Method*, 1696, and in Lane's grammar of 1700 were quoted above, p. 480.

By the middle of the eighteenth century *subject* is well established in the conventional form of words, 'Subject or Nominative Case', but the working term in quite half the grammars is still *nominative*, and *subject* is still associated particularly with logic: 'When a Sentence is regular and orderly, Nature's Substance, the Logician's Subject, and the Grammarian's Substantive are all denoted by that Case, which we call the Nominative.'[3] (But Harris is here forcing his terms to display their roots in the wrong place: *substantive* was never used as an equivalent of *subject* and *nominative*.)

At the end of the century Benjamin Rhodes refers to a number of terms which he considers synonymous: 'The Noun, or pronoun, which is the doer, is called the nominative case—(Though some grammarians call it the Leading state: others the agent: but these different terms have all the same meaning.)'[4] It is noticeable that Rhodes does not include *subject*.

Agent, for the syntactical, as well as the material, category, became common during the second half of the eighteenth century, frequently linked also with *subject*. Its popularity probably sprang from Lowth, who listed 'The Parts of a Sentence'[5] as *agent, attribute* and *object*.[6] Even as careful a writer as Lowth, it may be noted, defined the agent, just called part of a *sentence*, as 'the *thing* chiefly spoken of'. L. Murray is a good guide to the popularity of a term. In his first edition he follows Lowth, with *agent* rather than *nominative*; by 1802 he has changed it to *subject*. Roughly, over the whole period, *nominative* is slightly more frequent than *subject*, and both are much more frequent than *agent*.

---

[1] Wilkins, 1668, p. 304.   [2] Cooper, 1685, p. 140.
[3] Harris, 1751, p. 280.   [4] Rhodes, 1795, p. 35.
[5] He changed it in the 2nd edn to 'The Principal Parts...'.
[6] Lowth, 1762, p. 102.

The term *object* was slower to arrive. It was used by Lewis in the passage quoted above, p. 475, but not as the name of a precise syntactical category. It is used as a syntactical category by Lane: 'A Verb Active Transitive is that which admits Various Objects, or (which is the same) Various Accusatives.'[1] And later he gives 'I call *thee*, I call *him*', as instances of 'the Accusative of the Object'.[2] Gildon and Brightland still use a periphrasis. The third constituent of a sentence is: '...another Name...which signifies, or denotes the Thing, to which the Action of the Word [i.e. verb] does immediately relate'.[3] It is not till 1735 that another grammar uses *object*, although as a material rather than as a syntactical category: '[after the verb] a Word usually follows which expresseth the object of Affirmation, and is commonly a Name, called the Accusative Case...'[4] In 1739 there is an unambiguous reference to 'the noun on which the action of the verb passes, call [*sic*] the Object',[5] and after the middle of the century *object* becomes much more common than *accusative*.

PREDICATE

The sentence 'Man is mortal' can be regarded in two ways. A logical analysis is to divide it into three parts: subject, copula and predicate. A grammatical analysis is to divide it into two: subject and predicate (...*is mortal*). This latter division, whereby the grammatical predicate is a syntactical and not a logical category, does not appear in the English grammars before 1800. The Oxford English Dictionary quotes one instance, before 1638, of *predicate* being used, in non-technical writing, to include the verb, but gives no other before the nineteenth century. Our grammatical *complement* is not distinguished as a category, nor is the term used, before 1800. When Harris wishes to refer to the word *pleasure* in 'Happiness is Pleasure' he calls it the predicate.[6] Otherwise this part of the sentence is just called that which follows the verb *to be*. In 'A foolish son is the heaviness of his mother' *heaviness* is described as 'a substantive noun, singular number, nominative case, following the verb *is*'.[7]

[1] Lane, 1700, p. 39.
[2] op. cit. p. 87.
[3] G–B, 1711, p. 144.
[4] Collyer, 1735, p. 5.
[5] D. Turner, 1739, p. 23.
[6] Harris, 1751, p. 230.
[7] Fenning, 1771, p. 123.

GAULTIER'S METHODS OF ANALYSIS

The Abbé Gaultier, whose system of parts of speech was described above, p. 239, brought together into one teaching method parsing, sentence analysis, rudimentary clause analysis, and what we now call précis. His work may legitimately be noticed here because the first of his two most influential books was written in English, and published in England in 1800, and his system was a step in the development of modern elementary analytical techniques. While Gaultier was a refugee in London he wrote, and had published in English, *A Method of Making Abridgments; or, easy and certain rules for analysing authors*, 1800–1. The preface explains how the 'method of abridgment' grew out of a method of sentence analysis:

Whilst he [the author] was contriving how to fix the attention of Children on the analysis of each principal part of a sentence, he found, after a few trials, that to paint in different colours the several parts of the sentences, according to his general division of Grammar, would be a useful, and even an amusing exercise.

He therefore directed them to put, 1st, The Nominative Case, or the subject, in *deep blue*; and its modifications, viz. the adjectives which are joined to the nominative, or expressions which supply the place of the adjectives, in *light blue*. 2dly, The Verb, or the attribute, in *deep red*; and the oblique cases governed by the verb, in *light red*. 3dly, The Modifications of Verbs, or the words which determine their signification, as adverbs, adverbial expressions, or some conjunctions, in *yellow*.

...He observed, and the Children also, that in every sentence which they had analysed by means of colours...there was never to be found more than two or three general *modifications*, besides the *subject*, and the *attribute*; and consequently that in the most diffuse sentence, and one that formed, even by itself, a long paragraph, there never could be discovered by the analysis more than four or five distinct ideas.

It was this last conclusion alone that led the Author to conceive the first plan of abridgments. For, since it was no longer a problem that *every sentence or paragraph, of whatever length it might be, was composed of but few ideas*, it was easy for him to see, that *if those ideas could be generalised*, and comprised in *very short expressions, the result would be an abridgment of all the thoughts contained in the sentence or paragraph*.

He then directed all his endeavours to find out by what means this *compression* could be effected, and soon discovered those means in his former works for Children. He observed that the same rules which he had laid down to distinguish and analyse the *adjectives, oblique cases*, and *adverbs* of a sentence would be equally useful as the means of compressing sentences.

Syntactical categories

For, 1st, Whatever was in *light blue*, viz. the *modification of the subject*...
might be very often rendered by a simple *adjective*.
2dly, Whatever was in *light red*, viz. the *oblique cases*, completing the
signification of the attribute...might be very easily replaced by a single
noun. (E. C. Gaultier, 1800, pp. iv–viii.)

Similarly, adverbs or adverbial expressions were substituted for what
was underlined in yellow. Gaultier then prescribed three rules:
(i) analyse the paragraph; (ii) compress it; (iii) with the compressed
parts make the abridgment. What is meant by 'analysing the paragraph' he explains as follows:

If the paragraph consist of a simple or of a complex sentence, find out the
subject, attribute, and adjuncts.
   If the paragraph consist of a compound sentence, or several split
sentences, find out the principal, and then the subordinate sentences,
which either modify a noun, or determine the signification of the attribute.
(op. cit. pp. 17–18.)

In the sentence *We are wandering in a beautiful and romantic country*,
'*We* is the subject...*are wandering*, is the attribute...*In a beautiful
and romantic country* is an adjunct determinative of place, and expresses
where *we are wandering*.'[1]
   This is very familiar language.
   Soon after Gaultier returned to France in 1802, he extended the
analytical part of his scheme in a fresh work, *Méthode pour analyser la
pensée sans déranger l'ordre des mots qui l'expriment*, from the second
edition of which, 1806, this account is taken. Besides the coloured
underlining described in his earlier work he now suggests 'un tracé
de lignes et de colonnes portant un titre énonciatif de cinq parties
de la phrase ou de la période'.[2] (*Phrase* and *proposition* he treats as
synonyms; *période* he defines as 'un assemblage de plusieurs phrases,
soit simples, soit complexes, liées les unes aux autres par des conjonctions ou par des pronoms relatifs'.[3] He continues: 'Dans les
propositions composées il y a toujours une phrase à laquelle toutes
les autres se rapportent: elle s'appelle *phrase principale*; celles qui
dependent de la phrase principale s'appellent *subordonnées, incidentes,
relatives* ou *modificatives*.'[4] This was the most explicit statement yet
made of the now familiar analysis into main and subordinate
clauses.

[1] Gaultier, 1800, p. 19.
[2] *Méthode*, 2nd edn 1806, p. 5.
[3] op. cit. p. viii.
[4] ibid.

487

Within the sentence itself Gaultier makes five possible divisions, represented either by columns or by coloured underlining: subject, verb, direct object (le régime direct), indirect object and 'le déterminatif'. The last he describes as answering the questions When? How? Who? How many? In what circumstances? It seems always to be what we would call an adverbial clause. In addition there are 'modifications... les mots, les expressions, ou les phrases qui qualifient, complètent, ou déterminent le sens des mots'.[1] These can be attached to any of the five parts of the sentence. Two of Gaultier's examples, one analysing a simple, the other a complex sentence, show his system at work:

Subject	Verb	Régime
Le chagrin rongeur	monte sur	les chars ornés de bronze.[2]

Gaultier's willingness to take *monte sur* as a verb has been remarked already:[3] no school textbook dare advocate that now. *Rongeur* and *ornés de bronze*, as other examples show, would in a fuller analysis be separated as modifications of the subject and object.

The second of Gaultier's examples is a passage from Swift:

If the choice had been left to me, I would rather have trusted the refinement of our language, as far as it relates to sound, to the judgment of the women, than of illiterate court-fops, half-witted poets, and university boys: for it is plain, that women, in their manner of corrupting words, do naturally discard the consonants, as we do the vowels.

Gaultier analyses this as follows:

Subject I
Verb would rather have trusted
Direct Object the refinement of our language
Indirect Object to the judgment of the women, than of illiterate court-fops, halfwitted poets, and university boys
Determinative (*a*) If the choice had been left to me
　　　　　　　　(*b*) for it is plain, that women, in their manner of corrupting words, do naturally discard the consonants, as we do the vowels.
(Gaultier, *Méthode*, 2nd edn 1806, p. 103.)

Several things distinguish Gaultier's analysis from earlier procedures in, at any rate, English and Latin. His *modification* includes all adjectival expressions, whether words, phrases or clauses; his category *déterminatif*, on the other hand is not just one type of qualifying expression, but is identical with our adverbial clause.

---

[1] ibid.　　　　　[2] op. cit. p. xvii.　　　　　[3] Above, p. 446.

Gaultier also (though it is difficult to say how original he was in this) was using analysis not as part of the 'labelling' considered necessary in the elementary teaching even of one's own language, but as a means of understanding structure, and hence meaning.

En effet, par ce procédé, on leur facilite les moyens de comprendre ce qu'ils lisent...on leur enseigne plus clairement et les règles de la ponctuation et la méccanisme du langage; on les met a portée de distinguer le style de tout bon écrivain au point de l'imiter, et par conséquent de bien écrire: car décomposer c'est apprendre à recomposer. (op. cit. p. iii.)

The nature of Gaultier's advance, which it is not altogether easy for us to appreciate, can be seen by comparing his analysis of a sentence with that of Joseph Aickin, a century before:

A perfect Sentence is composed of the Substantive and Verb and the words following the Verbs, either by agreement or Government, then words joyned by concordance, apposition, the substantive with the preposition, the Infinitive mood, the Substantive put absolutely, Adverbs, Conjunctions added according to the nature of the discourse. As *The General pursuing fast the Enemy, fell unfortunately into their hands, where to our great sorrow, alas! by wicked men, he was shamefully put to death.* (Aickin, 1693, p. 19.)

Aickin's is the approach, based on the parts of speech, from which the eighteenth-century grammarians gradually began to free themselves. Gaultier's approach, based on some out of many possible syntactical categories, is one which we are only now beginning to improve on. Gaultier is, however, very rigid, and presses too pedantically the virtues of analytical coherence. Later in the *Méthode* he uses the opening of Paradise Lost to illustrate not only the 'abrégé' but also a still more compressed form of the original, the 'sommaire'. His analysis shows that 'la construction grammaticale [of Milton] n'est donc pas exacte. Nouvelle preuve que les pensées qui ne sont pas exprimées selon l'analyse ne peuvent s'analyser.'[1] Yet again Milton is to blame: already under suspicion for having written artificially he is now accused of grammatical inexactitudes.

[1] Gaultier, *Méthode*, 2nd edn 1806, p. 158.

17. PROTEST AND ACCEPTANCE

A good English grammar is an object which we may probably continue to wish for, till the ingenious men of our own country turn their thoughts to their native language.[1]

THE GRAMMATICAL INHERITANCE

The evidence[2] summarised in Part One shows that the continuity of the classical tradition, real and strong though it is, lies often in the names of the categories rather than in their contents. The emphasis customarily placed on the continuity of the tradition is misleading unless it is balanced by a recognition that the grammarians were also struggling with broader issues than the pedagogue's routine; that the categories were often unstable, and that this instability was caused by the struggle as well as by inadequacies in the categories themselves.

Then, as now, language could be a point of interaction between many branches of knowledge. Part of Priscian's greatness is that he thinks in terms which are logical and literary as well as grammatical. But such flexibility cannot last. Categories harden. Our whole conception of grammar for a vernacular has been deeply and, it may be argued, disastrously influenced by the fact that it was formed before there was any science of language. The hardening of categories, the increasing autonomy of logic and rhetoric, and the lack of any science of language, forced on grammar a preoccupation with the classification and analysis of words alone. Once logic and rhetoric were conceived as disciplines distinct from grammar fresh patterns of interaction were unlikely. Grammar was doomed to be trivial: a necessary descriptive procedure in the elementary study of a foreign tongue, but irrelevant, sterile and dull when applied to a vernacular. This restricted scope of grammar was partly caused by, and in turn fostered, a common enough human tendency: to make the world tidy and safe; to catalogue and classify; to knock into a comfortable and familiar shape, and above all to name, whatever threatens us

---

[1] *Mon. Rev.* 49. 1772. 93.
[2] In this chapter page references in the text are all to the present work.

with emergent individuality. The opposite tendency is to question and to explore; to move the pieces of experience into unfamiliar patterns, to accept incompleteness and uncertainty. The last general expression of such a questioning tendency within the tradition came from the speculative grammarians. The grammarians of the renaissance repudiated their predecessors' logico-metaphysical speculation, and there were by then few questions which they themselves could feel any need to ask. Interaction between these related branches of knowledge was more difficult. Questions about language as a social activity, the affective elements in language, much that we would call the psychology of language—all this belonged, if anywhere, to rhetoric. If questions could be asked about the validity and meaningfulness of an utterance, or about the functions of different types of utterance, this too was rhetoric, or logic. The symbolic nature of language, which the speculative grammarians had begun to consider,[1] was lost sight of, and by the time the first English grammars were written only a little was left even of the old lip-service paid to a unified conception of grammar in which literary criticism and exposition were kept in relation to the history and classification of words and discourse. Of those who still questioned the most conspicuous was Sanctius, and he was almost entirely destructive. He could see, and did not hesitate to mock, the weakness of the traditional categories, but he could only suggest, rather vaguely, greater reliance on logical criteria. The one advance which the renaissance grammarians had made was one they could not appreciate: they greatly extended the use of syntactic criteria. Position in a sentence had been used by Dionysius Thrax and by Priscian as a criterion in the definition of some of the undeclined parts. The renaissance grammarians extended the criterion to the declined parts but did not recognise the significance of what they were doing. They could have distinguished syntactic from other criteria only if they had possessed a conception of language and of linguistic analysis for which the time had not yet come.

What the English grammarian inherited, therefore, can be summed up as follows:

(i) A very broad concept 'grammar' and the memory, fossilised in its conventional definition, of a time when there had been the

---

[1] cf. Martin of Dacia, p. 7: 'Omne quod potest esse signum rei significatae, etiam potest esse de consideratione grammatici.'

ideal, if not the actuality, of a unified literary and linguistic discipline;

(ii) a set of labelled grammatical categories (accompanied by frequently overlapping definitions) the contents of which were both stereotyped and variable;

(iii) a very few analytical procedures, almost all restricted to units no larger than the single word;

(iv) the almost unquestioned assumption that this classical equipment must be more than adequate for modern languages because the classical languages were richer and more expressive than modern ones;

(v) examples of enterprise, insight and originality within the tradition, available for those who could find or recognise them.

THE DOMINANCE OF LATIN

One of the questions originally asked in this study was 'what happened when Latin grammar was applied to English?'. It can now be seen that the question was wrongly framed. Because Latin was not just one out of many languages, but was a living international language of the highest possible status (Hebrew was put in a special class by its heavenly associations), its grammar was not just one grammar out of many: it *was* grammar. There could be no question of 'applying Latin' grammar to English. If Latin 'had' a grammar it was not for English to have anything different. It could have only the same, and less of it. The universality of Latin appeared also in the semantic definitions which were sometimes preferred, for elementary teaching, to definitions based on form. If a noun was the name of a thing which could be seen, felt, heard or understood (p. 55) or if a verb expressed action, passion or being (p. 60) this would be as true in English as in Latin. Such attempts at elementary definitions of Latin categories were a powerful influence on the development of English grammar. It was assumed that children learnt by applying a previously memorised definition; the definition, in order to be useful, must be in terms they could understand without knowing Latin; the definition of a category in English, therefore, often seemed to be the definition of an English category. It was this feature of elementary teaching which the basic grammars, in particular, exploited (pp. 281 f.). The ideal of universal grammar had two sources, one of which worked against, the other for, the development of a grammar for English. In so far as universal grammar was just a rationalisation and extension of the prestige of Latin (which, in the seventeenth century, before the appearance of the Port Royal grammar, it often was) it delayed the development of a genuinely linguistic approach to English. In so far as universal grammar was the application of logic to language it can be argued that, even though it gave no help of a strictly linguistic kind, it did direct attention to the structure of discourse and to the existence of units larger than the word—attention which is of great importance even at an elementary stage, but possible (at the elementary stage) only in the study of a vernacular. When to these pressures is added the lack, at the end of the sixteenth century, of any knowledge of the historical development of English it can be readily understood that English grammar could not have begun in any other form than as a dilution of Latin grammar.

We must now consider one of the central questions of this enquiry. What was the attitude of the early grammarians? Was there any protest about the 'application' of Latin to English, any movement of reform?

It is difficult to realise how overwhelming the dominance of Latin was. R. F. Jones has documented the conflicting criticisms and hopes which centred on English at the end of the sixteenth century.[1] These concerned mostly its vocabulary and its capacity to provide adequate and elegant expression.

Pluperfect Latinisms. There is also evidence of a rather different kind. The odd plural of 'grammatical adjectives' has been described (p. 312). A similar specifically grammatical illustration, only one instance of which seems to have been remarked before,[2] will show forcefully how the prestige of Latin could lead to the manifest distortion of English, not only in the early grammars but throughout the eighteenth century. This cultural curiosity (more strange, even, than the declension of the article quoted in chapter 11) is the invention of the forms *to had loved* and *might had loved*. They seem to have originated with Lily,[3] in a feeling, possibly, that *amavisse* was so closely related to the pluperfect subjunctive *amavissem* that it must contain

---

[1] *The Triumph of the English Language,* 1953.
[2] Poldauf, p. 68. [3] Lily, *Shorte Intro.* 1567, sig. B 5 recto.

some 'pluperfect' component, especially as there were already infinitives for present, future and perfect. Bullokar follows Lily, with a preter infinitive *to loved* and a pluperfect *to had loved*.[1] Greaves also gives this pluperfect infinitive to English,[2] as does George Mason in 1622.[3] During the eighteenth century Lily's example is repeated by Reay Sabourn in his Latin grammar,[4] and in nine English grammars.[5] The form *might had loved*, assigned either to the subjunctive or to the potential, is no less frequent in the tables. It is actually used in the text by John Hewes, speaking of masters who are harsh with their pupils' mistakes: 'It may bee, that being then of a more quicke wit and capacitie (as their yeares also might had better helped thereto) they now expect the like of others without difference.'[6]

Similar Latinisms are frequent in the paradigms of the English grammars:

1671	*could had turned*
	might had turned[7]
1690	*I might have had been* (fuissem)
	He would have had been praised (laudatus esset)[8]
1695	*That I might had called* (plup. subj.)[9]
1706–88	*Might had* (*loved*)[10]
1732	*Ought to had been called*[11]
1770	*I might have had loved*
	I might have had been loved[12]
1791	*I may have had fought* (plup. pot.)[13]
1795	*If I may then have had loved*[14]

Forms with *might had*...are the commonest, and are particularly associated with the pluperfect potential, as can be seen not only from these illustrations but from the comments of more cautious grammarians: one says of the potential, 'The Preterpluperfect and Future Tenses...are better out than in, it being no good Sence to say, *I might*

---

[1] Bullokar, 1586, pp. 358 and 362. [2] Greaves, 1594, p. 15.
[3] G. Mason, *Grammaire Angloise*, 1622, p. 42.
[4] Sabourn, *An Epitome of Grammar*, 1733, p. 33.
[5] Owen, 1732, p. 17; Saxon, 2nd edn 1737, p. 63; J.J., 1752, p. 25; Martin, 1754, p. 108; Henson, 1756, p. 15; Swaine and Sims, 1761, p. xiii; Bell, 1769, p. 225; Metcalfe, 2nd edn 1771, p. 49; Johnston, 1772, p. 16.
[6] Hewes, 1624, sig. B 1 recto. [7] Lye, 1671, p. 121.
[8] Clare, 1690, pp. 73, and 74. [9] Lane, 1695, p. 19.
[10] Owen, 1732, p. 17; *English Accidence*, 1733, p. 62; J.J., 1752, p. 24; Metcalfe, 1771, p. 49; Bell, 1769, p. 224; Smetham, 1774, p. 155; Binns, 1788, p. 264; *Key to Spelling*, 1788, p. 26.
[11] Owen, 1732, p. 17. [12] Hodgson, 1770, p. 75.
[13] Clarke, 14th edn 1791, p. 82. [14] Rhodes, 1795, p. 22.

had loved, &c.'[1] and another: 'The Pluperfect Tense in this Mode, is best expressed by the Perfect; as, *I might have loved*.'[2]

These pluperfect categories are not Latinisms; they have no more existence in Latin than in English. They are the product of sub-servience to Latin combined with an unthinking insistence that systems of moods and tenses should be exhaustively symmetrical. It is easy to see how they could have arisen in the sixteenth century, when modern English was raw and experimental, but it is strange and depressing that they could still be put forward in the year of Keats's birth.

LATIN DOMINANCE RESISTED

Three arguments. If the dominance of Latin lasted a long time it was also resisted early, continuously, and on several grounds. What may be called the grammatical argument is the one which most concerns us here, but two others are closely related to it: the priority argu-ment, which attacks the custom of teaching Latin before English, and the curriculum argument, which maintains that no Latin is needed in the education of 'ordinary' children.

In its positive form the grammatical argument was a claim for the independent status of English as a language, with its own grammar and methods of teaching. Mulcaster has already been quoted[3] as stating, as early as 1582, the fundamental principle that 'grammar' for a vernacular was different from 'grammar' for an unknown language, and John Brinsley in 1612 and 1627 argued at length that English should be taught as a subject in its own right.[4] In 1611 an anonymous translator of Cicero had argued that 'our naturall tongue...ought much more then it is, to bee Grammatically knowne, and after the course here set downe for the Latine, parsed and examined, and in all Schoole exercises...daily practised'.[5] The fullest and most emphatic of these early claims for English was made by George Snell, whose importance has been recognised only by R. F. Jones.[6] Not only would instruction in English grammar make the learning of Latin and other languages easier but:

---

[1] *English Scholar Compleat*, 1706, p. 9.
[2] Kitson, 1798, p. 85.   [3] Above, p. 164.
[4] Above, p. 154.
[5] *Certaine Epistles of Tully Verbally Translated*, 1611, sig. A 4 verso, quoted by R. F. Jones, *The Triumph of the English Language*, 1953, pp. 300–1.
[6] op. cit. pp. 293 ff.

It shall bee esteemed, of all that understand, to bee a verie excellent and useful skil, in one that knoweth nothing but meer English, to bee able, out of his Grammar, for the English tongue, to give a warrantable rule and reason, for everie word and sentence which hee speaketh, and to justifie the same for sound and approved...

...It seem's little better then a brutish and reasonless Reason, for a man to bee able to saie no more for the defens and justification of the speech which hee useth, then this, I speak so and so, becaus I hear and see that all others do speak, as I speak, and do write as I write: and for a truth, this idiotish reason is all the reason that anie man can give, for anie thing that hee writeth, unless by help of a wit more then ordinarie, hee can applie the Rules of his Latine Grammar, to maintein the rights of his English speech.

Let the English youths bee taught to learn and approve their own language, by rules of Grammar, made fit for that purpose; and they may speak English as intelligently as ever the Romanes did speak Latine: and better then anie other people, since the Romanes lost the perfection both of their Empire, and of their Eloquence...

...everie illiterate plow man can allege the constant use and custome of others, to uphold and justifie his own manner of words, pronunciation and writing: but shall one that hath been bred up at School, bee able to know no better caus, nor to yield stronger reason for the speech which hee useth, then illiterate ones can?...The neglect of this teaching of English by Grammar, is the nurs and cherisher of manie, and verie hurtful mischiefs, not onely among the common sort of Scholars, but even among them also, who otherwise are famously reputed for learning. (George Snell, *The Right Teaching of Useful Knowledge*, 1649, pp. 28–34.)

The positive and the negative sides of the grammatical argument, in later writers, usually went together. Wallis says that he wrote his grammar 'so that our own country people may see further into the workings of their native language', and he continues by complaining of his predecessors 'all forcing this English tongue of ours to conform too much to the Latin pattern'.[1]

After Wallis the protests are more frequent:

It must be acknowledged sure, that every Speech and Language hath an Idiom proper to itself: or shall the English onely be denyed that Priviledge or Prerogative? or be constrained to learn from a Forreign Language that Idiom which is proper to our own?...It is sufficiently known, that a great part of the English Tongue hath no dependence at all upon the Latin. (Newton, 1669, preface.)

[1] Wallis, sig A 7 verso: 'unde...nostrates veram nativae suae linguae rationem penitius perspiciant...omnes enim ad Latinae linguae normam hanc nostram Anglicanam nimium exigentes'.

The daily obstructions and difficulties, that occur in teaching and Learning our Mother Tongue, proceed from the want of an English Grammar, by Law establish'd...Since then all other Tongues, and Languages are taught by Grammar, why ought not the English Tongue to be taught so too. (Aickin, 1693, preface.)

English masters, Aickin goes on, cannot be more respected and better paid 'till it be found that the English Tongue is copious enough of it self, to express every thing and notion; but more chiefly till people do see that it may be perfectly acquired, without being beholden to the Latine'.[1] A tolerant conservative view is expressed in a Latin grammar which prides itself on being written in English throughout:

From the learned Languages we derive that Art and Skill which enables men for the highest Employments; for which reason the study of them will be necessary, as long as good Sense is esteemed in the world; but yet after all the Greek and Roman Authors are read, the main of all our business is perform'd in our own Language: in English we eat and drink, buy and sell; in English we live, and when all's done at last must die in English. (*The Royal Grammar Reformed*, 1695, p. 20.)

Early in the eighteenth century the anonymous writer of a Latin grammar, to which an English grammar is prefixed, acknowledges—with something of a jerk—that learning Latin and Greek is not in itself sufficient to give control of the vernacular: 'Courteous Reader, Thou hast here presented to thee so much Latin and Greek as will well suffice to make thee a compleat Master of English; or, at least, as will help thee to Write, Speak and Spell it properly (as far as Latin and Greek help).'[2] The curriculum argument is put forward by John Newton also: 'I am bold to say, that it would certainly be more advantageous, not onely for Children, but for the Common Wealth, if in stead of the Rudiments in the Latin tongue, they might be taught the Arts of Astronomy, Rhetorick, and Logick in their own.'[3] The priority argument, often implicit in the others, appears separately in Miege: 'All Young People that are designed for any Thing of good Education should begin with the Grounds of their Language.'[4] Daniel Duncan, also, makes it the principal reason for his book:

to give Children an Idea of their Mother Tongue, in every Part of Speech, before they enter upon learning of Latin. Which Method (in the Author's

[1] Aickin, 1693, preface, sig. A 3 verso. [2] *English Scholar Compleat*, 1706, preface.
[3] Newton, preface, sig A 8 verso. [4] Miege, 1688, sig. A 2 verso.

humble Opinion) would make to Boys the rational Part of Grammar (thus abstracted from the Notion of any dead or foreign Language) much easier to learn. (Duncan, 1731, p. vii.)

The author of *The English Accidence* argues that if pupils learn English before Latin 'it will (if their parents can afford it) make them learn *latin* or any other language *three times sooner*, than they do now without the knowledge of the grounds, excellency and beauty of the *English* tongue'.[1] Similar arguments are repeated countless times during the following fifty years, and not only by professed supporters of English teaching.

A. Lane. The curriculum argument is not common before the end of the seventeenth century and is absent even from the long and interesting preface in which Lane discusses the place of English. Lane's *A Key to the Art of Letters, or, English a Learned Language*, 1700, is a turning-point in the development of the English grammars. It is in many ways conservative, and later writers scorned it for keeping so narrowly to the categories of Latin. Yet, together with the English grammar in his earlier *A Rational and Speedy Method*, 1695, it is the first of those advocating a vernacular system of parts of speech, and Lane's whole approach is intended to raise the status of English. His preface begins: 'To write an English Grammar for English Youth, may seem to many, at first view, a very superfluous and ridiculous thing.' But, he continues, grammar '...is every where misunderstood, and consequently misapply'd, ever since the Latin Tongue ceas'd to be a living Language.'[2] He describes the consequent troubles of both children and masters, who

are so miserably toyl'd and perplex'd in teaching and learning Grammar, that almost all learned and ingenious Persons shun to be Schoolmasters, but whom necessity drives to those Workhouses for the necessary subsistance of Life...(Lane, 1700, p. viii.)

The consideration of these Distresses every where...has engaged the Endeavours of many Learned and Excellent Men of several Nations to study, and find out various new Methods, and compose various new Forms of Grammar; but all to little or no purpose: for the old difficulties still continue under all their new Methods. (op. cit. p. ix.)

Lane is the first writer since Mulcaster to see the central point in all these grammatical 'distresses':

---

[1] *English Accidence*, 1733, p. vi.   [2] Lane, 1700, pp. vii and viii.

The principal End and Use of Grammar is universally mistaken by all the European Nations, who think it to be nothing else but an Instrument to acquire some unknown Tongue: Whereas the true End and Use of Grammar is to teach us how to speak and write well and learnedly in a Language already known, according to the unalterable Rules of right Reason, which are the same in all Languages how different soever they be. (op. cit. p. x.)

The rest of the preface, and the bulk of the grammar itself, shows Lane's limitations. He had arrived at a fundamental truth by an unreliable path. He based his argument on universal grammar, whereas the sounder base is a linguistic fact: that the pupils at Mile End Green to whom he taught English grammar already had a measure of control over the language which made possible a depth and refinement of understanding unattainable in any other language, and demanded completely different analytical procedures. It follows from Lane's reliance on universal grammar that what the pupil learns in English grammar can be applied directly to Latin, and he demonstrates how a boy who knows no Latin can take the sentence *Pater amat filium* and

after the Master has construed it to him in the natural order, he will tell him as readily as if he had been seven years at Latin, that *Pater* is a Noun Substantive of the Nominative Case, of the Masculine Gender, and of the Singular Number; that *amat* is a Verb Active Transitive of the third Person Singular of the Present Tense... [etc.] (op. cit. p. xii.)

But if Lane fails to see that the boy's 'success' is achieved only by a breach of the principle stated earlier in the preface about the nature of a vernacular grammar he is not imperceptive about how language functions. He answers an objection that his methods, when carried over to Latin, will not enable his pupils to manage 'the many Idioms, and burdensome Exceptions that are in the Latin Tongue'. Lane's reply is a rare and early reference to the importance of context:

If no words, whether Analogous or Anomalous, be minded any where but in the contexture of good Sense; they will of course insinuate themselves into the Memory by frequent reading, as they do in the Mother-Tongue by frequent conversation.

We do not put our Children to toil themselves in the Mother-Tongue with a task of words, whether regular or irregular; and yet they equally understand them all. And if the Child be ask'd how he came by so many words, he can tell you no more than if you should convey something into his Pocket by stealth, and then ask him how it came there. (op. cit. p. xiii.)

Vernacular approaches. During the first decades of the eighteenth century protests against the dominance of Latin come, as would be expected, from those advocating a vernacular approach:

I believe it is pretty plain, that the Rules of our Tongue are only to be drawn from our Tongue it self, and as it is already in Use...and that we are to have no manner of Regard to the Proprieties of other Tongues, either Ancient or Modern. (G–B, 1711, preface.)

Several Authors have attempted to force our Language (contrary to its Nature) to the Method and Rules of the Latin Grammar...Latin Rules, when applied to our Language are no better than a useless and ridiculous Medley, serving rather to puzzle and confound, than instruct, the English Scholar...The speaking or writing English properly...may be done sooner, with far less Trouble and to as good, if not better Purpose, by a *Grammar in our own Language.* (Loughton, 1734, preface.)

The English Language ought to be learnt by an English Grammar...free from the Embarrassment of the Latin Terms and Rules. (*Easy Intro.* 1745, preface.)

The learning a Grammar of the Latin Tongue, rather than one adapted to the English, only for the English, is...absurd. (*New English Grammar*, 1746, preface.)

If to be Master of any Language, so as to write it with *Propriety* and *Exactness*, is to understand it *grammatically*; it must certainly be a *nearer* or *more concise Way*, to the Perfection of *ours*, to learn the *English Grammar itself*, than to go about to study the *Latin One*, &c. merely to come at the Knowledge of *our own* from the Nature of *theirs.* (Fisher (1749), preface to 3rd edn 1753.)

The Peculiarities of our Language can never be found out, merely by learning a Grammar that is adapted to the Latin. (S. Butler, *An Essay upon Education, c.* 1750, p. 107.)

A Soldier or Seaman residing sometime abroad might learn the Language of the Country in which he so resides, and supposing Latin a living Language might attain it in the same Manner; and yet I believe nobody can imagine he would be more capable by that Means of writing English properly than he was before: Wherefore if Latin is a necessary Help to writing our own Language, it is not meerly the Understanding it, but our Manner of getting that Understanding which furnishes this Help...In order to write English properly, it is necessary (not to learn Latin, or any foreign Language but) to learn the English Language by Grammar. (Gough, 1754, preface, p. xi.)

But it was by no means only the explicit reformers who protested. John Ash, whose tenfold system of parts of speech was an extension rather than a repudiation of the Latin practice, nevertheless wanted more attention to be paid to the distinctive features of English. Ash's grammar was so influential, and his preface describes so fairly the position at the middle of the century, that it is worth quoting at length:

The Importance of an English Education is now pretty well understood; and 'tis generally acknowledged, that...an intimate Acquaintance with the Proprieties, and Beauties of the English Tongue, wou'd be a very desirable, and necessary Attainment; far preferable to a Smattering of the more learned Languages.

But then, it has been suppos'd, even by Men of Learning, that the English Tongue is too vague, and untractable to be reduc'd to any certain Standard, or Rules of Construction; and, that a competent Knowledge of it cannot be attain'd without an Acquaintance with the Latin...

This vulgar Error...might perhaps arise from a too partial Fondness for the Latin, in which, about two Centuries ago, we had the Service of the Church, the Translation of the Bible, and most other Books, few, of any value, being then extant in the Mother Tongue.

But now the Case is happily alter'd. Nor do I think the Error above mention'd would have been so long indulg'd, under the Blessings of the Reformation, had it not been for the many fruitless Attempts, which have been made, to fix the Grammatical Construction of the English Tongue.

Many Gentlemen, who have wrote on the Subject, have too inconsiderately adopted various Distinctions of the learned Languages, which have no Existence in our own: Many, on the other hand, convinc'd by this Impropriety, have been too brief, at least, too general in their Definitions, and Rules, running into the quite opposite Extreme: And all of them, I think, have too much neglected the Peculiarities of the Language on which they wrote. (Ash, 1760, preface.)

Like Ash, the author of *A Real English Grammar* attempts a historical explanation of the dominance of Latin. He begins his preface: 'It has been for some ages a received Maxim, that no Englishman can speak or write his native Language with propriety (that is Grammatically) who has not learned Latin.'[1] More attention ought to have been given to the fact 'that the definitions, and the nature of the dependence of the several parts of Speech on each other, may be learned in any Language': that is, to universal grammar. Only the idioms need to be learnt in each particular language. More attention was not paid to universal grammar because when the world recovered from 'the universal deluge, that overwhelmed the Power of the Romans [and] destroyed their Language' veneration which was due to the subject-matter which had been preserved by the monks was given

[1] *A Real English Grammar*, 1764, p. iii.

to the Latin and Greek languages in which that subject-matter had been preserved: 'A Learner must throw away his time, who is made to study a Language entirely new to him, and for which he will have no sort of occasion in any future scheme of life, only to attain to the knowledge of principles common to all Languages, and which may be with more perspicuity, laid before him in his own.'[1] The author seeks to explain why reform has not been more successful:

The peculiarities of the English Language seem not to have been yet considered in a proper light: Some, who have essayed to give us instructions, appear not to have been masters of the subject...Some...seem to be in the state of the man, who is put to perform a different action at one and the same time with each Hand; in this case the hand, that is least used, does insensibly, and contrary to the will of its owner, imitate the action of its fellow. Thus they, who have been used from their youth to give their greatest attention to any one Language and its rules, cannot avoid inadvertently applying these rules, so deeply imprinted on their minds by habit, if they happen to consider another when they are grown up to man's estate. (*A Real E.G.* 1764, pp. vi–vii.)

The author continues by giving as examples of Latinism the cases of English substantives and the voices of verbs. He then proceeds to champion English: 'Our Language has been totally neglected and in general despised by our learned men, who have constantly affected to value themselves more on a critical knowledge of any other (particularly the Latin) than of their own.'[2] He supposes Cicero to return to eighteenth-century England, believing at first, from the respect paid to it, that Latin must be the language of parliament and the courts:

How much he must be disappointed when informed, that notwithstanding all this Sputter, it is not used in our public Assemblies nor in common conversation; that in all our Academies, so plentifully endowed, there is no Professor to instruct Men in the Language, in which they write, speak, plead, preach and debate...that the simplicity of our Language, which ought to invite us, is offered as the reason, why we despise and neglect to cultivate it. (*A Real E.G.* 1764, pp. xviii–xix.)

Ash's middle position is also that of Goldsmith's preface to Wiseman's grammar a few years later:

It has been asserted...that in order to produce a complete Grammar of our language, we should imitate the Latin in the formation of our Cases, Moods, and Tenses; whilst others, on the contrary, affirm that the English

---

[1] op. cit. p. vi.   [2] op. cit. p. xv.

tongue has no similitude whatever with the Latin in this respect, and therefore they are for preventing our making use of the common technical terms usually employed in Grammars of our language: We have taken the liberty to dissent from both...This Grammar will serve to shew that our language may be reduced to system, without the necessity of adhering so closely to the Latin as has hitherto been thought necessary; but, at the same time, care has been taken not to dissent so far from that standard language as to discard those grammatical terms borrowed from it, and which have acquired...a prescriptive right to be admitted into our own. (Wiseman, 1764, preface by Goldsmith.)

Goldsmith also refers to a view more popular in our day than his: some people, 'endeavour to palliate their own indolence' by maintaining that 'English may very well be learned without any Grammar whatsoever'; but in this 'they most certainly are deceived'.[1] Ash's argument is used also by William Ward, who admits 'there is probably no language so different from the English as the Latin is', and that 'if an English Grammar were to be made for the sole Purposes of those who propose to learn, and to use no Language but the English only, it might be put into a different Form from that of the Grammars of the learned Languages'.[2] But as you can never be sure that you may not later wish to learn another language: 'Why then may not those grammatic Forms of Nouns and Verbs, which produce the same Effects in different Languages, be called by the same grammatic Names?'[3] This conservative attitude fails to recognise that the teacher's difficulties lie in the categories themselves, not just in their names. It is this failure which made the reforming movement ineffective and makes present-day reform difficult. Too few of the reforming grammarians, and they only in moments of insight, could detach their thinking from the categories in which they had learnt to think about language. There was consequently not much practical difference between a reforming grammarian like Loughton and a conservative grammarian, like Ash, who admitted that the influence of Latin was too strong; the English grammarians who stand most clearly distinct are the Latinists like W. Turner,

[1] Not unnaturally this view is not expressed by the writers of English grammars. Nevertheless Priestley, five years after the publication of his own grammar, wrote to Caleb Rotherham: 'I question whether it will signify much to teach any English grammar. Making the scholars compose dialogues, themes, etc., correcting their bad English and making occasional remarks, I always found of most real use.' *Life and Correspondence of Joseph Priestley*, ed. J. T. Rutt, 1. 64, quoted by Irene Parker, *Dissenting Academies in England*, 1914, p. 117.

[2] W. Ward, 1767, preface. pp. iv and vii.   [3] op. cit p. vii.

Henson, Shaw and Trinder. This explains why the protests against Latin continue during the rest of the century, after the earlier promise of reform had come to little or nothing:

It is possible I may be thought to have leaned too much from the Latin idom...but I think it is evident that all other grammarians have leaned too much to the analogies of that language. (Priestley, (1761), 2nd edn 1768, preface.)

> Why should we Things of living Use neglect,
> To treat dead Languages with such Respect?...
> For, if in English, Two and Two make Four,
> In Latin, or in Greek they make no more. (Clarke (1772), 1791, p. 92.)

A practice still more ridiculous [than teaching Latin grammar but not English] has universally prevailed, till very lately...that of straining the English Tongue, without any reason or necessity, to be subservient to the puzzling rules, exceptions, and intricacies, of the Latin Grammar. (Smetham, 1774, preface.)

Our grammarians have been still endeavouring to frame the English language according to the rules of foreign languages, or to square it by their form and structure, which is as great a blunder as to fabricate a ship in the form of a horse. (*Only True Guide*, 1779, p. 1.)

Children...if they chance to be instructed in the principles of their native tongue...learn them from some system that does little more than fetter it with the rules of construction drawn from another language. (Fell, 1784, preface.)

[Members of the learned professions] having...improperly begun the study of the Latin grammar, before they had the least acquaintance with the grammatical principles of their own tongue, are too much inclined to torture the English language into a compliance with the Roman idiom. (Coote, 1788, preface.)

By the end of the century the protest is no longer made with vehemence; there is no one to convert, although no change has been made. The protest has been absorbed into the fabric of English grammar and sterilised by acceptance. Thomas Coar admits, sweetly and reasonably: 'I am...aware that I may have been misguided, as well as other writers on English Grammar, by the custom of connecting in my mind Grammar, and Latin Grammar.'[1] Final and crippling respectability was given to the protest by its inclusion in the third edition of Lindley Murray's grammar:

The English tongue is, in many respects, materially different from the learned languages; and it is necessary to regard these peculiarities, when

---

[1] Coar, 1796, preface.

we are forming a system of English Grammar. It is therefore very possible to be mistaken ourselves, and to mislead and perplex others, by an undistinguishing attachment to the principles and arrangement of the Greek and Latin Grammarians... We are apt to think, that the old names must precisely stand for the things which they anciently signified. But if we rectify this mistake, and adjust the names to the peculiar nature of the things in our own language...we shall be clear and consistent in our own ideas; and, consequently, better able to represent them intelligibly to those whom we wish to inform. (L. Murray, introduced into the 3rd edn, 1797, p. 91.)

Meantime the curriculum argument had been providing further support for a vernacular education: 'It is our Mother Tongue that is likely in the practice to be most useful...It being a Vulgar Error... to think, that to learn over the Grammar and some few Latine Books before a Boy goes to a Trade, are things so very necessary to his reading or writing true English.'[1] The vulgar error is by several writers attributed to parents as a class, and by Daniel Farro especially to

the self-conceited unthinking Tradesmen and Yeomen, who having been much more conversant and busied (very necessarily too) about coarse and earthy Matter, than Literature and Elegance, they must need, and too ambitiously, direct their Aim in the Education of their Children, intirely at the dead Languages; and when they hear their Children (they themselves not knowing what they say) only rehearse the Declensions and Conjugations of the Latin for a few modern British Words, they confide that...their Issue are compleat modern British Scholars, understanding the full extent of their native Language. (Farro, 1754, p. 242.)[2]

The curriculum argument persisted throughout the eighteenth century, less often in the grammars, more often in the numerous minor works on general education:

British Scholars, in order to be made Roman Orators, are finished compleat Blockheads; and without the least Regard to natural Capacity, are chained to the Oars of Declensions and Conjugations, until they are rendered unfit for Commerce, Trade, or even mechanical Employments. The Importance and Advantages accruing from an Acquaintance with the Classics, is universally allowed; but at the same Time it were to be wished, a proper Attention were paid to certain Arts and Sciences no less

[1] John Hawkins, *The English School-Master compleated* (1692), 1694, preface.

[2] A. Murray, 1787, is equally abusive about the 'inexcusable infatuation' of parents who insist that their children learn Latin, 'for which they will have no more necessary use, in the line of life the Parents intend them for, than the language of the Hottentots or Chinese' (p. x).

necessary, and useful, particularly the Elements of the English Tongue. (Joel, 1770, preface.)

Learning boys Latin, who are to be brought up to trade and business, or to the mechanical, is merely wasting a very precious portion of their time to no purpose, which would be spent to far greater advantage...in acquiring a grammatical knowledge of their own tongue, reading at school the best English classics, writing, accompts, geography, and the most useful branches of the mathematics. (Buchanan, *A Plan of an English Grammar-School Education*, 1770, p. 142.)

There can be no doubt that during the seventeenth and eighteenth centuries the grammarians *did* protest—more, perhaps, than has been realised—against the dominance of Latin. The grammatical and the priority arguments are the most significant; the curriculum argument is the most readable, but is only another aspect of a long-standing utilitarian tradition.

Did the protests lead to action? This is another unsatisfactory question. Most of the protests *were* action: the grammarians who have just been quoted are the small minority who were thoughtful enough, or cared enough, to make an explicit protest in general terms. It is necessary to distinguish these explicit protests from the evidence of dissastisfaction and discomfort which is the principal subject-matter of the preceding chapters. It has been shown how unstable the categories were: how their criteria were shifting and uncertain; how their contents could vary even when their definitions were the same; how the definitions and the criteria could be inconsistent with each other. Much of this instability was caused by the inappropriateness of the categories themselves. Some was caused by the writers' ignorance of the best practice of their own day, some by their lack of a linguistic knowledge which was not available to them. Nevertheless, much of the instability—it is impossible to say how much—must have some other cause. The tradition, as was shown in Part One, was less stable than it is often said to be, but it was very much more stable than the English tradition which took over from it. Further instability would arise from the use with a largely uninflected language of categories evolved to fit inflected languages: the stresses which this could set up have been apparent. But these stresses would have been much less noticeable if the English grammarians had been content with their inheritance. They are as evident as they are because the grammarians were dissatisfied, and tried, with widely varying degrees of awareness, to modify the system. What is evidence for the existence of stresses within the system is very often evidence also for the grammarians' dissatisfaction.

A MOVEMENT OF REFORM

In chapter 8 it was shown that the grammarians gave their approval to fifty-six different systems of parts of speech—perhaps the most surprising fact to emerge from this enquiry. Even among those which kept most closely to the Latin (p. 521), there are twenty different systems. If grammarians, few of whom are trying to make any change, disagree amongst themselves to this extent the categories they are using must be unstable. Equally, there could not be so many 'Latin' systems unless, consciously or not, many individual adjustments and modifications were being made. James Douglas's manuscripts (p. 222) show just such modifications. First he says there are ten parts of speech; then he moves the participle under the verb, and says there are nine; then he goes back to the old practice of combining adjective and substantive in the one category noun, and says there are eight. And in all these three versions he keeps also to the view that the parts of speech can be reduced to three: noun, verb and particle. He makes no protest. He expresses no dissatisfaction with the tradition or its categories, but his actions imply it. Douglas provides a particularly clear instance of conscious but unformulated dissatisfaction. Dr Johnson provides an instance of the opposite kind. He does not enumerate his parts of speech; he does not even say how many there are; he does not even discuss all those he obviously recognises. *Noun Substantive* and *Adjective* he discusses in sections headed by these terms. He refers always to *adjectives*, never to *noun adjectives*, and the arrangement and tone of his discussion suggest almost without doubt that he thinks of substantive and adjective as distinct parts of speech. The only cause for hesitation is that he uses the term *noun substantive* (once only) rather than *noun* or *substantive* alone. Nevertheless the evidence is far stronger for assuming that he regards them as two parts of speech than as one. It then appears that Dr Johnson is the first grammarian (apart from Douglas in his second draft) to propose this system of parts of speech—No. 10. It is disconcerting to find that Dr Johnson is an innovator in a matter over which he expressed conservative views; it would be absurd to suggest that he felt dissatisfaction but could not express it. What then do the facts signify? Johnson's treatment of the parts if speech, like the more explicit systems of most other Latinate grammarians, is the product of many marginal judgments: whether the substantive and adjective are two primary parts of speech or one; whether the participle is a primary part of speech or included within the verb; whether the article stands alone or is treated as an adjective. None of these judgments *by itself* constitutes an innovation; none of them requires a considered opinion such as it would take to put four parts of speech into a primary category of particle. Johnson's classification may be evidence of instability in the categories but not of dissatisfaction, even latent dissatisfaction, on his part.

It is not easy to say, therefore, how far the grammarians' protests led to action. There are conscious reforms, discussed by their authors, such as the tense-schemes of Groups IV and V (pp. 408 ff.); most of the individual systems of parts of speech (Appendix One); and many of those among the vernacular systems (pp. 525–7). There are modifications which could not have been made unwittingly, but are put forward without comment. These are numerous and varied: calling the verb an affirmation; making the article an adjective; saying that adverbs and conjunctions are so alike that it is scarcely worth while to distinguish between them; approving an alternative system of parts of speech; saying that English has no passive verbs, or no moods, or only two tenses. Each modification of this kind is significant: it implies a conscious departure from the tradition, even if it is also a decision just to copy from some 'modern' grammar. There are modifications which are so slight that they may not be apparent to the author and are no evidence for his opinions. They are compatible with a happy traditionalism or with scarcely acknowledged doubts; they are of no significance individually, but of considerable importance collectively. Such are the grammarians' struggles with the neuter verb (chap. 12) and with the pronoun (chap. 10), the many variations in the definition of the substantive (chap. 9), and countless small judgments of classification, like Dr Johnson's. Only the two first kinds of modification are significant as action. Both are combined in those grammars which have been referred to many times in this study as supporting a vernacular system. The authors form a real, if tentative, movement which has not been commented on before.

These reforming grammars have two features in common: (i) a fourfold system of parts of speech (Systems 31–41) comprising substantive, adjective, verb and particle. The pronoun is almost always included within the substantive; the particle includes at least the adverb, conjunction and preposition. A distinctive feature of this fourfold classification is that it makes the adjective a primary part. (ii) the second characteristic is an attempt at a vernacular terminology, if only for one or two categories.

Only twenty-five grammars contain both these features. Their authors have a policy: to give English a grammar more suited to it and less subservient to Latin. Although they are few in number and scattered over sixty years they represent a tendency for which there is clear evidence, and it is no exaggeration to call it, if not a reforming movement, at least a movement of reform:

Reforming grammars advocating both the fourfold system and a vernacular terminology

1711 Gildon and Brightland, *A Grammar of the English Tongue*; seven later editions to 1759.

1734 William Loughton, *A Practical Grammar of the English Tongue*; seven later editions to 1755.

1737 Solomon Lowe, *English Grammar Reformd*.

1737 Samuel Saxon, *The English Schollar's Assistant*, 2nd edn.

1745 *An Easy Introduction to the English Language*; eight later editions to 1787.

1746 *A New English Grammar*; another edition in 1760.

1750 Anne Fisher, *A New Grammar*, 2nd edn; over forty editions to 1800.

1750? *An English Grammar*.

1753 *A Pocket Dictionary*, and three later editions to 1779.

1754 Daniel Farro, *The Royal Universal British Grammar and Vocabulary*; three editions in that year.

1754 James Gough, *A Practical Grammar of the English Tongue*, 2nd edn; six other editions to 1801.

1754 Thomas Wise, *The Newest Young Man's Companion*; at least ten editions to 1778.

1755 Solomon Lowe, *The Critical Spelling Book*; a second edition in 1770.

1755 *A Spelling Dictionary*; about fifteen later editions to 1798, but it is not certain that they all contain the grammar.

1760 Daniel Bellamy, *A New Complete English Dictionary*; three other editions to 1764.

1765 John Entick, *The New Spelling Dictionary*; nearly thirty later editions to 1791.

1771 *A New and Improved Spelling Dictionary*.

1773 *The Court Letter-Writer*.

1773 John Carter, of Leeds, *A Practical English Grammar*, and perhaps an edition in 1775.

1774 James Barclay, *A Complete and Universal English Dictionary*; three later editions to 1799.

1774 Thomas Smetham, *The Practical Grammar*; two other editions by 1775.

1775? Thomas Cooke, *The Universal Letter-Writer* (No. 55 of Appendix VI, below) at least five later editions to 1809.

1776? Daniel Farro, *The Royal Golden Instructor*. It keeps close to the grammar of 1754.

1790? Thomas Cooke, *The Universal Letter-Writer* (No. 56 of Appendix VI, below). It keeps close to the grammar of 1775.

1790? David Fordyce, *The New and Complete British Letter-Writer*.

The movement of reform is expressed centrally in these twenty-five grammars, first issued between 1711 and, with virtually one exception, 1775. They appear in at least 170 editions by 1809.

The characteristics which these twenty-five grammars have in common represent two lines of reform. Their fourfold system has no intrinsic connection with the vernacular movement. It is put forward first by A. Lane in his two grammars of 1695 and 1700 (p. 254) in terms which are, in this form, new to the English tradition. Lane's four parts of speech correspond to four kinds of words: substantives, verbs, and the 'manners' of each; and the four kinds of words correspond to four constituents of experience: things, actions and the qualities of each. If a source has to be located for this classification it is almost certainly the Port Royal grammar, beyond which stands Wallis, and behind him Gill. The vernacular terminology does not come from Lane but from Gildon and Brightland who, much more than Lane, were directly under the influence of the Port Royal grammar. *Name*, *affirmation*, and to a lesser extent *manner*, they take from Port Royal, though only *affirmation* was a real novelty. Their use of *quality* for *adjective* does not come from Port Royal. In the Port Royal grammar *affirmation* is used not instead of *verb* (as it is by Gildon after his first edition) but as the key term in describing the verb's function. The reforming movement among the English grammars seems, therefore, to have its most obvious source in two of the Port Royal principles: the application of logic to grammar, and the use of everyday, non-technical terms in which to describe the categories. But the Port Royal grammar was not the only route by which these principles entered the English grammatical tradition.

Gill, in 1619, had used a threefold system including the particle. A logical approach to grammar had been an almost constant accompaniment, and sometimes a central part of, the earlier tradition, and went back to its beginnings. The vernacular approach was 'modern'. Its first spokesman among the English grammars was John Wallis. Although he wrote in Latin he maintained that English needed a grammar of its own, and the lead he gave lasted a hundred years. But even Wallis only represented the best thought of his time. The vernacular approach was supported by pressures of great power and complexity—pressures patriotic, protestant, utilitarian and rationalistic.

As the two approaches, the logical and the vernacular, are separable, so there are grammars in which they occur separately. Those thirteen grammars, especially, which use the four-fold system without a vernacular terminology must be considered part of the movement of reform:

1695   A. Lane, *A Rational and Speedy Method*; another edition in 1698.
1700   A. Lane, *A Key to the Art of Letters*; two later editions to 1706.
1704   *Right Spelling very much improved.*
1726   J. T. Philipps, *An Essay towards an Universal and Rational Grammar*;[1] two later editions to 1741.
1735   Dyche and Pardon, *A New General English Dictionary*; at least twenty later editions to 1800.
1739   Daniel Turner, *An Abstract of English Grammar and Rhetoric*; another edition in 1741.
1748   Benjamin Martin, *Institutions of Language.*
1752   J. J., *Prittle-Prattle.*
1758   Mr S. Johnson, *A Compleat Introduction to the Art of Writing Letters.*
1760?   Samuel Hammond, *A Complete and Comprehensive Spelling Dictionary.*
1765   Samuel Edwards, *An Abstract of English Grammar.*
1767?   Charles Johnson, *The Complete Art of Writing Letters*; six editions by 1779, but it is not known whether the grammar is in all editions.
1777   H. Ward, *A Short but clear System of English Grammar.*

---

[1] Philipps shows what divided these grammarians from those using the vernacular terms: 'All these together [his four primary parts] the Grammarians in obscure terms call'd Noun, Pronoun, Participle, Verb, Adverb, Preposition, Conjunction, Interjection. I dare say a Child would learn many hundred Latin Words, before he can understand these eight Terms: Nevertheless we are oblig'd to make Use of these Terms, tho' obscure in themselves, that the Learner may not be ignorant of the Grammatical Language.' (2nd edn 1731, p. iv.) The same argument is common today.

Reforming terminology. Those grammars which use vernacular terms without adopting this fourfold system are not necessarily part of the movement of reform. Many of them adopted one or two vernacular terms without in any way modifying their Latinate approach. The new term was chosen not because it was English but because it was simple to teach: a good reason, but distinct from the grounds on which the reforming movement was based. The only one of these grammarians whose work is wholly in the reforming spirit is John Collyer, 1735, who refers to the fourfold system as being advocated by 'some modern Grammarians', but does not adopt it. His enthusiasm is entirely for the vernacular terms, which he puts forward in greater profusion than any other writer. These terms have been recorded at the end of each chapter, but it will be useful to see them collected together, with one or two which have not yet been referred to:

(Substantive)	*Name* (p. 316) Lane, 1695; G–B, 1711; frequently thereafter.
(Adjective)	*Quality* (p. 318) G–B, 1711; not uncommon.
(Pronoun)	*Personal name* (p. 348) Lane, 1695; not frequent.
	Proname (p. 348) G–B refer to it; its use is very rare.
	For-noun (p. 319) Possibly by Sampson, 1790.
	Representative (p. 348) Collyer, 1735; occasionally in later grammars; not necessarily considered a vernacular term.
	Alternative (p. 322) Used only by Kirkby, 1746.
	Deputy-name (p. 347) Used only by Douglas, *c.* 1720.
(Verb)	*Affirmation* (p. 392) G–B, 1712; frequently thereafter.
(Adverb)	*Added word* (p. 450) G–B, 1711, only.
	Manner (p. 451) Used virtually as a synonym for *adverb* by Collyer.
(Conjunction)	*Joining word* (p. 454) G–B, 1711, and Collyer only.
(Preposition)	*Foreplaced word* (p. 461) G–B, 1711, only.
	Forename ⎱ (p. 461) ⎧It is not certain what these terms *For-verb* ⎰ ⎩referred to.
(Interjection)	*Exclamation* Collyer seems to suggest that this should be the vernacular name of the category.
(Imperative)	*Commanding mood* ⎱ A. Murray only.[1]
(Infinitive)	*Unlimited mood* ⎰
(Auxiliary)	*Helper* 'I chuse to call them *Helpers*, rather than *Auxiliary* or *Helping* Verbs, because when they are thus used, they are not properly Verbs.' (Collyer)[2]
	Helping Verb A common simplification in Latin and

[1] A. Murray, 2nd edn 1787, p. 32.
[2] p. 53 n; also in *Remarks on the English Tongue*, 1776, p. 17.

English grammars throughout the period, but especially popular with the reforming grammarians.

(Syntax)   *Sentences* (p. 186) By many writers the division of grammar into Letters (Syllables), Words, Sentences, was looked on as an 'English' form of the division into Orthography, Etymology, and Syntax, but it appears also in Latin grammars.

(Nominative)   *Foregoing or leading state*⎱ Wallis, in order to avoid saying
(Accusative)   *Following state*   ⎰ that English pronouns possessed cases, had called their variations *formae* or *status*, the one *rectus*, the other *obliquus*. Gildon anglicised *status* as *state*. Greenwood, also in 1711, called the nominative and accusative 'foregoing' and 'following' states, and in the next year Gildon, in the second edition, called the forms of the pronoun 'leading state' and 'following state'. The reforming grammarians adopted these terms, usually from Gildon, and many others welcomed them because they were self-explanatory. (There were difficulties: interrogative forms pushed John Williams, about 1780, into the Gilbertian statement that 'leading words...come properly behind'.) These terms occur in about fifty grammars throughout the eighteenth century.

(Accusative)   *Patient or*   ⎱ J. T. Philipps alone: the accusative is
               Passive Case⎰ 'more properly call'd the *Patient* or *Passive* Case'.[1]

(Nominative)   *Antecedent*⎱ Used only by Gough.[2]
(Accusative)   *Consequent*⎰

(Nominative   *Explicit*⎫
and Subject)   ⎬ Used only in *The Practice* and by John Kirkby.
(Accusative   *Implicit*⎭
and Object)

Kirkby calls the two 'states' of the pronouns 'first' and 'second'. In the first state the pronoun is said to be 'explicit', in the second 'implicit'. These terms then become equivalent to *subject* and *object*, so that Kirkby can say, 'The Infinitive Mood may be an Explicit to a Verb'.[3] *Explicit* is used in the same sense in *The Practice*, though it seems to be sometimes a second thought.[4] In *The Practice* *implicate*, not *implicit*, is used for *object*, and *implicate state* sometimes for *accusative*.[5] *Pure state* is found in *The Practice* for the uninflected (nominative) form of a pronoun.[6] This corresponds to *leading state*, mentioned above.

---

[1] Philipps (1726), 2nd edn 1731, p. ix.   [2] Gough, 1754, p. 103.
[3] Kirkby, 1746, p. 117.   [4] *Practice*, pp. 153–4.
[5] op. cit. p. 142.   [6] op. cit. p. 162.

(Tense)   *Time* (p. 394) *Tense* had been anglicised in the sixteenth century, and this was an obvious term for the reformers to use.

The centre of the reforming movement lies in the grammars which use both the fourfold system of parts of speech and a vernacular terminology. Closely supporting the reform are those who use the fourfold system but not the terminology. Related to these, but often with quite different motives, are those who use a vernacular terminology but some other system of parts of speech. The logical side of the reform is introduced by Lane in 1695; Gildon and Brightland add the vernacular terms in 1711 and 1712. The movement of reform is active between 1730 and 1775.[1] It is advocated positively in thirty-eight grammars and affects, in small ways, at least as many again. It is not much of a movement, but in the heavy atmosphere surrounding eighteenth-century English grammar even a small movement needed quite an effort.[2]

OTHER CONSTRUCTIVE ACHIEVEMENTS

Many constructive and influential grammarians were bigger than, and stood outside, the reforming movement. Many who were not influential nevertheless struggled for better control over the language, for better descriptive and analytical procedures. To the first class belong, for example, Paul Greaves; Alexander Gill; John Wallis; John Wilkins; Mark Lewis; James Greenwood; James Harris; John Ash; James White; Robert Lowth; Joseph Priestley; William Ward; James Beattie; James Pickbourn; John Horne Tooke; Lindley

---

[1] 'In 1738 the English master in Ayr was deposed because he was "not known in the New Method". In 1746 a schoolmaster was appointed in Irvine to teach English "after the modern way".' (William Boyd, *Education in Ayrshire through Seven Centuries*, London 1961.) It is not known what this 'new method' was. Boyd supposes that it 'involved a systematic study of the grammar of the language' and quotes an unnamed source as saying that 'in 1769 the teaching of English grammar was "a branch almost new"'. The earliest of the grammars in Appendix vi to be printed in Scotland is James Corbet's, in Glasgow, 1743, which contains no suggestion that English grammar was an innovation in the west of Scotland.

[2] That the reforming grammarians were seen as such quite early on is shown by one of the writers in *The Many Advantages of a good Language*, 1724, sponsored by Thomas Wilson, Bishop of Sodor and Man: 'Have our late Grammarians done well in reducing the Number [of the parts of speech] to Four, and changing their Names? As Eight is a convenient Number, altho' not strictly natural or necessary, yet had we not better agree with our Latin and Greek Grammars, and with our Nabors also, than change the present State of our Grammars without great Reason?' (p. 75).

Murray, and John Dalton. Among the second belong Christopher Cooper; the authors of *The True Method* and of *The English Scholar Compleat*; Hugh Jones; Daniel Duncan; John Kirkby; James Douglas; the author of *The Practice*; Anselm Bayly; James Swaine and Joseph Sims; Samuel Edwards; the author of *A Real English Grammar*; Rowland Jones; Mark Anthony Meilan; James Burnett; Lord Monboddo; John Fell; Alexander Murray; Daniel Pape; J. Cook; P. W. Fogg; James Anderson; 'Mica'; the author of the article on 'Grammar' in the third edition of the *Encyclopaedia Britannica*; Patrick Lynch; H. Groombridge, and John Sedger. The evidence for their dissatisfaction, and for their attempts to modify particular categories, lies in the preceding chapters. Together they are powerful witnesses both to the instability of the system and to its capacity for development.

If one is forced to claim that the seventeenth- and eighteenth-century grammarians have hitherto been under-estimated this is not to say that they have noticeable linguistic talent. Detailed search among such a large number of works would naturally reveal flashes of insight and enterprising quirks. But cumulatively even these are of interest. They balance and support the better-known discussions of usage during the last thirty years of the eighteenth century, and suggest that the grammatical tradition, though not as lively as the rhetorical and lacking a single figure to compare with George Campbell, was not dead—only drowsy. It could be active in protest and small ingenuities, if not in systematic reform. There is no single reason why its capacity for development remained largely unfulfilled, but there was certainly no greater obstacle to grammatical advance than that persistent confusion between form and meaning which complicated the use of every category described in this work.

The positive achievement is less organised and less articulate than the movement of protest. This is natural. The dominance of Latin caused much constructive energy to be diverted into attacks on the past. Richard Johnson is a particular instance of an acute, scholarly critic who did not succeed in systematising his positive ideas because he was continually enraged by the absurdities of the authorised grammar. Only the exceptional schoolmasters like Lewis, Lane, William Ward or Pickbourn could see beyond the urgency of protest to the greater need for experiment and change. It was a little easier for the bishops, professors and country gentlemen to take a broad view. Not only were they more highly placed; they did not have to teach Latin to schoolboys.

The achievement is more substantial than it may seem at first. The true status of a vernacular grammar was seen by Mulcaster (p. 164) and by Lane (p. 498). The fourfold system of Lane and the other reforming grammarians substantially anticipates the four word-classes of a modern structural grammarian, C. C. Fries.[1] The category *particle*, used by the reforming writers and many others (p. 535) preserves much of the old and important distinction between 'logical' words and 'full' words. The importance of relation, an idea fundamental to any analysis of a vernacular, is preserved by Wallis, by Newton (p. 370), Gildon and Brightland, and especially by Harris (pp. 456–7) and William Ward (pp. 378–9 f., 457–8). It is implicit in the analogies with algebra made by W. Ward (p. 458), the *Encyclopaedia Britannica* (B) (p. 428), Sedger (p. 370 n.) and by Gregory (p. 428). The separation of criteria achieved by Linacre is preserved (to no avail) by John Ward and a few others (p. 373). A flexible approach to the units of analysis appears in the formation of new parts of speech (p. 212); in the traditional view of the adverb and interjection as contracted sentences (pp. 449, 464, 479); in Lewis's thinking about subordination (p. 475); in W. Ward's fuller treatment of coalescence (p. 287); in Wallis's widely adopted respective and possessive adjectives (pp. 307–10); in the remarks of William Scott (p. 455) and William Ward (p. 457) on the function of the prepositional phrase, and even in Sedger's eccentric treatment of the preposition (p. 445). The affective elements in speech are just recognised in Rowland Jones's comments on the interjection (p. 462), in the references by Harris (p. 323) and Gregory (p. 428) to gesture in the discussion, started by Harris, about the speaker's 'energy' or intention (pp. 367–8) and they are implicit in the widely used concept of assertion (p. 366). The importance of situation and context is referred to by Harris (p. 323) and Lane (p. 499), and the importance of an empirical approach to grammar is maintained by Priestley and others (p. 192). But perhaps the most important anticipation of reform is one of the commonest features of the grammars, quite unremarked at the time, and only now known to have been so frequent: the use of syntactic criteria in defining the parts of speech. If only the grammarians could have understood the significance of

---

[1] *The Structure of English*, New York, 1952.

what they were doing they could have given English grammar much-needed techniques of its own. But, as is shown by the illustrations in chapters 9–12, they saw these syntactic definitions only as a usefully 'visual' form of explanation.

It is not through timidity, nor even through modesty, that so little has been said here about the cultural and philosophical background to these 273 grammars. They are surprisingly, distressingly, self-contained. In them grammar had become such an impacted discipline that it could scarcely be modified from outside. The grammarians responded to the specifically educational ideas of Comenius and Locke, and to specifically grammatical writings such as the Port Royal grammar and Richard Johnson's *Grammatical Commentaries*. But there are few references to Locke's *Essay*, and no sign that it influenced the treatment of the parts of speech or the categorical framework generally. In the eighteenth century the idea of universal grammar had lost the connection with logic which made it linguistically important and was used by the grammarians merely to assure their pupils that in studying one language they were being prepared to learn them all. Utilitarian and rationalist views strongly affected eighteenth-century education and influenced much that was written about language. But grammar and language were far apart. It was the rare individual, Harris or William Ward, who allowed the enlightening power of reason to affect his grammatical categories. The popularity of vernacular terms, and the great increase in the number of grammars towards the end of the century, are closely related to the development of nonconformist and commercial schooling and to the growing concern for the education of girls. But there is no evidence (and little likelihood) that these movements affected the *categories* in the grammars, with which we are here concerned. Yet the categories have been shown to be unstable. The paradox of the grammars is their combination of crass stability with constant internal restlessness and change. This restlessness, these minor but not insignificant modifications, are not the product (even indirectly) of philosophy but of unpretentious experience in the classroom. The further paradox follows: that the schoolmasters were more aware than they knew that something was wrong with the system they had inherited.

Otto Funke and Ivan Poldauf have tried to relate the grammars to a philosophical background. It is possible to value their work highly but at the same time to regret its lack of illustration and evidence. In the eighteenth century, especially, there is a gap (because there was *then* a gap) between the grammars and the intellectual movements of the time. 'Influence' is notoriously difficult to isolate and measure. Unless it can be well supported by evidence it remains questionable and of little value; it may titillate hypotheses but adds nothing to knowledge. We need a history of the philosophy of language in the seventeenth and eighteenth centuries, but it must be based on a closer study than has yet been made of the considerable linguistic literature.

From the outside the grammars look impressively, if monotonously, stable. From another point of view they are sadly fossilised. Such stability, such a uniform (if monotonous) façade, has given authority to our grammatical tradition, and teachers have respectfully preserved the façade from the decay which should have destroyed it. Our respect has been misplaced: it should have been given to those ill-informed, dissatisfied, protesting, and sometimes perceptive schoolmasters who were making the first attempts to give English a grammar of its own, and to teach English children how to control the English language.

APPENDICES

INDEX

APPENDIX I

SYSTEMS OF PARTS OF SPEECH
(see above, pp. 209 ff.)

No. 6   1670   1 grammar   (p. 219)

Substantive (incl. pronoun)   Adverb
Adjective   Conjunction
Verb   Preposition (incl. article)

No. 7   1710–97   13 grammars   (p. 220)

Noun (adjective incl. article)   Adverb
Pronoun   Conjunction
Verb   Preposition
Participle   Interjection

No. 8   1712   1 grammar   (p. 222)

Noun   Adverb (incl. interjection)
Pronoun   Conjunction
Article   Preposition
Verb
Participle

No. 9   1720–1799   53 grammars   (p. 223)

Substantive   Adverb
Adjective   Conjunction
Article   Preposition
Pronoun   Interjection
Verb
Participle

No. 10   1720–1800   45 grammars   (p. 225)

Substantive   Adverb
Adjective   Conjunction
Article   Preposition
Pronoun   Interjection
Verb (incl. participle)

No. 11   1735–90   2 grammars   (p. 228)

Substantive   Adverb
Adjective (incl. article and participle)   Conjunction
Pronoun   Preposition
Verb   Interjection

No. 12   1739   1 grammar   (p. 228)

Substantive (incl. pronoun substantive)   Adverb
Adjective (incl. pronoun adjective and   Conjunction
   participle)   Preposition
Verb   Interjection

Appendix I

No. 13   1756–64   2 grammars   (p. 229)

Noun
Pronoun (incl. article)
Verb
Participle

Adverb
Conjunction
Preposition
Interjection

No. 14   1760   1 grammar   (p. 230)

Substantive (incl. pronoun substantive)
Adjective (incl. article; participle; pro-
   noun adjective)
Verb

Adverb (incl. interjection)
Conjunction
Preposition

No. 15   1761–98   6 grammars   (p. 231)

Substantive
Adjective (incl. article)
Pronoun
Verb (incl. participle)

Adverb
Conjunction
Preposition
Interjection

No. 16   1763–9   2 grammars   (p. 233)

Substantive (incl. pronoun)
Adjective (incl. article)
Verb
Participle

Adverb
Conjunction
Preposition
Interjection

No. 17   1768–71   2 grammars (1 author)   (p. 233)

Substantive
Adjective (incl. participle)
Article
Pronoun
Verb

Adverb
Conjunction
Preposition
Interjection

No. 18   1777–98   2 grammars   (p. 234)

Substantive (with article)
Adjective
Pronoun
Verb
Participle

Adverb
Conjunction
Preposition
Interjection

No. 19   1786–94   3 grammars   (p. 235)

Substantive
Adjective (incl. article)
Pronoun
Verb
Participle

Adverb
Conjunction
Preposition
Interjection

No. 20 1801 1 grammar (p. 235)

Noun (incl. interjection; adjective incl.   Adverb
  article)   Conjunction
Pronoun   Preposition
Verb (incl. participle)

Number of grammars using Latin systems 203

MODIFIED SYSTEMS BEFORE 1700

No. 21 1594 1 grammar (p. 236)

Noun (adjective incl. article)   Adverb (incl. preposition
Pronoun   and interjection)
Verb (incl. participle)   Conjunction

No. 22 1619–1720 2 grammars (p. 237)

Noun (incl. pronoun)
Verb (incl. participle)
Particle (compr. adverb; conjunction; preposition; article; interjection)

No. 23 1633 1 grammar (p. 239)

Noun (incl. pronoun; article, with   Adverb (incl. conjunction
  substantive)   and interjection)
Verb (incl. participle)   Preposition

No. 24 1652 1 grammar (p. 240)

Words of action
Words of quality
Words of help

No. 25 1653 1 grammar (p. 241)

Substantive   Adverb
Adjective   Conjunction ⎫ perhaps as
Pronoun   Preposition ⎬ particle
Verb (incl. participle)   Interjection ⎭

No. 26 1661 1 grammar (p. 241)

Noun

No. 27 1668 1 grammar (p. 247)

Integral
Grammatical particle
Cross-categories

No. 28   1685   1 grammar   (p. 251)

Noun (article, preposition and pronoun with substantive; adjective incl. participle)
Verb

Adverb (incl. interjection and preposition)
Conjunction

No. 29   1686   1 grammar   (p. 253)

Noun (incl. pronoun; adjective incl. article)
Verb (incl. participle)

Adverb (incl. interjection and preposition)
Conjunction

No. 30   1696   1 grammar   (p. 253)

Substantive (incl. pronoun substantive)
Adjective (incl. pronoun adjective)
Verb (incl. participle)

Adverb
Conjunction
Particle (compr. article; preposition; interjection; auxiliary verb, etc.)

Number of grammars before 1700 using a modified system   11

VERNACULAR SYSTEMS

No. 31   1695–1700   2 grammars (1 author)   (p. 254)

Substantive (incl. 1st and 2nd person pronouns)
Adjective (incl. 3rd person pronouns and article)
Verb (incl. participle)
Particle (compr. adverb; conjunction; preposition)

No. 32   1704   1 grammar   (p. 255)

Substantive (with article; incl. pronoun)
Adjective
Verb (incl. participle)
Particle (compr. adverb; conjunction; preposition)

No. 33   1711–76   7 grammars   (p. 255)

Substantive (incl. pronoun)
Adjective (incl. article and participle)
Verb
Particle (compr. adverb, incl. interjection; conjunction; preposition)

No. 34 1726 1 grammar (p. 256)
Substantive (incl. pronoun)
Adjective (incl. article and participle)
Verb
Particle (compr. adverb; conjunction; preposition)

No. 35 1735–75 11 grammars (p. 257)
Substantive (with article; incl. pronoun)
Adjective
Verb (incl. participle)
Particle (compr. adverb; conjunction; preposition; interjection)

No. 36 1737–77 8 grammars (p. 258)
Substantive (incl. pronoun)
Adjective (incl. article)
Verb (incl. participle)
Particle (compr. adverb; conjunction; preposition; interjection)

No. 37 1737 1 grammar (p. 260)
Substantive (with article)
Adnoun (compr. adjective; pronoun; participle)
Verb
Particle (compr. adverb; conjunction; preposition; interjection)

No. 38 1739–52 3 grammars (p. 260)
Substantive (incl. pronoun substantive)
Adjective (incl. pronoun adjective and participle)
Verb
Particle (compr. adverb; conjunction; preposition: interjection)

No. 39 1760–74 2 grammars (p. 261)
Substantive (incl. pronoun)
Adjective (incl. participle)
Verb
Particle (compr. adverb; conjunction; preposition incl. article; inter-
jection)

No. 40 1765 1 grammar (p. 261)
Substantive (incl. pronoun)
Adjective (incl. participle and article)
Verb
Particle (compr. adverb; conjunction; preposition; interjection)

Appendix I

No. 41   1790   2 grammars   (p. 262)

Substantive (with article)
Adjective
Verb
Particle (compr. adverb; conjunction; preposition; interjection; pronoun)

Number of grammars using a vernacular system   39

MODIFIED SYSTEMS AFTER 1700

No. 42   1724   1 grammar   (p. 262)

Noun (incl. pronoun and participle)
Verb
Particle (compr. article; adverb; conjunction; preposition; interjection)

No. 43   1746   2 grammars   (p. 263)

Substantive (incl. pronoun)
Adjunctive (compr. adjective, incl. article; verb, incl. participle)
Particle (compr. adverb; conjunction; preposition; interjection)

No. 44   1751–71   3 grammars   (p. 264)

Substantive (incl. pronoun)
Attributive (compr. (i) verb; adjective; participle
                    (ii) adverb, incl. interjection)
Definitive (incl. article)
Conjunctive (compr. conjunction and preposition)

No. 45   1754   1 grammar   (p. 265)

Noun (incl. pronoun)
Verb (incl. participle)
Adverb
Particle (compr. conjunction; interjection; preposition incl. article)

No. 46   1756–72   2 grammars (1 author)   (p. 265)

Noun (incl. pronoun, which incl. article)
Verb (incl. participle)
Particle (compr. preposition; adverb; conjunction; interjection)

No. 47   1760   1 grammar   (p. 266)

Substantive (incl. pronoun substantive)
Adjective (incl. pronoun adjective)
Verb (incl. participle)
Adverb
Particle (compr. article; conjunction; preposition; interjection)

527

No. 48   1761   1 grammar   (p. 267)

Noun (substantive incl. pronoun; adjective incl. participle)
Verb
Particle (compr. adverb; conjunction; preposition, incl. article; interjection)

No. 49   *c.* 1760–79   2 grammars   (p. 267)

Substantive
Adjective
Pronoun
Verb (incl. participle)
Particle (compr. article; adverb; conjunction; preposition; interjection)

No. 50   1771   1 grammar   (p. 268)

Substantive (incl. pronoun substantive)
Adjective (incl. article; pronoun adjective; some participles)
Verb (incl. some participles)
Adverb (with verbs only)
Comparative (with adjectives and adverbs)
Particle (compr. conjunction; preposition; interjection)

No. 51   1774–86   2 grammars   (p. 269)

Substantive (incl. pronoun and article)
Verb (incl. participle; adjective; adverb; conjunction; preposition; interjection)

No. 52   1775   1 grammar   (p. 271)

Noun
Pronoun
Verb
Particle (compr. adverb; conjunction; preposition; interjection)

No. 53   1793   1 grammar   (p. 271)

Noun (incl. pronoun)
Article
Verb (incl. participle)
Particle (compr. adverb; conjunction; preposition; interjection)

No. 54   1793   1 grammar   (p. 271)

Article	Adjunct
Name	Relation
Definitive	Conjunction
Substitute	Interjection
Quality	Number
Existence	

No. 55   1797–8   2 grammars   (p. 273)
   Substantive
   Adjective
   Verb

No. 56   1797   1 grammar   (p. 273)
   Noun (incl. pronoun; article)
   Verb (incl. preposition; conjunction; interjection; participle)
   Adverb

Number of grammars after 1700 using a modified system   22

TABLES SHOWING THE FORM TAKEN
BY EACH PART OF SPEECH
(see above, p. 211.)

	Forms taken by the category NOUN	No. of grammars
	Always a primary part of speech, comprising:	
1	Substantive; adjective	31
2	Substantive (with article); adjective	39
3	Substantive (incl. pronoun); adjective	3
4	Substantive; adjective (incl. article)	14
5	Substantive; adjective (incl. participle)	2
6	Substantive (with article, preposition, pronoun); adjective	1
7	Substantive; adjective (incl. article); interjection	1
8	Substantive; adjective; pronoun	1
9	Substantive (incl. pronoun); adjective (incl. participle)	1
10	Substantive (with article); adjective; pronoun	3
11	Substantive; adjective; pronoun (incl. article)	2
12	Substantive; adjective; pronoun; participle	1
13	Substantive; adjective; pronoun; article	1
14	Common; proper; pronoun (substantival and adjectival cross-categories)	1
15	As only part of speech	1
		102

	Forms taken by the category SUBSTANTIVE	
	As a primary part of speech:	
1	Alone	117
2	With article	5
3	Including pronoun	26
4	Including pronoun substantive	9
5	Including 1st and 2nd person pronouns	2
6	With article; including pronoun	13
		172

Appendix II

As a secondary part of speech:

a	Within Noun (see Noun 1, 4, 5, 7, 8, 11, 12, 13)	52
b	Within Noun, with article (see Noun 2, 10)	42
c	Within Noun, incl. pronoun (see Noun 3, 9)	4
d	Within Noun, with article, preposition, pronoun (see Noun 6)	1
e	As a cross-category within Noun (see Noun 14)	1
f	With Word of Action (see System 24)	1
		101

Forms taken by the category ADJECTIVE

No. of grammars

As a primary part of speech:

1	Alone	123
2	Incl. pronoun adjective	1
3	Incl. participle	2
4	Incl. article	19
5	Incl. participle and article	11
6	Incl. 3rd person pronoun and article	2
7	Incl. pronoun adjective and participle	6
8	Incl. pronoun adjective, participle and article	2
		166

As a secondary part of speech:

a	Within Noun (see Noun 1, 2, 3, 6, 8, 10–13)	82
b	Within Noun, incl. article (see Noun, 4, 7)	15
c	Within Adjunctive, incl. article (System 43)	1
d	Within Noun, incl. participle (see Noun 5, 9)	3
e	Within Verb (see Verb 4)	1
f	Within Attributive (System 44)	3
g	Within Adnoun (System 37)	1
		106

Forms taken by the category PRONOUN

As a primary part of speech:

1	Alone	199
2	Including article	2
		201

As a secondary part of speech:

a	Within Noun (see Noun 10, 12–14)	6
b	Within Substantive (see Substantive 3–6)	49
c	Within Particle (see Particle 3, 11)	3
d	Within Adjective (see Adjective 6, 7, 8)	9
e	Within Word of Help (System 24)	1
f	Within Adnoun (System 37)	1
g	Within Noun and including article (see Noun 11)	2
		71

As a tertiary part of speech:

h	Within substantive (see Noun 3)	3
k	With substantive (see Noun 6, 9)	2
		5

	No. of
Forms taken by the category ARTICLE	grammars

As a primary part of speech:

1	Alone	132

As a secondary part of speech:

a	With Substantive (see Substantive 2, 6)	18
b	Within Noun (see Noun 13)	1
c	Within Adjective (see Adjective 4, 5, 6, 8)	34
d	Within Pronoun (see Pronoun 2)	2
e	Within Preposition (see Preposition 2)	1
f	Within Particle (see Particle 2, 7, 10, 12)	8
g	Within Definitive (System 44)	3
		67

As a tertiary part of speech:

h	With substantive (see Noun 2, 6, 10)	43
k	Within adjective (see Noun 4, 7; Adjunctive, System 43)	16
l	Within pronoun (see Noun 11)	2
m	Within preposition (see Particle 4, 8)	4
		65

Appendix II

Forms taken by the category VERB

As a primary part of speech:

1	Alone	165
2	Including participle	97
3	Incl. conjunction; preposition; interjection; participle	1
4	Incl. conjunction; preposition; interjection; participle; adjective; adverb	1
5	With derived adverb (System 27)	1
		265

As a secondary part of speech:

a	Within Word of Action (System 24)	1
b	Within Attributive (System 44)	3
c	Within Adjunctive, incl. participle (System 43)	2
		6

Forms taken by the category PARTICIPLE   No. of grammars

As a primary part of speech:

1	Alone	138

As a secondary part of speech:

a	Within Noun (see Noun 12)	1
b	Within Verb (see Verb 2, 3, 4)	99
c	Within Adjective (see Adjective 3, 5, 7, 8)	21
d	Within Attributive (System 44)	3
e	Within Adnoun (System 37)	1
		125

As a tertiary part of speech:

f	Within adjective (see Noun 5)	2

Forms taken by the category ADVERB

As a primary part of speech:

1	Alone	205
2	Incl. interjection	4
3	Incl. interjection and preposition	2
4	Incl. interjection and conjunction	1
		212

As a secondary part of speech:

a	Within Verb (see Verb 4)	I
b	With Verb (see Verb 5)	I
c	Within Particle (see Particle 1–4, 6, 10, 13)	47
d	Within Particle and incl. interjection (see Particle 5)	7
e	Within Attributive and incl. interjection (System 44)	3
f	Within Word of Help (System 24)	I
g	Within Sub-Quality (System 50)	I
		61

No. of grammars

Forms taken by the category CONJUNCTION

As a primary part of speech:

1	Alone	209

As a secondary part of speech:

a	Within Verb (see Verb, 3, 4)	2
b	Within Adverb (see Adverb 4)	I
c	Within Particle (see Particle 1–9, 13)	56
d	Within Conjunctive (System 44)	3
e	Within Word of Help (System 24)	I
		63

Forms taken by the category PREPOSITION

As a primary part of speech:

1	Alone	205
2	Including article	I
		206

As a secondary part of speech:

a	Within Verb (see Verb, 3, 4)	2
b	Within Particle (see Particle 1–3, 5–7, 9, 10, 12)	53
c	Within Particle and incl. article (see Particle 4, 8)	4
d	Within Adverb (see Adverb 3)	2
e	Within Conjunctive (System 44)	3
		64

As a tertiary part of speech:

f	With substantive (see Noun 6)	I

		No. of grammars
Forms taken by the category INTERJECTION		

As a primary part of speech:

1	Alone	195

As a secondary part of speech:

a	Within Noun (see Noun 7)	1
b	Within Verb (see Verb 3, 4)	2
c	Within Adverb (see Adverb 2, 3, 4)	7
d	Within Particle (see Particle 1–4, 7–11)	46
		56

As a tertiary part of speech:

e	Within adverb (see Particle 5)	7

Forms taken by the category PARTICLE

Always a primary part of speech, comprising:

1	Adverb; conjunction; preposition; interjection	31
2	Adverb; conjunction; preposition; interjection; article	5
3	Adverb; conjunction; preposition; interjection; pronoun	2
4	Adverb; conjunction; preposition (incl. article); interjection	3
5	Adverb (incl. interjection); conjunction; preposition	7
6	Adverb; conjunction; preposition	4
7	Conjunction; preposition; interjection; article	1
8	Conjunction; preposition (incl. article); interjection	1
9	Conjunction; preposition; interjection	1
10	Article; auxiliary verb; some adverbs; interjection; preposition	1
11	(Substitutive particle) compr. pronoun and interjection (System 27)	1
12	(Connexive particle) compr. preposition and article (System 27)	1
13	('Other' particle) compr. underived adverb and conjunction (System 27)	1
		59

APPENDIX III

INDEX OF AUTHORS AND
SYSTEMS
(see especially chapter 8)

GREEK AND LATIN GRAMMATICAL WORKS CONSULTED: AN ALPHABETICAL LIST

The following grammatical works have been used in summarising the tradition. The customary attributions and dates are given, even where they are doubtful. The only exception is the grammar attributed to Duns Scotus: it now seems certain that it was written by Thomas of Erfurt.[1]

1 ÆLFRIC, *c.* 955–1020. *Grammatica*, ed. Julius Zupitza (*Ælfric's Grammatik und Glossar*), Berlin 1880.

2 ALBERTUS MAGNUS, 1193–1280. *Quaestiones de Modis Significandi*, Wynkyn de Worde (1515?).

3 ALCUIN, 735–804. *Grammatica*, ed. J.-P. Migne, *Patrologia Latina*, 101, Paris 1863. cols. 849–902.

4 ALEXANDER of Villedieu, *c.* 1170–*c.* 1250. *Doctrinale* (written 1199) ed. Dietrich Reichling (Monumenta Germaniae Pedagogica, XII), Berlin, 1893.

5 ANSELM, 1033–1109. *Dialogus de 'grammatico'*, ed. J.-P. Migne, *Patrologia Latina*, 158, Paris 1863, cols. 561–2.

6 ANTONIO of Lebrixa (Antonius Nebrissensis), 1444–1522. *Grammatica*, Laurentius Hyllare (Paris) 1521.

7 APOLLONIUS DYSCOLUS, second century A.D. *De Pronomine*; *De Adverbio*; *De Coniunctione*; *De Constructione*, ed. R. Schneider and G. Uhlig, 3 vols. Leipzig 1878–1910.

8 ARISTOTLE, 384–322 B.C. *Categories and De Interpretatione*, ed. L. Minio-Paluello, Oxford 1949.
transl. E. M. Edghill, Oxford 1928.

9 ARISTOTLE, *Topics*, and *De Sophisticis Elenchis*, ed. W. D. Ross, Oxford 1958.
transl. W. A. Pickard-Cambridge, Oxford 1928.

10 ARISTOTLE, *Rhetoric*, ed. H. Roemer, Leipzig 1888.
transl. W. Rhys Roberts, Oxford 1924.

11 ARISTOTLE, *Poetics*, ed. Ingram Bywater, 2nd edn, Oxford 1911.
transl. Ingram Bywater, Oxford 1924.
transl. L. J. Potts as *Aristotle on the Art of Fiction*, Cambridge 1953.

---

[1] Grabmann, T. E., pp. 11 f.

12 BACON, Roger, 1214?–1294. *Summa Gramatica*, ed. R. Steele, Oxford 1940 (Opera hactenus inedita Rogeri Baconi, Fasc. xv), pp. 1–190.

13 BACON, Roger. *Sumule Dialectices*, ed. R. Steele, Oxford 1940 (*Opera hactenus inedita Rogeri Baconi*, Fasc. xv), pp. 191–359.

14 BACON, Roger. *Greek Grammar*, ed. Edmond Nolan and S. A. Hirsch, Cambridge 1902.

15 BEDE, 673–735. *Cunabula grammaticae artis Donati*, ed. J.-P. Migne, *Patrologia Latina*, 90, Paris 1863, cols. 613–32. (Bede's authorship is doubtful.)

16 BEDE. *De Octo Partibus Orationis*, ed. J.-P. Migne, *Patrologia Latina*, 90, Paris, 1863, cols. 632–42 (authorship doubtful).

17 BEKKER, for scholiasts on Dionysius Thrax; see No. 26 below.

18 BOETHIUS of Dacia, d. before 1284. *Tractatus de modis significandi*. Extracts in M. Grabmann, *Thomas von Erfurt*, Munich 1943, pp. 80–1.

19 CHARISIUS, Flavius Sosipater, late fourth century A.D. *Ars Grammatica*, ed. H. Keil, *Grammatici Latini*, vol. I, Leipzig, 1857.

20 CHRYSIPPUS, *c.* 280–207 B.C. Quoted by Diogenes Laertius, q.v. See also von Arnim, *Stoicorum Veterum Fragmenta*, 4 vols. Leipzig 1905–1924, vols. 2 and 3.

21 DESPAUTER, Jean (Jan van Pauteren) d. 1520. *Rudimenta...pueris utilissima et omnino necessaria...cum quaestiunculis de Poenitentia.* 2nd edn Paris 1527 (first printed 1512).

22 DIOGENES BABYLONIUS, *c.* 240–152 B.C. Quoted by Diogenes Laertius, q.v. See also von Arnim, *Stoicorum Veterum Fragmenta*, vol. 3.

23 DIOGENES LAERTIUS, third century A.D. *Lives and Opinions of eminent Philosophers*, ed. and transl. R. D. Hicks, 2 vols. (Loeb Classical Library) 1925.

24 DIOMEDES, late fourth century A.D. *Ars Grammatica*, ed. H. Keil, *Grammatici Latini*, vol. I, Leipzig 1857.

25 DIONYSIUS of Halicarnassus, first century B.C. *De Compositione Verborum*, ed. and transl. W. Rhys Roberts, London 1910.

26 DIONYSIUS THRAX, second century B.C. *Grammar*, ed. G. Uhlig, *Dionysii Thracis Ars Grammatica*, Leipzig 1883.
       ed. I. Bekker, *Anecdota Graeca*, vol. II, Berlin 1816, pp. 627–43. Page refs. are to Uhlig; scholiasts cited as *Bekker*.

27 DONATUS, Aelius, fourth century A.D. *De partibus orationis ars minor*, ed. H. Keil, *Grammatici Latini*, vol. IV, Leipzig 1864.

28 DONATUS, Aelius, *Ars Grammatica*, ed. H. Keil, *Grammatici Latini*, vol. IV, Leipzig 1864.

29 EBERHARD of Bethune, fl. 1200. *Graecismus*, ed. J. Wrobel, *Corpus grammaticorum medii aevi*, vol. I, Breslau 1887.

30 *Glose super Priscianum maiorem.* Twelfth-century manuscript, quoted by R. W. Hunt, 'Studies on Priscian in the 11th and 12th Centuries', *Med. and Ren. Studies*, I. 1941. 194–231; II. 1950. 1–56. (Cited as Hunt I and Hunt II.)

31 HUGO of St Victor, d. 1141. *De Grammatica*, ed. Jean Leclerq, *Archives d'histoire doctrinale et littéraire du moyen age*, XIV, Paris 1943–5, 263–322.

32 JOHANNES AVICULA de Lotharingia, early fourteenth century? *Summa de modis significandi*. Quoted by M. Grabmann, *Mittelalterliches Geistesleben*, I. Munich 1943. 136.

33 JOHANNES of Dacia, late thirteenth century. *Summa Grammaticalis*. Quoted by M. Grabmann, *Thomas von Erfurt*, Munich 1943, p. 69.

34 JOHN of Salisbury, c 1120–80. *Metalogicon* (completed 1159), ed. C. C. J. Webb, Oxford 1929.
trans. Daniel D. McGarry, Berkeley 1955.

35 ISIDORE of Seville, c. 570–636. *Etymologiae*, ed. W. M. Lindsay, Oxford 1911.

36 LILY, William, 1486?–1523. The compilation most briefly known as Lily's grammar is of mixed authorship, uncertain origin and varying title. The clearest guide to its long and complex history is J. P. Tuck, 'The Latin Grammar attributed to William Lily', *Research Review*, University of Durham Institute of Education, No. 2, 1951. 33–9. Three modern editions have been used:

a (cited as) LILY, 1527; the English accidence and the English syntax in the combined edition of 1527 reprinted from the Peterborough Cathedral Library copy by S. Blach, 'Shakespeares Lateingrammatik', *Jahrbuch der deutschen Shakespeare-Gesellschaft*, XLIV. 1908. 65–117; XLV. 1909. 51–100.

b (cited as LILY, 1566) *The Royal Grammar*, 1566, reprinted from the Bodleian copy by S. Blach, ibid.

c (cited as) LILY, *Shorte Intro.* 1567 (the part written in English)
LILY, *Brev. Inst.* 1567 (the part written in Latin) *The Royal Grammar*, 1567, reproduced in facsimile by V. J. Flynn, from the copy in the Folger Shakespeare Library, as *A Shorte Introduction of Grammar*, Scholars' Facsimiles and Reprints, New York 1945.

37 LINACRE, Thomas, c. 1460–1524. *Progymnasmata grammatices vulgaria*, London (1525?). First printed about 1512?

38 LINACRE, Thomas. *De Emendata Structura Latini Sermonis*, London 1524.

39 MARTIANUS CAPELLA, fifth century A.D .(written between 410 and 439). *De nuptiis Philologiae et Mercurii et de septem artibus liberalibus*, ed. U. F. Kopp, Frankfurt-am-Main 1836.

40 MARTIN of Dacia, d. 1304. *Modi significandi*, ed. H. Roos, *Martini de Dacia Opera (Corpus Philosophorum Danicorum Medii Aevi*, II) Copenhagen, 1961. Extracts in H. Roos, *Die Modi Significandi des Martinus de Dacia (Beiträge zur Geschichte der Philosophie und Theologie des Mittelalters*, XXXVII. 2), Munster 1952.

41 MATTHEW of Bologna (Matthaeus Bononiensis) late thirteenth century. *Quaestiones de modis significandi*. Quoted by M. Grabmann, *Mittelalterliches Geistesleben*, I. Munich 1943, 138.

42 MICHEL de Marbais, *c.* 1300. *Summa modorum significandi.* Quoted by Thurot, *Notices et Extraits,* Paris 1868.

43 *Notae super Priscianum et super rhetoricam.* Twelfth-century MS quoted by R. W. Hunt, 'Studies on Priscian in the 11th and 12th Centuries', *Med. and Ren. Studies,* I. 1941. 194 f.

44 PEROTTUS, Nicholas (Nicolo Perotti) 1430–80. *Rudimenta Grammatices* (written 1468, first printed 1473), Venice 1486.

45 PETER of Spain, d. 1277, *Summulae Logicales,* Tractatus VII, *De Proprietatibus Terminorum.* Text and translation in J. P. Mullally, *The Summulae Logicales of Peter of Spain,* Notre Dame, Indiana 1945.

46 PETER HELIAS, *c.* 1150. *Summa super Priscianum.* Extracts printed by R. W. Hunt, 'Studies on Priscian in the 11th and 12th Centuries', *Med. and Ren. Studies,* I. 1941. 194 f. and by Thurot, *Notices et Extraits,* Paris 1868.

47 PLATO, *c.* 429–347 B.C. *Protagoras; Cratylus; Sophist.* Quoted from Burnet's text in the Oxford edition, with reference to Jowett's translation, 4th edn 1953.

48 PRISCIAN, *c.* 500 A.D. *Institutiones Grammaticae,* ed. Martin Hertz, 2 vols, Leipzig 1855 (*Grammatici Latini,* ed. H. Keil, vols. II and III).

49 PROTAGORAS, fifth century B.C. Quoted by Aristotle and Diogenes Laertius (H. Diels, *Die Fragmente der Vorsokratiker,* 5th edn Berlin 1934–7, II. 253–71).

50 QUINTILIAN, first century A.D. *Institutio Oratoria,* Bk I, ed. F. H. Colson, Cambridge 1924.

51 RADULPHUS BRITO (Raoul de Hotot), late thirteenth century. *Tractatus de modis significandi.* Quoted by M. Grabmann, *Thomas von Erfurt,* Munich 1943, 91–2.

52 RAMUS, Petrus (Pierre de la Ramée), 1515–72. *Grammaticae libri quattuor,* 3rd edn Paris 1560. First published 1559.

53 RAMUS, Petrus. *Rudimenta grammaticae latinae,* Frankfurt 1595.

54 SACERDOS, M. Plotius, third century A.D. *Grammatica,* ed. H. Keil (*Grammatici Latini,* vol. VI), Leipzig 1874.

55 SANCTIUS (Francisco Sanchez of Brozas), 1523–1601. *Minerva, seu de causis linguae Latinae commentarius,* Utrecht 1795. First published 1587.

56 SEXTUS EMPIRICUS, fl. A.D. 180. *Adversus Mathematicos,* transl. R. G. Bury (Loeb Classical Library), 1949. Bk I, *Adversus Grammaticos.*

57 SIGER of Courtrai, d. 1341. *Summa Modorum Significandi* (written *c.* 1300) ed. G. Wallerand, *Les Œuvres de Siger de Courtrai* (*Les Philosophes Belges,* VIII), Louvain 1913.

58 SMARAGDUS, *c.* 800. *Liber in partibus Donati.* Verse prefaces printed by Ernst Dummler, *Poetae Latini aevi carolini* (Monumenta Germaniae Historica), I. 605–15, Berlin 1881.

59 SULPITIUS, Ioannes (Giovanni Sulpizio) late fifteenth century. *Grammatica,* Paris 1495. First printed 1475.

60 TATWINE, d. 734. *Ars grammatica.* Extracts, ed. August Wilmanns, *Rheinisches Museum für Philologie,* n.s. XXIII. 1868. 398–401.

61 THEODORE of Gaza, *c.* 1400–75. *Introductivae grammatices libri IV*, Paris 1516. First printed 1495.

62 THOMAS of Erfurt, fl. 1325. *Grammatica Speculativa*, ed. P. Fr. Mariani Fernandez Garcia, Quaracchi 1902. Formerly attributed to Duns Scotus. Cited as *TE*.

Also in *Gymnasium Speculativum*, Paris 1605, pp. 861–932, a collection of philosophical works made by Augustinus Gothutius. Cited as *TE*, 1605.

63 VARRO, M. Terentius, 116–27 B.C. *De Lingua Latina*, Bks V–X, ed. and transl. Roland G. Kent (Loeb Classical Library) 1938.

64 VICTORINUS, Maximus, 4th century A.D. *Ars Grammatica*, ed. H. Keil, *Grammatici Latini*, VI, Leipzig 1874.

65 VICTORINUS, Gaius Marius, date unknown, *De Arte Grammatica* and *Ars Grammatica*, ed. H. Keil, *Grammatici Latini*, VI, Leipzig 1874.

66 WHITTINTON, Robert, fl. 1520. *De Octo partibus orationum opusculum*, Wynkyn de Worde, 1519. First printed 1515?

APPENDIX V

GREEK AND LATIN
GRAMMATICAL WORKS CONSULTED:
A CHRONOLOGICAL LIST

Protagoras	Fifth Century B.C.
Plato	c. 429–347 B.C.
Aristotle	384–322 B.C.
Chrysippus	c. 280–207 B.C.
Diogenes Babylonius	c. 240–152 B.C.
Dionysius Thrax	Second Century B.C.
Varro	116–27 B.C.
Dionysius of Halicarnassus	First Century B.C.
Quintilian	First century A.D.
Sextus Empiricus	fl. A.D. 180.
Apollonius Dyscolus	Second century A.D.
Diogenes Laertius	Third century A.D.
Sacerdos	Third century A.D.
Donatus	Fourth century A.D.
Charisius	Late fourth century A.D.
Diomedes	Late fourth century A.D.
Gaius Marius Victorinus	Fourth century A.D.
Maximus Victorinus	Unknown
Martianus Capella	Fifth century A.D.
Priscian	c. 500
Isidore of Seville	c. 570–636
Tatwine	d. 734
Bede	673–735
Alcuin	735–804
Smaragdus	c. 800
Ælfric	c. 955–1020
Anselm	1033–1109
Hugo of St Victor	d. 1141
Peter Helias	c. 1150
John of Salisbury	c. 1120–1180
Notae⎫ *Glose*⎭	Eleventh–twelfth century
Alexander of Villedieu	c. 1170–c. 1250

EBERHARD OF BETHUNE	*c.* 1200
ALBERTUS MAGNUS	1193–1280
PETER OF SPAIN	d. 1277
BOETHIUS OF DACIA	d. before 1284
MARTIN OF DACIA	Late thirteenth century
ROGER BACON	1214?–1294
MICHEL DE MARBAIS	*c.* 1300
JOHANNES OF DACIA	Late thirteenth century
RADULPHUS BRITO	Late thirteenth century
MATTHEW OF BOLOGNA	Late thirteenth century
SIGER DE COURTRAI	d. 1341
JOHANNES AVICULA	Early fourteenth century?
THOMAS OF ERFURT	fl. 1325
THEODORE OF GAZA	1400–75
PEROTTUS	1430–80
SULPITIUS	Late fifteenth century
DESPAUTER	d. 1520
LINACRE	*c.* 1460–1524
WHITTINTON	fl. 1520
ANTONIO OF LEBRIXA	1444–1522
LILY	1468?–1523
RAMUS	1515–72
SANCTIUS	1523–1601

APPENDIX VI

ENGLISH GRAMMARS CONSULTED:
AN ALPHABETICAL LIST

1 James Douglas, 1675–1742, surgeon, botanist.
Grammatical Manuscripts, *c.* 1720?, in Glasgow University Library:
   No. 585 (fols. 460, unnumbered): 'The Parts of English Speech'.
   No. 586 (fols. 358): 'The Pronunciation of the Vowels'—which in
   fact includes the consonants also.
   No. 587*a* (fols. 379, unnumbered) 'The Parts of Speech in the
   English Language'.
   No. 587*b* (fols. 66, unnumbered) 'The Fourth Part of Grammar
   called Syntax'.
Blackburn Cabinet Papers:
   Bundle 1.6 (fols. 87½, unnumbered) 'A Fair Copy of the paradigms
   of the regular and irregular English verbs in four conjugations'.
   Bundle 1.7 (fols. 293, unnumbered) The wrapper is headed
   'English Grammar Perfect as far as the Syntax' and the title inside
   is 'The Parts of Speech in the English Language'.
   Bundle 3.3 (fols. 88, with 3 blank leaves, all unnumbered) 'An
   Essay towards a new grammar of the English tongue, in which all
   the declinable parts of speech are delineated in proper paradigms'.
   The exact relation between these manuscripts has yet to be established. No. 586 and fols. 1–47 of No. 587*a* are concerned solely with
pronunciation. Bundles 1.6 and 3.3 take the form of tables of declension and conjugation: there are no definitions and no discussion of the
parts of speech. No. 587*b* discusses the syntax of each part of speech,
punctuation, abbreviations, spelling, handwriting and the parts of a
book.
   The parts of speech themselves are discussed in Nos. 585, 587*a*
(fols. 48 f.) and Bundle 1.7. Of these No. 585 is the earliest. In its
original form it referred to ten parts of speech, including the participle.
A first revision altered the wording, but not the number of the parts of
speech; a second revision struck out the participle and reduced the
number to nine. No. 587*a* and Bundle 1.7 reduce the number again
to eight, and both these manuscripts incorporate alterations made to
No. 585. Bundle 1.7 incorporates some alterations made to 587*a*

(e.g. the addition of a potential mood: 587 fol. 218 verso; 1.7 fol. 110 recto) but in other places the same corrections have been made on both 587*a* and 1.7 (e.g. 587*a*, fol. 61 recto and 1.7, fol. 11 recto, where the word *it* is omitted in both manuscripts).

A possible sequence is that 587*a*, a major revision of 585, was revised and recopied as 1.7; that 1.7 was itself revised; that 587*a* was revised a second time, but whether before or after the revision of 1.7 cannot yet be said. The differences between 587*a* and 1.7 affect the grammatical categories in only a few places, and the manuscripts are here taken as being of equal authority, except with reference to the classification of the parts of speech.

Glasgow University Library tentatively dates the manuscripts (in a printed catalogue of 1908) at 1700, when Douglas was 25. Accompanying Bundle 3.3 is a letter, dated 7 July 1740, from Solomon Lowe (see Nos. 159 and 160 below) to Douglas, commending 'yr Grammatical Lists and Paradigms...the world wants such a thing, & I dare say, would be very thankfull for it'. It is not possible to say how continuous was Douglas's interest in grammar, so the manuscripts are here given an arbitrarily middle date, *c.* 1720?

2 John EVELYN, 1620–1706.
   The English Grammar. BM Add. MS. 15950. fols. 94–8, *c.* 1650.
   The grammar carries the sub-title 'The first key', and the Latin grammar which follows is subtitled 'The second key'.

   The English grammar begins: 'Herein I have (after a manner) wholy followed B. Jonson'. In the margin has been added, apparently in the same hand, though with a thicker pen: 'This is now more accurately set forth by Dr. Wallis'.

   This work is not mentioned in de Beer's edition of Evelyn's Diary, nor in Geoffrey Keynes's bibliography. The date is the British Museum's conjecture.

3 Warren HASTINGS, 1732–1818.
   Of the English Verbs. BM Add. MS. 39891. fols. 166–74, *c.* 1800?
   No reference seems to have been made before to this slight manuscript. It is 'an attempt to explain the Construction of the English Verbs upon the Principles which appertain to them independently of any Practice of Speech but their own'.

   The manuscript is undated, and Sir Keith Feiling, author of the standard biography of Hastings, writes (privately), 'I can only *guess* that it was compiled in England, not in India, that is, after 1785'. The work would then belong among 'the extraordinarily variegated hobbies, whims and side-issues' which Hastings pursued in old age. An arbitrary date of 1800 is assigned to the work here.

4 *The Practice of Speaking and Writing English.* Brotherton Collection, Leeds University, MS. Lg. 1. (See No. 142.)

This grammar has carried, since Sotheby's sale on 28–9 June 1865, the conjectural attribution to Captain John Stevens, d. 1726. It has not hitherto been noticed that much of the grammar is identical with John Kirkby's *A New English Grammar*, 1746. The system of parts of speech used in both grammars is unique, and many terms, definitions and illustrations are word for word the same. On the present evidence it seems likely that *The Practice of Speaking and Writing English* was written after 1746. It is here provisionally dated *c.* 1750?.

Cited as *Practice c.* 1750?.

5 Thomas TOMKIS, Scholar of Trinity College, Cambridge, 1599. *De Analogia Anglicani Sermonis Liber Grammaticus*. BM. MS. 12 Reg. F. xviii. fols. 1–15, 1612.

The manuscript is dated 1612. The relation between Tomkis's grammar and Ben Jonson's needs investigation. In many places Tomkis's Latin exactly corresponds to Jonson's English. This cannot arise from a common Latin source, such as Ramus, because the correspondence is particularly close in the section on the articles and includes, there and elsewhere, English examples such as 'the onelie hee or shee of the towne' and, in the section on compound words, at least five examples, including *tennis-court-keeper*, *foote-bal-player* and *hand-kercher*. No common English source suggests itself, and the question is roused whether Tomkis saw the first, and full, form of Jonson's grammar, or whether Jonson saw Tomkis's.

PRINTED WORKS

6 Alexander ADAM, 1741–1809, Rector of the High School, Edinburgh. *The Principles of Latin and English Grammar*. Edinburgh 1772; 4th edn 1793.

7 Joseph AICKIN, 'Schoolmaster in Fisher-street, near Red Lion Square...lately one of the masters of the Free-School of London-derry'. *The English Grammar*. London 1693. (Alston 1, No. 34.)

Page references are to the second part of the grammar.

8 James ALDERSON, Master of the English Academy, Ashford, Kent. *English Grammatical Exercises*. London 1795.

9 James ANDERSON. *Remarks on Grammar* (and under similar titles): a series of short articles in his weekly periodical *The Bee*, Edinburgh, between February and October 1792.

Remarks on Grammar	No. 62 (vol. VII, 271–82)
Exercises in Practical Grammar	No. 68 (vol. VIII, 179–84)
	No. 85 (vol. X, 146–52)
	No. 86 (vol. X, 177–82)

Grammatical Disquisitions

No. 88 (vol. x, 239–45)
No. 89 (vol. x, 274–85)
No. 90 (vol. x, 311–18)
No. 94 (vol. xi, 120–30)
No. 96 (vol. xi, 193–204)
No. 97 (vol. xi, 240–50)
No. 98 (vol. xi, 266–74)

10   William ANGUS, 'Teacher of English and Geography in Glasgow'.
An Epitome of English Grammar. Glasgow 1800. (Alston i, No. 529.)

11   *The Art of Teaching in Sport.* London [1770?]; 1785. (Alston i, Nos.
366 and 367.)

12   John ASH, 1724(?)–1779, Minister at Pershore (see No. 13).
Grammatical Institutes, Worcester 1760; as *The Easiest Introduction to
Dr Lowth's English Grammar,* London 1768; as *Grammatical Institutes,*
5th edn London 1771; 1779; 1796. (Alston i, Nos. 153, 157, 158, 164,
187.)
    The edition of 1768 contains an 'advertisement', signed *John
Ryland* and dated 12 September 1767, which gives some information
about the grammar. It was written by Ash, a friend of Ryland's, for
Ash's five-year-old daughter. It was printed privately and had been
used by Ryland in his own school for the preceding six years. Ryland
refers to himself as the editor of this new impression.

13   John ASH (see No. 12).
The New and Complete Dictionary of the English Language. 2 vols. London
1775; 2nd edn 1795. (Alston v, Nos. 288 and 289.)
    The grammar prefixed to the dictionary includes almost all the
material of No. 12, usually verbatim.

14   Nathan BAILEY, 1691–1742, Under-master at the Grammar School,
Norwich, and Joseph Nicol SCOTT.
A New Universal Etymological English Dictionary. London 1755; 1764.
(Aslton v, Nos. 173 and 175.)
    The grammar, which is not referred to on the title-page, was added
after Bailey's death to this much-revised form of his *Universal Etymo-
logical English Dictionary,* 1721. See Starnes and Noyes, chap. 22.

15   James BARCLAY, 'Curate of Edmonton, in Middlesex, and many
years Master of an Academy in Goodman's Fields, and at
Tottenham'.
A Complete and Universal English Dictionary. London 1774; 1792.
(Alston v, Nos. 284 and 286.)
    The grammar prefixed to this dictionary is practically identical
with that of Bellamy, 1760, No. 27.

16 Isaac BARKER, Schoolmaster in Whitby.
An English Grammar. York [1733?]. (Alston I, No. 63.)
The grammar is avowedly based on Greenwood.

17 Frederick BARLOW, Vicar of Burton.
The Complete English Dictionary. London [1772?]. (Alston I, No. 282.)

18 Alexander BARRIE, 'Teacher of English'.
A Spelling and Pronouncing Dictionary of the English Language... to which are added, the principles of English grammar. Edinburgh 1794. (Alston IV, No. 910.)
    In 1808 the grammar was added to Barrie's *The Tyro's Guide to Wisdom and Wealth*, in its fifth edition, the title-page to which suggests that the grammar had by then been published separately.

19 M. BAYLEY.
An Universal Etymological Dictionary. Edinburgh 1764. (Alston V, No. 234.)
    Except for its opening paragraphs the grammar is identical with those in Fenning, 1761 (No. 94), J. Johnson, 1763 (No. 133) and the *Universal Dictionary*, 1763 (No. 250). Alston regards M. Bayley as a piratical fiction.

20 Anselm BAYLY, 1719–94, Sub-dean of the Chapel Royal (see Nos. 21, 22, 23.)
An Introduction literary and philosophical to Languages: especially to the English, Latin, Greek and Hebrew, exhibiting at one view their grammar, rationale, analogy and idiom. In three parts... Parts the first and second. London 1756; as, *An Introduction to Languages*, literary and philosophical... [adds part three] London, 1758.
Cited as Bayly, 1756.

21 Anselm BAYLY (see Nos. 20, 22, 23).
A Practical Treatise on singing and playing with just expression and real elegance, being an essay on I Grammar, II Pronunciation, III Singing. London 1771.
Cited as Bayly, 1771.

22 Anselm BAYLY (see Nos. 20, 21, 23).
The English Accidence. London 1771. (Alston I, No. 294.)
Cited always from No. 23.

23 Anselm BAYLY (see Nos. 20, 21, 22).
A Plain and Complete Grammar of the English Language: to which is prefixed the English accidence: with remarks and observations on 'A short Introduction to English Grammar'. London 1772. (Alston I, No. 313.)
Cited as Bayly, 1772.

24 James BEATTIE, 1735–1803.
Dissertations Moral and Critical. On memory and imagination. On dreaming. The theory of language...London 1783. The dissertation on the theory of language was reprinted, with some few changes, as *The Theory of Language.* In two parts. Part I. Of the Origin and general Nature of Speech. Part II. Of Universal Grammar. London 1788.

25 Cave BECK, 1623–1706?, Master of the Free Grammar School, Ipswich.
The Universal Character, by which all the nations in the world may understand one anothers conceptions, reading out of one common writing their own mother tongues. An invention of general use, the practise whereof may be attained in two hours space, observing the grammatical directions. Which character is so contrived, that it may be spoken as well as written. London 1657. (Alston VII, No. 286.)

26 John BELL, 'late teacher of grammar and the mathematics'.
A Concise and Comprehensive System of English Grammar. 2 vols. Glasgow 1769. (Alston I, No. 287).

27 Daniel BELLAMY, d. 1788, Minister of Kew and Petersham.
A New Complete English Dictionary. London 1760; as, *A New, Complete, and Universal English Dictionary,* 4th edn London 1764. (Alston V, Nos. 225 and 226.)
    The grammar prefixed to the dictionary is entitled 'The Compendious British Grammarian: or, an easy introduction to the study of the English tongue'. The grammar is practically identical with that of Barclay, 1774, No. 14.
    Alston treats as the principal author John Marchant, who signed the preface to the 1760 edn but is not mentioned on the title-page.

28 John BENTICK, Schoolmaster.
The Spelling and Explanatory Dictionary of the English Language. London 1786. (Alston V, No. 335.)

29 John BETTESWORTH, 'Master of the Academy in Quaker's Buildings, W. Smithfield'.
The English Grammar Epitomis'd. [London] 1778. (Alston I, No. 348.)

30 Alexander BICKNELL, d. 1796.
The Grammatical Wreath. London 1790. (Alston I, No. 450.)

31 John BINNS, 'Schoolmaster, at Bretton, near Wakefield, Yorkshire'.
The Youth's Guide, to the English language, in four parts...IV. A compendious English grammar. [Leeds?] 1788. (Alston I, No. 442.)

32 Richard BLOME, d. 1705.
The Gentleman's Recreation. London 1686.

33 T. BOWEN, Master of an Academy at Walsall.
The Rudiments of English Grammar. Walsall 1799. (Alston I, No. 521.)

34 Edmund Philip BRIDEL, 'Master of an Academy, Stoke Newington, Middlesex'.
An Introduction to English Grammar. London 1797. (Alston 1, No. 499.)

35 *The British Letter-Writer...* to which is added a plain and easy English Grammar. London [1765?].

36 George BROWN.
The New English Letter-Writer... including also a new English grammar. London [1779?].

37 Richard BROWN, Schoolmaster in Rugby, Coventry, Westminster and York.
The English School Reformed; containing... an accidence adapted to our English tongue. London 1700; 3rd edn 1707; 7th edn 1722; 11th edn 1736.
There has been some doubt about the identity of R. Brown. In the preface to this work Brown refers to 'the Method I formerly publish'd, these seven Years past' which is here improved, and has had an accidence added to it. He does not name the earlier work, but it is presumably *The English Examiner*, 1692, by Richard Browne, a spelling book which the *English School Reformed* closely resembles. A third work by the same author is *The English Expositor Improv'd*, 1707, which is the 10th edition of John Bullokar's *The English Expositor* (first issued in 1616) and the first to be revised by Brown (Starnes and Noyes, p. 25).
In 1692 the author is 'Richard Browne...late English and Writing Master of Rugby...but now of the city of Coventry'. In 1700 he is 'R. Brown, in Westminster' (title-page above). In 1707 he is 'R. Browne, Author of the *English School Reform'd*' (title-page of *The English Expositor Improved*). In 1722 he is 'R. Brown, formerly Master of a Boarding School in Greek-Street, in St. Ann's Westminster, but now Master of a private School in York' (above, title-page of 3rd edn).
Watt, followed by DNB and Poldauf (p. 92), attributes an English grammar, 1692, to one Richard Browne, physician, of Queen's College, Oxford, and Oakham, author of *Medica Musica*. There is no trace of a grammar of this date, nor any indication that Brown the schoolmaster and Brown the physician could be the same person. The attribution is wrong, through a natural confusion. Goold Brown (1857) gives an English grammar, 1692, to a Richard Browne, but it is not clear whether he is following Watt or loosely calling *The English Examiner* a grammar.

38 James BUCHANAN, Master of Loughbury House, Camberwell, Surrey, (see Nos. 39 and 40).
The Complete English Scholar. In three parts. Containing a new, short and familiar method of instructing children and perfecting grown

persons in the English tongue, and of learning grammar in general, without the help of Latin. London 1753. (Alston 1, No. 143.)

39 James BUCHANAN (see Nos. 38 and 40).
The British Grammar. London 1762. (Alston 1, No. 208.)
The grammar was published anonymously.

40 James BUCHANAN (see Nos. 38 and 39).
A Regular English Syntax. London 1767; 1769. (Alston 1, Nos. 279 and 280.)
The first 66 pages—'An Introduction to English Syntax'—cover briefly the orthography and etymology included in No. 38 and, more fully, in No. 39.

41 Henry St John BULLEN, 'First assistant master at the Grammar School, Bury St Edmund's'.
The Rudiments of English Grammar. Bury St Edmunds 1797. (Alston 1, No. 501.)

42 William BULLOKAR, *c.* 1530–*c.* 1590.
William Bullokar's Pamphlet for Grammar. London 1586. (Alston 1, No. 1.)
For the ghostly status of Bullokar's *Bref Grammar*, and the misleading form of the Bodleian copy reprinted by Max Plessow, 'Geschichte der Fabeldichtung in England bis zu John Gray', *Palaestra*, 52. 1906, see Alston. In the present work references are to Plessow's reprint, and Bullokar's orthography is modernised.

43 John BURN.
A Practical Grammar of the English Language. Glasgow 1766; 8th edn 1802. (Alston 1, 271.)

44 Charles BUTLER, *c.* 1560–1647. Master of Basingstoke School.
The English Grammar, or the institution of letters, syllables, and words, in the English tongue. Oxford 1633; 1634. (Alston 1, Nos. 5 and 6.)
References in the present work are to the edition by A. Eichler, *Neudrucke frühneuenglischen Grammatiken*, vol. 4. i, Halle 1910. Butler's orthography has been modernised.

45 John CARTER, 'Teacher of the English language'.
A Practical English Grammar. Leeds 1773. (Alston 1, No. 316.)

46 John CARTER.
A Short and Easy Introduction to English Grammar. 5th edn Ipswich 1797. (Alston 1, No. 503.)
This is a different work from No. 45 and, so far as is known, by a different author.

47 William CLARE.
A Compleat System of Grammar English and Latin: wherein that most excellent art is plainly, fully and distinctly taught, and practically manag'd thro' every part thereof. In a method which renders it easie

to all capacities, and by the use whereof the learner may attain to the perfect knowledge of the Latin tongue in less than one quarter of the time usually spent therein, and those who have lost their Latin may hereby soon repair it. London 1690; 1699.

48 John CLARKE, of Grantham.
The Rational Spelling Book, or, an easy method of initiating youth into the rudiments of the English tongue. Containing I. Orthography in general. II. A complete, concise and easy English Grammar. III. The rudiments of English grammar rendered easy, familiar, and pleasant, being concisely delivered, for the help of memory, in familiar and entertaining verse. IV. Proper exercises and lessons, in prose and verse, fables, prayers, graces, sentences, &c. London [1772?]; 14th edn 'published from a MS. copy revised by the late John Entick, A.M.', Dublin 1791. (Alston IV, Nos. 722 and 724.)

49 Thomas COAR.
A Grammar of the English Tongue. London 1796. (Alston I, No. 495.)
    According to Henry Thompson, *History of Ackworth School*, London 1879, p. 104, this grammar was written by some of the staff at Ackworth, and Coar was only the publisher. See No. 88.

50 John COLLYER, Schoolmaster in Nottingham.
The General Principles of English Grammar; especially adapted to the English tongue. With a method of parsing and examination. For the use of schools. Nottingham 1735. (Alston I, No. 72.)

51 *The Complete Letter-Writer*...to which is prefix'd a plain and compendious English grammar. London 1755; 3rd edn 1756; 4th edn 1757; 12th edn Dublin 1768.

52 *A Comprehensive View of English Grammar.* London 1794. (Alston I, No. 474*a*; V, No. 334.)

53 J. COOK.
The Westminster Spelling-Book. London 1792; vol. 2, 'to which is added a concise English grammar', 1793. (Alston IV, No. 891.)
    Published anonymously.

54 Thomas COOKE (see Nos. 55 and 56).
The Universal Letter-Writer...to which is added...a new plain, and easy grammar of the English language. London [1771?]. Cited as Cooke, 1771?

55 Thomas COOKE (see Nos. 54 and 56).
[Later editions of No. 53 in which the grammar is radically changed and must be regarded as a distinct work.] London [1775?]; 1788; Gainsborough 1801; London 1809.
    An edition of 1819 gives the author as 'The Rev. F. Cooke, A.B.' and omits the grammar: 'We have not sacrificed a considerable

portion of the work to a tedious grammar'. Still later editions of *The Universal Letter-Writer* include abridgements of Cobbett's grammar (1860) and Lindley Murray's (1863). Cited as Cooke, 1775?

56 Thomas COOKE (see Nos. 54 and 55).
[An undated edition of *The Universal Letter-Writer* contains a grammar different from either No. 54 or No. 55.] London [1790?]. Cited as Cooke, 1790?

57 Christopher COOPER, *c.* 1655–98, Master of the Grammar School at Bishops Stortford (see No. 58).
Grammatica Linguae Anglicanae. London 1685; ed. J. D. Jones, *Neudrucke frühneuenglischer Grammatiken,* vol. 5, Halle 1911. (Alston 1, No. 29.)
   Page references are to J. D. Jones's edition.

58 Christopher COOPER (see No. 57).
The English Teacher, or the discovery of the art of teaching and learning the English tongue. London 1687; reprinted by Bertil Sundby as *Christopher Cooper's English Teacher,* 1687, *Lund Studies in English,* 22, Lund 1953.
   This is, with some additions, a translation of No. 57, but the whole of the etymology is omitted because Cooper is here concerned primarily with phonology. There is very little strictly grammatical material in *The English Teacher.*

59 Charles COOTE, 1761–1835.
Elements of the Grammar of the English Language, written in a familiar style: accompanied with notes critical and etymological; and preceded by an introduction, tending to illustrate the fundamental principles of universal grammar. London 1788. (Alston 1, No. 445.)

60 James CORBET, Schoolmaster.
An Introduction to the English Grammar. Glasgow 1743. (Alston 1, No. 90.)

61 John CORBET.
A Concise System of English Grammar. Shrewsbury 1784; 3rd edn 1788. (Alston 1, Nos. 377 and 379.)

62 *The Court Letter Writer*...to which is prefixed, a complete grammar of the English language. London 1773.

63 William CRAKELT, 1741–1812. Master of Northfleet Grammar School, Kent.
A Comprehensvie Grammar of the English Tongue [in] *Entick's New Spelling & English Dictionary.* London 1795; 1800. (Alston v, No. 270.)
   This grammar, much of which comes from Ash, 1775 (No. 12) was first added to the 1795 edition of Crakelt's revision of John Entick's *New Spelling Dictionary,* 1765 (No. 87) in place of Entick's own grammar. (Alston v, No. 267.)

64 Abraham CROCKER, Writing Master at Ilminster from 1765 till *c.* 1782.
A Practical Introduction to English Grammar and Rhetoric. Sherborne [1772]; London 1775. (Alston I, Nos. 309 and 310.)

65 George DALGARNO, *c.* 1626–87, Schoolmaster in Oxford.
Ars Signorum, vulgo character universalis et lingua philosophica. Qa poterunt, homines diversissimorum idiomatum, spatio duarum septimanarum, omnia animi sua sensa (in rebus familiaribus) non minus intelligibiliter, sive scribendo, sive loquendo, mutuo communicare, qam linguis propriis vernaculis. Praeterea, hinc etiam poterunt juvenes, philosophiae principia, et veram logicae praxin, citius et facilius multo imbibere, qam ex vulgaribus philosophorum scriptis.
London 1661; reprinted for the Maitland Club, Edinburgh 1834. Page references are to the reprint. (Alston VII, No. 289.)

66 John DALTON, 1766–1844, Schoolmaster and chemist.
Elements of English Grammar: or a new system of grammatical instruction, for the use of schools and academies. Manchester and London 1801; 2nd edn Birmingham and London 1803.

67 Edward DEARLE, 'Schoolmaster, Golden-Lane'.
A Sure Guide for all Youth. 2nd edn London 1792. (Alston IV, No. 882.)
A short English grammar appeared first in this edition.

68 Ellin DEVIS.
The Accidence; or first rudiments of English grammar. London 1775; 3rd edn 1777; 5th edn 1786; 7th edn (?) 1793; 8th edn 1795; 9th edn 1797. (Alston I, Nos. 320, 321, 323, 325, 326, 327.)
Published anonymously. There were few significant changes in the grammar after the third edition. The author is described in the *Monthly Review,* LII. 1775. 464, as 'Mrs. Davis, a teacher at Cambden-house school'. The 1775 edition is dedicated to 'Mrs. Terry, of Campden-House, Kensington'.

69 Thomas DILWORTH, 'Schoolmaster in Wapping'.
A New Guide to the English Tongue: In five parts. Containing...III. A short, but comprehensive grammar of the English tongue, delivered in the most familiar and instructive method of question and answer; necessary for all such persons as have the advantage only of an English education. London 1740; 19th edn 1757. (Alston IV, Nos. 423 and 434.)

70 Dorothea DU BOIS.
The Lady's Polite Secretary to which is prefixed a short, but comprehensive, grammar of the English language. London [1771].
The author is described on the title-page as 'the Right Hon. Lady Dorothea Du Bois'.

71 Daniel DUNCAN, 'Master of Islington School'.
A New English Grammar. London 1731. (Alston I, No. 61.)

72 Thomas DYCHE, 'School-Master at Stratford le Bow', and William PARDON.
*A New General English Dictionary...*to which is prefixed a compendious English grammar. London 1735; 3rd edn 1740; 4th edn Dublin 1744; 6th edn London 1750. (Alston v, Nos. 143, 145, 147, 149.)
This is the first English dictionary to contain a grammar. There can be no certainty that the grammar was written by Dyche, who had died before the dictionary was completed, but *A Practical Grammar of the English Tongue* by Thomas Dyche is announced in the *London Magazine*, I. 1732. 211. No copy is known (Alston I, No. 62).

73 *An Easy Introduction to the English Language*; or, a compendious grammar for the use of young gentlemen, ladies and foreigners. Being the second volume of *The Circle of the Sciences.* London, for John Newbery, 1745; 2nd edn as: '*Grammar made familiar* and easy to young gentlemen, ladies, and foreigners. Being the first volume of the Circle of the Sciences', London, 1748; 3rd edn 1769; 4th edn 1776; as: '*Grammar and Rhetorick,* being the first and third volumes of The Circle of the Sciences, considerably enlarged and greatly improved, 1776'. (Alston I, Nos. 91, 92, 95, 97.)
The grammar is sometimes attributed to Newbery. The 1776 edition of *Grammar and Rhetorick* (Alston I, No. 97) contains two grammars. The first is here cited as *Easy Introduction* 1776; the second is treated as a separate work (No. 82) and cited as *English Grammar,* 1776.
The grammar in No. 73 is in most places identical with the grammar in two other publications by Newbery: the *Pocket Dictionary,* 1753 (No. 202) and the *Spelling Dictionary,* 1755 (No. 235).

74 *An Easy, Short and Systematical Introduction to the English Grammar,* London 1794. (Alston I, 475.)
Cited as *Easy S.S.I.,* 1794.

75 Mrs M. C. EDWARDS, 'Of Brentford Butts'.
A Short Compendium of English Grammar, Brentford 1796. (Alston I, No. 496.)

76 Samuel EDWARDS, 'Schoolmaster, in Golden-lane'.
An Abstract of English Grammar, including rhetoric and pronunciation. Dublin 1765. (Alston I, No. 260.)

77 *The Elementary Principles of English Grammar,* collected from various authors; but chiefly from Dr Priestley. Bridport 1785; n.p. 1798. (Alston I, Nos. 404 and 405.)
The dedication to the 1785 edition is signed 'M.A.'. There is no dedication, nor any reference to M.A., in the 1798 edition.

78 James ELPHINSTON, 1721–1809, Master of an academy in Kensington.
    The Principles of the English Language digested: or, English grammar reduced to analogy. 2 vols. London 1765; as: '*The Principles of the English Language,* digested for the use of schools, 1766', an abridgement. (Alston 1, Nos. 261 and 262.)
    According to Nichols, 1812, III. 32 n., the grammar was written about 1753. The abridgement keeps the framework of the whole grammar but shortens the syntax particularly.

79 *Encyclopaedia Britannica* (see No. 80).
    s.v. 'Grammar', vol. 2, Edinburgh 1771; 2nd edn vol. 5, 1780.
    There is no change in the second edition but the article is completely rewritten in the third edition, here treated as a separate work.
    Cited as *Enc. Brit.* (A).

80 *Encyclopaedia Britannica* (see No. 79).
    s.v. 'Grammar', 3rd edn vol. 8, Edinburgh 1797; 4th edn vol. 10, 1810.
    This is a different work, using different categories from No. 79.
    Cited as *Enc. Brit.* (B).

81 *The English Accidence,* being the grounds of our mother tongue; or, a plain and easy introduction to an English grammar. London 1733. (Alston 1, No. 64.)

82 *An English Grammar* (see No. 73).
    This is the second grammar, placed after the elementary grammar, on pp. 55–71 of *Grammar and Rhetorick,* 1776.
    Cited as *English Grammar,* 1776.

83 *An English Grammar.* St John's in Antigua [1750?]. (Alston 1, No. 108.)

84 *The English Scholar Compleat*: containing I. An English grammar, or rather accidence, treating of the parts of English speech, and what belongs to them, which is the meaning of the word *accidence.* II. A catalogue of all the chief Latin roots from whence English–Latin words are derived. III. An explanation of such words...IV. Several select Latin sentences, met oft-times in English writers unexplain'd, made English. V. An history of select proper names. VI. An English rhetorick. VII. A catalogue of all such Greek roots, as Greek–English words are derived from...as also of all significant words of common use in our language, deriv'd from other tongues...
    Compos'd for the use of an English School, at the Cock and Swan in Cannon-Street: and very useful for most people under academics. With a letter in Latin to all Latin-Masters, recommending it to the use of several in their schools.
    London 1706. (Alston 1, No. 39.)

85 *English Syntax Rules*, composed for the use of Sutton Academy, Nottinghamshire. Mansfield 1798. (Alston I, No. 514.)

The English Tutor, 1747 (see *A New English Grammar*, 1746, No. 184).

86 John ENTICK, 1703?–1773, Schoolmaster in Stepney (see No. 87).
Speculum Latinum: or, Latin made easy to scholars, by an English grammar only; neither tedious, nor obscure; composed on natural principles, and instructing the young beginner in Latin, by English rules, adapted to the meanest capacities, for the use and benefit of schools and families. London 1728. (Alston I, No. 60.)
For the sense in which this can be regarded as an English grammar see p. 162 above.
Cited as Entick, 1728.

87 John ENTICK (see No. 86).
The New Spelling Dictionary...to which is prefixed, a grammatical introduction to the English tongue. London 1765; enl. by Rev. William Crakelt, 1784; 1787. (Alston v, Nos. 238, 258, 261; IV, No. 678.)
The original grammar is dropped from the edition of 1791. Following editions, which contain an entirely new grammar, are here treated separately under CRAKELT, 1795 (No. 63).
Cited as Entick, 1765.

88 *An Essay towards an English Grammar* for Ackworth School. York 1800. (Alston I, No. 531.)
Attributed by Cambridge University Library to John Binns and Thomas Coar.

89 Mrs EVES, 'Crescent School, Birmingham'.
The Grammatical Play-thing, or, winter evening's recreation, for young ladies from four to twelve years old. Birmingham 1800. (Alston I, No. 532.)
The book is intended to accompany a game with cards, counters and a board.

90 Daniel FARRO, Master of a school in Red Lion Court, Watling Street, London, and later at No. 6, The Horse fair, Bristol (see No. 91).
The Royal Universal British Grammar and Vocabulary. Being a digestion of the entire English language into its proper parts of speech. Compiled and calculated for equal ease, both for the master and scholar. In a method entirely new.
In which an exact parallel is observed between the names, qualities and affirmations, according to Being, Doing, and Suffering, in the English or modern British language, and the declension of the nouns, both substantive and adjective; the pronouns and conjugations of verbs in the Latin and other languages; the regular words of each

part of speech are distinctly separated from the irregular; and plain, and concise rules are given precedent to the full and entire scope of examples.

The whole being delivered in the most approv'd and entertaining manner; viz, by proper queries and answers. In this work the etymology of the English language is illustrated, and rendered very facile; the various acceptations of the same word are carefully distinguished; the proper accents accurately marked; and children may be taught the formation of more than ten thousand sentences, by marginal insertions, apposed to that part of speech term'd qualities; which have not increased the volume two pages. London 1754; 2nd edn 1754; 3rd edn 1754. (Alston I, Nos. 145, 146, 147.)

Cited as Farro, 1754.

91 Daniel FARRO (see No. 90).
The Royal Golden Instructor for youth...being a copious abridgement of the Royal Universal British Grammar and Vocabulary...Lessons are formed after all the parts of speech for parsing and challenging the foregoing instructions...Practice in art removes difficulty. [Bristol?] [1776?] (Alston I, No. 148.)

Cited as Farro, 1776?

92 John FELL, 1735–97. Congregational Minister at Thaxted; classical tutor at Mile End Academy.
An Essay towards an English Grammar. With a dissertation on the nature and peculiar use of certain hypothetical verbs in the English language. London 1784. (Alston I, No. 380.)

The grammar appeared anonymously. The preface, written as if by the 'Editor' speaking for 'the author', is said by DNB to be by Richard ('Conversation') Sharp, a former pupil of Fell's.

93 Daniel FENNING, 'Late schoolmaster of Bures in Suffolk' (see Nos. 94 and 95).
The Universal Spelling-Book:...containing...a very easy and approved guide to English Grammar, by way of question and answer. London 1756; 4th edn 1760; [1767?]; 21st edn 1776. (Alston IV, Nos. 650, 631, 639.)

The grammar differs entirely from either No. 94 or No. 95.

Cited as Fenning, 1756.

94 Daniel FENNING (see Nos. 93 and 95).
The Royal English Dictionary...to which is prefixed a comprehensive grammar of the English tongue. London 1761; 2nd edn 1763; 3rd edn 1768. (Alston V, Nos. 227, 228, 229.)

The grammar is unchanged throughout the first three editions, and is identical with those in Bayley, 1764 (No. 19); J. Johnson, 1763 (No. 133), and *An Universal Dictionary*, 1764 (No. 250). It is different from both No. 93 and No. 95.

Cited as Fenning, 1761.

95 Daniel FENNING (see Nos. 93 and 94).
A New Grammar of the English Language. London 1771; 1793; Romsey 1800. (Alston I, Nos. 295, 301, 303.)
    Cited as Fenning, 1771.

96 Anne FISHER, d. before 1801; wife of Thomas Slack, printer, of Newcastle-upon-Tyne (see Nos. 97 and 265).
A New Grammar. 2nd edn Newcastle-upon-Tyne 1750; 3rd edn London 1753; 4th edn Newcastle-upon-Tyne 1754; 5th edn 1757; 8th edn 1763; 11th edn 1768. (Alston I, Nos. 109, 111, 112, 113, 116, 120.)
    The first two editions of the grammar were published anonymously. In a third edition of 1751 the author is given as D. Fisher; in the third edition of 1753, and subsequently, the author is A. Fisher. Poldauf, p. 110, and Parker, p. 127, erroneously say that Mrs Slack is G. Fisher. Kennedy makes no attempt to separate A. Fisher from G. Fisher. George Fisher seems to have been an American writing-master and the author of *The Instructor, or Young Man's Best Companion,* 1748 and numerous editions to 1853. See L. C. Karpinski, 'The Elusive George Fisher, Accomptant', in *Scripta Mathematica,* 3. 1935. p. 4.
    J. Wilson's revision of *A New Grammar,* under the title *Fisher's Grammar Improved,* Congleton 1792, (Alston I, No. 135) fundamentally changed it, and it is here treated as a new work, No. 265.
    Cited as Fisher, 1750.

97 Anne FISHER (see No. 96).
The New English Tutor:...also, a practical abstract of English grammar. This work is beautified with elegant cuts, representing such vices as children are most addicted to, and such virtues as should be first inculcated: likewise several fable cuts, with striking lessons, referring to each particular passion, &c. 3rd edn Newcastle 1774. (Alston IV, No. 699.)
    The first edition was probably in 1763. The grammar adopts a different system of parts of speech from that in No. 96.
    Cited as Fisher, 1774.

98 Peter Walkden FOGG, Master of a private school in Stockport (see No. 99).
Elementa Anglicana: or, the principles of English grammar displayed and exemplified, in a method entirely new. Vol. 1, Stockport 1792.
    Cited as Fogg, 1792.

99 Peter Walkden FOGG (see No. 98).
Elementa Anglicana: or, the principles of English grammar displayed and exemplified, in a method quite original. Vol. 2, Stockport 1796; combined with vol. 1, 1797.

This is more than a continuation of volume 1: there is a considerable change of plan. More than half the book is given to twenty-seven 'Dissertations grammatical and philological' which are independent of the first volume and repeat some of its substance.

Cited as Fogg, 1796.

100   David FORDYCE.
The New and Complete British Letter-Writer...with a concise and familiar English grammar. London [1790?]

101   William FRANCIS, of Hook.
A Concise Introduction to English Grammar. Marlborough 1790. (Alston 1, No. 450.)
The last half of the book is 'A poetical epitome of English grammar' which repeats in verse form the principal definitions in the main grammar.

102   J.G., of the Literary and Commercial Seminary, Bristol.
An Easy Introduction to the English Language...to which is prefixed, a sketch of grammar, for children under seven years old. Bristol 1796. (Alston 1, No. 497.)
The grammar is mostly from Ash.

103   Jane GARDINER, of Beverley (1799); of Elsham Hall (1808).
The Young Ladies' English Grammar; adapted to the different classes of learners. With an appendix, or abbreviation of the grammar. York 1799; as '*English Grammar* adapted to...', 2nd edn London 1808; 3rd edn 1809. (Alston 1, No. 525.)

104   Robert GENTLEMAN, 'a dissenting Minister at Kidderminster'.
The Young English Scholar's Pocket Companion. In six parts. Part I. A compendious English grammar. 2nd edn Kidderminster 1797.
The first edition was probably published in 1788 (*Monthly Review*, 81. August 1789. 173).

105   Charles GILDON, 1665–1724, and John BRIGHTLAND, d. 1717.
A Grammar of the English Tongue, with notes, giving the grounds and reason of grammar in general. London 1711; 2nd edn 1712; 3rd edn 1714; 4th edn 1721. (Alston 1, Nos. 42, 44, 45, 46.)
The grammar was published anonymously. For the question of authorship see references listed in Alston 1, No. 42, to which should be added: Rae Blanchard, *The Correspondence of Richard Steele*, 1941, p. 523 n.; G. Scheurweghs & E. Vorlat, 'Problems of the History of English Grammar', *English Studies*, 60. 1959. 140.
Gildon's authorship was stated as early as 1718 (*Evening Post*, No. 1411, August 16–19, quoted by R. H. Griffith, *Notes and Queries*, 194. 1949. 362–5.). Brightand's role was certainly that of sponsor and it is probable that he was, with others, associated with the writing

of the grammar. The grammar is often called 'Brightland's Grammar' or 'Bickerstaff's' or 'Steele's'.

Much of the work derives from Wallis and the Port Royal grammar, but it is not entirely a hack work. Its system of parts of speech had few precedents and could have been adopted only as the result of considered choice, perhaps from Lane, 1700.

Cited as G–B, 1711, etc.

106 Alexander GILL, 1565–1635, High Master of St Paul's School.
Logonomia Anglica. Qua gentis sermo facilius addiscitur. London 1619; 2nd edn 1621; ed. Otto L. Jiriczek, *Quellen und Forschungen*, 90, Strassburg, 1903. (Alston I, Nos. 3 and 4.)

Quoted here from the second edition, with page references to Jiriczek's reprint. The text, where quoted, does not differ materially from that of the first edition. The changes which Gill made in the second edition were either concerned with phonology or were designed to simplify the notation in which his English was printed.

107 William GORDON, 'Teacher of the Mathematics'.
Every Young Man's Companion: containing directions for spelling, reading, and writing English. London 1755. (Alston IV, No. 624.)

The grammar is very sketchy: the parts of speech are neither enumerated nor defined, and it is not possible even to infer a system of classification.

108 James GOUGH, 1712–80, and John GOUGH, 1721–91, 'Master of the Boarding-School, Lisburn'.
A Practical Grammar of the English Tongue. Dublin 1754; 3rd edn Dublin 1764; 6th edn 1792. (Alston I, Nos. 194 and 196.)

Alston (I, No. 193) records a second edition of 1760. The first edition was not known to Alston when the first volume of his bibliography was published.

109 Paul GREAVES.
P. Gr. Grammatica Anglicana. Praecipue quatenus a Latine differt, ad unicam P. Rami methodum concinnata. In qua perspicue docetur quicquid ad huius linguae cognitionem requiritur. Authore P. G. Cambridge 1594; ed. Otto Funke, *Wiener Beiträge zur englischen Philologie*, 60, Vienna 1938. (Alston I, No. 2.)

The attribution to Greaves (or Graves) first made by Ames in 1790, has been confirmed by the title-page of a copy in Cambridge University Library (G. Scheurweghs and E. Vorlat, 'Problems of the History of English Grammar', *Eng. Studies*, 40. 1959. 135–43.)

110 James GREENWOOD, d. 1737, Sur-master, St Paul's School (see No. 111.)
An Essay towards a Practical English Grammar, describing the genius and nature of the English tongue. Giving likewise a rational and plain

account of grammar in general, with a familiar explanation of its terms. London 1711; 2nd edn 1722; 3rd edn 1729; 4th edn 1740; 5th edn 1753. (Alston I, Nos. 52–6.)

 Cited as Greenwood, 1711.

111 James GREENWOOD (see No. 110).
The Royal English Grammar. London 1737; 2nd edn 1744; 4th edn 1750. (Alston I, Nos. 76, 77, 79.)

 An abridgement of No. 110. Cited as Greenwood, 1737.

112 H. GROOMBRIDGE, 'Lecturer on Elocution, Geography, &c'.
The Rudiments of the English Tongue; or, a plain and easy introduction to English grammar. Bath 1797. (Alston I, No. 504.)

113 Charles HALLIFAX.
Familiar Letters...to which are prefixed, a short and comprehensive grammar [etc.] 5th edn London [1765?].

114 Samuel HAMMOND, Master of the Bluecoat School, Nottingham.
A Complete and Comprehensive Spelling Dictionary...to which is prefix'd, a compendious English grammar; with a history of the language. Nottingham [1760?]. (Alston IV, No. 690.)

115 S. HARLAND, 'Schoolmaster in Norwich'.
The English Spelling-Book revis'd. 3rd edn 1719. (Alston IV, No. 292.)

116 James HARRIS, 1709–80.
Hermes: or, a philosophical inquiry concerning language and universal grammar. London 1751; 4th edn 1786.

 The text of the 4th edn is practically the same as that of the first.

117 Ralph HARRISON, 1748–1810. Minister of Cross Street Chapel, Manchester; professor of classics, Manchester Academy.
Institutes of English Grammar, Manchester 1777; 6th edn London, 1794; 9th edn 1805.

118 E. HARROLD.
A Short Introduction to English Grammar: adapted to the use of schools. With an appendix, containing I. Grammatical figures, and examples of the ellipsis. II. Observations upon transposition, with examples. III. Observations upon the derivation of words. IV. Examples of grammatical analysis. V. Ungrammatical English, to be corrected by way of exercise. 3rd edn Birmingham 1787; 4th edn 1791; 1792; 5th edn 1798. (Alston I, Nos. 435–8.)

119 James HAYWOOD, Schoolmaster.
A Short Introduction to the English Tongue. Sheffield 1800; 2nd edn 1805. (Alston I, No. 536.)

 Considerable changes were made in the second edition.

120 John HENSON, Master of the Free Grammar School, Nottingham.
A Compendium of English Grammar, containing chiefly the two parts, etymology and syntax: in which the rules and examples...will give [children] a sufficient knowledge of grammar in general, whereby they may be prepared for learning the Latin, French, or any other language, without burden to the memory. Nottingham [1760?] (Alston I, No. 198.)

121 John HEWES.
A Perfect Survey of the English Tongue, taken according to the use and analogie of the Latine. And serveth for the more plaine exposition of the grammatical rules and precepts, collected by Lillie, and for the more certaine translation of the English tongue into Latine. Together with sundry good demonstrations, by way of sentences in either tongue. Written and collected by Io: Hewes, Master of Arts. London 1624; as *A Survey...*, with slight changes, 1632.
    The Dedicatory Epistle in the second edition is dated 'Jan. 1, 1624, The Charterhouse'.

122 John HEWLETT, 1762–1844, Master of the Academy, Newington Green in 1787; of Shacklewell School in 1798.
An Introduction to Reading and Spelling. 4th edn London 1798. (Alston IV, No. 859.)
    The first edition appeared in 1786 but no copy has been located of any edition before the 4th (Alston IV, Nos. 857 and 858).

123 Isaac HODGSON, d. by 1787, 'Master of the Grammar School in Southampton'.
A Practical English Grammar. London 1770; 5th edn 1787. (Alston I, Nos. 289, 291.)

124 John HORNSEY, d. 1820. Master of the Academy, King Street, Scarborough.
A Short English Grammar...To which are added, rules, illustrated with examples, for the structure, precision, and unity of sentences. York 1793. (Alston I, No. 468.)
    Hornsey expresses his obligations to Lowth's grammar, for which this is designed as a preparation.

125 John HOUGHTON, 'Master of a private grammar-school at Namptwich, in Cheshire'.
A New Introduction to English Grammar. Salop 1766. (Alston I, No. 278.)
    Based on, and designed as a preparation for, Lowth's grammar.

126 James HOWELL, 1594?–1666.
A New English Grammar, prescribing as certain rules as the language will bear, for forreners to learn English. London 1662.
    The material of the grammar is derived very largely from Jonson.

127 Alexander HUME, Rector of Edinburgh High School, 1596–1606.
Of the Orthographie and Congruitie of the Britan Tongue: a treates, noe
shorter then necessarie for the schooles. Ed. H. B. Wheatley, EETS
No. 5, from BM MS. Bibl. Reg. 17A. xi, 1865.
The grammar was written about 1617.

128 Thomas HUNTLEY.
A Short System of English Grammar. Cirencester 1793. (Alston 1, No.
470.)

129 J. IRELAND, 'Curate of Tynemouth, and Master of a Grammar
School, North Shields'.
Beauties in Prose and Verse...to which is added, a practical English
Grammar. Newcastle 1784.

130 [J.J.]
Prittle prattle. Or, a familiar discourse on the persons I, Thou, He or
She, We, Ye or You, and They. Designed for the use and benefit of the
youth of the people called Quakers, who have not had the opportunity of learning a grammar. London 1752. (Alston 1, No. 142.)
   The author describes himself as for some years secretary and steward
to William Penn.

131 Thomas JOEL, Schoolmaster.
An Easy Introduction to the English Grammar. Composed for the con-
veniency of children under seven years of age. Chichester 1770.
(Alston 1, No. 292.)

132 Charles JOHNSON.
The Complete Art of Writing Letters...to which is prefixed, a com-
pendious and useful grammar of the English language. 6th edn
London 1779.
   The first edition may have been in 1767 (Gabrielson, 1929,
p. 143).

133 J. JOHNSON.
The New Royal and Universal Dictionary...To which is prefixed, a
grammar of the English language. 2 vols. London 1763. (Alston v,
No. 233.)
   A pirated dictionary. The grammar is identical with those in
Fenning, 1761 (No. 94), M. Bayley, 1764 (No. 19) and *An Universal
Dictionary*, 1763 (No. 250).

134 S. JOHNSON.
A Compleat Introduction to the Art of Writing Letters...to which is
prefixed, a short but useful grammar of the English language.
London 1758.
   This is one of the works which has been suggested as the 'foolish
piece' to which Dr Johnson referred (Boswell's *Life*, ed. Hill and
Powell, v. 295 and 553, 8 October 1773).
   Cited as Mr S. Johnson, 1758.

135   Samuel JOHNSON, 1709–1784.
A Dictionary of the English Language... to which are prefixed a history of the language, and an English grammar. 2 vols. London 1755. (Alston v, No. 177.)
Some additions were made to the grammar in the fourth edition, 1773, but they are not relevant here.
Cited as Dr S. Johnson, 1755.

136   William JOHNSTON, of Tunbridge Wells.
A Pronouncing and Spelling Dictionary: to which is now added, a short, and plain grammar of the English language. 2nd edn London 1772.
The dictionary first appeared in 1764 but the grammar was not added till the second edition. It was also issued separately as *A Short Grammar of the English Language*, London 1772 (Alston i, No. 312).

137   Hugh JONES, 'lately Mathematical Professor at the College of William and Mary, at Williamsburgh in Virginia'.
An Accidence to the English Tongue. London 1724. (Alston i, No. 59.)
Cited as H. Jones, 1724.

138   Rowland JONES, 1722?–1774 (see No. 139).
Hieroglyfic: or, a grammatical introduction to an universal hieroglyfic language; consisting of English signs and voices. With a definition of all the parts of English, Welsh, Greek and Latin languages; some physical, metaphysical, and moral cursory remarks on the nature, properties, and rights of men and things. And rules and specimens for composing an hieroglyfic vocabulary of the signs or figures, as well as the sounds of things, upon rational and philosophical principles, and the primitive meaning of names. London 1768.
This is a development of Jones's *The Origin of Languages and Nations*, 1764, and is itself developed in No. 139 (Alston vii, No. 296).
Cited as R. Jones, 1768.

139   Rowland JONES (see No. 138).
The Circles of Gomer, or, an essay towards an investigation and introduction of the English, as an universal language, upon the first principles of speech, according to its hieroglyfic signs, argrafic, archetypes, and superior pretensions to originality; a retrieval of original knowledge; and a re-union of nations and opinions on the like principles, as well as the evidence of ancient writers; with an English grammar, some illustrations of the subjects of the author's late essays, and other interesting discoveries. London 1771.
The first 27 pages of the work are 'An Universal Grammar'. (Alston vii, No. 298.)
Cited as R. Jones, 1771.

140 Ben JONSON, 1572–1637.
The English Grammar made by Ben Johnson. For the benefit of all strangers, out of his observations of the English language now spoken, and in use. Ed. C. H. Herford, Percy and Evelyn Simpson, *Works*, vols. 2, 8, 9, 11 (1925–52). (Alston 1, Nos. 8–12.)

The grammar was written before 1623, in which year the MS. was destroyed by fire. Herford and Simpson suggest the early 1630s as a date for the present version, which was first published in 1640.

141 *A Key to Spelling*, and introduction to the English grammar. London 1788. (Alston 1, No. 446.)

142 John KIRKBY, Tutor to Edward Gibbon, 1744–5 (see No. 4).
A New English Grammar, or, guide to the English tongue, with notes: wherein a particular method is laid down to render the English pronunciation both more fixed among ourselves, and less difficult to foreigners. And a sufficient number of suitable examples are inserted to every figure of speech both grammatical and rhetorical, with an explanation of all the terms. The whole being the result of many years careful observation, as well upon the peculiarities of our own, as its conformity with other languages especially; the Latin. Its agreements with which being all here particularly distinguished; to anticipate, as much as possible, the labour of such as are designed for that study. To which is added a brief Latin grammar upon the same foundation. London 1746. (Alston 1, No. 100.)

Gibbon, writing, he says, with Kirkby's works before him, refers to this book as an *English and Latin Grammar*, London 1746; a true description, but not the title. Gibbon praises the grammar, but writes as if he found Kirkby's *Automathes* more interesting.

143 Roger KITSON, Master of an Academy at St Andrew's, Norwich. *A Short Introduction to English Grammar*. Norwich 1798. (Alston 1, No. 515.)

144 John KNOWLES.
The Principles of English Grammar. Liverpool 1785; 4th edn London 1796. (Alston 1, Nos. 417, 420.)

145 A. LANE, d. between 1700 and 1705. Master of the Free School, Leominster; later of a private school at Mile-end-Green, Stepney (see No. 146).
A Rational and Speedy Method of attaining to the Latine Tongue. In two parts. The first containing such precepts as are common to all languages. The second contains what is more peculiar to the Latin tongue. London 1695; 2nd edn 1698.

There is no significant change in the second edition. Cited as Lane, 1695.

146   A. LANE (see No. 145).
A Key to the Art of Letters: or, English a learned language, full of art, elegancy and variety. Being an essay to enable both foreigners, and the English youth of either sex, to speak and write the English tongue well and learnedly, according to the exactest rules of grammar. After which they may attain to Latin, French, or any other foreign language in a short time, with very little trouble to themselves or their teachers. With a preface shewing the necessity of a vernacular grammar. London, 1700; 1705. (Alston 1, Nos. 36 and 37.)
   An expansion of the first part of No. 145.
   Cited as Lane, 1700.

147   Mark LEWIS, Schoolmaster; at one time probably in Mr Bret's 'reformed school' at Tottenham (see Nos. 148, 149, 150).
[*Institutio*] *Grammaticae Puerilis*: or the Rudiments of the Latin and Greek tongues. Fitted to children's capacities, as an introduction to larger grammars. By M. Lewis of Tottenham High-Cross. London 1670.
   The title-page of the BM copy is cropped, top and bottom. This makes the title look like *Grammaticae Puerilis*, which is improbable. The top of the page of the Cambridge University Library copy is also cropped, but the librarian says that the traces suggest *Institutio*, rather than *Rudimenta* (which the English title would suggest) as the missing word.
   The date 1674 given by R. F. Jones, 1953, p. 292 n., and by Susie Tucker, 1961, p. 65 n. is that of the second form of the *Essay* (No. 148 below) and not of the *Institutio*. The passage they quote occurs in three works (*Institutio*, preface; *Essay*, 1674, p. 3; *Vestibulum*, 1675, sig. A 3 verso.)
   The *Institutio* contains '*An Apologie for a grammar printed about twenty years since*, by M. Lewis and reprinted for the use of a private school'. This earlier grammar has not been identified.
   Cited as Lewis, *Institutio*, 1670.

148   Mark LEWIS (see Nos. 147, 149, 150).
An Essay to facilitate the education of youth, by bringing down the rudiments of grammar to the sense of seeing, which ought to be improv'd by Syncrisis. Fitted to children's capacities, for the learning, especially of the English, Latin and Greek tongues: but may be as a general grammar, and a foundation to any tongue: in three parts, an accidence, a middle-grammar, and a critical, or idiomatical grammar. By M. Lewis of Tottenham. London [1670?]. Another edition? London 1674.
   This work exists in two versions. What seems to be the earlier is in the British Museum, but lacks the title-page. The second version, copies of which are in the Bodleian and in Wisconsin University

Library, is in two parts, separately paginated. Pp. (17) to (22) repeat the substance, but not the wording, of the early Essay; pp. 1–5 contain the English grammar, so headed but in fact a basic or universal grammar; pp. 6–17 contain the accidence, the first of the three parts mentioned in the title; pp. 18–60 contain a fuller grammar, with some syntax and prosody—the 'middle' grammar of the title. The critical or idiomatical grammar does not seem to have been included. Both the Bodleian and the Wisconsin copies end on p. 60.

The two versions are cited as Lewis, *Essay*, 1670? and Lewis, *Essay*, 1674.

149   Mark LEWIS (see Nos. 147, 148, 150).
Plain, and short Rules for pointing Periods, and reading sentences grammatically, with the great use of them. London [1675?].
   Both the Bodleian and British Museum copies lack their title-pages. Cited as Lewis, *Rules*, 1675?

150   Mark LEWIS (see Nos. 147, 148, 149).
Vestibulum Technicum: or, an artificial Vestibulum. Wherein the sense of Janua Linguarum is contained, and most of the leading words chapter by chapter, are compiled into plain, and short sentences, fit for the initiation of children. Each part of speech is distinguished by the character it is printed in (a method never used before) and a sufficient grammar is brought down to the sense of seeing, in regard of the thing signified, contained in two pages. London 1675.
   The lengthy preface discusses not only Lewis's teaching methods and his support for Comenius but also the parts of speech. The copy in the BM (the only copy located) is incomplete, ending on the first page of chapter 1.
   Cited as Lewis, *Vestibulum*, 1675.

151   *Lily's Accidence Improved*: or, a complete introduction in English prose to the several parts of Latin grammar: together with an abstract of English grammar. New edn London, 1793.
   The seventh edition appeared in 1788. (*Monthly Review*, 80. Feb. 1789. 184).

152   Francis LODOWYCK (see No. 153).
A Common Writing: whereby two, although not understanding one the others language, yet by the helpe thereof, may communicate their minds one to another. Composed by a well-willer to learning. Oxford 1647. (Alston VII, No. 280.)

153   Francis LODOWYCK (see No. 152).
The Ground-Work, or foundations laid, (or so intended) for the framing of a new perfect language: and universal or common writing. And

presented to the consideration of the learned. By a well-willer to learning. n.p. 1652.

This is generally accepted as Lodowyck's work, and the expression 'a well-willer to learning' seems to link No. 152 to it. The two works are closely related in substance. (Alston VII, No. 281.)

154 William LOUGHTON, 'School-Master, at Kensington'.
A Practical Grammar of the English Tongue: or, a rational and easy introduction to speaking and writing English correctly and properly; peculiarly adapted to the nature and genius of the language, and free from the hard and unnecessary terms of the Latin Rudiments. The whole treated of in expressive terms and familiar style, and in the most natural and instructive method, viz. that of question and answer. Designed for the use of schools: and tho' calculated chiefly for such as require only an English education, may yet be a useful foundation to those who are design'd for higher studies. London 1734; 2nd edn 1735; 3rd end 1739; 4th edn 1740; 5th edn 1744. (Alston I, Nos. 65–9.)

The changes made after the first edition are almost all in the subsidiary contents.

155 Mrs LOVECHILD, pseud. of Lady (Eleanor) Fenn, d. 1813 (see Nos. 156, 157, 158).
The Child's Grammar. Dublin 1799. (Alston I, No. 522.) 20th edn London 1810.
Cited as Lovechild, *CG*, 1799.

156 Mrs LOVECHILD (see Nos. 155, 157, 158).
The Mother's Grammar. London [1815?]. (Alston I, No. 518.)
The work is referred to in Mrs Lovechild's *Parsing Lessons for Young Children*, 1798.
Cited as Lovechild, *MG*, 1798?

157 Mrs LOVECHILD (see Nos. 155, 156, 158).
Parsing Lessons for Young Children. London 1798. (Alston I, No. 519.)
The grammatical parts of Nos. 155 and 156 are recapitulated.
Cited as Lovechild, *PY*, 1798.

158 Mrs LOVECHILD (see Nos. 155, 156, 157).
Parsing Lessons for Elder Pupils. London 1798; 2nd edn 1803. (Alston I, No. 520.)
The grammatical parts of Nos. 155 and 156 are recapitulated.
Cited as Lovechild, *PE*, 1798.

159 Solomon LOWE (see No. 160).
English Grammar Reformed into a small compass and easy method for the readier learning and better understanding of the English tongue by way of introduction to other languages. London 1737. (Alston I, No. 85.)

160   Solomon L O W E (see N9. 159).
The Critical Spelling Book. London 1755; 2nd edn 1770. (Alston IV,
Nos. 622 and 623.)
      This work reproduces No. 158; there is no substantial change in the
second edition.

161   Robert L O W T H, 1710–87, Bishop of London.
A Short Introduction to English Grammar, London, 1762; 2nd edn, 1763;
1767; 1771; 1775; 1786; (Alston I, Nos. 212, 213, 219, 222, 226, 239).
      In the preface to the second edition of his *Rudiments of English
Grammar* Priestley says that Lowth's grammar was published 'about
a month' after his (Priestley, 1768, p. xxiii). All the editions of
Lowth's grammar published in his lifetime were anonymous.

162   Thomas L Y E, 1621–84, Headmaster of Bury St Edmunds School in
1647.
The Child's Delight. Together with an English grammar. London
1671. (Alston I, No. 28.)

163   Patrick L Y N C H, 'School-Master, Carrick-on-Suir'.
The Pentaglot Preceptor...Vol. I. Containing a complete grammar of
the English Tongue. Carrick 1796. (Alston I, No. 498 a.)

164   T. M., 'a private tutor'.
The Grammarian's Vade-Mecum; or, pocket companion containing the
general terms of grammar in the French and English languages.
London 1774.

165   William M'I L Q U H A M.
A Comprehensive Grammar. Glasgow 1781; as, *A Compendious Grammar,*
3rd edn 1789; 5th edn 1797; 6th edn 1802. (Alston I, Nos. 370, 372,
373.)
      Substantial changes were made by the third edition, and again
by the fifth. No copies of the second and fourth editions have been
traced.

166   Michael M A I T T A I R E, 1668–1747. Second Master, Westminster;
then ran a private school at Mile-end.
The English Grammar; or, an essay on the art of grammar, applied to
and exemplified in the English tongue. London 1712. (Alston I,
No. 57.)

167   David M A N S O N, Schoolmaster.
A New Pocket Dictionary...to which are prefixed, a practical grammar; with directions for reading; the laws of versification; the
explanation of prepositions and terminations; and examples of bad
English, to be corrected by the rules of syntax. And a plan for the
improvement of children in virtue and learning, without the use of
the rod. With the present state and practice of the play-school in
Belfast. Belfast 1762. (Alston v, No. 231 a.)

168 Charles MARRIOTT, 'Rector of Drayton-cum-Longdale'.
The New Royal English Dictionary...to which is prefixed, a copious grammar of the English language. 2 vols London 1780. (Alston V, No. 311.)

169 Charles MARSHALL, Vicar of Brixworth, Northamptonshire, and Master of Aldersgate Ward School.
An Introduction to the English tongue...containing...an introduction to English grammar. 6th edn London [1790?]. (Alston IV, No. 774.)
The first edition to contain the grammar.

170 Benjamin MARTIN, 1704–82 (see No. 171).
Institutions of Language; containing a physico-grammatical essay on the propriety and rationale of the English tongue. London 1748. (Alston I, No. 103.)
The grammar was reissued in 1749 with Martin's dictionary, *Lingua Britannica Reformata* (Alston V, No. 163) but omitted from the second edition, 1754, perhaps because in that year Martin issued his *Introduction to the English Language*, of which Part Two was a more systematic English grammar.
Cited as Martin, 1748.

171 Benjamin MARTIN (see No. 170).
An Introduction to the English Language and Learning. In three parts. Part 1. A spelling-book of arts and sciences; containing...Part 2. The rudiments of English grammar. With the rules of orthography, construction, emphasis, and a just elocution. Part 3. Lessons on all the above-mentioned sciences; containing...With a preface, shewing, that nothing short of the method here taken can be sufficient for a plan of a genuine English education. London 1754. (Alston I, No. 149.)
Cited as Martin, 1754.

172 J. L. MAYNE, 'Exeter College, Oxford'.
A Compendious English Grammar, with ungrammatical exercises, to be corrected according to rule: also exercises in false English. Birmingham 1799. (Alston I, No. 526.)

173 Mark Anthony MEILAN, b. 1743; d. after 1816. 'Private teacher of the English language', 1772; Master of an Academy in Hoxton, 1776.
A Grammar of the English Language, intended for the use of young gentlemen and ladies passed [*sic*] the first principles of letters. London [1771?]. (Alston I, No. 304.)
Meilan's *An Introduction to the English Language*, 2 vols. London 1803, is an entirely fresh work which nowhere refers, even indirectly, to the earlier grammar.

174 *The Merchant Maiden Hospital Magazine.* Containing...Instructions for teaching the English grammar. Edinburgh 1779.
Cited as *Merchant Maiden*, 1779.

175 Blanch MERCY.

A Short Introduction to English Grammar. 2 vols. London 1799. (Alston I, No. 527.)

The second volume, which survives only in a second edition printed at Carlisle, 1801, is the 'instructress's book' and 'contains the manner of exercising and interrogating the scholars throughout their lessons and exercises'.

176 Thomas MERRIMAN, 'Schoolmaster in Reading'.

A Compendious English Grammar. Reading 1750. (Alston I, No. 141.)

177 Lister METCALFE, Curate of Middleham, and then of Muker, both in Yorkshire.

The Rudiments of the English Tongue... after the plan of Mr Ruddiman's Latin Rudiments. 2nd edn Newcastle upon Tyne 1771; 3rd edn 1777. (Alston I, Nos. 305 and 306.)

The grammar is much changed in the third edition, and the title-page omits the reference to Ruddiman.

178 'MICA'.

Observations on Grammar. 'The Bee', No. 115 (vol. 13, pp. 225-32). Edinburgh 1793.

This short article is included here because it attempts a fresh system of parts of speech designed for English.

179 Guy MIEGE, 1644-1718?

The English Grammar. London 1688; 2nd edn 1691. (Alston I, Nos. 31, 33.) As *A Compleat Guide to the English Tongue*, London 1689? (Alston I, No. 32.)

180 James Burnett, Lord MONBODDO, 1714-99.

Of the Origin and Progress of Language. Vol. 2, Edinburgh 1774.

Volume two, which comprises Books 1-3 of Part 2 of the whole work, includes a discussion of the parts of speech and of syntax.

181 Alexander MURRAY, Schoolmaster.

An Easy English Grammar. 2nd edn London 1787. (Alston I, No. 423.) The first edition, no copy of which has been located, was published in 1785.

182 Lindley MURRAY, 1745-1826 (see No. 183).

English Grammar. York 1795; 2nd edn 1796; 3rd edn 1797. (Alston I, Nos. 480, 481, 482)

183 Lindley MURRAY (see No. 182).

An Abridgment of Murray's English Grammar. York 1797; 2nd edn London 1798; 3rd edn 1799. (Alston I, Nos. 505-7.)

184 *A New English Accidence,* by way of short question and answer, built upon the plan of the Latin grammar, so far as it agrees with and is

consistent with the nature and genius of the English tongue. Designed for the use and benefit, and adapted to the capacity of young lads at the English school. In order to teach them the grounds of their mother tongue, and fit them for the more easy and expeditious attaining the grammar of the Latin, or any other language. London 1736. (Alston I, No. 75.)

The grammar is based on Greenwood. In spite of its title it contains a short syntax.

185 *A New English Grammar*, by question and answer; with notes. Containing concise, but plain and comprehensive rules, for speaking or writing English correctly: free from all unnecessary difficulties; and the most useful rules distinguished by the print, from the less useful. To which is added, a suitable appendix. Compiled from the best authorities, methodized and interspersed with new observations. London 1746, incorporated in *The English Tutor*, London 1747; as, *The English Grammar, by question and answer*, 2nd edn 1760. (Alston I, Nos. 101 and 102.)

The first form of the grammar, 1746, has a separate title-page and is separately paginated. It was presumably also issued separately.

186 *A New and Improved Spelling Dictionary*...to which is added...a compendious English grammar. London 1771. (Alston IV, No. 719.)

187 *Newbery's New Spelling Dictionary of the English Language*...to which is prefixed, a new and concise introduction to English grammar. London 1788. (Alston IV, No. 578.)

An edition of No. 235 containing a grammar radically different from those in earlier editions.

188 John NEWTON, 1622–78 (see No. 189).
School Pastime for Young Children: or the rudiments of grammar, in an easie and delightful method, for teaching of children to read English distinctly, and to write it truly. In which, by way of preface, a new method is propounded, for the fitting of children first for trades, and then for the Latin, and other Languages, by John Newton, Doctor in Divinity, and one of his Majesties Chaplains. London 1669. (Alston I, No. 27.)

The long and interesting preface ends with an address 'To the Teachers of English': one of the earliest references to such people. Page references are to the grammatical 'catechism' which follows p. 40, with fresh numbering.

Cited as Newton, 1669.

189 John NEWTON (see No. 188).
The English Academy: or, a brief introduction to the seven liberal arts ...chiefly intended for the instruction of young scholars, who are acquainted with no other than their native language; but may also

be very useful to other persons that have made some progress in the studies of the same arts. London 1677; 2nd edn 1693.

There is no change in the grammatical material in the second edition.

Cited as Newton, 1677.

190 J. NICHOLSON, 'Mathematician'.
The Rudiments or first Principles of English Grammar. Newcastle, [1793]. (Alston I, No. 471.)

191 R. OLIPHANT.
A Compendium of English Grammar drawn up for the use of the young ladies at the boarding school, Newcastle upon Tyne. Newcastle, 1781. (Alston I, No. 374.)

192 *The Only True Guide to English Grammar.* Dumfries 1779. (Alston I, No. 365.)

Alston records a note in the copy belonging to the Library Company of Philadelphia that the author is John M. Ray.

193 *Outlines of English Grammar.* Worcester 1791. (Alston I, No. 457.)

194 Edward OWEN, 1728–1807, Rector of Warrington and Master of the Grammar School.
A Short System of English Grammar. London 1777. (Alston I, No. 344.)

195 J. OWEN.
The Youth's Instructor in the English tongue...[containing] a compendious grammar of the English tongue. London 1732. (Alston IV, No. 357*a*.)

196 Daniel PAPE, of Morpeth.
A Key to English Grammar, by which it has been proved, by experience, that a boy, with a tolerable capacity, and of ten years of age only, may, in a few months, be taught to write the English language properly and correctly, though totally unacquainted with the Latin and Greek languages. Newcastle 1790. (Alston I, No. 451.)

Martin, 1824, p. 271, refers to an English Grammar by the Vicar of Penn, Staffs, called Pape, in an edition of 1806. He says the book can now be bought for three shillings a dozen, not because it is a bad book but because Lindley Murray is so popular.

197 William PERRY, Master of the Academy, Kelso, 1774; Master of the Academy, Edinburgh, 1776 (see Nos. 198 and 199).
The Man of Business, and Gentleman's Assistant...together with an essay on English grammar. Edinburgh 1774.

In a 3rd edition, Edinburgh 1777, the grammar is omitted.

Cited as Perry, 1774.

198 William PERRY (see Nos. 197 and 199).
The Royal Standard English Dictionary...to which is prefixed a comprehensive grammar of the English language. Edinburgh, 1775. (Alston v, No. 290.)

Much of the grammar closely resembles that in No. 197 and is almost identical with that in No. 199.

Cited as Perry, 1775.

199 William PERRY (see Nos. 197 and 198).
The Only Sure Guide to the English Tongue...to which is added, a comprehensive grammar of the English language. Edinburgh 1776. (Alston iv, No. 734.)

Cited as Perry, 1776.

200 Jenkin Thomas PHILLIPS, 'Preceptor to His Royal Highness Prince William, Duke of Cumberland'.
An Essay towards an Universal and Rational Grammar. London 1726; as, *A Rational Grammar*, 2nd edn 1731; 3rd edn 1741.

The essay is a universal grammar prefixed to a Latin grammar. The universal grammar is based on that of Port Royal; the Latin grammar is based on those of Shirley and Milton.

201 James PICKBOURN, 'Master of a boarding-school at Hackney'.
A Dissertation on the English Verb; principally intended to ascertain the precise meaning of its tenses. London 1789.

202 *A Pocket Dictionary*, or complete English expositor...with a compendious grammar. London 1753; 2nd edn 1758; 3rd edn 1765. (Alston v, Nos. 165–7.)

The grammatical material is substantially the same as that of *An Easy Introduction*, 1745 (No. 73) and of the *Spelling Dictionary*, 1755 (No. 235).

203 Joshua POOLE, d. before 1657, Usher at Mr Francis Atkinson's school, Ludgrove, Monken Hadley, Middlesex.
The English Accidence: or, a short, plaine, and easie way, for the more speedy attaining to the Latine tongue, by the help of the English. Set out for the use and profit of young children, & framed so, as they may bee exercised in it, as soon as they can but indifferently read English. London 1646; 1655; as, *The Youth's Guide*: or, *English Accidence*, 1662; 1670. (Alston i, Nos. 12a–12d.)

204 Richard POSTLETHWAITE, Rector of Newendon, Essex.
The Grammatical Art Improved. London 1795. (Alston i, No. 492.)

205 Joseph PRIESTLEY, 1733–1804 (see No. 206).
The Rudiments of English Grammar. London 1761; 1768; 3rd edn 1772; 1798. (Alston i, Nos. 199, 200, 203, 207.)

Many changes are made in the early editions, especially in the syntax.

206 Joseph PRIESTLEY (see No. 205).
A Course of Lectures on the Theory of Languages, and Universal Grammar.
Warrington 1762.

207 *The Pupil's Friend*...together with the most essential parts of the
English grammar. 3rd edn Gosport 1799.
    The author is Master of the Naval and Military Academy, Cold
Harbour, Gosport.

208 W.R.
A Series of Letters on English Grammar, published in the *Oxford
Magazine*, London, between July 1768, and September 1769.
                  Letters 1–6 in vol. I   1768
                  Letters 7–9 in vol. II   1769
                  Letter 10 in vol. III   1769

209 Matthew RAINE, Master of the Free Grammar School, Hartforth.
English Rudiments; or, an easy introduction to English grammar.
Darlington 1771; 2nd edn 1776. (Alston I, Nos. 307 and 308.)

210 *A Real English Grammar*; in which the nature of the several parts of
speech, and of their dependence on each other is set forth in a plain
and familiar manner fitted for the use of boys, &c. which will enable
them to speak and write their native language with grammatical
propriety. Dublin 1764. (Alston I, No. 258.)

211 *Remarks on the English Tongue*, for the instruction of youth. Eton
1776. (Alston I, No. 329.)
    Based on Lowth.

212 Benjamin RHODES.
A Concise English Grammar, Birmingham 1795. (Alston I, No. 493.)

213 *Right Spelling very much Improved*, London 1704. (Alston IV, No. 219.)
    Identical with *The Expert Orthographist*, 1704 (Alston IV, No. 218)
which is a revised edition of *The Writing Scholar's Companion*, 1695
(Dobson I, 358, but cf. Alston IV, No. 179). *Right Spelling* contains in
part two, pp. 25–32, a brief English grammar, which does not appear
in *The Writing Scholar's Companion*.

214 James ROTHWELL, d. 1798. 'Master of the Free School of Black-
rod'.
A Comprehensive Grammar of the English Language. Warrington 1787,
2nd edn 1797. (Alston I, Nos. 439 and 440.)
    The work ends with 'An Epitome of English Grammar' in verse.
There are numerous small additions throughout the second edition.

215 *Rudiments of Constructive Etymology and Syntax.* London 1795; 2nd edn
1797. (Alston I, Nos. 490 and 491.)

216   *Rudiments of English Grammar.* Falmouth 1788. (Alston I, No. 448.)

217   Nicholas SALMON, of 23 St John's Square, Clerkenwell.
The First Principles of English Grammar, methodically exhibited and explained, upon a plan entirely new, tending to render the knowledge of them useful in the study of other languages. The constant objects in view are to exercise the judgement of youth, to lessen the labour of the tutor, and to improve the practice of teaching English grammar. London 1798. (Alston I, No. 516.)

218   Samuel SAXON.
The English Schollar's Assistant; or, the rudiments of the English tongue. 2nd edn Reading 1737. (Alston I, No. 86.)

219   William SCOTT, 'Teacher of Elocution and Geography in Edinburgh' (see Nos. 220 and 221).
A New Spelling, Pronouncing, and Explanatory Dictionary of the English Language;...to which is prefixed...elements of English grammar. Edinburgh 1786; 1802. (Alston V, No. 308.)
      The first edition, no copy of which is known, was published in 1777. The grammar is identical with that in No. 220.
      Cited as Scott, 1786.

220   William SCOTT (see Nos. 219, 221).
Lessons in Elocution...with an appendix containing the principles of English grammar. Edinburgh, 3rd edn 1789; 15th edn 1801.
      The grammar is identical with that in No. 219.
      Cited as Scott, 1789.

221   William SCOTT (see Nos. 219, 220).
A Short System of English Grammar. Edinburgh 1793. (Alston I, No. 472.)
      The author here describes himself as 'Teacher of the English language, Edinburgh'. The grammar is confessedly based on Lowth and is very different from that in Nos. 219 and 220.
      Cited as Scott, 1793.

222   John SEALLY, 'Member of the Roman Academy'.
The Lady's Encyclopaedia. 3 vols. London 1788.
      Volume two contains an English grammar.

223   John SEDGER, teacher at Dr Barrow's Academy, Soho Square.
The Structure of the English Language; exhibiting an easy and familiar method of acquiring a grammatical knowledge of its constituent parts. London 1798.
      Dr Barrow subscribed for six copies before publication, but Mr Dempster, of Raleigh House Academy, Mitcham, subscribed for 50 copies. Eighty-eight subscribers subscribed for 326 copies between them.

Appendix VI

224 William SEWELL, 'Schoolmaster'.
English Grammar Methodized. Bristol 1789. (Alston 1, No. 449 *a*.)

225 John SHAW, 'Head-master of the Free Grammar School, at Rochdale'.
A Methodical English Grammar. London 1778; 4th edn 1793. (Alston 1, Nos. 353, 355.)

226 Thomas SHERIDAN, 1687–1738, Schoolmaster in Dublin.
An Easy Introduction of Grammar in English for the understanding of the Latin tongue. Dublin 1714.

227 *A Short English Grammar.* London 1794. (Alston 1, No. 476.)

228 *A Short and Easy Introduction to English Grammar.* London 1786. (Alston 1, No. 433.)
The title-page adds, 'First drawn up for the use of Miss Davies's boarding-school, Tryon's Place, Hackney'.

229 *Short and Easy Rules for attaining a knowledge of English grammar.* London 1800. (Alston 1, No. 535.)

230 *A Short Grammatical Introduction to the English Tongue.* Sheffield 1793. (Alston 1, No. 467 suggests James Haywood, No. 119 above, as author.)

231 *A Short Introduction to Grammar.* Stockton upon Tees 1793.

232 Thomas SMETHAM, 'Master of the Academy at Southgate, and late Master of the Boarding School at Ponders End'.
The Practical Grammar; or, an easy way to understand English. In which the rules are laid down in a manner entirely new; and the whole rendered so easy, familiar, and entertaining, that a child of only eight years of age may be perfectly initiated into a knowledge of the English tongue, with the greatest expedition and pleasure. To which is added, a poetical epitome of grammar, for the help of the memory, with a supplement, containing examples of bad English to be turned into good, with the good opposite, in order to illustrate every rule of syntax, or the composition of sentences; and a short English grammar, upon the plan of the Latin, for the use of such as are designed for the study of that language...London 1774. (Alston 1, No. 317.)

233 J. SMITH.
Grammatica Quadrilinguis. London 1674. (Alston 11, No... 143.)

234 James SMITH, 'Master of the Public Grammar-School at Holt'.
A Compendium of English Grammar...the whole designed principally for Children before they enter upon Latin grammar; and for such as have not the advantage of a classical education. 3rd edn Norwich 1778 (Alston 1, No. 349.)

235 *A Spelling Dictionary of the English Language* (see No. 187). 5th edn London 1755; 12th edn Dublin 1769. (Alston IV, Nos. 565, 573.)
   Alston (IV, No. 566) incorrectly says that the grammar appeared first in the sixth edition. The grammar is practically identical with that in *An Easy Introduction* (No. 73) and *A Pocket Dictionary* (No. 202). As Starnes and Noyes say (chap. 20), the grammar in these closely related works is compiled with discrimination, using particularly Dyche, 1735 (No. 72).

236 Thomas SPENCE, d. 1814, 'Teacher of English in Newcastle'.
   The Grand Repository of the English Language. Newcastle upon Tyne 1775.

237 George STAPLETON, 'Late English Preceptor at Paris and at Brussels'.
   The Road to Knowledge; or young man and woman's best friend:... Consisting of a concise, yet comprehensive grammar of the English language...[etc.]. London 1797.

238 John STIRLING, Master of St Andrew's School, Holborn, 1735; Vicar of Great Gaddesden, 1740.
   A Short View of English Grammar. In a method intirely new...London 1735; 2nd edn 1740. (Alston I, Nos. 73 and 74.)

239 Joshua STORY.
   An Introduction to English Grammar. Newcastle 1778; 3rd edn 1783; 5th edn 1793 (Alston I, Nos. 356, 358, 359.)
   There are many changes by the 3rd edn, deriving especially from Harris's *Hermes*.

240 R. STUBBS, Grammar-Master, Monmouth Boarding School.
   Rules and Exercises on English-Grammar. Hereford 1777. (Alston I, No. 347a.)

241 James SWAINE and Joseph SIMS.
   Cryptography. Or a new, easy, and compendious system of short-hand. London 1761. (Alston VIII, No. 239.)
   The work includes 'An Epitome of English Grammar', pp. iii–xv.

242 Mrs TAYLOR.
   An Easy Introduction to General Knowledge and Liberal Education. Warrington 1791.
   The work, which includes 'Elements of English Grammar', is 'for the use of the young ladies at Strangeways Hall, Manchester'.

243 John Horne TOOKE, 1736–1812.
   EPEA PTEROENTA or, The Diversions of Purley. Part I, London 1786; 2nd edn of Part I and 1st edn of Part II, 1798; rev. by Richard Taylor, from the author's MS., 2 vols. 1829.
   Page references are to Taylor's edition of 1829.

244 William Martin TRINDER, 1747–1818, Doctor and parson, of Romford, Essex.
An Essay on the English Grammar. London 1781. (Alston I, No. 375.)

245 *The True Method of Learning the Latin Tongue by the English*, and of obtaining the more perfect knowledge of the English by the Latin; containing a grammar for both the languages in a short, sure and easie way. London 1696.
   Kennedy 2607*a* attributes this to Adam Littleton, with the date 1697, but the work was published anonymously and Littleton died in 1694.

246 John TRUSLER, 1735–1820, 'eccentric divine, literary compiler and medical empiric' (DNB).
An English Accidence; or, abstract of grammar. London [1790?]. (Alston I, No. 450*b*.)

247 Daniel TURNER, 1710–98, Baptist minister at Abingdon.
An Abstract of English Grammar and Rhetoric. London 1739. (Alston I, No. 87.)

248 William TURNER, 1658–1726, Master of the Free School at Stamford, Lincs.
A Short Grammar for the English Tongue. London 1710. (Alston I, No. 40.)

249 *The Tutor; or Epistolary Guide*...to which are prefixed a new introduction to English grammar...[etc.]. London 1772. (Alston IV, No. 727.)

250 *An Universal Dictionary* of the English language...to which is prefixed a grammar of the English language. Edinburgh 1763. (Alston V, No. 234.)
   The grammar in this work is identical with those in Bayley, 1764 (No. 19), Fenning, 1761 (No. 94) and J. Johnson, 1763 (No.133).

251 George Neville USSHER.
The Elements of English Grammar, methodically arranged for the use of those who study English grammatically without a previous knowledge of the learned languages: and illustrated by rules and lessons of parsing adapted to the capacities of young beginners. Designed particularly for the use of ladies boarding schools. Glocester 1785, 2nd edn 1786. (Alston I, Nos. 426 and 427.)
   The first edition was published anonymously.

252 *A Vocabulary*, or pocket dictionary. To which is prefixed, a compendious grammar of the English language. Birmingham 1765. (Alston V, No. 237.)

253   John WALLIS, 1616–1703.
Grammatica Linguae Anglicanae. Oxford 1653; 2nd edn 1664; 4th edn 1674; 5th edn in vol. 3 of *Opera Mathematica*, 1699; London and Leipzig 1765.

In the preface to the 5th edition Wallis gives his own account of the changes in the principal editions: 'In secunda...adjeci nonnulla, nec tamen multa...In Quarta 1764, auctiora multa sunt...Quinta haec, quam praecedentes, est adhuc auctior.' The additions, which have been closely examined by Lehnert, are nearly all in the illustrations, in the chapter on poetry, and in the praxis first included in the fourth edition.

254   H. WARD, Master of an Academy in Whitehaven.
A Short but clear System of English Grammar. Whitehaven 1777. (Alston 1, No. 346.)

255   John WARD, 1679–1758, Professor of Rhetoric at Gresham College; had a school in Tenter Alley, Moorfields, in 1710.
Four Essays upon the English Language, viz. I. Observations on the orthography. II. Rules for the division of syllables. III. The use of the articles. IV. The formation of the verbs, and their analogy with the Latin. To these is subjoined a catalogue of the English verbs, formed through their radical tenses. London 1758. (Alston 1, No. 152.)

256   William WARD, 1708–72, Master of Beverley Grammar School, from 1751 (see No. 257).
An Essay on Grammar, as it may be applied to the English language. In two treatises. The one speculative, being an attempt to investigate proper principles. The other practical, containing definitions and rules deduced from the principles, and illustrated by a variety of examples from the most approved writers. London 1765; 1779. (Alston 1, Nos. 264, 266.)

The *Essay* is an elaborate work, in which Ward is said to have been helped by Laurence Whitaker, one of his assistants (Poldauf, p. 139). Pages 1–296 are occupied by the 'speculative' part, the rest by the practical. The form of the work possibly derives from Mark Lewis's statement, 'The Speculative Part of Grammar ought to be left to riper years, and the Practical Part may be made very short and easie'. (*Essay*, 1670? p. 1.)

257   William WARD (see No. 256).
A Grammar of the English Language, in two treatises. The first, containing rules for every part of its construction; with a praxis both of true and false English, shewing how the rules are to be applied in resolving the true, and in rectifying the false. The second, shewing the nature of the several parts of speech and the reasons for every part of construction. York 1767. (Alston 1, No. 269.)

258   Samuel WELLS, 'Writing Master in Cheltenham'.
The Construction of the English Language; or, a short, easy and compre-
hensive grammar, for the use of English schools. Cheltenham 1760.
(Alston I, No. 197.)

259   John WESLEY, 1703–91.
A Short English Grammar. Bristol 1748. (Alston I, No. 104.)

260   Jeremiah WHARTON.
The English-Grammar. London 1654; 1655. (Alston I, Nos. 25, 26.)

261   James WHITE, d. about 1812, Schoolmaster in Cecil Street, Strand,
then in Dublin.
The English Verb; a grammatical essay, in the didactic form. London
1761.

262   John WILKINS, 1614–72.
An Essay towards a Real Character and a Philosophical Language. London
1668. (Alston VII, No. 290.)

263   John WILLIAMS, Vicar of Catherington, Hants. (see No. 273).
The First Principles of English Grammar, in verse. [Salisbury?] [1780?]
(Alston I, No. 368.)
   Dedicated to James Harris.

264   George WILSON, 'Teacher at an Academy in London'.
The Youth's Pocket Companion: or, universal preceptor. Containing...
a plain and easy grammar of the English language. 2nd edn London
1759,
   First published perhaps in 1756, the date of a commendatory letter
in the second edition.

265   J. WILSON, Vicar of Biddulph, and Master of the Free Grammar
School, Congleton.
Fisher's Grammar Improved; or an English grammar in which Fisher's
plan is preserved, and the work made more perfect by various
amendments in orthography and prosody from Sheridan and others;
and in etymology and syntax principally from Lowth. Congleton
1792. (Alston I, No. 135.)
   See Nos. 96 and 97.

266   Thomas WISE, 'Accomptant'.
The Newest Young Man's Companion, containing a compendious English
grammar...Berwick, 1754; 3rd edn 1758; 8th edn 1774; 11th edn
1778.
   Much of the grammar is identical with Dyche, 1735. There is no
significant change in the grammar in the later editions.

267   Charles WISEMAN.
A Complete English Grammar on a new plan. For the use of foreigners, and such natives as would acquire a scientifical knowledge of their own tongue. In two parts. Containing, I. An exact analysis and proper division of sound, so far as it regards pronunciation, in all its variety, according to the true genius and idiom of the English language. II. The eight parts of speech distinctly considered, with the declension of articles, nouns, pronouns &c. and the conjugation of verbs, both regular and irregular, at full length; by which means, any one may learn English grammatically, in the same easy, familiar, and regular manner as the French and other modern languages.
The whole interspersed with several short praxes and remarks at the end of every part of speech. To which are added, similar comparisons of the Old English, Scotch, and Welsh tongues, with the modern English; as also, examples for those who understand Latin, Italian, French, Spanish, Portuguese, &c. shewing the affinity of the English to these languages, and the natural gradation of change, from one to another. London 1764. (Alston 1, No. 257.)
The preface is by Oliver Goldsmith, whose receipt to Newbery for £127, the fee for writing, among other works, the 'Preface to Wiseman's Grammar', is dated 7 June 1766. (K. C. Balderston, *A Census of the Manuscripts of Oliver Goldsmith*, New York 1926, p. 32.)

268   James WOOD.
Grammatical Institutes; or, a practical English grammar. Newcastle 1777. (Alston 1, No. 347.)

269   George WRIGHT, 'Teacher of English and the Mathematics'.
The Principles of Grammar, or youth's English directory. Sunderland 1794. (Alston 1, No. 477.)
Only the initial G. appears on the title-page. The name George is given in an advertisement for this work in a book of cuttings relating to Newcastle typography collected by John Bell and Samuel Longstaffe, and now in the Public Library, Newcastle-upon-Tyne.

270   Thomas WRIGHT, Master of a seminary at South-Town, near Great Yarmouth (see No. 271).
A Miscellany. [Great Yarmouth?] [1795?]
Pages 51–8 contain 'A Poetical Epitome of English Grammar', and pages 59–105 contain other grammatical and stylistic material. Cited as T. Wright, *Miscellany*.

271   Thomas WRIGHT (see No. 270).
An English Grammar. [Great Yarmouth?] [a. 1795?] (Alston 1, No. 534.)
The work is advertised in Wright's *Miscellany* as *The Elements of English Grammar*. Cited as T. Wright, *Grammar*.

272 Richard WYNNE, 1719–99, 'Rector of St. Alphage, London'.
An Universal Grammar, for the use of those who are unacquainted with
the learned languages, and are desirous of speaking and writing
English, or any other modern language, with accuracy and precision.
London 1775.

273 *The Young Mathematician's Logic*, upon the plan of Dean Aldrich's
celebrated Aristotle's Logic...To which is annexed, critical remarks
upon grammar in general. By the author of *Education of Children and
Young Students in all its Branches*. London 1760. (Alston VII, No. 247.)
    The Bodleian copy carries a MS. ascription to the Rev. John
Williams, Vicar of Catherington. See No. 263.

APPENDIX VII

ENGLISH GRAMMARS: A CHRONOLOGICAL LIST, BY DECADES, OF THE EARLIEST EDITIONS CONSULTED

(D = Dictionary; E = English; G = Grammar; Gl. = Grammatical; L = Language; T = Tongue).

BULLOKAR	*Pamphlet for G.*	1586
GREAVES	*Grammatica Anglicana*	1594
TOMKIS	*De Analogia Anglicanae Sermonis* (MS.)	1612
HUME	*Of the Orthographie...*	*c.* 1617
GILL	*Logonomia Anglica*	1619
HEWES	*A Perfect Survey*	1624
BUTLER	*The E.G.*	1633
JONSON	*The E.G.* (written *c.* 1630?)	1640
POOLE	*The E. Accidence*	1646
LODOWYCK	*A Common Writing*	1647
EVELYN	*The E.G.* (MS.)	*c.* 1650
LODOWYCK	*The Ground-Work*	1652
WALLIS	*Grammatica Linguae Anglicanae*	1653
WHARTON	*The E.G.*	1654
BECK	*The Universal Character*	1657
DALGARNO	*Ars Signorum*	1661
HOWELL	*A New E.G.*	1662
WILKINS	*An Essay towards a Real Character*	1668
NEWTON	*School Pastime*	1669
LEWIS	*(Institutio) Grammaticae Puerilis*	1670
LEWIS	*Essay*	1670?
LYE	*The Child's Delight*	1671
SMITH	*Grammatica Quadrilinguis*	1674
LEWIS	*Plain & Short Rules*	1675?
LEWIS	*Vestibulum Technicum*	1675
NEWTON	*The E. Academy*	1677

COOPER	*Grammatica Linguae Anglicanae*	1685
BLOME	*The Gentleman's Recreation*	1686
COOPER	*The E. Teacher*	1687
MIEGE	*The E.G.*	1688
CLARE	*A Compleat System of G.*	1690
AICKIN	*The E.G.*	1693
LANE	*A Rational & Speedy Method*	1695
The True Method of Learning the Latin T. by the E.		1696
BROWN	*The E. School Reformed*	1700
LANE	*A Key to the Art of Letters*	1700
Right Spelling very much Improved		1704
The E. Scholar Compleat		1706
W. TURNER	*A Short G.*	1710
GILDON AND BRIGHTLAND	*A G. of the E.T.*	1711
GREENWOOD	*An Essay towards a Practical E.G.*	1711
MAITTAIRE	*The E.G.*	1712
SHERIDAN	*An Easy Intro. of G.*	1714
HARLAND	*The E. Spelling-Book Revis'd* (3rd edn)	1719
DOUGLAS	[Grammatical MSS.]	*c.* 1720?
HUGH JONES	*An Accidence to the E.T.*	1724
PHILIPPS	*An Essay towards an Universal...G.*	1726
ENTICK	*Speculum Latinum*	1728
DUNCAN	*A New E.G.*	1731
J. OWEN	*The Youth's Instructor*	1732
BARKER	*An E.G.*	1733?
The E. Accidence		1733
LOUGHTON	*A Practical G. of the E. T.*	1734
COLLYER	*The General Principles of G.*	1735
DYCHE	*A New General E.D.*	1735
STIRLING	*A Short View of E.G.*	1735
A New E. Accidence		1736
SAXON	*The E. Schollar's Assistant* (2nd edn)	1737
GREENWOOD	*The Royal E.G.*	1737
LOWE	*E.G. Reform'd*	1737
D. TURNER	*An Abstract of E.G.*	1739
DILWORTH	*A New Guide to the E.T.*	1740
JAMES CORBET	*An Intro. to the E.G.*	1743
An Easy Intro. to the E.L.		1745
KIRKBY	*A New E.G.*	1746
A New E.G.		1746
MARTIN	*Institutions of L.*	1748
WESLEY	*A Short E.G.*	1748

An E.G.		*c.* 1750?
FISHER	*A New E.G.*	1750
MERRIMAN	*A Compendious E.G.*	1750
The Practice of Speaking & Writing E. (MS.)		*c.* 1750?
HARRIS	*Hermes*	1751
J.J.	*Prittle prattle*	1752
BUCHANAN	*The Complete E. Scholar*	1753
A Pocket Dictionary		1753
FARRO	*The Royal Universal British G.*	1754
GOUGH	*A Practical G. of the E.T.*	1754
MARTIN	*An Intro. to the E.L.*	1754
WISE	*The Newest Young Man's Companion*	1754
BAILEY	*A New Universal Etymological E.D.*	1755
The Complete Letter-Writer		1755
GORDON	*Every Young Man's Companion*	1755
DR S. JOHNSON	*A D. of the E.L.*	1755
LOWE	*A Critical Spelling Book*	1755
A Spelling D. of the E.L.		1755
BAYLY	*An Intro. . . to Languages*	1756
FENNING	*The Universal Spelling Book*	1756
MR S. JOHNSON	*A Compleat Intro. to . . . Writing Letters*	1758
J. WARD	*Four Essays upon the E.L.*	1758
G. WILSON	*The Youth's Pocket Companion* (2nd edn)	1759
ASH	*Grammatical Institutes*	1760
BELLAMY	*A New Complete E.D.*	1760
HAMMOND	*A Complete . . . Spelling D.*	1760?
HENSON	*A Compendium of E.G.*	1760?
WELLS	*The Construction of the E.L.*	1760
The Young Mathematician's Logic		1760
FENNING	*The Royal E.D.*	1761
PRIESTLEY	*The Rudiments of E.G.*	1761
SWAINE AND SIMS	*Cryptography*	1761
WHITE	*The E. Verb*	1761
BUCHANAN	*The British G.*	1762
LOWTH	*A Short Intro. to E.G.*	1762
MANSON	*A New Pocket D.*	1762
PRIESTLEY	*A Course of Lectures on the Theory of L.*	1762
J. JOHNSON	*The New Royal & Universal D.*	1763
BAYLEY	*An Universal Etymological D.*	1764
An Universal D. of the E.L.		1764
A Real E.G.		1764
WISEMAN	*A Complete E.G.*	1764
The British Letter-Writer		1765?
S. EDWARDS	*An Abstract of E.G.*	1765
ELPHINSTON	*The Principles of the E.L.*	1765

ENTICK	*The New Spelling D.*	1765
HALLIFAX	*Familiar Letters*	1765?
A Vocabulary or Pocket D.		1765
W. WARD	*An Essay on G.*	1765
BURN	*A Practical G. of the E.L.*	1766
HOUGHTON	*A New Intro. to E.G.*	1766
BUCHANAN	*A Regular E. Syntax*	1767
W. WARD	*A G. of the E.L.*	1767
R. JONES	*Hieroglyfic*	1768
W.R.	*Letters on E.G.*	1768–9
BELL	*A Concise & Comprehensive System of E.G.*	1769
The Art of Teaching in Sport		1770?
HODGSON	*A Practical E.G.*	1770
JOEL	*An Easy Intro. to the E.G.*	1770
BAYLY	*The English Accidence*	1771
BAYLY	*A Practical Treatise...*	1771
COOKE	*The Universal Letter-Writer*	1771?
DU BOIS	*The Lady's Polite Secretary*	1771
Encyclopaedia Britannica (A)		1771
FENNING	*A New G. of the E.L.*	1771
R. JONES	*The Circles of Gomer*	1771
MEILAN	*A G. of the E.L.*	1771?
METCALFE	*The Rudiments of the E.T.* (2nd edn)	1771
A New & Improved Spelling D.		1771
RAINE	*E. Rudiments*	1771
ADAM	*The Principles of Latin & E.G.*	1772
BARLOW	*A Complete E.D.*	1772?
BAYLY	*A Plain & Complete G. of the E.L.*	1772
CLARKE	*The Rational Spelling Book*	1772?
CROCKER	*A Practical Intro. to E.G.*	1772
JOHNSTON	*A Pronouncing & Spelling D.*	1772
The Tutor		1772
JOHN CARTER	*A Practical E.G.*	1773
The Court Letter-Writer		1773
BARCLAY	*A Complete & Universal E.D.*	1774
FISHER	*The New E. Tutor* (1763?) 3rd edn	1774
T.M.	*The Grammarian's Vade-Mecum*	1774
MONBODDO	*Of the Origin & Progress of L.*	1774
PERRY	*The Man of Business...*	1774
SMETHAM	*The Practical G.*	1774
ASH	*The New & Complete D. of the E.L.*	1775
COOKE	*The Universal Letter-Writer*	1775?
DEVIS	*The Accidence*	1775
PERRY	*The Royal Standard D.*	1775
SPENCE	*The Grand Repository of the E.L.*	1775

WYNNE	*An Universal G.*	1775
FARRO	*The Royal Golden Instructor*	1776?
An E.G.		1776
PERRY	*The Only Sure Guide*	1776
Remarks on the E.T.		1776
HARRISON	*Institutes of E.G.*	1777
E. OWEN	*A Short System of E.G.*	1777
STUBBS	*Rules & Exercises on E.G.*	1777
H. WARD	*A Short...System of E.G.*	1777
WOOD	*Gl. Institutions*	1777
BETTESWORTH	*The E.G. Epitomis'd*	1778
SHAW	*A Methodical E.G.*	1778
J. SMITH	*A Compendium of E.G.* (3rd edn)	1778
STORY	*An Intro. to E.G.*	1778
G. BROWN	*The New E. Letter-Writer*	1779?
C. JOHNSON	*The Complete Art of Writing Letters*	1779
The Merchant Maiden Hospital Magazine		1779
The Only True Guide to E.G.		1779
MARRIOTT	*The New Royal E.D.*	1780
WILLIAMS	*The First Principles of E.G.*	1780?
M'ILQUHAM	*A Comprehensive E.G.*	1781
OLIPHANT	*A Compendium of E.G.*	1781
TRINDER	*An Essay on the E.G.*	1781
BEATTIE	*Dissertations Moral & Critical*	1783
JOHN CORBET	*A Concise System of E.G.*	1784
FELL	*An Essay towards an E.G.*	1784
IRELAND	*Beauties in Prose & Verse*	1784
The Elementary Principles of E.G.		1785
KNOWLES	*The Principles of E.G.*	1785
USSHER	*The Elements of E.G.*	1785
A Short & Easy Intro. to E.G.		1786
BENTICK	*The Spelling & Explanatory D.*	1786
SCOTT	*A New Spelling...D.* (1777)	1786
TOOKE	*Diversions of Purley*	1786 and 1798
A. MURRAY	*An Easy E.G.* (2nd edn)	1787
HARROLD	*A Short Intro. to E.G.* (3rd edn)	1787
ROTHWELL	*A Comprehensive G. of the E.L.*	1787
BINNS	*The Youth's Guide*	1788
COOTE	*Elements of the G. of the E.L.*	1788
A Key to Spelling		1788
Newbery's New Spelling D.		1788
Rudiments of E.G.		1788
SEALLY	*The Lady's Encyclopaedia*	1788
PICKBOURN	*A Dissertation on the E. Verb*	1789
SCOTT	*Lessons in Elocution* (3rd edn)	1789

SEWELL	*E.G. Methodized*	1789
BICKNELL	*The Gl. Wreath*	1790
COOKE	*The New & Complete Universal Letter-Writer*	1790?
FORDYCE	*The New & Complete British Letter-Writer*	1790?
FRANCIS	*A Concise Intro. to E.G.*	1790
MARSHALL	*An Intro. to the E.T.*	1790
PAPE	*A Key to E.G.*	1790
TRUSLER	*An E. Accidence*	1790?
Outlines of E.G.		1791
TAYLOR	*An Easy Introduction*	1791
ANDERSON	*Remarks on G.*	1792
DEARLE	*A Sure Guide for all Youth*	1792
FOGG	*Elementa Anglicana* (1)	1792
J. WILSON	*Fisher's G. Improved*	1792
COOK	*The Westminster Spelling Book*	1793
HORNSEY	*A Short E.G.*	1793
HUNTLEY	*A Short System of E.G.*	1793
Lilly's Accidence Improved		1793
A Short Intro. to G.		1793
'MICA'	*Observations on G.*	1793
NICHOLSON	*The Rudiments of E.G.*	1793
SCOTT	*A Short System of E.G.*	1793
A Short Gl. Intro. to the E.T.		1793
BARRIE	*A Spelling & Pronouncing D.*	1794
A Comprehensive View of E.G.		1794
An Easy Short...Intro. to the E.G.		1794
A Short E.G.		1794
G. WRIGHT	*The Principles of G.*	1794
ALDERSON	*E. Gl. Exercises*	1795
CRAKELT	*A Comprehensive G. of the E.T.*	1795
L. MURRAY	*E.G.*	1795
POSTLETHWAITE	*The Gl. Art Improved*	1795
RHODES	*A Concise E.G.*	1795
Rudiments of Constructive Etymology		1795
T. WRIGHT	*An E.G.*	before 1795?
T. WRIGHT	*Miscellany*	*c.* 1795?
COAR	*A G. of the E.T.*	1796
MRS EDWARDS	*A Short Compendium of E.G.*	1796
FOGG	*Elementa Anglicana* (2)	1796
J.G.	*An Easy Intro. to the E.L.*	1796
LYNCH	*The Pentaglot Preceptor*	1796
BRIDEL	*An Intro. to E.G.*	1797
BULLEN	*The Rudiments of E.G.*	1797
J. CARTER	*A Short & Easy Intro. to E.G.* (5th edn)	1797
Encyclopaedia Britannica (B)		1797

GENTLEMAN	*The Young E. Scholar's Pocket Companion* (2nd edn)	1797
GROOMBRIDGE	*The Rudiments of the E.T.*	1797
L. MURRAY	*An Abridgement of Murray's E.G.*	1797
STAPLETON	*The Road to Knowledge*	1797
English Syntax Rules		1798
HEWLETT	*An Intro. to Reading & Spelling* (4th edn)	1798
KITSON	*A Short Intro. to E.G.*	1798
LOVECHILD	*Parsing Lessons for Young Children*	1798
LOVECHILD	*Parsing Lessons for Elder Pupils*	1798
SALMON	*The First Principles of E.G.*	1798
SEDGER	*The Structure of the E.L.*	1798
BOWEN	*The Rudiments of E.G.*	1799
GARDINER	*The Young Ladies' E.G.*	1799
LOVECHILD	*The Child's G.*	before 1799
MAYNE	*A Compendious E.G.*	1799
MERCY	*A Short Intro. to E.G.*	1799
The Pupil's Friend (3rd edn)		1799
ANGUS	*An Epitome of E.G.*	1800
An Essay towards an E.G.		1800
EVES	*The Gl. Plaything*	1800
HASTINGS	*Of the E. Verbs* (MS.)	*c.* 1800?
HAYWOOD	*A Short Intro. to the E.T.*	1800
Short & Easy Rules		1800
DALTON	*Elements of E.G.*	1801
LOVECHILD	*The Mother's G.* (1798?)	1815?

APPENDIX VIII

OTHER WORKS CONSULTED

MANUSCRIPT WORKS

Gwendoline K. COOKE, *English Grammarians, 1450–1650. A Critical Survey.* M.A. Dissertation, University of London 1938.

Thomas HAYWARD, *The English Institutions*, written after 1625. BM MS. Sloane 2609.

L. G. HELLER, *English Linguistic Terminology, 995–1645.* Unpublished dissertation, Columbia University, New York 1960.

Clara May PARKER, *The Development of Textbooks in English Grammar for Secondary Schools in Relation to the Latin Tradition.* Unpublished Ph.D. dissertation, University of Texas 1930.

Priscilla TYLER, *Grammars of the English Language to 1850: with special emphasis on school grammars used in America.* Unpublished dissertation, Western Reserve University 1953.

S. WATANABE, *Studien zur Abhängigkeit der frühneuenglischen Grammatiken von den mittelalterlichen Lateingrammatiken.* Unpublished dissertation, Münster 1958.

PRINTED WORKS

Hans AARSLEFF, *The Study of Language in England, 1780–1860*, Princeton University Press, Princeton, N.J. 1967.

David ABERCROMBIE, 'Forgotten Phoneticians', *Trans. Philol. Soc.* 1948, reprinted in *Studies in Phonetics and Linguistics*, 1965, 45–75.

William ADIE, *A New Spelling Book*, Paisley 1769.

G. A. AITKEN, 'Steele, and some English Grammars of his Time', *Walford's Antiquarian Mag.* 8. 1885. 166–70.

C. G. ALLEN, 'The Sources of "Lily's Latin Grammar"'; a review of the facts and some further suggestions', *The Library*, 5th ser. 9. 1954. 85–100.

R. C. ALSTON, *A Bibliography of the English Language from the Invention of Printing to the Year 1800*, vol. I, *English Grammars Written in English*, E. J. Arnold and Son, Leeds 1965.

vol. II, *Polyglot Dictionaries and Grammars*, Bradford 1967.

vol. IV, *Spelling Books*, Bradford 1967.

vol. V, *The English Dictionary*, E. J. Arnold and Son, Leeds 1966.

vol. VII, *Logic, Philosophy, Epistemology, Universal Language*, Bradford 1967.

vol. VIII, *Treatises on Short-hand*, E. J. Arnold and Son, Leeds 1966.

John ANCHORAN, see COMENIUS.

Basil ANDERTON, *Local Catalogue*, Newcastle-upon-Tyne Public Libraries, Newcastle-upon-Tyne 1932.

Antoine ARNAULD and Claude LANCELOT, see *Grammaire Générale*.

Antoine ARNAULD and P. NICOLE, *La Logique, ou l'Art de Penser*, 2nd edn Paris 1664.

    Logic; or the Art of Thinking, London 1685; 2nd edn 1693.

von ARNIM, ed., *Stoicorum Veterum Fragmenta*, 4 vols. Leipzig 1905–24. Cited as SVF.

Roger ASCHAM, *The Scholemaster* (1570), ed. E. Arber, London 1870.

Francis BACON, *The Advancement of Learning* (1605), ed. W. Aldis Wright, 5th edn Oxford 1900.

    De Augmentis Scientiarum (1623), Bk 6, chap. 1, ed. J. Spedding et al., vol. 1, London, 1872.

Roger BACON, *Opus Maius*, ed. J. H. Bridges, 2 vols. Oxford 1897. (*Pars Tertia* is 'De Utilitate Grammaticae'.)

    Opus Maius, transl. R. B. Burke, Philadelphia 1928.

Nathan BAILEY, *English & Latin Exercises*, London 1706; 3rd edn 1713; 5th edn 1720; 18th edn 1798.

[Robert BAKER] *Reflections on the English Language*, London 1770.

K. C. BALDERSTON, *A Census of the Manuscripts of Oliver Goldsmith*, New York 1926.

Jonathan BANKS, *Januae Clavis: or Lilly's Syntax Explained*, London 1679.

F. A. BARBOUR, 'History of English Grammar Teaching', *Educational Rev*. New York, 12. 1846. 487–507.

Johannes BARBOUR, *An Epitome of Grammatical Principles*, Oxford, 1668.

K. BARWICK, 'Remmius Palaemon und die Römische Ars Grammatica', *Philologus, Zeitschrift für das Klassische Altertum*, suppl. vol. 15, Part 2, pp. 1–272.

I. BEKKER, *Anecdota Graeca*, vol. 2, Berlin 1816.

Bellum Grammaticale: or, the Grammaticall Battel Royal. In reflections on three English Grammars, publish'd in about a year last past, London 1712.

Folke BERGSTROM, 'John Kirkby (1746) on English Pronunciation', *Studia Neophilologica*, 27. 1955. 65–104.

S. BLACH, 'Shakespeares Lateingrammatik', *Jahrb. der deutschen Shakespeare-Gesellschaft*, 44. 1908. 65–117; 45. 1909. 51–100.

Hugh BLAIR, *Lectures on Rhetoric & Belles Lettres*, 3 vols., 4th edn London 1790.

Rae BLANCHARD, *The Correspondence of Richard Steele*, Oxford 1941.

R. R. BOLGAR, *The Classical Heritage & its Beneficiaries*, Cambridge 1958.

Henry BRADLEY, 'On the Text of Abbo of Fleury's Quaestiones Grammaticales', *Proc. Brit. Acad*. 10. 1921–3. 173–80.

[John BRIGHTLAND?] *Reasons for an English Education*, London 1711.

John BRINSLEY, *A Consolation for our Grammar Schooles* (1622), ed. T. Pollock, Scholars' Facsimiles & Reprints, New York, 1943.

Ludus Literarius (1612), ed. E. T. Campagnac from 2nd edn 1627, Liverpool 1917.

The Posing of the Parts (2nd edn 1615), unnumbered edn London 1665.

Goold BROWN, *The Grammar of English Grammars*, 2nd edn New York 1857.

Richard BROWNE, *The English Examiner*, London 1692.

The English Expositor Improv'd, 10th edn London 1707.

Thomas Gunter BROWNE, *Hermes Unmasked; or the Art of Speech founded on the Association of Words & Ideas*, London 1795.

William F. BRYAN, 'Notes on the Founders of prescriptive English Grammar', *Manly Anniversary Studies in Lang. & Lit.* Chicago 1923, pp. 383–93.

Charles BRYANT, *A Key to Letters*...Bk 2, For the Use of Schools, Norwich [1769].

James BUCHANAN, *A Plan of an English Grammar-School Education*, Edinburgh 1770.

Edward BURLES, *Grammatica Burlesa: or, a new English Grammar*, London 1652 [a Latin Grammar].

[S. BUTLER] *An Essay upon Education*, London *c.* 1750.

Is.C., *The London New Method & Art of Teaching Children to Spell & Read*, London 1733.

George CAMPBELL, *The Philosophy of Rhetoric* (1776), 11th edn Edinburgh 1841.

Henry CARE, *The Tutor to True English*, London 1687.

I. CASSANDER (pseud. of John Bruckner), *Criticisms on The Diversions of Purley*, London 1790.

Certaine Grammar Questions for the Exercise of young Schollers in the learning of the Accidence, n.p. [1602?].

Ephraim CHAMBERS, *Cyclopaedia*, London 1728; 2nd edn 1738; 4th edn 1741; adds. by Abraham Rees, 1779 (s.v. 'Grammar').

B. M. CHARLESTON, *Studies on the Syntax of the English Verb*, Berne 1941.

C. W. CHILTON, 'Lindley Murray, a forgotten figure', *Studies in Education* (Univ. Hull, Inst. of Education), 2. 1954. 144–50.

Noam CHOMSKY, *Cartesian Linguistics*, New York 1966.

William CLARE, *Via Naturalis qua Lingua Latina facile percipitur*, London 1688.

John CLARKE, *A New Grammar of the Latin Tongue*...To which is annexed a dissertation on Language, London 1733.

Elisha COLES, *Syncrisis, or the most natural & easie method of learning Latin: by comparing it with English*, London 1675.

F. H. COLSON, 'The Analogist & Anomalist Controversy', *Class. Quart.* 13. 1919. 24–36.

J. A. COMENIUS. *The Gate of Tongues Unlocked & Opened* [a translation of *Janua Linguarum Reserata*, 1628–31], 2nd edn enlarged by John Anchoran, London 1633.

Janua Linguarum Reserata... *The Gate of Languages unlocked*, formerly translated by Tho. Horn: afterwards much corrected by John Robotham: now carefully reviewed by W. D., London 1673.

Orbis Sensualium Pictus, tr. Charles Hoole, London 1659.

E. R. CURTIUS, *European Literature & the Latin Middle Ages* (1948), transl. W. R. Trask, London 1953.

Thomas COOKE, *Tales, Epistles, Odes, Fables, &c...to which are added Proposals for perfecting the English Language,* London 1729.

Edmund COOTE, *The Englishe Schoolemaister,* London, 1596.

Simon DAINES, *Orthoepia Anglicana: or, the first principall part of the English Grammar* (1640) ed. M. Rösler & R. Brotanek, *Neudrucke frühneuenglischer Grammatiken,* Halle 1908.

R. C. DALLAS, 'Biographical Memoirs of James Elphinston', *Gent. Mag.* 79(2). November 1809. 1057–1063.

B. DEMOTT, 'The Sources and Development of J. Wilkins' Philosophical Language', *JEGP,* 57. 1958. 1–14.

P. M. G. DICKSON, *The Sun Insurance Office, 1710–1960,* London 1960.

E. J. DOBSON *English Pronunciation, 1500–1700,* 2 vols. Oxford 1957.

Robert DODSLEY, *The Preceptor; containing a general course of education,* 2 vols., 3rd edn London 1758.

Paul DOTTIN, *Robinson Crusoe examin'd & criticis'd, or a new edition of Charles Gildon's famous pamphlet,* London and Paris 1923.

John DRUMMOND, *A Grammatical Introduction to the modern pronunciation & Spelling of the English tongue,* Edinburgh 1767.

Thomas DYCHE, *A Guide to the English Tongue* (1707), 2nd edn London 1710; 14th edn 1729; 45th edn 1764.

J. E., *Grammaticus Analyticus...teaching three things necessary to the acquiring the Latine tongue:* London 1670.

Henry EDMUNDSON, ΣΥΝ ΘΕѠ, *Lingua Linguarum. The Natural Language of Languages...Contrived & built upon Analogy,* London 1658.

E. EGGER, *Apollonius Dyscole:essai sur l'histoire des théories grammaticales dans l'antiquité,* Paris 1854.

James ELPHINSTON, *Fifty Years' Correspondence,* vol. 8, London 1794.

Bert EMSLEY, 'James Buchanan & the Eighteenth Century regulation of English usage', *PMLA,* 48. 1933. 1154–1166.

'English Grammars', *Notes & Queries,* 7th ser. 6. 1888. 121, 243, 302, 453; 7. 1889. 54.

Encyclopédie, s.v. 'Grammaire', vol. 7, 1757.

An English Introduction to the Latin Tongue, London 1683.

Nils ENKVIST, 'Paul Greaves, Author of *Grammatica Anglicana*', *Neuphilologische Mitteilungen,* 59. 1958. 277–9.

John EVANS, *The Palace of Profitable Pleasure. Containing...whatsoever is necessary to be learned of an English Scoller,* London 1621.

Exercises Instructive and Entertaining in False English, 6th edn Leeds 1797. (Attributed by Kennedy, No. 5492, to John Carter and by Leeds Ref. Lib. to John Binns, who printed it.)

Appendix VIII

H. M. FLASDIECK, 'Zur Verfasserschaft der Grammatik von J. Bright-land', *Anglia, Beiblatt*, 39. 1928. 324–7.

Richard FLECKNO, *Miscellania*, London 1653 (pp. 75–107 contain 'A Discourse of Languages. And particularly of the English Tongue').

Jolly B. FLORIAN, *An Essay on an Analytical Course of Studies*, London 1796.

P. B. R. FORBES, 'Greek Pioneers in Philosophy and Grammar', *Class. Rev.* 47. 1933. 105–12.

John FREE, *An Essay towards a History of the English Tongue*, London 1749.

C. C. FRIES, 'The Periphrastic Future with *shall* and *will* in modern English', *PMLA*, 40. 1925. 963–1024 (for lists of grammars).

'The Rules of Common School Grammars', *PMLA*, 42. 1927. 221–37.

Otto FUNKE, 'Sprachphilosophische Probleme bei Bacon', *Eng. Studien*, 61. 1926/7. 24–56.

'Zum Weltsprachenproblem in England im 17. Jahrhundert', *Anglistische Forschungen*, 69. 1929.

Englische Sprachphilosophie im späteren 18. Jahrhundert, Berne 1934.

'Grammatica Anglicana von P.Gr., 1594', *Wiener Beiträge zur engl. Philol.* 60. 1938. pp. xi–li.

'William Bullokar's Bref Grammar for English, 1586', *Anglia*, 62.1938. 116–37.

'Ben Jonson's English Grammar, 1640', *Anglia*, 64.1940,117–34.

Die Frühzeit der englische Grammatik...von Bullokar bis Wallis, Berne 1941.

'On the System of Grammar', *Archivum Linguisticum*, 6. 1954. 1–19.

'On the Sources of John Wilkins' Philosophical Language (1668)', *Eng. Studies*, 40. 1959. 208–14.

A. GABRIELSON, 'Elisha Cole's *Syncrisis*, 1675, as a Source of Information on Seventeenth Century English', *Engl. Studien*, 70. 1935. 149–52.

'A Few Notes on Gil's *Logonomia Anglica*, 1619', *Studia Neophilologica*, 14. 1941/2. 331–9.

'Professor Kennedy's Bibliography of Writings on the English Language. A Review with a list of additions and corrections', *Studia Neophilologica*, 2. 1929. 117–68.

L. E. C. GAULTIER, *Jeu de Grammaire*, 2nd edn London 1794.

Méthode pour analyser la pensée sans déranger l'ordre des mots qui l'expriment, ou mécanisme de la décomposition des phrases rendu sensible aux yeux, 2nd edn Paris 1806.

Leçons de Grammaire, suivant la méthode des tableaux analytique, synthetique, & celui du mécanisme de la grammaire françoise, Paris 1787.

A Method of making Abridgments; or, easy and certain rules for analysing authors. Part 1, London 1800; Part 2, London 1801.

A General & Rational Grammar with the reasoning, the general agreement & particular differences of languages. Translated from the French of Messrs. de Port Royal, London 1753.

E. L. GILES, 'John Newton on Education', *Notes & Queries*, 175. 1938. 22–4.

H. A. GLEASON, *Linguistics and English Grammar*, New York 1965.

Martin GRABMANN, *Mittelalterliches Geistesleben*, Munich, 3 vols.: I, 1926; II, 1936; III, 1956 .(Cited as Grabmann, MG.)

   Thomas von Erfurt und die Sprachlogik des mittelalterlichen Aristotelismus, Munich 1943. (Cited as Grabmann, TE.)

C. F. GRAHAM, 'On English Grammars', *Class. Museum*, 2. 1845. 404–10.

Grammaire Générale et Raisonnée, contenant les fondements de l'art de parler, Paris, 1660; 2nd edn 1664; 4th edn 1679 (by Antoine Arnauld and Claude Lancelot).

Thomas GRANGER, *Syntagma Grammaticum*, or an easie and methodicall explanation of Lillie's Grammar, London 1616.

Emmanuel GREEN, *Bibliotheca Somersetensis*, 3 vols. Taunton 1902.

Richard GREEN, *The Works of John & Charles Wesley. A Bibliography.* London 1896.

Thomas GREEN, *The Royal Spelling Dictionary of the English Language,* London 1765.

Ormerod GREENWOOD, 'The Curious History of English Grammar', *The Listener*, 42. 1949. 13–14.

James GREGORY, 'Theory of the Moods of Verbs', *Trans. Royal Soc. of Edinburgh* 1790, pp. 1–58.

R. H. GRIFFITH, 'Isaac Bickerstaff's "Grammar"', *Notes & Queries*, 194. 1949, 362–5.

P.H., *A New English Introduction to the Latin Tongue*, London 1735.

Samuel HAMMOND, *The Young English Scholar's Guide*, London 1744.

Nicholas HANS, *New Trends in Education in the Eighteenth Century*, London 1951.

[George HARRIS], *Observations upon the English Language, in a letter to a Friend*, London [1752].

[John HART], *A Methode or comfortable beginning for all unlearned*, whereby they may bee taught to read English, London 1570.

B. HAURÉAU, *Notices et Extraits* de quelques manuscrits latins de la Bibliothèque Nationale, 6 vols. Paris 1890–3.

A. J. HAWKES, *Lancashire Printed Books*: a bibliography of all the books printed in Lancashire down to the year 1800, Wigan 1925.

John HAWKINS, *The English Schoolmaster compleated*, 2nd edn 1694.

W. C. HAZLITT, *A Handbook to Early English Literature*, etc., 7 vols. London 1867–1903.

Schools, School-books and Schoolmasters, London 1888.

D. P. HENRY, 'Saint Anselm's *De "grammatico"*', *Philosoph. Quart.* 10. 1960. 115–26.

   '*Why "grammaticus"?*', *Archivum Latinitatis Medii Aevi*, 28. 1958. 165–80.

[William HICKES?], *Grammatical Drollery*, London 1682.

Richard HOGARTH, *Grammar Disputations...Disputationes Grammaticales*, London 1712. (A bilingual Latin grammar.)

John HOLMES, *A New Grammar of the Latin Tongue*, 12th edn London 1782.

F. HOLTHAUSEN (a short note, on Farro, 1754), *Anglia, Beiblatt*, 30. 1918. 213–15.

Charles HOOLE, *The Common Rudiments of Latine Grammar* (London 1657), edn of 1659.
An Easie Entrance to the Latine Tongue, London 1649.
The Latine Grammar fitted for the use of schools, London 1651.
See also COMENIUS.

W. S. HOWELL, *Logic and Rhetoric in England, 1500–1700*, Princeton 1956.

Alexander HUME, *Grammatica nova*, Edinburgh 1612.
Prima Elementa grammaticae, Edinburgh 1612.

R. W. HUNT, 'Studies on Priscian in the Eleventh & Twelfth Centuries', *Med. & Ren. Studies*, 1. 1941. 194–231 (cited as Hunt I): 2. 1950. 1–56 (cited as Hunt II).
'Hugutio & Petrus Helias', *Med. & Ren. Studies*, 2. 1950. 174–8 (cited as Hunt II*b*).

John HUNTER, 'A Grammatical Essay on the Nature, Import, and Effect of certain Conjunctions'. *Transactions of the Royal Society of Edinburgh*, [1784].

L. JEEP, *Zur Geschichte der Lehre von den Redeteilen bei den lateinischen Grammatikern*, Leipzig 1893.

Otto L. JIRICZEK, 'Alexander Gill', *Studien zur vergleichenden Literaturgeschichte*, ed. Max Koch, 2. 1902, 129–45.

Ralph JOHNSON, *The Scholar's Guide from the Accidence to the University*, London, 1665.

Richard JOHNSON *Grammatical Commentaries*, London 1706.
Noctes Nottinghamicae; or, cursory, objections against the syntax of the common grammar (1714), Nottingham 1718.

Bassett JONES, *Herm'aelogium*; or an essay at the rationality of the art of speaking. As a supplement to Lillie's Grammar, philosophically, mythologically, & emblematically offered, London 1659.

J. JONES, *A Step towards an English Education*...together with an essay on the great usefulness of an English Grammar, 2nd edn Bristol 1740.

John JONES, *Practical Phonography*, London 1701, ed. E. Ekwall, Neudrucke frühneuenglischer Grammatiken, vol. 2, Halle 1907.

R. F. JONES, *The Triumph of the English Language*, London 1953.
'Science and English Prose Style in the third quarter of the seventeenth century', *PMLA*, 45. 1930, 977–1009.
'Science and Language in England of the mid-seventeenth century', *J. Eng. & Germ. Philol.* 31. 1932. 315–31.

Rowland JONES, *The Io-Triads; or the Tenth Muse*, London 1773.

Ernst KAPP, *Greek Foundations of Traditional Logic*, New York 1942.

A. G. KENNEDY, 'The Authorship of *The British Grammar*', *Mod. Lang. Notes*. 41. 1926. 388–91.
A Bibliography of Writings on the English Language from the beginning of printing to the end of 1922, Cambridge, Mass. 1927, repr. 1961.

W. KENRICK, *A New Dictionary of the English Language*, to which is prefixed a rhetorical grammar, London 1773.

K. L. KERN, *Die englische Lautentwicklung nach 'Right Spelling', 1704, und anderen Grammatiken um 1700*, Darmstadt 1913.

G. L. KITTREDGE, *English Grammars of Five Centuries*, Boston 1911. (A reissue, with one less illustration, of his *Some Landmarks in the History of English Grammar*, with illustrations from the collection of George A. Plimpton, Boston 1906.)

Marianne KNORRECK, *Der Einfluss des Rationalismus auf die englische Sprache. Sprache & Kultur*, vol. 30, Breslau 1938.

Vicesimus KNOX, *Liberal Education* (1781), 8th edn 2 vols. London 1786.

H. KÖKERITZ, 'Alexander Gil, 1621, on the Dialects of South & East England', *Studia Neophilologica*, 11. 1938/9. 277–88.

G. P. KRAPP, 'English Grammar; Grammatical Study', in *A Cyclopedia of Education*, ed. Paul Monroe, vol. 3, New York 1912, pp. 133–5.

[B. LAMY], *The Art of Speaking*: written in French by Messieurs du Port Royal...Rendred into English, London 1676.

Grace W. LANDRUM, 'The First Colonial Grammar in English', *William & Mary Quart. Hist. Mag.* 19. 1939. 272–85. (On Hugh Jones, 1724.)

P. LEHMANN, *Zu den sprachlogische Traktaten des Mittelalters (Mitteilungen aus Handschriften)*, *Sitzungsberichte der Bayerischen Akademie der Wissenschaft*, Part 2, Munich 1944.

M. LEHNERT, 'Die Abhängigkeit frühneuenglischer Grammatikern', *Engl. Studien*, 72. 1937. 192–206.

Die Grammatik des englischen Sprachmeisters John Wallis, 1616–1703, Breslau 1936.

S. A. LEONARD, *The Doctrine of Correctness in English Usage, 1700–1800* (*Univ. Wisconsin Studies in Lang. & Lit.* No. 25), Madison 1929.

Richard LLOYD, *The Latine Grammar*, London 1653 (included in the following).

The Schoole-master's Auxiliaries, 1654.

John LOCKE, *An Essay concerning Human Understanding* (1690), ed. A. C. Fraser, Oxford (1894), 1959.

Solomon LOWE, KOINA KAINⲰΣ, *An Appendix to Grammar*, London 1719.

A Grammar of the Latin Tongue, London 1726.

The Occasional Critique: on Education. Proposing a new scheme of grammar, and method of instruction, London 1728 (enlarged edn as *The Whetstone...1732*); also *The Occasional Critique*, No. IV, 1736, an expanded form of the 1728 issue.

Max LOWISCH, *Zur englischen Aussprache von 1650–1760 nach frühenglischen Grammatiken*, Kassel 1889.

W. T. LOWNDES, *The Bibliographer's Manual*, 6 vols. London 1885–1903.

R. L. LYNAM, *English Grammar in American Schools before 1850*, U. S. Education Bureau Bulletin, 1921. No. 12, Washington, D.C. 1922.

Duncan MACINTOSH and his two Daughters, *A Plain, rational essay on English Grammar*, Boston 1797; 2nd edn London 1808.

R. McKEON, 'Aristotle's Conception of Language', *Class. Philol.* 41. 1946. 193–206; 42. 1947. 21–50.

Henry MACNAB, *A Plan of Reform*, in the Mode of Instruction, at present practised in English schools, Glasgow 1786.

MADDEN, see SKEAT.

Lewis MAIDWELL, *Nova grammatices experimenta*: or, some new essays of a natural and artificial grammar, London 1707.

Max MANITIUS, *Geschichte der lateinischen Literatur des Mittelalters*, 3 vols. Munich 1911–31.

William MARSDEN, *Catalogue of Dictionaries, vocabularies, grammars & alphabets*, London 1796.

Thomas MARTIN, *An Explanation of Accidence and Grammar*, London 1754.

Thomas MARTIN, *A Philological Grammar of the English Language...* containing many original observations...on the comparative merits of more than one hundred treatises on English grammar, London 1824.

George MASON, *Grammaire Angloise* (1622), ed. R. Brotanek, Neudrucke frühneuenglischer Grammatiken, vol. 1, Halle 1905.

J. C. MAXWELL, 'Charles Gildon and the quarrels of the Ancients and Moderns', *Rev. Engl. Studies*, n.s. 1. 1950. 55–7.

Sanford B. MEECH, 'Early Application of Latin Grammar to English', *PMLA*, 50. 1935. pp. 1012–1032.

M. A. MEILAN, *An Introduction to the English Language*, 2 vols. London 1803.

T[homas] M[ERRIOTT], *Grammaticall Miscellanies*, Oxford 1660.

J. L. MOORE, *Tudor-Stuart Views on the Growth, Status and Destiny of the English Language* (*Studien zur englischen Philologie*, Part 41), Halle 1910.

Leo MOREL, *De Johannis Wallisii Grammatica Linguae Anglicanae*, Paris 1895.

Richard MULCASTER, *The First Part of the Elementarie* (1582), ed. E. T. Campagnac, Oxford 1925.

J. P. MULLALLY, *The Summulae Logicales of Peter of Spain*, Publications in Med. Studies, No. 8, Univ. Notre Dame, Indiana 1945.

David MURRAY, *Some Early Grammars & other School Books in Use in Scotland*, Royal Philosophical Society, Glasgow 1905–6.

Gilbert MURRAY, 'The Beginnings of Grammar', *Proc. Class. Assoc.* 1931, reprinted in his *Greek Studies*, Oxford 1946, pp. 171–91.

R. NARES, *Elements of Orthoepy*, London 1784.

William NELSON, 'The Teaching of English in Tudor Grammar Schools', *Studies in Philol.* 49. 1952. 119–43.

H. NETTLESHIP, 'The Study of Grammar among the Romans in the First Century A.D.', *J. Philol.*, 15. 1886, reprinted in his *Lectures & Essays, 2nd Series*, London 1895, pp. 145–71, as *Latin Grammar in the First Century*.

John NEWTON, *An Introduction to the Art of Logick*, London 1671.
An Introduction to the Art of Rhetorick, London 1671.

John NICHOLS, *Literary Anecdotes of the Eighteenth Century*, 9 vols. London 1812–15.

Appendix VIII

John A. NIETZ, *Old Textbooks*, University of Pittsburgh 1961.

N. E. OSSELTON, *Branded Words in English Dictionaries before Johnson*, Groningen Studies in English, 7, Groningen 1958.

Edward OWEN, *The Common Accidence methodised & enlarged*, London 1804.

L. J. PAETOW, *The Arts Course at Medieval Universities*, with special reference to grammar & rhetoric, Univ. Illinois, *Univ. Studies*, 3, No. 7, 1910.

Eloise PAFORT, 'A Group of Early Tudor School-Books', *Library*, 4th ser. 26. 1946. 227–61.

D. J. PALMER, *The Rise of English Studies*, O.U.P. for the University of Hull 1965.

Irene PARKER, *Dissenting Academies in England*, Cambridge 1914.

William PETTY, *Advice of W.P. to Mr. Samuel Hartlib* (1648), *Harl. Misc.* 6. 1810. 1–14.

V. J. PEYTON, *The History of the English Language*: deduced from its origin, & traced through its different stages & revolutions, London 1771.

J. T. PHILLIPS, *A Compendious Way of teaching antient & modern languages*, 2nd ed London 1723.

Ivan POLDAUF, *On the History of some Problems of English Grammar before 1800*, Prague 1948.

Port Royal Grammar, see *Grammaire Générale et Raisonnée*.

A Posing-Book for Scholars in Short Questions and Answers, London 1688.

Carl PRANTL, *Geschichte der Logik im Abendlände*, 4 vols. Leipzig 1855–70.

R. QUINTANA, 'Notes on English Educational Opinion during the Seventeenth Century', *Studies in Philol.* 27. 1930. 265–92.

C.R., 'English Grammar & English Grammarians', *Gent. Mag.* 117. 1840. 365–73; 473–81; 119. 1841. 478–85; 585–91.

R.R., *An English Grammar: or a plain exposition of Lilie's Grammar in English*, London 1641.

John RICE, *A Lecture on the importance & necessity of rendering the English language a peculiar branch of female education*, London 1773.

J. RIES, *Was ist ein Satz?* (Marburg 1894), 2nd rev. edn Prague 1931.

R. H. ROBINS, *Ancient & Medieval Grammatical Theory in Europe*, London 1951.

'Noun & Verb in Universal Grammar', *Language*, 28. 1952. 289–98.

A Short History of Linguistics, London 1967.

'Dionysius Thrax and the Western Grammatical Tradition', *Trans. Philol. Soc.* 1957. 67–106.

John ROBINSON, *The Art of Teaching the orthography, accent & pronunciation of the English language by imitation*, London 1800.

Heinrich ROOS, *Die Modi Significandi des Martinus de Dacia*, Beiträge zur Geschichte der Philosophie und Theologie des Mittelalters, vol. 37, Part 2, Munster 1952.

S. ROSCOE, *Newbery-Carnan-Power*, a provisional check-list of books for the entertainment, instruction and education of children and young people, issued under the imprints of John Newbery and his family in the period 1742–1802. Privately printed, 1966.

Margarete RÖSLER, 'Veraltete Wörter in der *Grammatica Anglicana* von 1594', *Engl. Studien*, 53. 1919. 168–95.

The Royal Grammar Reformed... for the better understanding of the English: and more speedy attainment of the Latin tongue, London 1695.

Reay SABOURN, *An Epitome of Grammar*: or, a short introduction to the Latin tongue, Newcastle-upon-Tyne, 1733.

C. E. A. SACHS, 'Studien zur Geschichte der englischen Grammatik', (*Herrigs*) *Archiv für das Studium der neueren Sprachen*, 23. 1858. 406–14.

[William SALISBURY], *Two Grammatical Essays*, London 1768.

Vivian SALMON, 'Language Planning in Seventeenth Century England; its Contexts and Aims', in C. E. Bazell and others, *In Memory of J.R. Firth*, London 1966, pp. 370–97.

J. E. SANDYS, *A History of Classical Scholarship from the Sixth Cent. B.C. to the end of the Middle Ages*, 3rd edn Cambridge 1921.

G. SCHEURWEGHS & E. VORLAT, 'Problems of the History of English Grammar', *Eng. Studies*, 40. 1959. 135–43.

Bernhard SCHMITZ, *Encyclopädie des philologischen Studiums der neuern Sprachen*, 2nd edn Leipzig 1876; appendix, 1877; 1st suppl. 2nd edn 1897; 2nd suppl. 1881.

Eduard SCHWYZER, *Griechische Grammatik* (Handbuch der Altertumswissenschaft), 3 vols Munich 1939–53.

A. E. SHAW, 'The Earliest Latin Grammars in English', *Trans. Bibl. Soc.* 5. 1901. 39–65.

Samuel SHAW, *Grammatica Anglo-Romana*, London 1687.

Thomas SHERIDAN, *A General Dictionary of the Eng. Lang.*... to which is prefixed a rhetorical grammar, 2 vols. 2nd edn London 1789.

A Dissertation on the causes of the difficulties which occur in learning the English tongue, London 1762.

James SHIRLEY, *Grammatica Anglo-Latina. An English and Latin Grammar.* London 1651.

Manuductio: or, a leading of children by the hand through the principles of grammar, 2nd edn London 1660.

The Rudiments of Grammar, London 1656.

Via ad Latinam Linguam complanata, London 1649.

Short Questions upon the Eight Parts of Speech, with the Concords in English. Fitted to the weake capacity of yong Schollers, London n.d. (BM query 1640; Kennedy gives 1629 and calls it an English Grammar.)

W. W. SKEAT, 'English Grammars', *Notes & Queries*, ser. 7, 6. 1888. 121–2; 243–4; 302–3. Reprinted in his *Student's Pastime*, 1896, with slight omissions.

W. SLOANE, *Children's Books in Seventeenth Century England & America*, New York 1955.

Adam SMITH, *Considerations concerning the first formation of languages*, *Philol. Miscellany*, 1. 1761. 440–79, reprinted in the 3rd edn, London

1767, of his *The Theory of Moral Sentiments*, as 'A Dissertation on the Origin of Languages'.

H. L. SMITH, K. DUGDALE, B. F. STEELE and R. S. McELHINNEY, *One Hundred Fifty Years of Grammar Textbooks*, Bloomington, Indiana 1946.

Joseph SMITH, *A Descriptive Catalogue of Friends' Books*, 2 vols. London 1867; supplement, 1893.

Sir Thomas SMITH, *De Recta et Emendata Linguae Anglicanae Scriptione Dialogus* (Paris 1568), ed. O. Deibel, Neudrucke frühneuenglischer Grammatiken, vol. 8, Halle 1913.

George SNELL, *The Right Teaching of Useful Knowledge*, London 1649.

Thomas STACKHOUSE, *Reflections on the nature and property of languages in general*, and on the advantages, defects, and manner of improving the English Tongue in particular, London 1731.

De Witt T. STARNES, *Renaissance Dictionaries: English–Latin & Latin–English*, Austin, Texas 1954.

  and Gertrude E. Noyes, *The English Dictionary from Cawdrey to Johnson, 1604–1755*, Chapel Hill, N. Carolina 1946.

[Richard STEELE], *The Tatler*, No. 234, 7 October 1710.

H. STEINTHAL, *Geschichte der Sprachwissenschaft bei den Griechen und Römern* (1863), 2nd edn Berlin 1890.

Alexander STEPHENS, *Memoirs of J. H. Tooke*, 2 vols. London 1813.

John STIRLING, *A Short View of Latin Grammar*, London 1737.

John STOCKWOOD, *A Plaine & Easie Laying Open* of the meaning & understanding of the rules of construction in the English Accidence, London 1590.

Nathaniel STRONG, *England's Perfect Schoolmaster* (1674), 3rd edn London 1681; 9th edn London 1706.

Ch. SVOBODA, 'La Grammaire Latine depuis le moyen âge, jusqu'au commencement du XIXe siècle', *Rev. des Etudes Lat.* 3. 1925. 69–77.

Elizabeth J. SWEETING, *Early Tudor Criticism, linguistic & literary*, Oxford 1940.

Jonathan SWIFT, *A Proposal for Correcting, Improving, and Ascertaining the English Tongue* (1711), *Works*, ed. Herbert Davis, vol. 4, Oxford.

  The Tatler, No. 230, 28 September 1710.

Christopher SYMS, *An Introduction to, or, the art of teaching, the Latine speach*, Dublin 1694.

Charles THUROT, *Notices et Extraits* de divers manuscrits latins pour servir à l'histoire des doctrines grammaticales du moyen âge. (Notices et extraits des mss. de la bibl. impériale et autres bibliothèques, vol. 22, Paris 1874, Part 2, dated 1868.)

J. P. TUCK, 'The Beginning of English Studies in the Sixteenth Century', *Research Review*, Univ. Durham Inst. Education, No. 7. September 1956. 65–73.

  'The Latin Grammar attributed to William Lily', *Research Review*, Univ. Durham Inst. Education, No. 2. 1951. 33–9.

'The use of English in Latin Teaching in England in the Sixteenth Century', *Research Review*, Univ. Durham Inst. Education, No. 1. 1950. 22–30.

Susie I. TUCKER, *English Examined*, Cambridge 1961.

G. H. TURNBULL *Hartlib, Dury & Comenius*, London 1947.

Sir Thomas URQUHART, *Logopandecteison*, or an introduction to the universal language, London 1653.

M. USSHER, *A Pronouncing Grammar & Spelling-book*, Gloucester 1794.

Vindex Anglicus; or the perfections of the English language. Defended, and asserted, [Oxford] 1644.

Emma VORLAT, *Progress in English Grammar, 1586–1753*, 4 vols. mimeographed, A. Peiffer, Luxembourg 1964.

William WALKER, *A Treatise of English Particles*; shewing much of the variety of their significations and uses in English, and how to render them into Latine, London 1655; 5th edn 1673; 7th edn 1679.

G. WALLERAND, *Les Oeuvres de Siger de Courtrai* (Les Philosophes Belges, vol. 8), Louvain 1913.

John WALLIS, *Institutio Logicae*, Oxford 1687.

[William WARD], *Short Questions upon the Eight Parts of Speech*, London n.d. [1628?].

Foster WATSON, 'Curriculum & Textbooks of the English Schools in the first half of the Seventeenth Century', *Trans. Bibliog. Soc.* 6. 1903. 159–267.

   The English Grammar Schools to 1660: their curriculum & practice, Cambridge 1908.

   'English Grammar, historical development', *A Cyclopedia of Education*, ed. P. Monroe, New York 1912, vol 3, 132–3.

R. WATT, *Bibliotheca Britannica*, 4 vols. Edinburgh 1824.

[Thomas WATT], *Grammar made Easy*, containing Despauter's Grammar Reform'd & rendred plain & obvious to the capacity of youth, 5th edn Edinburgh 1742.

Isaac WATTS, *The Improvement of the Mind*, or, a Supplement to the Art of Logic (1741), 2 vols. London 1795.

Noah WEBSTER, *Dissertations on the English Language*, Boston 1789.

   A Letter to the Governors, Instructors and Trustees of the Universities and other Seminaries on the Errors of English Grammars, New York 1798.

W. H. WELLS, *Wells's School Grammar*, Andover, U.S. 1847 (stereotype edn. of first issue in 1846).

   Chronological Catalogue of English Grammars issued prior to 1801, Chicago 1878 (= pp. 3–9 of his *Historical Authorship of English Grammar*, Chicago 1878).

Charles WELSH, *A Bookseller of the last century* [John Newbery], London 1885.

John WILLIAMS, *Thoughts on the Origin & on the most rational and natural Method of Teaching the Languages*, London 1783.

[Thomas WILSON], *The many Advantages of a good Language to any Nation*, London 1724.

Appendix VIII

William WOTTON, *Reflections upon ancient & modern learning* (1694), chap. 5, 'Of Ancient & Modern Grammar', in J. E. Spingarn, *Critical Essays of the 17th Century*, vol. 3, Oxford 1908, pp. 223–6.

Louis B. WRIGHT, *Middle-Class Culture in Elizabethan England*, Chapel Hill, N. Carolina 1935; reissued by Cornell U.P. 1958.

E. YOUNG, *The Compleat English Scholar* (1675), 18th edn London 1710.

R. E. ZACHRISSON, *English Pronunciation at Shakespeare's Time*, as taught by William Bullokar, Uppsala 1927.

'Notes on some early English & French Grammars', *Anglia, Beiblatt*, 25. 1914. pp. 245–53.

Review of C(hristian) Müller's 'Die englische Lautentwicklung nach Lediard, 1725, und anderen Grammatikern'; *Anglia, Beiblatt*, 28. 1917. 68–82.

ADDENDA

R. C. ALSTON, *A Bibliography of the English Language*, vol. VI, *Rhetoric, Style, Elocution, Prosody, Rhyme, Pronunciation, Spelling Reform*. Bradford 1969.

George DALGARNO, *Didascalocophus*, Oxford 1680.

Rowland JONES, *The Philosophy of Words*, London 1769.

A. C. PARTRIDGE, *Tudor to Augustan English*, London 1969.

INDEX

Index

Hunt, R. W., 14, 16–17, 30n., 58, 70n., 98n.
Hunter, John, 446–7
Huntley, Thomas, *A Short System of English Grammar*, 218, 567; cited, 348

ibn-Khallikan, 53n.
identity, 129
implicit, construction, 128
implicit, for *object*, 513
impositio, 16
indefiniteness, 68–70, 346, 361
individuation, 358–9
inflexion, 112, 376, 467
instability, of categories, *see* stability
integral, as part of speech, 247–9, 252
interjection, in the tradition, 49, 51, 53, 76–81, 107; in the English grammars, 461–5, 535; classification, 464–5; repudiated, 461–2; and adverb, 49, 51, 73, 77, 81, 201, 206–7, 211, 212, 219, 256; and conjunction, 212; and noun, 236, 461; and verb, 273, 461; as sentence equivalent, 219, 462, 516
intransitive, *see* transitivity *and* verb, transitive
intrinsic, pronoun, 99–101; mode, 125
inventio, 16–17
Ireland, J., *Beauties in Prose and Verse*, 223, 567
irregularity, of pronoun, 68; of usage, 361; of verb, 435–9
Isidore of Seville, 29, 35, 62, 70, 87, 139

J., J., *Prittle Prattle*, 388, 494n., 511, 567; cited, 260–1
Joannes Josse de Marville, 15
Joel, Thomas, *An Easy Introduction to the English Grammar*, 214, 567; cited, 321, 377, 505–6
Johannes Aurifaber, 15
Johannes Avicula, 21
John of Salisbury, 29–30, 88
Johnson, Charles, *The Complete Art of Writing Letters*, 257, 347, 511, 567; cited, 185, 403
Johnson, J., *The New Royal and Universal Dictionary*, 214, 303n., 329, 567
Johnson, Ralph, 192–3, 292, 294, 400, 435
Johnson, Mr S., *A Compleat Introduction to the Art of Writing Letters*, 257, 511, 567; cited, 294, 351
Johnson, Dr S., 200n.; *A Dictionary of the English Language*, 225–6, 300, 303, 309, 327, 383, 386, 438, 439, 507–8, 568; cited, 186
Johnston, William, *A Pronouncing and Spelling Dictionary*, 225, 494n., 568; cited, 294

joining word, as part of speech, 454, 512
Jones, Hugh, *An Accidence to the English Tongue*, 212, 316, 347, 349, 390, 391, 568; cited, 187, 262–3, 313
Jones, J., 182
Jones, R. F., 493, 495
Jones, Rowland, 276, 568; *The Circles of Gomer*, cited, 178, 233, 344, 420, 439; *Hieroglyfic*, 178; cited, 195, 233, 389, 391, 420, 462; *The Io-Triads*, 195; *The Philosophy of Words*, 389
Jonson, Ben, *The English Grammar*, 194, 218, 354, 362, 375, 569; cited, 187, 201, 298, 321, 357, 363, 373, 382, 409–10, 439–40

Key to Spelling, A, 218, 569; cited, 494
Kilwardby, Richard, 17, 22
Kirkby, John, *A New English Grammar*, 213, 280, 302, 347, 389, 390, 393, 569; cited, 208, 263, 264, 308, 322, 325, 345, 365, 371, 446, 513
Kitson, Roger, *A Short Introduction to English Grammar*, 223, 569; cited, 327, 495
Knowles, John, *The Principles of English Grammar*, 223, 569; cited, 292, 293, 332, 474

Lancelot, Claude, *see Grammaire Générale et Raisonnée*
Lane, A., 510; *A Rational and Speedy Method of Attaining to the Latin Tongue*, 348, 386, 498–9, 511, 569; cited, 171, 254, 452, 494; *A Key to the Art of Letters*, 171, 186, 336, 348, 390, 452, 498–9, 511, 570; cited, 254, 300, 305, 308, 319, 329, 364, 375, 449, 461, 471, 476, 481, 485
language, 9, 16f., 30, 32, 82, 167–8, 198, 441, 466, 491; change in, 172; conventional nature of, 173; origin of, 15–16, 71, 175, 323; study of, 130, 167–8, 338; symbolic function of, 173, 178; *see also* grammar, universal
Latin, *see* English and Latin
Lehnert, M., 172n.
Leonard, S. A., 425
Lewis, Mark, 158, 205, 211, 275, 326, 461n., 570–1; *Essay* (1670?), 159, 214, 219–20; cited, 206, 281–2, 285, 293, 327n., 444, 479; *Essay* (1674), 158n., 214, 215, 310, 344; cited, 159, 205–6, 213, 219, 282, 308, 352, 425, 462, 464, 474; *Institutio*, cited, 158–9, 205–6, 285, 351, 464n.; *Vestibulum Technicum*, 158n.; cited, 206, 308; *Plain and Short Rules*, 3, 469n.; cited 220, 473, 475

Index